Intergenerational Justice

The International Library of Justice
Series Editor: Tom Campbell

Titles in the Series:

Global Justice
Christian Barry and Holly Lawford-Smith

Justice and the Capabilities Approach
Thom Brooks

Theories of Justice
Tom Campbell and Alejandra Mancilla

Distributive Justice
Julian Lamont

Procedural Justice
Larry May and Paul Morrow

Intergenerational Justice
Lukas H. Meyer

Intergenerational Justice

Edited by

Lukas H. Meyer
University of Graz, Austria

ASHGATE

© 2012 Lukas H. Meyer. For copyright of individual articles please refer to the Acknowledgements.

All rights reserved. No part of this publication may be reproduced, stored in a retrieval system or transmitted in any form or by any means, electronic, mechanical, photocopying, recording or otherwise without the prior permission of the publisher.

Wherever possible, these reprints are made from a copy of the original printing, but these can themselves be of very variable quality. Whilst the publisher has made every effort to ensure the quality of the reprint, some variability may inevitably remain.

Published by
Ashgate Publishing Limited
Wey Court East
Union Road
Farnham
Surrey GU9 7PT
England

Ashgate Publishing Company
Suite 420
101 Cherry Street
Burlington
VT 05401-4405
USA

www.ashgate.com

British Library Cataloguing in Publication Data
Intergenerational justice. – (The library of essays on justice)
   1. Justice. 2. Reparations for historical injustices.
   3. Intergenerational relations.
   I. Series II. Meyer, Lukas H.
   320'.011-dc23

Library of Congress Control Number: 2011942701

ISBN 9780754629856

Printed and bound in Great Britain by
TJ International Ltd, Padstow, Cornwall.

Contents

Acknowledgements vii
Series Preface ix
Introduction xi

PART I   FOUNDATIONS

1   Jan Narveson (1967), 'Utilitarianism and New Generations', *Mind*, **76**, pp. 62–72.   3
2   John Rawls (1971), extract from 'Distributive Shares', in *A Theory of Justice*, second revised edition, Cambridge, MA: Harvard University Press, 1999, section 44, pp. 251–8.   15
3   Derek Parfit (1984), 'The Non-Identity Problem', in *Reasons and Persons*, Oxford: Clarendon Press, pp. 351–79, 522–523.   23
4   David Heyd (2009), 'The Intractability of the Nonidentity Problem', in Melinda A. Roberts and David T. Wasserstein (eds), *Harming Future People: Ethics, Genetics and The Nonidentity Problem*, Dordrecht: Springer, pp. 3–25.   55
5   Lukas H. Meyer (2004), 'Surviving Duties and Symbolic Compensation', in *Justice in Time. Responding to Historical Injustice*, Baden-Baden: Nomos, pp. 173–83. (originally published in French, 2003, 'Obligations Persistantes et Réparation Symbolique', *Revue Philosophique de Louvain*, **101**, pp. 105–22).   79
6   John Broome (1994), 'Discounting the Future', *Philosophy and Public Affairs*, **23**, pp. 128–56.   91
7   Dieter Birnbacher (2009), 'What Motivates Us to Care for the (Distant) Future?', in Axel Gosseries and Lukas H. Meyer (eds), *Intergenerational Justice*, Oxford: Oxford University Press, pp. 273–300.   121

PART II   SUBSTANTIVE PRINCIPLES OF INTERGENERATIONAL JUSTICE

8   Seana Valentine Shiffrin (1999), 'Wrongful Life, Procreative Responsibility, and the Significance of Harm', *Legal Theory*, **5**, pp. 117–48.   151
9   Brian Barry (1999), 'Sustainability and Intergenerational Justice', in Andrew Dobson (ed.), *Fairness and Futurity. Essays on Environmental Sustainability*, Oxford: Oxford University Press, pp. 93–117, 291.   183
10   John Rawls (1999), extract from: 'Nonideal Theory', in *The Law of Peoples*, Cambridge, MA: Harvard University Press, sections 15 and 16, pp. 105–20.   209
11   Lukas H. Meyer and Dominic Roser (2009), 'Enough for the Future', in Axel Gosseries and Lukas H. Meyer (eds), *Intergenerational Justice*, Oxford: Oxford University Press, pp. 219–48.   225

12	Axel Gosseries (2009), 'Three Models of Intergenerational Reciprocity', in Axel Gosseries and Lukas H. Meyer (eds), *Intergenerational Justice*, Oxford: Oxford University Press, pp. 119–46.	255
13	Gustaf Arrhenius (2008), 'Life Extension versus Replacement', *Journal of Applied Philosophy*, **25**, pp. 211–27.	283
14	Stephen M. Gardiner (2003), 'The Pure Intergenerational Problem', *The Monist*, **86**, pp. 481–500.	301
15	Simon Caney (2010), 'Climate Change and the Duties of the Advantaged', *Critical Review of International Social and Political Philosophy*, **13**, pp. 203–28 (reprinted in Matt Matravers and Lukas H. Meyer (eds) (2011), *Democracy, Equality, and Justice*, London: Routledge, pp. 203–28).	321

PART III NORMATIVE SIGNIFICANCE OF HISTORICAL INJUSTICES AND THEIR CONSEQUENCES

16	David Lyons (1977), 'The New Indian Claims and Original Rights to Land', *Social Theory and Practice*, **4**, pp. 249–72.	349
17	Jeremy Waldron (1992), 'Superseding Historic Injustice', *Ethics*, **103**, pp. 4–28.	373
18	Janna Thompson (2000), 'The Apology Paradox', *Philosophical Quarterly*, **50**, pp. 470–75.	399
19	George Sher (2005), 'Transgenerational Compensation', *Philosophy & Public Affairs*, **33**, pp. 181–201.	405
20	Rahul Kumar (2003), 'Who Can Be Wronged?', *Philosophy & Public Affairs*, **31**, pp. 98–118.	425
21	Daniel Butt (2007), 'On Benefiting from Injustice', *Canadian Journal of Philosophy*, **37**, pp. 129–52.	445
22	Lukas H. Meyer and Dominic Roser (2010), 'Climate Justice and Historical Emissions', *Critical Review of International Social and Political Philosophy*, **13**, pp. 229–53 (reprinted in Matt Matravers and Lukas H. Meyer (eds) (2011), *Democracy, Equality, and Justice*, London: Routledge, pp. 229–53).	469

Name Index 495

Acknowledgements

The editor and publishers wish to thank the following for permission to use copyright material.

Cambridge University Press for the essay: Seana Valentine Shiffrin (1999), 'Wrongful Life, Procreative Responsibility, and the Significance of Harm', *Legal Theory*, **5**, pp. 117–48. Copyright © 1999 Cambridge University Press.

Harvard University Press for the essays: John Rawls (1971), 'The Problem of Justice' extract from 'Distributive Shares', in *A Theory of Justice*, second revised edition, Cambridge, MA: The Belknap Press of Harvard University Press, 1999, section 44, pp. 251–8. Copyright © 1971, 1999 by the President and Fellows of Harvard University College; John Rawls (1999), extract from: 'Nonideal Theory', in *The Law of Peoples*, Cambridge, MA: Harvard University Press, sections 15 and 16, pp. 105–20. Copyright © 1999 by the President and Fellows of Harvard College.

The Monist for the essay: Stephen M. Gardiner (2003), 'The Pure Intergenerational Problem', *The Monist*, **86**, pp. 481–500. Copyright © 2003 *The Monist: An International Quarterly Journal of General Philosophical Inquiry*, Open Court Publishing Company, Chicago, IL.

Oxford University Press for the essay: Jan Narveson (1967), 'Utilitarianism and New Generations', *Mind*, **76**, pp. 62–72; Derek Parfit (1984), 'The Non-Identity Problem', in *Reasons and Persons*, Oxford: Clarendon Press, pp. 351–79, 522–523. Copyright © Derek Parfit; Dieter Birnbacher (2009), 'What Motivates Us to Care for the (Distant) Future?', in Axel Gosseries and Lukas H. Meyer (eds), *Intergenerational Justice*, Oxford: Oxford University Press, pp. 273–300; Lukas H. Meyer and Dominic Roser (2009), 'Enough for the Future', in Axel Gosseries and Lukas H. Meyer (eds), *Intergenerational Justice*, Oxford: Oxford University Press, pp. 219–48; Axel Gosseries (2009), 'Three Models of Intergenerational Reciprocity', in Axel Gosseries and Lukas H. Meyer (eds), *Intergenerational Justice*, Oxford: Oxford University Press, pp. 119–46.

Florida State University/Social Theory and Practice for the essay: David Lyons (1977), 'The New Indian Claims and Original Rights to Land', *Social Theory and Practice*, **4**, pp. 249–72.

Springer Science + Business Media for the essay: David Heyd (2009), 'The Intractability of the Nonidentity Problem', in Melinda A. Roberts and David T. Wasserstein (eds), *Harming Future People: Ethics, Genetics and The Nonidentity Problem*, Dordrecht: Springer, pp. 3–25. Copyright © Springer Science + Business Media BV 2009.

Taylor & Francis for the essay: Simon Caney (2010), 'Climate Change and the Duties of the Advantaged', *Critical Review of International Social and Political Philosophy*, **13**, pp. 203–28 (reprinted in Matt Matravers and Lukas H. Meyer (eds) (2011), *Democracy, Equality, and Justice*, London: Routledge, pp. 203–28). Reprinted by permission of the publisher (Taylor

& Francis Ltd, www.tandfonline.com); Lukas H. Meyer and Dominic Roser (2010), 'Climate Justice and Historical Emissions', *Critical Review of International Social and Political Philosophy*, **13**, pp. 229–53 (reprinted in Matt Matravers and Lukas H. Meyer (eds) (2011), *Democracy, Equality, and Justice*, London: Routledge, pp. 229–53). Reprinted by permission of the publisher (Taylor & Francis Ltd, www.tandfonline.com).

University of Calgary Press for the essay: Daniel Butt (2007), 'On Benefiting from Injustice', *Canadian Journal of Philosophy*, **37**, pp. 129–52.

University of Chicago Press for the essay: Jeremy Waldron (1992), 'Superseding Historic Injustice', *Ethics*, **103**, pp. 4–28. Copyright © 1992 by the University of Chicago. All rights reserved.

John Wiley and Sons for the essays: John Broome (1994), 'Discounting the Future', *Philosophy and Public Affairs*, **23**, pp. 128–56; Gustaf Arrhenius (2008), 'Life Extension versus Replacement', *Journal of Applied Philosophy*, **25**, pp. 211–27. Copyright © 2008 Society for Applied Philosophy; Janna Thompson (2000), 'The Apology Paradox', *Philosophical Quarterly*, **50**, pp. 470–75. Copyright © 2000 The Editors of the Philosophical Quarterly; George Sher (2005), 'Transgenerational Compensation', *Philosophy & Public Affairs*, **33**, pp. 181–201. Copyright © 2005 Blackwell Publishing, Inc.; Rahul Kumar (2003), 'Who Can Be Wronged?', *Philosophy & Public Affairs*, **31**, pp. 98–118. Copyright © 2003 by Princeton University Press.

Every effort has been made to trace all the copyright holders, but if any have been inadvertently overlooked the publishers will be pleased to make the necessary arrangement at the first opportunity.

Series Preface

Justice is one of the most enduring and central concepts within applied philosophy, and generates a vast and varied literature. This six-volume *International Library of Justice* series meets a number of distinct needs. The first volume, *Theories of Justice*, edited by Tom Campbell and Alejandra Mancilla, comprises a selection of some of the most important essays on the general theory of justice published over recent decades. One interesting aspect of this literature is the renewed attention that is being given to the notion of desert within theories of justice. Two further volumes, edited by Larry May and Paul Morrow, and Julian Lamont, respectively, deal with two traditional topics in justice that have undergone significant development in recent years – namely procedural justice, particularly with respect to constitutional law, and distributive justice, taking in important recent work on egalitarianism. Another two volumes, edited by Christian Barry and Holly Lawford-Smith, and Lukas H. Meyer, respectively, focus on the application of justice to less familiar areas, such as global institutions as they bear upon contemporary problems relating to extreme poverty and intergenerational justice. The sixth volume, *Justice and the Capabilities Approach*, edited by Thom Brooks, concentrates on the recent influential work by Amartya Sen and Martha Nussbaum on the relevance the concept of human capabilities in the formulation of policy on distributive justice, especially in developing countries.

Given the political priority that accrues to those matters that are categorized as having to do with justice, there is a tendency to extend the term beyond its distinctive uses and incorporate a very wide range of social values that relate to the proper ordering of social and political relationships. While the editors of each volume have striven to resist this inflation of the term 'justice' to cover all aspects of right human relationships, inevitably there is, in each volume, a substantial overlap with the bodies of literature concerned with the ideals of equality, reciprocity and humanity.

One such overlap arises with respect to rights, particularly human rights. Indeed, in some fields the discourse of justice has been largely overtaken by that of rights. The significance of this shift in emphasis within political rhetoric, which is one of the themes that features in *Theories of Justice*, recurs within the subsequent selections, raising interesting questions concerning contemporary political priorities and differing institutional approaches to social order.

The volumes in this series will assist those engaged in scholarly research by making available some of the most important contemporary essays on particular topics within the contemporary discourse of justice. The essays are reproduced in full, with the original pagination for ease of reference and citation.

The editors have been selected for their eminence in the study of law, politics and philosophy. Each volume represents each editor's selection of the most seminal recent essays in English on an aspect of justice. The Introductions present an overview of the issues in that particular volume, together with comments on the background and significance of the selected essays.

TOM CAMPBELL
Series Editor
Professorial Fellow, Centre for Applied Philosophy and Public Ethics (CAPPE),
Charles Sturt University, Canberra

Introduction

Overview

The subject matter of 'justice between generations' or 'intergenerational justice' is the transgenerational respect for the rights of and the fulfillment of duties vis-à-vis future and past generations. This reflects a broad understanding of justice (see Mill, 1863, ch. 5), according to which justice applies to intergenerational relations if future or past generations can be viewed as holding legitimate claims or rights[1] against present generations, who in turn have correlative duties to future or past generations. All those born within a certain period of time belong to one generation. In the philosophical literature, 'justice between generations' typically refers to the relations between non-contemporaries whose lifetimes do not overlap. In contrast, 'justice between age groups' refers to the relations of people whose lifetimes do overlap (Laslett and Fishkin, 1992).

One of the legitimate claims of future generations vis-à-vis present generations appears to be a claim of distributive justice: Depending on the understanding of the relevant principles of distributive justice to be applied, if there is an intergenerational conflict of interests, present generations may be obliged by considerations of justice not to pursue policies that create benefits for themselves but impose costs on those who will live in the future. John Rawls first discussed systematically the distributive duties of justice vis-à-vis future generations (Rawls, 1971 and Chapter 2). Rawls refers to the question of the just savings rate investigated by Frank P. Ramsey (1928). Besides Rawls, Jan Narveson (1973 and Chapter 1), Brian Barry (1977, 1989, 1995 and Chapter 9), Derek Parfit (1976, 1982, 1984, 1986 and Chapter 3), and David Heyd (1992, 2009 and Chapter 4) have contributed most to an understanding of the ethics of intergenerational relations.

The philosophical field of research can be divided into three areas: First, considerations concerning the very possibility of intergenerational justice, in particular concerning the question of whether (distant) future people can be bearers of rights vis-à-vis currently living people; second, interpretations of the significance of historical injustice; and, third, investigations into what substantively is owed to future (and past) people and what weight we should give to fulfilling our intergenerational obligations. As considerations of intergenerational justice are of central importance in providing an interpretation of what ought to be done in responding to the global problem of climate change, 'Climate Justice' has become a field of applied intergenerational justice. This volume collects essays that, taken together, provide insights into all these fields of research.[2]

---

[1] In the following I will speak of moral rights and legitimate claims interchangeably, but nothing hinges on this as long as it is understood that having a legitimate claim implies another person or persons standing under the correlative duty to respond to the claim.

[2] Previously published collections on (aspects of) intergenerational ethics include Sikora and Barry (1978), Partridge (1981b), Fotion and Heller, (1997), Laslett and Fishkin (1992), Dobson (1999),

The Non-Identity Problem: Harming Future People

A central problem of the first area of research noted above is the non-identity problem. The non-identity problem systematically raises doubts about the possibility of currently living people harming future persons' interests and, thus, threatens to undermine the very possibility of future people being bearers of welfare rights vis-à-vis currently living people.[3] A person is treated unjustly if she wrongfully suffers harm by being hindered in the pursuance of basic interests and by having her rights violated. The harmed person may have a just claim to compensation. According to our common understanding of harm – the hypothetical-historical understanding – an action harms a person only if owing to the action she is worse off at some later time than had the action not been carried out. The non-identity problem relies on the claim that currently living people cannot harm future people in that way. Many, if not most, actions carried out by currently living people will affect not only the conditions of life of future people but also the very composition of future people – that is, the number, existence and identity of future people; this is also true for actions that are typically regarded as harmful for future people. However, if not carrying out the seemingly harmful action meant that the seemingly harmed person did not exist, then this person cannot be considered harmed by the action having been carried out. This is at the heart of the non-identity problem (see Parfit, Chapter 3; also: Woodward, 1987; Buchanan et al., 2000; Benatar, 2006). The person who in her very existence depends upon the seemingly harmful action being carried out cannot be considered worse off owing to the action than had the action not been carried out. For then the person would not exist – and for the sake of argument we assume she has a life worth living.

In response to the non-identity problem, some hold that 'contingent future people' – that is, people whose existence as such persons is dependent upon currently living people's actions – cannot be the bearers of rights vis-à-vis currently living people and their carrying out such acts (De George, 1981; Heyd, 1992; Heyd, Chapter 4). Others argue that, while currently living people cannot harm future people, they can violate contingent future people's rights: the violation of some rights of a person may best be understood as not presupposing a set-back of her interests (Kumar, Chapter 20). Other philosophers make attempts at reducing the practical significance of the non-identity problem. First, they limit the relevant acts to those which are not only likely but necessary conditions of the existence of the affected person (see, as discussed by Kumar, Roberts, 1998, §§ 3.4 and 3.5; also: Simmons, 1995; Gosseries, 2004b, ch. 2). Second, they make an attempt at delineating a notion of harm for which the non-identity problem does not arise (Shiffrin, Chapter 8). According to the threshold notion of harm, an action is then harmful for a person if as a consequence of the action the person falls below a normatively defined threshold of well-being – this is being understood as a sufficient notion of harm only (Meyer, 2003). The non-identity problem does not arise

---

Meyer (2004a), Ryberg and Tännsjö (2004), Miller and Kumar (2007), Gosseries and Meyer (2009), and Roberts and Wasserstein (2009).

[3] Some theorists have denied that future people can have rights (or legitimate claims) vis-à-vis currently living people on different grounds: Owing to the fact that they will live in the future or that currently living people cannot relate to future people as individuals or that non-contemporaries cannot cooperate with each other. Also it has been claimed that, for future people to have rights vis-à-vis us, we would have to ascribe a right to existence to them. For a discussion of these questionable views, see Meyer (2008), § 2.

because, according to the threshold notion of harm, identifying the harm caused does not rely on a hypothetical comparison with the situation in which the harmful act was not carried out. Relying on such a notion of harm will limit the significance of the non-identity problem to differing degrees depending upon how the threshold is substantively defined.

Historical Injustices and Their Consequences

People living today can be considered as indirect victims of injustices committed against other people in the past. Owing to the consequences of these past injustices, the indirect victims suffer harm.[4] The non-identity problem can also threaten to undermine indirect victims' claims to an apology (Thompson, Chapter 8; Brooks, 1999) or to compensation for the consequences of historical injustice committed against other people in the past (Meyer, 2003, pp. 149–58). For these injustices can belong to the (necessary) conditions of the existence and identity of those who today make these claims. Then they cannot be considered harmed by these actions according to the common (the hypothetical-historical) understanding of harm. However, the indirect victims can claim compensation according to the threshold understanding of harm when, owing to the consequences of the historical injustice, they are worse off than they, today, ought to be.

Also, the successors of the original victims can claim compensation for the harm they suffered since conception, namely owing to the consequences of an additional harmful wrong they themselves suffered: the consequences of the fact that the direct victims or previous indirect victims were not (fully) compensated (Sher, Chapter 19). So understood, the indirect claims to compensation can rely on the hypothetical-historical understanding of harm: They would have been better off had their parents or (great-)grand-parents been fully compensated. The flipside of this way of understanding the claims of indirect victims is that the descendants of the perpetrators may be thought to stand under the correlative obligations to provide measures of compensation to the indirect victims. Often the descendants of perpetrators can be considered as beneficiaries of the wrongs committed by their predecessors. '[I]f it is accepted that they ... have rectificatory obligations to others, then they are innocent only insofar as they act reasonably promptly to fulfil the said obligations' (Butt, Chapter 21, p. 467 below). If they fail to fulfill their obligations they commit the additional wrong of not providing compensation to the indirect victim in time.

Further main issues in this second area of research noted above are the supersession of historical claims and the question whether currently living people can have duties vis-à-vis deceased persons. If the validity of property rights (or all moral claim rights, including property rights) depends upon their contributing to their bearers being able to realize certain values (for example, the value of living an autonomous life), then their validity may depend upon the circumstances.[5] Accordingly, the (long-)lasting effects of historical injustices, not the injustices themselves, to be sure, can be justified owing to changed circumstances. For example, even if today's structure of ownership and distribution of property rights were

---

[4] For interpretations of the normative significance of the consequences of past wrongs, see also Ackerman (1997) and Pogge (2004).

[5] For an alternative, namely backward-looking and procedural understanding of property entitlements, see Nozick (1974).

correctly interpreted as the result of, inter alia, historical injustices, say wrongful takings, today's distribution of property rights may still be considered legitimate if, under current conditions, the distribution can be shown to contribute sufficiently well to the realization of the relevant values (Lyons, Chapter 16). Then the historical injustices would be 'superseded' (Waldron, Chapter 17 and 2004). However, even in the case of distant historical injustices it is very difficult to show that the consequences of these injustices have been superseded owing to changed circumstances; this depends on our understanding of the grounds of property rights, on our understanding of what changes of circumstances are necessary for the supersession to occur and if we find these changes to have occurred (Patton, 2004; Meyer 2007).

Duties vis-à-vis Past People

For the sake of the argument let us assume that an historical injustice has been superseded and that the past wrong has no identifiable harmful effects on currently living or future people. Then nobody stands under any obligations to provide measures of compensation for the historical injustice. Even if that were so, we still face the fact that past people were victims of this injustice. The question then is whether this fact is normatively significant. Many find it intuitively plausible that present generations can have duties to deceased victims owing to the wrongs committed against them (by others) in the past: for example, that currently living people ought publicly to acknowledge them as victims of injustice. Whether this view can be defended – that is, that we have duties to past generations that are grounded in past deeds – seems to depend upon the normative status of deceased persons and, in particular, deceased victims of injustice.

The most straightforward defence would consist of showing that deceased people have rights vis-à-vis currently living people. However, this seems to presuppose that people continue to exist after their physical death and that they may be affected by (and affect) events of this world. These assumptions about the ontological status of previously living people are at least as controversial as their converse (Mulgan, 1999, pp. 54–5). Neither of these assumptions seems qualified to serve as starting points of a philosophical defence of duties vis-à-vis past people.

Some philosophers have argued that we can defend the view without relying on either assumption. Rather, they assume that upon a person's death any causal interaction between her and the physical world as we know it ceases completely. Thus neither can deceased people be bearers of interests or rights, nor can those presently alive harm or wrong deceased people. Nevertheless, currently living people can have duties vis-à-vis deceased people, or so they argue. According to one understanding, people's future-oriented interests that concern what are for them posthumous states of affairs can be violated when these people are alive (Pitcher, 1984; Feinberg, 1984; also: Feinberg, 1977, pp. 301–2; Feinberg 1980; Partridge, 1981a). However, in this explanation the posthumous harm – for example, the posthumous defamation of a past victim of an injustice as having deserved to be treated in that way – must have occurred before the death of the person. This seems to presuppose a deterministic understanding of the occurrence of the harmful action. It is also questionable whether the interpretation is an interpretation of posthumous harm as such rather than of harm to living people that is caused by posthumous events (Waluchow, 1986; Gosseries, 2004b). According to a second explanation, currently living people can have (imperfect) duties vis-à-vis deceased people without the deceased holding correlative rights. Rather, the future-oriented rights that the deceased had while alive imply the reasons for attributing duties to people living today. These duties survive the deaths of the bearers of the correlative rights (Wellman, 1995; Meyer, Chapter 5, pp. 80–84 below; Meyer 2005, ch. 3). A further question is whether we can plausibly interpret practices of public commemoration of historical injustices at least in part as reflecting surviving duties towards the deceased victims of these injustices (Meyer 2004b; Meyer, 2005, chs 4 and 5; Thompson, 2009, chs 4–7).

Saving for Future People

I now turn to the third area of philosophical research noted above, namely to substantive questions of intergenerational justice. As already mentioned, legitimate claims of future generations vis-à-vis present generations can be understood as claims of distributive justice so that currently living people may not use up all resources for their own sake or simply impose the costs of their undertakings on those who will live in the future. John Rawls first systematically analyzed the distributive duties of justice vis-à-vis future generations. He discusses what we owe to future people as a matter of the just savings rate. Here, savings include all resources to which future people will have access no matter whether currently living people planned to set them aside for them or not. Rawls justifies the savings rate as the result of a decision taken in the hypothetical decision situation, that is, his 'original position'. Rawls first assumed that all generations are being represented in the original position. However, the relations between non-contemporaries do not reflect the 'circumstances of justice' (Rawls, 1971, pp. 148–52): Currently living people cannot cooperate with previously living people; the latter can benefit and harm the former but not the other way around. There are ways to extend the notion of reciprocity to fit the relations between people belonging to differing generations, most obviously when the time spans of the generations overlap (Gosseries, Chapter 12). However, these extensions have their limits and it would be extremely far-fetched to think of all generations standing in a normatively significant relation of reciprocity towards each other. This is the source of what has been dubbed the 'pure intergenerational problem' (Gardiner, Chapter 14).

In any case, Rawls suggests an alternative understanding of the intergenerational original position: The representatives all belong to one and the same generation but when their generation will exist they do not know (Rawls, Chapter 2, pp. 18–19 below). For contemporaries the circumstances of justice hold. However, as their representatives in the intergenerational original position so conceived cannot know whether previous generations saved for them, Rawls first stipulated a motivational assumption according to which representatives care about their successors and thus will want to save for them no matter whether previous generations saved for them or not (ibid., p. 19). In his later work Rawls gives up this motivational assumption and understands the problem that previous generations did not fulfill their duties as specified by the just savings principle as a problem of non-ideal theory (Rawls, Chapter 10, esp. pp. 211 and 221–2). For ideal theory strict compliance with the principles as adopted in the original position is assumed. Thus the savings rate as adopted in the original position has ideal validity for all generations (Rawls, 1993, pp. 385–6). To be sure, holding the savings principle to be ideally justified in this sense does not necessarily suffice to motivate an agent to act accordingly and, a fortiori, when she knows that past societies did not and many current societies do not comply with the principle. Rawls does not address the question of what other than the purely moral motivation to do the morally right thing may in fact sufficiently motivate people to care for the well-being of distant future people. Practically speaking, this is the most important issue (Birnbacher, Chapter 9; also: Birnbacher, 1988, pp. 140–79; Jonas, 1979, pp. 63–4).

Rawls distinguishes two phases of societal development for the application of his distributive principle of just savings. Currently living people have reason to save positively for future people (so that future people will have more resources at their disposal than they themselves) if such savings are necessary 'to establish (reasonably) just basic institutions... and to secure a social world that makes possible a worthwhile life for all its citizens' (Rawls, Chapter 10, p. 211 below) – in the so-called accumulation phase. When just basic institutions have been established, positive saving is no longer required. Saving then serves the maintenance of just institutions in a sustainable manner (Barry, Chapter 9). In that second stage – known as the steady-state stage – people ought to leave their descendants at least the equivalent of what they received from the previous generation, namely, as Rawls understands it, 'the conditions needed to establish and to preserve a just basic structure over time' (Rawls, 2001, p. 159).

Rawls' savings principle provides us with a particularly sensible substantive interpretation of intergenerational sufficientarianism. Sufficientarianism requires that we ought to be concerned with the absolute level of well-being of persons by giving high priority to fulfilling the claim of all people, including future people, to live under conditions that allow them to have a sufficiently good or decent life (Meyer and Roser, Chapter 11). However, how many people will live in the future needs to be taken into account in determining the just savings rate (Heyd, 1992; Dasgupta, 1994; Casal and Williams, 1995; Gosseries, 2001). A growing population can bring about that if, as Rawls requires of us in that second stage, we were to leave our descendants the equivalent of what we received from the previous generation, future generations may not be able to maintain a just basic structure of institutions: As more people are likely to use up more resources in fulfilling their basic needs, less resources would be left for the preservation of just institutions. One response to this problem is to adjust to the size of the future population how much currently living people ought to hand down to or preserve for future people (Barry, Chapter 9).

The issue of how to understand the significance of the expected size of the future population for specifying obligations of distributive intergenerational justice brings us back to the non-identity problem, this time with respect to the possibility of currently living people benefiting future people: Insofar as their population policies influence people's procreational choices, do policy-makers have reasons to make an attempt at increasing or decreasing the size of the population out of regard for possible future persons? (Analogously at the individual level: When potential parents make decisions about having children or not, do they have reasons out of regard for the interests of their possible future children to bring them into existence or to refrain from doing so?) Many have contributed to the debate on whether and how an asymmetry of our procreational duties can be justified (Narveson, Chapter 1; Narveson, 1973; Parfit, 1976; Govier, 1979, p. 111; Heyd 1992, pp. 96–7, 102, 105–6, 241–2; Mulgan, 2006, ch. 6). The claimed asymmetry is the following: While prospective parents have no obligation to procreate out of regard for the interests of possible future children, even if they can expect that their would-be children will be very happy, they have an obligation not to beget children who are going to be miserable (and analogously for policy-makers: while out of regard for the interests of possible future people they have no obligation to increase the number of happy lives, they have an obligation to hinder the bringing into existence of seriously miserable people). There is also a related problem: Many, if not most, of us hold we ought to help people to extend their lives as long as they are worth living or, in other words, that we have an obligation to increase the length of existing happy lives. But it is less than obvious that this claim is compatible with holding that we have no obligation to increase the number of happy lives (Arrhenius, Chapter 13). Whether we can hold both views coherently will depend upon our understanding of the normative relevance of the non-identity problem for benefiting persons: The non-identity problem concerns not only the possibility of harming possible future people but, in an analogous way, the possibility of benefiting possible future people. If benefiting a person means to act in such a way that she is better off at some later time had we not carried out the action, and if not carrying out the seemingly beneficial action means that the seemingly better-off person did not exist, then this person cannot be considered benefited by the action having been carried out. Then out of regard for the interests of possible future people we could not hold an obligation to bring happy people into existence, but out of regard for the interests of existing persons we might hold an obligation to benefit them by, for example, extending their happy lives (Parfit, 1984, pp. 487–90).

Satisfying people's basic needs or protecting their basic human rights can count as a minimal demand of justice. Accordingly the establishment and preservation of conditions under which basic needs can be satisfied is a minimal demand of intergenerational justice (Brundtland et al., 1987, p. 47). Here I will presuppose that future people can legitimately claim that much and that currently living people hold the corresponding duties of justice vis-à-vis future people. However, according to 'pure time preference' temporally distant benefits are less important than temporally close benefits and, normatively speaking, protecting the just claims of future persons is less important than protecting the current or less distant claims of contemporaries (or future persons) even if everything else – except the time of the realization of these claims – remains the same. Thus, even though future people are considered to be bearers of just claims vis-à-vis currently living people, their claims ought to have little or close to no weight in our practical deliberation – how much depends on the 'discount rate' to be applied. Typically, philosophers reject pure time preference since from the perspective of those who ought to count equally, namely the bearers of just claims, nothing seems to speak in favour of holding that, for example, satisfying their basic needs is less important for them when they happen to be in a dire situation in fifty years' time rather than now (see, for example, Parfit, 1984, pp. 480–86; Cowen and Parfit, 1992).

However, we may have reasons for valuing temporally distant benefits less than temporally close ones without implying that this must be so due to pure time preference (Broome, Chapter 6; Parfit, 1984, pp. 487–90; Caney, 2009; Meyer and Roser, 2011). For example, because many commodities are less valuable for wealthy people than for poor people, wealth is a circumstance that affects the value of benefits. If future people really can be expected to be wealthier, then it is this correlation (and not time itself) that explains that we have more reason to confer the commodities to people who are temporally closer to us – and if, in fact, the situation were reversed, we should discount in favour of future people. Discounting based on such a wide understanding of time preference – for which we might have a good number of reasons – is compatible with rejecting pure time preference.

Climate Change and Intergenerational Justice

Intergenerational justice in both time dimensions – namely what currently living people owe to future people and how to interpret the normative significance of what past people did – is of central importance in providing an interpretation of what ought to be done in responding to climate change. Among key features of climate change are the following (IPCC, 2007): So-called greenhouse gases in the atmosphere affect the climate on planet earth. Since industrialization, humankind has added to their concentration significantly, in particular through carbon dioxide emissions. People realize numerous benefits when they engage in emission-generating activities, such as developing infrastructure, producing industrial goods as well as food, driving cars or engaging in deforestation. It is very probable that the effects of the emissions of these human activities will be harmful overall rather than beneficial. As far as the harmful effects are concerned, it does not matter where on the globe the emissions causing them occur. And much of the climate change that is caused by emissions materializes with a time lag of several decades after the occurrence of those emissions. From the perspective of intergenerational justice the most important fact is that, even though industrialization in the developed countries is responsible for a large part of the build-up in greenhouse gases, people in the developing countries – in particular those living in the future – will suffer disproportionally more from climate change. Developed countries, despite hosting a clear minority of the world's population, were responsible for more than three times as many emissions between 1850 and 2002 than developing countries (Baumert et al., 2005, p. 32). At the same time, people of the developing countries – in particular those living in the future – will suffer disproportionally more from climate change. Developing countries are more vulnerable to climate change due to geographical factors (such as higher temperatures, even before climate change), higher reliance on agriculture, which is an especially vulnerable sector, and lower adaptive capacities (IPCC, 2007, esp. § 3.3). We face an asymmetry: the asymmetry of, on the one hand and on the side of the developed countries, having main historical and causal responsibility for climate change as well as large benefits from emission-generating activities and small damages from the resulting climate change and of, on the other hand and on the side of the developing countries, having comparatively little historical and causal responsibility as well as small benefits from emission-generating activities but large (current as well as future) damages from the resulting climate change. This asymmetry suggests that, normatively speaking, the problem of climate change can be understood as a distributive intergenerational problem with a significant historical dimension.

First, let us look at the intergenerational dimension with respect to the future. Here the question of intergenerational justice is concerned with the duties of present generations (of both developing and industrialized countries) towards future generations in view of the fact that the present emissions affect the environmental conditions of the future. This can be understood as a question of distributive intergenerational justice. In order for a question of distributive justice to arise, a certain amount of a given good must be available for distribution. The given good in question here is benefits from emission-generating activities. Emitting itself is not beneficial but rather the activities which have emissions as their necessary by-product. Nature by itself does not set a 'natural' stopping point for our emitting greenhouse gases. This is different in many other cases of distributive justice where the good in question is strictly (or somewhat) limited, such as land or GDP. So, if there is to be a maximum limit on emissions, it has to be determined by us – it cannot be taken as given. The most straightforward justification of a maximum limit on emissions follows the lines of the section 'Saving for Future People' above:[6] Assuming that future people will suffer serious harm in terms of the violation of their basic rights when temperatures rise above a certain level and, further, that currently living people can hinder such temperature rise by limiting their emissions to a certain amount, a global cap on emissions is required for currently living people to be able to fulfil their minimal duties of justice vis-à-vis future generations. In imposing a global cap on emissions, currently living people will help to establish or preserve conditions of life for future people that will allow them to have a sufficiently good or decent life. Of course, this line of reasoning presupposes both that currently living people can harm future people and that the protection of future persons' basic rights (or the fulfilment of their basic needs) gives them reason to act. That is, justifying a global cap on emissions as a matter of intergenerational justice[7] presupposes a response to the non-identity problem along the lines in the section above on 'The Non-Identity Problem' so that future people can have welfare claim rights vis-à-vis currently living people. It also presupposes the rejection of 'pure time preference' so that protecting the just claims of future persons cannot be considered to be insignificant, normatively speaking, as explained in the section 'Saving for Future People' above.

A second important question of climate justice concerns the division of emission rights (given that they are to be limited) and other burdens and benefits among the present generations, in particular between developing and industrialized countries. On the face of it this is a question of global distributive justice, but it is a question which, some philosophers have argued, must take into account intergenerational relations, namely the differing levels of both past emissions and future vulnerabilities (Caney, Chapter 15). A number of objections have been raised against taking into account past emissions. Colloquially put, some of the important and often raised objections are (see also Posner and Weisbach, 2010, ch. 5): First, I cannot be responsible for the sins of my ancestors; second, my ancestors cannot be blamed for their emissions since until recently people did not know about their harmful effects for future people; and, third, in any case, people living today would not exist as the persons they are had previously living people not engaged in the emission-generating activities as they did and thus nobody is better or worse off owing to the emissions of previously living people. However, it is questionable whether these objections justify not taking into account all past emissions and their consequences from the perspective of distributive justice. If we are concerned with the distribution of benefits from emission-generating activities during the whole lifespan of individual people, then we should take into account currently living people's benefits from their own emission-generating activities since their birth. Also, and again since their birth or conception, currently living people have benefited from past people's actions that have emissions as a side-product and, as indicated above, highly unequally so. These ways of taking into account the consequences of (some of the) past emissions is not open to the first and the second objection as stated. Also, the non-identity problem, on which the third objection is

---

[6] The following essays in this volume provide detailed analyses to work out the following sketch of an argument: Barry (Chapter 9), Meyer and Roser (Chapter 11), Gardiner (Chapter 14) and Caney (Chapter 15). See also Wolf (2009) and the contributions in Gardiner et al. (2010).

[7] Other considerations, such as considerations of international justice and the significance of the relations between humans and the rest of nature, may play a role in determining such a quota. On the former, see Gosseries (2007); on the latter, see, for example, von der Pfordten (1996).

based, is not relevant as the two ways of taking past emissions into account concern the distributive effects of emission-generating activities since after the identities of people have been determined, namely since their birth or conception (Meyer and Roser, Chapter 22).

While climate change has a historical dimension it can hardly be described as a typical case of historical injustice, as the second objection correctly points out. Climate change does not raise most of the issues we face when we seek adequate ways of responding to typical cases of historical injustices, such as the Nazi genocide committed against the European Jews, the enslavement of millions of Africans in the Americas or the forceful expulsion of indigenous peoples from their territories during the colonization of the Americas and Australia.[8] The case of climate change differs from these standard instances of historical injustice in a number of ways. First, the activity that constitutes the problem (that is, emission-generating activities and their long-term consequences) is not something that is wrong per se (such as genocide or slavery), but rather is only wrongful when done excessively. Second, until recently (though it is debatable until when exactly – La Rovere et al., 2002; Gosseries, 2004a[9]) people could not be blamed for not knowing about the long-term harmful consequences of the emissions they generated as a by-product of their activities. Third, in the case of climate change the situation is that earlier (and past) generations of one region (the North) directly affect(ed) something to the detriment of later (and currently living) generations of the other region (the South). When it comes to the harmful consequences of climate change, so far at least we have very few past victims (and indirect victims) and, owing to the first two observations, those harmed are likely not to have been wronged. Fourth, the case of climate change also differs from standard cases of historical injustice in that it is not a problem of people within a limited (and often short) period of time having been wronged and others having committed the wrongs or wrongfully benefiting. Also, those who are mainly responsible for causing climate change and those who suffer under it do not belong to specific political communities. Rather, victims, wrongdoers and beneficiaries are dispersed (but unequally so) among different communities and generations.

As climate change differs from the standard cases of historical injustice, we do not face the main issues of responding to historical injustice as introduced above in the sections 'Historical Injustices and Their Consequences' and 'Duties vis-à-vis Past People': First, as emissions mostly cause damage with a time lag of many decades and as the normatively relevant damages have materialized recently, or will harm future people, we will not have to investigate the status of so-called indirect victims or the direct victims' descendants and their claims to compensation and restitution. Also, the issue of supersession – that is, that the consequences of an historical injustice are legitimate today owing to changed circumstances – does not arise. Second, as we have no or, at most, very few past victims of wrong-doing, we do not have to engage with the issue of currently living people's duties towards them.

However, the normative situation will change if currently living people do not fulfil their intergenerational duties of justice vis-à-vis future people with respect to climate justice. Currently living people have such duties if it is the case that they can be said to know not only

---

[8] For detailed philosophical interpretations of historical injustice in general, see Thompson (2003), Meyer (2004a), Meyer (2005) and Schefczyk (2011).

[9] Gosseries lists and discusses some salient dates which might serve as an alternative to 1990: 1840 (as proposed by the Brazilian Proposal), 1896 (first scientific text on the greenhouse effect by Svante Arrhenius), 1967 (first serious modelling exercises) and 1995 (second IPCC report).

about the seriously harmful consequences of their emission-generating activities for future people, but also about effective measures to protect future people's basic rights and if they can implement these policies at reasonable costs to themselves.[10] Failing to fulfil their duties vis-à-vis future people would then constitute harmful wrong-doing. This finding is particularly relevant for the inhabitants of industrialized countries: Almost any argument on climate justice points in the direction of ascribing higher duties of reducing the harmful consequences of climate change to the industrialized countries (for example, Shue, 1993; Singer, 2002, ch. 2; Page, 2006; Caney, Chapter 15; Meyer and Roser, Chapter 22).

References

Ackerman, B.A. (1997), 'Temporal Horizons of Justice', *Journal of Philosophy*, **94**, pp. 299–31.
Barry, B. (1977), 'Justice between Generations', in P.M.S. Hacker and J. Raz (eds), *Law, Morality and Society. Essays in Honor of H.L.A. Hart*, Oxford: Clarendon Press, pp. 268–84.
——— (1989), *Theories of Justice. A Treatise on Social Justice, Vol. I*, London: Harvester-Wheatsheaf.
——— (1995), *Justice as Impartiality. A Treatise on Social Justice, Vol. II*, Oxford: Clarendon Press.
Baumert, K., Herzog, T. and Pershing, J. (2005), *Navigating the Numbers: Greenhouse Gas Data and International Climate Policy*, Washington: World Resources Institute.
Benatar, D. (2006), *Better Never to Have Been. The Harm of Coming Into Existence*, Oxford: Clarendon Press.
Birnbacher, D. (1988), *Verantwortung für zukünftige Generationen*, Stuttgart: Reclam.
Brooks, R.L. (ed.) (1999), *When Sorry Isn't Enough. The Controversy over Apologies and Reparations for Human Injustice*, New York and London: New York University Press.
Brundtland, G.H. et al. (1987), *Our Common Future: The World Commission on Environment and Development*, New York: Oxford University Press.
Buchanan, A., Brock, D.W., Daniels, N. and Wikler, D. (2000), *From Chance to Choice. Genetics and Justice*, Cambridge: Cambridge University Press.
Caney, S. (2009), 'Climate Change and the Future. Discounting for Time, Wealth, and Risk', *Journal of Social Philosophy*, **40**, pp. 163–86.
Casal, P. and Williams, A. (1995), 'Rights, Equality and Procreation', *Analyse und Kritik*, **17**, pp. 93–116.
Cowen, T. and Parfit, D. (1992), 'Against the Social Discount Rate', in P. Laslett and J.S. Fishkin (eds), *Justice Between Age Groups and Generations*, New Haven and London: Yale University Press, pp. 144–61.
Dasgupta, P. (1994), 'Savings and Fertility', *Philosophy and Public Affairs*, **23**, pp. 99–127.
De George, R. (1981), 'The Environment, Rights, and Future Generations', in E. Partridge (ed.), *Responsibilities to Future Generations. Environmental Ethics*, New York: Prometheus Books, pp. 157–66.
Dobson, A. (ed.) (1999), *Fairness and Futurity. Essays on Environmental Sustainability*, Oxford: Oxford University Press.
Feinberg, J. (1977), 'Harm and Self-Interest', in P.M.S. Hacker and J. Raz (eds), *Law, Morality and Society. Essays in Honor of H.L.A. Hart*, Oxford: Clarendon Press, pp. 284–308.
——— (1980), 'The Rights of Animals and Unborn Generations', in J. Feinberg, *Rights, Justice, and the Bounds of Liberty. Essays in Social Philosophy*, Princeton: Princeton University Press, pp. 159–84.

---

[10] For an analysis of the economic costs, see, for example, Stern (2007); for philosophical investigations into the ability of currently living people's to fulfill their duties vis-à-vis future people, see Birnbacher (Chapter 7); and see especially Gardiner (2011).

—— (1984), *The Moral Limits of the Criminal Law, Vol. 1, Harm to Others*, Oxford: Oxford University Press.
Fotion, N. and Heller, J.C. (eds) (1997), *Contingent Future Persons. On the Ethics of Deciding Who Will Live, or Not, in the Future*, Dordrecht, Boston and London: Kluwer Academic Publishers.
Gardiner, S.M. (2011), *A Perfect Moral Storm. The Ethical Tragedy of Climate Change*, Oxford: Oxford University Press.
Gardiner, S., Caney, S., Jamieson, D. and Shue, H. (2010), *Climate Ethics, Essential Readings*, New York: Oxford University Press.
Gosseries, A. (2001), 'What Do We Owe the Next Generation(s)?', *Loyola of Los Angeles Law Review*, **35**, pp. 293–354.
—— (2004a), 'Historical Emissions and Free Riding', *Ethical Perspectives*, **11**, pp. 36–60.
—— (2004b), *Penser la justice entre les générations. De l'affaire Perruche à la réforme des retraites*, Paris: Aubier.
—— (2007), 'Cosmopolitan Luck Egalitarianism and Climate Change', *Canadian Journal of Philosophy*, supp. vol. 31, pp. 279–309.
Gosseries, A. and Meyer, L.H. (eds) (2009), *Intergenerational Justice*, Oxford: Oxford University Press.
Govier, T. (1979), 'What Should We Do About Future People?', *American Philosophical Quarterly*, **16**, pp. 105–13.
Heyd, D. (1992), *Genethics: Moral Issues in the Creation of People*, Berkeley: University of California Press.
—— (2009), 'A Value or an Obligation: Rawls on Justice to Future Generations', in A. Gosseries and L.H. Meyer (eds), *Intergenerational Justice*, Oxford: Oxford University Press, pp. 167–88.
IPCC (Intergovernmental Panel on Climate Change) (2007), *Climate Change 2007. Synthesis Report. Contribution of Working Groups I, II and III to the Fourth Assessment Report of the Intergovernmental Panel on Climate Change*, ed. R.K. Pachauri and A. Reisinger, Geneva: IPCC.
Jonas, H. (1979), *Das Prinzip Verantwortung. Versuch einer Ethik für die technologische Zivilisation*, Frankfurt: Insel Verlag.
La Rovere, E., de Valente de Macedo, L. and Baumert, K. (2002), 'The Brazilian Proposal on Relative Responsibility for Global Warming', in K. Baumert, O. Blanchard, S. Llosa and J. Perkaus (eds), *Building on the Kyoto Protocol: Options for Protecting the Climate*, Washington: World Resources Institute, pp. 157–73.
Laslett, P. and Fishkin, J.S. (eds) (1992), *Justice Between Age Groups and Generations*, New Haven and London: Yale University Press.
Meyer, L.H. (2003), 'Past and Future. The Case for a Threshold Conception of Harm', in L.H. Meyer, S.L. Paulson and T.W. Pogge (eds), *Rights, Culture, and the Law. Themes from the Legal and Political Philosophy of Joseph Raz*, Oxford: Oxford University Press, pp. 143–59.
—— (ed.) (2004a), *Justice in Time. Responding to Historical Injustice*, Baden-Baden: Nomos.
—— (2004b), 'Surviving Duties and Symbolic Compensation', in L.H. Meyer (ed.), *Justice in Time. Responding to Historical Injustice*, Baden-Baden: Nomos, pp. 178–82.
—— (2005), *Historische Gerechtigkeit*, Berlin: de Gruyter.
—— (2008), 'Intergenerational Justice', in E.N. Zalta (ed.), *The Stanford Encyclopedia of Philosophy* (Spring 2008), at http://plato.stanford.edu/entries/justice-intergenerational/.
—— (2007), 'Historical Injustice and the Right to Return', in E. Benvenisti, C. Gans and S. Hanafi (eds), *Israel and the Palestinian Refugees*, Berlin, Heidelberg and New York: Springer, pp. 295–306.
Meyer, L.H. and Roser, D. (2011), 'The Timing of Benefits of Climate Policies. Reconsidering the Opportunity Cost Argument', *Jahrbuch für Wissenschaft und Ethik*, **16**, pp. 35–70.
Mill, J.S. (1969), 'Utilitarianism' (1861), in J.M. Robson (ed.), *Collected Works of John Stuart Mill, Vol. X: Essays on Ethics, Religion and Society*, Toronto: University of Toronto Press, pp. 203–60.

Miller, J. and Kumar, R. (eds) (2007), *Reparations: Interdisciplinary Inquiries*, Oxford: Oxford University Press.

Mulgan, T. (1999), 'The Place of the Dead in Liberal Political Philosophy', *Journal of Political Philosophy*, **7**, pp. 52–70.

────── (2006), *Future People. A Moderate Consequentialist Account of our Obligations to Future Generations*, Oxford: Clarendon Press.

Narveson, J. (1973), 'Moral Problems of Population', *The Monist*, **57**, pp 62–86.

Nozick, R. (1974), *Anarchy, State, and Utopia*, Oxford: Blackwell.

Page, E. (2006), *Climate Change, Justice and Future Generations*, Cheltenham: Edward Elgar.

Parfit, D. (1976), 'On Doing the Best for Our Children', in M.D. Bayles (ed.), *Ethics and Population*, Cambridge: Schenkman, pp. 100–115.

────── (1982), 'Future Generations: Further Problems', *Philosophy & Public Affairs*, **11**, pp. 113–72.

────── (1984), *Reasons and Persons*, Oxford: Clarendon Press.

────── (1986), 'Comments', *Ethics*, **96**, pp. 832–72.

Partridge, E. (1981a), 'Posthumous Interests and Posthumous Respect', *Ethics*, **91**, pp. 243–64.

────── (ed.) (1981b), *Responsibilities to Future Generations. Environmental Ethics*, New York: Prometheus Books.

Patton, P. (2004), 'Colonization and Historical Injustice. The Australian Experience', in L.H. Meyer (ed.), *Justice in Time. Responding to Historical Injustice*, Baden-Baden: Nomos, pp. 159–72.

Pitcher, G. (1984), 'The Misfortunes of the Dead', *American Philosophical Quarterly*, **21**, pp. 183–8.

Pogge, T.W. (2004), 'Historical Wrongs. The Two Other Domains', in L.H. Meyer (ed.), *Justice in Time. Responding to Historical Injustice*, Baden-Baden: Nomos, pp. 117–34.

Posner E.A. and Weisbach, D. (2010), *Climate Change Justice*, Princeton and Oxford: Princeton University Press.

Ramsey, F.P. (1928), 'A Mathematical Theory of Savings', *The Economic Journal*, **38**, pp. 543–59.

Rawls, J. (1971), *A Theory of Justice*, Oxford: Oxford University Press; 2nd rev edn, Cambridge, MA: Harvard University Press, 1999.

────── (1993), *Political Liberalism*, New York: Columbia University Press.

────── (2001), *Justice as Fairness*, Cambridge, MA: Harvard University Press.

Roberts M.A. (1998), *Child versus Childmaker: Future Persons and Present Duties in Ethics and the Law*, Lanham: Rowman & Littlefield.

Roberts, M.A. and Wasserstein, D.T. (eds) (2009), *Harming Future People: Ethics, Genetics and the Nonidentity Problem*, Dordrecht: Springer.

Ryberg, J. and Tännsjö, T. (eds) (2004), *The Repugnant Conclusion. Essays on Population Ethics*, Dordrecht, Boston and London: Kluwer Academic Publishers.

Schefczyk, M. (2011), *Verantwortung für historisches Unrecht. Eine philosophische Untersuchung*, Berlin and New York: de Gruyter.

Shue, H. (1993), 'Subsistence Emissions and Luxury Emissions', *Law and Policy*, **15**, pp. 39–59.

Singer, P. (2002), *One World: The Ethics of Globalization*, New Haven and London: Yale University Press.

Sikora R.I. and Barry, B. (eds) (1978), *Obligations to Future Generations*, Philadelphia: Temple University Press.

Simmons, A.J. (1995), 'Historical Rights and Fair Shares', *Law and Philosophy*, **12**, pp. 149–84, 178–9.

Stern, N. (2007), *The Economics of Climate Change. The Stern Review*, Cambridge: Cambridge University Press.

Thompson, J. (2003), *Taking Responsibility for the Past*, Cambridge: Polity.

────── (2009), *Intergenerational Justice: Rights and Responsibilities in an Intergenerational Polity*, New York and London: Routledge.

Von der Pfordten, D. (1996), Ökologische *Ethik. Zur Rechtfertigung menschlichen Verhaltens gegenüber der Natur*, Reinbek bei Hamburg: Rowohlt.

Waldron, J. (2004), 'Redressing Historic Injustice', in L.H. Meyer (ed.), *Justice in Time. Responding to Historical Injustice*, Baden-Baden: Nomos, pp. 55–77.

Waluchow, W.J. (1986), 'Feinberg's Theory of "Preposthumous" Harm', *Dialogue*, **25**, pp. 727–34.

Wellman, C. (1995), *Real Rights*, New York, Oxford: Oxford University Press.

Wolf, C. (2009), 'Intergenerational Justice, Human Needs, and Climate Policy', in A. Gosseries and L.H. Meyer (eds), *Intergenerational Justice*, Oxford: Oxford University Press, pp. 347–76.

Woodward, J. (1986), 'The Non-Identity Problem', *Ethics*, **96**, pp. 804–31.

——— (1987), 'Reply to Parfit', *Ethics*, **97**, 800–17.

Part I
Foundations

[1]
UTILITARIANISM AND NEW GENERATIONS
By Jan Narveson

ONE of the stock objections to utilitarianism goes like this: "If utilitarianism is correct, then we must be obliged to produce as many children as possible, so long as their happiness would exceed their misery." It has always seemed to me that there is a certain air of sophistry about this argument, and in this paper, I shall endeavor to demonstrate this by exposing the fallacies upon which it is founded. I shall also consider in its own right the question of the nature and extent of our duties in the line of procreation, if any, on the utilitarian principle. To this end, three preliminary matters must be explained.

To begin with, there are two radically different questions here, of which the first is the crucial one. On the one hand, there is the question of whether we should produce person X because X would be happy if produced. Let us call this the question of the 'direct effects' upon the general happiness; clearly, it is what is in point. The other question is this: should we produce person X, if we can foresee that X's existence will have a favorable effect on the happiness of other people besides X, e.g. his parents, or people who might benefit from his activities. Later on, I shall suggest that the appearance of plausibility to the objection probably stems from a subtle confusion between these two different questions. I shall spend most of my time on the first question, reserving the second until the final section of the paper.

In the second place, there is some difference of opinion about the way in which the utilitarian theory is to be formulated. Those who have put the objection are assuming that according to the utilitarian, there is a certain sort of mental state called "pleasure" or "happiness", of which it is our obligation to produce as much as possible, by whatever means. Let us call this the "greatest total happiness" formulation. But it is obviously not the one which Bentham and Mill had in mind. Their formulations, as everybody knows, have it that the "greatest happiness of the greatest number" is the end of morality. This view Smart and Flew call the "greatest average happiness" view, though as I shall show below this characterization is somewhat misleading. Now, it supposedly follows directly from the "total" view that we have a duty to produce children if they would be happy; though I am inclined to think that the view involves a further confusion which, if taken account of, might clear even it of this charge to some extent. But at any rate, it is much less clear that the classical view has any such implication. For that we are to aim at the greatest happiness *of* the greatest number, does not imply that we are to aim at the greatest happiness *and* the greatest number. In order to make this perfectly clear, note that the classical utilitarians' view may be put this way : everyone should be as happy as possible. Cast into modern logical form, this reads, " For all persons x, x should be as happy as possible ", and this is equivalent to, " if a person exists, he should be as happy a possible ". This last shows clearly that the classical formulation does not imply that as many happy people as possible should be brought into existence.

The third point is to be clear about the general idea of the utilitarian theory about morality. It is often thought that according to that theory, if we like jam, then we have a duty to eat jam. This is nonsense. The whole point of the utilitarian theory is that people should be permitted, in so far as possible, to do as they please. As in all moral theories, utilitarianism picks out as duties those acts which you should be constrained to do. You may or may not like doing your duty, but if you do not, that is irrelevant. Now, it makes sense to say that you have a duty to do something which you happen to enjoy doing anyway ; but it does not make sense to say that you have a duty to do something *on the ground that* you like it. To assert a duty is to deny the permissibility of the opposite. Consequently, if you say that I have a duty to do whatever I like, there is nothing whose permissibility I am denying : if I liked doing A, I still could not have a duty to do A, since I could also do not-A if I liked.

What *is* true is that for the classical utilitarian, the sole ground of duty is the effects of our action on other people, and from this it follows that whenever one has a duty, it *must* be possible to say on whose account the duty arises—i.e. *whose* happiness is in question. In deciding what we are to do, the only consideration which is morally relevant, according to utilitarianism, is how others would be affected. If we cannot envisage effects on certain people which would ensue from our acts, then we have no moral material to work on and we can do as we like.

II

We are now in a position to throw light on the problem before us. The oddity in this kind of question, of course, consists in the fact that if a person is not born, he does not exist. I am neglecting the question about the point at which a person comes into existence. Those who would wish to consider embryos as a kind of person may simply replace ' born ' and ' birth ' with ' conceived ' and 'conception' throughout. And as we all know, non-existent people are not just a special kind of people; therefore, unborn people are also not just a special kind of people. Further, " people " are among the things you can point to, see, hear, and so forth. There is no such thing as an " abstract person ", though we may indeed talk in the abstract about people (concrete).

Consider now the sentential form, " if x were born, x would be happy; therefore, x ought to be born ". We assume the utilitarian principle as the suppressed major premiss. Now, there are two types of logical expression which can be substituted for 'x' in such an argument, namely, proper names and descriptions. Let us examine each in turn. To begin with, no sensible proposition can be formed of the consequent in the minor premiss of an argument of this form, by replacing the blanks (x's) with proper names, since, for example, " Hiram Jones ought to be born " makes no sense. If 'Hiram Jones' refers, then he already is born and there is no open question left as to whether he " ought to be born"; and if, on the other hand, it does not refer, then it is not (logically) a proper name, there being nothing for it to name.

Notice, incidentally, that the point just made does not depend upon the temporality of personal existence. The name 'Hiram Jones' refers, logically speaking, no matter when Jones is alive. But whether or not Jones lives in the future, it is still true of him, whenever he may live, that he was born, and consequently it is in any case nonsense to say that he ought to be born.

Nor am I denying that we may sensibly ask, once he *is* born, whether he *should have been* born. This is in many cases an interesting question, though not a very practical one under the circumstances. Some people should not have been born; and as there are other people whose existence is a good thing, we may say of them that they, in the same sense, " should have been born " ; though of course they *were*, and it is not a point of much practical importance so far as it concerns the individual the desirability of whose birth is in question. Hitler should not have been born, Churchill should have been born, and there are other cases where it is debatable—though I admit that all such questions, are, as we say, " merely theoretical ". What I am claiming is that, if we regard 'Hitler' and 'Churchill' as proper names, Hitler's mother and Churchill's mother could not have presented themselves, prior to their conceptions, with sensible questions of the form, " ought we to give birth to Hitler? ", " Ought we to give birth to Churchill? " The latter appear to be parallel to, " ought I to spank Adolph? ", " Ought I to spank Winston? " ; but they plainly are not.

Suppose, on the other hand, that we complete the argument-forms by replacing our 'x' with descriptions. Thus we might say, "someone should be born who would bring peace to the world"; and supposing that we could know that *our* boy, if born, would bring peace to the world, we might argue that this is a good reason for bringing him into existence. As indeed it is, but we have shifted our question here, and are no longer answering the one we set out to discuss. For we began by resolving to discuss the question, whether the *direct* effects of bringing someone into the world could be a reason for so doing, and "bringing peace into the world" is not of this kind. I said at the outset that the distinction between direct and indirect effects in reference to this question was a vital one, and I am about to show why. So far, then, the question is whether we could argue as follows: "our boy, if born, would be very happy; therefore we ought to produce him." In order to show why this argument is not sanctioned by the principle of utility, whereas the former perhaps is, we must turn again to the third point argued above.

III

Three possible outcomes of an act are of interest from the utilitarian point of view. The act either will (1) increase the general happiness, (2) decrease the general happiness, or (3) have no effect on the general happiness. Neglecting such interesting but here irrelevant questions as how you decide which in fact will result, there is an important question as to just which of the three is such as to give rise to a duty, if any; but let us say for purposes of the present discussion that, in cases where the different things we can do would some of them eventuate x in (1), others in (2), and others in (3), it is our duty to avoid (2) and prefer (1). In other words, it is only with increases and decreases in the general happiness that we are morally concerned if we are utilitarians. And this means that when we specify the individuals who would be affected by our actions, as we must on the utilitarian view, the characteristic about those people with which we are morally concerned is whether their happiness will be increased or decreased. If an action would have no effects whatever on the general happiness, then it would be morally *indifferent*: we could do it or not, just as we pleased. Hence whether to do it or not would be a non-moral question, which could only be solved by non-moral considerations. If I were to have a candy bar, this would normally have no effect on the happiness of others; hence whether I am to do it or not is entirely a question, according to the utilitarians, of whether I want to or not, which is not a question about what I morally ought to do but rather one about what I *like* to do. Now, to which of these types does our present question belong: is it a moral or a non-moral one? I will show that it is ordinarily a *non-moral* one, and that in the case where it is a moral one, then it is because of its indirect effects. "Direct effects," I shall show, can only give rise to the duty *not* to have children and can never give rise to a duty to have them. Having children, in other words, is normally a matter of moral indifference. Let us see why this is so.

In order to show that the general happiness would be increased by our having a child, the argument would have to go as follows. Imagine that the total number of people is N, and that the total happiness is H, the average happiness therefore being $N/H = 1$. Now suppose that we have good evidence that any child produced by us would be twice as happy as that, giving him a value of 2. Then the average happiness after he is born will be $\frac{N+2}{H+1}$, which would be somewhat larger, therefore, than before. Does this give us a moral reason to produce children? No. We have committed a fallacy.

Suppose that we live in a certain country, say, Fervia, and we are told by our king that something is about to happen which will greatly increase the general happiness of the Fervians: namely that a certain city on Mars, populated by extremely happy Martians will shortly become a part of Fervia. Since these new Fervians are very happy, the average happiness, hence the "general happiness" of the Fervians will be greatly increased. Balderdash. If you were a Fervian, would you be impressed by this reasoning? Obviously not. What has happened, of course, is simply that the base upon which the average was calculated has been shifted. When the Fervians are told that their happiness will be affected by something, they assume that the happiness of those presently understood by them as being Fervians will be increased. The king has pulled the wool over their eyes by using, in effect, a fallacy of four terms: 'Fervians' refers to one group of people on one occasion—"The general happiness of the Fervians$_1$ will be increased ",—and another on another occasion—" Hence, the general happiness of the Fervians$_2$ has been increased ". Because the Fervians$_2$ are a different group from the Fervians$_1$, although including the latter, it is a mere piece of sophistry to say that an increase in the happiness of the Fervians has come about as a result of this new acquisition of Martian citizenry. The fraud lies in the fact that no *particular* Fervian's happiness has been increased; whereas the principle of utility requires that before we have a moral reason for doing something, it must be because of a change in the happiness of some of the affected persons.

The argument that an increase in the general happiness will result from our having a happy child involves precisely the same fallacy. If you ask, " whose happiness has been increased as a result of his being born? ", the answer is that nobody's has. Of course, his being born might have indirect effects on the general happiness, but that is quite another matter. The " general populace " is just as happy as it was before; now, what of our new personnel? Remember that the question we must ask about him is not whether he is happy, but whether he is happier as a result of being born. And if put this way, we see that again we have a piece of nonsense on our hands if we suppose that the answer is either " yes " or " no ". For if it is, then with whom, or with what, are we comparing his new state of bliss? Is the child, perhaps, happier than he used to be before he was born? Or happier, perhaps, than his alter ego? Obviously, there can be no sensible answer here. The child cannot be happi*er* as a result of being born, since we would than have a relative term lacking one relatum. The child's happiness has not been increased, in any intelligible sense, as a result of his being born; and since nobody else's has either, directly, there is no moral reason for bringing him into existence.

IV

But, you say, would not the world be better off than it was before, even though in your sense the general happiness has not been increased as a result of his being born? As Smart has put it,

> . . . would you be quite indifferent between (a) a universe containing only one million happy sentient beings, all equally happy, and (b) a universe containing two million happy beings, each neither more or less happy than any in the first universe? Or would you, as a humane and sympathetic person, give a preference to the second universe? I myself cannot help feeling a preference for the second universe. But if someone feels the other way I do not know how to argue with him. It looks as though we have yet another possibility of disagreement within a general utilitarian framework.[1]

This being the remark of one of the few thorough-going proponents of the utilitarian theory extant, it is in order to point out what is wrong here. It is true, of course, that utilitarianism is supposed

[1] J. J. C. Smart, *Outline of a System of Utilitarian Ethics* (Melbourne, 1961), p. 18.

to appeal to "sympathetic and benevolent" men (—as well as everyone else !). And no doubt a person who was sympathetic and benevolent by nature might be inclined to prefer Smart's second universe to his first. But I suggest that if he does, the inclination is morally irrelevant; and the reason Smart would not know how to argue with a person preferring the first or being indifferent, is that there is no moral argument at issue here. How large a population you like is purely a matter of taste, except in cases where a larger population would, due to indirect effects, be happier than the first, the latter possibility to be discussed below. And having children is also purely a matter of taste, for the same reason, and with the same exception.

Consider what a person who would claim that the larger universe is the better "because there is more happiness in it", is asserting. According to utilitarianism, as I pointed out earlier, all obligations and indeed all moral reasons for doing anything must be grounded upon the existence of persons who would benefit or be injured by the effects of our actions. From this it follows that a man's objective moral goodness is a function of the number of people whom he benefits or injures, for any given population of the universe. But the man who says "the more happiness, the better" is going far beyond this view. For he is saying that if the universe does not contain the possibility of your doing good or harm, then it is your duty to go out of your way to create situations in which you *could* do good (or harm). To put it another way: the existence of duties and of moral reasons for doing things depends, in the utilitarian conception, upon the existence of people. Consequently, one can increase the number of situations in which one has duties and moral reasons, as opposed to merely personal reasons, for doing things by increasing the population. But on whose view of morality is it our duty to go out of the way to create duties for ourselves? We believe that it is our duty to keep promises; must we also insist that, as a corollary, we must make as many promises as possible?

Such a view, incidentally, might lead to some weird consequences. Imagine a universe in which everyone is perfectly happy on account of his own efforts, so that nobody ever has a moral reason to do anything therein. Our so-called "utilitarian" who argues that we must increase the population for moral reasons, would have to say that such a universe is less desirable than one in which many people could be made happier by the efforts of others, and this in turn would, I suppose, have to be reckoned a worse one than one in which there were some sufferers whose suffering could be relieved by others ! But that such is not the utilitarian view should, I think, be perfectly evident. Quite the contrary : given a universe, it follows from utilitarianism, at least as Mill and Bentham construed it, that it would be best off if everyone in it were perfectly happy by his own efforts, and worse off if people had to constrain themselves from self-seeking by assisting others.

It must always be borne in mind that I am not arguing that there is no reason of *any* kind for preferring larger to smaller universes or vice versa. In the first place, within suitable limits, a larger population has a better chance for securing happiness to all than a smaller one owing to the necessities of industrialization and economic organization, and other such things. And in the second place, there is no reason on earth why people cannot *like* larger universes better than smaller ones. I am only pointing out that we must not confuse matters of taste with matters of morality. Those who argue that if they like larger populations better than small ones and therefore have a moral duty to make the population as large as possible, are in fact saying that they have a duty to make *themselves* happier : for the reason they must give for their actions is that the effect of them is to get something that they like. And this, as argued earlier, is wrong. There can be no question, on utilitarian principles, of a " duty " to do what one likes.

V

On the other hand, however, I now wish to argue that it does follow from utilitarian principles that, if we could predict that a child would be miserable if born, then it is our duty *not* to have it. This result, I admit, will look rather peculiar in view of my preceding argument ; but the peculiarity can be overcome if we consider certain logical points about duty-fulfilling and duty-transgressing.

As is generally accepted today, every statement describing a particular duty on a particular occasion must be backed up by a general principle of some kind, from which the particular one follows by application. Such is certainly the case with utilitarianism, at any rate. Now let us suppose, as is plausible, that two of our utilitarian duties are to avoid inflicting misery on people, and to reduce misery where it exists. The first of these is a general principle which might be put into logically precise form in some such manner as this : " each person x is such that for each person y, x should not inflict suffering on y ", while the second would be, " each person x is such that for each person y, if y is suffering, then x should reduce y's suffering ". Now, as we know, all general statements of a hypothetical form "(x) Fx ⊃ Gx)", are equivalent to universal disjunctions, "(x) (− Fx v Gx)". And this means that there are two ways of acting in accordance with either of these duties: either there is no person x upon whom to inflict suffering, or if there is, then to avoid inflicting it on him, in the first case; and in the second, either x is not suffering, or we reduce his suffering. I am, of course, neglecting complications such as supervening duties; also I am assuming that a duty to reduce suffering is a duty to *try* to reduce it.

On the other hand, there is only one way in which such a principle may be infringed, and that is by the occurrence of a state of affairs described by a true existentially quantified statement. Thus, I can infringe the first duty if the following statement is true: "there is someone on whom I have inflicted misery", and in the other case, "someone$_x$ is suffering and someone$_y$ has failed to reduce x's suffering".

From this analysis, it will again be evident that we cannot have a duty to produce children just because the latter would be happy. For even if it were our duty to make everyone as happy as possible, we would be guilty of no transgression of it if we were not to add to the population, though we would transgress it by making somebody less happy than he otherwise might have been. In other words, the duty being "each y is such that for each x, y should make x as happy as possible"; and if, say, "the son of Jones" does not exist, then it is not the case that Jones is failing to make his son as happy as possible. Or, to sum it up: true affirmative existential statements are not necessary to fulfil duties, but *are* necessary to *infringe* them.

Now let us suppose that we are contemplating having a child, who would, we know, be miserable. For example, suppose that we know he would have a hereditarily-acquired painful disease all his life; or that we are poverty-stricken unemployables living in a slum. In both these cases, we can reasonably predict that any child of ours would be miserable. Now, these miseries will be unavoidable if we produce the child; and consequently, a counter-instance to a duty statement will be true, namely: " a child of Smith's is miserable and the Smiths could have prevented this." This would violate the second duty. But quite likely it would violate the first too, for although one does not inflict pain on someone by giving birth to him even though he is in pain ever after, since if you cannot make someone happy by bearing him, you also cannot make him miserable by doing so, nevertheless in many such cases, *e.g.* the slum-dwelling case, you will actually have inflicted misery on the child, by underfeeding him, exposing him to disease, filth, and ugliness, making him associate with equally wretched persons, and so forth, and thus you will also have transgressed the first duty. And in both cases, you could have avoided these evils by not having the child in question.

If, therefore, it is our duty to prevent suffering and relieve it, it is also our duty not to bring children into the world if we know that they would suffer or that we would inflict suffering upon them. And incidentally, I think this also is a strong argument against those who think that it is our *duty* to make everyone as happy as possible. For this is a duty we could infringe by having a child who we know would not be as happy as possible. And of how many people can't *this* be foreseen? Frankly, I do not think there is any such duty on utilitarian principles, but it is something to think about for those who do.

VI

Finally, we may briefly consider the moral relevance of indirect effects on the " general happiness ". Clearly, it will often be the case that we can foresee good or bad effects on the existing population by the production of new people. If we assume, as seems reasonable enough to me, that an advanced civilization is likely to be happier than a primitive one, and that industrialization is necessary to advanced civilization, then it is obvious that a fairly substantial population will be necessary to achieve these desirable ends. On the other hand, as we also know, too large a population tends to have adverse effects from the agricultural point of view. With too much pressure on food supply, inferior lands have to be put into cultivation, and yield per man-hour tends to go down ; withal, if the pressure is too severe, as it is in some parts of the world today, one of two evils will set in : either some people will starve or be severely shorted in their diets while others have enough, so that the various evils resulting from inequality will set in, or everyone will have less than enough. In all likelihood, there is an optimum population for any particular piece of land at a given state of advancement in agricultural technology, as the economists tell us. A further consideration is the aesthetic effects of over- or under-population. If population is very dense, people will be crowded together, and will have little solitude. Further, little land will be available for parks and natural scenery. If it is too thin, on the other hand, human intercourse is much reduced, and the interesting by-products of cities, such as the ability to maintain art galleries and concert halls, and the support of architecturally interesting buildings, will be missed.

Now it seems to me clear that all of these considerations are of the sort which will provide what, in the narrowest sense, may be called " utilitarian " reasons for changing the sizes of populations. The only question of interest is which of these would give rise to genuine duties, and which merely to something less. My final suggestions, which the reader may take or leave, follows here.

Many critics of utilitarianism will object that according to this latest turn, we have a right to increase slave populations in order to benefit the rest. This is false, I believe, but the discussion of it would occupy too much space to be included here. Other objections of the same kind also seem to me misguided.

It is obvious that there can be good reasons for producing children, and also that there can be good ones for not producing them. But when are these sufficiently stringent to give rise to a duty rather than merely to a moral inducement? My own answer, which I cannot defend here, would be that whenever the production of new children would either result in misery for them, or would result in substantial decreases in the happiness of other people, it is one's duty not to have them. If, for example, one's child would be a burden upon the public, then it seems to me one has no right to produce him. It therefore seems to me that the public has the right to prohibit the having of children in such cases.

Is it *ever* one's duty to have children? I can think of only one case where it might. If it can be shown that the populace will suffer if its size is not increased, then it seems to me that one could perhaps require efforts in that direction, and punish those who could comply but do not. But I am inclined to think that such a situation is exceedingly rare.

There is one final question which might bring the whole issue into a sort of focus. This is : is there any *moral* point in the existence of a human race, as such? That is to say, would a universe containing people be morally better off than one containing no people? It seems to me that it would not be, as such, at any rate on utilitarian grounds. We might *prefer*, like Smart, a universe containing people to one that does not contain them, particularly since we presumably would not be able to occupy the second one ourselves ; but is this, then, a moral preference? It seems to me, again, that it is not, and that the effort to make it one is a mistake. Given people to have them toward, there will be duties ; but if we are not given them, questions of duty will not arise. And it is not a question of duty whether we should create new duties. Our duty is to fulfil them, once they are raised.

University of New Hampshire

[2]

DISTRIBUTIVE SHARES

John Rawls

THE PROBLEM OF JUSTICE BETWEEN GENERATIONS

We must now consider the question of justice between generations. There is no need to stress the difficulties that this problem raises. It subjects any ethical theory to severe if not impossible tests. Nevertheless, the account of justice as fairness would be incomplete without some discussion of this important matter. The problem arises in the present context because the question is still open whether the social system as a whole, the competitive economy surrounded by the appropriate family of background institutions, can be made to satisfy the two principles of justice. The answer is bound to depend, to some degree anyway, on the level at which the social minimum is to be set. But this in turn connects up with how far the present generation is bound to respect the claims of its successors.

So far I have said nothing about how generous the social minimum should be. Common sense might be content to say that the right level depends upon the average wealth of the country and that, other things equal, the minimum should be higher when the average increases. Or one might say that the proper level is determined by customary expectations. But these suggestions are unsatisfactory. The first is not precise enough since it does not say how the minimum depends on average wealth and it overlooks other relevant aspects such as distribution; while the second provides no criterion for telling when customary expectations are themselves reasonable. Once the difference principle is accepted, however, it follows that the minimum is to be set at that point which, taking wages into account, maximizes the expectations of the least advantaged group. By adjusting the amount of transfers (for example, the size of supplementary income payments), it is possible to increase or decrease the prospects of the more disadvantaged, their index of primary goods (as measured by wages plus transfers), so as to achieve the desired result.

Now offhand it might seem that the difference principle requires a very high minimum. One naturally imagines that the greater wealth of those better off is to be scaled down until eventually everyone has nearly the same income. But this is a misconception, although it might hold in special circumstances. The appropriate expectation in applying the difference principle is that of the long-term prospects of the least favored extending over future generations. Each generation must not only preserve the gains of culture and civilization, and maintain intact those just institutions that have been established, but it must also put aside in each period of time a suitable amount of real capital accumulation. This saving may take various forms from net investment in machinery and other means of production to investment in learning and education. Assuming for the moment that a just savings principle is available which tells us how great investment should be, the level of the social minimum is determined. Suppose for simplicity that the minimum is adjusted by transfers paid for by proportional expenditure (or income) taxes. In this case raising the minimum entails increasing the proportion by which consumption (or income) is taxed. Presumably as this fraction becomes larger there comes a point beyond which one of two things happens. Either the appropriate savings cannot be made or the greater taxes interfere so much with economic efficiency that the prospects of the least advantaged in the present generation are no longer improved but begin to decline. In either event the correct minimum has been reached. The difference principle is satisfied and no further increase is called for.

These comments about how to specify the social minimum have led us to the problem of justice between generations. Finding a just savings principle is one aspect of this question.[20] Now I believe that it is not

---

20. This problem is often discussed by economists in the context of the theory of economic growth. For an exposition see A. K. Sen, "On Optimizing the Rate of Saving," *Economic Journal,* vol. 71 (1961); James Tobin, *National Economic Policy* (New Haven, Yale University Press, 1966), ch. IX; and R. M. Solow, *Growth Theory* (New York, Oxford University Press, 1970), ch. V. In an extensive

44. Justice between Generations

possible, at present anyway, to define precise limits on what the rate of savings should be. How the burden of capital accumulation and of raising the standard of civilization and culture is to be shared between generations seems to admit of no definite answer. It does not follow, however, that certain significant ethical constraints cannot be formulated. As I have said, a moral theory characterizes a point of view from which policies are to be assessed; and it may often be clear that a suggested answer is mistaken even if an alternative doctrine is not ready to hand. Thus it seems evident, for example, that the classical principle of utility leads in the wrong direction for questions of justice between generations. For if one takes the size of the population as variable, and postulates a high marginal productivity of capital and a very distant time horizon, maximizing total utility may lead to an excessive rate of accumulation (at least in the near future). Since from a moral point of view there are no grounds for discounting future well-being on the basis of pure time preference, the conclusion is all the more likely that the greater advantages of future generations will be sufficiently large to outweigh most any present sacrifices. This may prove true if only because with more capital and better technology it will be possible to support a sufficiently large population. Thus the utilitarian doctrine may direct us to demand heavy sacrifices of the poorer generations for the sake of greater advantages for later ones that are far better off. But this calculus of advantages, which balances the losses of some against benefits to others, appears even less justified in the case of generations than among contemporaries. Even if we cannot define a precise just savings principle, we should be able to avoid this sort of extreme.

Now the contract doctrine looks at the problem from the standpoint of the original position and requires the parties to adopt an appropriate savings principle. It seems clear that as they stand the two principles of justice must be adjusted to this question. For when the difference principle is applied to the question of saving over generations, it entails either

---

literature, see F. P. Ramsey, "A Mathematical Theory of Saving," *Economic Journal*, vol. 38 (1928), reprinted in Arrow and Scitovsky, *Readings in Welfare Economics;* T. C. Koopmans, "On the Concept of Optimal Economic Growth" (1965) in *Scientific Papers of T. C. Koopmans* (Berlin, Springer Verlag, 1970). Sukamoy Chakravarty, *Capital and Development Planning* (Cambridge, M.I.T. Press, 1969), is a theoretical survey which touches upon the normative questions. If for theoretical purposes one thinks of the ideal society as one whose economy is in a steady state of growth (possibly zero), and which is at the same time just, then the savings problem is to choose a principle for sharing the burdens of getting to that growth path (or to such a path if there is more than one), and of maintaining the justice of the necessary arrangements once this is achieved. In the text, however, I do not pursue this suggestion; my discussion is at a more primitive level.

Distributive Shares

no saving at all or not enough saving to improve social circumstances sufficiently so that all the equal liberties can be effectively exercised. In following a just savings principle, each generation makes a contribution to those coming later and receives from its predecessors. There is no way for later generations to help the situation of the least fortunate earlier generation. Thus the difference principle does not hold for the question of justice between generations and the problem of saving must be treated in some other manner.

Some have thought the different fortunes of generations to be unjust. Herzen remarks that human development is a kind of chronological unfairness, since those who live later profit from the labor of their predecessors without paying the same price. And Kant thought it disconcerting that earlier generations should carry their burdens only for the sake of the later ones and that only the last should have the good fortune to dwell in the completed building.[21] These feelings while entirely natural are misplaced. For although the relation between generations is a special one, it gives rise to no insuperable difficulty.

It is a natural fact that generations are spread out in time and actual economic benefits flow only in one direction. This situation is unalterable, and so the question of justice does not arise. What is just or unjust is how institutions deal with natural limitations and the way they are set up to take advantage of historical possibilities. Obviously if all generations are to gain (except perhaps the earlier ones), the parties must agree to a savings principle that insures that each generation receives its due from its predecessors and does its fair share for those to come. The only economic exchanges between generations are, so to speak, virtual ones, that is, compensating adjustments that can be made in the original position when a just savings principle is adopted.

Now when the parties consider this problem they do not know to which generation they belong or, what comes to the same thing, the stage of civilization of their society. They have no way of telling whether it is poor or relatively wealthy, largely agricultural or already industrialized, and so on. The veil of ignorance is complete in these respects. But since we take the present time of entry interpretation of the original position (§24), the parties know that they are contemporaries; and so unless we modify our initial assumptions, there is no reason for them to agree to any saving

---

21. The remark of Alexander Herzen is from Isaiah Berlin's introduction to Franco Venturi, *Roots of Revolution* (New York, Alfred Knopf, 1960), p. xx. For Kant, see "Idea for a Universal History with a Cosmopolitan Purpose," in *Political Writings,* ed. Hans Reiss and trans. H. B. Nisbet (Cambridge, The University Press, 1970), p. 44.

44. Justice between Generations

whatever. Earlier generations will have either saved or not; there is nothing the parties can do to affect that. So to achieve a reasonable result, we assume first, that the parties represent family lines, say, who care at least about their more immediate descendants; and second, that the principle adopted must be such that they wish all earlier generations to have followed it (§22). These constraints, together with the veil of ignorance, are to insure that any one generation looks out for all.

In arriving at a just saving principle (or better, limits on such principles), the parties are to ask themselves how much they would be willing to save at each stage of advance on the assumption that all other generations have saved, or will save, in accordance with the same criterion. They are to consider their willingness to save at any given phase of civilization with the understanding that the rates they propose are to regulate the whole span of accumulation. It is essential to note that a savings principle is a rule that assigns an appropriate rate (or range of rates) to each level of advance, that is, a rule that determines a schedule of rates. Presumably different rates are assigned to different stages. When people are poor and saving is difficult, a lower rate of saving should be required; whereas in a wealthier society greater savings may reasonably be expected since the real burden of saving is less. Eventually, once just institutions are firmly established and all the basic liberties effectively realized, the net accumulation asked for falls to zero. At this point a society meets its duty of justice by maintaining just institutions and preserving their material base. The just savings principle applies to what a society is to save as a matter of justice. If its members wish to save for other purposes, that is another matter.

It is impossible to be very specific about the schedule of rates (or the range of rates) that would be acknowledged; the most that we can hope from these intuitive considerations is that certain extremes will be excluded. Thus we may assume that the parties avoid imposing very high rates at the earlier stages of accumulation, for even though they would benefit from this if they come later, they must be able to accept these rates in good faith should their society turn out to be poor. The strains of commitment apply here just as before (§29). On the other hand, they will want all generations to provide some saving (excluding special circumstances), since it is to our advantage if our predecessors have done their share. These observations establish wide limits for the savings rule. To narrow the range somewhat further, we suppose the parties to ask what is reasonable for members of adjacent generations to expect of one another at each level of advance. They try to piece together a just savings sched-

Distributive Shares

ule by balancing how much they would be willing to save for their more immediate descendants against what they would feel entitled to claim of their more immediate predecessors. Thus imagining themselves to be fathers, say, they are to ascertain how much they should set aside for their sons and grandsons by noting what they would believe themselves entitled to claim of their fathers and grandfathers. When they arrive at the estimate that seems fair from both sides, with due allowance made for the improvement in circumstances, then the fair rate (or range of rates) for that stage is specified. Once this is done for all stages, the just savings principle is defined. Of course, the parties must throughout keep in mind the objective of the accumulation process, namely, a state of society with a material base sufficient to establish effective just institutions within which the basic liberties can all be realized. Assuming that the savings principle answers to these conditions, no generation can find fault with any other when it is followed, no matter how far removed they are in time.

The question of time preference and matters of priority I shall leave aside until the next sections. For the present I wish to point out several features of the contract approach. First of all, while it is evident that a just savings principle cannot literally be adopted democratically, the conception of the original position achieves the same result. Since no one knows to which generation he belongs, the question is viewed from the standpoint of each and a fair accommodation is expressed by the principle adopted. All generations are virtually represented in the original position, since the same principle would always be chosen. An ideally democratic decision will result, one that is fairly adjusted to the claims of each generation and therefore satisfying the precept that what touches all concerns all. Moreover, it is immediately obvious that every generation, except possibly the first, gains when a reasonable rate of saving is maintained. The process of accumulation, once it is begun and carried through, is to the good of all subsequent generations. Each passes on to the next a fair equivalent in real capital as defined by a just savings principle. (It should be kept in mind here that capital is not only factories and machines, and so on, but also the knowledge and culture, as well as the techniques and skills, that make possible just institutions and the fair value of liberty.) This equivalent is in return for what is received from previous generations that enables the later ones to enjoy a better life in a more just society.

It is also characteristic of the contract doctrine to define a just society as the aim of the course of accumulation. This feature derives from the

44. Justice between Generations

fact that an ideal conception of a just basic structure is embedded in the principles chosen in the original position. In this respect, justice as fairness contrasts with utilitarian views (§41). The just savings principle can be regarded as an understanding between generations to carry their fair share of the burden of realizing and preserving a just society. The end of the savings process is set up in advance, although only the general outlines can be discerned. Particular circumstances as they arise will in time determine the more detailed aspects. But in any event we are not bound to go on maximizing indefinitely. Indeed, it is for this reason that the savings principle is agreed to after the principles of justice for institutions, even though this principle constrains the difference principle. These principles tell us what to strive for. The savings principle represents an interpretation, arrived at in the original position, of the previously accepted natural duty to uphold and to further just institutions. In this case the ethical problem is that of agreeing on a path over time which treats all generations justly during the whole course of a society's history. What seems fair to persons in the original position defines justice in this instance as in others.

The significance of the last stage of society should not, however, be misinterpreted. While all generations are to do their part in reaching the just state of things beyond which no further net saving is required, this state is not to be thought of as that alone which gives meaning and purpose to the whole process. To the contrary, all generations have their appropriate aims. They are not subordinate to one another any more than individuals are and no generation has stronger claims than any other. The life of a people is conceived as a scheme of cooperation spread out in historical time. It is to be governed by the same conception of justice that regulates the cooperation of contemporaries.

Finally, the last stage at which saving is called for is not one of great abundance. This consideration deserves perhaps some emphasis. Further wealth might not be superfluous for some purposes; and indeed average income may not, in absolute terms, be very high. Justice does not require that early generations save so that later ones are simply more wealthy. Saving is demanded as a condition of bringing about the full realization of just institutions and the equal liberties. If additional accumulation is to be undertaken, it is for other reasons. It is a mistake to believe that a just and good society must wait upon a high material standard of life. What men want is meaningful work in free association with others, these associations regulating their relations to one another within a framework of just basic institutions. To achieve this state of things great wealth is not necessary. In fact, beyond some point it is more likely to be a positive hindrance, a meaningless distraction at best if not a temptation to indulgence and emptiness. (Of course, the definition of meaningful work is a problem in itself. Though it is not a problem of justice, a few remarks in §79 are addressed to it.)

We now have to combine the just savings principle with the two principles of justice. This is done by supposing that this principle is defined from the standpoint of the least advantaged in each generation. It is the representative men from this group as it extends over time who by virtual adjustments are to specify the rate of accumulation. They undertake in effect to constrain the application of the difference principle. In any generation their expectations are to be maximized subject to the condition of putting aside the savings that would be acknowledged. Thus the complete statement of the difference principle includes the savings principle as a constraint. Whereas the first principle of justice and the principle of fair opportunity are prior to the difference principle within generations, the savings principle limits its scope between them.

Of course, the saving of the less favored need not be done by their taking an active part in the investment process. Rather it normally consists of their approving of the economic and other arrangements necessary for the appropriate accumulation. Saving is achieved by accepting as a political judgment those policies designed to improve the standard of life of later generations of the least advantaged, thereby abstaining from the immediate gains which are available. By supporting these arrangements the required saving can be made, and no representative man in any generation of the most disadvantaged can complain of another for not doing his part.

So much, then, for a brief sketch of some of the main features of the just savings principle. We can now see that persons in different generations have duties and obligations to one another just as contemporaries do. The present generation cannot do as it pleases but is bound by the principles that would be chosen in the original position to define justice between persons at different moments of time. In addition, men have a natural duty to uphold and to further just institutions and for this the improvement of civilization up to a certain level is required. The derivation of these duties and obligations may seem at first a somewhat farfetched application of the contract doctrine. Nevertheless these requirements would be acknowledged in the original position, and so the conception of justice as fairness covers these matters without any change in its basic idea.

[3]

THE NON-IDENTITY PROBLEM

Derek Parfit

THERE is another question about personal identity. Each of us might never have existed. What would have made this true? The answer produces a problem that most of us overlook.

One of my aims in Part Four is to discuss this problem. My other aim is to discuss the part of our moral theory in which this problem arises. This is the part that covers how we affect future generations. This is the most important part of our moral theory, since the next few centuries will be the most important in human history.

119. HOW OUR IDENTITY IN FACT DEPENDS ON WHEN WE WERE CONCEIVED

What would have made it true that some particular person would never have existed? With one qualification, I believe

The Time-Dependence Claim: If any particular person had not been conceived when he was in fact conceived, it is *in fact* true that he would never have existed.

This claim is not obviously true. Thus one woman writes:

It is always fascinating to speculate on who we would have been if our parents had married other people.[1]

In wondering who she would have been, this woman ignores the answer: 'No one'.

Though the Time-Dependence Claim is not obviously true, it is not controversial, and it is easy to believe. It is thus unlike the Reductionist View about personal identity over time. This is one of several competing views, and is hard to believe. The Time-Dependence Claim is not about personal identity over time. It is about a different though related subject: personal identity in different possible histories of the world. Several views about this subject are worth discussing. But the Time-Dependence Claim is *not* one of these views. It is a claim that is true on *all* of these views.

As I have said, the claim should be qualified. Each of us grew from a particular pair of cells: an ovum and the spermatozoon by which, out of millions, it was fertilized. Suppose that my mother had not conceived a child at the time when in fact she conceived me. And suppose that she had conceived a child within a few days of this time. This child would have grown from the same particular ovum from which I grew. But even if this child had been conceived only a few seconds earlier or later, it is almost certain that he would have grown from a different spermatozoon. This child would have had some but not all of my genes. Would this child have been me?

We are inclined to believe that any question about our identity must have an answer, which must be either Yes or No. As before, I reject this view. There are cases in which our identity is indeterminate. What I have just described may be such a case. If it is, my question has no answer. It is neither true nor false that, if these events had occurred, I would never have existed. Though I can always ask, 'Would I have existed?', this would here be an empty question.

These last claims are controversial. Since I want my Time-Dependence Claim not to be controversial, I shall set aside these cases. The claim can become

> (TD2) If any particular person had not been conceived within a month of the time when he was in fact conceived, he would in fact never have existed.

I claim that this is *in fact* true. I do *not* claim that it is *necessarily* true. The different views about this subject make competing claims about what is necessary. It is because I claim less that my claim is not controversial. Those who disagree about what *could* have happened may agree about what *would in fact* have happened. As I shall argue, the holders of all plausible views would agree with me.

These views make claims about the *necessary properties* of each particular person. Some of a person's necessary properties are had by everyone: these are the properties that are necessary to being a person. What concerns us here are the *distinctive* necessary properties of each particular person. Suppose I claim that P is one of Kant's distinctive necessary properties. This means that Kant could not have lacked P, and that only Kant could have had P.

According to

> *The Origin View*, each person has this distinctive necessary property: that of having grown from the particular pair of cells from which this person in fact grew.[2]

This property cannot be *fully* distinctive. Any pair of identical twins *both* grew from such a pair of cells. And any fertilized ovum might have later split, and produced twins. The Origin View must be revised to meet this problem. But I need not discuss this revision. It is enough for my purposes that, on this view, Kant could not have grown from a different pair of cells.

119. How Our Identity Depends On When We Were Conceived

It is irrelevant that, because there can be twins, it is false that *only* Kant could have grown from this pair of cells.

Holders of the Origin View would accept my claim that, if Kant had not been conceived within a month of the time when he was conceived, he would in fact never have existed. If he had not been conceived in that month, no child would in fact have grown from the particular pair of cells from which he grew. (This claim makes an assumption both about the distinctive necessary properties of this pair of cells, and about the human reproductive system. But these assumptions are not controversial.)

According to certain other views, Kant could have grown from a different pair of cells. On

The Featureless Cartesian View, Kant was a particular Cartesian Ego, which had *no* distinctive necessary properties.

On this view, a person's identity has no connections with his physical and mental characteristics. Kant might have been me, and vice versa, though, if this had happened, no one would have noticed any difference. It is at worst mildly controversial to claim, as I did, that we should reject *this* version of the Cartesian View.

Two other views are closely related. On

The Descriptive View, each person has several distinctive necessary properties. These are this person's most important distinctive properties, and they do not include having grown from a particular pair of cells.

In the case of Kant, these properties would include his authorship of certain books. One version of this view does not claim that Kant must have had *all* these properties. Anyone with most of these properties would have been Kant.

On

The Descriptive Name View, every person's name means 'the person who . . .'. For us now, 'Kant' means 'the person who wrote the *Critique of Pure Reason,* etc'. A particular person's necessary properties are those that would be listed when we explain the meaning of this person's name.

Both this and the Descriptive View might be combined with the other version of Cartesianism. Kant might be claimed to be the Cartesian Ego whose distinctive necessary properties include the authorship of certain books. But the two Descriptive Views need not add this claim.[3]

One objection to the Descriptive Views is that each person's life could have been very different. Kant could have died in his cradle. Since this is possible, the authorship of certain books cannot be one of Kant's necessary properties.

One reply to this objection retreats to a weaker claim. It could be said:

Though this property is not necessary, it is distinctive. Kant might not have written these books. But, in any possible history in which a single person wrote these books, this person would have been Kant.

I need not discuss whether this, or some other reply, meets this objection. Even if the objection can be met, my Time-Dependence Claim is true.

On both Descriptive Views, Kant could have grown from a different pair of cells, or even had different parents. This would have happened if Kant's mother had not conceived a child when she conceived him, and some other couple had conceived a child who later wrote the *Critique of Pure Reason*, etc. On the Descriptive Views, this child would have been Kant. He would not have been *called* Kant. But this does not worry holders of these views. They would claim that, if this had happened, Kant would have had both different parents and a different name.

Though they believe that this might have happened, most holders of the Descriptive Views would accept my claim that it would *not in fact* have happened. If they claim that it *would* have happened, they must accept an extreme version of Tolstoy's view, stated in the epilogue of *War and Peace*, that history does not depend on the decisions made by particular people. On this view, if Napoleon's mother had remained childless, history would have provided a 'substitute Napoleon', who would have invaded Russia in 1812. And, if Kant's mother had remained childless, history would have provided another author of the *Critique of Pure Reason*. This view is too implausible to be worth discussing.

There is another way in which holders of the Descriptive Views might reject my claim. They might claim that Kant's necessary properties were far less distinctive. They might for instance merely be: being his mother's first child. This claim meets the objection that each person's life might have been very different. But this claim is also too implausible to be worth discussing. I am the second of my mother's three children. This claim implies absurdly that, if my mother had conceived no child when she in fact conceived me, I would have been my younger sister.

Consider next the possible history in which the Descriptive Views seem most plausible. Suppose that Kant's mother had not conceived a child when she conceived him, and that one month later she conceived a child who was exactly like Kant. This child would have grown from a different pair of cells; but by an amazing coincidence, of a kind that never actually happens, this child would have had all of Kant's genes. And suppose that, apart from the fact and the effects of being born later, this child would have lived a life that was just like Kant's, writing the *Critique of Pure Reason*, etc.

On the Descriptive Views, this child would have been Kant. Holders of the Origin View might object:

> Kant was a particular person. In your imagined possible history, you have not shown that you are referring to *this* particular person. In this imagined history, there would have been someone who was *exactly like*

119. *How Our Identity Depends On When We Were Conceived*

this person. But exact similarity is not the same as numerical identity, as is shown by any two exactly similar things.

These remarks explain why the Origin View refers to the particular pair of cells from which a person grew.

A fifth view also makes such a direct reference. On

> *The Backward Variation View,* this reference need not be to the point of origin, or to the cells from which a person grew. The reference can be made at any time in this person's life. By making such a reference, we can describe how this person might have had a different origin.

Consider a holder of this view who, in 1780, is attending one of Kant's lectures. This person might claim:

> Kant is the person standing *there*. Kant might have had different parents, and lived a different life up until the recent past. For this to have been what happened, all that is needed is that this different life would have led Kant to be now standing there.

This view must make some further claims. But it meets the objection that, to justify a claim of identity, we need more than similarity. Holders of the Origin View therefore need a different objection to the Backward Variation View. For my purposes, I need not decide between these views.

On the Backward Variation View, Kant might have had a different origin. But holders of this view would accept my claim that, in fact, this would not have happened. They would agree that, if Kant had not been conceived within a month of the time when he was conceived, he would in fact never have existed.

I have now described all of the views about our identity in different possible histories.[5] I discuss in endnote 6 how these views are related to the different views about our identity over time. On all of the plausible views, my Time-Dependence Claim is true. This claim applies to everyone. You were conceived at a certain time. It is in fact true that, if you had not been conceived within a month of that time, *you* would never have existed.

120. THE THREE KINDS OF CHOICE

Unless we, or some global disaster, destroy the human race, there will be people living later who do not now exist. These are *future people*. Science has given to our generation great ability both to affect these people, and to predict these effects.

Two kinds of effect raise puzzling questions. We can affect the identities of future people, or *who* the people are who will later live. And we can affect the number of future people. These effects give us different kinds of choice.

The Non-Identity Problem

In comparing any two acts, we can ask:

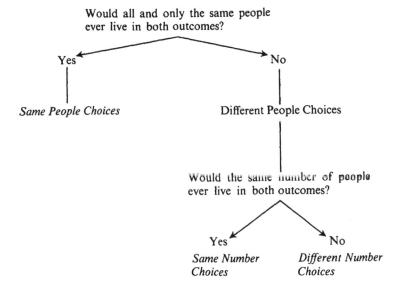

Different Number Choices affect both the number and the identities of future people. Same Number Choices affect the identities of future people, but do not affect their number. Same People Choices affect neither.

121. WHAT WEIGHT SHOULD WE GIVE TO THE INTERESTS OF FUTURE PEOPLE?

Most of our moral thinking is about Same People Choices. As I shall argue, such choices are not as numerous as most of us assume. Very many of our choices will in fact have some effect on both the identities and the number of future people. But in most of these cases, because we cannot predict what the particular effects would be, these effects can be morally ignored. We can treat these cases as if they were Same People Choices.

In some cases we can predict that some act either may or will be against the interests of future people. This can be true when we are making a Same People Choice. In such a case, whatever we choose, all and only the same people will ever live. Some of these people will be future people. Since these people will exist whatever we choose, we can either harm or benefit these people in a quite straightforward way.

Suppose that I leave some broken glass in the undergrowth of a wood. A hundred years later this glass wounds a child. My act harms this child. If I had safely buried the glass, this child would have walked through the wood unharmed.

121. *How Important Are The Interests Of Future People?*

Does it make a moral difference that the child whom I harm does not now exist?

On one view, moral principles cover only people who can *reciprocate*, or harm and benefit each other. If I cannot be harmed or benefited by this child, as we can plausibly suppose, the harm that I cause this child has no moral importance. I assume that we should reject this view.[7]

Some writers claim that, while we ought to be concerned about effects on future people, we are morally justified in being less concerned about effects in the further future. This is a common view in welfare economics, and cost-benefit analysis. On this view, we can *discount* the more remote effects of our acts and policies, at some rate of *n* per cent per year. This is called the *Social Discount Rate*.

Suppose we are considering how to dispose safely of the radio-active matter called *nuclear waste*. If we believe in the Social Discount Rate, we shall be concerned with safety only in the nearer future. We shall not be troubled by the fact that some nuclear waste will be radio-active for thousands of years. At a discount rate of five per cent, one death next year counts for more than a billion deaths in 500 years. On this view, catastrophes in the further future can now be regarded as morally trivial.

As this case suggests, the Social Discount Rate is indefensible. Remoteness in time roughly correlates with some important facts, such as predictability. But, as I argue in Appendix F, these correlations are too rough to justify the Social Discount Rate. The present moral importance of future events does *not* decline at a rate of *n* per cent per year. Remoteness in time has, in itself, no more significance than remoteness in space. Suppose that I shoot some arrow into a distant wood, where it wounds some person. If I should have known that there might be someone in this wood, I am guilty of gross negligence. Because this person is far away, I cannot identify the person whom I harm. But this is no excuse. Nor is it any excuse that this person is far away. We should make the same claims about effects on people who are temporally remote.

122. A YOUNG GIRL'S CHILD

Future people are, in one respect, unlike distant people. We can affect their identity. And many of our acts have this effect.

This fact produces a problem. Before I describe this problem, I shall repeat some preliminary remarks. I assume that one person can be worse off than another, in morally significant ways, and by more or less. But I do not assume that these comparisons could be, even in principle, precise. I assume that there is only rough or partial comparability. On this assumption, it could be true of two people that neither is worse off than the other, but this would not imply that these people are exactly equally well off.

'Worse off' could be taken to refer, either to someone's level of happiness, or more narrowly to his standard of living, or, more broadly, to the quality of

The Non-Identity Problem

his life. Since it is the broadest, I shall often use the phrase 'the quality of life'. I also call certain lives 'worth living'. This description can be ignored by those who believe that there could not be lives that are not worth living. But, like many other people, I believe that there could be such lives. Finally, I extend the ordinary use of the phrase 'worth living'. If one of two people would have a lower quality of life, I call his life to this extent 'less worth living'.

When considering future people, we must answer two questions:

(1) If we cause someone to exist, who will have a life worth living, do we thereby benefit this person?

(2) Do we also benefit this person if some act of ours is a remote but necessary part of the cause of his existence?

These are difficult questions. If we answer Yes to both, I shall say that we believe *that causing to exist can benefit.*

Some people answer Yes to (1) but No to (2). These people give their second answer because they use 'benefit' in its ordinary sense. As I argued in Section 25, we ought for moral purposes to extend our use of 'benefit'. If we answer Yes to (1) we should answer Yes to (2).

Many people answer No to both these questions. These people might say: 'We benefit someone if it is true that, if we had not done what we did, this would have been worse for this person. If we had not caused someone to exist, this would *not* have been worse for this person.'

I believe that, while it is defensible to answer No to both these questions, it is also defensible to answer Yes to both. For those who doubt this second belief I have written Appendix G. Since I believe that it is defensible both to claim and to deny that causing to exist can benefit, I shall discuss the implications of both views.

Consider

The 14-Year-Old Girl. This girl chooses to have a child. Because she is so young, she gives her child a bad start in life. Though this will have bad effects throughout this child's life, his life will, predictably, be worth living. If this girl had waited for several years, she would have had a different child, to whom she would have given a better start in life.

Since such cases are becoming common, they raise a practical problem.[8] They also raise a theoretical problem.

Suppose that we tried to persuade this girl that she ought to wait. We claimed: 'If you have a child now, you will soon regret this. If you wait, this will be better for you.' She replied: 'This is my affair. Even if I am doing what will be worse for me, I have a right to do what I want.'

We replied: 'This is not entirely your affair. You should think not only of

122. A Young Girl's Child

yourself, but also of your child. It will be worse for him if you have him now. If you have him later, you will give him a better start in life.'

We failed to persuade this girl. She had a child when she was 14, and, as we predicted, she gave him a bad start in life. Were we right to claim that her decision was worse for her child? If she had waited, this particular child would never have existed. And, despite its bad start, his life is worth living. Suppose first that we do *not* believe that causing to exist can benefit. We should ask, 'If someone lives a life that is worth living, is this worse for this person than if he had never existed?' Our answer must be No. Suppose next that we believe that causing to exist *can* benefit. On this view, this girl's decision benefits her child.

On both views, this girl's decision was not worse for her child. When we see this, do we change our mind about this decision? Do we cease to believe that it would have been better if this girl had waited, so that she could give to her first child a better start in life? I continue to have this belief, as do most of those who consider this case. But we cannot defend this belief in the natural way that I suggested. We cannot claim that this girl's decision was worse for her child. What is the objection to her decision? This question arises because, in the different outcomes, different people would be born. I shall therefore call this the *Non-Identity Problem*.[9]

It may be said:

In one sense, this girl's decision *was* worse for her child. In trying to persuade this girl not to have a child now, we can use the phrase 'her child' and the pronoun 'he' to cover *any* child that she might have. These words need not refer to one particular child. We can truly claim: 'If this girl does not have her child now, but waits and has him later, *he* will not be the same particular child. If she has him later, he will be a different child.' By using these words in this way, we can explain why it would be better if this girl waits. We can claim:

(A) The objection to this girl's decision is that it will probably be worse for her child. If she waited, she would probably give him a better start in life.

Though we can truly make this claim, it does *not* explain the objection to this girl's decision. This becomes clear after she has had her child. The phrase 'her child' now naturally refers to this particular child. And this girl's decision was *not* worse for *this* child. Though there is a sense in which (A) is true, (A) does not appeal to a familiar moral principle.

On one of our familiar principles, it is an objection to someone's choice that this choice will be worse for, or be against the interests of, any other particular person. If we claim that this girl's decision was worse for her child, we cannot be claiming that it was worse for a particular person. We cannot claim, of the girl's child, that her decision was worse for *him*. We must admit that, in claim (A), the words 'her child' do not refer to her child.

(A) is not about what is good or bad for any of the particular people who ever live. (A) appeals to a new principle, that must be explained and justified.

If (A) seems to appeal to a familiar principle, this is because it has two senses. Here is another example. A general shows military skill if, in many battles, he always makes his the winning side. But there are two ways of doing this. He might win victories. Or he might always, when he is about to lose, change sides. A general shows no military skill if it is only in the second sense that he always makes his the winning side.

To what principle does (A) appeal? We should state the principle in a way that shows the kind of choice to which it applies. These are Same Number Choices, which affect the identities of future people, but do not affect their number. We might suggest

The Same Number Quality Claim, or *Q*: If in either of two possible outcomes the same number of people would ever live, it would be worse if those who live are worse off, or have a lower quality of life, than those who would have lived.

This claim is plausible. And it implies what we believe about the 14-Year-Old Girl. The child that she has now will probably be worse off than a child she could have had later would have been, since this other child would have had a better start in life. If this is true, Q implies that this is the worse of these two outcomes. Q implies that it would have been better if this girl had waited, and had a child later.

We may shrink from claiming, of this girl's actual child, that it would have been better if he had never existed. But, if we claimed earlier that it would be better if this girl waits, this is what we must claim. We cannot consistently make a claim and deny this same claim later. If (1) in 1990 it *would be* better if this girl waits and has a child later, then (2) in 2020 it *would have been* better if she had waited and had a child later. And (2) implies (3) that it would have been better if the child who existed had not been her actual child. If we cannot accept (3), we must reject (1).

I suggest that, on reflection, we can accept (3). I believe that, if *I* was the actual child of this girl, I could accept (3). (3) does not imply that my existence is *bad*, or intrinsically morally undesirable. The claim is merely that, since a child born later would probably have had a better life than mine, it would have been better if my mother had waited, and had a child later. This claim need not imply that I ought rationally to regret that my mother had *me*, or that she ought rationally to regret this. Since it would have been better if she had waited, she ought perhaps to have some moral regret. And it is probably true that she made the outcome worse for herself. But, even if this is true, it does not show that she ought rationally to regret her act, all things considered. If she loves me, her actual child, this is enough

122. *A Young Girl's Child*

to block the claim that she is irrational if she does not have such regret.[10] Even when it implies a claim like (3), I conclude that we can accept Q.

Though Q is plausible, it does not solve the Non-Identity Problem. Q covers only the cases where, in the different outcomes, the same number of people would ever live. We need a claim that covers cases where, in the different outcomes, different numbers would ever live. The Non-Identity Problem can arise in these cases.

Because Q is restricted, it could be justified in several different ways. There are several principles that imply Q, but conflict when applied to Different Number Choices. We shall need to decide which of these principles, or which set of principles, we ought to accept. Call what we ought to accept *Theory X*. X will solve the Non-Identity Problem in Different Number Choices. And X will tell us how Q should be justified, or more fully explained.

In the case of the 14-Year-Old Girl, we are not forced to appeal to Q. There are other facts to which we could appeal, such as the effects on other people. But the problem can arise in a purer form.

123. HOW LOWERING THE QUALITY OF LIFE MIGHT BE WORSE FOR NO ONE

Suppose that we are choosing between two social or economic policies. And suppose that, on one of the two policies, the standard of living would be slightly higher over the next century. This effect implies another. It is not true that, whichever policy we choose, the same particular people will exist in the further future. Given the effects of two such policies on the details of our lives, it would increasingly over time be true that, on the different policies, people married different people. And, even in the same marriages, the children would increasingly over time be conceived at different times. As I have argued, children conceived more than a month earlier or later would in fact be different children. Since the choice between our two policies would affect the timing of later conceptions, some of the people who are later born would owe their existence to our choice of one of the two policies. If we had chosen the other policy, these particular people would never have existed. And the proportion of those later born who owe their existence to our choice would, like ripples in a pool, steadily grow. We can plausibly assume that, after one or two centuries, there would be no one living in our community who would have been born whichever policy we chose. (It may help to think about this question: how many of us could truly claim, 'Even if railways and motor cars had never been invented, I would still have been born'?)

How does this produce a problem? Consider

Depletion. As a community, we must choose whether to deplete or conserve certain kinds of resources. If we choose Depletion, the quality of life over the next two centuries would be slightly higher than it would have been if we had chosen Conservation. But it would later, for many centuries, be much lower than it would have been if we had chosen Conservation. This would be because, at the start of this period, people would have to find alternatives for the resources that we had depleted. It is worth distinguishing two versions of this case. The effects of the different policies would be as shown below.

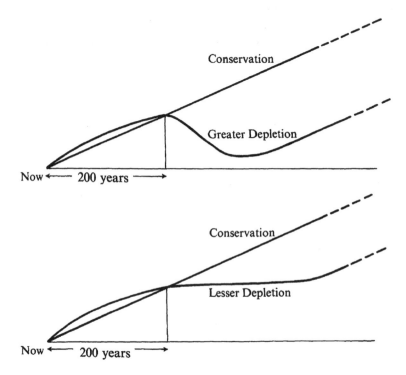

We could never know, in such detail, that these would be the effects of two policies. But this is no objection to this case. Similar effects would sometimes be predictable. Nor does it matter that this imagined case is artificially simple, since this merely clarifies the relevant questions.

Suppose that we choose Depletion, and that this has either of the two effects shown in my diagram. Is our choice worse for anyone?

Because we chose Depletion, millions of people have, for several centuries, a much lower quality of life. This quality of life is much lower, not than it is now, but than it would have been if we had chosen Conservation. These people's lives are worth living; and, if we had chosen Conservation, these

123. *How Lowering The Quality Of Life Might Be Worse For No-one* 363

particular people would never have existed. Suppose that we do not assume that causing to exist can benefit. We should ask, 'If particular people live lives that are worth living, is this worse for these people than if they had never existed?' Our answer must be No. Suppose next that we do assume that causing to exist can benefit. Since these future people's lives will be worth living, and they would never have existed if we had chosen Conservation, our choice of Depletion is not only not worse for these people: it *benefits* them.

On both answers, our choice will not be worse for these future people. Moreover, when we understand the case, we know that this is true. We know that, even if it greatly lowers the quality of life for several centuries, our choice will not be worse for anyone who ever lives.

Does this make a moral difference? There are three views. It might make all the difference, or some difference, or no difference. There might be no objection to our choice, or some objection, or the objection may be just as strong.

Some believe that *what is bad must be bad for someone*. On this view, there is no objection to our choice. Since it will be bad for no one, our choice cannot have a bad effect. The great lowering of the quality of life provides no moral reason not to choose Depletion.

Certain writers accept this conclusion.[11] But it is very implausible. Before we consider cases of this kind, we may accept the view that what is bad must be bad for someone. But the case of Depletion shows, I believe, that we must reject this view. The great lowering of the quality of life must provide *some* moral reason not to choose Depletion. This is believed by most of those who consider cases of this kind.

If this is what we believe, we should ask two questions:

(1) What is the moral reason not to choose Depletion?

(2) Does it make a moral difference that this lowering of the quality of life will be worse for no one? Would this effect be *worse*, having greater moral weight, if it *was* worse for particular people?

Our need to answer (1), and other similar questions, I call the Non-Identity Problem. This problem arises because the identities of people in the further future can be very easily affected. Some people believe that this problem is a mere quibble. This reaction is unjustified. The problem arises because of superficial facts about our reproductive system. But, though it arises in a superficial way, it is a real problem. When we are choosing between two social or economic policies, of the kind that I described, it is *not true* that, in the further future, the same people will exist whatever we choose. It is therefore *not true* that a choice like Depletion will be against the interests of future people. We cannot dismiss this problem with the pretence that this *is* true.

We partly answer question (1) if we appeal to Q. On this claim, if the

364 *The Non-Identity Problem*

numbers would be the same, it would be worse if those who live have a lower quality of life than those who would have lived. But the problem can arise in cases where, in the different outcomes, there would be different numbers of people. To cover these cases we need Theory X. Only X will explain how Q should be justified, and provide a full solution to our problem.

124. WHY AN APPEAL TO RIGHTS CANNOT WHOLLY SOLVE THE PROBLEM

Can we solve our problem by appealing to people's rights? Reconsider the 14-Year-Old Girl. By having her child so young, she gives him a bad start in life. It might be claimed: 'The objection to this girl's decision is that she violates her child's right to a good start in life'.

Even if this child has this right, it could not have been fulfilled. This girl could not have had *this* child when she was a mature woman. Some would claim that, since this child's right could not be fulfilled, this girl cannot be claimed to violate his right. The objector might reply: 'It is wrong to cause someone to exist if we know that this person will have a right that cannot be fulfilled.' Can this be the objection to this girl's decision?[13]

Some years ago, a British politician welcomed the fact that, in the previous year, there had been fewer teenage pregnancies. A middle-aged man wrote in anger to *The Times*. He had been born when his mother was only 14. He admitted that, because his mother was so young, his early years had been hard for both of them. But his life was now well worth living. Was the politician suggesting that it would have been better if he had never been born? This suggestion seemed to him outrageous.

The politician was, implicitly, suggesting this. On the politician's view, it would have been better if this man's mother had waited for several years before having children. I believe that we should accept this view. But can we plausibly explain this view by claiming that this angry man had a right that was not fulfilled?

I believe that we cannot. Suppose that I have a right to privacy. I ask you to marry me. If you accept, you are not acting wrongly, by violating my right to privacy. Since I am glad that you act as you do, with respect to you I *waive* this right. A similar claim applies to the writer of the angry letter to *The Times*. On the suggestion made above, this man has a right to be born by a mature woman, who would give him a good start in life. This man's mother acted wrongly because she caused him to exist with a right that cannot be fulfilled. But this man's letter shows that he was glad to be alive. He denies that his mother acted wrongly because of what she did to him. If we had claimed that her act was wrong, because he has a right that cannot be fulfilled, he could have said, 'I waive this right'. This would have undermined our objection to his mother's act.

It would have been better if this man's mother had waited. But this is not because of what she did to her actual child. It is because of what she could

124. *Why An Appeal To Rights Cannot Wholly Solve The Problem* 365

have done for any child that she could have had when she was mature. The objection must be that, if she had waited, she could have given to some other child a better start in life.

Return now to the Case of Depletion. Suppose that we choose Greater Depletion. More than two centuries later, the quality of life is much lower than it would have been if we had chosen Conservation. But the people who will then be living will have a quality of life that is about as high as ours will on average be over the next century. Do these people have rights to which an objector can appeal?

It might be claimed that these people have a right to their share of the resources that we have depleted. But people do not have rights to a share of a particular resource. Suppose that we deplete some resource, but invent technology that will enable our successors, though they lack this resource, to have the same range of opportunities. There would be no objection to what we have done. The most that could be claimed is that people in each generation have a right to an equal range of opportunities, or to an equally high quality of life.[14]

If we choose Greater Depletion, those who live more than two centuries later will have fewer opportunities, and a lower quality of life, than some earlier and some later generations. If people have a right to equal opportunities, and an equally high quality of life, an appeal to these rights may provide some objection to our choice. Those who live more than two centuries later could not possibly have had greater opportunities, or a higher quality of life. If we had chosen otherwise, these people would never have existed. Since their rights could not be fulfilled, we may not violate their rights. But, as before, it may be objected that we cause people to exist with rights that cannot be fulfilled.

It is not clear that this is a good objection. If these people knew the facts, they would not regret that we acted as we did. If they were glad to be alive, they might react like the man who wrote to *The Times*. They might waive their rights. But, since we cannot assume that this is how they would all react, an appeal to their rights may provide some objection to our choice.

Can this appeal provide an objection to our choice of *Lesser* Depletion? In this case, those who live more than two centuries later have a much higher quality of life than we do now. Can we claim that these people have a *right* to an *even higher* quality of life? I believe that, on any plausible theory about rights, the answer would be No.

It will help to imagine away the Non-Identity Problem. Suppose that our reproductive system was very different. Suppose that, whatever policies we followed, the very same people would live more than two centuries later. The objection to our choice would then be that, for the sake of small benefits to ourselves and our children, we prevent many future people from receiving very much greater benefits. Since these future people would be better off than us, we would not be acting unjustly. The objection to our choice would have to appeal to the Principle of Utility.

The Non-Identity Problem

Could this objection appeal to rights? Only if, like Godwin, we present Utilitarianism as a theory about rights. On Godwin's view, everyone has a right to get what the Principle of Utility implies that he should be given. Most of those who believe in rights would reject this view. Many people explain rights as what *constrain*, or *limit*, the Principle of Utility. These people claim that it is wrong to violate certain rights, even if this would greatly increase the net sum of benefits minus burdens. On such a theory, some weight is given to the Principle of Utility. Since such a theory is not Utilitarian, this principle is better called the *Principle of Beneficence*. This principle is one part of such a theory, and the claim that we have certain rights is a different part of this theory. I shall assume that, if we believe in rights, this is the kind of moral theory that we accept.

Return to the case where we imagine away the Non-Identity Problem. If we reject Godwin's view, we could not object to the choice of Lesser Depletion by appealing to the rights of those who will live in the further future. Our objection would appeal to the Principle of Beneficence. The objection would be that, for the sake of small benefits to ourselves and our children, we deny, to people better off than us, very much greater benefits. In calling this an objection, I need not claim that it shows our choice to be wrong. I am merely claiming that, since we deny these people very much greater benefits, this provides *some* moral reason not to make this choice.

If we now restore our actual reproductive system, this reason disappears. Consider the people who will live more than two centuries later. Our choice of Lesser Depletion does not deny these people *any* benefit. If we had chosen Conservation, this would not have benefited these people, since they would never have existed.

When we assume away the Non-Identity Problem, our reason not to make this choice is explained by an appeal, not to people's rights, but to the Principle of Beneficence. When we restore the Non-Identity Problem, this reason disappears. Since this reason appealed to the Principle of Beneficence, what the problem shows is that this principle is inadequate, and must be revised. We need a better account of beneficence, or what I call Theory X.

One part of our moral theory appeals to beneficence; another part appeals to people's rights. We should therefore not expect that an appeal to rights could fill the gap in our inadequate Principle of Beneficence. We should expect that, as I have claimed, appealing to rights cannot wholly solve the Non-Identity Problem.[15]

125. DOES THE FACT OF NON-IDENTITY MAKE A MORAL DIFFERENCE?

In trying to revise our Principle of Beneficence—trying to find Theory X— we must consider cases where, in the different outcomes, different numbers of people would exist. Before we turn to these cases, we can ask

125. Does The Fact Of Non-Identity Make A Moral Difference?

what we believe about the other question that I mentioned. Our choice of Depletion will be worse for no one. Does this make a moral difference?

We may be able to remember a time when we were concerned about effects on future generations, but had overlooked the Non-Identity Problem. We may have thought that a policy like Depletion would be against the interests of future people. When we saw that this was false, did we become less concerned about effects on future generations?

When I saw the problem, I did not become less concerned. And the same is true of many other people. I shall say that we accept the *No-Difference View*.

It is worth considering a different example:

> *The Medical Programmes*. There are two rare conditions, *J* and *K*, which cannot be detected without special tests. If a pregnant woman has Condition J, this will cause the child she is carrying to have a certain handicap. A simple treatment would prevent this effect. If a woman has Condition K when she conceives a child, this will cause this child to have the same particular handicap. Condition K cannot be treated, but always disappears within two months. Suppose next that we have planned two medical programmes, but there are funds for only one; so one must be cancelled. In the first programme, millions of women would be tested during pregnancy. Those found to have Condition J would be treated. In the second programme, millions of women would be tested when they intend to try to become pregnant. Those found to have Condition K would be warned to postpone conception for at least two months, after which this incurable condition will have disappeared. Suppose finally that we can predict that these two programmes would achieve results in as many cases. If there is Pregnancy Testing, 1,000 children a year will be born normal rather than handicapped. If there is Preconception Testing, there will each year be born 1,000 normal children rather than a 1,000, different, handicapped children.

Would these two programmes be equally worthwhile? Let us note carefully what the difference is. As a result of either programme, 1,000 couples a year would have a normal rather than a handicapped child. These would be different couples, on the two programmes. But since the numbers would be the same, the effects on the parents and on other people would be morally equivalent. If there is a moral difference, this can only be in the effects on the children.

Note next that, in judging these effects, we need have no view about the moral status of a foetus. We can suppose that it would take a year before either kind of testing could begin. When we choose between the two programmes, none of the children has yet been conceived. And all those who are conceived will become adults. We are therefore considering effects, not on present foetuses, but on future people. Assume next that the handicap in question, though it is not trivial, is not so severe as to make life doubtfully worth living. Even if it can be against our interests to have been born, this is not true of those born with this handicap.

Since we cannot afford both programmes, which should we cancel? Under one description, both would have the same effect. Suppose that Conditions J and K are the only causes of this handicap. The incidence is now 2,000 among those born in each year. Either programme would halve the incidence; the rate would drop to 1,000 a year. The difference is this. If we decide to cancel Pregnancy Testing, it will be true of those who are later born handicapped that, but for our decision, they would have been cured. Our decision will be worse for all these people. If instead we decide to cancel Pre-Conception Testing, there will later be just as many people who are born with this handicap. But it would not be true of these people that, but for our decision, they would have been cured. These people owe their existence to our decision. If we had not decided to cancel Pre-Conception Testing, the parents of these handicapped children would not have had *them*. They would have later had different children. Since the lives of these handicapped children are worth living, our decision will not be worse for any of them.

Does this make a moral difference? Or are the two programmes equally worthwhile? Is all that matters morally how many future lives will be lived by normal rather than handicapped people? Or does it also matter whether these lives would be lived by the very same people?

We should add one detail to the case. If we decide to cancel Pregnancy Testing, those who are later born handicapped might know that, if we had made a different decision, they would have been cured. Such knowledge might make their handicap harder to bear. We should therefore assume that, though it is not deliberately concealed, these people would not know this fact.

With this detail added, I judge the two programmes to be equally worthwhile. I know of some people who do not accept this claim; but I know of more who do.

My reaction is not merely an intuition. It is the judgement that I reach by reasoning as follows. Whichever programme is cancelled, there will later be just as many people with this handicap. These people would be different in the two outcomes that depend on our decision. And there is a claim that applies to only one of these two groups of handicapped people. Though they do not know this fact, the people in one group could have been cured. I therefore ask: 'If there will be people with some handicap, the fact that they are handicapped is bad. Would it be *worse* if, unknown to them, their handicap could have been cured?' This would be worse if this fact made these people worse off than people whose handicap could *not* have been cured. But this fact does not have this effect. If we decide to cancel Pregnancy Testing, there will be a group of handicapped people. If we

125. Does The Fact Of Non-Identity Make A Moral Difference? 369

decide to cancel Pre-Conception Testing, there will be a different group of handicapped people. The people in the first group would not be worse off than the people in the second group would have been. Since this is so, I judge these two outcomes to be morally equivalent. Given the details of the case, it seems to me irrelevant that one of the groups but not the other could have been cured.

This fact *would* have been relevant if curing this group would have reduced the incidence of this handicap. But, since we have funds for only one programme, this is not true. If we choose to cure the first group, there will later be just as many people with this handicap. Since curing the first group would not reduce the number who will be handicapped, we ought to choose to cure this group only if they have a stronger claim to be cured. And they do not have a stronger claim. If we *could* cure the second group, they would have an equal claim to be cured. If we chose to cure the first group, they would merely be luckier than the second group. Since they would merely be luckier, and they do not have a stronger claim to be cured, I do not believe that we ought to choose to cure these people. Since it is also true that, if we choose to cure these people, this will not reduce the number of people who will be handicapped, I conclude that the two programmes are equally worthwhile. If Pre-Conception Testing would achieve results in a few more cases, I would judge it to be the better programme.[16]

This matches my reaction to our choice of Depletion. I believe that it would be bad if there would later be a great lowering of the quality of life. And I believe that it would not be *worse* if the people who later live would themselves have existed if we had chosen Conservation. The bad effect would not be worse if it had been, in this way, worse for any particular people. In considering both cases, I accept the No-Difference View. So do many other people.

I have described two cases in which I, and many others, accept the No-Difference View. If we are right to accept this view, this may have important theoretical implications. This depends on whether we believe that, if we cause someone to exist who will have a life worth living, we thereby benefit this person. If we believe this, I cannot yet state the implications of the No-Difference View, since these will depend on decisions that I have not yet discussed. But suppose we believe that causing someone to exist cannot benefit this person. If this is what we believe, and we accept the No-Difference View, the implications are as follows.

I have suggested that we should appeal to

Q: If in either of two possible outcomes the same number of people would ever live, it will be worse if those who live are worse off, or have a lower quality of life, than those who would have lived.

Consider next

The Non-Identity Problem

The Person-Affecting View, or *V*: It will be worse if people are affected for the worse.

In Same People Choices, Q and V coincide. When we are considering these choices, those who live are the same in both outcomes. If these people are worse off, or have a lower quality of life, they are affected for the worse, and vice versa.[17] Since Q and V here coincide, it will make no difference to which we appeal.

The two claims conflict only in Same Number Choices. These are what this chapter has discussed. Suppose that we accept the No-Difference View. In considering these choices, we shall then appeal to Q *rather than* V. If we choose Depletion, this will lower the quality of life in the further future. According to Q, our choice has a bad effect. But, because of the facts about identity, our choice will be bad for no one. V does not imply that our choice has a bad effect. Would this effect be worse if it *was* worse for particular people? If we appealed to V rather than Q, our answer would be Yes. But, since we believe the No-Difference View, we answer No. We believe that V gives the wrong answer here. And V gives the wrong answer in the case of the Medical Programmes. Q describes the effects that we believe to be bad. And we believe that it makes no moral difference whether these effects are also bad according to V. V draws moral distinctions where, on our view, no distinctions should be drawn.

In Same People Choices, Q and V coincide. In Same Number Choices, where these claims conflict, we accept Q rather than V. When we make these two kinds of choice, we shall therefore have no use for V.

There remain the Different Number Choices, which Q does not cover. We shall here need Theory X. I have not yet discussed what X should claim. But we can predict the following. X will imply Q in Same Number Choices.

We can also predict that X will have the same relation to V. In Same People Choices, X and V will coincide. It will here make no difference to which we appeal. These are the choices with which most of our moral thinking is concerned. This explains the plausibility of V. This part of morality, the part concerned with beneficence, or human well-being, is usually thought of in what I shall call *person-affecting* terms. We appeal to people's interests—to what is good or bad for those people whom our acts affect. Even after we have found Theory X, we might continue to appeal to V in most cases, merely because it is more familiar. But in some cases X and V will conflict. They may conflict when we are making Same and Different Number Choices. And, whenever X and V conflict, we shall appeal to X *rather than* V. We shall believe that, if some effect is bad according to X, it makes no moral difference whether it is also bad according to V. As before, V draws a moral distinction where, on our view, no distinction should be drawn. V is like the claim that it is wrong to enslave whites, or to deny the vote to adult males. We shall thus conclude that this part of morality, the part concerned with beneficence and human well-being, cannot be explained

125. *Does The Fact Of Non-Identity Make A Moral Difference?* 371

in person-affecting terms. Its fundamental principles will not be concerned with whether our acts will be good or bad for those people whom they affect. Theory X will imply that an effect is bad if it is bad for people. But this will not be *why* this effect is bad.

Remember next that these claims assume that causing to exist cannot benefit. This assumption is defensible. If we make this assumption, these claims show that many moral theories need to be revised, since these theories imply that it must make a moral difference whether our acts are good or bad for those people whom they affect.[18] And we may need to revise our beliefs about certain common cases. One example might be abortion. But most of our moral thinking would be unchanged. Many significant relations hold only between particular people. These include our relations to those to whom we have made promises, or owe gratitude, or our parents, pupils, patients, clients, and (if we are politicians) those whom we represent. My remarks do not apply to such relations, or to the special obligations which they produce. My remarks apply only to our Principle of Beneficence: to our general moral reason to benefit other people, and to protect them from harm.

Since my remarks apply only to this principle, and we shall have changed our view only in some cases, this change of view may seem unimportant. This is not so. Consider once again this (too grandiose) analogy: In ordinary cases we can accept Newton's Laws. But not in all cases. And we now accept a different theory.

126. CAUSING PREDICTABLE CATASTROPHES IN THE FURTHER FUTURE

In this section, rather than pursuing the main line of my argument, I discuss a minor question. In a case like that of Depletion, we cannot wholly solve the Non-Identity Problem by an appeal to people's rights. Is this also true in a variant of the case, where our choice causes a catastrophe? Since this is a minor question, this section can be ignored, except by those who do not believe that Depletion has a bad effect. Consider

> *The Risky Policy.* As a community, we must choose between two energy policies. Both would be completely safe for at least three centuries, but one would have certain risks in the further future. This policy involves the burial of nuclear waste in areas where, in the next few centuries, there is no risk of an earthquake. But since this waste will remain radio-active for thousands of years, there will be risks in the distant future. If we choose this Risky Policy, the standard of living will be somewhat higher over the next century. We do choose this policy. As a result, there is a catastrophe many centuries later. Because of geological changes to the Earth's surface, an earthquake releases radiation, which kills thousands of people. Though they are killed by this catastrophe,

these people will have had lives that are worth living. We can assume that this radiation affects only people who are born after its release, and that it gives them an incurable disease that will kill them at about the age of 40. This disease has no effects before it kills.

Our choice between these two policies will affect the details of the lives that are later lived. In the way explained above, our choice will therefore affect who will later live. After many centuries there would be no one living in our community who, whichever policy we chose, would have been born. Because we chose the Risky Policy, thousands of people are later killed. But if we had chosen the alternative Safe Policy, these particular people would never have existed. Different people would have existed in their place. Is our choice of the Risky Policy worse for anyone?

We should ask, 'If people live lives that are worth living, even though they are killed by some catastrophe, is this worse for these people than if they had never existed?' Our answer must be No. Though it causes a predictable catastrophe, our choice of the Risky Policy will be worse for no one.

Some may claim that our choice of Depletion does not have a bad effect. This cannot be claimed about our choice of the Risky Policy. Since this choice causes a catastrophe, it clearly has a bad effect. But our choice will not be bad for, or worse for, any of the people who later live. This case forces us to reject the view that a choice cannot have a bad effect if this choice will be bad for no one.

In this case, the Non-Identity Problem may seem easier to solve. Though our choice is not worse for the people struck by the catastrophe, it might be claimed that we harm these people. And the appeal to people's rights may here succeed.

We can deserve to be blamed for harming others, even when this is not worse for them. Suppose that I drive carelessly, and in the resulting crash cause you to lose a leg. One year later, war breaks out. If you had not lost this leg, you would have been conscripted, and killed. My careless driving therefore saves your life. But I am still morally to blame.

This case reminds us that, in assigning blame, we must consider not actual but predictable effects. I knew that my careless driving might harm others, but I could not know that it would in fact save your life. This distinction might apply to our choice of the Risky Policy. Suppose we know that, if we choose this policy, this may in the distant future cause many accidental deaths. But we have overlooked the Non-Identity Problem. We mistakenly believe that, whichever policy we choose, the very same people will later live. We therefore believe that our choice of the Risky Policy may be very greatly against the interests of some future people. If we believe this, our choice can be criticized. We can deserve blame for doing what we *believe* may be greatly against the interests of other people. This criticism stands even if our belief is false—just as I am as much to blame even if my

126. *Causing Predictable Catastrophes In The Further Future*

careless driving will in fact save your life.

Suppose that we cannot find Theory X, or that X seems less plausible than the objection to doing what may be greatly against the interests of other people. It may then be better if we conceal the Non-Identity Problem from those who will decide whether we increase our use of nuclear energy. It may be better if these people believe falsely that such a policy may, by causing a catastrophe, be greatly against the interests of some of those who will live in the distant future. If these people have this false belief, they may be more likely to reach the right conclusions.

We have lost this false belief. We realize that, if we choose the Risky Policy, our choice will *not* be worse for those people whom the catastrophe later kills. Note that this is not a lucky guess. It is not like predicting that, if I cause you to lose a leg, this will later save you from death in the trenches. We know that, if we choose the Risky Policy, this may in the distant future cause many people to be killed. But we also know that, if we had chosen the Safe Policy, the people who are killed would never have been born. Since these people's lives will be worth living, we *know* that our choice will not be worse for them.

If we know this, we cannot be compared to a careless driver. What is the objection to our choice? Can it be wrong to harm others, when we know that our act will not be worse for the people harmed? This might be wrong if we could have asked these people for their consent, but have failed to do so. By failing to ask these people for their consent, we infringe their autonomy. But this cannot be the objection to our choice of the Risky Policy. Since we could not possibly communicate with the people living many centuries from now, we cannot ask for their consent.

When we cannot ask for someone's consent, we should ask instead whether this person would later regret what we are doing. Would the people who are later killed regret our choice of the Risky Policy? Let us suppose that these people know all of the facts. From an early age they know that, because of the release of radiation, they have an incurable disease that will kill them at about the age of 40. They also know that, if we had chosen the Safe Policy, they would never have been born. These people would regret the fact that they will die young. But, since their lives are worth living, they would not regret the fact that they were ever born. They would therefore not regret our choice of the Risky Policy.

Can it be wrong to harm others, when we know *both* that if the people harmed knew about our act, they would not regret this act, *and* that our act will not be worse for these people than anything else that we could have done? How might we know that, though we are harming someone, our act will not be worse for this person? There are at least two kinds of case:

(1) Though we are harming someone, we may also know that we are giving to this person some fully compensating benefit. We could not know this unless the benefit would clearly outweigh the harm. But, if this is so, what we are doing will be better for this person. In this kind of case, if we

are also not infringing this person's autonomy, there may be no objection to our act. There may be no objection to our harming someone when we know both that this person will have no regrets, and that our act will be clearly better for this person. In English Law, surgery was once regarded as justifiable grievous bodily harm. As I argued in Section 25, we should revise the ordinary use of the word 'harm'. If what we are doing will not be worse for some other person, or will even be better for this person, we are not, in a morally relevant sense, harming this person.

If we assume that causing to exist can benefit, our choice of the Risky Policy is, in its effects on those killed, like the case of the surgeon. Though our choice causes these people to be killed, since it also causes them to exist with a life worth living, it gives them a benefit that outweighs this harm. This suggests that the objection to our choice cannot be that it harms these people.

We may instead assume that causing to exist cannot benefit. On this assumption, our choice of the Risky Policy does not give to the people whom it kills some fully compensating benefit. Our choice is not *better* for these people. It is merely *not worse* for them.

(2) There is another kind of case in which we can know that, though we are harming someone on the ordinary use of 'harm', this will not be worse for this person. These are the cases that involve overdetermination. In these cases we know that, if we do not harm someone, this person will be harmed at least as much in some other way. Suppose that someone is trapped in a wreck and about to be burnt to death. This person asks us to shoot him, so that he does not die painfully. If we kill this person we are not, in a morally relevant sense, harming him.

Such a case cannot show that there is no objection to our choice of the Risky Policy, since it is not relevantly similar. If the catastrophe did not occur, the people killed would have lived for many more years. There is a quite different reason why our choice of the Risky Policy is not worse for these people.

Could there be a case in which we kill some existing person, knowing what we know when we choose the Risky Policy? We must know (*a*) that this person will learn but not regret the fact that we have done something that will cause him to be killed. And we must know (*b*) that, though this person would otherwise have lived a normal life for many more years, causing him to be killed will be neither better nor worse for him. ((*b*) is what we know about the effects of our choice of the Risky Policy, if we assume that, in doing what is a necessary part of the cause of the existence of the people killed by the catastrophe, we cannot be benefiting these people.)

Suppose that we kill some existing person, who would otherwise have lived a normal life for many more years. In such a case, we could not *know* that (*b*) is true. Even if living for these many years would be neither better nor worse for this person, this could never be predicted. There cannot be a case where we kill some existing person, knowing what we know when we choose the Risky Policy. A case that is relevantly similar must involve

126. *Causing Predictable Catastrophes In The Further Future*

causing someone to be killed who, if we had acted otherwise, would never have existed.

Compare these two cases:

Jane's Choice. Jane has a congenital disease, that will kill her painlessly at about the age of 40. This disease has no effects before it kills. Jane knows that, if she has a child, it will have this same disease. Suppose that she can also assume the following. Like herself, her child would have a life that is worth living. There are no children who need to be but have not been adopted. Given the size of the world's population when this case occurs (perhaps in some future century), if Jane has a child, this will not be worse for other people. And, if she does not have this child, she will be unable to raise a child. She cannot persuade someone else to have an extra child, whom she would raise. (These assumptions give us the relevant question.) Knowing these facts, Jane chooses to have a child.

Ruth's Choice. Ruth's situation is just like Jane's, with one exception. Her congenital disease, unlike Jane's, kills only males. If Ruth pays for the new technique of in vitro fertilization, she would be certain to have a daughter whom this disease would not kill. She decides to save this expense, and takes a risk. Unluckily, she has a son, whose inherited disease will kill him at about the age of 40.

Is there a moral objection to Jane's choice? Given the assumptions in the case, this objection would have to appeal to the effect on Jane's child. Her choice will not be worse for this child. Is there an objection to her choice that appeals to this child's rights? Suppose we believe that each person has a right to live a full life. Jane knows that, if she has a child, his right to a full life could not possibly be fulfilled. This may imply that Jane does not violate this right. But the objection could be restated. It could be said: 'It is wrong to cause someone to exist with a right that cannot be fulfilled. This is why Jane acts wrongly.'

Is this a good objection? If I was Jane's child, my view would be like that of the man who wrote to *The Times*. I would regret the fact that I shall die young. But, since my life is worth living, I would not regret that my mother caused me to exist. And I would deny that her act was wrong because of what it did to me. If I was told that it *was* wrong, because it caused me to exist with a right that cannot be fulfilled, I would *waive* this right.

If Jane's child waived his right, that might undermine this objection to her choice. But, though *I* would waive this right, I cannot be certain that, in all such cases, this is what such a child would do. If Jane's child does not waive his right, an appeal to this right may perhaps provide some objection to her choice.

Turn now to Ruth's choice. There is clearly a greater objection to *this* choice. This is because Ruth has a different alternative. If Jane does not have a child, she will not be able to raise a child; and one fewer life will be lived. Ruth's alternative is to pay for the technique that will give her a different child whom her disease will not kill. She chooses to save this expense, knowing that the chance is one in two that her child will be killed by this disease.

Even if there is an objection to Jane's choice, there is a greater objection to Ruth's choice. This objection cannot appeal only to the effects on Ruth's actual child, since these are just like the effects of Jane's choice on Jane's child. The objection to Ruth's choice must appeal in part to the possible effect on a different child who, by paying for the new technique, she could have had. The appeal to this effect is not an appeal to anyone's rights.

Return now to our choice of the Risky Policy. If we choose this policy, this may cause people to exist who will be killed in a catastrophe. We know that our choice would not be worse for these people. But, if there is force in the objection to Jane's choice, this objection would apply to our choice. By choosing the Risky Policy, we may cause people to exist whose right to a full life cannot be fulfilled.

The appeal to these people's rights may provide some objection to our choice. But it cannot provide the whole objection. Our choice is, in one respect, unlike Jane's. Her alternative was to have no child. Our alternative is like Ruth's. If we had chosen the Safe Policy, we would have had different descendants, none of whom would have been killed by released radiation.

The objection to Ruth's choice cannot appeal only to her child's right to a full life. The same is therefore true of the objection to our choice of the Risky Policy. This objection must in part appeal to the effects on the possible people who, if we had chosen differently, would have lived. As before, the appeal to rights cannot wholly solve the Non-Identity problem. We must also appeal to a claim like Q, which compares two different sets of possible lives.

It may be objected: 'When Ruth conceives her child, it inherits the disease that will deny it a full life. Because this child's disease is inherited in this way, it cannot be claimed that Ruth's choice kills her child. If we choose the Risky Policy, the causal connections are less close. Because the connections are less close, our choice kills the people who later die from the effects of released radiation. That we kill these people is the full objection to our choice.'

This objection I find dubious. Why is there a greater objection to our choice because the causal connections are less close? The objection may be correct in what it claims about our ordinary use of 'kill'. But, as I argued in Section 25, this use is morally irrelevant. Since that argument may not convince, I add

The Risky Cure for Infertility. **Ann** cannot have a child unless she takes a certain treatment. If she takes this treatment, she will have a son, who will be healthy. But there is a risk that this treatment will give her a rare

126. *Causing Predictable Catastrophes In The Further Future*

disease. This disease has the following features. It is undetectable, and does not harm women, but it can infect one's closest relatives. The following is therefore true. If Ann takes this treatment and has a healthy son, there is a chance of one in two that she will later infect her son in a way that will kill him when he is about forty. Ann chooses to take this treatment, and she does later infect her son with this fatal disease.

On the objection stated above, there is a strong objection to Ann's choice, which does not apply to Ruth's choice. Because the causal connections are less close, Ann's choice kills her son. And she knew that the chance was one in two that her choice would have this effect. Ruth knows that that there is the same chance that her child will die at about the age of 40. But, because the causal connections are so close, her choice does not kill her son. According to this objection, this difference has great moral relevance.

This is not plausible. Ruth and Ann both know that, if they act in a certain way, there is a chance of one in two that they will have sons who will be killed by a disease at about the age of forty. The causal story is different. But this does not make Ann's choice morally worse. I believe that this example shows that we should reject this last objection.

The objector might say: 'I deny that, by choosing to take the Risky Cure, Ann kills her son'. But, if the objector denies this, he cannot claim that, by choosing the Risky Policy, we kill some people in the distant future. The causal connections take the same form. Each choice produces a side-effect which later kills people who owe their existence to this choice.

If this objection fails, as I believe, my earlier claim is justified. It is morally significant that, if we choose the Risky Policy, our choice is like Ruth's rather than Jane's. It is morally significant that, if we had chosen otherwise, different people would have lived who would not have been killed. Since this is so, the objection to our choice cannot appeal only to the rights of those who actually later live. It must also appeal to a claim like Q, which compares different sets of possible lives. As I claimed earlier, the appeal to rights cannot wholly solve the Non-Identity Problem.

127. CONCLUSIONS

I shall now summarize what I have claimed. It is in fact true of everyone that, if he had not been conceived within a month of the time when he was conceived, he would never have existed. Because this is true, we can easily affect the identities of future people, or *who* the people are who will later live. If a choice between two social policies will affect the standard of living or the quality of life for about a century, it will affect the details of all the lives that, in our community, are later lived. As a result, some of those who later live will owe their existence to our choice of one of these two policies. After one or two centuries, this will be true of everyone in our community.

The Non-Identity Problem

This fact produces a problem. One of these two policies may, in the further future, cause a great lowering of the quality of life. This would be the effect of the policy I call Depletion. This effect is bad, and provides a moral reason not to choose Depletion. But, because of the fact just mentioned, our choice of Depletion will be worse for no one. Some people believe that a choice cannot have bad effects if this choice will be worse for no one. The Case of Depletion shows that we must reject this view. And this is shown more forcefully by the Case of the Risky Policy. One effect of choosing this policy is a catastrophe that kills thousands of people. This effect is clearly bad, even though our choice will be worse for no one.

Since these two choices will be worse for no one, we need to explain why we have a moral reason not to make these choices. This problem arises because, in the different outcomes, different people would exist. I therefore call this the Non-Identity Problem.

I asked whether we can solve this problem by appealing to people's rights. I argued that, even in the case of the Risky Policy, the objection to our choice cannot appeal only to people's rights. The objection must in part appeal to a claim like Q, which compares different possible lives. And we cannot plausibly appeal to rights in explaining the objection to our choice of Lesser Depletion. Even after the great lowering of the quality of life, those who will be living will be much better off than we are now. These people cannot be claimed to have a *right* to the even higher quality of life that different people would have enjoyed if we had chosen Conservation. If we imagine away the Non-Identity Problem, the objection to our choice would appeal to our Principle of Beneficence. To solve the Non-Identity Problem, we must revise this principle.

One revised principle is Q, the Same Number Quality Claim. According to Q, if in either of two outcomes there would be the same number of people, it would be worse if those who live are worse off, or have a lower quality of life, than those who would have lived. We need a wider principle to cover cases where, in the different outcomes, there would be different numbers of people. This needed principle I call Theory X. Only X will fully solve the Non-Identity Problem.

Does the fact of non-identity make a moral difference? When we see that our choice of Depletion will be worse for no one, we may believe that there is less objection to our choice. But I believe that the objection is just as strong. And I have a similar belief when I compare the effects of the two Medical Programmes. This belief I call the No Difference View. Though I know of some people who do not accept this view, I know of more who do. If we accept the No Difference View, and believe that causing to exist cannot benefit, this has wide theoretical implications. We can predict that Theory X will not take a person-affecting form. The best theory about beneficence will not appeal to what is good or bad for those people whom our acts affect.

In what follows, I shall try to find Theory X. As I have claimed, this attempt will raise some puzzling questions.

Notes

1 RAVERAT.
2 See KRIPKE, BOGEN, FORBES (1).
3 See the discussion of these views, and the suggested references, in KRIPKE.
4 Suggested to me by D. Wiggins, who also cites H. Ishiguro.
5 Some people claim that there are no distinctive essential properties. This implies that, for each of these people, it is an empty question whether, if his parents had never married, *he* would never have existed. Though I believe that there could be empty questions about our identity, I doubt whether, on reflection, these people would believe *this* question to be empty. (There are, in the special case of monovular twins, some empty questions here. I hope to discuss this point elsewhere.)
6 What is the relation between this subject and personal identity over time? On the Origin View, it is an essential property of each person that he grew from a particular fertilized ovum. This view could be combined with the Physical Criterion. On the most plausible version of this criterion, one essential property of each person is that he has enough of his particular brain to support fully conscious life. It might be claimed that it is an essential property of any particular brain that it grew from a particular fertilized ovum.

The Physical Criterion need not be combined with the Origin View. A believer in this criterion might accept the Backward Variation View. I described how, on this view, Tolstoy might have had a different origin. In this imagined different possible history, the Physical Criterion would have been fulfilled. Similarly, we could accept the Origin View but reject the Physical Criterion. We might combine the Origin View with the wide versions of the Psychological Criterion. We would then believe that it is essential to me that I grew from a particular pair of cells, and that I therefore started living in a particular body. But we would also believe that my life could continue in a different body. This would happen, for instance, if I was Teletransported.

Consider next the Psychological Criterion, which appeals to psychological continuity. Those who believe in this criterion might agree that my life could have gone quite differently. And between me in my actual life and myself in this different possible life there might be very little psychological continuity. Suppose that my parents had taken me to Italy when I was three years old, and that I had become an Italian. There would then be the following relation between me now and myself as I might now have been. Both in my actual life and in this different possible life I would now be psychologically continuous with myself in my actual life when I was three. This relation would be weak. There are few direct psychological connections between me now and myself when I was three. If we compare my actual life with this different possible life, the two lives might not in adulthood contain even a single common memory.

Some believers in the Psychological Criterion might claim that these are not two possible lives of the same particular person—that the child who would have gone to Italy at the age of three would have been, not me, but a different person. This claim revises our ordinary view about personal identity.

This revision is both technically difficult and unnecessary. The point can be made more simply. If I had gone to Italy at the age of three, my life would have been very different. And we may believe that this fact has various practical and moral implications. But this belief need not be expressed by denying the identity between me in my actual life and myself in this different possible life. We can admit that this relation is identity. We can make our point by claiming that, when we are comparing such very different possible lives, the fact of personal identity does not have its ordinary significance. See ADAMS (3).

7 For the reasons given by Brian Barry's 'Circumstances of Justice and Future Generations', in SIKORA AND BARRY.
8 See *Teenage Pregnancy in a Family Context: Implications for Policy Decisions*, edited by Theodora Ooms (née Parfit), Temple University Press, Philadelphia, 1981.
9 This problem has been called by Kavka *The Paradox of Future Individuals*. See KAVKA (4).
10 I follow ADAMS (3).
11 See T. Schwartz, 'Obligations to Posterity', in SIKORA AND BARRY.
13 This form of the objection is suggested in TOOLEY.
14 See B. Barry, 'Intergenerational Justice in Energy Policy', in MACLEAN AND BROWN ; see also BARRY (2).
15 For a further discussion, see J. WOODWARD, 'The Non-Identity Problem', in *Ethics*, July 1986.
16 J. McMahan has suggested to me that, if the handicap greatly affected the nature of these people's lives, it may not be clear that someone with a lifelong handicap would have been better off if he had been born normal. Some may doubt whether, in the relevant sense, these two very different lives would have been lived by the same person. And ADAMS (3) suggests that, even if such a person would have been better off, this need not imply that it would be irrational for him not to regret his handicap. If we accept either claim, the example is not what we need. We can avoid these questions by supposing that the handicap affects these people only when they are adults. The handicap might be, for example, sterility.
17 There may seem to be one exception. If my life is worth living, killing me affects me for the worse, but does it cause me to be worse off, or to have a lower quality of life? As I use the phrase, I do have 'a lower quality of life'. This is true if my life goes less well than it could have gone, or if what happens in my life is worse for me. Both are true when, with a life worth living, I am killed.
18 One example is the plausible theory advanced in SCANLON (3). Scanlon argues that the best account of moral motivation is not that given by Utilitarians, who appeal to universal philanthropy. Our fundamental moral motive is instead 'the desire to be able to justify one's actions to others on grounds that they could not reasonably reject'. Scanlon sketches an attractive moral theory built upon this claim. On this theory, an act is wrong if it will affect someone in a way that cannot be justified—if there will be some complainant whose complaint cannot be answered. On this theory, the framework of morality is essentially person-affecting. Unfortunately, when we choose a policy like Greater Depletion, there will be no complainants. If we believe that this makes no moral difference, since the objection to our choice is just as strong, we believe that it is irrelevant that there will be no complainants. The fundamental principle of Scanlon's theory draws a distinction where, on our view, no distinction should be drawn. Scanlon's theory therefore needs to be revised.

Similar remarks apply to many other theories. Thus BRANDT (2) suggests that to the phrase 'is morally wrong' we should assign the descriptive meaning 'would be prohibited by any moral code which all fully rational persons would tend to support, in preference to all others or to none at all, for the society of the agent, if they expected to spend a lifetime in that society' (p. 194). It seems likely that, on the chosen code, an act would not be wrong if there are no complainants. Similar remarks apply to GERT, to J. Narveson, *Morality and Utility*, and to G. R. Grice, *The Grounds of Moral Judgement*, and they may apply to MACKIE (2), RICHARDS, HARMAN, GAUTHIER (4), RAWLS, and others.

523a *Bibliography*

BIBLIOGRAPHY

ADAMS (3): R. M., 'Existance, Self-Interest, and the Problem of Evil', *Nous* 13, 1979.
BARRY (2): B., 'Justice Between Generations', in P. M. S. Hacker and J. Raz, eds., *Law, Morality, and Society: Essays in Honour of H. L. A. Hart,* Oxford, Clarendon Press, 1977.
BOGEN : J., 'Identity and Origin', *Analysis* 26, Apr. 1966.
BRANDT (2): R. B., *A Theory of the Good and the Right,* Oxford, Clarendon Press, 1979.
FORBES (1): G., 'Origin and Identity', *Philosophical Studies* 37, 1980.
GAUTHIER (4): D., *Morals By Agreement* (provisional title), Oxford, Clarendon Press, forthcoming.
HARMAN: G., *The Nature of Morality,* Oxford University Press, 1977.
KAVKA (4): G., 'The Paradox of Future Individuals', *Philosophy and Public Affairs* 11, No.2, Spring 1982.
KRIPKE: S. A., 'Naming and Necessity', in G. Harman and D. Davidson, eds., *Semantics of Natural Language,* Dordrecht, Reidel, 1972.
MACKIE (2): J. L., *Ethics,* Harmondsworth, Penguin Books, 1977.
MACLEAN AND BROWN: D. MacLean and P. G. Brown, eds., *Energy and the Future,* Totowa, N.J., Rowman and Littlefield, 1983.
RAVERAT: G., *Period Piece,* London, Faber and Faber, 1952.
RAWLS: J., *A Theory of Justice,* Cambridge, Mass., Harvard University Press, 1971.
RICHARDS: D. A. J., *A Theory of Reasons for Action,* Oxford, Clarendon Press, 1971.
SCANLON (3): T. M., 'Contractualism and Utilitarianism', in SEN AND WILLIAMS.
SIKORA AND BARRY: R. I. Sikora and B. Barry, eds., *Obligations to Future Generations,* Philadelphia, Temple University Press, 1978.
TOOLEY: M., *Abortion and Infanticide,* Oxford, Clarendon Press, 1983.

[4]
The Intractability of the Nonidentity Problem

David Heyd

Abstract The author, in this paper and elsewhere, defends a person-affecting approach to morality, according to which an act that harms *no one* cannot be wrong, together with the argument from the nonidentity problem that any act that adversely affects only those future persons who owe their existence to that act's being performed cannot properly be said to harm those future persons. Extending the logic of the nonidentity problem to cases involving not just strict numerical identity but "biographical identity" as well, the author argues that agents do nothing wrong when they raise a child under, or return a child to, a particular biographical identity, since a new biographical identity, even if more advantageous, would not make the one child better off but instead replace the one child with another child—a biographically nonidentical child—altogether.

Keywords Biographical identity · Person-affecting approach · Nonidentity problem.

1.1 The Logical and Metaphysical Dimensions of the Problem

Ethics and metaphysics have always been bound together in a philosophically problematic way. From the first chapter of Genesis and in many of the pre-modern metaphysical systems, the very existence of the world and its inner order were explained in terms of some ultimate good. No less prevalent was the attempt to explicate the concepts of the good life and moral virtue, justice and rights, in terms of human essential nature. But with the loss of confidence in, and consensus on, an overall metaphysical picture of the world, philosophers tried to articulate moral theories with no metaphysical foundations. Moral and political constructivism, of the kind articulated by Kant and Rawls, aimed at severing the classical bond of ethics and metaphysics. But it is far from certain that even constructivism can succeed

D. Heyd (✉)
The Hebrew University of Jerusalem, Jerusalem, Israel
e-mail: david.heyd@huji.ac.il

in such complete separation. For even if a system of rights and duties, principles of justice and concepts of the good can be purely constructed by reason, some metaphysical assumptions cannot be avoided. For example, both Kant and Rawls are committed to metaphysical individualism, i.e. the non-arbitrary consideration of individuals as the basic building blocks of the normative system. The concept of the individual person cannot itself be constructed.

One sphere in which metaphysics forces itself on moral theory is what I have referred to in the past as "genethics," namely the cluster of problems relating to the creation of new people: the determination of their very existence, their number and their identity. These problems can be divided into two categories or levels: the species and the individual. Questions such as the value of the existence of human beings (think of God's ante-diluvian and post-diluvian reflections) or the ethics of shaping the human genome (of the kind Jürgen Habermas is concerned with in his *The Future of Human Nature*)[1] belong to the first category. The issues of family planning, sex selection and demographic policies, which decide which individuals will exist and how many, belong to the second. But on both levels of discussion, some metaphysical questions cannot be avoided: in the case of the species, what are the contours of human nature (if there is any such essential nature)? In the case of individuals, how is a human being identified as a particular person and to what extent is such individuation relevant to the morality of procreation?

The nonidentity problem is one of the most succinct metaphysical challenges to moral theory. In retrospect, it seems surprising that it was not addressed by philosophers till the 1970s. The obvious explanation is that the numerical identity of those to whom moral judgment applies was naturally taken for granted and that only once humanity has acquired far-reaching control over procreation (by means of birth control, demographic planning and genetic screening) did the problem of nonidentity impose itself on moral theory. It is to the immense credit of Derek Parfit that he was the first to take up the challenge and not only articulate the problem but also show how fundamental and inescapable it was. Unlike the identity problem of the kind Locke was thinking of in the context of his discussion of responsibility and punishment, the *nonidentity* problem raises the question of the general limits of moral judgment.

The nonidentity problem can be mapped on a two-tier structure. On the first level lies the question whether the identity of persons is at all a relevant issue to moral judgments concerning the good, the right and the just. If the answer to this question is positive, a second-level question must be addressed, namely what kind of identity is presupposed by such judgments? The first question is conceptual, relating to the logic and conditions of moral judgment. The second is metaphysical and concerns the nature of those entities that are considered the carriers of value and rights. The first, preliminary question is the focus of the deep debate between the "impersonalist" and the "person-affecting" approaches to the nature of value in general. But then, once this debate is decided, the metaphysical question of what are the objects of value judgments and who are their subjects arises. More specifically, if we adopt a person-affecting view of morality, who are the relevant "persons" (affected)? I will first discuss the first question (in Section 1.2) and then proceed to make some comments on the second (in Section 1.3).[2]

1.2 Four Strategies for Responding to the Nonidentity Problem

The nonidentity problem presents ethical theory with a major challenge: if the consequences of our "genethical" choices are such that the affected future people are different in number or in identity from those who would have been affected had our choice been different, can we apply our moral principles (whether utilitarian or deontological, right-based or duty-based) to these choices? Although most of our moral choices remain unaffected by the nonidentity problem,[3] modern science and technology have created a long list of important decisions in which nonidentity is an intriguing theoretical obstacle. Wrongful life cases, demographic policies, intergenerational justice, genetic engineering, sex selection through PGD are all concerned with future people under problematic identity. And, as philosophers have lately noted, there are also backward-looking cases like affirmative action or compensation and apology for past crimes which raise the problem of nonidentity.[4] Should we compensate someone for wrongs done to her ancestors when it can be proved that *she* would not have existed had the wrong not taken place?

There are four principal ways to deal with the challenge of nonidentity:

1. Denying it is a problem to begin with.
2. Aspiring to solve it in some (yet unknown) integrative moral theory in the future.
3. Attenuating it so as to make it more palatable to our moral intuitions and theories.
4. Biting the bullet, i.e. accepting all the implications of the nonidentity problem.

The first strategy characterizes the view called "impersonalism," which holds that value is not human-dependent but an attribute of the world. The second response is associated with Parfit's own approach and his search for "Theory X," combining person-affecting and impersonal intuitions, both of which are impossible to give up. The third way tries to adhere to a person-affecting view by interpreting it in a wide sense or by supplementing it with impersonal features. The fourth reply to the challenge consists of embracing all the consequences and ramifications of the nonidentity problem, including those which may be less appealing to our common intuitions, and doing so by adhering to a strict person-affecting view.

I will try in Sections 1.2.1, 1.2.2 and 1.2.3 below to examine in some detail the flaws of the first three responses and discuss in Section 1.2.4 the inescapable superiority of the fourth, thus demonstrating that nonidentity matters and makes genethical choices categorically different from choices regarding present or actual people. This discussion belongs to the conceptual analysis of the nonidentity problem. In Section 1.3, I will address the metaphysical question of the kind and scope of a person's identity and explore the way in which this can serve to support the person-affecting approach.

A preliminary methodological comment might be worth making. The nonidentity problem is *sui generis*. It is unique in the sense that analogies from other contexts of moral judgment can be of little help. Since it relates to the sphere of the very creation of subjects and objects of moral values and rights, applying theories of value and rights to the act of their creation is logically puzzling like any bootstrapping feat.

Our established notions of legal harm and benefit cannot serve as guides in the genethical sphere, since the whole point of the challenge of the nonidentity problem is to show that they *presuppose* the existence of identifiable persons.[5] We may nevertheless think of two possible analogies from which we might derive some insight on the matter—*divine* creation and *self*-creation, which are both "genethical" in their nature. The former, which is not discussed here, is an abstract and pure theological test case which has some interesting results with which I have dealt elsewhere.[6] The latter has to do with the unique human capacity to control one's own identity to some degree and in that respect create oneself. It will turn out below (1.3) to be a useful analogy in the discussion of the nonidentity problem.

1.2.1 Denying the Problem

The first response on our list to the nonidentity problem is the denial of its relevance. Even if goodness, justice and freedom can be attributed to the world only through the mediation of human beings who are their subjects, there is value in promoting goodness, justice and liberty in the world, independently of human beings. This might sound strange, since goodness, justice and liberty cannot exist without human beings. But this is exactly the genethical challenge to moral theory: is there a value, or even a duty, to create "carriers" of those values, namely human beings, so as to have goodness, justice and liberty in the world? Is a human-less world any worse than a human-populated one? Impersonalists answer the question in the positive. They attribute value "to the world." A world of million happy people is better than a world with no people at all. And it is also better than a world with half a million equally happy people, even if these are completely different people. The question of the identity of the people in two alternative worlds which are compared for their value does not arise. *Who* is made happier by some beneficent act is unimportant as long as it creates more happiness in the world than any alternative act.

There is no direct way to rebut this view of value. Philosophers have brought up various examples that seem to make this approach unattractive, if not plainly absurd, like the famous "Repugnant Conclusion" or the duty to bring children to the world whenever that serves to increase the "total" happiness. But impersonal utilitarians are unperturbed by the nonidentity problem, since for them, even if the repugnant conclusion is an embarrassment, nonidentity is not; for whenever we have to choose between two options with the same number of people created in each option, we should follow the impersonal balance of utility and ignore the (different) identity of the individuals affected. But even the somewhat less disturbing case of the duty to promote the "average" happiness creates problems for the impersonalist, since it might imply serious restrictions on reproduction and a demand that each generation become more selective in the creation of new people than its predecessors. When it comes to justice, the impersonalist encounters even a harder conflict with commonsense moral thinking. For justice seems to be an ideal *for* human beings rather than some good *tout court*. Thus, when Rawls, in his later writings, argues that the principle of justice to future generations only requires the preservation of the justice of the basic structure of future society (rather than any particular intergenerational distribution), it is not clear what kind of value justice is. On the one hand, it seems that it is good only if there are human beings for whom it is good. On the other hand, we could shape the interests of our descendants (either by educational or by genetic means) so that they do not appreciate the value of justice (e.g. are not concerned with fairness). Would such a decision be, according to Rawls, morally permissible? And if not, would it not commit him to an impersonal view of justice?

Impersonalism dismisses the charge of nonidentity by simply denying the person-affecting nature of value (rights, justice, equality, etc.). It is the world in general which is made better by good deeds, regardless of who are the carriers or subjects of that value. Indeed, value can be attributed to the natural world independently of human beings, as some advocates of the principle of biodiversity claim, and as long as human beings are around on the planet and exercise control over it, they have a duty to preserve the variety of species and the sustainability of the environment independently of its value for human beings. But these are views which are difficult to defend, and philosophers often appeal to non-moral (aesthetic or religious) notions of shame or loss ("it would be a pity if...") as substitute for the moral grounding of such duties and values.

The impersonalist must identify what makes the world better (impersonally). It could be, as classical utilitarianism suggested, positive states of mind (such as pleasant experiences). But these do not lend themselves to easy individuation (can one answer the question "how many positive experiences did you have today?"). In response, the impersonalist could suggest that rather than aggregate positive and negative psychological states, we should aim to increase the overall happiness in the world by making people happier *and* by creating happy people. But this approach assumes that there is an objective way, independent of first-personal evaluations, to assess the overall balance of the happiness of a single person as well as to compare it to the balance of happiness of another person. This difficulty forces the impersonalist back either to the weighting and aggregation of individual experiences or to the way individual persons assess the happiness of their lives from their point of view. The first possibility raises the above mentioned problem of individuation of depersonalized experiences; the second makes the impersonalist vulnerable to the nonidentity problem. Impersonal utilitarianism tries to avoid both the classical problem of personal identity (the unity behind a series of discrete experiences) and the new problem of nonidentity (the incomparability of utilities of an actual person with those of possible, non-identical alternative persons). But such avoidance comes with a price.

1.2.2 Hoping for Future Solution

Derek Parfit is at pains to salvage his fundamental impersonalist intuitions from the challenge of the nonidentity problem. An action can make the world worse without wronging any actual human being. Unwilling to give up impersonalism but recognizing the force of the constraints of identity of the persons affected by human action, Parfit tries to do justice to both. But after having meticulously examined various options, he admits that he has failed. All he is left with is a *hope*, an aspiration to find a "Theory X" which would integrate our conflicting intuitions and resolve the tension between the Repugnant Conclusion and the nonidentity problem.[7] The final section of *Reasons and Persons* expresses a hope (which is reminiscent of the Kantian "dialectic" hope in being only partly grounded in reason) that "non-religious ethics," which at present is only at an early stage, would make *progress* in the future and develop moral reasoning that would provide us with such Theory X.[8] But can we even hope for such a theory?

Parfit suggests in that final section that the difference between killing 100% of humanity and killing 99% of it is much larger (i.e. is worse) than that between killing 99% of the humanity and killing no one. This is a very bold impersonalist statement, which Parfit justifies in terms of the loss of overall happiness involved in the cessation of all future human life on the planet and the loss of the potential of progress in art and science *and* (surprisingly!) in moral reasoning. The problem is that although Parfit explicitly dissociates himself from any religious conception of ethics, his approach seems to be committed to some teleological view. For, happiness (as well as justice, artistic beauty and scientific truth) is either good for actual human beings or for the world (a kind of realization of an essential potential which it would be wrong to curtail). But once there are no human beings who can satisfy their desires and perfect their abilities, can we say, without making strong teleological assumptions, that the world would lack something that could be good? It is hard to see how progress in science, art and ethics is valuable independently of human beings for whom such progress is a genuine interest, source of satisfaction or ideal. After all, the world has no interests. Parfit, who follows Sidgwick on that matter, is wrong in arguing that the destruction of humanity is the worst conceivable crime due to "the vast reduction of the possible sum of happiness."[9] Voluntary collective suicide of human beings is in my view less of a "crime" (if it is a crime at all) than the deliberate murder of people. Or to put the argument against the impersonalist analysis in person-affecting terms: there are no crimes against humanity; only crimes against humans.

So it seems that the hope for a Theory X is misguided since as Parfit himself has shown pure impersonalism with no regard for person-affecting considerations leads to absurd results but person-affecting considerations involve the insurmountable problem of nonidentity. There seems to be nothing that we don't know "yet" about the matter and which through progress in moral reasoning we would be able to discover. The nonidentity problem is not a scientific or a mathematical problem which will be solved through further research or reasoning. It seems more likely that it will be dissolved rather than solved, and that this will happen when our notions of identity change and adapt to the new forms of control we can expect to acquire in genetics and in social policy over future human beings. So although this is a matter of speculation, it seems that the "solution" will occur on the level of the metaphysics of the subject of moral judgment rather than on the level of the logic of the ascription of value.

So although Parfit was the first to recognize the acuteness of the nonidentity problem, he aligned himself with the impersonalist position, at least in the sense that he resisted the option of a fully person-affecting view of morality. But unlike the impersonalist denial of the challenge, Parfit believes that moral theory cannot be complete without addressing it.

1.2.3 Accommodating Nonidentity

We turn now to the third response. As is typical of sharp moral dilemmas, philosophers as well as lay people feel the pull of both horns. Most of us shirk the counterintuitive implications of pure impersonalism (like the duty to create a huge number of barely worthwhile human lives as long as the *overall* level of happiness in the world is promoted through their sheer numbers). But limiting moral judgment to actual, identifiable individuals makes us feel equally uneasy. Parfit recognizes this conflict but leaves us only with the hope of some future theoretical solution. But many philosophers in the past two decades have suggested solutions to the nonidentity problem. They may be categorized into two groups: the first, those who believe that we should accept combined personal and impersonal considerations in moral judgment, at least in those rare "genethical" cases; the second, those who deny that such a compromise is coherent and advocate a revised form of person-affecting theory that can accommodate at least most of the difficult challenges of the impersonalist. I shall discuss the two in turn in the following Sections 1.2.3.1 and 1.2.3.2.

1.2.3.1 Combining Person-Affecting with Impersonalist Approaches

The authors of *From Chance to Choice* admit that they do not have a full solution to the nonidentity problem and that it is a very complex issue which can be decided only in the light of a broad spectrum of questions that lie beyond genetics.[10] Nevertheless they do commit themselves to the view that despite the general validity of the person-affecting approach, there are cases in which an appeal to impersonalist principles is inevitable (such as the creation of "wrongful life" in personal reproductive decisions or the so-called "different number choices" in population policies). They accept Parfit's argument that the child in his famous example of the 14-year-old girl who decides to conceive is not harmed, and they also claim that it is not wronged (even though the mother acts wrongly). They argue, in conclusion, for a principle according to which it is wrong to create *any* child who would suffer from a serious disability if that can be avoided without a high cost to the parents and without affecting the number of future people.[11] The adolescent girl should wait till she can conceive *another* child, later on, who will be happier than the one she contemplates conceiving now. They concede that this is a "non-person-affecting" principle.

This, however, is at most an *ad hoc* solution, which might appease our intuitive objections to some implications of the person-affecting view, but is not theoretically satisfying in the sense that it does not provide a principled way of relating person- and non-person-affecting principles (as the authors admit[12]). Its *ad hoc* nature is manifest in the authors' claim that the impersonalist principle is to be introduced only when the suffering or the defect of the future child is "serious." But nonidentity is not a matter of the *degree* of harm or pain but a conceptual constraint regarding the conditions for making any moral judgment. And hence the authors' evaluation that causing a handicap to an existing child is a *more* serious moral wrong than causing the birth of a similarly handicapped child remains theoretically unexplained and appears more like a compromise which tries to pacify the challenge of nonidentity.

Being similarly committed to the importance of identity in moral judgment but equally reluctant to accept the full implications of the nonidentity problem, David DeGrazia, like the authors of *From Chance to Choice*, opts for a middle way. He takes seriously the nonidentity problem and argues that although intentionally conceiving a handicapped child rather than a healthy one is wrong, it is not a wrong *to* the child.[13] But then what kind of wrong is it? One way to describe it (which he correctly ascribes to me) is that the parents wrong themselves or society. But since DeGrazia strongly rejects that kind of explanation of the wrong, all he is left with are impersonal considerations which suppress the nonidentity problem. Consequently, like the authors of *From Chance to Choice*, DeGrazia suggests supplementing the person-affecting principles with an impersonal one: in Same People choices, apply person-affecting considerations; in Same Number choices, apply impersonal considerations. But this solution seems again to be *ad hoc*, an attempt to explain our intuitions about the wrongness of the choice of the 14-year-old girl without embracing a fully impersonalist view. DeGrazia himself admits that he does not have a theoretical explanation for the relationship between the person-affecting and the impersonal supplementary principles in ethical theory and that when it comes to Different Number Choices the right way for ethical theory to approach them "remains mysterious."[14] Even if he is right in considering the person-affecting principle as having more moral weight than the impersonal, how, for example, would he compare the one-time wrongness done to an actual individual with the impersonal bad consequences created to a thousand future, non-identifiable people who are going to be born as the result of some social choice we make? Can the two be compared in the first place?

Jeff McMahan is also working within a generally person-affecting view. In the end of his detailed critical examination of Peter Singer's "replaceability argument," he reaches the conclusion that choosing between an existing (suffering) newborn and another future (happy) child can be made on person-affecting grounds. That is to say, Singer's problem of infanticide should be decided in terms of the interests of existing people (weighing the interests of the existing child in going on living and those of the parents and society) rather than on impersonal grounds of the kind Singer appeals to (according to Singer, infanticide can be justified in terms of the overall increase in the impersonal balance of happiness in the world achieved by the "replacement" of the suffering newborn with a future healthy child).[15] But then McMahan is very sensitive to the "notorious" difficulty to defend the asymmetry between the duty to prevent the birth of a suffering child and the absence of a parallel duty to cause the birth of a happy child. If consistency is sought on this matter, we will be forced to accept that the fact that a person would have a good life serves as a reason to cause that person to exist, even though this reason is weak, weaker than that assumed by Singer.[16] But again, one may wonder why there should be a difference between the weight of the reasons to avoid the conception of a suffering child and those of the reasons for creating a happy child. McMahan himself asserts that he doubts whether the person-affecting and the impersonal intuitions we have can ever be reconciled. I contend that the consistent solution to the asymmetry problem is to deny that there are moral reasons (relating to the rights and interests of the future child) either to create it (happy) or not to create it (suffering).

1.2.3.2 Widening the Scope of the Person-Affecting Approach

It seems then that if pure impersonalism is incompatible with some of our fundamental moral views and if there is no way to incorporate it with person-affecting principles in one integrated theory (either in Parfit's sense of Theory X or in some compromise of the kind examined in the previous section), we are left with the option of the person-affecting approach. But the nonidentity problem presents us with a serious challenge, which threatens to undermine some equally fundamental views in the morality of procreation, demographic planning and environmental policies. Many philosophers have tried to meet the challenge without abandoning the person-affecting view or resorting to impersonalist supplements.

One strategy is to view future possible people *as if* they were all actual, or, in Parfit's terms, to consider "different people choices" as if they were "same people choices." Tim Mulgan believes that such an "as if" approach would lead to overall better reproductive choices from an impersonal point of view, thus avoiding the trap of the nonidentity of possible people which seems to lend us permission to create whomever we want. But Mulgan himself is aware that like any "as if" policy of this kind, this approach can work only if people are not aware of it! So even if this manipulative strategy is pragmatically useful, it obviously cannot serve as a theoretical response to the challenge of nonidentity. In any case Mulgan's idea indirectly proves how strong our person-affecting intuitions are and that the impersonalist consequentialist results of the kind Mulgan wishes to attain are best served by a person-affecting illusion.[17] Like the attempts to integrate person-affecting and impersonalist principles, discussed above, Mulgan wishes to give moral standing to both actual and possible people. But since he believes the former have *more* moral weight than the latter, he recommends that we think "as if" all future people are actual.

Another strategy to save the person-affecting approach from the challenge of nonidentity is taking *types* of people rather than individuals as the objects of evaluation in genesis choices. It is usually agreed that harm can be done only to actual people who have undergone some loss due to the harm done *to* them and hence that wrongful conception cases cannot make strict legal sense in tort law.[18] But some philosophers, like Rahul Kumar, argue that a child born in such circumstances can be said to have been *wronged*, even if not harmed. Although the child is not worse off than he could have been, his or her respect has been violated since wronging (in contrast to harming) is a matter of the agent's character rather than of the consequence for the other party. But why is not wronging subject to the same constraint of the identity of its "victim" in exactly the same way as harming is? Kumar answers that one can be wronged as a *type* of person, so that I have similar duties to my future (unidentified) children as I have to my students (whoever they are). And society in general has such duties towards future generations, when the type of person to which these duties are owed is the rational, autonomous individual of a Scanlonian contract. Such a person-type has a legitimate expectation of respect that should not be violated even if no harm can be identified to any person-token.[19]

This is an interesting attempt to preserve the person-affecting view while escaping the paradoxical implications of the nonidentity problem. However, it faces some serious difficulties. First, if wronging (in contrast to harming) has to do exclusively with the character of the *agent*, how can it affect the "receiver" of the action in any way, including the violation of her respect or dignity? And if it does affect her, does it not involve making her "worse off" than she was or could have been? This suggests that we either view wronging as having the same structure as harming in the effects on another party or consider it as a matter of the agent's character and accordingly judge it in terms of the way the agent alone is affected. In both cases the person-affecting view is upheld but only on the basis of assuming the identity of an actual person (agent or victim) who is affected by the action. Secondly, Kumar's contractualist abstraction of actual individual people into idealized types of agents who have some universal properties is indeed a powerful theoretical tool in the device of a hypothetical contract, but it turns out to be based on confusion between a hypothetical contract and a contract between hypothetical people. Teachers and students can form contractual agreements like employers and employees, but the contract is not between types of people but between actual individual people, present or future, known or unknown (albeit of a certain type).

To examine this confusion more closely, consider Jeffrey Reiman's proposal for the solution of the nonidentity problem within a person-affecting view. According to his view, "future people have rights irrespective of which particulars they turn out to be."[20] Reiman correctly points out that Rawls' veil of ignorance hides the property of one's temporal position (namely, to which generation one belongs) in the same way as it conceals sex, race and social position. But then he proceeds to argue that in the original position what matters morally speaking are only the *properties* future individuals are going to have rather than their particular, i.e. *numerical identity*.[21] This, I believe, is a wrong reading of Rawls' idea of the original position, or indeed of any social contract.

The social contract can only be made by *actual* people, who in order to create fair conditions for their bargaining, place themselves under a virtual veil of ignorance. This veil conceals all their particular properties (that might prejudice the way they choose the principles of justice), but *cannot* hide the fact of their very existence (or actuality). Indeed, the contract can (and should) also include future people who do not exist *yet*, but they must be *particular* individuals who are going to live anyway. Or, in other words, the hypothetical contract cannot take place between *possible* people and cannot include principles for their own creation or the choice of their identity.[22] Indeed, Reiman says that the contractors "represent all and only those people who, from this moment on, will ever exist: people who are currently living, and future people who do not yet exist but who one day will,"[23] but according to his own argument he cannot mean by that all numerically identifiable people who will actually live. For his whole point is to show how by deciding to cause the creation of a handicapped child rather than of "an individual" with better properties, we violate the rights of "the individual". But there is no one "individual" here, whose rights are allegedly violated, but rather two numerically distinct individuals: one who is a healthy individual and *another* who is handicapped. The Rawlsian contractors are not abstract, identity-less place-holders, but particular individuals. We should not confuse the level of the background conditions of the contract (actual people trying to agree on principles of justice) with the level of the procedure of the contract itself (the veil of ignorance as a device of representation). On the first level the motive to "enter" a contract is the wish to promote *my* interests and prospects (not that of a numerically distinct individual even if she is like me in all her properties). Numerical identity is a condition for ascribing not only rights but also the interest in having a normal functioning.[24] Thus, in contrast to Reiman's thesis that according to Rawls *any* future individual has rights against us, I maintain that Rawls' contract creates rights only for actual people who are either living or are going to live anyway in the future, i.e. whose identity is fixed (in the strong numerical sense). The idea that people have the right to be born healthy or with normal capabilities is incoherent, for no contractor would choose a principle of justice which would lead to the birth of someone else in his or her stead (even if that individual would be better off). Creating children with the good properties might be a noble goal, but it can only be grounded in an impersonal (rather than contractual) conception of justice.

For Parfit, the only way around the nonidentity problem was impersonal, through a principle of beneficence. Rights, unlike overall welfare, seem to be more typically linked to metaphysically identifiable people who are the subjects of the rights. An attempt to save the person-affecting approach and avoid impersonalism lies therefore in showing that the wrongness of conceiving a child at the age of fourteen *is* connected with rights. James Woodward argues that since the violation of rights (again, unlike harm) does not necessarily involve a decline for the worse in one's welfare, future people can claim that their rights have been infringed by the act of their "wrongful" creation even if their inborn and foreseeable handicap is offset by an otherwise happy and worthwhile life.[25] His main argument for this claim is from analogy: when an air company refuses for racist reasons to sell a ticket to a member of a minority group, the person may claim that his rights were infringed even if it turns out that he benefited from the refusal due to a crash in which all the passengers of the plane were killed. But the analogy does not work since it ignores what we referred to above as the *sui generis* nature of genesis choices. The crucial difference is that the individual discriminated against is a fully identifiable person *at whom* the offensive refusal was directed, while the possible child of the 14-year-old girl is not. The issue of the overall balance of good and bad, or the weighting of the infringement of rights vs. the benefit in welfare, is irrelevant to the logical question of the conditions that make *any* such ascriptions possible. Similarly, it is wrong to compare the 14-year-old girl's action to that of a person making to another person a promise he cannot fulfill. For in the first case, that of creating a new person, parents do not make any promise to anyone (but only assume a future responsibility). Methodologically, the use of these analogies simply begs the question of the relevance of identity to the ascription of rights.[26]

Another attempt (similar to Reiman's) to save the person-affecting approach from the quandary of nonidentity is through widening the scope of what is considered "person" so as to include all people affected by our acts "whoever they turn out to be." Melinda Roberts offers a sophisticated version of such a person-affecting theory. She contrasts it to my own narrow person-affecting approach that considers only actual existing people or future individuals who are going to exist "anyway" as objects of our moral duties.[27] According to Roberts, planting a piece of broken glass in my garden is wrong in being potentially harmful to future (yet non-existent) children, whether they are my neighbor's children (over whose creation I have no control) or my own (over whose creation I have control), i.e. whether they are (future) actual or merely possible people. But the nonidentity problem is a challenge to the person-affecting view in more specific circumstances, as Roberts seems to concede, namely when the act of planting the broken glass is *itself* the cause of the conception of a *particular* child. In such cases, known as wrongful conception, there is no way in which the particular child who gets injured could have been born without being injured by the glass. Of course, this is a bit far-fetched, but Roberts herself is willing to consider such a possibility,[28] and it is exactly the case of Parfit's 14-year-old girl or many of the legal complaints for wrongful conceptions. So I agree that the identity condition does not imply any knowledge of the actual identity of a future person and not even the total lack of control over his or her creation. It only applies to cases in which, in Roberts' language, a world with a particular person existing and without a certain adverse condition affecting him is *not* "accessible," or in simple words, the person would not and could not have existed without that adverse condition taking place.[29]

Roberts' thesis is that the nonidentity problem applies only to "two-alternative" situations (a child can be either born in defect or not born at all), but not to "three-alternative" situations (a child can be born in defect, not be born at all, or be born healthy). This sounds plausible, even compelling. For example it can demonstrate why giving birth to a child in order to sell him as a slave (Kavka's case) is wrong: the same child could be born without being sold as a slave (such a possible world is "accessible").[30] Roberts' original point is that it even can show in person-affecting, non-Parfitian terms why a depletion policy is wrong: for there *is*, at least theoretically, an alternative in which the same child could have been born better off without the depletion policy being implemented. However, it appears that Roberts must view the 14-year-old girl as a "two-alternative" example. For, if the girl waits before conceiving the child, there is logically no way in which the *same* child could have been better off. From the point of view of nonidentity, what is the difference between this case and creating a child with a genetic defect which Roberts concedes belongs to the "two-alternative" category? Since Roberts agrees that "two-alternative" choices are immune to moral criticism in terms of the wrongness *to* the child due to nonidentity, the disagreement about the response to Parfit's puzzles relates only to the scope of cases which belong to that category. Roberts' argument is convincing in that, due to causal possibilities regarding the coming to be of children and to metaphysical considerations relating to their individuation, the scope of the "two-alternative" choices is not as wide as we might have thought. But she shares the narrow person-affecting view (even though not easy to swallow) that conceiving a handicapped child, even if a healthy sibling could have been created in its place (by PGD), should not be considered as wronging the child.[31]

Impersonalists like Parfit believe that there is no difference between the moral standing of the child claiming damages for having been born in defect as the result of neglect during pregnancy and that of the child who is born as the result of negligent counseling before conception. Person-affecting philosophers tend to judge the cases as different, but feel uneasy about it. One way in which they justify the difference is by appealing to cases in which life is *very* bad or even not worth living. Thus, some of them hold that life as such can be good or bad for a person and that if it is bad on the whole, it would be wrong to create that person. They consider non-existence as having zero value to the person and life with certain serious defects as having negative value.[32] Since zero is better than a negative value, non-existence can be said to be better for the person than living in severe handicap. The problem with this analysis is that non-existence is given *a value* (zero), although there is no one to ascribe it to. Non-existence is neither good nor bad nor neutral for anyone, since good and bad can be ascribed only to metaphysically identifiable individuals. But zero is the balance or cutting point on a scale between good and bad. We cannot say that someone who has no bank account can be considered as having a zero balance! For there is no person or bank account to which we can ascribe the value zero.[33] Again, the nonidentity problem is *sui generis* in the sense that the comparison (whatever its merits) between having a bank account with a debit and having no bank account to begin with does not serve as an analogy to the comparison between life with great suffering and no life to begin with. Indeed, we can think of a world in which some actually existing individual (including myself) does not exist. But this person cannot say that such a world would have been better for him, because no value whatsoever can be ascribed to that person.

1.2.4 Embracing the Implications of Nonidentity

We have so far shown why the attempts to either combine impersonalism and person-affecting principles or to re-interpret person-affecting principles in a way which would overcome the nonidentity problem fail. Pure impersonalism cannot be said to fail in a similar way, that is to say, it is a coherent and systematic approach to "genethical" choices and avoids the issue of nonidentity by denying its relevance to the evaluation of people's coming into existence, their numbers and their identity. But the price of impersonalism is high: it leads to the Repugnant Conclusion, it implies a duty to procreate (happy children) and it commits us to the judgment that the world after the evolution of humanity is a better place than the world preceding it. To many people these are unpalatable consequences. The alternative to impersonalism with which we are thus left is the fourth strategy in the list of responses to the nonidentity problem, namely adhering to a strict person-affecting view.

The advocate of a strict person-affecting view is not indifferent to wrongful life cases and believes that there are moral reasons for avoiding the intentional creation of handicapped children or a reckless population policy. David Wasserman, for example, correctly points out that the moral constraints on the creation of children include the purpose for which the parents decide to have a child. Accordingly, it would be permissible to conceive a retarded child, even when another, healthy child could be created had the parents waited for a while or selected another embryo in a PGD procedure, as long as one of their *reasons* or motives included his own good. That is to say, although prospective parents cannot (logically) create a child "for its own sake", they are expected to be motivated by the prospect of parental giving and concern for their future child's good. Lack of sensitivity to the child's future suffering is morally repugnant since it violates the general expectation of parents.[34] For Wasserman, the parents are subject to duties derived from the "role morality of parents."[35] I would put it slightly differently. What counts in our moral judgment is the parents' moral profile, the kind of people they are, rather than the objective condition of the child (or the world). And it is of course also true that if parents are completely indifferent to the welfare of their planned future child, they are liable to become bad parents and to violate their parental duties *to* the child once she is born.

To reinforce Wasserman's approach, consider two couples: the first can *only* conceive a seriously ill child due to a permanent genetic condition from which they suffer; the second can conceive *now* a child who will be equally seriously ill, but if they postpone conception for a year, they will have a healthy child. Now, from the point of view of the child, there is no difference between the two cases, since both children are born into an equally painful life. But we do judge the parents' choice in the two cases differently, harshly condemning the second while approving or at least sympathizing with the first. This difference indicates that the judgment of procreative choices is made with regards to existing people, usually the parents. The first couple's choice is not merely excusable; it is morally understandable, even noble (if they are committed to take good care of the child once it is born). The second couple's choice is perverse, even "sick," and reflects a deformed character of people who are insensitive to pain and suffering or even derive satisfaction from it. The "positive" counterpart of that example is a case in which there are two options for giving birth to a healthy child. Our proverbial 14-year-old girl is offered two options to avoid the plight of her prematurely conceived child: wait another few years (as in Parfit's example) or let another (more mature) woman give birth to a child "instead of you." The latter offer sounds of course absurd, though from the point of view of the future child there is no difference between it and the first offer, since both children are going to be different from the originally planned child. The difference between the two options (which is of course significant) relates only to the girl, whose interests of satisfying motherhood can only be fulfilled by the first option.

Advocates of the strict person-affecting view, like myself, must face some consequences which are definitely counter-intuitive. They may nevertheless have reasons to "bite the bullet," so to speak. This could mean the willingness to take moral responsibility for action (or policy) based on the strict person-affecting view with all its ramifications for future children and future generations. It could alternatively mean a skeptical view regarding the theoretical possibility of a normative justification of procreative (genethical) prohibitions. This skeptical attitude is compatible with leaving the actual moral and political choice to be guided by intuitions and public perceptions even when these are confused and inconsistent. For anyone who is not a stringent impersonalist and who is convinced by the arguments against a diluted or compromised version of the person-affecting view, the strict or narrow person-affecting analysis seems to be the lesser theoretical evil in being both consistent and doing justice to some of our fundamental intuitions.[36]

It is important to note that conflicts of intuitions on the way to deal with the nonidentity problem can arise on two levels. They can refer either to the content of the intuition itself or to the way an agreed upon intuition is explained. Thus, the person-affecting intuition that the world was not made any better by the evolution of human beings stands in direct contrast to the opposite intuition held by the impersonalist (who would also bemoan the painless and voluntary disappearance of humanity). On the other hand, the wrongness of a free and intentional choice of a 14-year-old girl to conceive a child is a shared intuition by personalists and impersonalists alike. They only disagree about the *grounds* or the explanation of that intuition. To the former, the wrongness derives from the way the decision reflects on the mother's character, the irrationality of her act in terms of her own interests, or the burden it creates for society. For the latter, the wrongness lies in the bad consequences of the decision *tout court* (the world is made a worse place than it could have been). Unlike the direct conflict of intuitions of the first type, these differences in explanation are partly intuitive but partly theoretical. Hence there are better chances of engaging in a theoretical discussion about the second kind of conflicts than about the first.

But the appeal to intuitions in the morality of procreation (population policy, genetic engineering, etc.), although so central in the debate, is problematic. These intuitions are often confused due to the *sui generis* character of this problem and the difficulty in drawing analogies to it. Furthermore, they are not always sharp since the problem is not only theoretically unique but also historically new, and intuitions take time to form. Since much of the debate about remote examples such as Parfit's takes place among philosophers, it should not come as a surprise that the intuitions appealed to, even if clear, are heavily colored by theoretical considerations.

1.3 Numerical, Biographical and Autobiographical Identity

If moral judgments about the creation of people must be based on person-affecting considerations, the question remains as to the identity of persons. This raises the second-tier question about the *metaphysical* conditions of the relevance of the nonidentity problem. What is this "person," the identity of which is a constraint on the ascription of right and wrong in genethical choices? Who is the he or the she who counterfactually could have been better off had the choice been different? Logically, the person-affecting approach is not restricted to individualist conceptions of a person (as a carrier or subject of value). A collective, like a tribe or a nation, a family or a kibbutz, can be the object of duties and rights. But the nonidentity problem would equally apply to these entities: it would be incoherent to claim that it would have been better had one of these groups not existed in the first place and an alternative group created in its stead. For the same person-affecting question would arise: good for whom? However, beyond the problems of attributing the status of a moral subject to a collective, empirical circumstances make decisions on the creation or the identity (let alone the number) of future communities or collectives very rare (Moses in Egypt?).[37] So in the rest of this article the discussion will be limited to individual persons.

Since human beings are self-conscious and free, their identity is unique in being a combination of some general essential features and some constructed or self-constructed traits. Thus, my genetic makeup is essential to my personal identity, but being loyal to my nation might be essential "to me." Some theorists view the distinction between sex and gender as illustrating this double nature of identity. A person's identity begins to be formed at the moment of conception, but continues after birth through the powerful forces of socialization and education and later through the "big" choices the person makes for herself. The geneticist of the future definitely has control over the identity of people, but so do parents of young (or not so young) children, and later the individual adult who is forming and transforming her own personality.

Recent philosophical literature refers to this unique feature of human identity by distinguishing between numerical identity and narrative identity, or between personal identity in the traditional metaphysical sense (as in Leibniz or Kripke[38]) and biographical identity. (I will use the term "biographical," since it can refer both to the aspects of identity that are constructed by others and to those constructed by the self; furthermore, the term "narrative" in the description of a person's life is misleading in assuming that human life is similar in its construction to that of a story or a novel). In his fine discussion of the distinction, David DeGrazia points out that essential, numerical identity (*de re*) must precede and is assumed by "narrative" identity (*de dicto*).[39] Numerical identity is fixed by a particular event and at a certain moment (be it conception or some time around it). Biographical identity is gradually formed throughout the person's life, from childhood to adulthood, by parents, society and the person himself. But there is a point in constructing or self-constructing a biographical identity only *of* a numerically distinct entity (person) whose biography it is. Hence the logical precedence of the numerical over the biographical.

Narrative identity is taken (for example by DeGrazia) to relate to the way an individual forms her own identity as a person. And indeed this is an important constituent in what is important for us in continuing to be what we think we basically *are*. It is a first-person perspective on personal identity, a matter over which the subject has authority. It applies both prospectively (what kind of person I want to be) and retrospectively (how I interpret the kind of person I have been). But biographical identity is not only first personal and there is an important additional dimension of identity between the natural or essential identity of human beings and their autobiographical or first-person identity. Take, for instance, the dilemma facing charitable gentiles who saved Jewish children during the Holocaust. Should the children be raised as Christians (like their adopting parents)? Should they, after the end of the war, be "returned" to a Jewish environment (assuming that their biological parents died)? There is no question about the numerical identity of the children on the one hand, and they have not yet acquired the power to autonomously decide their own identity on the other. But they are definitely Jewish in some deep sense.

Now the application of the nonidentity problem to this case is not as clear as in pre-conceptive decisions like the 14-year-old girl exactly because it relates to biographical rather than to numerical identity. Consider how we should solve the dilemma if we take the principle of "the best interests of the child" as our decisive guide. There is a sense in which, given the numerical identity of the child, we can say that it would be in this child's best interest to stick to her Christian lifestyle to which she has been exposed during the war years. It would be definitely easier for her since she only vaguely remembers her Jewish origin or even forgot it altogether. Yet, there is a strong argument for judging the child's best interests as remaining Jewish since that is the way she was treated in her early phase of life. In other words, the *person* "affected" by the decision might be considered either this (numerically identified) *child* or this (biographically identified) *Jewish* child, in a way leading to two opposite conclusions. In the former case the religious or national identity of the child is created *ex nihilo*, with no moral constraints, like in the standard pre-conceptive "genethical" choices. Due to the "nonidentity" of the pre-war Jewish child and the post-war Christian child, there are no moral constraints on the decision to preserve the Christian lifestyle of the child.

When we move from biographical to *auto*biographical identity (which comes closer to the idea of narrative identity), the application of the nonidentity problem becomes even murkier but equally instructive. For human autonomy, usually exercised in the pursuit of the ends of a person of a certain kind, might, at least in extreme cases, serve to change the kind of people we are. Conversion is a conspicuous example and so is sex (or gender) change. At least from the first-person perspective, people report that they have become different persons, following the transformative change (although they obviously realize that they have not changed "numerically"). Autobiographical identity is a matter of identification, of what I find crucially important in my life, that without which my life would be meaningless or not worth living. Culture, religion and moral character are typical examples of such identity-fixing traits (which are not essential to my numerical identity).

The nonidentity problem, accordingly, casts doubt on the logical basis of complaints about biographical (and even autobiographical) identity. My claim here is that wrongful identity complaints are no more coherent than wrongful life suits due to the nonidentity condition. I cannot regret not having been born in the eighteenth century or to different parents because it would not have been (numerically) me. But equally it would not make sense for me to criticize my parents for having been *brought up* as an Israeli, secular Jew rather than as an English Anglican priest, even though from some abstract, impersonal perspective, the latter identity would have made my life easier or more successful according to some impersonal criterion. The reason is that it simply would not be me in some deep sense which suffices to make that comparison absurd or at least senseless from the point of view of what is good for me. Indeed, my parents could raise me (the numerically identical person) to become a different sort of person, but since the way I evaluate my good is partly informed by my biographical identity, such an alternative cannot be judged as better or worse for me.[40]

In that sense of biographical identity, I am in the position to make genethical choices about my own future in the same way as my parents did for me. A decision, for example, to convert to another religion or to immigrate to another country (and adopt another culture) must be based on person-affecting considerations, namely my *present* actual values rather the good of my "future self." For even though my numerical self can have alternative biographical identities, those cannot be fully compared to each other. How can Paul compare his life after the conversion on the way to Damascus with that preceding it: in terms of his previous Jewish values or in terms of his new Christian vision? Even if he believes there are objective (impersonal) reasons for preferring the post-conversion life, it is hard to justify that preference on person-affecting grounds. Or, to take a more mundane example, can a person regret having chosen a life-long career as a philosophy professor rather than embarking on that of a politician? After all, his present preferences are to much extent formed by the professional identity he actually formed and to have chosen otherwise cannot be considered as either better or worse for "him." The limits of our complaint to our past selves are logically similar to those we have towards our parents for having either bequeathed us with their genetic makeup or for having formed in us a particular cultural identity.

Since biographical and "narrative" identity is subjective and a matter of degree, these examples are naturally controversial and from a third-person point of view might be considered overblown. And indeed, from an objective point of view, it would be coherent to criticize even a major choice in another's life as a mistake in terms of *her* overall interests. Paul could thus argue that his post-conversion life better fitted his true or genuine identity (his character, dispositions, personality). But note that such a criticism would have to relate to some underlying features in one's identity which are fixed and stable throughout the person's life. In other words, *if* and to the extent that we take biographical identity seriously, we must concede that the evaluation of individuals' choices during their lives are susceptible to the challenge of nonidentity in the same way as wrongful life suits are in the case of the creation of numerical identity.

The metaphysical question of the identity of human beings should be clearly distinguished from the question of the beginning of the life of a person. Numerical identity is probably formed some time after conception (for example, after the moment of possible twinning of the fertilized egg), but that does not mean that this is the point in which a human organism becomes a person (which as many philosophers have shown depends on the acquisition of some advanced mental powers, consciousness, or some other traits). Therefore, the issue of wrongful life (or wrongful identity) should be set apart from that of abortion. It is perfectly consistent to hold that a woman has a right to abort her fetus but is prohibited from harming it. The reason is that the embryo, not being a person (yet) has no rights (including the right to life), but the future existing person will have a cause for complaint for having suffered harm during pregnancy since *he* could have been better off without suffering it.[41] He is definitely numerically the same entity as the embryo from which he developed. Nonidentity does not undermine this kind of grievance. In that respect, "person-affecting" is not restricted to "persons" as human beings with full moral standing.[42]

1.4 Conclusion

I hope to have shown in this article that the nonidentity problem is *intractable* in both the sense of being "stubborn" or difficult to handle and in the (etymological) sense of being impossible to "draw," extract or remove. Like most genuine philosophical questions, this is exactly what makes it fascinating and deep, in both theory and practice.

Acknowledgements Faculty and Fellows of the Department of Bioethics at the NIH were generous and very helpful with numerous incisive comments, oral and written, on this paper.

Notes

1. Habermas (2003).
2. I have dealt in the past more with the first than with the second question, but most of the arguments which I critically examine in this article were raised after my book was published. See Heyd (1992).
3. If we adopt a global consequentialist view, every action in the world can easily be seen as having some effect on the timing of conception of future people, which would mean that the challenge of nonidentity is much more pervasive than we usually think.
4. Thompson (2000), pp. 470–475.
5. Admittedly, this presupposition is not held by impersonalist theories of value. It should also be noted that the argument for the uniqueness of the nonidentity problem in terms of the person-affecting theory of value is circular and that one of the best arguments for that theory itself lies in our intuition about the nonidentity problem. So there is nothing logically inconsistent in impersonalism together with denial of the challenge of nonidentity. But once the person-affecting view is accepted, it becomes clear why for conceptual reasons there are no analogies to the ethics of creation of people.
6. Heyd (1997), pp. 57–70.
7. Parfit (1984), p. 405.
8. Parfit (1984), pp. 453–454.
9. Parfit (1984), p. 454.
10. Buchanan et al. (2000), p. 247. The nonidentity problem is discussed in pp. 245–255.
11. Buchanan et al. (2000), p. 244.
12. Buchanan et al. (2000), p. 250.
13. DeGrazia (2005), p. 274.

14. DeGrazia (2005), pp. 277 and 279. Parfit holds that there is no (moral) difference between not taking certain pre-conceptive measures to ensure the health of a future child and not taking similar measures after the child is born. I contend that there is a radical difference between the two. DeGrazia suggests that there is "a *slight* difference," thus trying to follow Parfit's acceptance of impersonalism without denying the grip of the nonidentity problem. However, I don't see how this kind of difference can be a matter of degree.
15. McMahan (2002), p. 357.
16. McMahan (2002), pp. 353–354.
17. Mulgan (2006), pp. 155–156. Mulgan advocates rule-utilitarianism as a middle position between impersonalism, which absurdly requires the creation of happy children, and the person-affecting view, which equally absurdly leaves us free to create a suffering child even if we can avoid it. But his solution seems to belong to the attempts at combining person-affecting and impersonalist principles of the kind discussed in the previous section. For a similar proposal that the government act *as if* future generations have rights over us, see Marc D. Davidson (forthcoming). Davidson's reason for his proposal is that most people believe that future people can be wronged, i.e. do not think in terms of the nonidentity problem.
18. For a view according to which the wrongful creation of life can be considered as a direct harm to the individual created, see Shiffrin (1999), pp. 117–148 and Harman (2004), pp. 89–113. Harman's argument is based on the elaborate moral weighting of reasons regarding the harms and benefits to the future person; but my claim is that any such weighting can take off the ground only once there *is* an identifiable individual as the subject of these benefits and harms. The act of giving life (of whatever quality) to a person is in itself neither a benefit nor a harm and the pain suffered by a person once she is born and throughout her life cannot be considered as caused by the parents' act of bringing her into the world.
19. Kumar (2003), pp. 99–118. Markie, like Kumar, tries to stick to the person-affecting view, without relinquishing the grounds for wrongful life complaints, by distinguishing between being wronged and being harmed. Unlike Kumar, he appeals to the results (the existence of a handicapped child) rather than to the character of the agent. But Markie is misled by the ambiguity of "result": the existence of such a child is a bad result "for the world (parents, society)" but not "for the child." Markie is thus pushed back to impersonal evaluation which is exactly what he wanted to avoid. Markie (2005), pp. 290–305.
20. Reiman (2007), p. 92.
21. Reiman (2007), p. 84.
22. I have elaborated this critical interpretation of Rawls in Heyd (2009, forthcoming). Reiman quotes *A Theory of Justice*, in which Rawls indeed requires real capital accumulation from one generation to the next as part of the duties of justice, but Rawls himself abandoned that view and the intergenerational application of the difference principle in his later writings in favor of a more modest requirement to maintain the institutions of justice. Rawls (2001), p. 159.
23. Rawls (2001), p. 79. Thus, unlike Reiman, I believe it does not make sense "to think that it is in [a person's] interest to be born with certain properties rather than others" independently of the person's particular identity. Numerical identity is a condition for any ascription of interests to a person.
24. This is the reason for my disagreement with the recently published solution to the nonidentity problem offered by Caspar Hare, who suggests that there may be harms done to people *de dicto* even if no harm was done to anyone *de re*. Thus, according to Hare, in the same way I can harm the 35th President of the U.S., I can harm "my future child," even though the identity of the particular person who is going to "fill" the relevant description is not fixed yet. I believe this cannot be the case since types of people (exemplifying some description) cannot have interests or rights (or be better or worse off). Only actual people can have them. One may have rights and interests *in virtue* of being of a certain type (or description), but the rights and interests relate to her *de re*. See Hare (2007), pp. 514–520.
25. Woodward (1986), pp. 804–831. Smolkin similarly believes that future (possible) people have rights, even if they cannot be said to have interests, arguing that rights are not dependent "substantively" on interests. But as he himself acknowledges, my own view is "formal" (or

1 The Intractability of the Nonidentity Problem 23

   logical) rather than substantive, denying the ascribability of both interests and rights to possible people, irrespective of the *degree* of suffering or disability. Smolkin (1994), p. 319; and Smolkin (2002), pp. 202ff.
26. For a similar analogy between creating a debt which cannot be repaid and "wrongful life," see Singer (1998), pp. 383–398.
27. Roberts (1998), p. 18.
28. Roberts (1998), p. 24.
29. It is hard to judge whether the world in which this particular child exists without the broken glass by which it will be injured is "accessible" to us or not since the example is a bit artificial. Surely, the parents could delay the moment of conception by engaging in an alternative, less deleterious activity than that of planting broken glasses. And of course they could, after conception, remove the glass (as the parents in Kavka's famous example could breach the contract and not give away their child to slavery after birth). But Parfit's real-life examples and much of the legal history of wrongful conceptions do not suffer from this ambiguity and hence highlight the nonidentity problem more clearly.
30. See Roberts' article in this collection, in which she solves the slave-child paradox by first distinguishing between the assessment of the procreative choice on the basis of its *actual* value and such an assessment on the basis of its (probable) *expected* value and then showing that the source of the sense of paradox lies in the fallacious mixing of the two kinds of assessments. In the first kind of assessment, we could think of an alternative in which the same child is born without becoming a slave; and in the second, the chances (at the moment of making the choice) for the coming into being of this particular child are anyway infinitesimally low due to the biology of the procreative act.
31. Roberts (1998), pp. 28–29.
32. Roberts (2003), pp. 159–185, particularly p. 168.
33. Roberts tries to solve the problem of comparability between a world in which a person has an anguished life and a world in which she does not exist by weighing "amounts": "what we are comparing is the *amount* of well-being that Nora's having certain properties and lacking certain others at α adds up to at α with the *amount of well-being* that Nora's *lacking all properties* at β adds up to at β" (p. 177). The question is, how can Nora be individuated or identified while "lacking *all* properties?" And how can all these absent properties add up to zero, as Roberts suggests, when she admits that zero is not a property of well-being that we can attribute to a non-existent person? Roberts (2003), p. 178.
34. Wasserman (2005), pp. 132–152. Wasserman, although leaning to the person-affecting approach, offers his solution to the challenge of wrongful life complaints in terms which seem to lie somewhere between the person-affecting and the impersonal.
35. This leaves Wasserman's account with some measure of ambiguity. For on the one hand he says that the completely selfish parents can be accused of moral insensitivity, but that their child, born out of this insensitivity, cannot have grounds for complaint for having been born with impairment (pp. 146–147); yet on the other hand he argues that parents who conceive a child for reasons that have nothing to do with the child's good "make themselves vulnerable to a complaint from the child for the unavoidable hardship in his life" (p. 151). The two statements are inconsistent. A purely person-affecting view, which accepts the relevance of nonidentity, can judge the act of the parents as a moral fault *only* in terms of the way it reflects on *their* character.
36. In Heyd (1992), I discussed in detail the superiority of the person-affecting view over its impersonalist rival in terms of a "global" assessment of the merits and flaws of both as general theories of value.
37. A similar argument would apply to animals. If they are considered as moral subjects of any kind, the nonidentity condition must equally constrain judgments about their creation in the same way as it does in the case of human beings.
38. Parfit's discussion of personal identity belongs to the former rather than the latter: although it is concerned with human consciousness (psychological continuity), it is not that part of the identity of persons which is constructed or self-constructed.

39. DeGrazia, (2005), pp. 28–29, p. 114 and Chapter 3. The force of DeGrazia's hierarchy of the two kinds of identity does not depend on the particular substantive details of the metaphysics of human and personal identity on which philosophers have varied views. Hence, I do not have to take a position here on the question whether prenatal genetic interventions in an embryo should be considered as "treatment" of an identifiable individual or as the creation of a new individual. This is a separate metaphysical issue which demonstrates that biographical identity may include also prenatal events in the individual's life (once it is numerically individuated but not yet having some fundamental features of her biographical identity, such as those which can be genetically molded in her). But I tend to agree with DeGrazia that such genetic manipulation after the third week of embryonic life does not change one's essential (numeric) identity (pp. 263–264).
40. I want to distinguish my analysis of biographical identity from the mechanism of "adaptive preferences" originally described by Jon Elster. Adaptive preferences are one kind of response to gaps between desires and the chances of their satisfaction, i.e. the re-formation of desires in the light of the conditions which would make them satisfiable. They are considered irrational since they do not reflect the genuine preferences of the person but rather the frustration of her inability to gratify them. In contrast, self-construction of identity (or conversion) is not necessarily an *adaptive* change in one's set of preferences but an authentic choice which is not tailor-made to fit external circumstances. Adaptive preferences are created *within* the existing biographical identity of a person. Conversions are changes *of* that identity.
41. Jeff McMahan doubts whether the (adult) person born out of a fetus that was harmed can be said to have been wronged, since he might have adapted to his condition and preferred it to not having been born at all or even to having been born without the harmful condition. See McMahan (2002), p. 301. But I think that the question of the preferences or degree of adaptability of the adult person is not what should decide the question of harm. The fact that *this* particular person could have been better off (in terms of opportunities) suffices to view the harm done to the fetus as harm to the ensuing adult person.
42. David DeGrazia eloquently makes this point by carefully distinguishing between persons and human animals and by using the term "individual-regarding" (rather than person-regarding) so as not to prejudge the issue of moral standing. See DeGrazia (2005), p. 263.

References

Buchanan, A., D. Brock, N. Daniels, and D. Wikler. 2000. *From chance to choice: Genetics and justice.* Cambridge: Cambridge University Press.
Davidson, M. 2008. Wrongful harm to future generations: The case of climate change. *Environmental Values* 17: 471–488.
DeGrazia, D. 2005. *Human identity and bioethics.* Cambridge: Cambridge University Press.
Habermas, J. 2003. *The future of human nature.* Malden, MA: Polity.
Hare, C. 2007. Voices from another world: Must we respect the interests of the people who do not, and will never, exist? *Ethics* 117: 498–523.
Harman, E. 2004. Can we harm and benefit in creating? *Philosophical Perspectives* 18: 89–113.
Heyd, D. 1992. *Genethics: Moral issues in the creation of people.* Berkeley: University of California Press.
Heyd, D. 1997. Divine creation and human procreation: Reflections on genesis in the light of genesis. In *Contingent future persons: On the ethics of deciding who will live, or not, in the future,* eds. N. Fotion and J.C. Heller, 57–70. Dordrecht: Kluwer.
Heyd, D. 2009. A value or an obligation: Rawls on justice to future generations. In *Justice between generations,* eds. L. Meyer and A. Gosseries. London: Oxford University Press.
Kumar, R. 2003. Who can be wronged? *Philosophy and Public Affairs* 31: 99–118.
Markie, P.J. 2005. Wrongful conception and harmless wrongs. *Ratio* 18: 290–305.

McMahan, J. 2002. *The ethics of killing*. Oxford: Oxford University Press.
Mulgan, T. 2006. *Future people: A moderate consequentialist account of our obligations to future generations*. Oxford: Clarendon Press.
Parfit, D. 1984. *Reasons and persons*. Oxford: Clarendon Press.
Rawls, J. 2001. *Justice as fairness: A restatement*. Cambridge, MA: Harvard University Press.
Reiman, J. 2007. Being fair to future people: The non-identity problem in the original position. *Philosophy and Public Affairs* 35: 69–92.
Roberts, M. 1998. *Child versus childmaker: Future persons and present duties in ethics and the law*. Lanham, MD: Rowman and Littlefield.
Roberts, M. 2003. Can it ever be better never to have existed at all? Person-based consequentialism and a new repugnant conclusion. *Journal of Applied Philosophy* 20: 159–185.
Shiffrin, S. 1999. Wrongful life, procreative responsibility, and the significance of harm. *Legal Theory* 5: 117–148.
Singer, P. 1998. Possible preferences. In: *Preferences*, eds. C. Fehige and U. Wessels 383–398. Berlin: De Gruyter.
Smolkin, D. 1994. The non-identity problem and the appeal to future people's rights. *Southern Journal of Philosophy* 32: 315–329.
Smolkin, D. 2002. Towards a rights-based solution to the non-identity problem. *Journal of Social Philosophy* 30: 194–208.
Thompson, J. 2000. The apology paradox. *Philosophical Quarterly* 50: 470–475.
Wasserman, D. 2005. The nonidentity problem, disability, and the role morality of prospective parents. *Ethics* 116: 132–152.
Woodward, J. 1986. The non-identity problem. *Ethics* 96: 804–831.

[5]

Surviving Duties and Symbolic Compensation[1]

Lukas H. Meyer

1. Introduction

Our obligations to provide measures of compensation for past injustices are often justified by appeal to the interests of contemporaries and future people: We should attempt to counteract the negative consequences of these past wrongs for the well-being of current and future people. However, such a forward-looking interpretation of the relevance of past injustices is incomplete when understood as a statement of how we ought to respond to the fact that past people were severely wronged. The true moral significance of past wrongs does not lie in their impact on currently living and future people's well-being; rather, the significance of past wrongs should be seen in the fact that *past* people *were* victims of these injustices. We need to enquire into the question of what we owe to the dead victims of past public evils. The forward-looking interpretation is misleading in suggesting that we owe them nothing – that, in the words of Max Horkheimer, "[p]ast injuries took place in the past and the matter ended there. The slain are truly slain."[2]

One could defend the claim that we are obliged to the past victims of injustices by attributing rights to them. To attribute rights to dead people may seem unproblematic if we assume that people continue to exist after their physical death, that they exist as people who can be affected by the events of this world or that they might even be able to act in ways that have an impact on what happens in the world. These assumptions about the ontological status of previously living people are at least as controversial as the as-

---

[1] For helpful discussion, comments and suggestions I should like to thank Brian Barry, Brian Bix, Axel Gosseries, David Heyd, Stanley L. Paulson, Walter Welsch, Andrew Williams, and two anonymous referees of *Revue Philosophique de Louvain* (which published the article under the title "Obligations Persistantes et Réparation Symbolique" in 101 (2003).

[2] "Das vergangene Unrecht ist geschehen und abgeschlossen. Die Erschlagenen sind wirklich erschlagen." In a letter to Walter Benjamin 1937, as quoted in R. Tiedemann, *Dialektik im Stillstand*, 107.

sumption that dead people do not exist as persons.[3] A presupposition that is equally compatible with at least some of the controversial and mutually exclusive presuppositions on the ontological status of dead people can be considered a suitable starting point for a philosophical investigation into the question of whether we can stand under duties to previously living people. In the following discussion I am proceeding on the assumption that dead people either do not exist (a1) or, if they do, that there is no connection between them and currently living (a2). The second assumption (a2) is meant to imply that for currently living people dead people are neither passive nor active subjects. In other words, I am proceeding on the assumption that the end of the physical existence of a human person, that is, his or her death, is the end of the possibility of this person acting in a way that she has an impact on the world as we know it and of events of this world or currently living persons' actions affecting the dead person (presupposition (A), that is: (a1) and (a2)).

2. Surviving Duties

Is this presupposition compatible with an interpretation of the claim that the true significance of past wrongs lies in the fact that past people were the victims of these injustices? The position of surviving duties is compatible with presupposition (A).[4] The duties survive the death of the bearer of the right[5]. While the bearer of the right does no longer exist, currently living people can stand under the correlative duties. The notion of surviving duties relies on the idea that the reasons for a person's right imply reasons for a duty under which other people stand after the death of the bearer of the right. If it is a moral right, then these reasons will also include general social reasons which are relevant not only for the bearer of the right but also for the bearer of the surviving duty, his contemporaries (and future people). For example, we all have reasons to protect people's trust that promises be kept and that people have the reputation they deserve. The reasons for the surviving duties also include the reasons that are necessary for showing that a particular person had the moral right.

For the following discussion I will assume:
(A*) Dead people have no interests or rights with respect to the state of affairs in the world as we know it.
(B) Currently living people can stand under duties.

Claim (B) seems unproblematic. Claim (A*) corresponds to presupposition (A) as introduced above. The position under consideration relies upon the following claims:
(C) Some rights are future-oriented in the sense that they impose duties in the future.
(c) Such rights can impose surviving duties: The rights imply duties that are (also) binding after the death of the bearer of the right if the appropriate bearer of the duty is identified.

I would like to comment on these claims by investigating the reasons for surviving duties with the help of an example of a person who wishes to establish posthumously a

---

[3] See T. Mulgan, "The Place of the Dead in Liberal Political Philosophy", 52-70, 54f.
[4] See C. Wellman, *Real Rights*, 155-7. For a critique of positions on "posthumous harm" that are compatible with presupposition (A) but do not support the claim under consideration, see A. Gosseries, *Intergenerational Justice*, ch. iv, "The Dead End of Intergenerational Justice. What Do We Owe Our Ancestors" (on file with author).
[5] Or of a person's legitimate claim. In the following I will speak of moral rights rather than moral claims, but nothing hinges on this as long as it is understood that people can stand under a duty to respond to the legitimate claims of others.

prize for the sciences. I will call the person Alfred Nobel even though the example and the variations on the example I will use in the following discussion make no claim to resemble the historical person Alfred Nobel to whose bequeathal we owe the Nobel Prize.

"A right implies a duty" means that a proposition about the right's validity implies a proposition that some duty exists. Such an implication relies upon the claim that the reasons for the right contain (some of) the reasons for the duty. In the case of rights that are future-oriented in the sense indicated, the reasons for the rights of people while alive are sufficient for holding currently living people under a duty, that is, a surviving duty. With respect to moral rights specifically moral reasons are among these reasons. Such reasons are meant to protect the conditions of a morally speaking valuable social life.

Suppose Alfred Nobel kept to himself his wish to establish posthumously a prize for the sciences. Although he accumulated the fortune necessary for the purpose, Nobel neglected to write it in his will. Hiking in isolated mountains together with his friend Barbara, Nobel has an accident and both he and his friend realize that he will die before they can call on somebody for help. He asks his friend to promise him that she will make sure that his fortune will be spent for the establishment of a prize for the sciences and that his wish to this effect will be acknowledged as if it had been written in his will.

Why should Barbara keep his promise? The particular strength of the position under consideration is to be seen in its connecting the surviving duty both to the previous right of the deceased person and to those general moral reasons which are relevant for the bearer of the duty and his contemporaries. First, the particular reasons which ground the right of the no longer existing person imply reasons for the validity of the surviving duty. Some of the reasons for a currently living person to stand under the duty towards the deceased person are implied by the reasons for attributing the corresponding right to the deceased person while alive. This is also the sense in which we stand under surviving duties *towards* the deceased person. For example, the surviving duty to keep a death-bed promise is valid, inter alia, for the reason that the promise was given to the deceased person and that is why the latter, while alive, had a moral right that the promise given to him be kept. If the duty is not understood to be binding due to the fact, inter alia, that the deceased person had the future-oriented right, surviving duties could not be distinguished from interpretations of, for example, death-bed promises according to which the duty to keep the promise is owed to our contemporaries alone (and possibly to people living in the future). The position under consideration differs from some consequentialist interpretations of, for example, death-bed promises by insisting that a surviving duty necessarily be based upon, inter alia, the reasons for the previous future-oriented right and that these reasons contain the specific reasons for the attribution of the previous right to the deceased person.[6]

So far I have investigated one type of reason for a current person to stand under a duty towards the deceased person. These reasons are implied by the reasons for attributing the corresponding right to the deceased person while alive. However, and second, there are other reasons too. These reasons are general in that they concern the protection or promotion of values important for the quality of social life. With respect to death-bed promises trust and the protection from betrayal are at stake. We all have reasons to protect the value of people having confidence that promises be kept. In so far as people can and do have an interest in future posthumous states of affairs of the world as we know it, and in so far as pursuing such interests can be of high importance to the well-being of

---

[6] Ernest Partridge discusses the example of Alfred Nobel and defends a rule-utilitarian reading of death-bed promises in his "Posthumous Interests and Posthumous Respect", 243f, 259-61.

people while alive,[7] it is important for people that others can bind themselves by promises or contracts to the effect that they will carry out certain actions after the promisee's death, and that when others have done so, that they can be confident that the promise will be kept. For the practice of such promises, trust is of special importance, for the promisee will not be able to determine whether the promise was kept. Thus, the practice of such promises is particularly dependent upon the protection of the value of people having confidence in promises being kept. At the same time, if such promises have often not been kept, this is likely to undermine the confidence in promises being kept generally. The right of the deceased person that the promise given will be kept is based on, among others, these reasons. Although the right and the person who is the bearer of the right has ceased to exist, the moral reasons are still valid and the duty of the person who gave the promise continues to be binding on the basis of these reasons. As these reasons are general moral reasons they are not only relevant for the individual bearer of the right but also for the surviving bearer of the correlative duty and his contemporaries. The death of the bearer of the right leaves these moral reasons unaffected and the surviving duty is based on these reasons in conjunction with the reasons that are implied by the particular reasons for the attribution of the correlative right to the deceased person while alive. Thus, contemporaries of a person who stands under a surviving duty have reason to impose sanctions on the person should he not keep his promise.

One might wonder whether this interpretation of surviving duties as currently living persons' duties towards deceased people is compatible with the presupposition that dead people are bearers of neither interests nor rights and that they cannot be affected by the actions of currently living people. At the very least, the position of surviving duties I am defending presupposes the possibility of the attribution of posthumous properties and, more particularly, of their change.

If Barbara were not to keep his promise, Nobel would have the posthumous property of being the person with respect to whom Barbara violated the duty to keep the promise she gave. Such posthumous predication is incompatible with the claim

(D) If X has the property P at a particular time t, then X exists at t.[8]

For our understanding of posthumous duties is to be compatible with the mortality assumption (a1), that is, with the assumption that dead people do not exist. The idea of surviving duties presupposes the possibility of posthumous predication of properties to no longer existing persons and, thus, the rejection of (D). More particularly the idea of surviving duties presupposes the possibility that previously living people undergo a change of properties after their death.

If a property is attributed to an entity at a particular point in time and it was not true of the entity at an earlier point of time, and it might not be true of the entity at a later point in time, then the entity undergoes change. For example, John forges the will of Nobel with the result that Nobel's fortune is spent contrary to his wishes. A short time later Barbara uncovers the fraud, Nobel's will is restored and his wishes are fulfilled. At first, the deceased Nobel is posthumously the person who is betrayed by John's forgery of his will; later on, it is true that Nobel has the property of being the person whose will is restored and whose wishes are fulfilled. How can Nobel undergo such changes if he is non-existent?

Here we can rely on an explanation of posthumous predication as introduced by David-Hillel Ruben. His explanation relies on two distinctions, namely, the distinction

---

7 See also L.H. Meyer, "More than They Have a Right to", 137-56, 141-43.
8 See W.J. Waluchow, "Feinberg's Theory of 'Preposthumous' Harm", 727-34.

between real and non-real changes and the distinction between relational and non-relational properties. The first distinction is the distinction between changes as ordinarily understood and changes that are only apparent: The change in a schoolboy if he comes to admire Socrates whom he did not admire before is an example of real change, whereas the change in Socrates when the schoolboy comes to admire him is an example of non-real change.[9] The second distinction concerns the distinction between non-relational properties and relational properties. For the non-relational property of an object one can ascribe the property without knowing anything else about other objects.[10] This does not hold true for the relational property of an object. The property that an object has as the result of a change of its color might be an example of a non-relational property while the property that Adam and Eve have each time they acquire a new descendant is an example of a relational property.[11]

In our example, John forges Nobel's will. This is an event, a change in the state of affairs that is based on non-relational changes in the person John. John undergoes a change and that brings about a non-relational property of John he did not have before. John violates a duty by acting contrary to the reasons that are valid for him. Not fulfilling his duty might cause feelings of guilt on his part – a non-relational change of the person John. What is more, his not fulfilling his duty can have certain consequences and this is the case in our example: When the forgery is uncovered John's contemporaries criticize his breach of duty. Doing so requires of them to act or to refrain from acting in certain ways. All these non-relational changes are real changes in the state of affairs.

However, John's violation of his surviving duty also entails relational changes. First, John's relations with Nobel undergo a change. Nobel now is a person with respect to whom John violated a duty under which John would not have stood had Nobel not been the bearer of the correlative right. Second, John's relations with his contemporaries undergo change. Because of his breach of duty John is now considered a person deserving of a sanction. According to the interpretation of surviving duties as sketched above, John has general moral reasons to fulfill his duty, and when he acts contrary to these reasons this is a matter of general moral concern.

Thus, I would like to maintain that Nobel can be a *relatum* of a relational change. Because Nobel is non-existent he cannot undergo non-relational changes. According to Ruben's analysis, for each relational change there is a simultaneous or earlier non-relational change to which the relational change is owed or on which the relational change depends.[12] We can distinguish several types of the relationship between relational and non-relational changes.[13] If a currently living person acts contrary to the surviving duty under which he stands, then only one of the *relata* which undergoes a relational change also undergoes a real change, namely, the currently living person – in our example, John. The other *relatum*, the deceased person, undergoes only a non-real change, namely, a relational change – in our example, Nobel. John, the person who violates the duty undergoes a real change and because of this he also undergoes a change in his relation

---

9   See D.-H. Ruben, "A Puzzle About Posthumous Predicaton", 211-36, 223-31. See also P. Geach, *Logic Matters*, 318-23; P. Geach, *God and the Soul*, 66f, 70-3, 98f; Michael Dummett discusses "phoney changes" in *Frege. Philosophy of Language*, ch. 14.
10 Ruben understands this be a sufficient condition. See D.-H. Ruben, "A Puzzle About Posthumous Respect", 217, fn. 7.
11 Ibid., 216f, 223. In the following I will speak of relational and non-relational changes. The former change brings about that an object has a relational property the object did not have before; the latter brings about that an object has a non-relational property the object did not have before.
12 Ibid., 230.
13 Ibid., 224, 231.

178 Lukas H. Meyer

to Nobel, the deceased person. Since the latter person is dead, he cannot undergo a real change but only non-real changes.

We are now in a position to qualify the claim (D), which we found to be incompatible with the idea of surviving duties. The claim reads: If X has the property P at a particular time t, then X exists at t. This holds true if the property in question is a matter of undergoing real change. The modified claim reads:

(D*) If X has the property P at a particular time t and the property is a matter of undergoing real change, then X exists at t.[14]

Only existing bearers of properties can have properties that indicate that the bearer undergoes real change; non-existing bearers of properties can have properties that indicate a change in their relations to other entities owing to real changes in the latter. It is true that real changes at time t presuppose existence at time t. However, this does not mean that non-existing entities cannot undergo non-real changes. In other words the posthumous attribution of non-real changes is possible. The idea of surviving duties presupposes the possibility of such attribution, namely of attributing the following property to a deceased person: being the person whose previous future-oriented right is now violated by a living person; the latter person breaches a surviving duty and thus undergoes a real change owing to which the relations between the living and the deceased person undergo a change without the deceased person's thereby undergoing a real change. The notion of dead people being wronged or harmed presupposes a real change in the dead person. If dead people cannot undergo real changes they cannot be harmed or wronged.

3. Carrying Out Acts of Symbolic Compensation in Fulfilling a Surviving Duty Towards the Dead Victims

Does the position of surviving duties help us in responding to the objection against the forward-looking understanding of the significance of historical injustices? I shall propose the idea that since people as members of ongoing societies can be said to have an obligation to compensate surviving and indirect victims of past injustices,[15] they may also have an obligation symbolically to compensate dead victims of past injustices, that is people who cannot be affected by our actions.

As I have argued above, we can stand under surviving duties towards past people even though neither can we change the value to them of any moment of their lives since they cannot be affected by what people do after their death nor can they be thought to be bearers of interests or rights. Until now I have discussed duties towards dead people with reference to (variations on) the example of Alfred Nobel and his bequeathal. Currently living people can act in ways that will constitute a violation of the surviving duties under which they stand owing to the rights past people had in the past. We stand under particular surviving duties towards past people owing to their future-oriented projects, the promises we made to them or the contractual obligations we entered with them. However, not all people have the opportunity or the wish to have a specific impact on posthumous states of affairs. Not all people pursue projects that are future-oriented in the relevant way and not all people oblige others to bring about what for them are posthumous states of affairs. Here I want to suggest that we can stand under surviving duties towards dead people owing to the fact that they were victims of historical in-

---

14 Ibid., 232, 236.
15 See L.H. Meyer, "Transnational Autonomy", 263-301, sect. 8.

justices. For us to show that currently living people can stand under such duties, we will have to assume that people generally have interests with respect to posthumous states of affairs. Indeed, people can be thought to generally have the interest to enjoy a good reputation both during their lifetime and posthumously. When people were violated in their rights and badly so, their posthumous reputation depends upon their being publicly acknowledged as victims of these wrongs and others being identified as the wrongdoers.

In acknowledging past people as victims of egregious wrongs we cannot affect their well-being. Also, such acknowledgement cannot be expressed vis-à-vis the dead victims, but only vis-à-vis currently living people in light of the wrongs past people suffered. However, if it is true that we stand under surviving duties towards past victims of historical injustice owing to the wrongs they suffered, then our fulfilling the duty by publicly acknowledging the past injustices they suffered will change the relation between us and the dead victims of historical injustice. It will be true of the past victims of these injustices that they have the posthumous property that we fulfilled our surviving duty towards them. To be sure, a change of the relation between a currently living person and a dead person does not bring about or rely upon a real change of the latter person. Rather the relational change is based upon the real change of the person who carries out the act.

For us to bring about the public acknowledgment of past people as victims of historical injustice can require different measures under different circumstances. Currently living people can express their acknowledgment of past people as victims of past wrongs in an indirect way, namely, by providing measures of compensation for those who are worse off than they should be owing to the effects of the past injustices suffered by their predecessors. The message of such measures of compensation can contain the acknowledgment that past people were victims of past wrong. Here I would like to suggest that we can understand efforts at finding appropriate forms of commemoration of today's dead victims as efforts at bringing about measures of symbolic compensation and restitution.

Establishing a memorial is the typical course of action where the effort is made to realize the symbolic value of compensating those victims who are no longer living. A memorial may be a public speech, a day in the official calendar, a conference, a public space or a monument – for example, a sculpture or an installation. Often these memorials are meant to commemorate crimes that previous members committed in the name of a political society whose currently living members now want to carry out actions of public symbolic compensation or restitution for these crimes towards the victims and their descendants. While there is still no established practice for such efforts at public symbolic compensation, such acts of symbolic compensation have been carried out since the 1970s in Germany and we have been observing the beginnings of an international practice of symbolic compensation.[16]

How can we understand this practice of symbolic compensation? Here I can only adumbrate the basic idea: the value of real compensation – the rectification or compensation at which we would aim if only it were possible – is imputed, at least in part, to the act of symbolic compensation.[17] The imputation of the value of real compensation to the acts of symbolic compensation is partly based upon the expressive value of acts of symbolic compensation. For those who carry out acts of symbolic compensation these acts make it possible to express attitudes towards the past victims – attitudes that are consti-

---

16 For a comparison of the memorials for the victims of the Shoa in Poland, Germany and Israel, see J.E. Young, "The Texture of Memory", 1799-811.
17 See R. Nozick's analysis of symbolic value in chs. 1 and 2 of his *The Nature of Rationality*.

tutive of acts of compensation. Acts of symbolic compensation make it possible for us to act in such a way as to express an understanding of ourselves as people who wish to, and would, carry out acts of real compensation if this were only possible. If successful we will have firmly expressed an understanding of ourselves as persons who would provide measures of real compensation to the previously living person or people if this were only possible.

Acts of symbolic compensation can be valuable for those who carry out the acts since doing so helps to express attitudes that are important for their self-understanding and, thus, for their identity. They understand themselves to be persons committed to support the just claims of those who have been injured and to be persons prepared to contribute to the establishment and maintenance of a just political society. Indeed, acts of symbolic compensation will not help us in fulfilling our duties towards the past victims of wrongs and thus in bringing about a change in our relationship to the dead victims unless we succeed in expressing that we are people who wish to, and would, carry out acts of real compensation if this were only possible. Carrying out acts of symbolic compensation can symbolize that one is a person who shares this identity, can be evidence of one's being such a person and, importantly, can have the consequence of helping one to secure the self-understanding of being such a person. The latter is a real consequence of such acts and can be of great importance to the person carrying out the act.[18]

However, we will not succeed in bringing about these consequences in carrying out acts of symbolic compensation if we aim to bring about these consequences as such. Carrying out an act of symbolic value as a means of bringing about certain consequences will change the character of the act and, thus, the reasons that speak on behalf of carrying out the act in the first place. It is certainly not the case that we will become a person of a certain identity simply in virtue of our carrying out an act in a specific situation in which a person of this identity would have carried out the act. Carrying out acts of symbolic compensation does not by itself cause one to become a person of this identity. While such consequences for the self-understanding of a person can be an important factor in explaining the person's acts, in choosing what to do the person cannot herself explicitly take into account this type of consequence without thereby diminishing or undermining this very effect of her act.

Carrying out acts of symbolic compensation will have consequences for others as well. There will often be surviving and indirect victims of past injustices. Acts of symbolic compensation can have consequences for the surviving victims, for the descendants of victims, and for the group whose previous members were harmed by the injustices: The public acknowledgment of the suffering of past people who were wronged by, say, a genocidal policy cannot be separated from the acknowledgment of those who survived the same policy and suffer as an effect of this policy or from those who suffer as indirect victims of the policy. Those who carry out acts of symbolic compensation will want to provide measures of real compensation to those who currently suffer as a result of the same past wrongs. The reasons for acts of symbolic compensation include the reasons for carrying out measures of real compensation where this is possible. Measures of symbolic compensation belong to the measures likely to have the effect of providing surviving victims with assistance in recovering or regaining the status of membership in their respective societies, such that they are once again able to lead lives under condi-

---

18   Elizabeth Anderson provides a theory of expressive reasoning and the relation between expressive reasoning and consequentialist reasoning in *Value in Ethics and Economics*. I would need to say a good bit more if I were going to bring what I say here to bear on Anderson's theory.

tions of justice. In so far as people were wronged as members of a group that continues to exist, the public acknowledgment of past victims also provides a measure of acknowledgment for the group whose previous members were wronged.[19]

Carrying out acts of symbolic compensation may hinder us from realizing other values, may have negative consequences or have consequences less positive than other courses of action – and this can be the case even if carrying out such acts can bring about positive consequences for others. First, carrying out acts of symbolic compensation can compete with acts that make possible the realization of important non-symbolic values. Of course, we may well find that realizing non-symbolic values is more important than realizing symbolic values. The conflict may be due to the fact that carrying out the act of symbolic compensation is costly, materially speaking. Indeed, establishing a monument or a museum as a measure of public commemoration of victims of past injustices can be costly. However, if we find ourselves in a situation in which we have to choose between carrying out such a measure of symbolic compensation and realizing another project that is meant to improve the conditions of the worst off by, say, establishing a medical facility for homeless people, there will often be alternative ways of expressing the value of symbolic compensation, some of which are likely to be less costly. For example, the establishment of a day of commemoration in the official calendar may well make it possible for us to realize the value of symbolic compensation and be less costly than the establishment of a museum or a monument. Depending upon the specific situation in which we find ourselves – depending upon, for example, what measures of public commemoration have been established –, a less costly alternative may be as good in expressing the value of symbolic compensation as the more costly one. In any case, there does not seem to be a general correlation between material expenditure in carrying out such an act and the success in symbolically realizing the value in question. If so, it then seems likely that a conflict of the sort referred to can be resolved or mitigated by choosing one of the less costly alternatives in carrying out acts of symbolic compensation.

Other conflicts might be more difficult to resolve. Carrying out acts of symbolic compensation may compete with realizing other symbolic values. Also, carrying out such actions can have consequences that undermine or threaten the self-understanding of groups that members of these groups want to preserve. For example, public acts of this sort may undermine the stability of a particular institution, say, the military, whose compliance with the rules of the new regime, yet to be established, may well be a condition of the success of a "transition to democracy". I doubt that one can say much in general in response to these types of conflicts. How we assess the conflicts depends upon, inter alia, how we assess the self-understandings of the groups and institutions that are said to be threatened. These self-understandings might well not deserve our respect. Our assessment will also depend upon who is negatively affected and in what ways and by whom as an effect of our carrying out actions of symbolic compensation. At the same time, it can be true that our success in realizing the symbolic value in question does not require our carrying out acts of a sort that have threatening negative consequences for others. Indeed, since such consequences are connected with our attempt at symbolically compensating people, this very connection may well undermine our chances of realizing the symbolic value in question, which in part depends upon the

---

19 The Roma (Gypsies) were victims of a racially motivated genocide committed by the Nazis – a truth that has been long denied with the result that most surviving victims as well as the descendants of those murdered were excluded from compensation and restitution. See L.H. Meyer, "Transnational Autonomy", 269.

182 *Lukas H. Meyer*

public acknowledgment of the past victims as victims of wrongs. We might often be able to find an alternative course of action that is more promising with respect to both our chance of realizing the symbolic value in question and diminishing the threatening consequences to others.

4. Concluding Remarks

I presented the interpretation of symbolic compensation as a response to an objection to the forward-looking understanding of the significance of historical injustices. According to the forward-looking interpretation past injustices matter only and insofar as they have an impact on the well-being of currently living and future people. The forward-looking interpretation of the relevance of historical injustices is incomplete: the significance of past wrongs should also be seen in the fact that *past* people *were* victims of these injustices.

Symbolic compensation as understood here provides an interpretation of our relating to the fact that past people were victims of injustices without presupposing that past people can be bearers of interests or rights today. Insofar as people while alive generally have an interest and a just claim to enjoy the reputation they deserve and insofar the reasons for their just claim can oblige us even after the bearer of the interest and the just claim has ceased to exist, our carrying out acts of symbolic compensation can be understood as fulfilling a surviving duty towards dead people who were wronged in the past, namely, the duty of restoring the posthumous reputation they deserve. Our measures of symbolic compensation, if successful, will change our relations to past victims of wrongs without changing the value to these past victims of any moment of their lives. Such a change of our relations to the past victims does not presuppose a real change in the past people. Rather, the relational change is based upon real change of the person who carries out the act. Bringing about this relational change can be important for the self-understanding of the people who carry out the acts. Carrying out acts of symbolic compensation can have positive consequences for surviving and indirect victims as well.

Bibliography

Anderson E., *Value in Ethics and Economics*, Harvard University Press, 1993.
Dummett, M., *Frege. Philosophy of Language*, Duckworth, 1973.
Geach, P., *God and the Soul*, Routledge and Kegan Paul, 1969.
Geach, P., *Logic Matters*, Basil Blackwell, 1981.
Gosseries, A., *Intergenerational Justice. Probing the Assumptions, Exploring the Implications*, 2000 (unpublished Ph.D. thesis, University of Louvain).
Meyer, L.H., "More than They Have a Right to. Future People and our Future-Oriented Projects", *Contingent Future Persons*, ed. N. Fotion and J.C. Heller, Kluwer Academic Publishers, 1997.
Meyer, L.H., "Transnational Autonomy. Responding to Historical Injustice in the Case of the Saami and Roma Peoples", *International Journal on Minority and Group Rights* 8 (2001).
Mulgan, T., "The Place of the Dead in Liberal Political Philosophy", *Journal of Political Philosophy* 7 (1999).
Nozick, R., *The Nature of Rationality*, Princeton University Press, 1993.
Partridge, E., "Posthumous Interests and Posthumous Respect", *Ethics* 91 (1981).
Ruben, D.-H., "A Puzzle About Posthumous Predicaton", *Philosophical Review* 97 (1988).
Tiedemann, R., *Dialektik im Stillstand. Versuche zum Spätwerk Walter Benjamins*, Suhrkamp, 1983.
Waluchow, W.J., "Feinberg's Theory of 'Preposthumous' Harm", *Dialogue* 25 (1986).
Wellman, C., *Real Rights*, Oxford UP, 1995.
Young, J.E., "The Texture of Memory. Holocaust Memorials and Meaning", *Remembering for the Future. Jews and Christians During and After the Holocaust*, Pergamon Press, 1988.

[6]

Discounting the Future

JOHN BROOME

I. INTRODUCTION

Should future goods be discounted? Should benefits that will come in the distant future count for less in our planning than benefits that will come in the present or near future? I am not thinking of the plans made by an individual on her own behalf, but of plans made on behalf of the public as a whole, particularly by governments. Should future goods be discounted by public authorities in their planning?

In cost-benefit analysis and other applications of welfare economics, economists typically do count future goods for less than present goods. To many philosophers this seems a reprehensible practice. How, they ask, can the mere date at which a good occurs make any difference to its value? Discounting seems to these philosophers a device for unjustly promoting our own interests at the expense of our descendants'. On the face of it, then, typical economists and typical philosophers seem to disagree. But actually I think there is more misunderstanding here than disagreement. Some economists do indeed disagree fundamentally with some philosophers, but most economists and most philosophers would be on the same side if they came to understand each other properly. I hope this article will contribute to a mutual understanding. My first purpose is to try and explain to philosophers what economists are doing when they discount the future and why they are doing it.

The basic point is very simple. When economists and philosophers think of discounting, they typically think of discounting different things. Economists typically discount the sorts of goods that are bought and sold in markets, which I shall call *commodities*. Philosophers are typically think-

---

This paper was written with the support of the Economic and Social Research Council, under grant number R 000 23 3334. Some of the work was done while I was a Visiting Fellow at the Centre for Applied Ethics, University of British Columbia. I am grateful to Wilfred Beckerman, Douglas MacLean, Carol Propper, and Tyler Cowen for taking the time to write very helpful comments, and to Jonathan Escott and Stefano Vettorazzi for some useful points.

ing of a more fundamental good, people's *well-being*. There are sound reasons to discount most commodities, and there may well be sound reasons not to discount well-being. It is perfectly consistent to discount commodities and not well-being.

However, it is also true that economists sometimes go too far in discounting; they discount where they ought not. There is some justice in the complaints of philosophers. A second purpose of this article is to say where economists overstep the mark.

Section II describes the idea of discounting well-being, but only in order to distinguish it from the discounting of commodities. I shall not discuss whether well-being ought or ought not to be discounted; that is not the subject of this article. Sections III–V explain the discounting of commodities and how it fits into the theory of cost-benefit analysis, and they explain what justification there is for it. Sections VI–VIII set limits to the justification.

II. THE PURE METHOD OF EVALUATION

In order to distinguish discounting commodities from discounting well-being, I shall start by explaining the idea of discounting well-being.

Suppose some public authority has to evaluate various alternative actions it might take. For instance, governments these days face a choice between allowing the emission of greenhouse gases to continue unchecked, or doing something to limit it. Let us ignore the uncertainty that in practice always surrounds the results of an action; let us suppose we know what the results of each alternative action will be. So if a particular action is taken, we know how history will then unfold. Particular people will be born, live for a particular time, and die. Each person who lives will have a particular level of well-being at each time in her life. If a different action is taken, history will unfold differently. Figure 1 shows schematically two alternative histories. Each half of the diagram shows one of them. The horizontal axis shows time and the vertical axis possible people. A vertical solid line marks the present. For each person who lives, a little graph shows her well-being from birth to death. Each half of the diagram represents a sort of two-dimensional grid, across which well-being is distributed. Time is one dimension and people the other. Different actions distribute well-being differently across the grid; indeed they may lead to the existence of different people. Alternative A in Figure 1 represents what will happen if

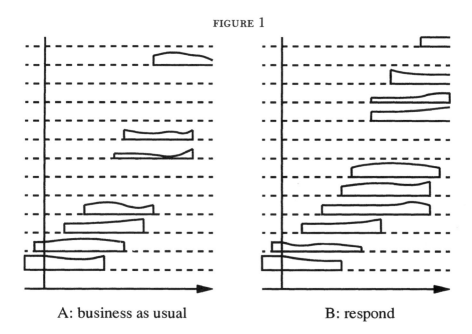

FIGURE 1

A: business as usual   B: respond

greenhouse gases are not controlled; alternative B what will happen if they are. B shows people worse off in the near future than they are in A, because of the cost of controlling the gases. But in the further future it shows more people living, and it shows them better off and longer lived. (I am not predicting that this will definitely be the result of controlling greenhouse gases; the diagram is only an illustration.)

An action, then, leads to a particular distribution of well-being across the two-dimensional grid of people and times. If alternative actions are open to us, we need to compare one distribution with another in order to decide which action is better. So we need to determine the value of each distribution. Well-being distributed across the grid must somehow come together to determine the overall value of the distribution. We need to know how: how is well-being *aggregated* across the grid? How is it aggregated across people and across time? Discounting is one part of this question: does well-being that comes later in time count for less in the aggregate than well-being that comes earlier? If later well-being is discounted, I shall call this *pure* discounting. Pure discounting means discounting well-being. A pure discount rate is the rate at which the value of well-being declines as we look forward in time from the present.

Discounting the Future

Economists often include pure discount rates in their theoretical work, allowing later well-being to be counted for less than earlier. But not many economists actually defend pure discounting. Often they include discount rates only for the sake of generality. The rate can always be set to zero, so that later well-being is not actually discounted at all. Frank Ramsey, wearing his economist's hat, decried the practice of discounting well-being, but nevertheless included discount factors in his work. He says: "It is assumed that we do not discount later enjoyments in comparison with earlier ones, a practice which is ethically indefensible and arises merely from the weakness of imagination; we shall, however, . . . include such a rate of discount in some of our investigations."[1] So the fact that discount rates appear in their formulas does not show that economists approve of them. Some do, but I think more do not.[2] Most philosophers are opposed to pure discounting, and I think many economists would be on their side; I do not think this is a major point of disagreement. I shall not consider the arguments for and against pure discounting in this paper. But in order to draw out the contrast with the type of discounting economists do in practice, I shall generally take for granted the majority view that the pure discount rate should be zero: future well-being ought not to be discounted.

Theoretical work is one thing. When they come to assessing real projects in practice, such as new roads or plans to control greenhouse gases, economists rarely deal in well-being at all. The direct way to evaluate a practical project would be to work out the distribution of well-being that would result from it and then find its overall value by aggregating well-being across the two-dimensional grid. I shall call this the pure method of evaluation. In practice it would be very difficult. It would require us, first, to work out how well off each person will be at each time in her life, as a result of the project. Even setting uncertainty aside, there are major difficulties in this. To begin with, there may be a fundamental difficulty in principle. In drawing Figure 1, I took it for granted that the well-being of a person at a time is a measurable quantity that can be compared between people and

---

1. Frank Ramsey, "A Mathematical Theory of Saving," *Economic Journal* 38 (1928): 543–49, reprinted in his *Foundations: Essays in Philosophy, Logic, Mathematics and Economics*, ed. D. H. Mellor (London: Routledge and Kegan Paul, 1978), p. 261.
2. One economist who comes down firmly against pure discounting is Robert Solow in "The Economics of Resources or the Resources of Economics," *American Economic Review Papers and Proceedings* 64 (1974): 1–14. On the other hand, there is a sustained argument in favor of pure discounting in Partha Dasgupta and Geoffrey Heal, *Economic Theory and Exhaustible Resources* (Cambridge: Cambridge University Press, 1979), pp. 255–82.

across times. This assumption is open to serious doubts that economists know well. Besides, there is in any case the great practical difficulty that information about people's well-being is hard to come by. A special problem is that the parts of a modern economy are so tightly interconnected that the effects of any economic action will be propagated to everyone throughout the economy. Remember that any economic project will have to be financed, perhaps by loans or taxes, and the financing will have its own complex repercussions. It would be impossible in practice to calculate all the effects on everyone.

Working out everyone's well-being at every time would only be the beginning of a pure evaluation. We would next have to aggregate all these amounts to arrive at the overall value of a project. To do so, we would need a theory of how this aggregation should be done. This would be an ethical theory, and it would not be easy to arrive at. One component of it would be the question of pure discounting: should future well-being be discounted? This alone is hard to settle.

Because of all these difficulties, economists have sensibly looked for a more practical method for evaluating projects. They want a shortcut through some of the difficulties. In particular, they want to avoid the need for difficult judgments about well-being and how to aggregate it. It is only a shortcut they are after. I think most economists would agree that the pure method would give the right answer if it could be applied.[3] The shortcut is not meant to supersede the pure method, but only to arrive at the right answer more easily. The eminent economist Joseph Stiglitz says as much:

> Any project can be viewed as a perturbation of the economy from what it would have been had some other project been undertaken instead. To determine whether the project should be undertaken, we first need to look at the levels of consumption of all commodities by all individuals at all dates under the two different situations. If all individuals are better off with the project than without it, then clearly it should be adopted (if we adopt an individualistic social welfare function). If all individuals are worse off, then clearly it should not be adopted. If some individuals are better off and others are worse off, whether we should adopt it or not depends critically on how we weight the gains and losses of different individuals. Although this is obviously the "correct" procedure to follow in evaluating projects, it is not a practical one; the problem of benefit-

3. Stephen Marglin is one exception. See the quotation in Section VII.

cost analysis is simply whether we can find reasonable shortcuts. In particular, we are presumed to have good information concerning the direct costs and benefits of a project, that is, its inputs and outputs. The question is, is there any simple way of relating the total effects, that is, the total changes in the vectors of consumption, to the direct effects?[4]

Economists have ended up taking a shortcut that leads them to deal in commodities rather than well-being. It leads them to discount future commodities, but not necessarily future well-being.

III. THE MARKET PRICE METHOD OF EVALUATION

In making an evaluation, the instinct of economists is to draw the information they need from the market. In this section, I shall explain the thinking that supports this instinct at a general level. I shall apply it to discounting in Section V.[5]

The market—specifically prices—provides us with information about the values people attach to different commodities. Take the two commodities labor and wine, for instance. Suppose labor is paid $10 per hour, and wine costs $5 per bottle. Each Sunday, in planning your week, you have to decide how much work to do that week and how much wine to buy. Having decided, you could always change your mind. For instance, you could work one hour more and buy two more bottles of wine, or you could work one hour less and buy two bottles fewer. But suppose you do not make these changes; you are in *equilibrium*—happy with your plans. This shows that two bottles are worth just as much to you as an hour of labor (or—as it appears from your point of view—an hour of leisure). More precisely, if your purchases were to change by two bottles, given what you are already planning to buy, that would be worth just as much to you as a change of one hour in your leisure time. Economists say two bottles of wine are worth as much to you as one hour of leisure *at the margin*. This expression means that an extra two bottles of wine, added to the bottles you already plan

---

4. Joseph Stiglitz, "The Rate of Discount for Benefit-Cost Analysis and the Theory of Second Best," in Robert Lind, et al., *Discounting for Time and Risk in Energy Policy* (Washington: Resources for the Future, 1982), p. 156.

5. I shall ignore several complications. In particular, I shall ignore the difference between the interest rates faced by consumers and producers, which is caused by taxation. There is a more detailed treatment in my *Counting the Cost of Global Warming* (Cambridge, UK: White Horse Press, 1992), chap. 3.

to buy, are worth an extra hour of leisure added to your planned leisure time.

I have explained, then, that the relative price prevailing in the market between wine and leisure must be exactly the same as the relative value to you of the two commodities at the margin. If it was any different, you would change your plans; you would work less and buy less wine, or else you would work more and buy more wine. When you are in equilibrium, the relative price must match the relative value to you.

For the same reason, the relative price of wine and labor must be the same as the relative value at the margin to anyone, and not just to you. But how can the relative value of wine and leisure be the same for everyone? Surely people differ in the values they attach to these things. The answer is that the prices are the same for everyone, and everyone adjusts themselves to the prices. Suppose you happen to value two bottles of wine above an hour of leisure. Then you will sign up for more work, earn some more money, and buy some more wine. If you still value two bottles of wine above an hour of leisure, you will sign up for more work still. But eventually, as you work longer and longer hours, the labor will begin to exhaust you, and you will have so much wine that its pleasures begin to pall. The value you attach to wine will fall, and the value you attach to leisure will rise. In saying this, I am assuming that wine and leisure have "diminishing marginal value" to you: the more of them you have the less you will value an extra unit. Economists generally make the plausible assumption that commodities have diminishing marginal value, and I adopt this assumption. You will reach an equilibrium where two bottles of wine are worth one hour of leisure to you at the margin. That is how your relative values at the margin come to match the relative prices in equilibrium. By the same process, so will everyone else's.

Relative prices, then, measure people's relative values. What do I mean by relative *values*? If a person's aim in life is to maximize her well-being, the value to her of a commodity is the well-being she derives from it. In that case, prices measure the relative amounts of well-being that commodities bring her at the margin. This means they provide data for evaluations of just the sort we are looking for; as I described pure evaluations, the data needed are people's well-being, and we are looking for a shortcut to a pure evaluation. But suppose a person's aim is not to maximize her well-being. In that case, the value to her of a commodity will not be the well-being she derives from it. But no matter, many economists would say: people should be free to choose their own aims in life. If they happen not to pursue their own well-being, that is their business. When it evaluates a project, a public authority should use the values people attach to commodities, whatever the aims that underlie these values may be.

There is a complication. Many of the things that concern public authorities when they evaluate projects are not bought and sold on the market, so they do not have a price.[6] Examples are public goods such as street lighting and safety equipment installed in nuclear power stations. (Even though they are not marketed, I shall call these "commodities.") How can we find the value to people of a nonmarketed commodity? We can use the price that people would be willing to pay for it if they had to, instead of its actual price. A person might be willing to pay something to have street lighting or safety equipment installed. The amount she is willing to pay for a commodity measures its value to her, compared with the value of other things she buys. It can be used as a measure of value to her in place of market price. People's willingness to pay for a commodity is not as easy to find as a market price, but in practice it can be worked out by various means.

How can prices, or willingness to pay, be used in evaluating a project? A project uses some commodities as inputs and produces others as outputs. Think of one that uses labor as input and produces wine as output. Suppose this project is profitable at market prices. That is to say, if prices are $10 for labor and $5 for wine, the project produces more than two bottles of wine as output for every hour of labor used as input. Now, everyone assigns the same value to two bottles as to one hour of labor at the margin. So everyone values the output of this project more than its input. Surely, then, the project is beneficial.

This simple thought is the basis of cost-benefit analysis. To decide whether a project is a good idea (by which I mean it is better to do it than not), first list all the commodities the project will use as inputs and all those it will produce as outputs. Value them all at market prices or, failing that, at people's willingness to pay for them. Call the value of an output a "benefit"

6. A smaller complication is this. I argued that the relative prices of commodities will measure their relative values to a person, at the margin. But the argument only works if the person buys or sells some amount of each commodity. If she chooses not to buy any of some commodity (and if she has none to sell), that commodity's price does not indicate its value to her. Evidently, its value to her is not more than its price, or else she would buy some, but it may be less than its price. Like the complication of nonmarketed commodities, this complication can also be dealt with by using the person's willingness to pay for the commodity in place of its price.

and the value of an input a "cost." If benefits exceed the costs, the project is profitable at market prices. In that case declare it a good idea. I shall call this the *market price method* for evaluating a project.

It seems plausible, but there is a snag. We need to ask how the project will be operated. Who will supply the inputs and who will get the outputs? One possibility is that the costs are borne by the same people as receive the benefits. In the example, the labor might be done by the people who eventually receive the output of wine. Each of these people might be employed on the project and paid for her labor in wine. The pay could be more than two bottles per hour, since the project produces more than two bottles per hour. Since each person values two bottles more than one hour of leisure, each would be benefited by the exchange. (Assume each person works only a little time on the project, so that the change is marginal.) All these people would benefit, and no one would be harmed. Undoubtedly, the project operated this way would be a good idea. If it were operated this way, we could sidestep all the theoretical problems of aggregating well-being across a grid like Figure 1. Since the project would make everyone better off, there would be no need to worry about aggregating well-being across people and time.

But in practice the benefits of a project often come to people who have not borne the costs, or all of the costs. When a road is built, some people have to suffer the noise it makes, while other people benefit. I can only fit this possibility into my simple example by making an exaggerated assumption. Assume the labor is coerced, without pay, and the wine produced is distributed to people who have not done the work. Have we any reason to suppose that the benefit to these people is greater than the cost to the workers? No. We know how each person individually values wine compared with leisure; that information is given us by the market prices. It happens that everyone values two bottles of wine equally with one hour of leisure. But we do not know how one person values wine compared with how another person values leisure; market prices do not convey that information. It may be that the workers value their sacrificed leisure more than the beneficiaries value their extra wine. In general, if some people bear the costs of a project and others get the benefits, we cannot tell from market prices whether the project is a good idea or not.

This is a fundamental difficulty in cost-benefit analysis. So long as a project harms some people and benefits others, valuing commodities by their market prices, or by willingness to pay, is not a reliable way to check whether the project is a good idea. The problem will be most severe if the people who are benefited are much better off, or much worse off, than the people who are harmed. When a person is in equilibrium, the price in money she pays for a commodity is the value of the commodity to her at the margin, divided by the value of money to her. For a given value of money, the price of a commodity is therefore a measure of the commodity's value to the person. Among people who are about equally well off, it is reasonable to assume the value of money to each of them is approximately the same. So among such people, prices may be reasonably good measures of values. On the other hand, money to a poor person is probably worth much more than money to a rich person. Between rich and poor, then, the prices of commodities are not good measures of their values. Of course, economists have ways of coping with this problem, which I shall not go into here.

This article is concerned with the distribution of resources between the present and the future. For the sorts of projects I am interested in, the people who benefit will often not in practice be the ones who bear the costs; they may well be in different generations. Furthermore, they may not be equally well off, because future generations may be much richer, or much poorer, than us. So one might expect the problem I have mentioned to be particularly acute for projects that cross generations. But actually it is not. The reason is that, in a way, the market price method ignores future generations. Their well-being is only taken into account to the extent that it is valued by the present generation. This is a major weakness in the method, which I shall discuss in Section VII. But it does happen to cancel out the fundamental weakness I have been describing. When the market price method deals with intertemporal questions, it treats them as questions about how the present generation values future commodities compared with present commodities, not as questions about how the values of the present generation compare with the values of future generations. Distribution between rich and poor generations is not really at issue. Consequently, I think it is reasonable to set aside this most fundamental problem with the market price method, and concentrate on difficulties that are specific to discounting.

IV. THE PRESENT PRICES OF FUTURE COMMODITIES

Before I can explain how to apply the market price method to discounting, I need to introduce a useful theoretical device: the idea of dated commodities and their prices. Suppose I have $100. I can use it to buy twenty bottles of wine at $5 each. Alternatively, I can put it in the bank. After a year I can get the money out, with interest. If the interest rate is 10%, I will have $110. If wine has meanwhile gone up to $5.25, I can then buy twenty-one bottles of wine. So $100 now will, in effect, buy me twenty-one bottles of wine in a year's time. We can think of wine in one year's time as a commodity on its own, separate from wine now, and its present price is $4.75 ($100/21, that is). This is what, in effect, I have to pay now in order to acquire a bottle of wine in a year's time. Since $4.75 is less than $5, the present price of future wine is less than the present price of present wine. In general, a commodity at any date—a *dated commodity*—has a present price. From now on, when I speak of the price of a future commodity, I mean its present price unless I say otherwise. The percentage difference between the present price of a present commodity and the present price of the same commodity next year (I mean, for instance, the 1994 price of the commodity in 1995, not the 1995 price of it) is called the commodity's *own interest rate*. In my example the own interest rate of wine is 5%.

Commodities typically have positive own interest rates. That is to say, future commodities are typically cheaper in the present than present commodities. If you have a particular sum of money, you can generally buy more of a future commodity with it than you can of a present commodity, by keeping the money in a bank and earning interest. The only exceptions are commodities whose current price (for instance, the 1995 price of the commodity in 1995) increases through time as fast as, or faster than, the rate of interest at the bank. These commodities have own interest rates that are zero or negative.

The relative price of commodities indicates the relative value people place on them. This is true among present commodities and also between present commodities and future commodities. In my example, the price of future wine, one year from now, is 5% below the price of present wine. Therefore, once people are in equilibrium—have made their plans, bought the amount of present wine they want, and set aside what they want in order to buy future wine—each person values present wine 5% above future wine at the margin.

How can this be? Future commodities are generally cheaper than present commodities, which implies that most people value future commodities less than present ones. But why should a person value a commodity less just because she will possess it in 1995 rather than 1994?

The answer to this question has two parts. The first is to explain why future commodities are generally cheaper than present ones anyway.

Oddly enough, this has little to do with the values of the people who buy present and future commodities. It has to do with the economy's productive technology, not with its consumption. Technology is, in a particular sense, *fertile*. It is a fact of technology that, to speak roughly, present commodities can be converted into a greater quantity of future commodities, if we choose.[7] Trees grow, for instance. If I fell my forests now, I shall harvest a particular quantity of timber. If I fell them next year, I shall harvest more. Let us say I shall harvest 5% more. The nature of my production process, then, gives me a choice between timber now and 5% more timber next year. This means that, when the economy is in equilibrium, the present price of next year's timber must be 5% below the price of this year's. If it were any higher, I would leave all my harvest to next year, and so would all my landowning colleagues. No timber would be put on the market this year. That would quickly drive up the price of this year's timber until it is 5% above the price of next year's. At that point I would begin harvesting again. Likewise, if the price of this year's timber rose higher than 5% above the price of next year's, the opposite would happen. The economy will only be in equilibrium when the price difference is 5%.

On the scale of a whole economy, things are much the same. Each year, some of the goods produced by the economy are consumed and some are reinvested, and the division between investment and consumption can be varied. If fewer commodities are consumed this year, more can be invested. The result will be more commodities produced next year, and next year's increase will exceed the decrease in consumption this year. Just as timber this year can, in effect, be converted by the production process into a greater quantity of timber next year, commodities in general this year can be converted into a greater quantity of commodities next year. This is what I mean when I say technology is fertile. A consequence is that next year's commodities must be cheaper than this year's. If they were not, producers would increase their investment this year, in effect switching their production to next year's commodities instead of this year's. This would increase the price of this year's commodities relative to next year's, until an equilibrium is reached with future commodities cheaper than present ones. Most commodities will therefore have positive own interest rates. This is a necessary consequence of the fertility of technology.

7. There is a fuller account of technological fertility in my *The Microeconomics of Capitalism* (London: Academic Press, 1983), particularly pp. 36–37.

Not every commodity will have a positive own rate of interest, though; I shall mention exceptions in Section VI. Nor need it always be true that most commodities will have a positive rate. Our technology may not always be fertile. If, for example, runaway global warming damages our productive abilities, or our resources are exhausted, future commodities may become more expensive than present ones. Own rates of interest may become generally negative. Still, with our present fertile technology, they are generally positive.

An economy's fertility may be affected to some extent by the decisions of consumers about saving. Suppose people decide to increase their savings, delaying some of their consumption to the future. In effect, they buy more future commodities in preference to present ones. This could raise the prices of future commodities compared with present ones, thereby reducing own interest rates. How could this happen? Only by causing a switch in the technical methods employed in the economy, to less-fertile methods. Here is a simple example. The change in consumers' behavior might induce the owners of forests to fell their trees at a more advanced age. But trees grow more slowly as they get older. So the change would cause the fertility of forestry to decline, and the equilibrium own interest rate of timber would be reduced. In ways like this, consumers might influence the fertility of technology. But for reasons I shall not go into here, I think their influence is small.[8] It is a fair approximation to think of fertility, and hence interest rates, as given independently of decisions about saving.

Tyler Cowen and Derek Parfit, on the other hand, stress the influence of savings on interest rates and suggest it is crucial to the argument about discounting.[9] I think not. My approximation is helpful for thinking about the problem, but it is not essential for the argument. We are concerned with interest rates established in the market, because these rates indicate the relative values people attach to present and future commodities. The important question is whether or not these rates are generally positive, because a positive rate implies that future commodities have a lower value than present ones. Insofar as savings influence interest rates, interest rates in the market will be determined by the mutual interaction of technology on the one hand and consumers' decisions about saving on the other.

---

8. Ibid.

9. Tyler Cowen and Derek Parfit, "Against the Social Discount Rate," in Peter Laslett and James S. Fishkin, ed., *Justice Between Age Groups and Generations* (New Haven: Yale University Press, 1992), pp. 144–61, esp. 151.

Discounting the Future

In present conditions, own interest rates will certainly emerge from this interaction generally positive. That is all that matters.[10]

If interest rates are positive, people attach less value to future commodities than to present ones. The second part of the answer to the question I posed earlier is to explain how this can happen. The explanation is that people must adjust themselves to the prices they face. Suppose next year's wine is as valuable to you as present wine. If it is cheaper than present wine, you will save your money and buy next year's wine rather than this year's. As you do this, and so find yourself with less wine this year, you will find you value this year's wine more and are less keen on buying yet more future wine. When you are in equilibrium, the relative values you attach to present and future wine at the margin must match their relative prices. Everyone will be in the same position. We shall all adjust our relative values, at the margin, to each commodity's own rate of interest. The process is exactly the same as the one I described in Section III for undated commodities.

This may still be mysterious. Even after adjustment, how can future wine be less valuable to you than present wine? Just because it comes in the future, how can that make it less valuable? I can think of three possible explanations. One is that the benefit you expect to get from wine declines with your advancing years: for any given quantity of wine, you expect to enjoy it less the older you are. I shall ignore this possibility in order to concentrate on the other two explanations, which I think are more impor-

---

10. Cowen and Parfit do not suggest market rates will be zero, but they do claim interest rates will be zero at the "optimum," when savings in the society are at the level they should be at. This is because they do not believe in discounting future commodities; they take present and future commodities to have the same value. So long as future commodities are cheaper than present commodities, they think savings are not as high as they should be. Savings should be increased, which means that more future commodities should be consumed instead of present ones. They think that increasing savings should eventually bring the price of future commodities up to the level of present ones. That is to say, interest rates should be brought down to zero. But this is mistaken. Under present environmental conditions, interest rates cannot generally be zero at the optimum. Suppose we grant that savings are at present too low. If they are increased, this will increase the rate of growth of the world economy. Long before interest rates are driven down to zero, the increased savings will bring about a positive rate of growth in per capita income: people will be getting richer as time passes. (Indeed, that may well be so already, even with savings at their present low level.) Consequently, the marginal value of commodities to people will be declining; as people get richer, they attach less value to extra commodities. Future commodities will be less valuable than present ones, then. Commodities ought to be discounted, that is to say, even at the optimum. Cowen and Parfit cannot legitimately take it for granted that they should not be.

tant. I shall assume that, at any time in your life, a particular quantity of wine will bring you the same well-being as it would at any other time.

The next possibility is illustrated by the indifference-curve diagram in Figure 2. Here I assume your aim is to maximize your own well-being. This means, among other things, that you do not discount your own future well-being compared with your present well-being; both count the same in your present values. Since I have already assumed that a particular quantity of wine brings you the same well-being in the future as in the present, your indifference curves must be symmetrical about the 45° line—the dotted line in the diagram. Your "budget line" in the diagram shows the options that are available to you, given whatever you have available to spend on wine. Your options are not symmetrical, because future wine is cheaper than present wine. This means the budget line is steeper than 45°. Out of all the options available to you on the budget line, you choose the one that puts you on the highest possible indifference curve. This is where an indifference curve touches the budget line. The diagram shows you will buy more future wine than present wine. This is how you end up valuing future wine less at the margin than present wine. All along, I have been assuming wine has a diminishing marginal value: the more of it you have, the less well-being an extra bottle will bring you. Since you have more future wine, you value extra bottles of it less.

Wine will presumably have a positive own interest rate throughout your life. Consequently, wine at later dates must always be less valuable to you at the margin than wine at earlier dates. If the explanation I have just given of how this happens is the right one, you must buy progressively more and more wine as your life continues. This point will become important in Section VIII.

The third possible explanation is illustrated in Figure 3. Here you yourself discount your future well-being; you value it less than your present well-being. Let us call this *imprudence* on your part. Imprudence skews your indifference curves toward present wine; the curves are not symmetrical about the 45° line, but steeper. Your budget line still has the same slope as before. In equilibrium you must value future wine less than present wine, since its price is less. If you are imprudent, that may happen even if you buy the same amounts of present and future wine. That is what the diagram shows: the point of tangency between the budget line and the highest indifference curve you can reach lies on the 45° line. This will

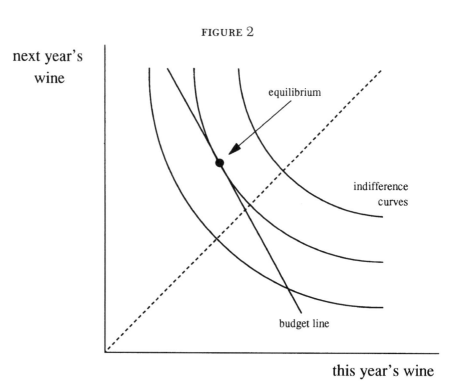

FIGURE 2

happen only by coincidence, because your degree of imprudence happens to match the own interest rate of wine. But it certainly can happen.

V. Discounting in the Market Price Method

Now back to cost-benefit analysis. In Section III, I described how the prices of commodities can be used in cost-benefit analysis. To evaluate a project, list the commodities it uses as inputs and the commodities it produces as outputs and evaluate them all at their market prices. Since market prices indicate their relative values to people, this seems a good basis for judging whether or not the project is a good idea.

Exactly the same idea extends to projects that have inputs and outputs at different dates. All the inputs and outputs can be evaluated at their market prices. In this case, these are the present prices of dated commodities. They measure the relative values of the dated commodities to people, so

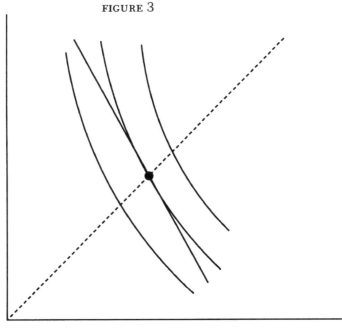

FIGURE 3

next year's wine

this year's wine

they seem a good basis for cost-benefit analysis. Generally, future commodities have lower present prices than present commodities. This process consequently discounts future commodities; it values them less than present commodities. This method provides a basis for discounting, then. The discount is applied to commodities, and not to well-being.

This is just the market price method of evaluation applied to the present and the future. Its great advantage is that the information it needs comes from the market. I said in Section II that economists were looking for a shortcut through the difficulties of the pure method. This is it. There is no need to inquire how much well-being each person derives from the project. Nor is there any need to engage in philosophical analysis to work out appropriate discount factors for future well-being. The market price method cuts through all that. Its discount factors come from the market like any other prices; they are simply the prices of future commodities compared with present ones. It may well be that future well-being ought not to be discounted at all. Even so, the market will value future commodities below present ones. So, if we are going to calculate with commodities at all, future commodities ought to be discounted.

There are, to be sure, some major, valid objections to the market price method. I shall come to them soon. But I think it is a mistake to object to the general idea of using this shortcut to evaluate projects. In his discussion of discounting in *Reasons and Persons*, Derek Parfit raises several accurate objections to the market price method,[11] but I think he underestimates the method's value. He says:

> It may be in several ways more convenient, or elegant, to calculate opportunity costs using a Social Discount Rate. But the conclusions that are established by such calculations could be re-expressed in a temporally neutral way. When describing the effects of future policies, economists could state what future benefits and costs there would be, at different times, in a way that used no discount rate. The arguments that appeal to opportunity costs could be fully stated in these terms. I believe that, on any important questions that we need to decide, this would be a better, because less misleading, description of the alternatives.[12]

Before responding to this remark, let me explain the idea of an "opportunity cost." The opportunity cost of something is what we could have instead, if we choose not to have this thing. The opportunity cost of timber today is the timber we could have next year if the trees were not felled today. Because trees grow, this opportunity cost is a greater amount of timber next year. That is why today's timber is more expensive than next year's timber; you have to give up a greater amount of next year's timber to get it. In general, because technology is fertile, the opportunity cost of commodities today is a greater quantity of commodities next year. That is why commodities today are more expensive than commodities next year—why next year's commodities are discounted, that is.

The opportunity costs of commodities are embedded in their prices. A cost-benefit analyst would simply value next year's timber below this year's in her calculations, next year's concrete below this year's, and so on, taking her valuations from market prices. What would Parfit have her do instead? He would have her trace through the economy all the effects on people's

[11]. Derek Parfit, *Reasons and Persons* (Oxford: Oxford University Press, 1984), pp. 480–86.
[12]. Ibid., p. 484.

well-being, at each time in the future, of using timber and concrete at particular dates. He would then have her add up these amounts of well-being, without discounting future well-being. Parfit, in fact, would like the economist to use the pure method of evaluation, without discounting well-being. But this would be a tremendously difficult operation, and normally pointless. The point of using prices is that, in a sense, they encapsulate all that information about the effects on people's well-being in an easily manageable and observable form. The market price method is a shortcut to the pure method, and it is a hundred times more practical.

In his discussion, Parfit concentrates on difficult cases where a cost-benefit analyst would be wrong to discount a particular future commodity. The existence of a stretch of beautiful countryside is one of his examples of a commodity, and Parfit is right that this one ought not to be discounted. I shall mention these cases in Section VI. The difficult cases lead Parfit to forget all the mundane cases where the discounting of future commodities is legitimate, and the only practical way of proceeding. Furthermore, as I shall explain in Section VI, even in these difficult cases the market price method would get the right answer if it was properly applied. This method actually tells us not to discount the future existence of a stretch of beautiful countryside.

Parfit raises a related point. He mentions, as a legitimate reason for valuing future commodities below present ones, that our successors will be better off than us. Being better off, they will derive less well-being from extra commodities than we will; this is the law of diminishing marginal value. So it is better, at the margin, for commodities to come to us than to them. However, says Parfit, the reason future commodities are less valuable is not that they exist in the future. It is that they are coming to people who are better off. It is deceptive to say we are discounting for time.[13]

In the theory I have developed so far, I have not yet mentioned our successors. Nevertheless, the situation depicted in Figure 2 allows me to say something about Parfit's point. That figure shows a person who consumes more wine next year than this year, because next year's wine is cheaper than this year's. Since most commodities are cheaper next year than this, she will consume more of most commodities next year than this. In a sense, she is better off next year because she has a greater consumption then. Consequently, the marginal value to her of all these commodities

---

13. Ibid.

is less next year than this. Her situation mimics within her single life the relation between us and our successors that Parfit talks about. So we can use this example to examine Parfit's point.

Future commodities are discounted compared with present ones: they have a lower present price. Correspondingly, the value to people of future commodities is less than the value of present ones. Is the discount a discount for time? Parfit says no: since future commodities are discounted because people have more future commodities than present ones, it is misleading to say the discount is for time. But I do not think it is misleading. It is commodities we are discounting, not well-being. Dated commodities are identified by their dates, and it happens that future commodities are cheaper than present ones. This can reasonably be called a discount for time. What *causes* future commodities to be cheaper than present ones is another matter. Evening phone calls are discounted compared with daytime phone calls. The cause of this discount is that fewer people use the phone in the evening; there is less pressure on the phone company's resources, so each call costs less to provide. Nevertheless, the discount is for the time you make the call. It is evening calls that the phone company markets at a discount, not calls when fewer people are using the phone.

As I explained in Section IV, the fertility of the economy's productive system is the chief cause of why future commodities are cheaper. The fact that people, like the person in Figure 2, end up assigning a lower value to future commodities than present ones is more an effect than a cause. People arrange their affairs so as to consume more in the future, and consequently they end up assigning less value to future commodities at the margin. But even if it was a cause, the discount would still be for time. Commodities are discounted by their own interests rates, and an interest rate is a discount for time.

VI. Commodities That Should Not Be Discounted

I have explained the thinking that underlies the market price method and said what is right about it. Now I come to what is wrong with it. A lot of sound objections have been raised, but I shall only mention three here.[14]

The first objection is not to the theory of the market price method, but to

---

14. There is a fuller catalog in my *Counting the Cost of Global Warming*, pp. 60–92.

the way the method is applied. I explained that a commodity in the future normally has a lower price than in the present. It is discounted, that is to say, and the appropriate discount is given by its own interest rate. According to the theory, each commodity should be discounted at its own rate. But in practice all commodities are generally lumped together and discounted at the same rate. Normally, they are all discounted at something called the "real" interest rate, which is a weighted average of the own interest rates of various commodities.

This may be an acceptable approximation for most commodities. Most commodities are produced within the economic system, and most have similar own interest rates, determined principally by the fertility of the technology. But some commodities have quite different rates. These include nonreproducible scarce resources, which are not produced at all. I explained in Section IV that most present commodities can, in a sense, be converted into a greater quantity of future commodities. That is why future commodities are generally cheaper than present ones. But this is true only of commodities that are produced within the economic system. Scarce resources cannot be converted into a greater quantity of future resources, and they therefore have own interest rates of zero or thereabouts.[15] It follows that they ought not to be discounted, even according to the theory of the market price method. Derek Parfit gives an example: a stretch of beautiful countryside that might be destroyed to build an airport.[16] The value of this scarce resource will remain the same through time; it will not decline like the value of produced commodities. It ought not to be discounted, and the theory underlying the market price method says it ought not to be discounted.

Parfit mentions another type of commodity that ought not to be discounted. Some industrial plants cause congenital deformities among people born in their neighborhoods. In valuing the plants, cost-benefit analysts often discount deformities that will happen in the distant future; they give them less significance than present ones. But Parfit says that is a mistake. A deformity caused at one time is just as bad as a deformity caused at another. It leads to the same loss of well-being, and since Parfit believes

15. This is known among economists as the "Hotelling rule," because it appears in H. Hotelling, "The Economics of Exhaustible Resources," *Journal of Political Economy* 39 (1931): 137–75.
16. Parfit, *Reasons and Persons*, p. 483.

well-being ought not to be discounted, he believes deformities ought not to be discounted either.[17]

Let us grant the premise that well-being ought not to be discounted. Then I am sure Parfit is right that deformities ought not to be discounted. But this example is theoretically tricky, and more needs to be said about it. Some commodities represent a constant quantity of well-being whenever they occur; let us call them constant-well-being commodities. Deformities are a negative constant-well-being commodity. For theoretical purposes, it is easier to work with positive commodities, so let us work with the converse of deformities: the positive commodity of saving people from deformities. Saving people's lives is plausibly another example of a constant-well-being commodity; on average, saving one person's life in one hundred years will presumably add just as much well-being to the world as saving one person's life now. Granted that well-being ought not to be discounted, constant-well-being commodities ought not to be discounted.

Some constant-well-being commodities are scarce resources, but some are not. Lifesaving is not, for instance. Lifesaving is actually a produced commodity. People's lives are saved by care in hospitals, by installing safety devices in factories, by propaganda against smoking, and in many other ways; these are all ways in which the commodity of lifesaving is produced by the economy. Furthermore, lifesaving participates in the general fertility of the productive system. It is like timber: a quantity of lifesaving in the present can be converted into a greater quantity in the future. We can, if we

---

17. Parfit makes a concession he ought not to make. He points out that we can compensate for some deformities by providing the victim with commodities as compensation. We must compensate for present deformities with present commodities. But we can compensate for future deformities by setting up a fund now to buy future commodities. The fund will grow over time with interest. Since the fund will grow, it will be cheaper to compensate for future deformities than present ones. Provided we set up the fund, says Parfit, this is a reason for valuing future deformities less than present ones. But there is a mistake in this reasoning. The fund earns interest because future commodities, in general, are cheaper in the present than present ones. That is what interest is: it is the fact that future commodities are cheaper in the present than present commodities. In equilibrium, they are therefore less *valuable* than present ones; they bring less benefit at the margin. A present deformity will require some quantity of present commodities as compensation. A future deformity will require a greater quantity of future commodities, because the future deformity is just as bad as the present one, but the future commodities are less valuable. The fund earns interest just as quickly as commodities decline in value, so it will just be able to provide compensation to the same value whenever it is spent. Consequently, future deformities can only be compensated for at exactly the same present cost as present deformities.

choose, use fewer resources on lifesaving today, invest them productively, and so have greater resources available next year, which we could use to save more lives next year. Because present timber can be converted into a greater quantity of future timber, future timber must be cheaper than present timber in equilibrium. Timber is therefore discounted. Surely, therefore, the same should be true of lifesaving. Future lifesaving is cheaper than present lifesaving; so lifesaving should be discounted. But this contradicts my earlier remark that it should not be discounted because it is a constant-well-being commodity. So there is a puzzle. Which is right?

The answer is that the earlier remark was right: if lifesaving is a constant-well-being commodity, it should not be discounted. Lifesaving in the future will make the same contribution to well-being as lifesaving in the present. Certainly, future lifesaving is cheaper than present lifesaving, but this is not a reason for valuing it less. The market prices of commodities only have a role in valuations because they measure the relative values of commodities to people. In equilibrium, they will do so, and up to now I have been assuming the economy is in equilibrium. But if lifesaving produces constant well-being and yet is cheaper in the future, we evidently do not have an equilibrium. With ordinary commodities like timber, there is a market that will move to equilibrium if it is working smoothly. But with lifesaving there is no such market. Nor is there one for saving people from deformities. We have no reason to discount these commodities at an interest rate that has been established in the market for marketed commodities.

There is more to the puzzle, though. If we can convert a quantity of lifesaving now into a greater quantity next year, and if lifesaving next year is just as valuable as lifesaving now, the conclusion we have to draw is that lifesaving should be deferred. We should withdraw resources from lifesaving today, and apply them to saving more lives next year. We should also defer lifesaving next year in order to save yet more lives the year after. We should defer lifesaving the year after in order to save still more the year after that, and so on. We will end up postponing all lifesaving to the indefinite future, which never comes. So, we will end up saving no lives at all. If lifesaving produces constant well-being and yet its price declines with time, this is the conclusion we must draw. But it is a ridiculous one. We have a paradox.

Here is one possible solution. Lifesaving may not be a constant-well-being commodity. Undoubtedly, saving some people's lives adds more well-being to the world than saving other people's. Saving a twenty-year-old with a long and happy future ahead of her adds more to well-being than saving a ninety-year-old with little left to look forward to. We may expect that, by and large, a society will first direct its resources to saving the people with most well-being to gain. As it progresses in its ability to save lives, it will start to save people with less and less to gain. In the future, therefore, where more lives are being saved, life-saving will, by and large, produce less well-being at the margin. Therefore, the more lifesaving is deferred to the future, the less well-being it will produce on average at the margin. Eventually, as lifesaving is deferred, there will come a point where the lower price of future lifesaving is matched by its lower benefit in terms of well-being. After that, it would be wrong to defer any more lifesaving. At that point, future lifesaving is on average genuinely less valuable than present lifesaving. Lifesaving should then be discounted.

It is possible that we are in this position already. If we are, lifesaving is not a constant-well-being commodity, and it should be discounted. But we have no reason to think this is so, because there is no market that can be expected to make it so. We cannot rely on a market interest rate. All we can do is consider directly what well-being will result from lifesaving at different dates. If we conclude that lifesaving will lead to the same amount of well-being at every date, as I assumed earlier, it should not be discounted. The same goes for saving people from deformities.

VII. Disenfranchised Generations

My second objection to the market price method is that for many projects most of the interested parties are not represented in the market. Many projects will affect future generations for centuries or millennia ahead. Nuclear waste will remain dangerous for many thousands of years, and projects for disposing of it must take account of that. Attempts to control global warming will bring their main benefits more than a century from now. But the only people whose values are registered in market prices are those who are alive now. This is surely a very serious gap.

One thing might lead you to disagree. I suggested in Section IV that the main determinant of interest rates is the economy's technology, specifically its fertility. If this is correct, then interest rates would not be much different even if, in some way, future generations came to be represented in the market. Imagine a trust for future generations was set up, able to borrow money against the potential earnings of future generations and empowered to buy resources for their use. Once the economy settled down to a new equilibrium, interests rates would not have changed much.

So is the disenfranchisement of future generations a significant fault in the market price method of evaluation, or is it not? If enfranchisement would not make much difference to interest rates, then surely not: the market price method uses interest rates that are about correct. But actually this reasoning is erroneous. Interest rates would be about the same in the new equilibrium, after the economy had settled down. But just after the new trust was set up, the economy would be very far from equilibrium. From the trust's point of view—representing future generations—future commodities would be much more valuable than they seem to us who are participating in the market now. The trust would use its funds to transfer many more resources to the future. It would buy up future commodities, making them more expensive and reducing their own interest rates. When the new equilibrium was achieved, their prices would drop again to their original level, and interest rates would be restored. But in the meantime many resources would have been transferred away from us for the use of future generations. It is only the disenfranchisement of future generations that gives us the share of the world's resources that we have.

With things as they are, then, in our present equilibrium, if we came to take account of the interests of future generations, we would use lower interest rates. We would discount the future less than we do now in the market. If public authorities took account of the interests of future generations, they would use lower interests rates than market rates in their decision making. This would transfer resources forward in time for the use of future people.

Should public authorities act this way? A. C. Pigou thought they should. He wrote:

> But there is wide agreement that the State should protect the interests of the future in some degree against the effects of our irrational discounting and of our preference for ourselves over our descendants. The whole movement for "conservation" in the United States is based on this conviction. It is the clear duty of Government, which is the trustee for unborn generations as well as for its present citizens, to watch over, and, if need be, by legislative enactment, to defend, the exhaustible natural resources of the country from rash and reckless spoliation.[18]

18. A. C. Pigou, *The Economics of Welfare*, 4th ed. (London: Macmillan, 1932), pp. 29–30.

Discounting the Future

On the other hand, some people think a public authority should adopt the values of its constituents. In a democracy, they think, public authorities are responsible to their electorate, which does not include generations not yet born. No doubt the present generation cares about future generations to some extent, and wishes to leave resources for their use. The value the present generation attaches to the well-being of future generations will have been embodied in present interest rates, and it would be wrong to give any further value to future generations. Stephen Marglin takes this view. He says: "I want the government's social welfare function to reflect only the preferences of present individuals. Whatever else democratic theory may or may not imply, I consider it axiomatic that a democratic government reflects only the preferences of the individuals who are presently members of the body politic."[19] Marglin and Pigou are arguing about what the job of a government is—an argument in political philosophy that I do not wish to join. I shall say something else instead.[20]

Besides the question of what a government ought to do, there is the separate question of which of its actions would have the best results. It is quite possible that the action a government ought to take is not the one that would have the best results. For instance, a government might have a duty to do what its electorate wants, and its electorate might want it to do something that would not have the best results. In this paper I concentrate on the question of what would have the best results. That was the question I posed in Section II. The problem I laid out was to compare alternative distributions of well-being across present and future people, to decide which is better. The market price method of evaluation came up as a possible shortcut toward achieving this aim. It was intended to avoid the very difficult process of comparing people's well-being directly, but was still meant to determine which distribution of well-being is better, weighing together the well-being of different people at different times. Marglin suggests, though, that a government's "social welfare function" should reflect

---

19. S. A. Marglin, "The Social Rate of Discount and the Optimal Rate of Investment," *Quarterly Journal of Economics* 77 (1963): 97. I would be misrepresenting Marglin if I did not point out that although he thinks the government should base its decisions on the preferences of the present generation, he does not think it should use market interest rates in its calculations. Because of something called the "isolation paradox," he thinks the market rate does not properly measure what the present generation would like to leave to its successors. I cannot go into the details of the isolation paradox here.

20. The point is developed in more detail in my *Weighing Goods* (Oxford: Blackwell, 1991), chap. 7. Parfit makes a similar point in *Reasons and Persons*, pp. 480–81.

only the preferences of the individuals who are presently members of the body politic. He sees the social welfare function as playing a particular role in a democratic political process: helping to determine what a government ought to do. He does not suggest the social welfare function measures the actual value of the alternative distributions. So his aim is different from the one I have been pursuing in this paper. I have been looking for a way of aggregating people's well-being to determine the overall value of alternative distributions, and for that purpose the well-being of future generations needs to be included.

VIII. IMPRUDENCE

Market prices indicate the relative values people set on different commodities. In Section III, I discussed what "values" means in this context. I said that if a person aims to maximize her well-being, the value of a commodity to her is the well-being she will derive from it. If people generally aim to maximize their well-being, then, market prices will indicate what well-being people expect to get from commodities. Prices will be some sort of a measure of well-being, and the market price method of evaluation has some chance of approximating the pure method.

But if people do not aim to maximize their well-being, this will not be so. Imprudence is an important instance. When I say a person is imprudent, I mean she discounts her own future well-being; she does not attach as much value to her future well-being as she does to her present well-being. Figure 3 shows indifference curves for an imprudent person. In the example I used for that diagram, future wine is 5% cheaper than present wine. In equilibrium the person must adjust her relative values to prices. She therefore values future wine 5% less than present wine, at the margin. But that does not mean an extra bottle of wine in the future would bring her 5% less well-being than an extra bottle in the present. As it happens, in the example I assumed it would bring her exactly the same well-being. So although future wine is discounted by 5% on the market, it does not bring 5% less well-being. The discount rate does not measure well-being.

In general, if people are imprudent, the market prices of commodities will not properly represent the commodities' effects on well-being. The market price method of evaluation will therefore not correctly indicate the results that would be reached by the pure method. Market interest rates will discount the future too quickly.

What is to be done about this? In Section III, I said that many economists would say "no matter." If people are imprudent, that is up to them. It is not the job of a public authority to overrule people's own decision making in these matters. So imprudence gives no reason to use a lower discount rate on commodities than the market's rate. Many economists believe that, if people are imprudent, this is a reason for the government to be imprudent too. On the other hand, Pigou thought otherwise. In the passage I quoted in Section VII, he says the government should protect the interests of the future, not only against our preference for ourselves over future generations, but also against our own "irrational discounting."

Once again, I shall decline to enter an argument about the job of the government; that is a matter for political theory. In this article, I have been asking what action would have the best results. The pure method of evaluation was intended to answer this question, and the market price method was intended as a shortcut to the pure method. If people are imprudent, the market price method will fail as a shortcut, because market prices will not measure people's well-being. Market interest rates will not correctly indicate which action will have the best results.

The practical importance of this point depends on whether people are typically imprudent. I know of no convincing evidence about that, one way or the other.[21] But it is theoretically important for the following reason. In Section IV, I explained that, for reasons of technology, future commodities would generally be cheaper in the market than present ones. This implies that consumers, when they are in equilibrium, must value future commodities less than present ones at the margin. I asked how that could happen, and I mentioned only two possible explanations of importance. The first is that the person might plan to consume more commodities in the future than in the present. This makes future commodities less valuable to her at the margin, because of their diminishing marginal value. Extra commodities will bring her less well-being in the future than in the present. So in this case future commodities ought definitely to be discounted in public evaluations; the positive market interest rates constitute a genuine reason for discounting. But this case can only occur if the person is increasing her consumption over time. It can only occur in a society generally if the economy is growing, so that people's consumption is generally increasing.

21. Mancur Olson and Martin Bailey, in "Positive Time Preference," *Journal of Political Economy* 89 (1981): 1–25, claim to have evidence that people are imprudent, but their argument is seriously flawed. See my *Counting the Cost of Global Warming*, p. 110n.21.

In a static economy, this cannot be the explanation of why people value future commodities less than present ones. In a static economy, only the second possible explanation is available, and that is imprudence. But if imprudence is the explanation, the fact that interest rates are positive in the market does not indicate that present commodities produce more well-being than future commodities. If well-being ought not to be discounted, market interest rates do not give us a good reason for discounting commodities in public decisions.

When it comes down to it, if well-being ought not to be discounted, the only justification there can be for discounting commodities is that future commodities produce less well-being than present ones. And that will only plausibly be the case if people will be better off in the future. Whatever happens, technology will almost always ensure that interest rates are positive, but these positive rates will justify discounting only if the economy is growing. This is a severe limitation on our right to discount future commodities.

IX. CONCLUSION

Within the market price method of evaluation, there are some good grounds for discounting future commodities. The method itself has its attractions, and it is much more practical than the pure method. But there are also some sound objections to the market price method. The most serious is that it does not take proper account of the well-being of future generations.

We cannot put our faith in the market price method in circumstances where the objections are important. It is certainly unreliable for evaluating long-term projects that have large effects on future generations. For instance, it is useless for projects aimed at mitigating global warming. For these projects, I think we have no alternative but to fall back on the pure method; no shortcut is available. We shall have to do our best to estimate the effects the projects will have on people's well-being. Then we shall have to decide whether future well-being should be discounted. I have avoided that question in this article. The market price method skirts around it, by fixing attention on the discounting of commodities. But it cannot be avoided in the end.[22]

22. My own tentative views about it are given in *Counting the Cost of Global Warming*, pp. 94–108.

[7]
What Motivates Us to Care for the (Distant) Future?

DIETER BIRNBACHER

1. The 'Motivation Problem'

'Motivation problem' is not a well-established term in future ethics or, for that matter, in any other branch of ethics. It is taken here as a convenient label for an inquiry into the conditions that have to be fulfilled in order to make a recommendation, norm, prescription or any other action-guiding statement effective in the sense of making the addressee of such a statement behave in conformity with it. Normative statements, whether in ethics, aesthetics, or technology cannot, by themselves, compel conformity. All they do is to prescribe, or recommend, a certain course of action. In order to make someone act accordingly they have to rely on further factors. In each case the rules formulated by the system appeal to certain dispositions of the addressee of these rules: self-interest, rationality, sensibility, and moral attitudes. Even if the prescription, or recommendation, is categorical, their addressee is in principle free to follow it or not.

Attempts to deal with the 'motivation problem' in ethics—sometimes called 'motivation *aporia*'[1]—date back to the beginnings of moral philosophy. The question of what factors are necessary and sufficient to act in conformity with a given rule has been extensively discussed in the ethical systems of Plato, Spinoza, Hume, and Kant, and these discussions keep reverberating through the recent debate between internalists and externalists about moral reasons. Internalists like Bernard Williams[2] thought that having moral reasons for an action is inseparable from being motivated to act in accordance with it, even though not necessarily to the extent that the action is actually carried out. Externalists like H. A. Prichard[3] claimed that having moral reasons for an action

---
[1] cf. Wieland 1989: 25 ff. [2] cf., e.g., Williams 1981, ch. 8.
[3] cf. Korsgaard 1986, section II.

and being motivated to carry it out are distinct items, so that a psychological mechanism independent of the acceptance of the moral rule is needed to explain action in conformity with it.

Though the problem of moral motivation is mostly formulated in terms of bridging the psychological gap between the *acceptance* of a rule, on the one hand, and of *acting* in accordance with it, on the other, a finer-grained analysis might distinguish two further steps in the transition from acceptance to action so that we get four items: *acceptance, adoption, application,* and *action*. In morality, a necessary condition of acting in accordance with a rule is that the addressee *accepts* the rule, in the sense of judging it to be right and justified. Second he must *adopt* the rule as a principle by which to guide his behaviour, to incorporate it, as it were, into his own identity. Third, he must *apply* it to situations of the appropriate kind, i.e. identify situations to which the rule is relevant, which, in the case of consequentialist rules, can require considerable effort. Fourth and finally, he must *act* as the respective rule says he should act in the given situation or, in cases where the rule commands a series of actions, to decide on a strategy reaching from the present into the future.

It is a moot question whether all four of these motivational steps are logically distinct. It is unclear, for example, whether the distinction between *acceptance* in the sense of judging a rule to be justified and *adoption* of a rule can coherently be upheld. Moral psychologists tend to insist on this distinction because empirical evidence strongly suggests that the capacity to make, for example, moral judgements is largely independent of the readiness to act in accordance with them.[4] In philosophy, internalists about moral motivation will dispute the distinction between accepting and adopting a moral rule and maintain the impossibility of purely intellectually accepting a moral rule without integrating it into one's moral outlook, at least to a certain extent. From this point of view, even accepting a rule cannot be conceived as a purely cognitive act but involves at least a modicum of affective identification. This, again, is taken to imply a motivation to act in accordance with the rule, if only to an extent that leaves it open whether the rule is actually followed. Some meta-ethical prescriptivists like Hare have even gone so far as to maintain that only action in conformity with a rule is sufficient proof that is has been accepted. Though they do not want to deny the reality of weakness of will, they insist that at least continued non-conformity is incompatible with saying that a rule has been accepted.[5] On this view, the motivation problem is not the problem of closing the gap between accepting a rule and following it, but rather it is the problem

---

[4] cf., e.g., Montada 1993: 268 and Baumgartner 2005: 114.   [5] cf. Hare 1963: 82 ff.

of the difference between merely asserting that one accepts a rule and really accepting it.

It is less controversial that these four motivational conditions are empirically interdependent and that, partly in consequence of this, there can be considerable problems in attributing a failure to act in accordance with a rule to any one of these in particular. A strongly internalized moral or prudential conviction will, as a rule, be accompanied by a more reliable conformity in action than a weaker moral or prudential belief. On the other hand, a moral or prudential principle will be more easily accepted if it corresponds to an already established way of acting. This interdependence is, however, far from perfect. Rule competence in the sense of being able to make valid normative judgements need not go together with rule competence in the sense of being able to rightly identify the situations in which these have to be applied. Even less does it imply moral performance in the sense of acting in conformity with these judgements. In cases where there are strong motives to deviate from an accepted rule, the empirically well-established theory of cognitive dissonance[6] predicts that even the capacity to identify the situations in which it should be applied will be considerably weakened. We not only fail to observe the principles we have adopted but even fail to see that we do so by unconsciously, or half-consciously, misrepresenting the situation to ourselves. The same motives that make us act in ways incompatible with our principles blind us about the nature, and, given the case, the consequences of our actions.

All this contributes to the complexities of attributing a failure to act in conformity with a professed rule retrospectively. In principle, a failure to follow one's practical beliefs can be attributed to weakness of will, to an insufficiently developed capacity to identify situations for which these beliefs are relevant, or to the fact that these beliefs are only asserted and not fully internalised. The fact that these factors are interdependent does not make it easier to pinpoint the exact source of defection.

2. Why Motivation to Care for the Future is a Special Case

Future ethics poses more stringent problems of motivation than other branches of practical philosophy because there is a more striking discrepancy between the motivation to accept principles of future ethics and the motivation to act in

[6] Festinger 1957.

accordance with them than in other areas of ethics. Furthermore, future ethics poses special difficulties in rightly identifying situations to which its principles are relevant. I will comment on these points in turn.

The motivation to *accept* future ethical principles is much less problematic than the motivation to *adopt* such principles because it is more or less natural to extend the principles relating to our dealings with present people to our dealings with future people. We live in a moral culture deeply impregnated with the universalistic moral tradition of the Enlightenment. Most people who accept a fundamental moral maxim like *neminem laede* as a rule of behaviour (Schopenhauer's 'principle of justice') will hardly object to generalizing this maxim in such a way that not only present but also future beings susceptible of being harmed are included in its domain. There does not seem to be a big difference between what motivates the unextended and what motivates the extended maxim. Once a maxim of non-harming is accepted it seems plausible to include potential future 'moral patients' in addition to potential present 'moral patients'. The point made by Henry Sidgwick at the end of the 19th century, that the temporal position of who is harmed by a present action cannot be relevant to its moral evaluation,[7] can be expected to seem compelling to most moralists.

Within the universalistic paradigm of morality, the irrelevance of the temporal position of a moral patient is indeed obvious. Though moral principles containing temporal relations (such as the principle to treat one's children better than one's grandchildren) are not—*pace* Hare[8]—incompatible with the meta-ethical principle of universalization, discrimination against future persons by excluding them from the range of moral principles seems incompatible with the ideal of impartiality characteristic of the universalistic paradigm. It is part and parcel of this paradigm that actions and their consequences are judged from a standpoint of maximal impartiality, a standpoint beyond personal preferences and the limited horizon of personal sympathies. One of the reasons for this is that only evaluations of a sufficiently impartial kind have a chance of making true the claim to universal assent, which is a condition equally characteristic of the universalistic paradigm. Given that the *moral* point of view is a point of view beyond all particular perspectives—the 'view from nowhere'—any attempt to defend a privileged treatment of present people (and, perhaps, people of the near future) over people in the more distant future, seems systematically misguided. It is no accident that for Kant, who endowed the universalistic paradigm of morality with his own metaphysical emphasis, it was more or less a matter of course that whoever is motivated to accept moral principles

---

[7] Sidgwick 1907: 381.   [8] Hare 1981: 100 ff.

in his dealings with present people is thereby also motivated to accept these principles in his dealings with future people, and to judge the good and bad of people in the future as no more and no less morally considerable than the good and bad of people in the present. In one of his late essays on the philosophy of history, he boldly asserted that 'human nature is so constituted that it cannot be indifferent to goods and bads that happen at the most distant epoch, if only they happen to our species and can be expected with certainty'.[9]

Roughly the same, however, holds at least for some variants of the particularistic, or communitarian, paradigm of morality for which the range of moral norms is restricted to the members of a certain group or community.[10] Though the moral norms recognized in such communities have only a limited range and do not extend to members of different communities, they generally include the future members of the community along with its present members.[11] Since the motivation to accept the norms of the community is, in this paradigm, not their plausibility judged from an impartial and rational perspective but group loyalty and adherence to the group's customs and traditions, these motivations extend as naturally to the future members of the community in question as the universalistic motivations to future mankind. Temporal universalization is, therefore, no exclusive feature of universalistic morality, despite the fact that intergenerational moral responsibility has always been a theme more prominent in universalistic systems of ethics such as Kantianism and Utilitarianism. The crucial difference between the universalistic and the particularistic paradigm, it seems, is not its tendency to go beyond temporal but to go beyond ethnic, social, and cultural limits.[12]

Universalists and particularists in ethics, then, go together in including future generations into the scope of their principles. Nevertheless, the 'motivation problem' tends to be more acute for universalists because of their indifference to psychological distance based on ethnic, social, or cultural differences. In successively extending the range of 'moral patients' that have to be taken into consideration in judging the morality of action, the Enlightenment has deeply challenged the anthropological drive towards keeping morality within

---

[9] Kant 1912: 27.

[10] For an early elaboration of this contrast combined with a speculation as to their psychological origins see Bergson 1932: 27 ff.

[11] An early example of such a theory is Golding 1981 who writes: 'Future generations are members of our moral community because, and insofar as, our social ideal is relevant to them, given what they are and their conditions of life.' (68). A more explicit conception of 'transgenerational communities' on the basis of what he calls 'moral similarity' is developed by De-Shalit in De-Shalit 1995, ch. 1.

[12] It may be, of course, that it is not really possible to go beyond temporal limits without at the same time going beyond these other limits, so that the long-term ethnic, social and cultural identity presupposed in such a view is an illusion.

the limits of emotional bonds. There can be no more conspicuous contrast than that between what universalistic ethical systems such as Kantianism and Utilitarianism expect of moral motivation and the evolutionary origins of morality in the low-distance-morality of the family, the clan and the tribe. While this origin is deliberately disavowed in the *principles* of these moralities, it stubbornly reappears in the limits of *motivation* documented by moral psychology. Moral emotions such as love of humanity, a sense of justice and international solidarity are readily affirmed in the abstract but rarely lived in the concrete.[13] Their motivational force is throughout inferior to competing low-distance emotions such as egoism, family bonds, group solidarity and patriotism. It has even to be doubted whether the whole of humanity, spread out in past, present and future, can at all be a proper object of love. Taken all in all, experience confirms Hume's sceptical view that

in general, it may be affirm'd, that there is no such passion in human minds, as love of mankind, merely as such, independent of personal qualities, of services, or of relation to ourself. 'Tis true, there is no human, and indeed no sensible, creature, whose happiness or misery does not, in some measure, affect us, when brought near to us, and represented in lively colours: But this proceeds merely from sympathy, and is no proof of such an universal affection to mankind, since this concern extends itself beyond our own species.[14]

Though the high-minded principles of a universalistic morality include the totality of peoples, cultures and generations, the limited possibilities of practised solidarity make our practical morality focus on small islands within an ocean of moral indifference. Even if, in theory, we recognize the rights of those most distant to us along with those nearer to us, this is rarely sufficient to make them effective. Even those who heroically postulated the universal brotherhood of men usually restricted the solidarity they demanded to an in-group of the righteous and excluded the unbrotherly, the tyrants, the heathens, or the capitalists. In the same Sermon of the Mount in which Jesus preaches the love of our enemies (Mt. 5, 44), he invokes the fire of hell on those who offend their brother by calling him a fool (Mt. 5, 22).[15]

Despite these differences in the problems of motivation facing universalistic and particularistic moralities, the motivational problems posed by obligations

---

[13] cf. Baumgartner 2005: 26 with relation to environmental values. See also Bierhoff 1990: 63 ff. and Bierhoff 2002:160 on the importance of sympathy for altruistic behaviour.

[14] Hume 1888: 481 ff.

[15] There may be other kinds of gap between the motivation to accept moral principles and the motivation to act accordingly which do not result from the fact that our principles are *stricter* than human nature allows but from the fact that they are *less strict* than human nature dictates. A pertinent case is the incest taboo.

towards the future, and especially towards the distant future (i.e. those generations that we have no chance to get into direct contact with during our lifetimes) are more or less alike, at least to the extent that particularistic moralities include distant future people as persons to whom the present generation owes moral concern. In our days, the moral imperative of taking the interests of future generations into account is firmly established in most parts of the industrialized world. Only few people in the more well-to-do countries of the world would deny that the present generation has responsibilities towards future generations. The diagnosis given by Tocqueville in the 19th century about North America that 'people want to think only about the following day'[16] is no longer true, neither of North America nor of Europe. On the contrary, the long-term preservation of the natural conditions on which human life depends and the preservation of a satisfactory quality of life seem to be widely recognized values, and the same seems to hold for what Hans Jonas has called the 'first commandment' of future ethics,[17] the imperative not to endanger the future existence of mankind.

Evidence for that comes from the international treaties on environmental protection and nature conservation that have been concluded in the last decades such as the CITES convention of 1973, the Montreal Protocol on the protection of the ozone layer of 1987, and the Kyoto protocol of 1997. It is further evidenced by empirical data. In a recent empirical study of attitudes to anthropogenic climate change, Russell et al. found that imposing climate changes on future generations by present energy use is predominantly judged to be morally unjust to these generations. They also found a clear correlation between the feeling of injustice and the expressed readiness to act in ways appropriate to reduce the risk of long-term climate change.[18] Similar results were found in a study of attitudes to the environment conducted by the American ecologists Minteer and Manning. The primary aim of this study, which was based on a representative sample of the population of Vermont, USA, was to find out what matters to people in policies of environmental protection.[19] One of the results was that there is a considerable pluralism of environmental values even within the relatively closed New England population. Not surprisingly, values with a religious background are more important to some than to others. The most interesting result was, however, that the three values which were the most often nominated and on which there is the highest degree of agreement were also the three values with the highest values in relative importance, namely 'future generations' (with the representative

---

[16] Tocqueville 1961: 156.   [17] Jonas 1979: 186.   [18] Russell et al. 2003: 167.
[19] Minteer and Manning 1999.

statement 'Nature will be important to future generations'), 'quality of life' (with the representative statement 'Nature adds to the quality of our lives (for example, outdoor recreation, natural beauty)'), and 'ecological survival' (with the representative statement 'Human survival depends on nature and natural processes'). This points to the conclusion that a justification of environmental protection can be expected to be the more successful the more it invokes anthropocentric but unselfish values of a roughly 'prudential' sort: the values of stewardship and of keeping nature intact for future generations.

However well-established such future ethical principles are, they compete with other, more present-oriented motivations, and it is far from guaranteed that the high-minded future ethical principles expressed by respondents are given priority in concrete practice. Empirical data strongly support the 'low cost hypothesis'[20] according to which moral principles concerning nature conservation will be the more easily observed the less this creates costs or opportunity costs for the individual. The difficulty is illustrated by the problems of keeping greenhouse emissions within the narrow limits of the Kyoto protocol. It must be doubted whether a tax on fossil fuels high enough to curb the further expansion of motorized traffic would be politically feasible except under conditions of acute crisis such as the oil crisis of the 1980s. An empirical study of a representative sample of the population of Baden-Württemberg in 2001 showed that though 50 per cent of the people interviewed associated the climate problem with a 'high' or even 'very high' catastrophe potential and 54 per cent saw great or very great societal dangers in it, this did not correlate with a willingness to find the causes for this problem in their own behaviour. Only 11 per cent associated the responsibility for climate change with their own ways of acting.[21] Similar data were reported from the US[22] exhibiting the same psychological pattern of denial.[23] If long-term objectives require changes in the habitual behaviours and consumption patterns of a society, we should be pessimistic about their prospects of being translated into action under non-critical conditions. Any attempt to change the fundamental behaviour patterns in a society by political initiatives seems doomed to failure if the necessity of these changes is only motivated by possible or future rather than by present dangers.[24]

---

[20] Baumgartner 2005: 87.   [21] Zwick 2001: 302.   [22] Leiserowitz 2006: 56.
[23] Stoll-Kleemann, O'Riordan, and Jaeger 2001: 111.
[24] These data suggest that the 'discounting' of future utility accepted in most economic models should be understood to refer to a motivational problem rather than to a valuational one. A person who discounts the gains or losses he expects for the future does not *underrate* the true size of these gains and losses, in the way a mountaineer underrates the height he has to climb in order to reach a shelter, but is

In the following, I will focus on temporally distant generations of humans and leave aside the question of temporally distant animals and other non-human beings. I will also leave aside overlapping generations for which the 'motivation problem' is less acute. There seem to be two principal factors to explain this relative weakness of motivation to act on one's own principles in the context of future ethics as far as temporally distant generations are concerned. The one is that actively taking responsibility for the distant future is more exclusively dependent on genuinely *moral* motives than other kinds of responsibility. The other is that the effectiveness of present action in altering the future course of events to the better is, in general, less *certain* than in other kinds of responsible behaviour.

3. Moral and Quasi-moral Motives to Care for the (Distant) Future

In principle, there are three kinds of motives from which a morally required act can be done: from moral motives, from quasi-moral motives, and from non-moral motives (or any combination of these). A morally required act is done from *moral* motives if it is done precisely because it is morally required, i.e. from conscientiousness or a feeling of duty. It is done from *quasi-moral* motives if it is done from altruistic motives such as love, compassion, solidarity, generosity or spontaneous impulses to care for others, i.e. from motives that often lead to the same courses of action as genuinely moral motives, without being dependent on the adoption of a particular system of morality. (Indeed, some systems of moral philosophy, like those of Hume and Schopenhauer, rely heavily, or even exclusively, on quasi-moral motivations in this sense.) Non-moral motivations comprise both self-centred and non-self-centred motivations that result in morally required action accidentally, such as the desire for self-respect, social integration and recognition, and the pursuit of personal ideals from which others happen to profit. (These are only the ideal types. In reality, there may be all kinds of combinations of these kinds of motive.)

According to psychological internalism, not only the adoption of a moral principle as a personal maxim, but even the judgement that a certain principle is right and proper implies a certain motivation to act in accordance with it. This is a rather strong position. Nevertheless, it seems more plausible than the externalist one that construes acceptance of a moral principle as a

---

less *motivated* to act in accordance with his expectations (cf. Birnbacher 2003: 45). This is obscured both by the expression 'myopia' and by Pigou's (1932: 25) metaphor of the defective 'telescopic faculty'.

purely cognitive act. To accept a moral principle means more than to accept a descriptive statement of fact. It implies that the principle in question is introduced, to a certain extent, not only into one's system of beliefs but also into one's system of motivation. Whoever accepts a moral principle has a reason to act in certain ways rather than in others. However, the internalist position is perfectly compatible with maintaining that the acceptance of moral principles is insufficient to motivate action in conformity with these principles in cases where competing motivations can be assumed to be present. Since this latter condition is fulfilled more often than not, pure acceptance of a moral principle is rarely sufficient for its practical observance. Even on internalist premises there are reasons to think that there have to be additional motivations, of another kind, to make moral principles effective.

This gives us at least part of an explanation for why there is a *special* 'motivation problem' in future ethics. Moral motives are usually too weak to effect appropriate action unless supported by quasi-moral and non-moral motives pointing in the same direction. Moreover, the quasi-moral motives potentially supporting moral motivation such as love and sympathy are significantly absent in this field because they essentially depend on face-to-face relations with their objects. Apart from some of the members of the generations of our children and grandchildren, future generations are faceless and invisible. Future people are objects of thought and calculation. They come into view only as abstract recipients of goods and potential victims of harms, as anonymous items, and do not offer themselves as concrete and experientially accessible objects of attitudes such as love, friendship, reverence, or solidarity. But it seems that our moral sensibilities are primarily attuned to 'identified' and not to 'statistical' beneficiaries and victims. As Calabresi and Bobbitt have shown, emotions are aroused primarily by people who are threatened by death or other harm under our eyes (the victims of mining accidents, the victims of earthquakes, the patient needing immediate help), and these emotions make us act for their survival and good health even in cases in which cold calculation would tell us that it would be more rational to use the resources for preventive measures.[25]

Our spontaneous quasi-moral motives are primarily directed to what lies next to our own person in terms of temporal, spatial and social distance. A bad conscience is much more likely with someone who behaves in a way harmful to people in his or her vicinity than to someone who behaves in a way harmful to people in the distant future. In this respect, Nietzsche's polemical concept

---

[25] Calabresi and Bobbitt 1978. Cf. also the list of conditions influencing the extent to which people are prepared to give money to alleviate distant needs in Unger 1996: 73. The most important of these conditions are also satisfied by situations in the distant future.

of *Fernstenliebe* (love of the most distant), the verbal opposite of *Nächstenliebe*, the love of one's neighbour, points to a real paradox.[26]

One important aspect of the necessary abstractness of future generations is that it is more difficult to present a vivid and realistic picture of future situations than of present situations in the media.[27] TV reports about disasters can be expected to stimulate a quite remarkable willingness to give money for their alleviation, provided these disasters are perceived as caused by external factors such as uncontrollable natural forces or military attacks from foreign states. It is much more difficult to present potential future disasters such as a rapid progress of desertification by changes in the global climate with a vividness and credibility that stimulates preventive action with comparable effectiveness.

4. Non-moral Motives to Care for the Future

Roughly the same holds for non-moral motivations potentially supportive of moral responsibilities to the distant future. There is not very much the future can do for a present moral agent, and those few things it can do lack motivation potential. Later generations can erect monuments for 'great men of the past', they can cultivate their memory by commemoration services, by re-editions of their works, or by naming streets, buildings or scientific discoveries after them. These manifestations of retrospective recognition and gratitude, however, are necessarily symbolical and do not actually effect the agent during his lifetime. Though there may be some motivating potential in the hope for posthumous fame (as in the notable case of Horace who prided himself of having created a work *aere perennius*), this is relevant only for a small elite, mainly for those occupying important positions in society, politics, religion or culture already during their lives. I personally doubt whether a less exclusive future-directed motivation such as the thought of being remembered by one's descendants is a particularly strong motivation to act for their benefit.

An even more important factor in weakening the motivation to act for the distant future is the impossibility of direct and indirect negative sanctions. While children and grandchildren are in a position to claim their legitimate share and to protest against future burdens (such as the burden of paying

---

[26] Nietzsche 1980: 77. A similar paradox is involved in Schopenhauer's attempt to extend the concept of *compassion* to cover an indefinite multitude of potential moral patients in the context of the *Mitleidsethik* (cf. Birnbacher 1990: 30 ff.). The more abstract the objects of compassion or pity become, the more the specific meaning of these concepts is lost.

[27] The importance of vivid representation as a precondition of sympathy with remote victims was already clearly stated by Hume, see the quotation above, p.280.

back international debts over a long period of time in the future), our grand-grandchildren necessarily remain silent. If they have a voice, it is only vicariously, through the advocacy of people who protect their interests and rights against the short-sighted loyalties of the present.

This, however, is only one of the obstacles lying in the way of future ethical motivation. The other is the *uncertainty* about which actions will have morally significant effects in the future. Though the general direction of future-oriented action may be clear (as, for example, reducing emissions of greenhouse gases in the case of the problem of global warming), there is more than one dimension of uncertainty to create doubts about whether future-oriented behaviour will really make a difference to future people. First, there is the uncertainty about the validity of the theories and scenarios on which the prognosis of future risks is based. Second, there is the uncertainty about whether and, if so, at what point of time alternative ways will be found to neutralize or to reduce future hazards. A third factor of uncertainty is the synergistic and cumulative nature of most long-term conservation strategies, both synchronically and diachronically. Potential impacts of present action are threatened by the potential lack of co-operation of present agents as well as by the potential lack of co-operation of future agents. The impact of present energy saving by one agent on future resources may be seen as negligible without the certainty that others join in. In order to attain their goal long-term strategies have to be undertaken by a series of successively co-operating generations. No single individual and no single collective can be sure, however, that its descendants will honour their efforts by carrying on the process into the distant future. There can be, in the nature of the case, no certainty that countervailing interests of later generations will not annul the beneficial effects of the efforts of the first generation.

Given these uncertainties (which apply especially to the distant future), the causal relevance of present action on future conditions is much less open to empirical control than the causal relevance of present action on spatially distant regions of the world. Acting for the future is inherently more risky than acting for the present or for the immediate future. It essentially involves the risk of squandering moral resources on projects that fail to achieve their intended aims by factors beyond the agent's control. That these risks have a considerable psychological impact on behaviour has been shown in several relevant areas. One of the preconditions for action motivation seems to be a relevant 'control belief', i.e. the belief that appropriate action will be effective in attaining the desired goal. Without relevant 'control beliefs', the motivation to enter upon a course of action can be expected to be unstable.[28]

[28] cf. for the case of air pollution Evans and Jacobs 1981: 116 ff.

Each of the factors listed above contributes to weaken the practical effectiveness of moral beliefs about obligations to the future. Some of these factors are specific to future ethics: future ethics has to do without the help of most of the quasi-moral and non-moral motivations that support the effectiveness of moral beliefs about obligations to present people. It further faces the problem that identifying actions by which the benefit of future generations can be secured is much more riddled with uncertainties than identifying actions by which the benefit of present people (or people in the near future) can be secured.

5. Indirect Motivations

This pessimistic picture is, however, too pessimistic to be realistic. It leaves out what, in future ethics, may be a far more potent motivational resource than the motivations discussed so far, *indirect* motivations. The distinction between direct and indirect motivations cuts across the distinction between moral, quasi-moral, or non-moral motivations introduced above. Indirect motivations can be moral, quasi-moral, or non-moral. Their distinctive mark is that they produce a certain value or good as a side-effect. In an intergenerational context, indirect motivations do not aim at the production of goods or the prevention of evils befalling future people, but aim at objectives in the present or in the near future. They are nevertheless indirect motivations to act for the distant future in so far as they can be assumed to work for the good of people in the long term and to contribute to the realization of the same ends as those underlying the principles of future ethics.

The advantage of indirect motivations from a practical point of view is their more reliable emotional basis and their potentially greater effectiveness in guiding behaviour. Differently from direct motivations, indirect motivations are supported by a broader range of emotional factors. This is not to say that a purely moral motivation to act responsibly towards the future is without emotions. These emotions, however, are necessarily abstract and impersonal. The future individuals (at least those in the far future) figure in them only as blanks. Indirect motivations, on the contrary, are able to make use of the full scope of quasi-moral motives, such as love, compassion, care, and solidarity, directed to objects accessible to experience.

The most well-known construction of an indirect motivation in future ethics is Passmore's idea of a 'chain of love'. 'Chain of love' means the intergenerational concatenation of each generation's love for its children and grandchildren. According to this model, each generation cares exclusively for the generation of its children and grandchildren, with the result that the sequence of limited responsibilities has the same or even better effects on the whole series of generations than postulates of a more future-oriented responsibility.[29] These advantages are both cognitive and motivational. Each generation is in a better position to judge what serves the well-being of the next generation than of what serves the well-being of the second or third generation coming after it. And each generation pursues the well-being of the next generation with higher intensity than that of the second or third generation coming after it because of the presence of stronger quasi-moral and non-moral motives.

The model can be interpreted and filled out in various ways, differing in the explanation given for why each generation cares for the generation of their children. One is to assume a natural and inborn propensity on the part of parents to make provisions for their children's future and to make sacrifices for their good. In this case, each generation is assumed to be motivated to care for its children independently of whether the generation of its own parents has similarly cared for itself. In a second variant the motivation is made to depend on a process of social learning. The motivation of the children's generation to care for their children is acquired by a process of model learning: each generation takes over the future-directed behaviour of their parents (and possibly grandparents) in their relations to their children (and grandchildren). The only external motivation necessary for triggering the concatenation of sympathies is the initial motivation of the first generation. Everything else follows, as it were, by chain reaction.

The chain of love-model is a quite powerful one. This is evident from the fact that even future disasters like a potential running out of a fundamental (non-substitutable) exhaustible resource such as energy can be modelled in such a way that even generations with a limited 'sympathy horizon' extending over no more than the two following generations have a reason to act so as to prevent or at least mitigate the future calamity. Even a generation not covered by the altruism of the first generation, such as the third generation coming after it, can be better off, in this model, than under the assumption that it is covered by the altruism of the first generation. This result essentially depends on the condition that though the aim of each generation's intergenerational sympathy is only the welfare of the directly following generations, this welfare is a compound of its own egoistic welfare and the altruistic welfare resulting from the anticipation of the welfare of subsequent generations. By aiming

---

[29] Passmore 1980: 88 ff.

at the welfare of the directly following generations, each generation thereby unintentionally sympathises with the welfare of the generations with which its directly following generations sympathise and therefore, by concatenation, with all future generations. Each generation aims at the welfare of no more than the two following generations. But in fact, as an unintended result, it promotes the welfare of the whole chain.

Assume, for example, that the compound welfare $U_{tot}s_n$ of each generation s_n is the sum of three utilities, its egoistic welfare $U_{ego}s_n$, a part of the compound welfare of the generation of its children, $U_{tot}s_{n+1}$, and a part of the compound welfare of the generation of its grandchildren, $U_{tot}s_{n+2}$.[30] Let the compound welfare of generation s_n, $U_{tot}s_n$ be defined as $U_{tot}s_n = U_{ego}s_n + 0.5\ U_{tot}s_{n+1} + 0.25\ U_{tot}s_{n+2}$, with 0.5 and 0.25 as 'sympathy factors' representing the degree to which the welfare of each generation depends on the welfare it perceives or anticipates subsequent generations to enjoy. It is easily shown that under these assumptions foreseen negative developments starting only during the lifetime of generation 4, which lies beyond the 'sympathy horizon' of generation 1, nevertheless have an impact on the welfare of generation 1.

Let us assume that after an initial period of growth, a foreseeable shortage occurs during the adult years of generation 4 leading to a decline in welfare of all subsequent generations (with generation 6 as the last generation):

generation	1	2	3	4	5	6
net welfare	2	3	3	1	1	1

As a consequence, the welfare of all earlier generations is affected:

generation	1	2	3	4	5	6
compound welfare	5.938	5.688	4.375	2	1.5	1

This distribution compares unfavourably with an alternative scenario in which generation 1 sacrifices part of its net welfare to invest in the prevention of the foreseeable shortage so that the level of net welfare rises instead of falling during the lifetime of generation 4. Think, for example, of heavy investments in the development of energy production from nuclear fusion in generation 1, resulting in a substitution of fossil fuels from generation 4 on.

---

[30] For a generalized model of iterated sympathy relations between subsequent generations see Dasgupta 1974: 413 ff.

generation	1	2	3	4	5	6
net welfare	1	3	3	4	4	4

In this case, the corresponding values for the compound welfare are:

generation	1	2	3	4	5	6
compound welfare	7.75	9.25	8.5	8	6	4

What makes the 'chain-of-love' model attractive is the weakness of the conditions on which it is based. It demands neither moral heroism nor dramatic sacrifices but only foresight and the effort to make each generation's sympathies for subsequent generations effective in future-oriented strategies. The motive of parents to see to the future of their children is a reliable motive mainly for two reasons: first, because it in fact seems 'natural' that parents have an interest in the future well-being of their children; and second, because many parents can be assumed to have an interest in securing assistance from their children in case they have to depend on them in old age.[31]

Furthermore, the model incorporates the empirical findings on the importance of model learning for intergenerational behaviour. How a generation behaves toward its immediate descendants seems to a large extent determined by the behaviour of the previous generation towards this generation. In a series of experiments on the distribution of a given quantity of resources between oneself and subsequent subjects (representing subsequent generations), Wade-Benzoni impressively showed that the preparedness to generosity toward future subjects heavily depends on the generosity experienced or attributed to the previous owner of the resource.[32] In conformity with Bandura's theory of social learning in moral contexts[33] the generosity or non-generosity of the previous owner from whom the initial stock of the resource has been inherited is interpreted as a social norm and mimicked by one's own preparedness to make sacrifices for the future. There is empirical evidence that even the form in which parents provide for the future of their children (i.e. by bequest, financial assistance, investment in their education etc.) is closely correlated with the kind of provisions their own parents made for them.[34]

At the same time, the chain-of-love model is hopelessly unrealistic as far as it construes whole generations as homogeneous, whereas, in reality, agency lies with politicians, economic planners, and the heads of families and dynasties

---

[31] See Becker and Murphy 1988: 5 ff. [32] Wade-Benzoni 2002. [33] Bandura 1969.
[34] Arrondel and Masson 2001: 417 ff.

WHAT MOTIVATES US TO CARE FOR THE (DISTANT) FUTURE? 289

with highly diverse possibilities of determining the welfare of subsequent generations. Well-to-do family heads usually bequeath their wealth to children who would be well-to-do even without the bequest, whereas older people with modest means usually have little to spare. The parts of the world in which future shortages are most likely to have an impact on the overall welfare of subsequent generations (and in which they do so already now) are also the least likely to have the means to make the investments necessary to prevent shortages in the future.

A second model of indirect motivations to care for the distant future was adumbrated by Passmore and then elaborated by Visser't Hooft.[35] In this model, indirect motivation is not aimed at *persons*, but at *goods* valued for their own sake, either natural or cultural. The idea of the model is that the long-term conservation of a certain good is best assured by establishing a tradition of valuing this good. This is plausible, first of all, for environmental goods such as beautiful landscapes and wilderness areas. It does not come as a surprise that, in an empirical study, Kals et al. found that emotional affinity towards nature proved to be an important predictor of the willingness to protect nature.[36] This is plausible, however, also for cultural goods such as forms of art, music, literature, philosophy, science, social virtues, and political institutions. Valuing these goods is closely linked, psychologically, to motivations to contribute to the conservation of these values and their manifestations. Whoever loves, for example, the music of Bach can be expected to have an interest in preserving this music from being lost or forgotten. That implies that he must be interested in conserving or even strengthening attitudes likely to respect the integrity of these values. He must be a conservative in respect to a certain form of life. It is hardly imaginable to subscribe to a cultural value like classical music, scientific truth or the democratic state without the hope that they will 'never die'. Indeed, Nietzsche's line according to which 'alle Lust will Ewigkeit' (all pleasure wants eternity)[37] seems to apply more to the objects of pleasure, satisfaction and valuation than to pleasure itself. It is not pleasure that we want to exist forever, but the objects of pleasure.

An anticipation of this model with respect to natural values is one of the pioneering conceptions of ecological ethics, Aldo Leopold's 'land ethic'. Leopold proposed the 'land ethic' because he was convinced that direct motives of nature conservation based on future ethical considerations are insufficiently effective in motivating ecologically correct action. Therefore, he thought, a functional substitute was needed; in his own words, 'a mode of guidance for meeting ecological situations so new or intricate, or involving

[35] Visser't Hooft 1999: 122. [36] Kals et al. 1999. [37] Nietzsche 1980: 404.

such deferred reactions, that the path of social expediency is not discernible to the average individual.'[38] Leopold's 'land ethic', though designed for ultimately anthropocentric purposes, has an ecocentric orientation. It expects the agent to see himself not as a conqueror but as part of nature and to define his role as serving nature instead of dominating it. It furthermore includes the cultivation of emotions such as love, respect and admiration of nature for its own sake.[39]

This characteristic indirectness of motivation is also present in some attempts within the communitarian school of social thought to incorporate future ethics into the communitarian framework. Philosophers in the communitarian tradition like De-Shalit have drawn attention to the close relations between the fact of being firmly embedded in a social group and the motivation to care for its future.[40] Concern about the future well-being of a group to which one has a close emotional relationship can be expected to be more reliable than the interest in the well-being of abstractions like humanity or future generations. Caring for the future of one's reference group can even be part of one's own moral identity. Whoever defines himself as German, Christian, or as a scientist, can hardly be indifferent to the future of the group to which his identity refers, though, with a plurality of identities and loyalties, their may be conflicts between the future-directed motivations associated with each. In a pioneering paper on the 'motivation problem' in future ethics, this source of motivation was called 'community bonding'.[41] The essential motivational factor in community bonding is the 'sense of belonging to some joint enterprise with others'. One's own contribution to the future is seen as a contribution to a common cause which one expects to be carried further by an indefinite number of subsequent generations of members of the same community.

Future-oriented motivations by specific loyalties are further supported by the fact that quite a number of collectives are either defined by a certain long-term project, as, e.g. 'movements' for x where x is a value or good of an intergenerational kind, or are so efficient in inculcating long-term objectives in their adherents that these have no room for long-term projects and ideals of their own. From the perspective of future ethics, such collective objectives are, however, a mixed blessing. They are too often directly averse to the well-being of future mankind, rationally conceived, as has been shown by the projects of imperialism, colonialism, and the world revolution.

This does not close the list of indirect motivations relevant to actively pursuing the good of future generations. There is one further indirect motivation to act for the future that can be expected to become even more important in the

---

[38] Leopold 1949: 203.   [39] Leopold 1949: 204, 209, 223.   [40] De-Shalit 1995.
[41] Care 1982: 207.

WHAT MOTIVATES US TO CARE FOR THE (DISTANT) FUTURE?

future, which is the motivation to give meaning to one's life by embedding it in a transgenerational context of solidarity. In the developed world, a spiritual vacuum has made itself felt that can be traced back both to the continuing historical process of secularization and to saturation with purely economic private and collective objectives. There is a high degree of preparedness to contribute to causes or projects that reach further than one's own person, one's own personal context, and one's own lifetime. Ernest Partridge has called such motives motives of 'self-transcendence'.[42] Future orientation and responsibility to the future offer themselves as the natural candidates for the longing for existential meaning in a secularized world. Acting for the future fits such motives most neatly because a commitment to the future makes the individual feel his own value and makes him feel embedded in a wider context of meaning which reaches from the past into the far future. By acting for the future, the individual is given the chance to see himself as an element in a chain of generations held together by an intergenerational feeling of community, which combines obligations in the direction of the future with feelings of gratitude in the direction of the past. However modest his contribution, he thereby situates himself in a context transcending the individual both in personal and temporal respects.

This motive will gain particular momentum when it is combined with the communitarian motive and supported by the feeling that one's own contribution is part of the objectives of a larger community. The best term to characterize such a feeling of transcending the bounds of one's existence seems to be *elevation*, a word characteristically used by Stendhal when he wrote, in an age more given to enthusiasm than ours: '... sacrifice du présent à l'avenir; rien *n'élève* l'âme comme le pouvoir et l'habitude de faire de tels sacrifices' (... sacrificing the present to the future; nothing elevates the soul like the power and the habit of such sacrifices).[43] Of course, at least part of the robustness of this motivation depends on the fact that it cannot be disappointed by experience. In this respect, motivations to act for the future resemble religious commitments of a more literally transcendent kind. Both are, for the present agent, unfalsifiable. Partly in consequence thereof, they are liable to be abused. Whether there will in fact be the temporally overarching community with shared objectives and values and shared feelings of solidarity implicitly assumed to exist in this motivation is highly uncertain. It is an open question whether our descendants will recognize, or honour by acting in accordance with them, the present generation's principles of intergenerational responsibility and visions of intergenerational justice. The more remote in time

---

[42] Partridge 1980: 204.   [43] Stendhal 1959: 246 ff. (my italics).

a later generation is situated and the more its principles are shaped by a long series of intermediary generations coming between ours and theirs, the less certain we can be that they will in fact be, as this motivation presupposes, part of the same moral community.[44] As historical examples of powerful ideologies like Marxism have shown, however, the risk of illusion does not necessarily detract from the strength of this motivation.

It should be mentioned that all four models discussed, though potentially quite effective in stimulating actions and omissions with long-term impact, have serious limits. The most important limit is the risk of wasting moral energies on the world's future that might more profitably be invested in solving the world's present problems. Each of these models might mislead the present generation in making provisions for the future that the future will not in fact need. It may, e.g., be doubted whether future generations would actually suffer from not having the chance to see live members of those biological species that will by that time have become extinct unless kept alive by the present generation's efforts. It is an open question whether the libraries of classical literature we try to preserve now will be of much use for the people of a distant future in which people's interests might have radically changed. On the other hand, there is a substantial risk that we are currently wasting resources that will prove to be much more vital for the basic needs of future people than we can possibly expect.

6. Self-binding as a Supportive Device

Hope for long-term policies does not come only from indirect motivations but also from *self-binding*. Self-binding functions either by raising the threshold to deviate from the road of virtue defined by one's own principles, or by limiting one's freedom to deviate from these principles. In either case, an attempt is made to control in advance the extent to which future motivations deviating from one's principles result in undesired behaviour, either by deliberately making deviations more difficult or less attractive, or by deliberately restricting future options. In the first case, the motivational mechanism is similar to the replacement of direct motives by indirect motives: whoever binds himself by a long-term contract and pre-commits himself to a certain course of action complements the direct motivation for long-term provisions or long-term beneficence by the indirect motivation to escape the short-term consequences of breaking or changing the contract.

[44] cf. Auerbach 1995: 79 ff.

The paradigmatic field of operation of self-binding mechanisms is the field of prudential maxims like paying one's debts, saving a portion of one's income, or not resuming smoking after having given it up. The agent pre-commits himself to live up to his maxims by delegating control to an external personal or institutional agency, thus protecting himself from his own opportunism. Self-binding must be attractive to anyone who thinks that he is inclined to impulses by which he risks jeopardizing his long-term objectives.

Self-binding can take various forms. *Internal* self-binding consists in self-binding relying on mechanisms internal to the agent. In the case of the individual, internal self-binding can assume the form of adopting maxims by which internal sanctions are activated to avoid opportunistic deviations from one's principles, so that deviations are 'punished' e.g. by feelings of guilt or shame. Feelings of guilt or shame are mobilized whenever the person does not live up to the obligations of his moral identity. Once these internal sanctions have been established, even the most extreme egoist has a reason to take these sanctions into account. In the case of collectives, internal self-binding can consist in establishing institutions within a society by which collective decisions are controlled and potentially revised. *External* self-binding consists in delegating these sanctions to an external agency, either by making it raise the threshold for deviations or by restricting the options open to oneself. Delegating the power to make one follow a rule according to the Ulysses-and-the-Sirens pattern can be thought of as a kind of self-paternalism, which, however, is without the moral problems characteristic of other forms of paternalism since the subject and object of paternalistic intervention are one and the same.

Self-binding is clearly relevant to future-oriented action. Given the psychological facts about time preference and the limited intergenerational sympathy horizon (which rarely exceeds the generations of children and grandchildren), self-binding is, in principle, a potent device in effectively caring for the future. A case for introducing such self-binding mechanisms in the context of future ethics was recently made by Baumgartner.[45] According to this author, future-oriented moral values can play the role of internal self-binding mechanisms if they are sufficiently firmly embedded in an individual's moral identity. The individual's moral identity is not a given. It can be modelled by morally significant experience and by a process of reflective working through of this experience. Self-binding is effected by moral experiences that are intense enough to have an impact on a person's moral identity.

The problem with individual self-binding, however, is that it is difficult to manipulate one's moral experience at will. Changes in fundamental value

[45] Baumgartner 2005: 283 ff.

orientation do not usually occur deliberately. It must be doubted, therefore, whether internal self-binding on the level of the *individual* is a good candidate for compensating for other kinds of future ethical motivation wherever these are lacking. A further problem is that even a conscience reliable enough to constitute a moral identity is not immune to corruption. Internal moral sanctions are often too weak to overcome temptation. On the whole, delegation of control to an external agency seems more effective.

This is true, however, only on the level of the individual. On the social level, internal self-binding might serve as a potent instrument of protecting collective long-term concerns from being weakened by myopic temptations, both by formal and informal means. The most important formal means are legal and constitutional safeguards; the most important informal means are educational policies. By educating the young generation in the spirit of sustainability and by creating an atmosphere in which foresight, cautious use of resources, nature conservation, and the long-term stability of social security are strengthened against countervailing short-term interests, society deliberately builds up pressure from below to keep its own opportunistic tendencies under control. This pressure then might act as a kind of 'social conscience' against the temptations of politicians to serve themselves or their constituencies at the cost of the future. This is not say that social self-binding mechanisms are by themselves supportive of sustainability and long-term objectives. On the contrary, in many welfare states the legal realities are such that long-term political objectives (such as lowering the national debt) are made more difficult by legally established social rights.

Compared to legal safeguards against social myopia, constitutional safeguards are clearly more reliable. They are not only less easy to change than simple laws, they can also be expected to pre-commit future generations of politicians and other decision-makers, thus contributing to continuity in the pursuit of transgenerational objectives.[46] Though there can be, in the nature of the case, no guarantee that they will remain in force during future generations, they provide as much certainty that the projects of today are carried on in the future as one can possibly hope for. Besides that, constitutions usually provide a certain degree of protection against politics being excessively dominated by short-term objectives, through both procedural and material safeguards. One of the procedural safeguards designed to control short-term orientation in political decision-making is the institution of indirect democracy, which requires that the members of the legislative organs are bound exclusively by their own conscience and/or party discipline and not by an imperative

[46] cf. Elster 1979: 95.

mandate. By assigning the control of the executive not to the constituencies themselves but to their elected representatives, potential pressure from the basis to prioritize short-term objectives over long-term objectives of preservation and development is effectively reduced. Again, this assignment of control will work in favour of long-term orientations only to the extent that the decisions taken by political representatives are in fact less myopic than those hypothetically taken by their constituencies. Whether this is so, is open to doubt.

Another procedural safeguard is the institution of an independent constitutional court with the power to control government policies by constitutional principles. Most constitutions contain material principles limiting the extent to which governments may indulge in 'obliviousness of the future'. In the German *Grundgesetz,* there are two articles to that effect: article 115 which limits the national debt to the sum total of national investments, and the recently introduced article 20a, which contains an explicit commitment to care adequately for the needs of future generations, especially by preserving resources and by protecting the natural environment.

There are other hopeful developments in establishing self-binding mechanisms by which collective agents keep their own myopia under control. In a number of political areas, such as economics, science, technology, environment, medicine and social security, there is a growing number of independent bodies whose counsel is heard, and often respected, in practical politics. Examples of such independent bodies are, on the one hand, research institutions, think tanks, and foundations designed to exist over longer periods of time and wholly or partly financed by the state, and, on the other hand, committees and commissions expected to work on more limited tasks. The intention in setting up these bodies is, partly, to make them act as a kind of collective 'future ethical conscience', a role which politics is often unable to play because of pressures of lobbying, party politics and election campaigns. Of course, there is no guarantee that the advice of these committees and commissions (even where it is unanimous) is respected. The advice coming from these bodies binds those to whom it is addressed as little as advice from a friend binds an individual. The alternative of endowing these bodies with executive or legislative powers, however, would not be compatible with basic democratic principles. The sovereignty of the people, or of its representatives, must not be usurped by experts.

Experience shows that it may take quite a long time until the warnings of experts from these bodies about future dangers have an impact on politics. In some cases, it takes twenty or thirty years until the warnings about long-term hazards are taken seriously by politicians, as, for example, in the case of climate changes caused by the emission of greenhouse gases. (One may well wonder how long it will take for the dangers inherent in the dramatic changes in the distribution of age groups to be fully recognized by political planners.) In part, these delays are not unreasonable given the fact that neither every warning is well-founded nor every catastrophe scenario realistic (think of such insufficiently founded warnings as the *Waldsterben* or the potentially fatal erosion of the oxygen content of the atmosphere). In part they are due, however, to the reluctance of politicians to meet new challenges and to confront their constituencies with truths they do not like.

7. External Self-binding Mechanisms

On the level of the individual, self-binding by an external agency is the more attractive the more firmly an individual wants to act on its long-term principles and the higher its risk of impulsiveness. An extreme case is the situation of gambling addicts, some of whom have gone so far as to demand legal possibilities to make gambling casinos restrict access to them on an international scale. A milder form of self-restraint by external self-binding would be to make one's decision to quit smoking public and to expose oneself to the mockery of friends in case of defection (cf. Bayertz 2004, 172).

Since time preference is a universal phenomenon, delegating responsibility for long-term provisions to an external agency like the state is often rational even for those who are less prone to succumb to their impulses. For one, control costs are shifted to an external institution. Self-restraint is wholly or partly replaced by restrictions coming from outside. Second, the individual can be more certain that his individual investment has an effect on the future in all cases where a cumulative effort is needed to make a difference. Third, it is more probable that the burdens of realizing long-term objectives are fairly distributed and that free riding on the idealism of others is ruled out. Fourth, there are advantages of a moral division of labour made possible by institutional solutions. Instead of each individual making its own provisions for the future, those with an intrinsic interest in the class of objects to be protected can be assigned the task of keeping them in good order, with environmentalists caring for the conservation of nature, and economists caring for the conservation of capital. Empirical surveys repeatedly show that a large proportion of citizens is interested in the conservation of nature but that very few are willing to actively contribute to it by voluntary work. In all such cases it is rational to lay these widely shared aims into the hands of those who are intrinsically motivated.

On the level of the collective, several external self-binding mechanisms with a clear relevance to future ethics are already in operation, some of them taking the form of international law and international contracts, others taking the form of transnational organizations and authorities. A model of an internationally effective agency able not only to give advice to national governments but also to implement their future directed policies independently of national politics is the European Central Bank. It functions independently of national governments and is bound exclusively by the criteria of the European Union Treaty. Important functions of an external control of government policies in the sphere of future objectives are international contracts like the Maastricht Treaty (concerning the limits set to the national debt) and the Kyoto Protocol (concerning the emission of greenhouse gases into the atmosphere). However, given the fact that governments are the key agents of most future hazards such as the destruction of large parts of tropical rain forest, the reduction of biodiversity, and the degradation of soils by intensive agriculture, there is still much to be done. There are quite a number of proposals about how this may be effected. One option that should be taken into consideration is the global court for future issues proposed, together with other options, by Weiss.[47] Such a court, even if it lacks the authority to check the 'obliviousness of the future' of national governments by issuing sanctions, would at least be able to protest against policies that endanger the interests of future people and to encourage the search for sustainable alternatives.

8. Conclusion

The 'motivation problem', the problem of bridging the psychological gap between the acceptance of a rule and acting in accordance with it, is not only a practical challenge to politicians and educators, but also a theoretical challenge to moral psychology and moral philosophy. The challenge is to identify factors that might help to motivate an agent not only to accept responsibility in the abstract but also to adopt it as a part of his moral identity and to take appropriate action. Though internalists about moral motivation are probably right in thinking that accepting a moral rule is more than a purely intellectual act of assent and involves some motivation to act in accordance with it, this motivation by itself is, in general, too weak to resist the temptations of more immediate and more controllable objectives.

---

[47] Weiss 1989: 121.

Motivation to make provisions for the more distant future is a particular challenge for any theory of moral motivation. Moral norms to care for the distant future do not only share the problems of motivation common to all moral norms but face particular difficulties resulting from the facelessness of future people and the inevitable abstractness of obligations to act for the future. Moreover, the motivation to act responsibly towards the future tends to be weakened by a number of uncertainties, among them the uncertainty about what our descendants will value, the uncertainty about whether present sacrifices will have an effect on future well-being, and the uncertainty about whether subsequent generations will co-operate in the long-term effort to preserve essential natural resources (such as energy resources) and important cultural resources (such as the democratic state).

The picture resulting from an exclusive consideration of direct motivations to act for the future is unduly pessimistic, however. It leaves out the important role of indirect motivations. In the context of future ethics, indirect motivations, whether moral, quasi-moral or non-moral, can be expected to have a more reliable emotional basis than direct motivations and to be more effective in guiding behaviour. Taking indirect motivations into account makes the prospects of future-oriented action appear much less gloomy. Among these are the love of one's children and grandchildren (and the expectation to receive something from them in exchange in a later period of life), group loyalties, the high valuation of transgenerational projects and ideals for their own sakes, and the satisfaction gained by embedding one's own limited existence into a 'self-transcending' chain of contributions to a transgenerational cause. These motivations hold at least a limited promise of effectively shaping the decisions of the present generation in a way compatible with widely shared principles of future ethics, especially if these motivations are supported by mechanisms of external self-binding on the level of the individual and by mechanisms of internal and external self-binding on the level of collectives like states and companies.

References

ARRONDEL, L., and MASSON, A. (2001), 'Family transfers involving three generations', *Scandinavian Journal of Economics*, 103: 415–44.

AUERBACH, B. E. (1995), *Unto the Thousandth Generation. Conceptualizing Intergenerational Justice* (New York: Peter Lang).

BANDURA, A. (1969), 'Social learning of moral judgements', *Journal of Personality and Social Psychology*, 11: 275–9.

BAUMGARTNER, C. (2005), *Umweltethik—Umwelthandeln. Ein Beitrag zur Lösung des Motivationsproblems* (Paderborn: Mentis).

BAYERTZ, K. (2004), *Warum überhaupt moralisch sein?* (Munich: Beck).

BECKER, G. S., and MURPHY, K. M. (1988), 'The family and the state', *Journal of Law and Economics*, 31: 1–18.

BERGSON, H. (1932), *Les deux sources de la moralité et de la religion* (Paris: Alcan).

BIERHOFF, H.-W. (1990), *Psychologie hilfreichen Verhaltens* (Stuttgart: Kohlhammer).

—— (2002), *Prosocial Behaviour* (Hove: Psychology Press).

BIRNBACHER, D. (1990), 'Schopenhauers Idee einer rekonstruktiven Ethik (mit Anwendungen auf die moderne Medizinethik)', *Schopenhauer-Jahrbuch*, 71: 26–44.

—— (2003), 'Can discounting be justified?', *International Journal of Sustainable Development*, 6: 42–51.

CALABRESI, G., and BOBBITT, P. (1978), *Tragic Choices* (New York: Norton).

CARE, N. S. (1982), 'Future generations, public policy, and the motivation problem', *Environmental Ethics*, 4: 195–213.

DASGUPTA, P. (1974), 'On some alternative criteria for justice between generations', *Journal of Public Economics*, 3: 405–23.

DE-SHALIT, A. (1995), *Why Posterity Matters. Environmental Policies and Future Generations* (London/New York: Routledge).

ELSTER, J. (1979), *Ulysses and the Sirens. Studies in Rationality and Irrationality* (Cambridge/Paris: Cambridge University Press).

EVANS, G. W., and JACOBS, S. (1981), 'Air pollution and human behavior', *Journal of Social Issues*, 37: 95–125.

FESTINGER, L. (1957), *A Theory of Cognitive Dissonance* (Stanford: Stanford University Press).

GOLDING, M. (1981), 'Obligations to future generations', in E. Partridge (ed.), *Responsibilities to Future Generations* (Buffalo (N. Y.): Prometheus Books), 61–72.

HARE, R. M. (1963), *Freedom and Reason* (Oxford: Clarendon Press).

—— (1981), *Moral Thinking: Its Levels, Method and Point* (Oxford: Clarendon Press).

HUME, D. (1888), *Treatise on Human Nature* (Oxford: Oxford University Press).

JONAS, H. (1979), *Das Prinzip Verantwortung. Versuch einer Ethik für die technologische Zivilisation* (Frankfurt/M.: Insel).

KALS, E., SCHUMACHER, D., and MONTADA, L. (1999), 'Emotional affinity toward nature as a motivational basis to protect nature', *Environment & Behaviour*, 31: 178–202.

KANT, I. (1912), 'Idee zu einer allgemeinen Geschichte in weltbürgerlicher Absicht', in *Werke* (Akademie-Ausgabe) (Berlin: Reimer), 8.

KORSGAARD, C. M. (1986), 'Skepticism about practical reason', *Journal of Philosophy*, 83: 5–25.

LEISEROWITZ, A. (2006), 'Climate change risk perception and policy preferences: The role of affect, imagery, and values', *Climatic Change*, 77: 45–72.

Leopold, A. (1949), 'The land ethic', in *A Sand County Almanac and Sketches Here and There* (New York: Oxford University Press), 201–26.

Minteer, B. A., and Manning, R. E. (1999), 'Pragmatism in environmental ethics: Democracy, pluralism, and the management of nature', *Environmental Ethics*, 21: 191–207.

Montada, L. (1993), 'Moralische Gefühle', in Edelstein,W., Nunner-Winkler, G., and Noam, G. (eds.), *Moral und Person* (Frankfurt/M.: Suhrkamp), 259–77.

Nietzsche, F. (1980), *Also sprach Zarathustra* (F. Nietzsche: *Sämtliche Werke. Kritische Studienausgabe*. Ed. Colli/Montinari, vol. 4, Munich/Berlin: dtv/de Gruyter).

Partridge, E. (1980), 'Why care about the future?', in E. Partridge (ed.), *Responsibilities to Future Generations* (Buffalo (N. Y.): Prometheus Books), 203–20.

Passmore, J. (1980), *Man's Responsibility for Nature. Ecological Problems and Western Traditions* (2nd edn., London: Duckworth).

Pigou, A. C. (1932), *The Economics of Welfare* (4th edn., London: Macmillan).

Russell, Y., Kals, E., and Montada, L. (2003), 'Generationengerechtigkeit im allgemeinen Bewußtsein?—Eine umweltpsychologische Untersuchung', in Stiftung für die Rechte zukünftiger Generationen (ed.), *Handbuch Generationengerechtigkeit* (Munich: ökom), 153–71.

Sidgwick, H. (1907), *The Methods of Ethics* (7th edn., London: Macmillan).

Stendhal (1959), *De l'Amour* (Paris: Garnier Frères).

Stoll-Kleemann, S., O'Riordan, T., and Jaeger, C. C. (2001), 'The pychology of denial concerning climate mitigation measures: Evidence from Swiss focus groups', *Global Envrionmental Change* 11: 107–17.

Tocqueville, A. de (1961), *De la Démocratie en Amérique* (Œuvres complètes, tome 1) (Paris: Gallimard).

Unger, P. (1996), *Living High and Letting Die. Our Illusion of Innocence* (New York: Oxford University Press).

Visser't Hooft, H. P. (1999), *Justice to Future Generations and the Environment* (Dordrecht: Kluwer).

Wade-Benzoni, K. A. (2002). 'A Golden Rule over time: Reciprocity in intergenerational allocation decisions', *Academy of Management Journal*, 45: 1011–28.

Weiss, E. B. (1989), *In Fairness to Future Generations: International Law, Common Patrimony, and Intergenerational Equity* (Tokyo/Dobbsferry (N. Y.): United Nations University/Transnational Publishers).

Wieland, W. (1989), *Aporien der praktischen Vernunft* (Frankfurt am Main: Klostermann).

Williams, B. (1981), *Moral Luck. Philosophical Papers 1973–1980* (Cambridge: Cambridge University Press).

Zwick, M. M. (2001), 'Der globale Klimawandel in der Wahrnehmung der Öffentlichkeit', *Gaia*, 10, 299–303.

Part II
Substantive Principles of Intergenerational Justice

[8]

WRONGFUL LIFE, PROCREATIVE RESPONSIBILITY, AND THE SIGNIFICANCE OF HARM

Seana Valentine Shiffrin
University of California at Los Angeles

A wrongful life suit is an unusual civil suit brought by a child (typically a congenitally disabled child)[1] who seeks damages for burdens he suffers that result from his creation. Typically, the child charges that he has been born into an unwanted or miserable life.[2] These suits offer the prospect of financial relief for some disabled or neglected children and have some theoretical advantages over alternative causes of action.[3] But they have had

---

1. In these cases, the disability is not usually caused by events after conception, such as prenatal damage. Rather, the disability, the underlying genetic condition, or the relevant circumstances of conception are essentially linked to the child's identity or existence. So, he must claim that his *life* was wrongfully caused, not only his disability. Jeff McMahan argues that some significant prenatal damage, occurring early in pregnancy, may affect the identity of the child. If he is correct, then such cases should be classified with the cases typically associated with wrongful life litigation. Jeff McMahan, *Wrongful Life: Paradoxes in the Morality of Causing People to Exist, in* RATIONAL COMMITMENT AND SOCIAL JUSTICE: ESSAYS FOR GREGORY KAVKA 208–47 (J. Coleman & C. Morris eds., 1998).

2. Usually these suits are brought on behalf of children and allege that their parents' doctors were at fault for failing to inform the parents of a likely defect (knowledge of which would have forestalled creation), failing to prescribe effective contraception, or failing to perform an abortion properly. *Cf.* Lori Andrews, *Legal Regulation of Genetic Testing, in* JUSTICE AND THE HUMAN GENOME PROJECT 64 (T. Murphy & M. Lappe eds., 1994), n.2 (citing evidence that most potential parents abort upon discovering their potential child will suffer a serious disability). But in some jurisdictions, the suit may be brought against the child's parents, alleging that the parents should not have conceived or should have aborted.

3. Wrongful life suits have three main advantages over their more commonly recognized counterparts, namely wrongful birth and wrongful conception suits. These other causes of action are brought by parents against their doctor. They allege that owing to fault of the doctor, the parents conceived or gave birth to an unintended, often disabled, child. Their underlying theory suggests that parents may sue at-fault doctors only for medical and other expenses incurred up to the child's majority; parents may not be legally responsible for their *adult* children's care and, consequently, may lack standing to sue for lifetime expenses. Wrongful life suits permit the child to sue for lifetime expenses. Second, parental–plaintiff causes of action require parents to claim that having this child was bad for them. Even if true, once the child exists, such allegations could cause the child and her caretakers psychological harm. By contrast, wrongful life suits do not require parents to make public, negative claims about the worthwhileness of their child's existence *to them*. Finally, wrongful life suits permit children to sue their *parents* for callous or negligent creation, whereas, their counterparts focus only upon *medical* misfeasance. The ability to sue one's parents has little practical impact where families

only mixed, mostly negative, success.[4] They have, however, spurred considerable philosophical interest.[5] This attention, though, has been primarily focused on issues about the coherence of complaining about one's existence or its essential conditions. These suits also raise important, but less well-probed, philosophical questions about the morality of procreation and, more generally, about the moral significance of imposed, but not consented to, conditions that deliver both significant harms and benefits.

This essay takes up these latter questions. As far as they go, the standard defenses of these suits are persuasive, but they have been overly limited in two important ways. First, its defenders uniformly regard the class of justified claims as limited to those brought by people whose burdens (e.g., their congenital disabilities) make their lives overall not worth living.[6] Many regard it as implausible to defend suits by children who, despite having significant burdens, nevertheless enjoy overall worthwhile lives. Why? The argument goes that those particular children could not have been born without their putatively identity-linked disabilities. If their lives are overall worthwhile, then the children cannot reasonably resent their disabilities. For without them, the children would not exist at all and could not enjoy their overall worthwhile lives.

Second, liability is defended as appropriate only in aberrant cases in which procreation results from negligence, recklessness, or maliciousness toward the risks of creating a significantly burdened child. Fully voluntary procreative activity is not considered a sufficient predicate for the cause of action. This reflects, I suspect, the general presumption that, typically, procreation is a straightforward, morally innocent endeavor.

I argue that these limits are wrongly understood as grounded in *philosophical* justificatory rationales. Quite possibly, they could be supported by

---

are intact and well-functioning, but may be practically significant in cases in which biological parents neglect their children or even fail entirely to exercise responsibility for them—as, most markedly, in cases of sales and donation of genetic material.

4. Only three states currently recognize the cause of action. Within these jurisdictions, the occasions of liability and the scope of damages have been significantly restricted. California originally approved suits even against parents who knew their child would be severely disabled, Curlender v. Bio-Science Labs, 106 Cal. App. 3d 811, 829 (1980), but the legislature subsequently precluded suits against parents. Cal. Civ. Code §43.6. Also, damages in wrongful life cases against physicians are limited to specific, not general damages. *See* Turpin v. Sartini 643 P.2d 954 (Ca. 1982) (declaring California rule); Gami v. Mullikan Medical Center, 18 Cal. App. 4th 870, 874 (1993) (reporting that New Jersey, Washington, and California all permit a cause of action for special damages).

5. *See, e.g.*, Dawn Danzeisen and Edward Reitler, *Tort Law: Wrongful Birth and Wrongful Life Actions*, 11 HARV. J. L. & PUB. POL'Y 861, 859–65 (1988); Joel Feinberg, *Wrongful Life and the Counterfactual Element in Harming, in* FREEDOM AND FULFILLMENT 3–37 (1992); Robert Goldstein, MOTHER-LOVE AND ABORTION: A LEGAL INTERPRETATION 50–1, 166–7 n.34 (1988); Frances Kamm, CREATION AND ABORTION 173–4 (1992); John Harris, WONDERWOMAN AND SUPERWOMAN, 79–97 (1992); David Heyd, GENETHICS 1–39 (1992); Nancy Jeckers, *The Ascription of Rights in Wrongful Life Suits*, 6 LAW & PHIL. 149–65 (1987); Jeff McMahan, *passim*, *supra* note 1; Bernard Williams, *Resenting One's Existence, in* MAKING SENSE OF HUMANITY (1995).

6. *See id.* and McMahan, *supra* note 1, and McMahan, *Cognitive Disability, Misfortune, and Justice*, PHIL. & PUB. AFF. 5 (Spring 1996).

more practical, political concerns about the feasibility and utility of policies of broad liability. Later, I canvass a few reasons why even these practical concerns may be exaggerated.[7] I suggest that it would not be unfair to impose liability in a wider range of cases, were it possible and advantageous to do so. These grounds for expanded liability have implications for an array of other family law issues (e.g., those concerning innovative reproductive arrangements). They also reveal continuties between these cases and more standard norms of parental responsibility, providing a justificatory account for quite standard practices of child support.

In Sections II and III, I scrutinize, in turn, the two main limitations of prior philosophical defenses of wrongful life liability. I discuss theoretical issues of general moral interest about the imposition of conditions that both harm and benefit. I go on to connect this discussion to the case of creating children. I argue for the philosophical defensibility of a broader-ranging liability based on a more equivocal moral assessment of procreation. This approach would permit liability assessments for significant burdens associated with being created—even in cases in which the life is worth living and in which those responsible for creating did not have, nor should they have had, special knowledge that the child's life would feature unusual or substantial burdens. In Section IV, I briefly discuss some practical concerns. In Section V, I sketch some implications that the view developed in the prior sections has for family law issues; these relate to anonymity in adoption, sales and donation of genetic material, so-called genetic and gestational surrogacy, and developments in reproductive technology.

II.

I begin from the (contested) assumption that it is possible that being created *can* benefit a person in part, or overall, should her life be sufficiently worth living, and that it is also possible that being created *can* harm a person.[8] I also assume that people do not exist in another form prior to

---

7. I confine my discussion to cases of fully voluntary procreation and I bracket concerns that a nonnegligible amount of procreation is not fully voluntary. I also bracket concerns that these burdens are not compensable. Sometimes, financial compensation can partly alleviate some burdens. Other goods, such as parental contact and information about one's family and the circumstances of one's creation, may also be valuable, albeit under-recognized, forms of relief. Apart from partly allaying the complainant's condition, recognition of liability may also have the salutary consequence of encouraging greater individual and cultural deliberation about the appropriate circumstances for and responsibilities attached to procreation.

8. For defenses, *see* Frances Kamm, *supra* note 5, at 173; Derek Parfit, REASONS AND PERSONS (1984), Appendix G. I also defend the view in *The Benefits of Existence,* unpublished manuscript. There is insufficient space to outline that defense here. The basic idea is that by being the direct cause of a person's being in a situation that intrinsically delivers harm, one harms that person; it is sufficient for this article, though, to assume that if one is the direct cause of a person's being in a situation that intrinsically delivers harm, then one is responsible for that person's suffering harm, even if one does not *harm* her.

conception. Therefore (nonexistent) potential children will undergo no harm if they are not created. Consider then a child who suffers from a serious, somewhat debilitating, untreatable, painful, congenital condition. Suppose that, nonetheless, her life is worth living and, therefore, that her life (the sheer elements of human existence and the particulars of her life) is an all-things-considered benefit to her. Does this mean that she should not be able to seek compensation for the burdens that are ineliminable aspects of this overall benefit?

Joel Feinberg has argued for precluding liability on the following grounds.[9] Assessing liability for the imposed burdens of this child's life would be like "holding a rescuer liable for injuries he caused an endangered person."[10] The rescuer may have to cause some injuries to save the endangered person. But, "the rescuer-defendant did not cause a condition that was harmful on balance, offset as it was by the *overriding benefit* of rescue. . . . [H]e cannot be said, therefore, to have harmed the [rescued person] (in the relevant full sense) at all."[11] Likewise, the benefits of existence are, by hypothesis, weighty enough to make the life worthwhile. In these cases, the benefits are, as in the rescue case, necessarily conjoined with the burdens imposed. The benefits offset the burdens and therefore the child lacks a good claim for recovery.

Despite its surface plausibility, this argument harbors implicit and questionable views about what harms and benefits are, their moral significance, and the symmetry of harms and benefits. First, I register some reservations about the rescue case's description. This introduces an extended treatment of more abstract, background issues about harms and benefits. This discussion will then support a distinction between the rescue case and wrongful life liability.

A. Comparative Models of Harm and the Rescue Case

There are two salient interpretations of Feinberg's argument. I suspect Feinberg holds the second position I describe, but the first position raises interesting issues and is appealed to frequently. First, Feinberg might be read as asserting that, in the rescue case, because on overall benefit has been conferred, namely the saving of a life, the injuries cannot be characterized as harm at all. I believe this idea, that one has not been harmed by the breaking of one's arm during an overall beneficial rescue, is mistaken. Notably, we still have the same impetus and the same sorts of reasons to alleviate the pain and to set the broken limb (i.e., the reasons typically

---

9. Jeff McMahan advances a similar argument in *Wrongful Life: Paradoxes, supra* note 1.
10. Feinberg, *supra* note 5, at 27.
11. *Id.* (emphasis added).

generated in response to harm). These reasons surface whether or not the person has been rescued from an even greater harm, harmed while receiving a greater benefit, or just has her arm broken for no compensating purpose.[12]

The tendency of some to believe otherwise, that the rescued person has not been harmed, may derive from the prominence of a certain comparative, symmetrical model of harms and benefits. To wit, many regard harms and benefits as though they represent two ends of a scale, like the scale of positive and negative numbers. Benefits are thought to be just like harms, except that harms are bad and benefits are good. On Feinberg's natural and attractive interpretation of this symmetrical picture, harms involve the setback of one's interests, whereas benefits involve the advancement of one's interests along a sliding scale of promotion and decline.[13] To evaluate whether an event has benefited or harmed a person, one compares, with respect to the fulfillment of his interests, either his beginning and his end points (historical models), or his end point and where he would have been otherwise (counterfactual models). If he has ascended the scale (either relative to his beginning point or alternative position), then he has been benefitted. If he moves down, then he has been harmed. Either way, one arrives at an all-things-considered judgment that either harm or benefit (but not both) has been bestowed. Thus, because he has been overall benefited, he has not been harmed.

There are many difficulties with this model. First, it fails to accommodate, much less explain, some deep asymmetries between benefits and harms. For instance, we often consider failing to be benefited as morally and significantly less serious than both being harmed *and* not being saved from harm.[14] This asymmetry is difficult to explain on a comparative model. For, within it, harming and failing to prevent harm do not *look* so different from failing to benefit. Variants that identify harm and benefit in terms of counterfactual comparison render them indistinguishable. The versions that draw historical comparisons between one's beginning and one's end point can, by contrast, mark some distinction between harming and failing

---

12. Of course, adherents of this view do not deny that the broken arm should be set. They can claim that it would be an important benefit to provide. My complaint is that thinking of it merely as a benefit can underemphasize its importance. Such characterizations are difficult to square with the moral priority of harm that manifests, in large part, in a strong priority, other things being equal, on avoiding or alleviating harms over bestowing benefits.

13. *See, e.g.,* Joel Feinberg, HARM TO OTHERS 31–65 (1984).

14. The asymmetry between our reactions to at least some cases of failing to benefit and failing to prevent harm suggests that the harm/benefit asymmetry cannot be explained fully by reference to the distinction between doing and allowing. Both failing to benefit and failing to prevent harm may be cases of allowings and not doings. Nonetheless, there is often a strong asymmetry between our reactions to the two, even if the relevant relative comparisons on a welfare scale that result are comparable—that is, even if the size of the benefit foregone is comparable to the size of the harm endured. Likewise, the asymmetry remains even if one compares active harming to the active removal of a benefit—both doings.

to benefit.[15] Nonetheless, the distance between the end points that make it a harm rather than a failure to be benefited may be rather too small to account for the strength of our asymmetrical reactions.

Second, even if the beginning points (or the available alternatives) are morally arbitrary and not deserved, such views nonetheless count as a person's being relegated to a particular position by an event as a harm but count that event's depositing another person in that exact same position as a benefit. Suppose A could have been or was at a higher status, $x + 2$, and is lowered to x, whereas B could have been or was at a lower status, $x - 2$, and is elevated to x. On comparative accounts, A will have been harmed and B benefited, even though they are identically situated.[16] The problem becomes more pronounced if A moves from $x + 2$ to $x + 1$, but B moves from $x - 4$ to $x - 3$. On comparative accounts, A is harmed and B is benefited, even though A is better off, all-things-considered. If this were so, why should harm, per se, in this sense, be a special subject of moral concern and have greater priority than failures to be benefited?

Of course, frequently a loss itself can represent a harm in the morally significant sense. But this is for reasons related more to a person's strong attachment to or personal investments in her higher position than to the sheer comparison between her present state and her prior or alternative state. But the comparative model does not trade upon A's investments or expectations in deeming her harmed. If being placed in a state can be either a harm or a benefit depending upon the affected person's prior or alternative positions, this again makes it mysterious why *harm* matters especially. Why should loss or setback of an interest *pro tanto* matter more than gain, especially if the resultant positions are identical and there are no relevant expectations and neither party is deserving?

A related manifestation of the model's difficulties lies in its failure to identify harm where it occurs. Contrary to this model's pronouncements, there may be an asymmetry between the criteria for benefits and harms. If an event makes someone very poorly off in absolute terms but, in doing so, it also somewhat advances a minor interest of hers, it seems strained to say

---

15. So can a different counterfactual account that identifies harm with a patient's being made worse off because of a (harming) *agent's* presence and benefits with improvements due to an agent's presence. Then, a patient could fail to be benefited by an agent's absence when her presence would have made him better off, but not harmed because the agent is not present. But it faces the problem that the historical accounts do—the conditions associated with harms and with failures to be benefited are not reliably distant enough from each other to make sense of there being a strong asymmetry between them. It also encounters other problems. It presupposes, by stipulation, that an agent cannot harm by omission, that natural events cannot harm, and even that an agent cannot fail (through absence or omission) to alleviate harm (because harm, on this view, depends on the agent's presence). Related appeals to action, *e.g.*, the distinction between doing and allowing, might be thought to buttress comparative accounts. I mention some difficulties for such appeals in *supra* note 14.

16. To question this result is not to say that if I *stole* 2 from A to give it to B, that their resultant states would be identical. The notion of *stealing* suggests the violation of a right and introduces considerations of desert that I mean to put aside. The right's violation might harm A even if the condition of being at level x does not, in itself, involve harm.

that she has been benefited. Rather, she has just been harmed, although an interest of hers has been partly advanced as well. But if it moves someone *very high* up the welfare scale or delivers a huge financial windfall to a person already comfortably well off, but simultaneously delivers a short episode of intense pain or a broken thumb, it seems the person has been both benefited and harmed; perhaps she is overall benefited, but nevertheless she is still harmed. This is some evidence for the view that whether harm has been done is not *entirely* a contextual, comparative matter. At least, that one has ascended the scale of overall interest satisfaction does not mean that one has not been harmed at all. (Whether one has been benefited, on the other hand, may be, in some circumstances, more dependent upon context.)

In light of these difficulties and others,[17] comparative models of harm and benefit should be reconsidered. It is beyond the scope of this article to present a complete, rival account, but I will make a few brief remarks about what one possible rival account might look like. Accounts that identify harms with certain absolute, noncomparative conditions (e.g., a list of evils like broken limbs, disabilities, episodes of pain, significant losses, death) and benefits with an independently identified set of goods (e.g., material enhancement, sensual pleasure, goal-fulfillment, nonessential knowledge, competitive advantage) would not generate these puzzles. Structurally, they would be better placed to accommodate these asymmetries. If one could, in addition, provide an account that explained what unified such items, why they were together classified as harm, one might make further inroads to support (and not just to make conceivable) the asymmetries.

The rival account I propose identifies a unifying connection between various conditions that represent harm. The main points of the essay do not hinge upon the details of this proposed account. They rely only on recognizing certain significant asymmetries between harms and benefits. Nonetheless, having an example of a noncomparative account may be useful. On my view, harm involves conditions that generate a significant chasm or conflict between one's will and one's experience, one's life more broadly understood,[18] or one's circumstances. Although harms differ from one another in various ways, all have in common that they render agents or a significant or close aspect of their lived experience like that of an endurer as opposed to that of an active agent, genuinely engaged with her circumstances, who selects, or endorses and identifies with, the main components of her life. Typically, harm involves the imposition of a state or condition that directly or indirectly obstructs, prevents, frustrates, or undoes an agent's cognizant interaction with her circumstances and her efforts to

---

17. I elaborate upon these difficulties and defend an alternate conception in greater depth in *Harm and Its Moral Significance*, unpublished manuscript.

18. By this I mean that the contents of one's life may well exceed the boundaries of one's conscious knowledge or even one's conscious experience. This has been thoroughly discussed in the literature on death. *See, e.g.,* Thomas Nagel, *Death, in* MORTAL QUESTIONS 1–11 (1979).

fashion a life within them that is distinctively and authentically hers—as more than merely that which must be watched, marked, endured or undergone.[19] To be harmed primarily involves the imposition of conditions from which the person undergoing them is reasonably alienated or which are strongly at odds with the conditions she would rationally will; also, harmed states may be ones that preclude her from removing herself from or averting such conditions. On this view, pain counts as a harm because it exerts an insistent, intrusive, and unpleasant presence on one's consciousness that one must just undergo and endure. Disabilities, injured limbs, and illnesses also qualify as harms. They forcibly impose experiential conditions that are affirmatively contrary to one's will; also, they impede significantly one's capacities for active agency and for achieving harmony between the contents of one's will and either one's lived experience or one's life more broadly understood.[20] Death, too, unless rationally willed, seriously interferes with the exercise of agency. By constraining the duration and possible contents of the person's life, it forces a particular end to the person—making her with respect to that significant aspect of her life merely passive.[21]

I will say more later about benefits, and an important equivocation over their identification. Briefly, though, I use the term "pure benefits" to refer to those benefits that are just goods and which are not also removals from or preventions of harm. The central cases of *pure* benefits involve the enhancement of one's situation or condition, or the fulfillment of nonessential, but

---

19. The requirement of active, genuine engagement with one's circumstances is meant to reflect the sense that living and choosing inauthentically, according to a significantly mistaken conception of one's situation, one's good, or one's moral responsibilities, may do one harm.

20. Can this theory of harm account for harm to animals since, arguably, they lack wills? It depends, in part, on the sort of creature. When an insect loses a leg, it has been damaged. Sometimes we speak of damage as a form of harm; but this sense does not represent the sort of harm that tends to carry heightened moral significance and regarding which there is a special moral priority. Other animals, like cats and dogs, appear to suffer pain and to have at least rudimentary beliefs, intentions, and desires. In some sense, they have wills that conflict with pain and broken limbs; having a will in the sense required by this account does not require being a full-blown, morally responsible agent with the capacity to form a life plan. But, because they have fewer capacities, animals may not be subject to certain harms (*e.g.*, the frustration of long-term projects). Possibly, their harms are less morally significant than the harms suffered by beings with more sophisticated wills.

21. Thus, I do not think that natural deaths, ordinary inabilities, naturally contracted diseases and natural susceptibility to illness are precluded from being harms just because they are natural or ordinary conditions. These things impose states that generate strong reasons, of the sorts typical with harm, to act to avert or relieve them. These reasons and their basic degree of strength are not eliminated just because the conditions predictably happen to most or all. In some cases, normalcy matters because of how it affects one's abilities, though. What would be an inability in one context (*e.g.*, deafness may encumber communication in a predominantly hearing environment) may not be an inability in another, where that condition is normal (*e.g.*, deafness in a sign-language culture). Of course, disabilities (as well as other sorts of harms) may enhance one's life in various respects, making it sharper and more directed. A loss of an ability or a threat to one's life, such as a heart attack, may come to make one value one's life more and provoke a greater level of engagement with it. The imposition of a disability may or may not be an *overall* harm. My point is just that they are, *pro tanto*, harms. In these cases, they are lesser harms that avert a greater harm or that catalyze a greater benefit.

perhaps important, interests. Such enhancement and fulfillment go beyond merely securing the minima that make one's life more than tolerable and susceptible to active identification. The list of goods mentioned earlier (material enhancement, sensual pleasure, goal-fulfillment, nonessential knowledge, competitive advantage) seems roughly right. Those items all involve goods, but the absence of them would not create the stark cleavage between one's will and one's experience, life, or circumstances that I suggest characterizes harm.[22]

To return to the rescue case, these considerations about harms and benefits suggest we should not deny that the (necessarily) broken limb is a form of harm. It imposes a condition of disability and inflicts pain. It seems to meet the criteria of harm, then, and does so irrespective of the concomitant benefits delivered alongside it; on these criteria, it can be harm even if, in some overall sense, the event makes the person better off. The rescued person has been harmed so as to prevent her suffering a greater harm. And, even if being saved is a sort of benefit, the fact that the rescued person enjoys an overall benefit does not mean that she is not also harmed.

One might suggest, however, that although the saved person suffers harm, the rescuer does not harm her at all. He breaks her arm to save her from a threat of greater harm. The threat of drowning or the terrible currents are responsible for the break; if anything, they harm her. That the rescuer's action is justified may seem to motivate this view; the rescuer does not cause harm because the threat of drowning and the terrible currents necessitate the break and are therefore responsible.[23] But as long as it is clear that the rescuer is not to blame, I am not sure what is gained by denying that the rescuer inflicts a lesser harm, whereas the denial seems in tension with recognizing *justified* harms and harming actions. Why deploy this "lesser harm" language at all? It registers that the rescuer's action was a serious one, in need of a special sort of justification. It also registers that the inflicted condition is serious and exerts significant moral force—the rescuee remains in need of attention or has gone through something difficult. It seems right to say both that the saved person has been harmed and that the rescuer has harmed her, although under special circumstances.[24]

---

22. The absence of *all* such benefits might, arguably, constitute a form of harm, but the absence of many possible benefits would not.

23. It is harder to start to make this argument in the cases I will go on to discuss where a broken arm is inflicted to bring about a greater, pure benefit, such as enhanced visual perception or large sums of (unneeded) money. For it is implausible to think that being without enhanced sight or without an extra $5 million *necessitates* a broken arm.

24. On related, but narrower, grounds, one might resist the claim that because existence may deliver harms, the creator who causes a person to exist causes her harm. One might object that placing someone in a condition where she will necessarily suffer harm is not the same as causing her harm. In some sense, the condition inflicts the harm, not the agent. But this observation seems tangential to assessments of responsibility. If an agent places a patient in the path of an evident, oncoming avalanche that will break her arm, it seems fair to say that the agent harms the patient; at the least (and sufficient for my purposes), the agent is accountable

So, the first characterization of the rescue case should be rejected. The rescue benefits the saved person but delivers a harm to him as well. But, it is a distinct question what moral significance this harm has and whether there should be compensation for it. It seems right that the rescued person should not be compensated for this necessary, lesser injury. More likely, this is what Feinberg means when he contends there has not been harm in the "relevant full sense." In these circumstances, the harms these injuries represent do not have the same moral significance that other impositions of harm have.

But we must take care how we identify this different moral significance. Another characterization of the rescue case seems prominent in Feinberg's thought, offering another diagnosis about what makes the harms inflicted by the rescuer special and of different moral significance than other inflictions of harm. Feinberg suggests that the bestowal of an overall *benefit* explains the rescuer's immunity. This then fuels his analogy to wrongful life cases. This analogy, however, illegitimately trades upon a common equivocation of "benefit." In the rescue case, the injury is necessarily inflicted to prevent greater harm. Although we sometimes speak as though removing someone from harm *benefits* that person, it does not follow that the *beneficial* aspect of the saving does the moral justificatory work for inflicting the lesser harm. Rather, I believe the fact that a greater *harm* is averted performs the justificatory service. A more closely tailored reading of the rescue case is that it illustrates that when a person is unavailable for consent, it can be justified both to inflict a lesser harm upon her to avert a greater harm, and to refrain from providing compensation or apologies for one's act.

This narrower interpretation raises the question whether unconsented-to harms inflicted as necessary incidents of the delivery of a *pure* benefit should be similarly assessed. I believe they should not. There is a substantial asymmetry between the moral significance of harm delivered to avoid substantial, greater harms and harms delivered to bestow pure benefits.

---

and responsible for the harm the patient suffers—even if the agent does not break the arm directly through his action, does not seek the harm and even tries to prevent it (as may happen in cases of deliberate action resulting in foreseen, but unintentional harm). The placement may be a case of justified harm (supposing, *e.g.,* it averts greater harm to the patient). But whether the agent causes or is responsible for the harm seems distinct from issues of justification and blameworthiness.

One might distinguish making someone worse off from placing her in a harmful condition where she is no worse off. Some suspect that moral obligations *to the patient* extend only to refraining from the former, not the latter. Often, that one has not made another worse off plays a large role in justifying or excusing conduct that places another in a harmful condition, *e.g.,* where one inflicts lesser harm to avert greater harm, or where one *must* harm one of two parties and the harm to one is overdetermined. But this cannot reliably serve as a sufficient excuse or justification: for example, usually one may not break an innocent's leg just because if one does not, another will. Further, one should not create a child whose life is overall not worth living, even though she is not made worse off. Of course, even if the *main* moral significance of harm derives from the qualities of the patient's resultant condition and not her prior or alternative states, making someone worse off may have some independent moral significance. Often, it aggravates an offense. Sometimes, when it involves the violation of a right and the wrongful imposition of one person's will on another, it will represent harm, even if the condition otherwise would not intrinsically be a harmful one.

Absent evidence that the person's will is to the contrary, it is permissible, perhaps obligatory, to inflict the lesser harm of a broken arm in order to save a person from significant greater harm, such as drowning or brain damage from oxygen deprivation. But, it seems wrong to perform a procedure on an unconscious patient that will cause her harm but also redound to her greater, *pure* benefit. At the very least, it is much harder to justify. For example, it seems wrong to break an unconscious patient's arm even if necessary to endow her with valuable, physical benefits, such as supernormal memory, a useful store of encyclopedic knowledge, twenty IQ points worth of extra intellectual ability, or the ability to consume immoderate amounts of alcohol or fat without side effects. At the least, it would be much harder to justify than inflicting similar harm to avert a greater harm, such as death or significant disability.

Such examples already suggest that we should not interpret the rescue case as demonstrating the principle that one may inflict a lesser harm on someone simply to benefit him overall, when he is unavailable to give or deny consent. Consider another and more fantastic example of inflicting a lesser harm for a greater benefit. The example differs from those just offered, in part by introducing benefits and harms of different currencies (whereas the prior examples dealt with physical benefits and physical harms). This is appropriate for my ultimate purpose, analogizing to wrongful life cases, because the benefits and harms presented by human existence are themselves of mixed currency. This example also incorporates other special features analogous to wrongful life cases, including the inability to communicate in advance with the beneficiaries, the risk of greater harm, and an inseparable connection between the harmful and beneficial aspects of the bestowal:

> Imagine a well-off character (Wealthy) who lives on an island. He is anxious for a project (whether because of boredom, self-interest, benevolence, or some combination of these). He decides to bestow some of his wealth upon his neighbors from an adjacent island. His neighbors are comfortably off, with more than an ample stock of resources. Still, they would be (purely) benefitted by an influx of monetary wealth. Unfortunately, due to historical tensions between the islands' governments, Wealthy and his agents are not permitted to visit the neighboring island. They are also precluded (either by law or by physical circumstances) from communicating with the island's people. To implement his project, then, he crafts a hundred cubes of gold bullion, each worth $5 million. (The windy islands lack paper currency.) He flies his plane over the island and drops the cubes near passers-by. He takes care to avoid hitting people, but he knows there is an element of risk in his activity and that someone may get hurt. Everyone is a little stunned when this million-dollar manna lands at their feet. Most are delighted. One person (Unlucky), though, is hit by the falling cube. The impact breaks his arm. Had the cube missed him, it would have landed at someone else's feet.

Unlucky may have his arm repaired for much less than $5 million and benefits from the extra cash. He admits that all-things-considered, he is better off for receiving the $5 million, despite the injury. In some way he is glad that this happened to him, although he is unsure whether he would have consented to being subjected to the risk of a broken arm[25] (and worse fates) if he had been asked in advance; he regards his conjectured *ex-ante* hesitation as reasonable. Given the shock of the event and the severity of the pain and disability associated with the broken arm, he is not certain whether he would consent to undergo the same experience again.

Despite Unlucky's concession that he has been overall benefited, Unlucky's case is morally disturbing in a way the rescue case is not. I suspect this is because the harm Unlucky undergoes is not, as it is for the rescued person, in the service of preventing his suffering a greater harm; rather, it is to bestow a great benefit. These differences affect how we should react. First, surely Wealthy owes Unlucky an apology for the injury he inflicted, although the rescuer owes none.[26] Already, this marks an asymmetry between harm bestowed to prevent harm and harm bestowed to confer a pure benefit.[27] Second, if Unlucky were to approach Wealthy and ask him to bear the costs of restorative surgery, it seems that, morally, Wealthy ought to do so. If Wealthy refuses, then Unlucky should have a cause of action against Wealthy for inflicting unnecessary bodily injury. It seems an inadequate defense that Wealthy had already given Unlucky $5 million and that this gift made Unlucky better off, even considering the broken arm. The fact that Wealthy was involved in benefiting (though nonconsensual) activity when he risked people's safety and broke Unlucky's arm should not shield him from liability for his voluntary, harmful, and risky behavior. Nor should Wealthy be insulated from liability because he could argue truthfully that *this* benefit could not have been bestowed without imposing the risk of the burden that was subsequently realized.[28]

The judgment that Wealthy should compensate Unlucky could be explained in two distinct ways. First, one might hold that Wealthy's action of

---

25. Some may think it clear, even rationally mandated, that they would agree to a high risk or even the certainty of a broken arm for this payoff. Of course, the example may be modified to the point where it is uncertain that consent would be granted; one may consent to a broken arm, but not to a broken leg, a gouged-out eye, or a year-long coma.

26. The rescuer is blameless and does not *owe* an apology. It would, however, be appropriate and good of him to feel and express regret for the injuries he caused.

27. To a close degree, these points also hold about harms inflicted to protect pure benefits. If the bricks were worthless, but dropped to protect (somehow) holdings of nonessential wealth, the deposits would have moral difficulties and require similar compensation. There may be differences in degree because there may be somewhat stronger reasons for inflicting harm to protect a vested benefit than to confer a new one. But as suggested in the text, loss alone, when distinguished from expectation, strong attachment, or identification, is insufficient to register as harm. I am grateful to Frances Kamm for prompting this point.

28. Perhaps the benefactor's intention distinguishes the rescue and the Wealthy case. The rescuer saves from duty or benevolence but Wealthy is probably relieving boredom; the benefit is merely a foreseen, welcome side effect. But procreators, like rescuers, have better intentions: they seek to benefit the child or, at least, to engage in a time-honored practice that has a generally beneficial side effect on the child and society. This suggestion ultimately exerts little force. It does not matter much, when assessing whether the rescuer should compensate for the unavoidable injuries, if the rescuer acted from benevolence, whimsy, or a desire to impress.

dropping the bullion at all was morally wrong, all-things-considered, because it risked and inflicted serious harm on nonconsenting individuals but was not in the service of a suitably important end (such as the prevention of greater harm to them). Consequently, he owes compensation to Unlucky because his action wrongfully caused Unlucky harm. A second, weaker position would also ground liability. It would hold that it would be wrong to drop the bullion unless the benefactor also willingly assumed responsibility for incidental harm inflicted in its delivery. On such a view, unconsented-to mixed benefactions (i.e., bestowals of significant harms alongside benefits) are all-things-considered morally permissible as long as any incidental harm is acknowledged and remedied. I am inclined toward the stronger position and believe that Wealthy acted immorally. This position better explains the sense that an apology is owed. But, on either explanation, Wealthy may be held accountable for the incidental harm he inflicts in the course of the delivery of the benefit.

It might be objected that liability seems justified because the $5 million does not really compensate for the harm. Perhaps, that is, Unlucky mistakenly regards the event as an all-things-considered benefit. If that were the source of the assessment that liability is justified, though, then the case might yield a very different result if the cubes were worth more, say a billion dollars. Would the greater monetary value alter our moral assessment? I do not think that Wealthy's duty alters as the worth of the cube varies (although the greater the size of the gift, the more our sense of Unlucky's character might decline if he continued to demand what we agree is owed to him by right). One way to explain this reaction is to claim that benefit and harm are "incommensurable" and, for that reason, cannot be treated as items on a spread-sheet or sliding scale. Although I have expressed doubts about the sliding-scale view of benefits and harms, simply saying that benefits and harms are incommensurable is not sufficiently illuminating. A further answer may be provided by appealing to the heightened moral importance of harm and its special badness, and the difference between the assessment of harm from the first- and third-person perspectives.[29] Some decisions involving a willingness to endure harm are permissible from the first-person

---

The motive will certainly affect our evaluation of his character, but it does not seem to influence our sense of whether he should compensate for the rescued person's loss. Likewise, with respect to liability, Wealthy's motive matters little. What matters is that he imposed risk and injuries on people without their consent and without the justifying reason that it was necessary to avoid a substantial harm. Nevertheless, if Wealthy's intention were altruistic, it might be wrong for Unlucky to demand that to which he had a right. When Unlucky is all-things-considered much better off, making such a demand would show a rigid, ungracious character. I discuss related issues, *infra*.

29. Thomas Scanlon, among others, has noted a related asymmetry: One may reasonably put much greater weight on a project from the first-person perspective than would reasonably be accorded to it from a third-party's viewpoint. A person may reasonably value her religion's mission over her health, but the state may reasonably direct its welfare efforts toward her nutrition needs rather than to funding her religious endeavors. Thomas Scanlon, *Preference and Urgency*, 72 J. PHIL. 655–69 (1975).

perspective that are not permissible or are more problematic from the third-person perspective. Harm is objectively bad in such a way that it is morally problematic to inflict (unsolicited) a significant level of it on another for the sake of conferring a benefit, although a person may reasonably decide to undergo the same level of harm to retain the same level of benefit. So, a related difficulty with the suggestion that $5 million is simply insufficient compensation is that if we accept it, we would then have to condemn Unlucky as irrational were he to choose to endure a broken arm for $5 million. Whether it would be irrational seems unclear and certainly less clear than the sense that it would be wrong for another to impose the broken arm on him.

Why is the imposition of harm by a third party special? One might appeal to epistemic difficulties. Prohibitions on inflicting harm may derive from the fact that outside parties often err or are uncertain whether a benefit really will outweigh a harm. This is often true but supplies an incomplete explanation—one that does not explain our reaction to Unlucky's case. Nor will it provide an explanation for the range of cases in which we would regard it as unreasonable for a third party to impose harm nonconsensually, but permissible and reasonable for the party who will endure the harm to elect to undergo it.

The analysis of harm I suggested provides a different answer. On this view, harm brings about a cleavage between a person's life and her will. When she actively decides to undergo a harmful condition, that cleavage is partially or perhaps entirely bridged by the operation of her will and control. The active engagement and operation of her will, in taking on and endorsing the imposition of harm, changes the significance of the harm into more of that associated with a mere cost. Thus, it may be permissible and rational for a person to agree to undergo a harm to receive a benefit, yet it may not be permissible for another party to impose the harm. (Or, on the weaker principle, it is not permissible to impose the harm without attempting specifically to remedy the harm.)

What if Wealthy claims that part of the $5 million was anticipatory compensation? His aim was to give only $3.5 million as a gift and to include an extra $1.5 million to compensate recipients for the risk and any damage they endured?[30] This seems sophistic. Suppose that just after Unlucky retrieves the cube from the ground, a thief runs up and snatches the cube from him. Most of us would, I think, hold that Wealthy should repair Unlucky's broken arm and should be liable for such repair. But our reac-

---

30. *See also* Restatement of Torts, §920: "When . . . tortious conduct has caused harm to the plaintiff . . . and in so doing has conferred a special benefit to . . . the plaintiff . . . , the value of the benefit conferred is considered in mitigation of damages, to the extent that this is equitable." My discussion may be read either as challenging this principle or offering a constrained reading of what constitutes equitable mitigation. Generally, the principle's actual applications depend on the more limited claim that I endorse: If harmful conduct averts greater *harm* to the plaintiff, then the averted harm should be considered in mitigation of damages.

tions would differ in a case that more straightforwardly involved the payment of compensation for harm. Suppose Unlucky sues Wealthy for an unrelated tort and wins (or settles). Wealthy hands Unlucky a suitcase of money as compensation that Unlucky accepts. As Unlucky walks off, a robber wrests the suitcase from him. Here, Unlucky cannot reasonably demand a replacement compensation package. These different reactions suggest there is some difference between the dropping of the bullion and the payment of compensation.

Perhaps the difference is that the "compensation-is-built-in" approach does not hold Wealthy seriously accountable for the risk and harm he imposed. In Wealthy's case, the supposed "compensation" is not offered specifically as compensation to the injured party but the same-size benefit is delivered to everyone, in advance—not as a reaction to harm. To act as compensation for a wrong, the event marking the accountability or responsibility should genuinely acknowledge the harm and be, in some way, separate from the delivery of the harm.[31] Indeed, it seems particularly problematic in the bullion case that the instrument of harm is supposed also to function as the instrument of compensation. This confluence further undermines the compensation's fully discharging moral accountability for the harm.

B. An Objection: Hypothetical Consent

One might object to the foregoing arguments by appealing to hypothetical consent in one of two different ways. First, one might object that the asymmetry between the cases does not reflect a difference between harms and benefits. Rather, hypothetical consent can be inferred in the rescue cases but not in Unlucky's case. While this may be true, I am not convinced that the appeal to hypothetical consent does the justificatory work. I suspect that the differing significance of harms and benefits grounds the different hypothetical consent results and makes them salient to us. On the same lights, the different significance that benefits, and particularly unchosen benefits, have grounds Unlucky's reasonable *ex post* ambivalence. Notably, there seems to be a harm/benefit asymmetry built into our approaches to hypothetical consent where we lack specific information about the individual's will. We presume (rebuttably) its presence in cases where greater harm is to be averted; in the cases of harms to bestow greater benefits, the presumption is reversed. One might claim that this is because the (predictive) likelihood of hypothetical or *ex post* consent is just higher in the harm cases than in the benefit cases. But this is an unsatisfying explanation.

---

31. This seems true when the harm is intentionally inflicted or inflicted through an intentional act aimed at the victim, *e.g.*, an action intended to benefit the victim. Where the harm is a foreseen but unintended side effect of a justified effort to benefit *third parties*, simultaneous compensation seems more acceptable.

Again, why is it more likely and why do we regard it as rational and as authorizing our other-regarding action? Mightn't it be because the special badness of harm makes consent the rational default position in the former case? So, regarding death, there is always some uncertainty that a patient would really want to avoid it and would be willing to endure a significant harm to avoid it. Complementary cases involving benefits of vast sums of money or suitably large conferrals of knowledge may approximate this degree of uncertainty. Yet even if the likelihoods of consent are the same, it still seems easier to justify imposing the lesser harm to avoid a patient's death than to bestow the benefit. It seems more likely that the differences between the cases are attributable to an antecedent asymmetry between the significance of harms and benefits.

Alternatively, one might challenge the view that Wealthy's actions are impermissible (even if he does not compensate). One might argue that, despite Unlucky's *ex post* hesitation, it is reasonable to infer Unlucky's hypothetical consent to his action (or that Unlucky's reported reaction renders the case's description atypical or implausible). I do not think it is clear that Unlucky would give his consent nor is it clear what test is relevant: that his consent is certain? rationally required? likely? Surely he is not rationally required to have or to risk having his arm broken for the money, were the bargain put to him directly. Many people reasonably refuse to endanger themselves for financial gain, even if they would value the rewards and even enjoy the benefit should their refusal not be honored. This also casts doubt on the certainty and the likelihood of Unlucky's consent.

But suppose his consent were likely. It is not clear what relevance this would have, especially to the liability question. For suppose it is as likely, or even more likely, that Wealthy would consent to liability if it were a condition of his activity. Why then would the fact that Unlucky might consent to no compensation entail that no compensation was owed? Could not an equally strong argument be made that compensation is owed, since Wealthy might consent to a compensation requirement? (And if Wealthy would not consent, shouldn't it matter whether his refusal would be reasonable?) It is not clear, then, that the question of what Unlucky *in particular* is *likely* to consent to should be determinative of the liability issue.

Further, I am not convinced of the principle that one may (without providing compensation) inflict serious harm (or risk) on a person to bring about her greater benefit if, based on the reactions of the general population, it is likely that she would consent. This deployment of hypothetical consent procedures is rather extreme. The hypothetical consent would be generic: It would not appeal to features of the individual or his attitudes toward risks and the relationship between harms and benefits. Generic hypothetical consent is, sometimes, regarded as appropriate—perhaps in the rescue case and perhaps to identify principles of justice. But in the rescue case, something of great objective significance is at stake. This may be what generates a reasonable presumption that action is warranted. In the political case, generic hypothetical consent may be appropriate because consideration of the contractors' individual features would introduce morally arbitrary factors.

But on an asymmetrical account of harms and benefits, generic hypothetical consent may be less appropriate in deciding whether to harm for an individual's pure benefit. In part, the difference is that harm matters more, objectively, and in part it is that the valuation of benefits and the role benefits play within a life are more individual matters. In contrast to harm's avoidance, it is more important to identify, personally, the choiceworthy benefits and to realize them through efforts involving oneself. Further, individuals quite reasonably have different responses to available benefits, to trade-offs between them, and in their willingness to endure harm to enjoy them. What may be desirable for some may be alien, burdensome, or intolerable for others. These different responses reflect very personal decisions that mark the individual's distinctiveness. Where large benefits are at stake, hypothetical consent arguments are more plausible when they draw on specific evidence about the affected patient's unique will and personality.

One may argue, though, that the likelihood of consent is much stronger in the procreation cases than in Unlucky's case. After all, a *very high* percentage of people claim to be glad to have been born. I am not sure what to make of such claims, as there are people who do regret being born and find the burdens of their lives too great. Others are strongly ambivalent: They find their burdens are not entirely canceled out by the goodness of their lives and regard these burdens as ineliminable serious problems and intrusions. Although sometimes these reactions are unreasonable, it is hard to dismiss all these familiar, if unusual, reactions as wholly irrational.

Further, the procreation case is more complicated because, in contrast to the Unlucky case, the condition bestowed is one that cannot be escaped without very high costs (suicide is often a physically, emotionally, and morally excruciating option). Generic hypothetical consent seems especially difficult to justify where the imposed conditions are difficult to exit, if the patient complains about the harms imposed. Thus, four factors make the appeal to hypothetical consent problematic: (1) the fact that great harm is not at stake if no action is taken; (2) but if action is taken, the harms suffered may be very severe; (3) the imposed condition cannot be escaped without high costs; and (4) the hypothetical consent procedure is not based on features of the individual who will bear the imposed condition. Even if the high likelihood of hypothetical consent (and *ex post* consent) does justify procreation, it is still unclear, especially given these factors, why those who take this risk should not bear liability if the risk's dangers are realized—that is, if the beneficiaries do suffer serious burdens about which they complain.

C. Wrongful Life Cases and Harming to Bestow a Pure Benefit

Thus, I am skeptical of moving from the claim that one may permissibly, without offering compensation, nonnegligibly harm another to save her from greater harm, to the purportedly analogous claim that one may permissibly, without compensation, subject a person to substantial harm or to nonnegligible risk of such harm to confer a pure benefit without that beneficiary's consent. This suggests that wrongful life cases should be distinguished from the rescue cases. While causing a person to exist may benefit that person, it does not save the potential person from any harm, much less from greater harm. Rather, if causing to exist does impose harms, the harms are part of a process that, at best, brings about a pure benefit. And benefits do not have the same moral significance and justificatory power as do harms. Causing another to exist may well be all-things-considered justified, but the conditions in which it may be justified seem different from those in which inflicting harm to prevent harm is justified. Specifically, this justification would yield a permission only if the bestower is accountable for harm that results.

There is a second, important dis-analogy between the rescue case and the wrongful life cases. If the rescuer fails, or refrains from rescuing, the drowning person will suffer a great harm. Her life will go for the worse, either through premature curtailment or impeded mental functioning. By contrast, if the benefit bestowed by creation is not conferred, the nonexistent person will not experience its absence; further, she has no life that will go worse. In this way, procreation also differs from the Wealthy case. In the Wealthy case, if Wealthy refrains from acting, in one sense, Unlucky will have a comparatively worse life (although he will not be harmed) because he will be without a sizable financial windfall. But, if procreation does not occur, there is no child whose life will go worse than it otherwise would had the benefit of existence been bestowed.

Thus, two distinctions are at play here. One is the distinction between the moral impetus to avoid and prevent harm versus the lesser, more confined, impetus to bestow benefits. The other is between the moral significance of failures to benefit existent people and nonexistent potential people. In most cases, the absence of a pure benefit is experienced by a person or, otherwise makes a difference in the content of his life. This difference plays a significant explanatory role in the strength of the moral impetus to bestow pure benefits. The contrast we can draw between *that* person's life with the benefit and without it, coupled with the urge to prevent inferior situations, I suspect, partly propels our sense of the moral impulse to bestow benefits.[32]

---

32. This is not to endorse comparative views of benefit. There are reasons to fret over such criteria—some similar to those rehearsed about comparative views of harm. Perhaps an event that does not improve a life *can* benefit a person. But, the *moral significance* of nonimproving benefits is importantly less. Harms may differ—a harm that does not make a life worse does not always have less or significantly less weight than harms that do worsen lives, marking another asymmetry between harms and benefits.

Wrongful Life **135**

In the case of procreation, though, this sort of moral reason for beneficence is not generated, because the potential beneficiary does not exist. Even if the failure to bestow a benefit were on a par with harm (as counterfactual comparative views contend), the failure to be created is a "harm" that would never, even indirectly or as an opportunity cost, affect an *ongoing* person's life. If the failure to impart them will have no influence on a life, benefits do not generate the same sort of moral reasons as those that compel us to avert and prevent harm that will affect a person. And they do not even generate the same reasons as are produced by pure benefits that would *improve* an ongoing life. Thus, this suggests a second reason why a permission to harm, without providing compensation, to prevent greater (experienced) harm, does not support the first limitation on wrongful life liability: The fact that the "harm" or absence of benefit represented by not procreating will not affect an existent person or her life in progress renders the benefit bestowed by creation far less morally significant.

Thus, both the asymmetry between harms bestowed to prevent greater harm and harms inflicted to bestow benefits, and the asymmetry between those benefits that do and those that do not improve a life, challenge the argument for requiring a wrongful life plaintiff to allege that he prefers not to have been created. Even if *that* plaintiff could not have been born and enjoyed the benefits of life without his particular, concomitant burdens, it does not follow that he should be the one to foot the bill for these burdens.[33] Because he did not assume them freely and they were not bestowed to prevent a greater harm or even an inferior situation, it may be entirely appropriate to lay responsibility upon the imposer.

III.

Suppose we resolve the issue of Section II one way or another, either expanding the set of justified complaints we recognize or affirming the dominant view that only those overall harmed have a valid complaint. A second, distinct issue concerns whether only those who acted negligently or worse toward the foreseeable burdens their children would incur should be liable, or whether all those significantly participating in voluntary procreation should be liable for the harm their children undergo.

The prevalent view is that liability should be restricted. A dim eye is cast on procreation done haphazardly, as it is with any acceptable activity done haphazardly. In general, though, it is not viewed as a suspect, harmful, or

---

33. One might try to distinguish the Wealthy case by claiming that it was physically possible for Wealthy to bestow this benefit in a nonrisky way but that this is not true of procreating. The example's details are meant to forestall this claim. Wealthy could not enter the island or bestow the benefit in a nonrisky way. Why should genetic impossibility be more morally significant than the obstructions Wealthy faces? The real charge behind the nonidentity problem is the idea that one may not complain about a burden unless it comparatively worsens one's state. The Wealthy example is meant to challenge this; it is unclear what other reason there is to think the metaphysical impossibility at issue is morally important.

hazardous activity. In unusual cases, parents and others central to creation demonstrate abnormal, culpable motives (e.g., they are severely negligent or reckless with respect to unwanted or unwise creation). In these *special* circumstances, moral disapproval is deemed appropriate. Defenders of wrongful life liability believe this disapproval may legitimately translate into a legitimate complaint by the child.[34]

Although the dominant perspective has an intuitive familiarity and plausibility, I believe it is mistaken. I suggest a different moral perspective toward routine procreation, what I will call the "equivocal view."[35] The view regards procreation as an intrinsically and not just epistemically a morally hard case. For it is not a morally straightforward activity, but one that ineliminably involves serious moral hazards. Although there is much to be said for it, it faces difficult justificatory hurdles because it involves imposing serious harms and risks on someone who is not in danger of suffering greater harm if one does not act. I then explore the implications of this perspective for the philosophically justified range of wrongful life suits. I argue that voluntary procreation should be sufficient to ground responsibility for the resultant harm children undergo because of their creation (should they complain), whether or not it is done particularly negligently or recklessly.[36]

If one shared all my intuitions about the Wealthy case, liability would not hinge upon whether he exercised due care in dropping the cubes. It should not matter with respect to his liability for compensatory damages whether he was negligent or reckless in his methods. (These factors, perhaps, are relevant to the assessment of punitive damages.) Even if he took the greatest care, he imposed risk of harm and injury on another without consent and without the justification that it was necessary to avoid a more substantial harm. Everyday procreation may be described in similar terms.

First, some preliminary observations. As previously noted, I assume it is both coherent and true that causing a person to exist *can* benefit and harm the resultant person. Furthermore, I assume that, in the vast majority of cases, causing a person to exist does actually provide an overall benefit to the resultant person. Nevertheless, even though procreators may benefit their

---

34. Whereas its opponents believe the child has no complaint. The disapproval is properly directed only at a defect in the character of the procreator or in the state of affairs that results, judged impersonally. *See, e.g.,* Dan Brock, *The Non-Identity Problem and Genetic Harms,* 9 BIO-ETHICS 269–75 (1995); John Harris, *supra* note 5; and David Heyd, GENETHICS (1992), ch. 1.

35. I summarize the main grounds for this view here. I defend it in depth in *Consent and the Morality of Procreation* (unpublished D. Phil. thesis, Oxford University, 1993). Independently, David Benatar has advanced some related arguments that causing to exist imposes burdens on children in *Why It Is Better Never to Come Into Existence,* 34 AM. PHIL. Q. 345–55 (July 1997).

36. The argument I offer supports parental liability (and responsibility generally) for the essential, burdensome aspects of the child's life—things like pain, disabilities, illnesses, moral burdens, the burdens posed by the necessity of death, and the typical risks of physical and psychological injuries that are run in a human life. I note here but bracket the question whether even partial parental responsibility is appropriate where an intermediate agent imposes some harm during the child's life. One might hold parents partly responsible for such harms, because they exposed their children to the risk of harms imposed by others, or one might hold the intermediate agent fully responsible.

progeny by creating them, they also impose substantial burdens on them. By being caused to exist as persons, children are forced to assume moral agency, to face various demanding and sometimes wrenching moral questions, and to discharge taxing moral duties. They must endure the fairly substantial amount of pain, suffering, difficulty, significant disappointment, distress, and significant loss that occur within the typical life. They must face and undergo the fear and harm of death. Finally, they must bear the results of imposed risks that their lives may go terribly wrong in a variety of ways.

All of these burdens are imposed without the future child's consent. This, it seems, is in tension with the foundational liberal, anti-paternalist principle that forbids the imposition of significant burdens and risks upon a person without the person's consent. Doing so violates this principle even if the imposition delivers an overall benefit to the affected person. Hence, procreation is a morally hazardous activity because in all cases it imposes significant risks and burdens upon the children who result. The imposition of significant burdens and risks is not a feature of exceptional or aberrant procreation, but of all procreation. Thus, restricting liability only to aberrant cases seems philosophically ad hoc; there may be practical reasons for doing so, but one could justifiably acknowledge a much more expansive philosophical base for liability. One way to think about this view of procreation as morally problematic is to say that procreation violates the consent rights of the child who results. Creating a person imposes significant burdens and harms on that child without the child's consent and without meeting the specifications of the relevant exceptions; most notably, such imposition is not necessary to avert the child from suffering a greater harm.

This characterization raises many issues, which I will only briefly discuss here, about the structure of consent rights. One issue concerns whether the argument assumes that we must predicate consent rights of future, currently nonexistent people, and whether we may do so. One might deny that nonexistent people could have rights, because they do not exist, while also objecting that they must have rights for it to be possible for our contemporary actions to violate their rights. But as Joel Feinberg has pointed out, hiding a nondefusable bomb attached to a nontamperable time clock of seven years in a kindergarten would be clearly wrong. In part, it would be wrong because it violates the rights to life of the children who will die, even though they do not now exist and do not yet possess rights to life. One's action sets into motion a chain of events that will lead to the violation of the rights that will come to be held.[37] Likewise, the equivocal view does not require the predication of contemporarily held consent rights. Instead, one need only claim that the procreative acts will set into motion a series of events that will impose a set of significant, burdensome conditions on the person; being subject to these unchosen harms, assuming they persist so long, will violate the person's consent rights at whatever point these rights

---

37. Feinberg, *supra* note 13, at 97.

vest. (If I enroll my toddler now in a nonreversible career path (through mental indoctrination or a severe servitude agreement), her autonomy rights may not yet be violated, because she does not yet possess them, but the action is wrong now because they will be violated, immediately, upon their vesting.) Our moral duties emanate from the force these future rights exert on us now, not from any right predicated to be held by nonexistent persons. If our actions now set into motion causal chains that will result in a right's being violated in the future, this action is, at best, morally problematic. That the effect is not imminent and the future rights holder is not present at the time of our action matters little. Immediacy carries little moral importance as such. It may matter when nonimmediate harm may be prevented by intervening action. But here that does not hold true—these burdens and risks are not contingent ones, but attend every life.

Another important issue concerns whether the consent right can be said to be violated given that the child was unable, owing to her nonexistence, to give her consent at the time the action did and had to occur. It may be claimed that nonconsensual, beneficial action is unobjectionable when the affected person is absent or unable to consent. I do not think the fact of absence can support a completely satisfactory defense for many of the reasons given in the discussion of generic hypothetical consent in Section II. Briefly, I believe that the generally recognized exceptions to consent requirements, such as the rescue case, are plausible only when and because they are necessary to save a person from enduring or experiencing more significant harm. It would not be permissible to perform the substantially burdening surgery on an unconscious patient just to deliver a large, pure benefit, even if it were the only chance to do so. There is a substantial difference between the rescue case and the case involving Unlucky. In both cases, the affected person cannot be consulted, but in the former case, nonconsensual action will avert greater harm, whereas in the latter, a large but unnecessary pure benefit is bestowed. In the case of procreation, as with Unlucky, inaction may forego a benefit, the benefit of life, but there is no harm to avert. As I suggested in Section II, it is implausible to treat this opportunity cost for a pure benefit as a harm, especially when no person's ongoing life will go worse because of the missed opportunities. Thus, for similar reasons, we cannot infer from judgments about what it is permissible to do in the rescue case to the case of procreation.[38]

---

38. This consent-right argument does not entail the rejection of paternalism toward children. Much paternalism aims to prevent greater harm to children, either as children or as later adults. This coheres with the general presumption that action may be taken to prevent or alleviate greater harm when a person is unavailable for consent. Some paternalism aims merely to provide benefits, though. This may be permissible (depending on how significant the harm and how much more substantial the benefit) where the harm and the benefits do not extend beyond the point at which the child gains consent rights (or the relevant ones at the relevant strength). I think we are, however, properly hesitant to impose significant harms or limitations that extend beyond the child's minority, if imposed only to provide pure benefits—especially if they will be difficult to reverse, should the child come to disapprove of them, and if we are without specific evidence that the child favors the imposed condition.

Wrongful Life **139**

I am not advancing the claim that procreation is all-things-considered wrong. It is consistent with these arguments to regard nonconsensual, burden-imposing actions as morally problematic but not always impermissible, or to regard procreation as a special case. All I mean to advance is the claim that because procreation involves a nonconsensual imposition of significant burdens, it is morally problematic and its imposer may justifiably be held responsible for its harmful results. Acknowledging such responsibility might help to explain why such action may be permissible. One might believe that imposing overall beneficial conditions that nonetheless involve significant burdens is permissible, when the beneficiary is unable to consent, if one attempts to alleviate or partially shoulder the burdens one imposes. Thus, one might hold that the unconsented-to burdens of life do not make it wrong to procreate per se, but rather wrong to procreate without undertaking a commitment to share or alleviate any burdens the future child endures.[39] I am not sure whether such justificatory arguments ultimately succeed, but it is not essential to the argument about liability that they be resolved. As long as the argument made the case that procreation had a *pro tanto* wrongful element, it would challenge the second common limitation on wrongful life litigation as overly restrictive. Voluntary procreation is not morally problematic only in unusual cases of negligent or reckless conception. In every case it involves a person imposing a risk upon another where the imposition is not necessitated by the need to avert greater harm.

Of course, one may agree that procreation is morally problematic without entertaining any notion of directly regulating it. Familiar arguments against state interference with rights of bodily autonomy and concerns about the terrific potential for state abuse would properly prevent consideration of such drastic measures. The equivocal view might, however, alter our understanding of the legal right to procreate. We would not see it as deriving directly from beliefs about the unproblematic nature of procreation. Rather, it would derive from more general rights against interference with one's body and sexuality and from deep skepticism about the possibility of benign use of government power in this context. Acknowledging a right to procre-

---

39. On this reading, the argument for parental responsibility and liability takes on a strict liability cast. Of course, a usual condition of strict liability is not present, namely that the activity is not normally engaged in. This condition, however, is theoretically difficult to justify where there is a large disparity in the type of burdens various people endure because of the activity. If one drew the stronger conclusion, that procreation is not fully justified by an assumption of responsibility for the burdens it imposes on the children, then the argument would operate more like one of intentional tort.

In many cases, another typical requirement of strict liability is not met: Usually, the genetic contribution to procreation is not a product placed on the market, except, notably, where the sperm (or eggs) is obtained from a sperm bank. Notably, the "donation" and provision of genetic material through such outlets should not be deemed (strict-liability exempt) "services," like blood provision. *See, e.g.,* West's Ann. Cal. Health & Safety Code § 1606. Blood provision is deemed a service to promote blood donations and transfusions. No analogous public urgency is associated with assisted reproduction. Although the inability to produce genetically related progeny is a very serious matter for some, its importance does not approach that of the risk of death, particularly since, generally, the ability to parent (via adoption) is available.

ate, then, would not lend itself to an endorsement of procreation; nor would it entail any duties to assist or facilitate procreative activity. Thus, it is consistent with acknowledging a legal right to procreation to think that those who do engage in procreation, thereby imposing burdens on another person and running risks with her life, could reasonably bear some legal duties to compensate her or otherwise help to shoulder the costs of this imposition.

Such a view would not necessitate a radical change of practice. In most cases, the burdens of the typical life are fairly manageable. Further, most parents generally maintain relationships of emotional and financial support with their children. These relationships help children cope with their burdens and permit children to confront, hold responsible, show gratitude toward, and receive comfort and instruction from those who have given them this burden-riddled mixed benefit. In fact, the arguments of this and the prior section together help to explain the legal mandate behind these relationships and, in particular, behind mandatory child support.[40] Whereas, for those who believe that bestowing life is normally and fairly reliably a tremendously beneficial activity, and for that reason alone permissible, it should present something of a puzzle why parents who initiate a child's creation (generally the biological parents) should owe (morally or legally) child support. After all, they have given the child more of a benefit than any others—if further benefits must be bestowed, should not the onus be on others to step in as further benefit providers?[41] If, however, we acknowledge that initiating parents have caused harm to their children or even violated their children's rights through creation, it becomes easier to explain the fairness of levying duties of support upon parents beyond the assumed enormous benefit that procreation bestowed and beyond the minima necessary to make life worth living.[42]

---

40. For discussions of the problem of justifying child support, *see* Scott Altman, *A Theory of Child Support*, USC Law School Working Paper No. 98–13 (1998), and John Eekelaar, *Are Parents Morally Obliged to Care for Their Children?* 11 Oxford J. Legal Stud. 340 (1991).

41. One may object that causing to exist *plus* minimal support is necessary for creation to bestow a benefit. Even so, this does not entirely solve the puzzle behind mandatory child support. Our expectations of parents go beyond provisions of minimal support. Many think they include duties to share resources more fully and for temporal periods beyond those necessary to ensure the child's functioning.

42. That children may be needy will not, alone, explain why the biological parents in particular are expected to fulfill the need. *Ex hypothesi*, with respect to *that* child, the parents have given it a great deal. So, shouldn't the general duties of benevolence and to respond to need weigh harder (or at least equally) upon others who have not benefited the child? One might explain parents' particular responsibility on the grounds that, otherwise, they will have imposed support responsibilities on others who did not consent to a child's creation. This argument has some, but incomplete, force. This explanation would ground a duty that biological parents owe to others to prevent their having to bear unsolicited financial expense. But it would fail to explain why biological parents also owe the support *to* their children and why their children may rightfully complain if the duty is shirked. Second, the concern about laying financial burdens on nonprocreating members of society is in some tension with the commonly held sentiment that creating people benefits the society by perpetuating it. For then it would seem that even nonprocreating citizens should assume large portions of the costs of the production and maintenance of this benefit.

This argument works most clearly to establish the theoretical soundness of entertaining a wider range of wrongful life suits against parents who initiate creation. They, most clearly, impose life upon their children. The case of doctors is more difficult because doctors are not the prime initiators of conception and because they have socially important duties to act as neutral, fairly noninterventionist agents who protect their patients' health. More needs to be said than there is room for to delineate the proper scope of physician liability—that is, whether doctors should be responsible for all cases in which they facilitate conception and birth or only when they act in dereliction of their medical duties. My tentative assessment is that when doctors act knowingly, recklessly or negligently, so that they cause the creation of a child that will suffer inequitable burdens;[43] or when they take unusual risks, for example, through experimentation with fertility drugs or reproductive technology meant to encourage or facilitate otherwise unlikely procreation, and the resulting child suffers from burdens attributable to the experimental techniques; or they fail to give sufficient information to prospective parents to permit them to make an informed choice about their procreative risks, doctors should bear some of the liability.[44] Otherwise, when doctors merely provide medical care to pregnant women and assist in delivery, liability should not be assessed. There the parents are fully responsible for the creation. To assess liability in those cases would create an enormous conflict between doctors' duties of care to patients and duties to future children.

IV.

This section moves beyond the theoretical argument for liability and comments on some more pragmatic concerns about such suits. Does the argument waged so far imply that *all* children may have causes of action? *In theory*, the answer is yes. However, four mitigating factors make an explosion of suits unlikely, even were this more expansive form of liability officially recognized.

First, the fact that most children experience their imposed lives as miraculous benefits suggests that few of those who have families that provide adequate support would want or need to sue. Second, for most children, there is little a court could provide that would make suits worthwhile. As noted above, most parents already provide support for their children to help them manage these burdens. For those with relatively minor burdens (in contrast to those born in difficult circumstances or with significant disabilities), parental support and acknowledgment of responsibility may be

---

43. Section IV discusses limiting liability to cases where children have inequitable burdens.
44. I note but leave aside the difficult issues concerning requirements to inform potential parents of emerging genetic testing measures. Permitting the parents to refuse invasive testing, though, should not give rise to a cause for action, for the same sorts of parental privacy and bodily autonomy rationales that ground a legal right to procreate and that should insulate doctors from liability for basic obstetric care.

all that is appropriate to expect. Attempts at further compensation may be worse for the child, as a good and full life generally requires learning and engaging in self-management of the typical burdens of life.

Third, additional moral and psychological barriers would typically forestall suits by children. An interesting, prevalent moral barrier, often occurring between friends and family members, prevents people from demanding what may be owed to them by right. In some cases, one may have a legitimate claim against another that the obligated person should voluntarily fulfill without request. Yet it would show a bad character and perhaps be wrong actually to make the claim. In some cases, a friend owes one money but it would be rude and petty to demand it. Or a friend may owe one gratitude or a display of admiration but it would be improper to ask for or elicit it. Likewise, demanding damages from one's parents where one has even only a decent relationship with them may exhibit rudeness, pettiness, and ingratitude; it may threaten the relationship, even if the substance of one's demand itself has some reasonable basis. These moral barriers are likely to forestall legal claims from being pressed except in those few but serious cases in which compensation is truly needed because the family relationship is either nonexistent or significantly inadequate.

Finally, courts could reasonably demarcate a narrower class of cases as judicially cognizable. We need not, and standardly do not, provide judicial relief for all moral claims. Courts might take into account the reasonable pragmatic aim of limiting litigation, the difficulties of assessing financial compensation in the everyday cases, and the general provision of care and other forms of nonfinancial, voluntary compensation that parents standardly provide their children. Such considerations might justify limiting wrongful life causes of action to those children who suffer disproportionately great burdens. Although everyone endures the burdens of moral agency, moderate stretches of pain, and the risks of suffering worse, some people are hampered by extra burdens—for example, ever-present significant pain, hindering disabilities, or life-threatening or shortening diseases. For these people, because their burdens are substantially stronger than those endured by the average individual, we might justifiably delineate them as the class eligible to pursue greater relief.[45]

It might be objected that when directed against parents, wrongful life suits unfairly penalize those parents whose offspring suffer greater disabilities than most but who acted no differently from parents whose offspring are better off. In some cases, this objection will be implausible where the

---

45. This delimiting approach has a distinct advantage over the even more limited theories of liability criticized; *see supra* note 3. These other theories require that courts find that a child's life is not worth living and either attempt to evaluate the degree to which life is worse than nonexistence or, like California, abandon the idea of actual damages. (These problems partially motivated some courts to reject wrongful life claims.) This suggested approach eliminates the need for such disturbing findings and simplifies damage assessment. All a court must find is that the child suffers from a disproportionate allocation of burdens. The court may award damages in much the same way as it awards damages to those who become disabled early in childhood.

plaintiff claims the parents neglected special, demonstrable risks that they, specifically, would bear an inordinately burdened child. Where the objection does exert force, though, there are two different lines of available, familiar response. One line maintains that this disproportionate burden is not unfair as each set of parents, *ex hypothesi,* freely undertook the risk that their child's life might be overburdened. An alternative insurance-oriented approach would tax all parents (perhaps progressively)[46] for their risk-taking and then distribute the proceeds to those children made worse off by procreation. This approach has the advantage of not unduly burdening the individual parents of a disproportionately burdened child, and by spreading costs it makes it more likely that burdened children will have adequate funds available to them. Although I am sympathetic to this approach, I will not attempt here to defend it. Importantly, the arguments for mandatory, parent-funded insurance schemes still rely on the same fount of argument that supports wrongful life liability without pooled risk.

V.

The equivocal view also has ramifications for a range of other procreative practices, including adoption, surrogacy, and the use of reproductive technology.

What difference might such a view make in our assessment of adoption issues? Standard treatments often suppose that the link between biological parents and children is morally privileged, because, for instance, biological parents deserve relationships with their children since they created them, because children inherit their genetic material, or because the biological relationship is culturally, psychologically, or even inherently significant. Prominent adoption advocates such as Elizabeth Bartholet criticize these views and argue for the equal moral importance of the bond between children and adoptive parents.[47]

The equivocal view takes a further step and partly inverts the hierarchy of biological parents over traditional adoptive parents—that is, those who care for children but do not initiate their creation. On the equivocal view, biological parents perform a morally mixed act by imposing the risks, burdens, and benefits of human existence on their children, whereas traditional adoptive parents do not impose the risks and burdens of existence on those children. In the main,[48] they respond to existent children's needs

---

46. Here, of course, there are hard issues about whether those with genetic histories or behavioral patterns predisposing their children to be disproportionately burdened should shoulder higher premiums.

47. *See, e.g.,* Elizabeth Bartholet, FAMILY BONDS: ADOPTION AND THE POLITICS OF PARENTING (1993).

48. They do, of course, impose a particular relationship on the child that may have significant burdensome aspects. Usually, though, this relationship averts the greater harm of the child's lacking all parental relations.

but do not engage in the morally mixed activity of creation toward them. This inversion might, for example, make some difference in our approach to custody disputes between biological parents who have abdicated responsibility (or for other reasons failed to develop a relationship) for the child and adoptive or foster parents who have cultivated a strong relationship with the child. In some cases, we might allow a long-term bond with foster or adoptive parents, created from voluntarily assumed responsibility, to count for more than we do now; we might regard the fact of a genetic relationship as more of a mixed blessing, especially if the genetic parents have experienced lapses in responsibility, rather than as a very strong presumptive factor.[49] This is not to denigrate family reunification goals. They often facilitate children having strong familial relationships with those best suited to serve their needs. They also serve the pragmatic aim of encouraging temporarily beset parents to turn to the foster care system for assistance. But reunification goals predicated on the importance of genetic ties should not necessarily trump custodial claims arising from strong, committed relationships developed by adoptive or foster parents.

The equivocal view also generates new reasons to resist rigid anonymity and indemnity protections in genetic and gestational "donation" contexts. Legislation that encourages genetic donation by shielding the identities of contributors of genetic material and immunizing them from support requirements and liability may be misguided.[50] Those parents who sponsor the creation and assume custody in an assisted reproductive relationship might legitimately waive their rights for child support and the like against genetic contributors, the agency that arranges the contribution, and against gestational carriers. But they should not be able to waive the rights of the *child* to support or damages should that child be in need. The person (partly) causally responsible for the child's burdens has a duty of responsibility to that child that should not be waivable by a parent. Anonymity provisions currently protect even donors who are reckless toward or even knowledgeable of high probabilities that their offspring would suffer from debilitating genetic conditions.[51] Why should the donor, an integral, voluntary, participant in the creation process, be able to avoid responsibility for

---

49. This could support a different outcome in the Baby Jessica case in which, after two years of adoptive care, an infant was returned to her biological father who had been unaware of the child's existence and did not consent to her adoption. *In re Clausen*, 502 N.W. 2d 649 (Mich. 1993), stay denied, 509 U.S. 1301 (1993).

50. *See, e.g.*, Cal. Civil Code §43.1.

51. These are not mere possibilities. A couple is currently suing a sperm bank, seeking the identity of a sperm donor who misreported his medical history and passed on an incurable kidney disease to the child who resulted from his sperm contribution. Julie Marquis, *Gift of Life, Questions of Liability*, L.A. TIMES, August 9, 1997, at A1. In another case, a man passed on the herpes virus to a surrogate and to the child she conceived, who suffers from severe disabilities. Rebecca Powers, *Surrogate Negligence Case Ready for Court*, THE DETROIT NEWS, Jan. 20, 1993, at 2. The Sixth Circuit found that the broker, lawyer, and doctors who facilitated the surrogacy arrangement had an affirmative duty of care and could be sued for negligence. Stiver v. Parker, 975 F.2d 261 (6th Cir. 1992).

Wrongful Life

the life he has created? The fact that the donor might not provide genetic material if he were susceptible to liability or support requirements, and hence the child might not have otherwise come into existence, is not, as we have seen, a sufficient reason to disclaim responsibility to the child for the burdens imposed by creation.

Should, then, biological parents who give their children up for adoption in the traditional manner (i.e., not through an arrangement crafted prior to conception) also continue to be financially responsible, as default supporters, for their children? In principle, the answer is yes, although two factors support waiving this responsibility and imposing more stringent duties on mere genetic contributors. First, traditional participants in the adoption system are less likely to have created intentionally; genetic contributors, however, almost uniformly have opted intentionally and, generally, voluntarily to participate in a creation arrangement. Further, unlike traditional biological parents who relinquish custody through the adoption system, genetic contributors often contribute to creation as part of a business or financial transaction. It seems only fitting that they should absorb the costs of their business activities. Second, it may facilitate adoptions that promote the child's best interests to waive support requirements; if biological parents remain susceptible for support payments, this may deter unfit parents from relinquishing custody; but in the genetic contribution context, liability may only deter creation in the first place, which will not harm the nonexistent, potential child.

Apart from financial liability, biological parents should assume moral accountability for the lives they create. As some argue, it *may* better promote children's psychological development and sense of stability to connect only with a single set of parents and not to have extra-familial relationships during childhood with nonparenting biological parents. Nevertheless, legal structures that permit biological parents, genetic donors, and gestational carriers to remain anonymous interfere with the child's opportunity to consult one's biological parents in adulthood. Those who participated in the initiation of a life should assume responsibility for it and should, at the least, be accessible to the child, at some point, to participate in a justificatory dialogue about the child's origins—that is, to discuss why the life was created, to relay familial history, and to listen to the child's account of his difficulties and burdens.

The equivocal stance also provides guidance for the resolution of disputes over genetic material, such as the dispute in *Davis v. Davis* about who should determine the fate of frozen embryos.[52] Where both genetic contributors cannot agree that (or where) the embryo should be implanted, the presumption should lie with affording the reluctant donor a veto against their use, on the grounds that if one of the parents does not want the child, is unwilling to assume responsibility for it, or judges that the

---

52. 842 S.W. 2d 588 (1992).

future child's interests are best served if it is not born, then that parent's decision should be deferred to. If burdens and the risk of further harm are imposed to bestow a benefit, without that person's consent, it should be done with the full confidence of each parent that such imposition is advisable and with their voluntary assumption of responsibility.[53] These grounds suggest, in contrast to the *Davis* court's holding,[54] that this veto should have dispositive force, even if one of the contributors lacks another means to create a biologically related child.

Finally, this approach has implications for the resolution of disputes arising out of so-called surrogacy arrangements. Many have argued that it is important to establish presumptive custody rules between contesting parties both seeking custody so as to forestall litigation, establish expectations, and protect children from prolonged disputes and possible severe interruptions in the continuity of care.[55] Less remarked upon is the importance of establishing presumptive rules demarcating duties of financial support and other forms of mandated responsibility in these complicated relationships. Without such clear rules in place, as these arrangements multiply, tragic scenarios in which the parties all attempt to disclaim custody and responsibility may more frequently occur. The sponsoring parents may divorce and one or both such parents may attempt to avoid both custodial and support obligations.[56] Or, emerging evidence of a child's disability (or perhaps race or sex)[57] may prompt sponsoring parents to renege on the agreement.

Frequently, all of the parties will have evinced improper attitudes by, in some ways, treating the child as an object of a bargain. Although the

---

53. It does not follow that fathers should be able to force their pregnant partners to abort. Here, child-regarding interests conflict with strong rights of bodily autonomy and concerns about gender domination. For much the same reasons that the state could not ban procreation, the state could not empower one parent to control the body of another. Support requirements could be imposed because the father voluntarily participated in activity that might create a child, the effects of which would not necessarily be reversible. Where one can revoke one's commitment to parenthood without harming a child or interfering with another's bodily integrity, however, that revocation should be respected. This also provides a further argument, in addition to bodily autonomy arguments, for recognizing surrogates' rights to abort, even if their contractual obligations may be otherwise fully enforceable.

54. *See* Davis, *supra* note 52, at 604 (suggesting that the absence of alternative means to procreate may be dispositive).

55. *See, e.g.,* Martha Field, SURROGATE MOTHERHOOD 126 (1990).

56. In a California case, two sponsoring, "intentional" parents took genetic material from two anonymous contributors. The resultant embryo was implanted in a separate gestational carrier. Before the child's birth, the sponsoring father filed for divorce and sought to avoid support obligations for the child. To further his position, he contended that his ex-wife, the sponsoring mother, lacked custody rights, although she avidly claimed them, because she was not the genetic or gestational mother. A trial court ruled that the child was entirely without legal parents. An appellate court reversed, finding the father liable for support and the sponsoring mother to be the child's parent. Buzzanca v. Buzzanca, 1998 WL 102105 (Ca. 1998).

57. One biological father rejected a child he produced through a surrogacy relationship because the child was male. *See, Surrogate Mother Stunned as Dad Rejects One Twin,* CHICAGO SUN TIMES, April 24, 1988, at 1. Another planned to reject a child from a surrogacy relationship because the child was disabled. *See* Powers, *supra* note 51.

equivocal view provides grounds for resisting attempts to break all the child's ties with the gestational mother and the genetic parents, it also provides grounds for establishing a presumptive, possibly defeasible, rule to choose between the parties. At least as a default, custody and support rights should rest with the sponsoring parents, on the grounds that they initiated the creation and made an early commitment to parent and provide for the child.[58] Of course, genetic contributors and carriers may come to want to assume that commitment (and, if in the child's best interests, they should both be permitted and required to fulfill some parental functions such as revealing their identity, supplying medical histories, and serving as default parental figures). Nonetheless, the fact that earlier they viewed the creation as a financial transaction, not a responsibility-generating event, provides grounds for presuming that the sponsoring parents have had a stronger and less wavering commitment to the child's best interests and thus might better serve them.

The sponsoring parents' primary role in initiating creation with the intent to care for the child also renders them the preferred holders of a presumptive duty of support. It is important that such obligations attach at conception so as to discourage sponsoring parents from rejecting children with unwanted traits at birth. Making sponsoring parents responsible for children who are created at their behest provides security for children. It also encourages more careful thought and commitment in the initiation of creation. Approaches that leave it indeterminate or rest primary responsibility with the carrier or genetic contributor are less likely to promote this result. Carriers and donors, although morally subject to some duties of support and parental contact, are unlikely to be adequately prepared to assume primary custody or support obligations. Resting primary responsibility with them in cases of conflict is unlikely to discourage many from entering the relationships since most such relationships do result, uneventfully, in the child's placement with the sponsoring parents; the opposite outcome may not be readily anticipated.[59] Further, carriers are expected to attempt to cultivate emotional distance from the children they carry, to facilitate uncontested transfers. Although carriers should assume responsibility for the children they create if the children are in need, because the carriers' role asks them actively to distance themselves from the children, it is unlikely to serve children to rest the default support responsibility with carriers. By contrast, locating the default duties with the sponsoring parents would not subject them to conflicting psychological demands. They, like

---

58. This rationale is similar to that voiced in Johnson v. Calvert, 851 P.2d 776 (Ca. 1993), but does not, as the California court does, deny that the gestational carrier is a natural mother of the child or contend that natural motherhood is the key factor for custody.

59. Marjorie Shultz also makes this point in her more parent-oriented argument for intent-based approaches to parenthood determinations. Marjorie Shultz, *Reproductive Technology and Intent-based Parenthood: An Opportunity for Gender Neutrality*, WIS. L. REV. 297, 324 (1990). *See also* John Hill, *What Does It Mean to Be a 'Parent'? The Claims of Biology as the Basis for Parental Rights*, 66 N.Y.U. LAW REV. 353 (1991).

traditional biological parents, would be expected to assume responsibility for the child they create—whether or not their marriage undergoes strain or the child has undesirable traits.

VI.

I have argued for a more equivocal stance toward procreation, one that recognizes that parents subject their future children to harm and substantial risk by bringing them into existence. Even if the creation is overall beneficial for the child, that is not alone a sufficient reason to refuse to impose liability. These arguments challenge some of the purported philosophical barriers against wrongful life liability and have implications for legal approaches to other issues involving parent–child relations.

Of course, strong and practical considerations exist against the imposition of wrongful life liability, but these considerations, and the practical alternatives to such liability, have been underscrutinized because of the perceived philosophical barriers to liability. Exploring these philosophical grounds for stronger norms of parental responsibility may orient the debate more toward assessing the most effective measures to promote children's welfare.[60]

---

60. I am grateful for the critical feedback of audiences at the USC Law Center and the UCLA Center for the Study of Women, and to members of a UCLA graduate seminar I taught about harm. For very useful conversations and written comments, I owe special thanks to Rick Abel, Scott Altman, Peter Arenella, Elizabeth Bartholet, Tyler Burge, Robert Goldstein, Mitu Gulati, Barbara Herman, Frances Kamm, Gillian Lester, Jeff McMahan, Michael Otsuka, Gary Schwartz, and Steven Shiffrin.

[9]

Sustainability and Intergenerational Justice

BRIAN BARRY

1. *The Question*

As temporary custodians of the planet, those who are alive at any given time can do a better or worse job of handing it on to their successors. I take that simple thought to animate concerns about what we ought to be doing to preserve conditions that will make life worth living (or indeed liveable at all) in the future, and especially in the time after those currently alive will have died ('future generations'). There are widespread suspicions that we are not doing enough for future generations, but how do we determine what is enough? Putting the question in that way leads us, I suggest, towards a formulation of it in terms of intergenerational justice.

A methodological principle to which I shall appeal more systematically in section 2 is that we shall make most headway in asking ethical questions about the future if we start by asking them about the present and then see how the results can be extended to apply to the future. The rationale for this procedure is that we are accustomed to thinking about relations among contemporaries and have developed a quite sophisticated apparatus to help us in doing so. We have no similar apparatus to aid our thoughts about relations between people living at different times. Rather than starting from scratch, then, my proposal is that we

This chapter was first published in *Theoria*, Vol 45 No 89 (June, 1997), pp. 43–65.

should move from the familiar to the unfamiliar, making whatever adaptations seem necessary along the way.

If we follow this precept, and start from relations among contemporaries, we shall immediately run into a contrast that virtually all moral systems draw, though they derive it differently and use different vocabularies, between what it would be desirable (virtuous, benevolent, supererogatory) to do for others and what it would be wrong not to do for them. We may be said to have a duty or an obligation to do things that it is wrong to do, though this entails taking the words outside their natural homes in, respectively, institutionally generated roles and constraints imposed within rule-governed activities (e.g. legal obligations or promissory obligations).

Another family of terms that fits in somewhere here is the one made up of 'just', 'unjust', 'justice', and 'injustice'. A broad conception would make 'unjust' roughly equivalent to 'wrong' or 'morally impermissible'. John Stuart Mill proposed a broad use in chapter 5 of *Utilitarianism*,[1] and I have myself employed a similarly broad conception of justice in a recent book.[2] However, we would not in normal usage describe murder or assault as unjust, even though they are paradigmatically wrong. Rather, we reserve terms from the 'justice' family for cases in which some distributive consideration comes into play. For the present purpose, it will make little difference whether we choose the broader or the narrower conception of justice. This is because the questions about intergenerational justice that are liable to create distinctive moral problems are very likely to be issues of justice in the narrow sense: cases where there is (or is believed to be) an intergenerational conflict of interest. Thus, suppose we could provide a benefit or avoid a loss to people in the future at some cost to ourselves, are we morally required to do it? This inter-temporal distributive question falls within the scope of justice in the narrow sense. It is quite true that we can also damage people in the future without benefiting ourselves. But such actions will normally be wrong in relation to contemporaries or at the very least recklessly imprudent. Thus, if the people living at a certain time devastate a large part of the world by fighting a nuclear war, that will obviously be bad for later generations (assuming that human life is not entirely wiped out). But its inflicting immense evils on subsequent people is of a piece, as it were, with its devastating effect on those alive at the time.

I qualified my equation of injustice and wrongness in the broad sense by saying only that they are roughly equivalent. I had in mind two ways in which we can behave wrongly but not unjustly. First, I take it to be uncontroversial that we can act wrongly in relation to non-human animals. It is, of course, controversial whether or not certain practices such as using them in medical experiments or raising them for food are wrong. But scarcely anybody would deny that some acts (e.g. torturing them for fun) are wrong. We can, I think, stretch 'duty' and 'obligation' further beyond their core applications to enable us to talk about duties or obligations to non-human animals. (Even here, though, the core applications exert a pull: we are especially liable to use the vocabulary of duty where a role-related responsibility is at issue.) In contrast, it does not seem to me that the concept of justice can be deployed intelligibly outside the context of relations between human beings. The reason for this is, I suggest, that justice and injustice can be predicated only of relations among creatures who are regarded as moral equals in the sense that they weigh equally in the moral scales.

The second way in which wrongness and injustice come apart is that it is possible to behave wrongly even where the interests of sentient beings are not involved. Here, it is controversial that there are really any cases in which we can treat 'nature' wrongly unless the interests of sentient beings are somehow affected. I shall defend the claim below (section 5) though I shall there argue that the common move of appealing to the 'independent value of nature' is a mistaken one. For the present purpose, however, I can bracket the validity of the claim. Let me simply say that *if* it is in some circumstances wrong to behave in a certain way in relation to 'nature', there is no entity that can properly be described as a victim of injustice.[3] I also believe, incidentally, that talking about duties or obligations to 'nature' is misguided. My reason for holding this will, I hope, become apparent when I explain the sense in which I think we can behave wrongly in relation to 'nature'.

To sum up the discussion this far, behaving unjustly to future generations is wrong but (even in the broad conception of justice) it is not the only thing that those currently alive can do in relation to the distant future that is wrong. Injustice is, however, such a manifestly important aspect of wrongness that it is well worth the amount of attention it gets from political philosophers. Further, if we define 'distributive justice' to correspond to the narrow conception of justice, which focuses on conflicts of interest, we may say that questions about intergenerational justice are characteristically questions about intergenerational distributive justice.

With that by way of preamble, I can now set out very quickly what I see as the question to be asked about the ethical status of sustainability. This is as follows: Is sustainability (however we understand the term) either a necessary or a sufficient condition of intergenerational distributive justice?

2. Distributive Justice

In accordance with the methodological maxim that I laid down at the beginning, I shall approach the question of the demands of intergenerational justice via the question of the demands of distributive justice among contemporaries. The premiss from which I start is one of the fundamental equality of human beings. (It is precisely because this premiss does not make moral standing depend on the time at which people live that principles of justice valid for contemporaries are *prima facie* valid for intergenerational justice too.) Fundamental equality is, as John Stuart Mill said, 'the first principle of morals'. 'Bentham's dictum, "everybody to count for one, nobody for more than one"' is, as he noted, a specific application of it to the utilitarian calculus, telling us that pains and pleasures of equal intensity are to be given the same value in the calculus, regardless of the identity of the person to whom they belong.[4] An application that is not tied to utilitarianism is that different treatments of different people must be justified by adducing some morally relevant ground for different treatment. This is, of course, not saying a great deal until we know what are to count as morally relevant reasons. But even if we simply say that they are grounds which we ought reasonably to expect the person affected to accept freely, we shall rule out many historically prominent forms of domination and systematic inequality of rights, which have rested on nothing but the power of the beneficiaries to impose them.[5]

I do not know of any way of providing a justification for the premiss of fundamental equality: its status is that of an axiom. I will point out, however, that it is very widely accepted, at least in theory, and attempts to provide a rationale for unequal treatment at least pay lip service to the obligation to square it with the premiss of fundamental equality. Moreover, it seems to me that there is a good reason for this in that it is very hard to imagine any remotely plausible basis for rejecting the premiss. In any case, it is presupposed in what follows.

In brief compass, then, I shall propose four principles which are, I claim, theorems of the premiss of fundamental equality. These are as follows:

1. *Equal rights.* Prima facie, civil and political rights must be equal. Exceptions can be justified only if they would receive the well-informed assent of those who would be allocated diminished rights compared with others.

2. *Responsibility.* A legitimate origin of different outcomes for different people is that they have made different voluntary choices. (However, this principle comes into operation fully only against a background of a just system of rights, resources and opportunities.) The obverse of the principle is that bad outcomes for which somebody is not responsible provide a prima-facie case for compensation.

3. *Vital interests.* There are certain objective requirements for human beings to be able to live healthy lives, raise families, work at full capacity, and take a part in social and political life. Justice requires that a higher priority should be given to ensuring that all human beings have the means to satisfy these vital interest than to satisfying other desires.

4. *Mutual advantage.* A secondary principle of justice is that, if everyone stands *ex ante* to gain from a departure from a state of affairs produced by the implementation of the above three principles, it is compatible with justice to make the change. (However, it is not unjust not to.)

What implications do these principles of justice have for justice between generations? Let me take them in turn.

1. *Equal rights.* I cannot see that this principle has any *direct* intergenerational application. For it would seem to me absurd to say, e.g. that it is unfair for a woman to have more rights in Britain now than a century ago, or unfair that a woman had fewer rights then. Surely, the principle of equal rights applies to contemporaries and only to contemporaries. However, the present generation may be able to affect the likelihood that there will be equal rights in the future. Thus, it seems to be a robust generalization that rights suffer at times when large challenges to a system demand rapid and co-ordinated responses. (To offer a relatively modest example, I would guess that all individual university teachers and departments have lost autonomy in the last twenty years.) The more environmental stress we leave our successors to cope with, therefore, the poorer prospects for equal rights.

2. *Responsibility.* This principle will clearly apply among people who are contemporaries in the future, as it does among people who are contemporaries today, to justify inequalities of outcome that arise from choice. But what place, if any, does it have in relations between different generations? People in the future can scarcely be held responsible for the physical conditions they inherit, so it would seem that it is unjust if people in future are worse off in this respect than we are. (This, of course, leaves open the question of what is the relevant criterion of being well off, and I shall take that up in the next section.) What future people may be held responsible for, however, is how many of them there are at any given time.

Clearly, if we take the view that the principle of responsibility applies to population size, it will have highly significant implications for the requirements of intergenerational justice. I shall pursue this further in section 4.

3. *Vital interests.* The fundamental idea that location in space and time do not in themselves affect legitimate claims has the immediate implication that the vital interests of people in the future have the same priority as the vital interests of people in the present. I shall take up the implications of this in section 4.

4. *Mutual advantage.* In theory, it would be possible for the principle of mutual advantage to have cross-generational implications. That is to say, it could be that there are intertemporally Paretian improvements to be made in comparison with a baseline constituted by the outcomes of the other principles working together. However, I think it quite implausible that there are. The scope of the principle in relation to the distant future is particularly limited because it is explicitly stated in terms of preferences, and the further into the future we look the less confidence we can have about the preferences that people will have.

An objection commonly made against a universalist theory of justice such as this one is that it does not provide an adequate account of motivation to conform to its demands. It is certainly true that it leaves a gap in a way that 'communitarian' accounts do not. Consider, for example, Avner de-Shalit's book *Why Posterity Matters.*[6] It seems to me that his account closes the gap only too successfully. For in essence what he is saying is that concern for people in the future is something we naturally have, to the extent that we see them as carrying on with projects that are dear to us, because that gives depth and meaning to our own lives. This is doubtless true to some degree, though it would seem more for some than for others, but (except to the extent that it can generate intragenerational obligations arising from the 'principle of fair play') it does not tell people that they have to do what they are not inclined to do anyway. Moreover, because it is a cross-generational form of communitarianism, it cannot offer any reason for people in rich countries to cut back so as to improve the prospects of future people in other communities. Yet that is, as it seems to me, the most important thing for a conception of intergenerational justice to deliver.

In almost all the world, there is discrimination against women: they have fewer legal rights than men, are poorly protected by the law, and even more by its administration, against domestic violence, they have restricted educational and occupational opportunities, and so on. In most countries there are (*de facto* or *de jure*) different grades of membership based on race, ethnicity, language, religion, or some other characteristic. Such practices have powerful beneficiaries and it might be said (and is by so-called communitarian political philosophers) that it is 'no use' applying universalistic criteria of justice and pointing out that according to these criteria practices such as these are unjust. The only 'useful' criticism is 'connected' criticism, which deploys already accepted ideas. But this means that criticism cannot get a foothold so long as those who discriminate on the basis of gender or ethnicity have an internally coherent rationale. Meanwhile, it remains none the less true that such practices are unjust. And even if that thought does not have any motivating effect on those within a country who are in a position to change things, it may motivate people outside to organize boycotts and lead international organizations to exclude such countries from the benefits of international trade and aid.

I believe that the core idea of universalism—that place and time do not provide a morally relevant basis on which to differentiate the weight to be given to the interests of different people—has an immense rational appeal. Its corollaries—the illegitimacy of slavery and the impermissibility of assigning women an inferior legal status, for example—have been acted on for the past two centuries in a significant part of the world, despite strongly entrenched interests and beliefs in opposition to them. In the past fifty years, concern for people who are distant in place and time has grown in a quite unprecedented way. The great question for the future is whether or not that concern will grow sufficiently to induce action of the kind called for by the demands of justice. But I can see no reason for supposing that those demands should be scaled back to match pessimistic predictions about the way in which that question will be answered, even if we believe pessimism to be a reasonable response to the evidence so far.

3. Sustainability

Many people who have thought seriously about the matter have reached the conclusion that the concept of sustainability is inherently incapable of carrying the burden it would have to bear if it were to constitute a basic building block in a theory of intergenerational justice. With due diffidence, as a non-expert, I should like to make two observations on the literature that I have read. I first note a tendency to elide an important distinction. I have in mind here on the one hand the problem of producing a definition of sustainability that is coherent and comprehensible, and on the other hand the problem of drawing out concrete policy implications from any such definition. It seems to me that the problem of application is undeniably enormous, but that this should not be allowed too readily to impugn the possibility of achieving a definition of the concept.

The other point that occurs to me about the pessimists is their propensity to cite disagreement about the concept of sustainability as a basis for dismissing it. But we need not despair so long as the disagreements reflect substantive differences of viewpoint. Thus, let us suppose that concern about sustainability takes its origins from the suspicion that I articulated at the beginning: the suspicion that we are shortchanging our successors. If we then take this to mean that we should not act in such a way as to leave them with less of what matters than we enjoy, and call that sustainability, it is clear that the content of sustainability will depend crucially on what we think matters. For example, one writer may assume that what matters is utility, understood as want-satisfaction. (Such a writer is unlikely to be anything other than an economist, but economists loom quite large in the literature of sustainability.) Others will disagree and propose some alternative. There is nothing either mysterious or discreditable about this. It is, in fact, exactly what we should expect.

The core concept of sustainability is, I suggest, that there is some X whose value should be maintained, in as far as it lies within our power to do so, into the indefinite future. This leaves it open for dispute what the content of X should be. I have already mentioned one candidate: utility, understood (as is orthodox in economics) as the satisfaction of wants or, as they are usually called, preferences. The obvious objection to this criterion is that wants are (quite reasonably) dependent on what is, or is expected to be, available. Perhaps people in the future might learn to find satisfaction in totally artificial landscapes, walking on the astroturf amid the plastic trees while the electronic birds sing overhead. But we cannot but believe that something horrible would have happened to human beings if they did not miss real grass, trees, and birds.

The want-satisfaction criterion does not enable us to explain what would be wrong with such a world. This sheds light on the oft-noted tendency of economists to be disproportionately located at the 'brown' end of the spectrum on environmental issues. For economists are also, as I have already noted, the most significant adherents of the want-satisfaction criterion. Combine that criterion with a faith in the adaptability of human preferences and you have a formula that can easily generate optimism about the future. For it will seem plausible that almost any environmental degradation that does not actually undermine productive capacity will be compensable by advances in technology that we can safely assume will continue to occur.

If I am right that substantive disputes about the concept of sustainability reflect disagreements about what matters, we can begin to see why what appear superficially to be technical questions of definition are so intractable. Consider especially the arguments in the literature about the status of 'natural capital'. For someone who adopts want-satisfaction as a criterion, all resources are in principle fungible: if plastic trees are as satisfying as real ones, there is no reason for worrying about the destruction of the world's trees so long as the resources exist to enable plastic replacements to be manufactured in sufficient numbers. Those who insist that 'natural capital' must be preserved are in effect denying the complete fungibility of all capital. But what is this disagreement actually about? On the interpretation I wish to offer, this is not a disagreement that turns on some matter of fact. It would be quite possible to agree with everything that might be said in favour of fungibility and still deny that it amounts to a case against the special status of 'natural capital'. For the case in favour of giving the preservation of nature an independent value is that it is important in its own right. If future people are to have access to what matters, and unspoilt nature is an essential part of what matters, then it follows that loss of 'natural capital' cannot be traded off against any amount of additional productive capacity. (I leave until section 5 the idea that nature might have value independently of its contribution to human interests, broadly conceived.)

What helps to obscure the point at issue is the terminology of 'capital' itself. For this naturally suggests that what is going on is a technical dispute about the conditions of production. On this understanding of the matter, the proponents of 'natural capital' are insisting that production has a natural base that cannot be run down beyond a certain point without putting future production in jeopardy. But the 'fungibility' school are not committed to denying this. They insist on fungibility *in principle*; whether or not everything can be substituted for *in practice* is a matter of fact on which they do not have to be dogmatic. But if I am right the real dispute is at the level of principle, and is not perspicuously represented in terms of the properties of different kinds of capital.

'Capital' is a term that is inherently located within economic discourse. A mountain is, in the first instance, just a mountain. To bring it under the category of 'capital'—of any kind—is to look at it in a certain light, as an economic asset of some description. But if I want to insist that we should leave future generations mountains that have not been strip-mined, quarried, despoiled by ski-slopes, or otherwise tampered with to make somebody a profit, my point will be better made by eschewing talk about 'capital' altogether.

Let us dismiss the hypothesis that X is want-satisfaction. What, then, is it? On the strength of the objection urged against want-satisfaction, it might appear that what should be maintained for future generations is their chance to live a good life as we conceive it. But even if 'we' agreed on what that is (which is manifestly not the case), this would surely be an objectionable criterion for 'what matters'. For one of the defining characteristics of human beings is their ability to form their own conceptions of the good life. It would be presumptuous—and unfair—of us to pre-empt their choices in the future. (This is what is wrong with all utopias). We must respect the creativity of people in the future. What this suggests is that the requirement is to provide future generations with the opportunity to live good lives according to their conception of what constitutes a good life. This should surely include their being able to live good lives according to our conception but should leave other options open to them.

This thought leads me to the suggestion (for which I claim no originality) that X needs to be read as some notion of equal opportunity across generations. Unfortunately, however, the concept of equal opportunity is notoriously treacherous. Although, therefore, I do believe this to be the right answer, I have to confess that saying this is not doing a lot more than set out an agenda for further study.

To summarize an extensive and in places technical literature with desperate brevity, there are two natural approaches to the measurement of opportunity, both of which rapidly turn out to be dead ends. One is to count opportunities. This has the obvious drawback that three options that are very similar (three apples of the same variety) will have to be said to give more opportunity than two more dissimilar options (an apple and an orange). But why is a greater range more valuable? A natural response might be that a choice between a number of apples is fine if you are an apple-lover but leaves you out of luck otherwise, whereas a choice between an apple and an orange gives you two shots at getting something you like. We might be tempted to move from this to the conclusion that what makes a range of options valuable is the want-satisfying property of the most preferred item in it. From there it is a short step to identifying the value of a set of opportunities with the utility of the most preferred option in it.

Notice, however, that if we follow this path we shall have insensibly changed the subject. We began by asking for a measure of the *amount* of opportunity provided by a set of options. What we have now done is come up with a measure of the value of the opportunities provided by a set of options. Even if we concede that the value of the most preferred element is for certain purposes an appropriate measure of the value of a set of options, it is strikingly counterintuitive as a measure of the amount of opportunity offered by a set of options. Thus, for example, it entails that opportunity is not increased by adding any number of desirable options to a singleton choice set, so long as none of those added comes as far up the agent's preference scale as the one option with which we began.

Another way of seeing the inadequacy of this measure of opportunity is to note that it takes preferences as given. But the whole reason for our taking opportunities to be constitutive of X was that we could not accept utility based on given preferences as the criterion of X. If preferences in the future are such that plastic trees (the only kind, let us suppose, that are available) give as much satisfaction to people then as real trees do now to us, the amount of opportunity in the future is not diminished. Thus, if we embrace the measure of opportunity that equates it with the utility of the most preferred item in the choice set, we shall simply be back at utility as the criterion of X. All that will have happened is that it will have been relabelled 'opportunity'.

The notion of a range of opportunity cannot be reduced either to the sheer number of opportunities or to the utility of the most preferred option. We must define it in a way that tracks our reasons for wishing to make it our criterion of X in the first place. That means taking seriously the idea that conditions must be such as to sustain a range of possible conceptions of the good life. In the nature of the case, we cannot imagine in any detail what may be thought of a good life in the future. But we can be quite confident that it will not include the violation of what I have called vital interests: adequate nutrition, clean drinking-water, clothing and housing, health care and education, for example. We can, in addition, at the very least leave open to people in the future the possibility of living in a world in which nature is not utterly subordinated to the pursuit of consumer satisfaction.

More work, as they say, needs to be done, but I cannot hope to undertake it within the bounds of this chapter. The most important contention that I have tried to establish in this section is that the concept of sustainability is irreducibly normative, so that disputes about its definition will inevitably reflect differing values.

If, as I maintain, the root idea of sustainability is the conservation of what matters for future generations, its definition is inescapably bound up with one's conception of what matters.

4. Sustainability and Intergenerational Justice

Having said something about intergenerational justice and something about sustainability, it is time to bring them together. We can be encouraged about the prospect of a connection if I am correct in my contention that sustainability is as much a normative concept as is justice. And I believe that there is indeed a close connection. It may be recalled that the question that I formulated at the end of section 1 asked if sustainability was either a necessary or a sufficient condition of intergenerational justice. It appears that sustainability is at least a necessary condition of justice. For the principle of responsibility says that, unless people in the future can be held responsible for the situation that they find themselves in, they should not be worse off than we are. And no generation can be held responsible for the state of the planet it inherits.

This suggests that we should at any rate leave people in the future with the possibility of not falling below our level. We cannot, of course, guarantee that our doing this will actually provide people in the further future with what we make possible. The next generation may, for all we can know, go on a gigantic spree and leave their successors relatively impoverished. The potential for sustaining the same level of X as we enjoy depends on each successive generation playing its part. All we can do is leave open the possibility, and that is what we are obliged by justice to do.

An objection sometimes raised to the notion that it would be unjust to let future generations fall below our standard (of whatever is to count as X) is that there is something arbitrary about taking the current position as the baseline (see Beckerman Ch. 3 in this volume). We are, it is argued, better off materially than our ancestors. Suppose we were to pursue policies that ran down resources to such an extent that people in future would be no better off than our ancestors were a hundred years (or two hundred years) ago. Why would that be unjust? What is so special about the present as the point of comparison? In reply, it must be conceded that the expression 'intergenerational justice' is potentially misleading—though perhaps it actually misleads only those who are determined to be misled. It is a sort of shorthand for 'justice between the present generation and future generations'. Because of time's arrow, we cannot do anything to make people in the past better off than they actually were, so it is absurd to say that our relations to them could be either just or unjust. 'Ought' implies 'can', and the only people whose fate we can affect are those living now and in the future. Taking the present as our reference point is arbitrary only in some cosmic sense in which it might be said to be arbitrary that now is now and not some other time. It is important, however, to understand that 'now' means 'now' in the timeless sense, not '1998'. Wilfred Beckerman suggested in a presentation to the seminar from which this chapter arose (see Beckerman in this volume) that there was something arbitrary in privileging 1998 from all dates in history as the benchmark of sustainability. So there would be. But in 1999 the benchmark will be 1999, and in 2099 it will be 2099. There are, as I have explained, excellent reasons for starting from now, whenever 'now' may be. But just as 'here' does not mean my flat (though that is where I am as I write this) so in the sentence 'We start from now' the meaning of 'now' is not rigidly designated.

We now have to face a question of interpretation so far left aside. This is: How are we to deal with population size? On one quite natural interpretation of the concept of sustainability, the X whose value is to be maintained is to be defined over individuals. The demands of justice will then be more stringent the larger we predict the future population to be. Suppose we were simply to extrapolate into the indefinite future growth rates of the order of those seen in past decades. On the hypothesis that numbers double every forty years or so, we shall have a world population after two centuries of around a hundred and fifty billion and in a further two centuries a population of five thousand billion. If the increase were spread evenly round the world, this would imply a population for the UK more than ten times the size of the whole current world population.

It is surely obvious that no degree of self-immiseration that those currently alive could engage in would be capable of providing the possibility of an equal level of X per head even that far inside the future. This would be so on any remotely plausible definition of X. (Indeed, we can be certain that some cataclysm would have occurred long before these numbers were reached.) But even far more modest increases in population would make it impossible to maintain X, if X is taken to include the preservation of so-called 'natural capital'.

This is worth emphasizing because the 'cornucopian' school of optimists about population, such as Julian Simon, cite in support of their ideas the alleged failures of early neo-Malthusians (from the mid-nineteenth century onward) to predict correctly the course of events. But I believe that the pessimists have already been proved right on a central point: the deleterious impact on the quality of life of sheer numbers. Thus, John Stuart Mill's forebodings a century and a half ago (in 1848 to be precise) have, it seems to me, proved quite uncannily prescient. All that he feared has already in large measure come to pass, and every bit of future population increase will make things that much worse.

Mill was quite prepared to grant the 'cornucopian' premiss that material conditions might be able to keep up with a greatly expanded population (or even more than keep up with it). But he still insisted that the population increase should be regretted. 'A population may be crowded, though all be amply supplied with food and raiment . . . A world from which solitude is extirpated, is a very poor ideal . . . Nor is there much satisfaction in contemplating the world with nothing left to the spontaneous activity of nature; with every rood of land brought into cultivation, which is capable of growing food for human beings; every flowery waste or natural pasture ploughed up, all quadrupeds or birds which are not domesticated for man's use exterminated as his rivals for food, every hedgerow or superfluous tree rooted out, and scarcely a place left where a wild shrub or flower could grow without being eradicated as a weed in the name of improved agriculture.'[7]

Treating future population as parametric is in effect assuming it to be beyond human control. But any such assumption is obviously false. I suggest, therefore, that the size of future population should be brought within the scope of the principle of responsibility. We must define intergenerational justice on the assumption that 'the increase of mankind shall be under the guidance of judicious foresight', as Mill put it.[8] If future people choose to let population increase, or by default permit it to increase, that is to be at their own cost. There is no reason in justice for our having any obligation to accommodate their profligacy. Concretely, then, the conception of sustainability that makes it appropriate as a necessary condition of intergenerational justice may be formulated as follows: Sustainability requires at any point in time that the value of some X per head of population should be capable of being maintained into the indefinite future, on the assumption that the size of the future population is no greater than the size of the present population.

It is worth emphasizing again that we always start from now, and ask what sustainability requires. The question is: What amount of X could be maintained into the indefinite future, given things as they are now, on the assumption that future population will be the same then as now? The way in which 'now' is always moving would not matter if (a) the demands of sustainability were correctly assessed in 1998; (b) sustainability were achieved in 1998 and maintained thereafter; and (c) the assumption of stable population control were in fact accurate. If all these conditions were met, we could substitute '1998' for 'now', but not otherwise.

We know that stabilization of population is perfectly possible as a result of voluntary choices made by individuals because a number of Western countries have already arrived at the position at which the (non-immigrant) population is only barely replacing itself, if that. Although they stumbled into it without any particular foresight, the formula is now known and can be applied elsewhere. Women have to be educated and to have a possibility of pursuing rewarding occupations outside the home while at the same time compulsory full-time education and stringent child-labour laws make children an economic burden rather than a benefit.

Unfortunately, however, many countries have such a large proportion of their population below the age of fifteen that their numbers would double before stabilizing even if every female now alive had only two children. Stabilizing population at its current level in these countries can be achieved only if women have only one child. So long as a policy restricting women to one child is operated consistently across the board, it does not contravene any principle of intragenerational justice, and is a requirement of intragenerational justice. Combined, as it has been in China, with a focus on medical care and education for children, there can be no question that it offers the next generation the best chance of living satisfactory lives, and removes a huge burden on future generations.

At this point, however, we must expect the response, already anticipated in general terms, that whether or not this is just it simply conflicts too strongly with religious objections to contraception and abortion and to powerful pronatalist norms, especially in many parts of the world where great importance is attached to having a male heir. If we are impressed by this, we shall have to say that justice demands more of people than they can reasonably be expected to perform. But what follows from that? At this point, it seems to me unavoidable to enter into the question that I have so far left on one side: the concrete implications of any criterion of sustainability. Suppose we believed that it would be fairly easy to provide the conditions in which X (e.g. some conception of equal opportunity) could be maintained into the indefinite future for a population twice the existing one. We might then treat as parametric the predicted doubling of world population and redefine sustainability accordingly. But my own conjecture is that the criterion of sustainability already proposed is extremely stringent, and that there is little chance of its demands being met. If I am right about this, all we can do is get as close to that as we can, which means doing everything possible to reduce population growth as well as everything possible to conserve resources and reduce depletion.

What then about the future? Suppose that the demographers' (relatively optimistic) projection for world population is correct, so that it stabilizes some time in the next century at double its current size. If we stick to the proposition that intragenerational justice is always a problem for the current generation (because they are the only people in a position to do anything about it), the implication is that sustainability should be redefined by each generation as the indefinite continuation of the level of X over the existing population, whatever it is. Whether people in the past have behaved justly or not is irrelevant. But if I am right in thinking that we are going to fall short of maintaining sustainability even on the basis of the continuation of current population size, it seems highly unlikely that people in the future will achieve it on the basis of a population twice as large. The only ray of light is that getting from a stable population to a gently declining one would not be difficult (nothing like as difficult as stabilizing a rapidly expanding population), and that the power of compound interest means that even a gradual decline in numbers would suffice to bring world population back well below current levels over a matter of a few centuries.

My conclusion, after this vertiginous speculation, is that we would be doing very well to meet the criterion of sustainability that I originally proposed. The more we fail, and the more that world population is not checked in coming decades, the worse things will be in the future and the smaller the population at which it will be possible to maintain tolerable living conditions. Perhaps the right way to look at the matter is to think of population and resources (in the largest sense) as the two variables that enter into sustainability: we might then say that sustainability is a function of both. Realistically, any given generation can make only a limited impact on either. But what can at least then be said is that if some generation is failing to meet the condition of sustainability (defined in the standard way over a fixed population), it can at least be more just than otherwise towards its successors by ensuring that the dwindling resources will have to spread around over fewer people.

Interpreted on some such lines as these, sustainability is, I suggest, adequate as a necessary condition of intergenerational justice. Is it also a sufficient condition? I feel strongly inclined to say that it is: if we were to satisfy it, we would be doing very well, and it is hard to see that we could reasonably be expected to do more. My only hesitation arises from the application of the vital interests. (I noted in section 2 that this needed later discussion.) Obviously, if we give the principle of vital interests priority over the principle of responsibility, we are liable to be back at a version of the absurd idea that we are obliged to immiserate ourselves to a level capable of sustaining a hugely larger population if we predict there will be one. For if we predict an enormously greater number of people in the future, meeting their vital interests trumps any objective we might have. I have not specified priority relations among the principles, and I do not think this can be done across the board. The principles are guides to thinking, not a piece of machinery that can be cranked to grind out conclusions. However, in this case it seems to me that giving the principle of vital interests priority produces such absurd results that this cannot possibly be the right thing to do.

Even if we make the principle of vital interests subordinate to the principle of responsibility, there is still a feature of the principle of vital interests that is worth attention. So far 'generations' have been treated as collective entities: the question has been posed as one of justice between the present generation as a whole and future generations as wholes. But the principle of vital interests forces us to focus on the fates of individuals. Suppose we leave future generations as collectivities with 'enough' between them to satisfy the criterion of sustainability, but it is distributed in such a way that the vital interests of many will predictably fail to be met? Does this possibility suggest that the criterion of sustainability has to be supplemented in order to count as a sufficient condition of intergenerational justice?

What I think it shows is that the distinction between intergenerational and intragenerational justice cannot be made absolute. I pointed out in section 1 that some things that would be wrong in relation to people in the future (e.g. fighting a nuclear war) would in the first instance be wrong among those alive at the time. Similarly, the primary reason for our being able to predict that the vital interests of many people in the world will not be met in the future is that they are not being met in the present. Formally, I suggest we have to say that maldistribution in the future is intragenerational injustice in the future. But we must recognize that intragenerational injustice in the future is the almost inevitable consequence of intragenerational injustice in the present.

5. Beyond Justice

If the current generation meets the demands of justice, is that enough? In the broad sense of justice, we would not be doing wrong in relation to human beings if we met the demands of justice. But we can (as I said in section 1) behave wrongly in relation to non-human animals even though this does not fall within the scope of justice. If we factor this in, what difference does it make? As far as I can see, its main effect is to reinforce the importance of keeping the lid on population, since the pressure on the habitats of the remaining wild non-human animals are already being encroached on at an alarming rate as a consequence of the growth of population that has already occurred.

The remaining question is the one that divides environmentalists into those for whom the significance of the environment lies solely in its contribution to human (or if you like animal) welfare from those for whom the environment has some significance beyond that. (Perhaps talking about 'the environment' is itself prejudicial since it suggests something in the background to another thing that is more important. But I take it that the distinction is familiar enough in a variety of descriptions.) I have to confess that I cannot quite decide what I think about this question because I find it hard to focus on the question when it is put, as it often is, as one about the 'independent value of nature'. Let me explain.

In *Principia Ethica*, G. E. Moore sought to discredit Sidgwick's claim that nothing can be said to be good 'out of relation to human existence, or at least to some consciousness or feeling'.[9] To this end, he asked his reader to consider

the following case. Let us imagine one world exceedingly beautiful. Imagine it as beautiful as you can; put into it whatever on this earth you most admire—mountains, rivers, the sea, trees, and sunsets, stars and moon. Imagine these all combined in the most exquisite proportions so that no one thing jars against another but each contributes to increase the beauty of the whole. And then imagine the ugliest world you can possibly conceive. Imagine it simply one heap of filth, containing everything that is most disgusting to us, for whatever reason, and the whole, as far as maybe, without one redeeming feature. Such a pair of worlds we are entitled to compare: they fall within Prof. Sidgwick's meaning, and the comparison is highly relevant to it. The only thing we are not entitled to imagine is that any human being ever has or ever, by any possibility, *can*, live in either, can ever see and enjoy the beauty of the one or hate the foulness of the other. Well, even so, supposing them quite apart from any possible contemplation by human beings; still, is it irrational to hold that it is better that the beautiful world should exist, than the one that is ugly?[10]

It is surely obvious that the question is loaded, because the two worlds are already unavoidably being visited by us, at least in imagination. It requires a self-conscious effort to avoid being affected by that. But if I make that effort conscientiously, I have to say that the whole question strikes me as ridiculous. In what possible sense could the universe be a better or a worse place on one supposition rather than the other? It seems to me an abuse of our language to assume that the word 'good' still has application when applied to such a context.

If adherence to the 'deep ecological' or 'dark green' position entails giving Moore the answer he wanted about the two worlds, I have to be counted out. But I wonder if all (or even many) of those who wish to endorse such a position feel thereby committed to attaching an intrinsic value to nature in the sense suggested by Moore. And, quite apart from that biographical question, there is the philosophical question: is there any way of being 'dark green' that does not entail being committed to Moore's preferred answer about the two worlds?

I am inclined to think that there is an attitude (which I share) that is distinguishable from the first position but is perhaps misleadingly expressed in terms of the intrinsic value of nature. This is that it is inappropriate—cosmically unfitting, in some sense—to regard nature as nothing more than something to be exploited for the benefit of human beings—or other sentient creatures, if it comes to that. There is an obvious sense in which this is still somehow human-centred, because it is about the right way for human beings to think about nature. But the content of that thought could be expressed by talking about the intrinsic value of nature.

It is important to observe that what I am saying here is not to be equated with the kind of environmental utilitarianism put forward by Robert Goodin in his *Green Political Theory*.[11] According to this, we do as a matter of fact care about unspoilt nature—for example, even the most carefully restored site of open-cast mining is 'not the same' as the original, any more than a perfect copy of a statue is 'the same' as the original. A sophisticated utilitarianism will therefore take our concerns about nature into account and set more stringent limits on the exploitation of the environment than would be set by our merely regarding the environment as a factor of production. This enables us to press 'green' concerns but still within a framework that makes human interests the measure of all things.

What I am saying is quite different from this. For it is a purely contingent matter whether or not people have the attitude to nature attributed to them by Goodin or, if they do, how far it weighs in their utility function compared with, say, cheap hamburgers from the cattle raised on pasture created from the ravaged Brazilian rain forest. The view that I am proposing says bluntly that people behave wrongly if they act out of a wrong attitude to nature. Although this is in a sense a human-centred proposition, it cannot be captured in any utilitarian calculus, however extensive its conception of human well-being.

6. Conclusion

I want to conclude by saying that I can understand and indeed sympathize with the impatience that will undoubtedly be felt by any environmental activist into whose hands this might fall. (Jonathon Porritt eloquently expressed such sentiments—and not only in relation to my contribution—during the final session of the Keele seminars on social justice and sustainability.) What the activist wants is ammunition that can be used in the fight for greater ecological awareness and responsibility. Fine-drawn analyses of sustainability such as those offered here are hardly the stuff to give the troops. But is it reasonable to expect them to be?

Let me make what may at first sight seem an eccentric suggestion. This is that it is not terribly difficult to know what needs to be done, though it is of course immensely difficult to get the relevant actors (governmental and other) to do it. I do not deny that there are large areas of scientific uncertainty, and probably always will be (e.g. about global warming), since the interacting processes involved are so complex. But what I am claiming is that virtually everybody who has made a serious study of the situation and whose objectivity is not compromised by either religious beliefs or being in the pay of some multinational corporation has reached the conclusion that the most elementary concern for people in the future demands big changes in the way we do things. These could start with the implementation by all signatories of what was agreed on at the Rio Conference.

Moreover, whatever is actually going to get done in, say, the next decade, to move towards a sustainable balance of population and resources is going to be so pathetically inadequate that it really does not matter how far it falls short. We know the direction in which change is required, and we know that there is absolutely no risk that we shall find ourselves doing more than required. It really does not make any practical difference whether we think a certain given effort represents 10 per cent of what needs to be done, or whether we think it is as much as 20 per cent. Either way, we have good reason to push for more. If I am right about this, it explains the feeling among practitioners that philosophical analyses have little relevance to their concerns. For whether we make the demands of justice more or less stringent, it is going to demand more than is likely to get done in the foreseeable future. What then is the use of pursuing these questions?

One obvious answer is that as political philosophers we are concerned to discover the truth, and that is an adequate justification for our work. The agenda of a scholarly discipline has its own integrity, which is worthy of respect. Distributive justice among contemporaries and within the boundaries of a state has been at the centre of the dramatic revival of political philosophy in the last quarter century. Extending the inquiry into the nature of distributive justice beyond these limits is a natural and inevitable development. But I think that there is also something to offer to those who are not interested in pursuing these questions for their own sake. It is surely at least something to be able to assure those who spend their days trying to gain support for measures intended to improve the prospects of future generations that such measures do not represent optional benevolence on our part but are demanded by elementary considerations of justice. What I have aimed to do here is show that the application of ideas about justice that are quite familiar in other contexts have radical implications when applied to intergenerational justice, and that there is no reason why they should not be.

Notes

1. J. S. Mill, *Utilitarianism* (Indianapolis: Bobbs-Merrill, 1971), ch. 5. Mill defines justice as equivalent to the performance of 'duties of perfect obligation', which presupposes 'a wrong done, and some assignable person who is wronged' (p. 47). This is close to my wide conception of justice (see below) in that it rules out obligations to non-human animals and obligations to 'nature'. However, the requirement that there should be assignable persons who are wronged would rule out the possibility of behaving unjustly with respect to future generations, since they can scarcely be regarded as assignable.
2. B. Barry, *Justice as Impartiality* (Oxford: Clarendon Press, 1995), esp. ch. 4.
3. In a paper presented to the first of the three seminars from which this book emerged, Andrew Dobson wrote of 'the privileging of human welfare over justice to nature'. But perhaps this was not intended to carry a lot of theoretical freight ('Sustainabilities: An Analysis and a Typology', paper presented to the Social Justice and Sustainability Seminars, Keele University, UK, (1996b), fo. 11). See also A. Dobson, *Justice and the Environment Conceptions of Environmental Sustainability and Dimensions of Social Justice* (Oxford: Oxford University Press, 1998).
4. Mill (1971), 55–6.
5. In *Justice as Impartiality* I have set out the criterion of reasonable agreement more fully and worked out some of its implications.
6. A. de-Shalit, *Why Posterity Matters: Environmental Politics and Future Generations* (London: Routledge, 1995).
7. J. S. Mill, *Principles of Political Economy*, ed. Donald Winch (Harmondsworth, Penguin Books, 1970 [1848]), Book IV, ch. 5, 115–16.
8. Ibid. 117.
9. G. E. Moore, *Principia Ethica* (Cambridge: Cambridge University Press, 1903), 81.
10. Ibid. 83–4.
11. R. Goodin, *Green Political Theory* (Cambridge: Polity Press, 1992).

[10]

Nonideal Theory

John Rawls

§15. Burdened Societies

15.1. Unfavorable Conditions. In noncompliance theory we have seen that the long-term goal of (relatively) well-ordered societies is somehow to bring the outlaw states into the Society of well-ordered Peoples. The outlaw states[32] of modern Europe in the early modern

---

32. Some may object to this term, yet these states were indeed outlaw societies. Their wars were essentially dynastic wars to which the lives and fundamental interests of most members of the societies were sacrificed.

period—Spain, France, and the Hapsburgs—or, more recently, Germany, all tried at one time to subject much of Europe to their will. They hoped to spread their religion and culture and sought dominion and glory, not to mention wealth and territory. These states were among the more effectively organized and economically advanced societies of their day. Their fault lay in their political traditions and institutions of law, property, and class structure, with their sustaining religious and moral beliefs and underlying culture. It is these things that shape a society's political will; and they are the elements that must change before a society can support a reasonable Law of Peoples.

In what follows I take up the second kind of nonideal theory, namely, societies burdened by unfavorable conditions (henceforth, *burdened societies*). Burdened societies, while they are not expansive or aggressive, lack the political and cultural traditions, the human capital and know-how, and, often, the material and technological resources needed to be well-ordered. The long-term goal of (relatively) well-ordered societies should be to bring burdened societies, like outlaw states, into the Society of well-ordered Peoples. Well-ordered peoples have a *duty* to assist burdened societies. It does not follow, however, that the only way, or the best way, to carry out this duty of assistance is by following a principle of distributive justice to regulate economic and social inequalities among societies. Most such principles do not have a defined goal, aim, or cut-off point, beyond which aid may cease.

The levels of wealth and welfare among societies may vary, and presumably do so; but adjusting those levels is not the object of the duty of assistance. Only burdened societies need help. Furthermore, not all such societies are poor, any more than all well-ordered societies are wealthy. A society with few natural resources and little wealth can be well-ordered if its political traditions, law, and property and class structure with their underlying religious and moral beliefs and culture are such as to sustain a liberal or decent society.

15.2. First Guideline for Duty of Assistance. The first guideline to consider is that a well-ordered society need not be a wealthy society. I recall here three basic points about the principle of "just savings" (within a domestic society) as I elaborated it in *A Theory of Justice*, §44.

15. Burdened Societies

(a) The purpose of a just (real) savings principle is to establish (reasonably) just basic institutions for a free constitutional democratic society (or any well-ordered society) and to secure a social world that makes possible a worthwhile life for all its citizens.

(b) Accordingly, savings may stop once just (or decent) basic institutions have been established. At this point real saving (that is, net additions to real capital of all kinds) may fall to zero; and existing stock only needs to be maintained, or replaced, and nonrenewable resources carefully husbanded for future use as appropriate. Thus, the savings rate as a constraint on current consumption is to be expressed in terms of aggregate capital accumulated, resource use forgone, and technology developed to conserve and regenerate the capacity of the natural world to sustain its human population. With these and other essential elements tallied in, a society may, of course, continue to save after this point, but it is no longer a duty of justice to do so.

(c) Great wealth is not necessary to establish just (or decent) institutions. How much is needed will depend on a society's particular history as well as on its conception of justice. Thus the levels of wealth among well-ordered peoples will not, in general, be the same.

These three features of the savings process discussed in *A Theory of Justice* bring out the similarity between the duty of assistance in the Law of Peoples and the duty of just savings in the domestic case. In each instance, the aim is to realize and preserve just (or decent) institutions, and not simply to increase, much less to maximize indefinitely, the average level of wealth, or the wealth of any society or any particular class in society. In these respects the duty of assistance and the duty of just savings express the same underlying idea.[33]

---

33. The main idea I express here draws on J. S. Mill's *The Principles of Political Economy*, 1st ed. (London, 1848), book IV, chap. 6, "The Stationary State." I follow Mill's view that the purpose of saving is to make possible a just basic structure of society; once that is safely secured, real saving (net increase in real capital) may no longer be necessary. "The art of living" is more important than "the art of getting on," to use his words. The thought that real saving and economic growth are to go on indefinitely, upwards and onwards, with no specified goal in sight, is the idea of the business class of a capitalist society. But what counts for Mill are just basic institutions and the well-being of what Mill would call "the labouring class." Mill says: ". . . the decision [between a just system of private property and socialism] will depend mainly on one consideration,

THE LAW OF PEOPLES

15.3. Second Guideline. A second guideline for thinking about how to carry out the duty of assistance is to realize that the political culture of a burdened society is all-important; and that, at the same time, there is no recipe, certainly no easy recipe, for well-ordered peoples to help a burdened society to change its political and social culture. I believe that the causes of the wealth of a people and the forms it takes lie in their political culture and in the religious, philosophical, and moral traditions that support the basic structure of their political and social institutions, as well as in the industriousness and cooperative talents of its members, all supported by their political virtues. I would further conjecture that there is no society anywhere in the world—except for marginal cases[34]—with resources so scarce that it could not, were it reasonably and rationally organized and governed, become well-ordered. Historical examples seem to indicate that resource-poor countries may do very well (e.g., Japan), while resource-rich countries may have serious difficulties (e.g., Argentina). The crucial elements that make the difference are the political culture, the political virtues and civic society of the country, its members' probity and industriousness, their capacity for innovation, and much else. Crucial also is the country's population policy: it must take care that it does not overburden its lands and economy with a larger population than it can sustain. But one way or the other, the duty of assistance is in no way diminished. What must be realized is that merely dispensing funds will not suffice to rectify basic political and social injustices (though money is often

---

viz., which of the two systems is consistent with the greatest amount of human liberty and spontaneity. After the means of subsistence are assured, the next in strength of personal wants of human beings is liberty, and (unlike physical wants which as civilization advances become more moderate and more amenable to control) it increases instead of diminishing in intensity as intelligence and the moral faculties are more developed." From the 7th and last edition of the *Principles* published in Mill's lifetime, paragraph 9 of §3 of chap. 1 of book II. What Mill says here is perfectly consistent with the Law of Peoples and its structure of political values, though I could not accept it as it stands. References to Mill's *Principles* are from the paperback edition, edited by Jonathan Riley, in Oxford World Classics (Oxford: Oxford University Press, 1994). The complete text of the *Principles* is now in *The Complete Works of John Stuart Mill*, vols. 2 and 3, Introduction by V. W. Bladen, ed. J. M. Robson (London: University of Toronto Press, Routledge and Kegan Paul, 1965).

34. Arctic Eskimos, for example, are rare enough, and need not affect our general approach. I assume their problems could be handled in an *ad hoc* way.

15. Burdened Societies

essential). But an emphasis on human rights may work to change ineffective regimes and the conduct of the rulers who have been callous about the well-being of their own people.

This insistence on human rights is supported by Amartya Sen's work on famines.[35] In his empirical study of four well-known historical cases (Bengal, 1943; Ethiopia, 1972–1974; Sahel, 1972–1973; and Bangladesh, 1974), he found that food decline need not be the main cause of famine, or even a minor cause. In the cases he studied, the drop in food production was not great enough to lead to famine given a decent government that cared for the well-being of all its people and had in place a reasonable scheme of backup entitlements provided through public institutions. The main problem was the failure of the respective governments to distribute (and supplement) what food there was. Sen concluded: "famines are economic disasters, not just food crises."[36] In other words, they are attributable to faults within the political and social structure, and its failure to institute policies to remedy the effects of shortfalls in food production. A government's allowing people to starve when it is preventable reflects a lack of concern for human rights, and well-ordered regimes as I have described them will not allow this to happen. Insisting on human rights will, it is to be hoped, help to prevent famines from developing, and will exert pressure in the direction of effective governments in a well-ordered Society of Peoples. (I note, by the way, that there would be massive starvation in every Western democracy were there no schemes in place to help the unemployed.)

Respecting human rights could also relieve population pressure within a burdened society, relative to what the economy of the society can decently sustain.[37] A decisive factor here appears to be the status

---

35. See Amartya Sen, *Poverty and Famines* (Oxford: Clarendon Press, 1981). Sen's book with Jean Drèze, *Hunger and Public Action* (Oxford: Clarendon Press, 1989), confirms these points and stresses the success of democratic regimes in coping with poverty and hunger. See their summary statement in chap. 13, p. 25. See also the important work of Partha Dasgupta, *An Inquiry into Well-Being and Destitution* (Oxford: Clarendon Press, 1993), chaps. 1, 2, and 5.

36. Sen, *Poverty and Famines*, p. 162.

37. I do not use the term "overpopulation" here since it seems to imply the idea of optimal population; but what is that? When seen as relative to what the economy can sustain, whether there is population pressure is a clear enough question. I am indebted to Amartya Sen on this point.

of women. Some societies—China is a familiar example—have imposed harsh restrictions on the size of families and have adopted other draconian measures. But there is no need to be so harsh. The simplest, most effective, most acceptable policy is to establish the elements of equal justice for women. Instructive here is the Indian state of Kerala, which in the late 1970s empowered women to vote and to participate in politics, to receive and use education, and to own and manage wealth and property. As a result, within several years Kerala's birth rate fell below China's, without invoking the coercive powers of the state.[38] Like policies have been instituted elsewhere—for example, in Bangladesh, Colombia, and Brazil—with similar results. The elements of basic justice have proven themselves essential for sound social policy. Injustice is supported by deep-seated interests and will not easily disappear; but it cannot excuse itself by pleading lack of natural resources.

To repeat, there is no easy recipe for helping a burdened society to change its political culture. Throwing funds at it is usually undesirable, and the use of force is ruled out by the Law of Peoples. But certain kinds of advice may be helpful, and burdened societies would do well to pay particular attention to the fundamental interests of women. The fact that women's status is often founded on religion, or bears a close relation to religious views,[39] is not in itself the cause of their subjection, since other causes are usually present. One may explain that all kinds of well-ordered societies affirm human rights and have at least the features of a decent consultation hierarchy or its analogue. These features require that any group representing women's fundamental interests must include a majority of women (§8.3). The idea is that any conditions of the consultation procedure that are necessary to prevent violations of the human rights of women are to be adopted. This is not a peculiarly liberal idea but one that is also common to all decent peoples.

38. See Amartya Sen, "Population: Delusion and Reality," *The New York Review of Books*, September 22, 1994, pp. 62–71. On Kerala, see pp. 70ff. China's birth rate in 1979 was 2.8; Kerala's 3.0. In 1991 these rates were 2.0 and 1.8 respectively.

39. I say this because many Muslim writers deny that Islam sanctions the inequality of women in many Muslim societies, and attribute it to various historical causes. See Leila Ahmed, *Women and Gender in Islam* (New Haven: Yale University Press, 1992).

15. Burdened Societies 111

We can, then, bring this idea to bear as a condition on offered assistance without being subject to the charge of improperly undermining a society's religion and culture. The principle here is similar to one that is always followed in regard to the claims of religion. Thus, a religion cannot claim as a justification that its intolerance of other religions is necessary for it to maintain itself. In the same way a religion cannot claim as a justification for its subjection of women that it is necessary for its survival. Basic human rights are involved, and these belong to the common institutions and practices of all liberal and decent societies.[40]

15.4. Third Guideline. The third guideline for carrying out the duty of assistance is that its aim is to help burdened societies to be able to manage their own affairs reasonably and rationally and eventually to become members of the Society of well-ordered Peoples. This defines the "target" of assistance. After it is achieved, further assistance is not required, even though the now well-ordered society may still be relatively poor. Thus the well-ordered societies giving assistance must not act paternalistically, but in measured ways that do not conflict with the final aim of assistance: freedom and equality for the formerly burdened societies.

Leaving aside the deep question of whether some forms of culture and ways of life are good in themselves, as I believe they are, it is surely a good for individuals and associations to be attached to their particular culture and to take part in its common public and civic life. In this way belonging to a particular political society, and being at home in its civic and social world, gains expression and fulfillment.[41] This is no small thing. It argues for preserving significant room for the idea of a people's self-determination and for some kind of loose or confederative form of a Society of Peoples, provided the divisive hostilities of different cultures can be tamed, as it seems they can be, by a society of well-ordered regimes. We seek a world in which ethnic hatreds leading to nationalistic wars will have ceased. A proper patriotism (§5.2) is an

---

40. See *Political Liberalism*, V: §6.
41. Ibid., V: §7.

attachment to one's people and country, and a willingness to defend its legitimate claims while fully respecting the legitimate claims of other peoples.[42] Well-ordered peoples should try to encourage such regimes.

15.5. Duty of Assistance and Affinity. A legitimate concern about the duty of assistance is whether the motivational support for following it presupposes a degree of affinity among peoples, that is, a sense of social cohesion and closeness, that cannot be expected even in a society of liberal peoples—not to mention in a society of all well-ordered peoples—with their separate languages, religions, and cultures. The members of a single domestic society share a common central government and political culture, and the moral learning of political concepts and principles works most effectively in the context of society-wide political and social institutions that are part of their shared daily life.[43] Taking part in shared institutions every day, members of the same society should be able to resolve political conflicts and problems within the society on a common basis in terms of public reason.

It is the task of the statesman to struggle against the potential lack of affinity among different peoples and try to heal its causes insofar as they derive from past domestic institutional injustices, and from the hostility among social classes inherited through their common history and antagonisms. Since the affinity among peoples is naturally weaker (as a matter of human psychology) as society-wide institutions include a larger area and cultural distances increase, the statesman must continually combat these shortsighted tendencies.[44]

What encourages the statesman's work is that relations of affinity are not a fixed thing, but may continually grow stronger over time as peoples come to work together in cooperative institutions they have de-

42. These are specified by the Law of Peoples.
43. Joshua Cohen, "A More Democratic Liberalism," *Michigan Law Review*, vol. 92, no. 6 (May 1994), pp. 1532–33.
44. Here I draw on a psychological principle that social learning of moral attitudes supporting political institutions works most effectively through society-wide shared institutions and practices. The learning weakens under the conditions mentioned in the text. In a realistic utopia this psychological principle sets limits to what can sensibly be proposed as the content of the Law of Peoples.

16. On Distributive Justice among Peoples

veloped. It is characteristic of liberal and decent peoples that they seek a world in which all peoples have a well-ordered regime. At first we may suppose this aim is moved by each people's *self-interest*, for such regimes are not dangerous but peaceful and cooperative. Yet as cooperation between peoples proceeds apace they may come to care about each other, and affinity between them becomes stronger. Hence, they are no longer moved simply by self-interest but by mutual concern for each other's way of life and culture, and they become willing to make sacrifices for each other. This mutual caring is the outcome of their fruitful cooperative efforts and common experiences over a considerable period of time.

The relatively narrow circle of mutually caring peoples in the world today may expand over time and must never be viewed as fixed. Gradually, peoples are no longer moved by self-interest alone or by their mutual caring alone, but come to affirm their liberal and decent civilization and culture, until eventually they become ready to act on the *ideals and principles* their civilization specifies. Religious toleration has historically first appeared as a *modus vivendi* between hostile faiths, later becoming a moral principle shared by civilized peoples and recognized by their leading religions. The same is true of the abolition of slavery and serfdom, the rule of law, the right to war only in self-defense, and the guarantee of human rights. These become ideals and principles of liberal and decent civilizations, and principles of the Law of all civilized Peoples.

§16. On Distributive Justice among Peoples

16.1. Equality among Peoples. There are two views about this. One holds that equality is just, or a good in itself. The Law of Peoples, on the other hand, holds that inequalities are not always unjust, and that when they are, it is because of their unjust effects on the basic structure of the Society of Peoples, and on relations among peoples and among their members.[45] We saw the great importance of this basic

---

45. My discussion of inequality is greatly indebted, as so often, to T. M. Scanlon.

structure when discussing the need for toleration of decent nonliberal peoples (§§7.2–7.3).

I note three reasons for being concerned with inequality in domestic society and consider how each applies to the Society of Peoples. One reason for reducing inequalities within a domestic society is to relieve the suffering and hardships of the poor. Yet this does not require that all persons be equal in wealth. In itself, it doesn't matter how great the gap between rich and poor may be. What matters are the consequences. In a liberal domestic society that gap cannot be wider than the criterion of reciprocity allows, so that the least advantaged (as the third liberal principle requires) have sufficient all-purpose means to make intelligent and effective use of their freedoms and to lead reasonable and worthwhile lives. When that situation exists, there is no further need to narrow the gap. Similarly, in the basic structure of the Society of Peoples, once the duty of assistance is satisfied and all peoples have a working liberal or decent government, there is again no reason to narrow the gap between the average wealth of different peoples.

A second reason for narrowing the gap between rich and poor within a domestic society is that such a gap often leads to some citizens being stigmatized and treated as inferiors, and that is unjust. Thus, in a liberal or decent society, conventions that establish ranks to be recognized socially by expressions of deference must be guarded against. They may unjustly wound the self-respect of those not so recognized. The same would be true of the basic structure of the Society of Peoples should citizens in one country feel inferior to the citizens of another because of its greater riches, *provided* that those feelings are justified. Yet when the duty of assistance is fulfilled, and each people has its own liberal or decent government, these feelings are unjustified. For then each people adjusts the significance and importance of the wealth of its own society for itself. If it is not satisfied, it can continue to increase savings, or, if that is not feasible, borrow from other members of the Society of Peoples.

A third reason for considering the inequalities among peoples concerns the important role of fairness in the political processes of the basic structure of the Society of Peoples. In the domestic case this concern is evident in securing the fairness of elections and of political opportu-

16. On Distributive Justice among Peoples

nities to run for public office. Public financing of political parties and campaigns tries to address these matters. Also, when we speak of fair equality of opportunity, more than formal legal equality is meant. We mean roughly that background social conditions are such that each citizen, regardless of class or origin, should have the same chance of attaining a favored social position, given the same talents and willingness to try. Policies for achieving this fair equality of opportunity include, for example, securing fair education for all and eliminating unjust discrimination. Fairness also plays an important role in the political processes of the basic structure of the Society of Peoples, analogous to, though not the same as, its role in the domestic case.

Basic fairness among peoples is given by their being represented equally in the second original position with its veil of ignorance. Thus the representatives of peoples will want to preserve the independence of their own society and its equality in relation to others. In the working of organizations and loose confederations of peoples, inequalities are designed to serve the many ends that peoples share (§4.5). In this case the larger and smaller peoples will be ready to make larger and smaller contributions and to accept proportionately larger and smaller returns. In addition, the parties will formulate guidelines for setting up cooperative organizations, and will agree to standards of fairness for trade as well as to certain provisions for mutual assistance. Should these cooperative organizations have unjustified distributive effects, these would have to be corrected in the basic structure of the Society of Peoples.

16.2. Distributive Justice among Peoples. Several principles have been proposed to regulate inequalities among peoples and prevent their becoming excessive. Two of these are discussed by Charles Beitz.[46] Another is Thomas Pogge's Egalitarian Principle,[47] which is similar in many respects to Beitz's second principle of redistributive justice.

---

46. Charles Beitz, *Political Theory and International Relations* (Princeton: Princeton Univerity Press, 1979).

47. Pogge's global egalitarian principle as set out in "An Egalitarian Law of Peoples," PAPA, 23:3 (Summer 1994) is not a statement of his own preferred view, but one that he sees as internal to *A Theory of Justice*. It states how he thinks the international system should be treated if it were treated as the domestic one is treated in *A Theory of Justice*.

These are suggestive and much-discussed principles, and I need to say why I don't accept them. But, of course, I do accept Beitz's and Pogge's goals of attaining liberal or decent institutions, securing human rights, and meeting basic needs. These I believe are covered by the duty of assistance discussed in the preceding section.

First let me state Beitz's two principles. He distinguishes between what he calls "the resource redistribution principle" and a "global distribution principle." The distinction between them is as follows: suppose first, that the production of goods and services in all countries is *autarkic,* that is, each country relies entirely on its own labor and resources without trade of any kind. Beitz holds that some areas have ample resources, and societies in such areas can be expected to make the best use of their natural riches and prosper. Other societies are not so fortunate, and despite their best efforts, may attain only a meager level of well-being because of resource scarcities.[48] Beitz views the resource redistribution principle as giving each society a fair chance to establish just political institutions and an economy that can fulfill its members' basic needs. Affirming this principle "provides assurance to persons in resource-poor societies that their adverse fate will not prevent them from realizing economic conditions sufficient to support just social institutions and to protect human rights."[49] He doesn't explain how the countries with sufficient resources are to redistribute them to resource-poor countries; but no matter.

The global distribution principle that Beitz discusses concerns a situation where production is no longer autarkic and there are flows of trade and services between countries. He believes that in this case a global system of cooperation already exists. In this instance Beitz proposes that a global difference applies (analogous to the principle used in the domestic case in *A Theory of Justice*), giving a principle of distributive justice between societies.[50] Since he believes that the wealthier countries are so because of the greater resources available to them, presumably the global principle (with its scheme of taxation, say) redistributes the benefits of greater resources to resource-poor peoples.

48. Beitz, *Political Theory and International Relations,* p. 137.
49. Ibid., p. 141.
50. Ibid., pp. 153–163.

16. On Distributive Justice among Peoples

However, because, as I have said, the crucial element in how a country fares is its political culture—its members' political and civic virtues—and not the level of its resources,[51] the arbitrariness of the distribution of natural resources causes no difficulty. I therefore feel we need not discuss Beitz's resource redistribution principle. On the other hand, if a global principle of distributive justice for the Law of Peoples is meant to apply to our world as it is with its extreme injustices, crippling poverty, and inequalities, its appeal is understandable. But if it is meant to apply continuously without end—without a target, as one might say—in the hypothetical world arrived at after the duty of assistance is fully satisfied, its appeal is questionable. In the latter hypothetical world a global principle gives what we would, I think, regard as unacceptable results. Consider two illustrative cases:

Case (i): two liberal or decent countries are at the same level of wealth (estimated, say, in primary goods) and have the same size population. The first decides to industrialize and to increase its rate of (real) saving, while the second does not. Being content with things as they are, and preferring a more pastoral and leisurely society, the second reaffirms its social values. Some decades later the first country is twice as wealthy as the second. Assuming, as we do, that both societies are liberal or decent, and their peoples free and responsible, and able to make their own decisions, should the industrializing country be taxed to give funds to the second? According to the duty of assistance there would be no tax, and that seems right; whereas with a global egalitarian principle without target, there would always be a flow of taxes as long as the wealth of one people was less than that of the other. This seems unacceptable.

Case (ii) is parallel to (i) except that at the start the rate of population growth in both liberal or decent societies is rather high. Both countries provide the elements of equal justice for women, as required by a well-ordered society; but the first happens to stress these elements, and its women flourish in the political and economic world. As a con-

---

51. This is powerfully (if sometimes a little too strongly) argued by David Landes in his book *The Wealth and Poverty of Nations* (New York: W. W. Norton, 1998). See his discussion of the OPEC countries, pp. 411–414. Landes thinks that the discovery of oil reserves has been a "monumental misfortune" for the Arab world (p. 414).

sequence, they gradually reach zero population growth that allows for an increasing level of wealth over time. The second society, although it also has these elements of equal justice, because of its prevailing religious and social values, freely held by its women, does not reduce the rate of population growth and it remains rather high.[52] As before, some decades later, the first society is twice as wealthy as the second. Given that both societies are liberal or decent, and their peoples free and responsible, and able to make their own decisions, the duty of assistance does not require taxes from the first, now wealthier society, while the global egalitarian principle without target would. Again, this latter position seems unacceptable.

The crucial point is that the role of the duty of assistance is to assist burdened societies to become full members of the Society of Peoples and to be able to determine the path of their own future for themselves. It is a principle of *transition*, in much the same way that the principle of real saving over time in domestic society is a principle of transition. As explained in §15.2, real saving is meant to lay the foundation for a just basic structure of society, at which point it may cease. In the society of the Law of Peoples the duty of assistance holds until all societies have achieved just liberal or decent basic institutions. Both the duty of real saving and the duty of assistance are defined by a *target* beyond which they no longer hold. They assure the essentials of *political autonomy:* the political autonomy of free and equal citizens in the domestic case, the political autonomy of free and equal liberal and decent peoples in the Society of Peoples.

This raises the question of the difference between a global egalitarian principle and the duty of assistance.[53] That principle is designed

---

52. Because these basic elements of equal justice for women (including liberty of conscience and freedom of religion) are in place, I assume that the rate of population growth is voluntary, meaning that women are not coerced by their religion or their place in the social structure. This obviously calls for more discussion than I can give here.

53. For a statement of Pogge's own view see his "Human Flourishing and Universal Justice," to appear in *Social Philosophy,* 16:1 (1999). Pogge tells me that here his view does have a target and a cutoff point. I mention in the text that this raises the question of how great the difference may be between the duty of assistance and Pogge's global egalitarian view in "Universal Justice." Without the details of his discussion before us, I cannot discuss it further here.

16. On Distributive Justice among Peoples 119

to help the poor all over the world, and it proposes a General Resource Dividend (GRD) on each society to pay into an international fund to be administered for this purpose. The question to ask about it is whether the principle has a target and a cutoff point. The duty of assistance has both: it seeks to raise the world's poor until they are either free and equal citizens of a reasonably liberal society or members of a decent hierarchical society. That is its target. It also has by design a cutoff point, since for each burdened society the principle ceases to apply once the target is reached. A global egalitarian principle could work in a similar way. Call it an egalitarian principle with target. How great is the difference between the duty of assistance and this egalitarian principle? Surely there is a point at which a people's basic needs (estimated in primary goods) are fulfilled and a people can stand on its own. There may be disagreement about when this point comes, but that there is such a point is crucial to the Law of Peoples and its duty of assistance. Depending on how the respective targets and cutoff points are defined, the principles could be much the same, with largely practical matters of taxation and administration to distinguish between them.

16.3. Contrast with Cosmopolitan View. The Law of Peoples assumes that every society has in its population a sufficient array of human capabilities, each in sufficient number so that the society has enough potential human resources to realize just institutions. The final political end of society is to become fully just and stable for the right reasons. Once that end is reached, the Law of Peoples prescribes no further target such as, for example, to raise the standard of living beyond what is necessary to sustain those institutions. Nor is there any justifiable reason for any society's asking for more than is necessary to sustain just institutions, or for further reduction of material inequalities among societies.

These remarks illustrate the contrast between the Law of Peoples and a cosmopolitan view (§11). The ultimate concern of a cosmopolitan view is the well-being of individuals and not the justice of societies. According to that view there is still a question concerning the need for further global distribution, even after each domestic society has achieved internally just institutions. The simplest illustrative case is to suppose that each of two societies satisfies internally the two principles of justice found in *A Theory of Justice*. In these two societies, the worst-off representative person in one is worse off than the worst-off representative person in the other. Suppose it were possible, through some global redistribution that would allow both societies to continue to satisfy the two principles of justice internally, to improve the lot of the worst-off representative person in the first society. Should we prefer the redistribution to the original distribution?

The Law of Peoples is indifferent between the two distributions. The cosmopolitan view, on the other hand, is not indifferent. It is concerned with the well-being of individuals, and hence with whether the well-being of the globally worst-off person can be improved. What is important to the Law of Peoples is the justice and stability for the right reasons of liberal and decent societies, living as members of a Society of well-ordered Peoples.

[11]
Enough for the Future

LUKAS H. MEYER AND DOMINIC ROSER

1. Introduction

What do we owe to future people as a matter of social justice? We follow a broad understanding of intergenerational justice: justice considerations are relevant to decisions that are likely to affect the existence, number and identity of future people if—with respect to these decisions—future generations can be viewed as holding legitimate claims or rights against present generations, who in turn stand under correlative duties to future generations. This chapter proposes a framework for the normative interpretation and assessment of intergenerational relations: we will delineate how to understand the welfare rights and distributive justice claims of future people vis-à-vis currently living people. We argue that we have strong and particular reasons for interpreting intergenerational justice in terms of a sufficientarian conception of justice. The sufficientarian interpretation of currently living people's duties of intergenerational justice (and future people's correlative rights) can guide our decision-making with respect to decisions that will have an impact on both the well-being of future people as well as the composition of future people, that is, on the number, existence, and identity of future people.

We will begin our discussion of intergenerational justice by distinguishing between sufficientarian and egalitarian conceptions of justice. We will then (in sections 3 and 4) argue in favour of a sufficientarian understanding of intergenerational justice in response to the so-called non-identity problem. Our argument here has two stages. First, we argue that by relying on a threshold conception of harm we can respond to the non-identity problem. Second, we argue that we have reasons to specify the threshold in terms of a sufficientarian understanding of justice. Finally, in section 5, we submit further reasons for intergenerational sufficientarianism.

2. Egalitarian and Sufficientarian Conceptions of Justice

According to Thomas W. Scanlon, egalitarian (or 'strictly egalitarian'—as we will call them) reasons are 'unspecific in not being concerned with the absolute level of benefits that individuals enjoy'. Rather, on the basis of these reasons inequalities are to be objected because relative differences between the states of persons are seen as something 'which is itself to be eliminated or reduced.'[1] Proponents of sufficientarianism, in contrast, hold the view that what primarily matters is that everybody is well off, i.e. has well-being above a certain given threshold which is considered 'sufficient' (this may or may not be a 'minimal' threshold). They also hold that one person being worse off than another is irrelevant if those persons are both well off. They reject the egalitarian understanding, at least for those people who are well off. Of course, equality and sufficiency are not the only promising distributive principles but, together with priority, they are deemed the most worthy of discussion in the contemporary debate. And so we will focus on these principles.

A strictly egalitarian position by which we understand a position that holds equality to be of intrinsic value is open to the so-called levelling-down-objection.[2] This objection is based on the fact that such an egalitarian understanding can recommend that the state of the better-off persons be worsened for the sake of equality even if this is not good for anyone. Indeed, most such strict egalitarians believe that a state of affairs in which nobody is well off but they are equally so, is better, in one respect, than a state in which some people are not well off and others are well off. For this such egalitarians assume that equality has intrinsic value. They will quickly want to add that, of course, equality at a low level of well-being is only better than inequality at a high level of well-being *in one respect*. In an all-things-considered view the other respects—such as the total sum of well-being—might easily outweigh the importance of equality. Thus also such a value-pluralist egalitarian might, when considering all things, prefer not to level down. But adding such value-pluralism to egalitarianism does not pull the sting out of the levelling-down-objection. For the objection already concerns the judgement that a state with equal but low well-being is better than a state with high but unequal well-being *in one respect*: the value-pluralist egalitarian, too, is committed

---

[1] Scanlon (2005: 6).
[2] If we follow Parfit (1997, 2000) deontological egalitarianism is not open to this objection. For a critical discussion of this claim, see Lippert-Rasmussen (2007).

to the view that in at least one respect the former state of affairs is better even though it is better for no one and worse for some. By claiming that a state of affairs can be better in some respect, even though it is better for no one, such a strictly egalitarian position must give up a person-affecting view, i.e. the view that the moral quality of a state of affairs must crucially depend on how the interests of (particular and actual) persons are being affected.[3]

The levelling-down-objection may seem to speak generally against egalitarian intuitions or, put more carefully, one may attempt to suggest a reformulation of these intuitions and without relying on the notion that what matters is equality as such. Derek Parfit's priority view is such a reformulation.[4] One plausible version of his priority view is:

Priority View: To benefit persons matters more the worse off the person is to whom the benefits accrue, the more people are being benefited and the greater the benefits in question.

According to the priority view equality, as such, does not matter. The view is thus not open to the levelling-down-objection. At the same time the priority

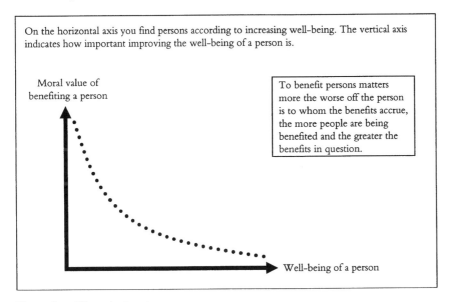

Figure 8.1. The priority view

---

[3] See also n 14 below. The term 'crucially' is of course less than precise and the reader is referred to Holtug (2007: 139–46) who carefully spells out how egalitarianism (and possibly prioritarianism) conflict with different versions of person-affecting views.

[4] See Parfit (1997: 213).

view clearly has a built-in tendency towards equality. To this extent it is correctly described as non-relational egalitarianism. The reason for this built-in tendency towards equality is found in the fact that the priority view accepts the following egalitarian condition: if X is worse off than Y, we have at least a *prima facie* reason for promoting the well-being of X rather than of Y. Even if prioritarians do not see anything intrinsically bad in social, economic, and other differences, their priority view is a derivatively egalitarian view. In the following, we will understand egalitarian conceptions of justice to include those that are based on strictly egalitarian reasons (reflecting the notion of the intrinsic value of equality) as well as those that give greater weight to benefiting less well-off persons, where these reasons apply quite apart from how well off these persons are.

The position of weak sufficientarianism qualifies the priority view. We can distinguish between weak and strong interpretations of sufficientarianism.[5] While, as we will explain below, the position of strong sufficientarianism qualifies the maximin view (i.e. lexical priority ought to be given to the worst off), the position of weak sufficientarianism can be understood as a qualified priority view: the latter claims that the priority to be given to the position of the not well off decreases to zero at a certain threshold of well-being, at which people are sufficiently well off, whereas the priority view claims that this is only the case if people's well-being is perfect, that is, when it simply cannot be improved further. Accordingly we can summarize the position of weak sufficientarianism as follows:

Weak Sufficientarianism: To benefit persons below the threshold matters more the worse off they are. Above the threshold there are no priorities. The priority to be given to the position of the not well off decreases to zero at the threshold and above the threshold there are no priorities. To benefit persons matters more the more people are being benefited and the greater the benefits in question.

As with the priority view, the position of sufficientarianism also holds that equality as such does not matter. And, likewise, sufficientarianism has a built-in tendency towards equality. However, this tendency is restricted in the following way: To benefit person X is more important than to benefit person Y, if X is below the threshold and if Y is better off than X. On a low level of well-being, equality is of derivative value. So, concerning the improvement of the position of those who are less well off than others, sufficientarianism holds both a positive and a negative thesis: it is more important to benefit people below the threshold than above the threshold (this being the positive thesis;

---

[5] So far the discussion has not led to a consensus on the concept of sufficientarianism. See, generally, Frankfurt (1987); Crisp (2003); Casal (2007).

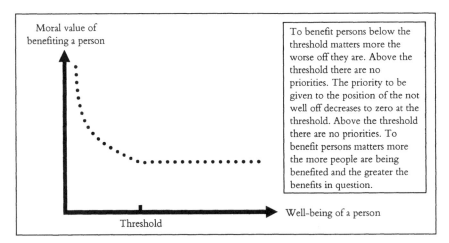

Figure 8.2. Weak sufficientarianism

in our versions of sufficientarianism people below the threshold get treated according to the priority view), and above the threshold the improvement of the position of the less well off is of no particular concern (this being the negative thesis).[6]

As explained, the position of weak sufficientarianism can be understood as a qualified priority view. The position of strong sufficientarianism, however, can be understood as a qualified maximin view. Strong sufficientarianism differs from weak sufficientarianism in how it interprets the priority of persons below the threshold. Strong sufficientarianism attributes much stronger priority, namely lexical priority, to those whose well-being is below the threshold (while according to weak sufficientarianism the priority decreases to zero at the threshold). This amounts to giving a person just below the threshold absolute priority over a person just above the threshold. Versions of sufficientarianism are stronger the greater the priority they attribute to those below the threshold. With a lexically prioritarian threshold strong sufficientarianism also rejects the view that it always matters more to benefit persons the more people are being benefited and the greater the benefits in question.

According to both weak sufficientarianism and the priority view, we ought to benefit those who are already well off if it is the case that, given the number of those benefited by our action and the extent of benefits accruing to them, we will do more good even if we take into account that benefiting

---

[6] For a general distinction between a positive and negative thesis for characterising sufficientarianism see Casal (2007: 297f.): 'The positive thesis stresses the importance of people living above a certain threshold, free from deprivation. The negative thesis denies the relevance of certain additional distributive requirements.'

people below the threshold has particular weight. This is what proponents of strong sufficientarianism reject and also those who defend the maximin principle.[7] In contrast to maximin strong sufficientarianism does not propose that the smallest improvement of the smallest number of the worst off ought to be given absolute priority over any improvement of people in the next worst off group. Strong sufficientarianism qualifies this view by making two assumptions:

Strong Sufficientarianism: First, the improvement in well-being of those whose level of well-being is below the threshold has absolute or lexical priority; and to benefit persons below the threshold matters more the worse off they are. Second, both below and above the threshold it matters more to benefit persons the more persons are being benefited and the greater the benefits in question. But: Trade-offs between persons above and below the threshold are precluded.

The position of strong sufficientarianism is absolutist in the sense that it attributes absolute or lexical priority to the improvement of the not well off. The position is single-level in so far as it attributes special moral significance to only one level of well-being.[8] As the position is single-level, it can be

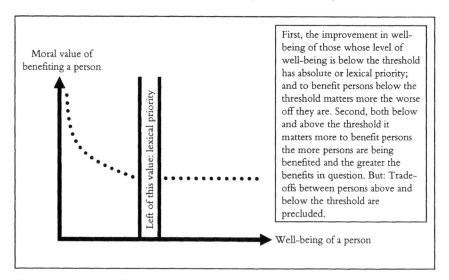

Figure 8.3. Strong sufficientarianism

---

[7] However, the maximin principle does not specify an absolute level of well-being for determining who ought to be given priority but rather demands that whoever is the worst-off be given lexical priority. Thus, maximin can demand the prioritarian treatment of people who are well off or very well off.

[8] Sufficientarian conceptions can be distinguished according to whether they specify one or more threshold values. For this and further differentiations see Meyer and Roser (2006: 235f.).

heterogeneous by specifying different principles of distribution below and above the threshold.[9]

To thresholds and especially such ones that designate an absolute priority—as is characteristic of the position of strong sufficientarianism—Richard Arneson[10] and others have objected that we cannot avoid an arbitrary specification of such priority thresholds. It can further be criticized, that such thresholds are incompatible with our distributive convictions' being non-heterogeneous—that is, that they all can be accounted for by means of one principle of distribution. The existence of thresholds where a tiny change (such as enhancing the well-being of an individual just below the threshold so as to place her just above the threshold) dramatically changes our evaluation of the total outcome, can be claimed to be alien to our moral intuitions.

So, if we cannot specify such a privileged level of well-being, as Arneson and others contend, the priority view seems to provide the best account of our basic intuition that we ought to give some priority to benefiting people who are not well off. According to the priority view a bad life in terms of well-being is rightly considered a morally bad state of affairs. At the same time we do not draw a categorical (qualitative) difference between a good and a bad life. Rather, formulations such as 'he fares badly' or 'she is doing well' are imprecise formulations that each refer (usually in a context-dependent manner) to a whole range of differing levels of well-being and where the border between the different levels does not have any special moral significance.

We therefore assume that the priority view is a plausible candidate for an adequate principle of distribution among contemporaries. However, in the following subsections 3 to 5 we show that we have special and strong reasons for a sufficientarian conception of intergenerational justice. We assume that one can justify a threshold, namely as specified by strong sufficientarianism, for intergenerational relations.[11]

---

[9] And any multi-level sufficientarianism can, of course, be even more heterogeneous by specifying a different distributional principle above every relevant threshold.

[10] See esp. Arneson (1999), (2000).

[11] The most promising approach for justifying a priority threshold relies upon the distinction between needs and (mere) wishes. Here, a short sketch of the argument may suffice: If person X has a need for something (needs something) that person Y wishes to have but does not need, then, *prima facie*, we ought to fulfil the needs of person X. But how do we distinguish between needs and mere wishes? Whether a need deserves the moral priority as indicated entirely depends upon whether the needy person would be badly off if the need in question is not fulfilled. Thus, an interpretation of the moral significance of needs suggests the commitment to a morally privileged priority line of well-being. If person X has the need for something that person Y wishes to have but does not need—in the sense that person X would not be well off if his need is not fulfilled, but person Y would still be well off if his wish is not fulfilled—then fulfilling the need of person X is *prima facie* more important than fulfilling the wish of Y. Of course, we would have to defend the argument as sketched against a good number of

Our discussion so far in section 2 enables us to specify what we will understand by egalitarian and sufficientarian conceptions of justice: Egalitarian conceptions comprise first those that include strictly egalitarian reasons for action as Scanlon understands them—reflecting the notion of equality as having intrinsic value—and, secondly, those conceptions that have a continuous tendency to lead to equality, and in particular the priority view. Conceptions of weak and strong sufficientarianism differ from both egalitarian understandings. Sufficientarian conceptions have a tendency to lead to equality only below the threshold. Above the threshold neither improving the position of the worse off nor even promoting equality as such are of concern. To simplify matters, we will identify sufficientarian justice with strong sufficientarianism. The conception of strong sufficientarianism differs most clearly from both egalitarian understandings. Furthermore, strong sufficientarianism differs from both weak sufficientarianism and the priority view in precluding trade offs between persons above and below the threshold.

We start our discussion by inquiring into particular reasons for holding that a sufficientarian understanding of justice is appropriate for the relations between currently living people and future non-contemporaries. We will then take up the question of the relevance of certain reasons often cited in favour of international sufficientarianism. These reasons, we hope to show, speak more strongly in favour of intergenerational than international sufficientarianism. We shall invite attention, too, to the fact that some of the more common instrumental reasons in favour of an egalitarian conception of justice are irrelevant in the intergenerational realm.

3. A Specific Case for Sufficientarianism (1): Responding to the Non-Identity Problem

A particular reason for holding a sufficientarian understanding of intergenerational justice relies upon a certain response to the so-called non-identity problem.[12] The non-identity problem rests upon the contingency of future people upon currently living people's decisions and actions. We know, of course, that when we harm future people's interests and violate their rights, specific persons are harmed. But the decision we make often counts as a

objections. Additionally, we would have to show that the argument will justify a substantial threshold that has absolute priority. For that we would also have to specify what activities or capabilities (or secure access to what goods) are necessary for a sufficiently good life.

[12] See Schwartz (1978); Kavka (1982); and esp. Parfit (1984), part IV.

necessary condition of the very existence of this genetically and numerically specific set of people at some future point in time. Consider a policy of making intensive and extensive use of exhaustible resources for the aim of increasing the welfare of currently living people. If the policy is criticized for harming future people on the ground that this policy will predictably worsen their conditions of life and, thus, is likely to violate their welfare rights, a defender of the policy could reply by saying: many, if not all of our actions have (indirect) effects not only on the conditions of life, but also on the composition of future persons, that is, on the number, existence, and identity of future persons. This is also true for actions that allegedly harm future persons. If the omission of the allegedly harmed action meant that the allegedly harmed person did not come into existence, then that person cannot be said to have been harmed by this action—or, at any rate, not according to the normal understanding of harm.[13] With respect to persons whose existence is dependent upon the allegedly harming action, they cannot be worse off owing to this action than they would have been had this action not been carried out, for in that case they would not have existed.

In responding to the non-identity problem and the skepticism linked to it with respect to the very possibility of future people having welfare rights vis-à-vis those currently living, we develop a two-stage argument. First, we introduce and defend a threshold notion of harm. Second, we argue that a (strongly) sufficientarian interpretation of the threshold is to be preferred.

A threshold understanding of harm (as an element of what we call the combined view of harm) allows us to justify the following propositions: The dependency (or contingency) of the number and specific identity of future people upon our decisions does not matter where the question is our potentially harming future people's interests and violating their rights. Considerations of justice, namely the welfare rights claims of future people vis-à-vis currently living people can guide us in choosing among long-term policies. Finally, such considerations can also guide prospective parents in deciding whether they ought to revise their decision to conceive out of regard for the children they would thereby beget.

These widely held convictions can be supported by an interpretation of harm that requires a subjunctive comparison with a threshold as its baseline (hereinafter: subjunctive-threshold interpretation). We presuppose a person-affecting view of ethics, which holds that the moral quality of an action has

[13] The common understanding is the subjunctive-historical interpretation of harm: An action (or inaction) at time t_1 harms someone only if the agent causes (allows) this person to be worse off at some later time t_2 than the person would have been at t_2 had the agent not interacted with (or acted with respect to) this person at all. For a detailed discussion see Meyer (2003: 147–49 and 155–58).

to be assessed on the basis of how it affects the interests of particular and actual persons. In the context of intergenerational justice, the person-affecting view has the implication that only the rights and interests of those persons whose identity is beyond manipulation by the acts (or social policies) under evaluation are to be regarded as morally relevant.[14] The person-affecting view stands in contrast to an impersonal view according to which the value of states of affairs is not reducible to their effects on the interests of actual people.

Some philosophers hold the view that future people whose existence depends upon currently living people's actions cannot have rights vis-à-vis the latter people's actions. Others argue that currently living people can violate the rights of future people even if the former cannot harm the latter.[15] If currently living people cannot affect the welfare of future people, future people cannot have welfare rights vis-à-vis currently living people. Or we can attempt to limit the practical significance of the non-identity problem. Some have suggested limiting the relevant actions to those that are not only likely but indeed necessary conditions of the existence of the concerned person.[16] Or, and this is the response we argue for, we may delineate an alternative understanding of harm, the so-called threshold conception of harm,[17] according to which future people can be said to be harmed by currently living people's actions even if these actions are among the necessary conditions of the existence, identity or number of future people. According to a threshold understanding of harm an action harms a person if as a consequence of that action the person falls under a normatively defined threshold—this is to be understood as a sufficient condition of harming a person.[18] The threshold understanding is unaffected by the non-identity problem, for here the finding of harm does not require a hypothetical comparison with the situation that would have occurred in the absence of the harming action. Such a notion of harm limits the practical significance of the non-identity problem to different degrees depending upon how the threshold is substantially defined.[19]

---

[14] For the person-affecting view see esp. Heyd (1992: 80–90 and passim). As Heyd we do not believe in a knock-down argument for the person-affecting and against the impersonal. Rather, by relying upon the method of wide reflective equilibrium the person-affecting view is to be assessed in comparison to an impersonal view, namely as an element of a philosophical account of, *inter alia*, intergenerational justice—taking into account their respective implications in dependence upon other assumptions (see Daniels (1979)).

[15] Kumar (2003).   [16] Roberts (1998).

[17] This understanding can be expressed in the formula: an action (or inaction) at time t_1 harms someone only if the agent thereby causes (allows) this person's life to fall below some specified threshold. See also Shiffrin (1999).

[18] Meyer (2003: 152–8).   [19] Meyer (2008: section 4).

The threshold interpretation of harm relies on the idea that we have a general duty to people not to cause them to be worse off than they ought to be. By our actions and omissions we can cause a person to be worse off than *that* person is entitled to be. The threshold interpretation of harm relies, *inter alia*, on our being able to specify a standard of well-being that enables us to assess the likely consequences of a long-term policy as harming future people. The threshold conception presupposes our being able to describe positively a level of well-being in such a way that a person's right is violated if we do not fulfill our negative duty to refrain from carrying out actions that would cause this person to fall below the specified standard. In addition, and in accordance with this understanding of harm, we can stand under the positive duty of seeing to it that persons reach a level of well-being at or above the threshold level of well-being. In so far as our specifying the relevant level of well-being reflects the idea of people *qua* people having rights vis-à-vis currently living people, our correlative duties set a normative framework that describes the level of protection owed to future people as bearers of general (human) rights.

In the following we will argue that a (strongly) sufficientarian interpretation of the threshold is to be preferred. While the threshold standard can substantively be defined in numerous ways we will argue that neither of the egalitarian conceptions of justice, by itself, can plausibly define the standard. But before we turn to this second stage of our argument for intergenerational sufficientarianism we would like to point out that the proposed solution to the non-identity problem also provides plausible guidance in the contexts of both procreational decision-making and population policies and with respect to the question whether we ought to bring into existence those people who are best off. Joined with the person-affecting view the threshold conception does not support the claim that if a possible person were to have a good enough life, but a different person could instead be brought into existence who would have an even better life, there is then an obligation to bring into existence the second child, rather than the first.[20] This is true for individual decisions about procreation as well as for collective policy decisions. Under the named conditions present generations have no obligation to bring into

---

[20] The priority view does not specify a threshold. Joined with the person-affecting approach the priority view will require that actual persons are to be taken into account according to how well off or less than well off they are—and likewise for future people from the time of their conception. This is also how we can interpret a strictly egalitarian understanding that takes equality to be intrinsically valuable: in conjunction with a person-affecting approach such an understanding will require that we diminish the relative differences among actual (future) people. However, such an egalitarian understanding that takes relative differences seriously can also be understood to specify a threshold such that future people have a claim to be not much worse off than either their contemporaries or the currently living people. For a discussion see below, section 4.

existence only those whose lives, among possible future persons, would be optimal, or even the obligation to bring into existence those whose lives would be comparatively better.

The following example illustrates this:[21] A woman knows that she is suffering from a particular disease which means that if she conceives a child now, that child will have a certain slight handicap, but will enjoy a life above the threshold, however specified. Fortunately, there is a treatment for this disease assuring that afterwards the woman will be able to conceive a perfectly healthy child. The treatment lasts three months. There is, thus, no way that this *particular* child can be born without the handicap. Can the woman be said to owe it to her child to postpone conception until after she has been treated for the disease? According to the threshold conception of harm, she cannot be said to owe this to her child.[22] She might, however, have good reasons to decide to receive the medical treatment and conceive later. These reasons will reflect her interests and those of her partner as well as the interests of other present and future people.[23] Such interests may well be important enough to give rise to an obligation on the part of the parents, namely, to postpone conception until after the treatment. We can then have obligations not to bring into existence persons whose lives, though still (far) above the threshold, are less worth living than the lives of others whom we might bring into existence in different circumstances, but these obligations are not grounded on considerations of harm to the future children in question.

To support the claim that parents *do* owe it to their prospective child to bring into existence the possible child who, among the options available to them, enjoys the highest level of well-being, we will have to rely on a different notion of harm—namely a notion of harm based upon the comparison of the state of a person to the counterfactual state of another person who could have been brought into existence instead.[24] Analogously, decisions concerning long-term policies are likely to have an impact on the size of the future population. Thus, if we wish to support a claim analogous to that just made with respect to the parents at the collective level, namely, that we owe it to

---

[21] This is a variation of Parfit's example of 'The 14-Year-Old Girl'. See Parfit (1984: 358, 364).

[22] See Meyer (1997a: 203–7); Woodward (1986: 815, n. 12); Woodward (1987: 808f.).

[23] According to the priority view people's claims to improvements in their well-being are the stronger, the worse off they are. If a person comes to existence and that person is not well off, others will stand under the corresponding duties. Conceiving a person who is likely not to be well off (due to genetic or other medical causes) will give rise to especially high demands on that person's future contemporaries. Analogously, a strictly egalitarian understanding requiring that relative differences be diminished will justify strong claims when a person comes into existence who is much worse off than most of his contemporaries.

[24] See Parfit's 'same number quality claim' (principle Q) in Parfit (1984: 360); Kavka (1982: 98f.).

possible future people to bring into existence those who will enjoy the highest level of well-being, we will also allow for different numbers.[25] The relevant understanding of harm can be expressed in the following formula: Having brought about a person's existence at time t_1, the agent thereby harms someone only if the agent causes this person to be worse off at some later time t_2 than other persons—whose existence the agent could have brought about instead—would have been at t_2 had the agent acted differently.[26]

If we follow this understanding of harm, a person whose quality of life is above the threshold will be considered harmed if there is a possible state of affairs in which, although this person would not have existed, another person or other persons would have existed and would have realized an even higher quality of life. According to the person-affecting approach and from the perspective of the allegedly harmed person, however, such a comparison makes no sense. We cannot simply proceed by drawing plausible intrapersonal comparisons of the life of this person and the counterfactual state of affairs in which, although this person would never have existed, another person or other persons would have existed.

The value of non-existence in the sense of never existing at all[27] cannot be compared with the value of the life of an actually existing person. As David Heyd argues: 'the comparison between life and nonexistence is blocked by two considerations: the valuelessness of nonexistence as such and the unattributability of its alleged value to individual subjects. The two considerations are intimately connected: one of the reasons for denying value to nonexistence *of* people is the very fact that it cannot be attached *to* people.'[28] A person can retrospectively prefer not to have been brought into existence, but it does not follow that this person would have been better off had he never been brought into existence.[29] To be sure, we can attribute to an existing person the state of 'nonexistence before conception' just as we can attribute to this person the state of 'having ceased to exist'.[30] This does not mean, however, that never existing at all can be understood as a (dis-)value vis-à-vis that person.

Those who claim, contrariwise, that we can meaningfully compare future states of affairs with different people (and different numbers of people)

---

[25] This can be true for procreative decisions also: Prospective parents might bring about more or less people (one child, twins, triplets etc.) depending upon their decisions.

[26] Compare the formulae in nn 13 and 17 above.

[27] Here we assume that comparing the state of an existing person with the state of the person had the person not been conceived amounts to comparing the state of an existing person with the state of the person had the person never existed at all.

[28] Heyd (1992: 37 and see 113).

[29] But see Roberts (1998: 151) (assigning zero-value to never having existed).

[30] See Meyer (1997a: 205); Meyer (2005: 95–99).

presuppose an impersonal approach: the value of states of affairs is not reducible to their effects on the interests of actual people; instead we can and have to compare possible future states of affairs with different people. Joined with an impersonal approach, the priority view (just like classical utilitarianism) leads to a repugnant conclusion, namely:[31] According to the priority view we aggregate the value realized for each possible world whereby the sum depends *inter alia* upon the number of persons who contribute to the realization of the value; thus, a possible world populated by persons all of whose lives are sufficiently good (according to a plausible threshold) or even better and very good, is to be judged worse than an alternative possible world populated by a large enough number of people whose lives are not sufficiently good but better than not-worth-living, even if only barely so. Principles with such features as these will recommend the creation of a large population whose people have lives worth living—and most theorists agree, this implication is repugnant and ought to be avoided.[32] A sufficiency principle specifying a minimal threshold for all people clearly does not imply the repugnant conclusion adumbrated here.[33]

We should also note that our argument for a threshold notion of harm is not meant to replace the more common notion of harm that requires a subjunctive comparison with a historical baseline.[34] Rather, we hold the view that the threshold notion of harm and the subjunctive-historical notion of harm can and are to be combined. According to the combined view the necessary condition for harming is the disjunction of the conditions of harming as set out by the threshold and the subjunctive-historical notion of harm.[35] The combined view is compatible with the response to the non-identity problem we argue for in this chapter: in assessing what we owe to future people we can employ the threshold interpretation of harm where the common understanding of harm does not apply. At the same time, the combined view allows us to rely on the common subjunctive-historical interpretation of harm whenever it is applicable, that is, when we will harm an actual person. In these cases the common notion provides us with a straightforward interpretation of the harm caused.[36]

---

[31] Parfit (1976); (1982); (1984), ch. 17.

[32] See Parfit (as in n. 31); Heyd (1992), ch. 2; and see the contributions in Ryberg und Tännsjö (2004).

[33] See also Blackorby et al. (2003: 354–60).

[34] See nn. 13 and 17, above, for the formulae of these notions of harm.

[35] The combined view can be expressed in the following formula: An action (or inaction) at time t_1 harms someone only if either the agent thereby causes (allows) this person's life to fall below some specified threshold; or the agent causes (allows) this person to be worse off at some later time t_2 than the person would have been at t_2 had the agent not interacted with (or acted with respect to) this person at all.

[36] For a detailed interpretation and defence of the combined view, see Meyer (2003: 152–8).

4. A Specific Case for Sufficientarianism (2): Specifying the Threshold of Harm

Responding to the non-identity problem as outlined in section 3—namely, by relying on a threshold notion of harm—does not by itself support a conception of intergenerational sufficientarianism. To be sure, the above-mentioned considerations as well as the interpretations of examples we submitted do suggest a specification of the relevant threshold as a *sufficientarian* standard. But for this substantive claim we need to provide further arguments.

Some have suggested defining the relevant sufficientarian standard in terms of absolute, noncomparative conditions.[37] One could hold a unitary view of the threshold according to which one and the same threshold would be applicable to all decisions. Even if we held that the same list of rights were attributable to all people (wherever and whenever they live), for example, those which are meant to protect basic capabilities of human beings, what these rights amount to will reflect contemporary social, economic, and cultural conditions.[38]

Specifying the standard by attributing equal minimal rights to people is only one possible interpretation of the threshold. We might, instead, want to define the threshold in accordance with either of the egalitarian conceptions introduced in section 2. First, strictly egalitarian considerations that address relative differences between people can help to specify the standard—and in at least two ways. We might hold that the standing of people relative to their contemporaries is important[39] and that the threshold notion of harm ought to reflect, say, the average level of well-being that people realize, or that future people will realize: the higher the average level of well-being the higher the threshold level of harm should be set. According to one interpretation of such an egalitarian reading, presently existing people harm future people by causing them to realize a (much) lower level of well-being than their own contemporaries.[40] In addition or alternatively, we might hold that the threshold level ought to reflect, say, the average level of well-being of the present generations upon whose decisions the existence, identity, and well-being of future people depend. According to such an interpretation,

---

[37] See Shiffrin (1999: 123f.); McMahan (1998: 223f.); and Meyer (1997a).
[38] See, e.g., Sen (1984); Nussbaum (2000b: 132f.).
[39] This would be the case since equality is of intrinsic value. See section 2 above, and see Marmor (2003); Steiner (2003). Responding to Marmor and Steiner, Raz (2003, 264f.) points out that what counts as sufficient might depend on how many people reach what levels of well-being and that this can be the case without our presupposing that equality is of intrinsic value. See also Gosepath (2004: 454–63); Brighouse and Swift (2006); Holtug and Lippert-Rasmussen (2007).
[40] Sher (1979: 389).

presently existing people harm future people by causing them to realize a (much) lower level of well-being than they enjoy themselves.[41] Still, even if egalitarian considerations that reflect a concern with the relative differences between people can contribute to the specification of the threshold, a plausible threshold is not going to be based on that concern, but will reflect primarily a concern with the absolute level of well-being of persons. Otherwise—this is an implication of the first interpretation—any level of well-being would be considered justified as long as all future people fare equally badly. This presupposes attributing intrinsic value exclusively to equality—an implausible view.[42] Moreover, to define the threshold standard of well-being of future people as the level of well-being achieved by currently living people (whatever it may be) is less than plausible, unless we were to attribute intrinsic value exclusively to intergenerational equality, so understood.[43] This view would deny that currently living people may stand under a duty of justice positively to save for future people so that they will achieve a sufficientarian level of well-being.[44]

The second way in which egalitarian considerations can help to identify the standard is to rely on the priority view for specifying the threshold. On this interpretation, future people fall under the threshold unless they are as well off as the priority view requires. However, this understanding is likely to be unreasonably demanding on the currently living. In the intergenerational context the priority view has most misleading implications even if it is coupled with the person-affecting approach. For, given the large number of future people whose level of well-being can be affected by the decisions and actions of currently living people, the priority view will make unreasonable demands on the currently living. In assessing alternative options we would have to weigh the claims to improvements as well as to take into account both the size of the benefit and the number of beneficiaries; if the number of future people is sufficiently large, we would then have to choose the option that improves their well-being even if both their claims to improvements in well-being are weak and the benefits they receive are small. If the number of future people

---

[41] See Barry (1999: 109). See also our remarks on the irrelevance of common instrumental justifications for more equality in section 5 below.

[42] See the above discussion regarding the levelling-down-objection. A monistic value egalitarianism will also have unacceptable implications when applied to contemporaries: the state of affairs in which all have lives barely worth living is to be preferred to a state in which all have good or very good lives but some are better off than others.

[43] See literature referred to in n. 39 above.

[44] Rawls (2001: 159) proposes a duty to save positively 'to make possible the conditions needed to establish and to preserve a just basic structure over time.' For discussion of the role of a principle of sufficiency in justifying this duty see Gaspart and Gosseries (2007: 200).

is sufficiently large, currently living people will stand under an obligation to improve the well-being of those future people even if in fulfilling that obligation the currently living people will lose (very) much in well-being and the improvements in well-being of future people will be small or even trivial.[45]

The objections to specifying the threshold in terms of the egalitarian conceptions as distinguished here present a particular reason for holding that the specification of the threshold ought to be informed by a sufficientarian understanding of justice, at least for intergenerational relations. In defining the relevant threshold we may also rely on considerations that reflect the significance of relative differences among future people or people who belong to different generations including the currently living. Considerations characteristic of the priority view may, also, be considered relevant for the specification of the threshold. It is implausible, however, to hold the view that we might define the relevant standard as reflecting solely egalitarian reasons of the two types distinguished: reasons for diminishing relative differences among people and those for the prioritarian weighting of claims to improvements in well-being. By defining a threshold of well-being according to which both currently and future living people are able to reach a sufficientarian conception allows us to avoid the misleading implications of both egalitarian conceptions. First, avoiding or reducing differences must not lead to a state of affairs in which people are worse off than they ought to be. Secondly, claims against currently living people are unreasonable if in fulfilling them the currently living people will bring about minimal or even trivial improvements of the well-being of future people but suffer losses themselves, causing them to fall under a plausible threshold level of well-being.

If these objections are valid, we have strong particular reasons for interpreting intergenerational justice in terms of a conception for which a sufficientarian threshold is of central significance. At the same time, the reasons for a sufficientarian understanding of intergenerational justice are not equally relevant for the relations among existing contemporaries—never mind whether we think of these contemporaries simply as people wherever they may live, or as members of a well-ordered liberal society, or as found in different basic political units. For the reasons reflect particular features of intergenerational

---

[45] The position of weak sufficientarianism can have this implication, too. For, even if we attribute particular weight to improving the well-being of people below the threshold, we might be able to do more good (in total) by benefiting many more people who are well-off already (compare, above, p. 224, last paragraph). This is an implication of both the priority view and the position of weak sufficientarianism even if the number of people to be considered is fixed; thus, it can arise in situations involving contemporaries only, as noted by Casal for the priority view (2007: 319f.).

relations: the non-identity problem simply does not arise in relations among existing contemporaries. The problem does not arise among institutionalised transgenerational legal entities such as Rawls's peoples or states understood as subjects of public international law, either. Also, as shown in sections 3 and 4 the (strength of) objections to egalitarian conceptions of intergenerational justice—to both the prioritarian conception and the conception relying on the notion that equality is of intrinsic value—reflect, in part, particular features of intergenerational relations. Thus, the reasons for a sufficientarian understanding of intergenerational justice are at least in part specific reasons and are not relevant for understanding either global justice or the notion of justice that holds among contemporary members of well-ordered societies.[46]

5. Further Reasons for Intergenerational Sufficientarianism

Next, we should like to turn to some of the often-cited reasons for a sufficientarian understanding of global justice. They concern, first, the prerequisites of implementing welfare rights, second, the possibility of measuring (relative) differences, and third, the significance of co-citizenship as well as instrumental justifications for an egalitarian distribution. We will ask whether these reasons are relevant to an understanding of intergenerational relations and whether they, in fact, speak more strongly on behalf of a sufficientarian conception of intergenerational relations than on behalf of such a conception of international relations. We hope to show that this is, indeed, the case. The reasons that are said to speak on behalf of a sufficientarian understanding of global justice turn out to be relevant to our understanding of intergenerational justice, and this owing to other special non-contingent features of intergenerational relations: the unchangeable power asymmetry as well as the impossibility of interaction between non-contemporaries, and not least of all our uncertainty as to how in particular our actions will affect future people. If so, there are weighty and specific reasons that speak on behalf of a sufficientarian conception of intergenerational justice and that are independent of the reasons we delineated in sections 3 and 4.

First, some authors[47] raise the criticism that the egalitarian understandings of global justice is negatively utopian: regulating world politics in accordance

---

[46] On the notion of well-ordered societies see Rawls (2001: 8f.); Rawls (1999).
[47] See Kersting (2001: 282–91); Miller (2005: 72f.).

with such demanding conceptions of justice—aiming either at globally establishing an equal distribution of well-being (and at a high level) or at giving weighted significance to globally improving the well-being of the not-well-off people—would require a world welfare state with far-reaching powers and authoritative means of implementation. For reasons familiar since Kant,[48] we cannot wish to live in a world state and in particular not in a world welfare state with regulatory powers. A world welfare state is likely to threaten seriously the liberty rights of all. We cannot hope to establish a sustainable well-ordered global state or its functional equivalent, or so the critics argue. On the other hand, a sufficientarian understanding is thought to specify a standard of distributive justice for international relations that could be implemented by means of co-ordinated efforts within a decentralized system (of a plurality) of basic political units. Of course, showing that a sufficientarian understanding of global justice is positively utopian would require further discussion. Here we just note that it is likely to be a less demanding goal of global justice.

We will not go into assessing the validity of the quasi-empirical claim that an egalitarian understanding of global justice is utopian in a negative sense, as its implementation will require a world state with far-reaching competencies and powers. Our point is simply the comparative one that we have additional and weighty reasons for believing that a world welfare state is a prerequisite for carrying out principles of intergenerational justice that require—in either of the ways specified—an egalitarian consideration of people whenever they live: solving so-called world problems[49] requires the global implementation of adequate measures. It is one thing, however, to aim at solving such problems without violating sufficiency standards; to aim at solving such problems and at the same time to pursue the goal of implementing an egalitarian conception of justice is quite another. The latter will demand a great deal both of currently living people (and as argued with respect to the priority view in section 4 possibly unreasonably much) and of international and intergenerational cooperation. Egalitarian solutions in particular will depend upon the reliable and stable

---

[48] See Kant (1795), (1784), (1793), and (1798), all in Kant (1968); but see Horn (1996); Höffe (1999); the so-called Clark-Sohn plan is the best-known post-World-War II proposal for the establishment of a world government. See Clark and Sohn (1960); see further, Suganami (1989) (who systematically compares and discusses alternative proposals for restructuring international society in accordance with its domestic counterparts).

[49] On 'world problems' see Opitz (2001). If we could realize intergenerational justice within well-ordered single states, we would not have to rely on a world state for its implementation. Here we do not discuss the problems of justice between age groups with respect to single-state cooperative schemes, e.g. social security systems. Rather, we take up problems of intergenerational justice among non-contemporaries. One such problem turns on the consequences of climate change and its normative implications.

cooperation of many influential actors in international politics; thus egalitarian solutions would require a world state or its functional equivalent:[50] If the solutions are meant to be just in accordance with an egalitarian conception and with respect to the claims of future people, a world welfare state is very likely presupposed. The implementation of measures aimed at securing the welfare rights of future people is particularly difficult. Non-contemporaries cannot give expression to and stand for their interests and they cannot impose sanctions on currently living people who do not carry out their obligations vis-à-vis them. Furthermore, the implementation of such measures is often dependent upon transgenerational cooperation. Both the fair representation of the interests of non-contemporaries and the securing of conditions of transgenerational cooperation require strong and stable institutions. Thus, if we hold that the implementation of an egalitarian understanding of global justice among contemporaries requires the institutions of a world welfare state, this will be true *a fortiori* for the implementation of an egalitarian understanding of global *and* intergenerational justice.[51] To the extent that we do not wish to live in a world state, the objection is valid for egalitarian conceptions of intergenerational relations; this is especially so for the reason that such a state would have to be enormously powerful in order to be able to implement egalitarian intergenerational obligations. At the same time, the particular reasons for the prerequisite of a world state, where intergenerational justice is concerned, reflect non-contingent features of intergenerational relations, namely, the unchangeable power asymmetry that holds between present and (remote) future generations and the impossibility of interaction between them.[52]

The second justificatory argument is connected with an argument on the level of practical validity. Some authors[53] claim that we cannot measure

---

[50] See Gardiner (2002: 406–416).

[51] Other factors may support the implementation of an egalitarian ideal in the intergenerational context, or, at the very least, there are amoral factors that contribute to the improvement of the well-being of future people. For example, many parents hope that their children will be better off than they themselves; this may contribute to the well-being of future people generally. Saving for future people comes with an interest yield, and this may induce an additional motivation for such savings. Also, if people are motivated to act in such ways that enhance their prospects of being better off in, say, 30 years, this may have the (unintended) side-effect of improving the well-being of future people in, say, 80 years.

[52] These features, one might well want to argue, require transgenerationally stable world state structures even for implementing the far less demanding conception of an intergenerational (minimal) sufficientarianism. However, our claim in this section is a comparative one: The world state or its functional equivalent is in all likelihood an institutional prerequisite if we are to fulfil intergenerational duties vis-à-vis (remote) future people and if (these) duties are interpreted in accordance with an egalitarian conception of justice, and less likely if we are to fulfil duties vis-à-vis (geographically distant) contemporaries and if (these) duties are interpreted in a non-egalitarian way.

[53] Miller (2005: 4–10); Brock (2005: 348–350).

globally what we would need to measure in order to be able to determine what in accordance with egalitarian conceptions of justice is owed to people who belong to different societies. We cannot say what an egalitarian justice, to quote David Miller, 'means in a culturally plural world'[54], for we can neither assess the relative differences among people who live in very different, historically formed cultural and social contexts, nor can we determine how well off they are in a way that bears on the prioritarian attribution of weighted claims to improvements in well-being. In response, we ought to consider whether the alleged difficulties of measurement are simply greater than the difficulties of measurement in single societies[55] or whether the difficulties of measurement are principally different and of a kind that they should be regarded as insuperable given the global pluralism of conceptions of the good and socially shared forms of life. Proponents of both egalitarian and non-egalitarian conceptions of justice agree that no problems principally different arise with respect to the measurement of some goods and especially the basic goods of survival when compared with the well-being of people wherever they might live. This is not to deny, of course, that the means necessary for supplying these goods vary and thus also the costs involved in providing and securing them; reaching, for example, the tolerable minimum of well-being in an OECD country requires secure access to a different set of goods than in a country of the so-called Third World. Applying a minimal sufficientarian threshold globally rather than within a single society does not, however, seem to entail principally different problems of measurement.

Problems principally different might arise, however, where we compare goods that are relevant for people's well-being above such a minimal threshold. People's well-being depends upon access to valuable options whose existence depends in turn upon collective and, often, also participatory goods whose supply is secured within bounded societies whose members share a particular historically and culturally formed understanding as to why these options are valuable to them.[56] Access to such options—professions, social roles, being a mother or a father, and societal activities in sports and culture—is of vital importance to the well-being and social status of members of a society. For realising the value of self-respect, backed by social recognition, depends upon having access to such options and having success in pursuing them.

It is, however, not obvious why we should face principally different problems when we compare access to such goods globally. Instead one might want to

---

[54] Miller (2005: 9).
[55] For an example of an author who focuses on the problems which already arise within a single society, see Rosenberg (1995).
[56] For an account see Meyer (2000).

argue that access to such options and success in pursuing them are goods whose comparative assessment in accordance with a conception of justice will rely upon a value that people can be said to hold in common transculturally, say, the value of self-respect. The sources of and the prerequisites for self-respect may well differ from society to society (this is true, for example, for the significance of belonging to certain professions) or culturally (this is true, for example, for such life options as having your own family), but not the significance of the value of self-respect. If the impact of life options on the value of self-respect counts from the perspective of justice[57] and if we are in a position to compare the impact of very different life options on the value of self-respect globally, then the great plurality of ways of life globally will not carry with it principled problems in measuring the relative well-being of people or the level of well-being they realize.

Further, Joseph Raz in particular holds that the value of such options even within a single (well-ordered liberal) society can be incommensurable in the strong sense of being incomparable: 'Two valuable options are incommensurable if (1) neither is better than the other, and (2) there is (or could be) another option which is better than one but is not better than the other.'[58] If so, the shared cultural-historical and social context within which these options exist does not guarantee their comparability for those who have access to these options. This might well not be decisive, however, if looked at from the perspective of an egalitarian understanding of justice. What counts is that people do have access to (morally acceptable) sources of self-respect quite apart from the options, whatever they may be, open to them in their particular cultural and social contexts. We may well be in a position to assess the impact of such options on the self-respect of people, even though, in other respects, these options are incommensurable.

It seems plausible both that problems of comparatively measuring the well-being of individuals both within single societies and globally will vary depending upon which goods we compare and that we will face problems of measurements more often in international relations given the far more far-reaching global pluralism of both conceptions of the good and available life options when compared with a reasonable pluralism within a single (Rawlsian well-ordered liberal) society. Thus, a conception of global egalitarian justice will be able to take into account only a selection of goods—which raises

---

[57] Of course we would have to show that the value of self-respect (or some other value) could play this central role for transculturally comparative judgements of justice. For self-respect as a central aspect of well-being or primary good, see Raz (1994: 24–26) and Rawls (2001: 58–61).

[58] Raz (1986: 325). Raz identifies incommensurability with the failure of transitivity. See also Raz (1991) und (1997), and Griffin's response (1991) to Raz.

questions about the meaningful applicability of the conception—or will have to make generalized assumptions about the significance of various goods for the realization, say, of the value of self-respect. The assumption, given that the value of self-respect is equally transculturally significant, is that we can rely upon the value of self-respect for comparative measurements of the well-being of people (or for the prioritarian assessment of weighted claims to improvements in well-being).

Comparatively to measure the well-being of people is even more difficult in intergenerational relations, however. For our knowledge of the relevant conditions of life of future people is limited and this epistemic situation of ours seems insuperable. At least two considerations support the view that in our efforts to carry out such measurements with respect to future people we face principally different problems:

- The particular way of life of future people is likely to depend in part upon those new and today unknown technologies to which they will have access. However, we cannot or can only with great difficulty predict technological developments.[59]
- The collective way of life of future people will depend, in part, upon their own individual and collective decisions. We are not in a position to predict how they will decide to organize their lives socially or how they will want to live individually and we cannot hope to determine these decisions either, that is, where we believe that the individual and collective autonomy of future people ought to be secured.[60] We also know that the decisions of their predecessors will have an impact on what options more remote future people will have as individuals and collectively; we cannot hope to determine the decisions of intervening generations either and for the same reason.

Thus, it might well be true that we are in no position to know what we owe to more remote future non-contemporaries in accordance with egalitarian conceptions of justice.[61] We are in no position to determine their pertinent relative differences, for the particular historically formed cultural and social contexts that the lives of remote future people will have are uncertain to us. We do know, however, that these particular contexts will be of decisive importance for the particular level of well-being that future people will enjoy.

---

[59] See Birnbacher (1988: 168f.). [60] See Meyer (1997b: 145–50).

[61] It might be well to stress, at this point, that the argument in favour of sufficientarianism in response to the non-identity problem and as the more plausible specification of the intergenerational threshold conception (sections 3 and 4) is independent of the epistemic considerations we have discussed in this section.

Accordingly, over and above the satisfaction of certain general or basic needs or preferences[62] which can be estimated with a certain level of reliability we cannot hope to determine today how well off future[63] people will be. We are in no position to know what impact our actions will have on the relative well-being of future people or their particular level of well-being, for their individual well-being will depend to a large part on socially shared understandings of what options are valuable as well as on who has access to them and how successful they are in pursuing them.[64]

Third, some of the reasons that have been advanced against an egalitarian conception of global justice and in favour of global sufficientarianism do speak in favour of intergenerational sufficientarianism. This is owing to further particular features of intergenerational relations. Some have argued that institutional relationships among citizens ought to be regulated by an egalitarian understanding of justice if and to the extent that such a conception legitimately regulates citizens' claims to benefits in a scheme of cooperation that is made possible by authoritative rules that the state will enforce, where necessary, by means of coercion.[65] Non-contemporaries cannot be regarded as co-citizens in the relevant sense, however; there is no interaction possible among non-contemporaries, and future people cannot take part in today's political decision-making. The legitimacy of principles of intergenerational justice

---

[62] See Barry (1977: 261f.) and (1989: 347).

[63] It can also be difficult to have a positive impact on the well-being of geographically distant people. However, in this instance we can learn from experience; the predictability of the consequences of our actions is not restricted due to the two reasons that characterise our epistemic situation with respect to more remote future people as mentioned in the text above (see nn. 56–7 and text).

[64] We would need to analyse more precisely what the problems of comparative measurement are, namely with respect to the subject-matter that we assess (in the sense of the so-called *Equality of What?*-debate). In the contemporary debate on justice the more common alternatives are to focus on resources or basic goods (see, e.g., Rawls (1971: 92–4); Dworkin (2000: 65–119)) or capabilities (see, e.g., Nussbaum (2000a: 78–80); Sen (1999)). As Pogge (2002) has convincingly shown, a highly advanced primary goods approach not only allows but requires us to take into account many of the factors Sen has identified as decisive for the quality of life people enjoy. Among these factors are: the significance of relative differences in access to goods for, e.g., self-respect; the significance of the particular social conditions (e.g., the availability of public goods—such as a tertiary educational system or advanced health care—or the crime rate within a society) for the value of claims and rights to, e.g., physical and psychic integrity of people and that they may move and reside freely within the territory of their societies; the significance of the quality of the natural environment and of its change; the value of having a job at a particular place and in a particular society. If, in our attempts comparatively to measure quality of life, we are to take into account these and similar factors and considerations, we will find that we cannot know for certain (or by relying on generalised hypotheses with little accuracy) how well off (more remote) future people will be (relative to their contemporaries). And this, in particular, for the reason that we would have to take into account that their conditions of life will depend, in part, upon their predecessors' decisions and actions.

[65] See for alternative interpretations of this view Dworkin (2000: 6); Blake (2002); Nagel (2005); Scanlon (2005: 10f.).

cannot depend upon future people's approval of these principles in any real sense. Further, there is no correlation between economic and political equality among non-contemporaries. This is one of the more common justifications for greater equality among citizens of one society: Large differences in wealth or income will make it possible for the rich to exercise impermissible power over the poor, which might, is indeed likely to, lead to unacceptable inequalities in people's liberty rights. There is, however, an unchangeable power asymmetry between non-contemporaries.[66] Furthermore, other instrumental advantages of equality among contemporaries are of very little, if any, relevance where relations among non-contemporaries are concerned. It makes no sense to claim that greater income equality among non-contemporaries will further intergenerational harmony, reduce intergenerational envy, or strengthen a sense of intergenerational solidarity or communal belonging.[67] And, finally, one further consideration might be noted: if we hold the view that the validity of calling for obligations of justice depends, in part, upon whether we can effectively fulfil them,[68] then, again, we have reasons for doubting that this is the case in calling for obligations of egalitarian justice vis-à-vis future people and, in particular, more remote future people. This is due, in part, to our dependency on transgenerational cooperation in fulfilling duties vis-à-vis more remote future people.[69]

6. Concluding Remarks

We have particular and strong reasons for understanding the justice claims of future people vis-à-vis currently living people in terms of intergenerational sufficientarianism. This view is developed in response to the non-identity problem and other considerations that reflect the normative significance of non-contingent features of intergenerational relations, which include the dependency of the number and identity of future people on currently living people's decisions, the uncertainty as to how current people's actions will affect the relative well-being of future people, the problems of measuring relative differences of well-being of people whose particular conditions of life differ to a large degree, and the impossibility of interaction between non-contemporaries and their not sharing membership in a common polity.

Of course, many of us have concerns for future people that cannot be accounted for by considerations of justice: Duties of intergenerational justice

---

[66] See Barry (1989: 189, 246).   [67] See Beckerman and Pasek (2001: 49f.).
[68] See Scanlon (1998: 224f.); for discussion see Wenar (2001: 80f.).
[69] See Gardiner (2002: 402–6); Birnbacher (1988: 157–64).

(and the correlative rights of future people) can account neither for the concern that there be future people at all nor that they share a particular way of life nor that future people should have a life well above the level of a sufficientarian level of well-being. We might want to argue that over and above what currently living people owe future people as a matter of justice, they can stand under additional duties to benefit future people so that they will be able to continue their way of life and enjoy a level of well-being that is above any plausible understanding of a sufficientarian threshold. But going into these issues is a matter for another occasion.[70]

Bibliography

ARNESON, R. J. (1999), 'Egalitarianism and Responsibility', *Journal of Ethics* 3: 225–47.
—— (2000), 'Luck Egalitarianism and Prioritarianism', *Ethics* 110: 339–49.
BARRY, B. (1977), 'Justice between Generations', in P. M. S. Hacker and Joseph Raz (eds.), *Law, Morality and Society. Essays in Honour of H. L. A. Hart* (Oxford: Clarendon Press), 268–84; reprinted in Barry, B. (1991), *Liberty and Justice. Essays in Political Theory 2* (Oxford: Clarendon Press), 211–41.
—— (1989), *Theories of Justice. A Treatise on Social Justice*, Band Vol. 1 (Berkeley: University of California Press).
—— (1999), 'Sustainability and Intergenerational Justice', in Andrew Dobson (ed.), *Fairness and Futurity. Essays on Environmental Sustainability* (Oxford: Oxford University Press), 93–117.
BECKERMAN, W., and PASEK, J. (2001), *Justice, Posterity, and the Environment* (Oxford: Oxford University Press).
BIRNBACHER, D. (1988), *Verantwortung für zukünftige Generationen* (Stuttgart: Reclam).
BLACKORBY, C., BOSSERT, W., and DONALDSON, D. (2003), 'The Axiomatic Approach to Population Ethics', *Politics, Philosophy and Economics*, 2: 342–81.
BLAKE, M. (2002), 'Distributive Justice, State Coercion, and Autonomy', *Philosophy & Public Affairs*, 30: 257–96.
BRIGHOUSE, H., and SWIFT, A. (2006), 'Equality, Priority, and Positional Goods', *Ethics*, 116: 471–97.
BROCK, G. (2005), 'The Difference Principle, Equality of Opportunity, and Cosmopolitan Justice', *Journal of Moral Philosophy*, 2: 333–51.
BUCHANAN, A. (2004), *Justice, Legitimacy, and Self-Determination. Moral Foundations for International Law* (Oxford: Oxford University Press).
CASAL, P. (2007), 'Why Sufficiency Is Not Enough', *Ethics*, 117: 296–326.
CLARK, G., and SOHN, L. B. (1960), *World Peace Through World Law*, 2nd edn (Cambridge: Harvard University Press).

[70] See Meyer (1997b) and (2005: chs. 4 and 5).

COHEN, J., and SABEL, C. (2006), 'Extra Rempublicam Nulla Justitia?', *Philosophy & Public Affairs*, 34: 147–75.

CRISP, R. (2003), 'Equality, Priority, and Compassion', *Ethics*, 113: 745–63.

DANIELS, N. (1979), 'Wide Reflective Equilibrium and Theory Acceptance in Ethics', *Journal of Philosophy*, 76: 256–82.

DWORKIN, R. (2000), *Sovereign Virtue. The Theory and Practice of Equality* (Cambridge: Harvard University Press).

FRANKFURT, H. G. (1987), 'Equality as a Moral Ideal', *Ethics*, 98: 21–43.

GARDINER, S. (2002), 'The Real Tragedy of Commons', *Philosophy & Public Affairs*, 30: 387–416.

GASPART, F. and GOSSERIES, A. (2007), 'Are Generational Savings Unjust?', *Politics, Philosophy & Economics*, 6: 193–217.

GOSEPATH, S. (2004), *Gleiche Gerechtigkeit. Grundlagen eines liberalen Egalitarismus* (Frankfurt: Suhrkamp).

GRIFFIN, J. (1991), 'Mixing Values', *Aristotelian Society*, Supplementary Vol. LXV: 101–18.

HEYD, D. (1992), *Genethics. Moral Issues in the Creation of People* (Berkeley: University of California Press).

HÖFFE, O. (1999), *Demokratie im Zeitalter der Globalisierung* (Munich: C.H. Beck).

HOLTUG, N. (2007), 'Prioritarianism', in N. Holtug and K. Lippert-Rasmussen (eds.), *Egalitarianism. New Essays on the Nature and Value of Equality* (Oxford: Oxford University Press), 125–56.

—— and LIPPERT-RASMUSSEN, K. (2007), 'An Introduction to Contemporary Egalitarianism', in N. Holtug and K. Lippert-Rasmussen (eds.). *Egalitarianism. New Essays on the Nature and Value of Equality* (Oxford: Oxford University Press), 1–38.

HORN, C. (1996), 'Philosophische Argumente für einen Weltstaat', *Allgemeine Zeitschrift für Philosophie*, 21: 229–51.

JULIUS, A. J. (2006), 'Nagel's Atlas', *Philosophy & Public Affairs*, 34: 176–92.

KANT, I. (1968), *Kants Werke*, vol. VIII (Akademie Werkausgabe, Wilhelm Weischedel (ed.), Berlin: Walter de Gruyter); the vol. contains: 'Zum Ewigen Frieden. Ein philosophischer Entwurf' (1795); 'Idee zu einer allgemeinen Geschichte in weltbürgerlicher Absicht' (1784); 'Über den Gemeinspruch: Das mag in der Theorie richtig sein, taugt aber nicht für die Praxis' (1793); 'Der Streit der Fakultäten' (1798). All essays in English translations in Kant (1970), *Kant's Political Writings*, Hans Reiss (ed.) (Cambridge: Cambridge University Press).

KAVKA, G. (1982), 'The Paradox of Future Individuals', *Philosophy & Public Affairs*, 11: 93–112.

KERSTING, W. (2001), 'Suffizienzorientierung versus Gleichheitsorientierung. Bemerkungen zur Konzeption einer internationalen Verteilungsgerechtigkeit', in K. G. Ballestrem (ed.), *Internationale Gerechtigkeit* (Opladen: Leske and Budrich), 278–315.

KUMAR, R. (2003), 'Who Can Be Wronged?', *Philosophy and Public Affairs*, 31: 99–118.

LIPPERT-RASMUSSEN, K. (2007), 'The Insignificance of the Distinction Between Telic and Deontic Egalitarianism', in N. Holtug and K. Lippert-Rasmussen (eds.), *Egalitarianism. New Essays on the Nature and Value of Equality* (Oxford: Clarendon Press), 101–24.

MARMOR, A. (2003), 'The Intrinsic Value of Economic Equality', in L. H. Meyer, S. L. Paulson, and T. W. Pogge (eds.), *Rights, Culture, and the Law. Themes from the Legal and Political Philosophy of Joseph Raz* (Oxford: Oxford University Press), 127–41.

MCMAHAN, J. (1998), 'Wrongful Life: Paradoxes in the Morality of Causing People to Exist', in J. Coleman and C. Morris (eds.), *Rational Commitment and Social Justice. Essays for Gregory Kavka* (Cambridge: Cambridge University Press), 208–47.

MEYER, L. H. (1997a), 'Can Actual Future People Have a Right to Non-Existence?', *Archives for Philosophy of Law and Social Philosophy, Beiheft 67: Rights*, 200–9.

—— (1997b), 'More Than They Have a Right to. Future People and Our Future Oriented Projects', in N. Fotion and J. C. Heller (eds.), *Contingent Future Persons. On the Ethics of Deciding Who Will Live, or Not, in the Future* (Dordrecht, Boston and London: Kluwer Academic Publishers), 137–56.

—— (2000), 'Cosmopolitan Communities', in A. Coates (ed.). *International Justice* (Aldershot and Brookfield: Ashgate), 89–110.

—— (2003), 'Past and Future. The Case for a Threshold Notion of Harm', in L. H. Meyer, S. L. Paulson, and T. W. Pogge (eds.), *Rights, Culture, and the Law. Themes from the Legal and Political Philosophy of Joseph Raz* (Oxford: Oxford University Press), 143–59.

—— (2005), *Historische Gerechtigkeit* (Berlin and New York: Walter de Gruyter).

—— (2008), 'Intergenerational Justice', in E. N. Zalta (ed.). *The Stanford Encyclopedia of Philosophy (Spring 2008 Edition)*. Available at <http://plato.stanford.edu/archives/spr2008/entries/justice-intergenerational/>.

—— and ROSER, D. (2006), 'Distributive Justice and Climate Change', *Analyse & Kritik*, 28: 223–49.

MILLER, D. (2005), 'Against Global Egalitarianism', *The Journal of Ethics*, 9: 55–79.

NAGEL, T. (2005), 'The Problem of Global Justice', *Philosophy & Public Affairs*, 33, 113–47.

NUSSBAUM, M. C. (2000a), *Women and Human Development. The Capabilities Approach* (Cambridge: Cambridge University Press).

—— (2000b), 'Aristotle, Politics, and Human Capabilities. A Response to Antony, Arneson, Charlesworthy, and Mulgan', *Ethics*, 111: 102–40.

OPITZ, P. J. (ed.) (2001), *Weltprobleme im 21. Jahrhundert* (Munich: Fink).

PARFIT, D. (1976), 'On Doing the Best for Our Children', in M. D. Bayles (ed.), *Ethics and Population* (Cambridge, Mass.: Schenkman), 100–15.

—— (1982), 'Future Generations. Further Problems', *Philosophy & Public Affairs*, 11: 113–72.

—— (1984), *Reasons and Persons* (Oxford: Clarendon Press).

Parfit, D. (1997), 'Equality and Priority', *Ratio*, 10: 202–21.

—— (2000), 'Equality or Priority?', in M. Clayton and A. Williams (eds.), *The Ideal of Equality* (New York: St. Martin's Press), 81–125.

Pogge, T. W. (1989), *Realizing Rawls* (Ithaca: Cornell University Press).

—— (2002), 'Can the Capability Approach be Justified?', in M. Nussbaum and C. Flanders (eds.), *Global Inequalities*, Special issue of *Philosophical Topics* 30: 167–228.

Rawls, J. (1971), *A Theory of Justice* (Oxford: Oxford University Press).

—— (1999), *The Law of Peoples* (Cambridge: Harvard University Press).

—— (2001), *Justice as Fairness. A Restatement* (Cambridge: Harvard University Press).

Raz, J. (1986), *The Morality of Freedom* (Oxford: Clarendon Press).

—— (1991), 'Mixing Values', *Aristotelian Society*, Supplementary Vol. LXV: 83–100.

—— (1994), 'Duties of Well-Being', in J. Raz, *Ethics in the Public Domain. Essays in the Morality of Law and Politics* (Oxford: Clarendon Press), 3–28.

—— (1997), 'Incommensurability and Agency', in Ruth Chang (ed.). *Incommensurability, Incomparability, and Practical Reason* (Cambridge: Harvard University Press), 110–28.

—— (2003), 'Responses', in L. H. Meyer, S. L. Paulson and T. W. Pogge (eds.), *Rights, Culture, and the Law. Themes from the Legal and Political Philosophy of Joseph Raz* (Oxford: Oxford University Press), 253–73.

Roberts, M. A. (1998), *Child versus Childmaker. Future Persons and Present Duties in Ethics and the Law* (Lanham: Rowman & Littlefield).

Rosenberg, A. (1995), 'Equality, Sufficiency, and Opportunity in the Just Society', *Social Philosophy and Policy*, 12: 54–71.

Ryberg, J., and Tännsjö, T. (eds.) (2004), *The Repugnant Conclusion. Essays on Population Ethics* (Dordrecht et al.: Kluwer).

Scanlon, T. M. (1998), *What We Owe To Each Other* (Cambridge: Harvard University Press).

—— (2005), *When Does Equality Matter?*, Ms. (presentation, British Academy, December 2005), 31pp.

Schwartz, T. (1978), 'Obligations to Posterity', in R. I. Sikora and B. Barry (eds.), *Obligations to Future Generations* (Philadelphia: Temple University Press), 3–13.

Sen, A. K. (1984), *Resources, Values and Development* (Cambridge: Harvard University Press).

—— (1999), *Choice, Welfare and Measurement* (Cambridge: Harvard University Press).

Sher, G. (1979), 'Compensation and Transworld Personal Identity', *Monist*, 62: 378–91.

Shiffrin, S. (1999), 'Wrongful Life, Procreative Responsibility, and the Significance of Harm', *Legal Theory*, 5: 117–48.

Steiner, H. (2003), 'Equality, Incommensurability, and Rights', in L. H. Meyer, S. L. Paulson, and T. W. Pogge (eds.), *Rights, Culture, and the Law. Themes from the Legal and Political Philosophy of Joseph Raz* (Oxford: Oxford University Press), 119–26.

SUGANAMI, H. (1989), *The Domestic Analogy and World Order Proposals* (Cambridge: Cambridge University Press).

WENAR, L. (2001), 'Contractualism and Global Economic Justice', *Metaphilosophy*, 32: 79–94.

WOODWARD, J. (1986), 'The Non-Identity Problem', *Ethics*, 96: 804–31.

—— (1987), 'Reply to Parfit', *Ethics*, 96: 800–17.

[12]
Three Models of Intergenerational Reciprocity

AXEL GOSSERIES

Introduction

Any theory of intergenerational justice needs to deal with a twofold question: what do we owe to the next generation, and why? Various accounts are available to answer this question, ranging from communitarian, utilitarian, libertarian to luck egalitarian or sufficientarian ones. In this chapter, I wish to focus on one family of theories, i.e. those relying on the idea of reciprocity, both to justify and define our obligations towards the next generation.[1] Personally, I do not consider reciprocity-based theories as the most defensible account of our intergenerational obligations, because of misfit with my other well-considered judgements as they apply among others in the intragenerational realm. Yet, even as a non-defender of such views, I consider it essential to explore them, both because I believe that they are more robust than one may think—which says something about what exactly would be wrong with them—and because they point at specificities as well as difficulties that other views have left unnoticed. If we are to criticize reciprocity-based accounts, we need to do so for the right reasons. This also explains why I will examine three—rather than merely one—types of reciprocity-based accounts of our intergenerational obligations, with the aim of increasing the level of generality and precision of our analysis.

Drafts of this chapter were presented in Bremen (GSSS, March 11, 2005), at the Ecole normale supérieure (Ulm, Paris, March 21, 2005), at the Katholieke Universiteit Leuven (May 20, 2005), at University College (London, September 22, 2005) and at the IEP of Lille (September 24, 2005). I wish to warmly thank these audiences as well as A.-P. André-Dumont, A. Autenne, J. Bichot, D. Casassas, J.-M. Chaumont, D. Cosandey, M. Fleurbaey, A. Gheaus, S.-K. Kolm, V. Muniz Fraticelli, F. Peter, G. Ponthière, G.-F. Raneri, Chr. Vandeschrick, Ph. Van Parijs, K. Wade-Benzoni, and two anonymous referees for comments and suggestions on earlier drafts.

[1] For reference work on reciprocity in general: Kolm (1984), (2000) & (2006). On intergenerational reciprocity more specifically: Barry (1989), Masson (1999).

Before proceeding, let me emphasize two points. First, I will rely on a relatively *narrow* definition of reciprocity here, and on two corollaries resulting respectively from the *multilateral* and *open* nature of the intergenerational context.[2] Let me explain. The idea of reciprocity refers here to a notion of equivalence in respective contributions, in the context of an exchange. Of course, equivalence does not mean that we should give back the very same object, but rather something of equivalent 'value'.[3] Moreover, whether an object should be seen as equally valuable will depend on a set of variables, including e.g. price fluctuations or environmental changes. Yet, it follows from a strict understanding of the reciprocity requirement that no one would be allowed or forced to end up being a net beneficiary or a net recipient. In a bilateral context, this entails a prohibition on any net transfers. In an intergenerational context, the idea that no one should end up being a net contributor or a net recipient calls for two important clarifications.

On the one hand, in a context involving more than two individuals, the prohibition on net transfers should not be applied in a segmented way to successive generations (i.e. 'is it complied with between generation 1 and 2?', '…between generation 2 and 3?', etc.). In other words, rather than operating such *direct* comparisons, one needs to construe the rule prohibiting net transfers as involving a comparison between one individual (or one generation) on the one hand, and *all* the other people (or generations) taken together, on the other. Hence, if a net transfer obtains between two persons (e.g. x and y), it may well be the case that another net transfer would have taken place between one of these two persons and a third one (e.g. y and z), such that neither x, nor y would end up being net contributors or net beneficiaries. The problem is that z may then end up being a net beneficiary, even under such an extended (and yet, narrow) interpretation of reciprocity.

Yet, the intergenerational context is not only multilateral (rather than merely bilateral). It is also *open ended towards the future*. This is crucial as to the ability of

---

[2] There are at least two good reasons to adopt such a narrow definition of reciprocity. First, this allows to concentrate on what I take to be at the heart of the very idea of reciprocity, on what makes it different from other notions such as impartiality, mutual advantage or solidarity. Second, as a way of methodological minimalism, I wish to show that even such a narrow notion of reciprocity allows to propose a relatively robust theory in the intergenerational realm. Let us note as well that the notion of reciprocity is used here in a non-Ralwsian way. See Rawls (2001: 77).

[3] When we talk about reciprocating the equivalent, we need to wonder each time: 'equivalent in which terms?' (e.g. of monetary value at time t, of potential for well-being for the beneficiary,…). While I leave the answer to this question open, it is clear that it may be of crucial importance, especially when people's preferences change with time, as we move from one generation to the next.

at least some of the reciprocity-based theories to propose an intergenerational model that would avoid any net transfer among generations. For in a *closed* context (involving a definite or finite number of people or generations), no matter how multilateral it may be, no one could be a net contributor without forcing at least some people into the position of net beneficiaries. This is not necessarily true in a context that is open towards the future, since each person (or generation) is able to pass on to the next person (or generation) her net benefit. This explains for example why a rule of reciprocity is not incompatible with the idea of transferring more to the next generation than what it received from the previous one. In short, it is possible for one generation, without violating the prohibition on net transfers, to be both a net beneficiary in relation with a given generation (admittedly not 'all generations considered'), and a net contributor with regard to the rest of all the other generations. It is thus worth noticing here that if the infinite/indefinite number of future people can be seen as a serious challenge for aggregative theories of intergenerational justice, and possibly as well to distributive ones,[4] it constitutes here—in contrast—the very feature which makes it possible to stick to a prohibition on net transfers while letting each generation free to transfer more to the next than it inherited itself.

Besides insisting both on the narrow interpretation of reciprocity that I will rely upon, as well as on the importance of the 'multilateral' and 'open-to-the-future' features of the intergenerational context, there is a second point I wish to make. It has to do with a rather sociological hypothesis: reciprocity-based intuitions of intergenerational justice would be especially popular among the general public,[5] even among those who, once dealing with intra-generational issues, would not be especially attracted towards such a theory. For, as stated above, it is to be expected that a theory prohibiting any net transfers among people would not necessarily be regarded as an extremely common account of what we owe each other. So, the sociological assumption is: reciprocity-based theories of justice are especially popular in the intergenerational realm, regardless of their level of popularity insofar as *intra*generational contexts are concerned. This hypothesis helps in justifying our focus on such theories. I do not provide empirical support for it here. I simply assume it.

Then, the question that arises is: if this were a sound sociological hypothesis, how would we explain the degree of attraction exerted by reciprocity-based accounts of intergenerational justice once compared with e.g. truly

---

[4] Lauwers & Vallentyne (2004).
[5] For one of the rare sources on this point: Wade-Benzoni (2002).

redistributive approaches of justice? Among possible answers, let me point at two of them. The first one underlines the mixed function of what we inherit from the previous generation. It serves as a source of obligation (as we shall see), explaining *why* we would owe something to other generations. It simultaneously serves as a source of inspiration as to *what* we owe other generations. We need such inspiration because we may owe something to the next generation, in some cases without having benefited from anything from this generation in the first place. This is what justifies the need for such a baseline.[6]

The second hypothesis as to the reasons why people may find intergenerational reciprocity views especially attractive has to do with a distinction among three sources of advantage or disadvantage: nature's action, the action of others, and one's own actions on oneself.[7] It may well be that when we envisage issues of intergenerational justice, we only consider two of these three sources. In other words, we would be considering that what we inherited would result either from what the previous generation transferred us, or from the activities from the members of our own generation. We would thus be overlooking the possibility of *exogenous* transfers, through the third source of advantages and disadvantages, i.e. nature. In the absence of such a third source of (dis)advantages, relying exclusively on a focus on the two other sources would make a commutative approach perfectly sufficient and a distributive approach redundant in most cases.[8] And yet, it makes perfect sense to consider the possibility of disadvantages resulting directly from natural events, even in an intergenerational context.[9] This being said, let me now move to a closer examination of intergenerational reciprocity as a theory of justice.

---

[6] See Wade-Benzoni (2002). Also Cigno (2005) ('family constitution') and Bichot (*in litt*, 9 Jan. 2006) ('imitation effect').

[7] As pointed out to me by one of the referees, in real life, these three sources of advantage/disadvantage do of course interact.

[8] In fact, this is not true for all distributive theories. Consider an egalitarian theory that is 'choice-sensitive', i.e. sensitive to responsibility, such as Dworkin's (2000). If a morally problematic disadvantage that affects me is a result from my choices, it is not society's job to compensate for it. And if it results from the action of identifiable third parties, it is these very people who are in charge of such compensation, as opposed to society as a whole. In contrast, let us imagine a distributive theory that would *not* deny a right to redistribution to a person who would be fully responsible for her extreme poverty, which is typically the case of a sufficientarian theory that would not be luck-sufficientarian. In such a society in which the disadvantages suffered by people would never result from causes different from free actions of its members (be it the very victim or a third party), such a distributive theory (sufficientarianism) would still operate in a way distinct from a commutative view, since the latter would be incapable of justifying redistributive transfers to the benefit of a very poor person who would be fully responsible for her situation. My thanks to G. Ponthière for having forced me to clarify this point.

[9] See Gosseries (2004).

1. Three Models

In order to focus on the core features of these theories, let us limit ourselves to four generations, defined as birth cohorts of 10 years each. G1 represents all those born during the first decade, G2, G3, and G4 all those born respectively during the second, the third, and the fourth decades. Among the different possible variants, let's single out three models of intergenerational reciprocity—not necessarily mutually exclusive if applied to different objects—each of them coming in two forms. One is the justificatory form, aiming at *justifying* the very *existence* of intergenerational obligations. The other form is substantive and it has to do with *defining* the *content* of such obligations.[10] Each of the three models that will now be presented comes in these two forms, i.e. substantive and justificatory.

Let us start with the first model, i.e. the *descending* one. According to its *justificatory* form, *G2 owes something to G3 because G1 transferred something to G2*. As to its *substantive* version, it states that *G2 owes at least as much to G3 as what it received itself from G1*. This descending model is the most standard of our three models. Its scope is the most *general* one, as it applies to all types of transfers from one generation to the next one. More importantly, together with the more limited ascending model described below, it relies on an idea of *indirect* reciprocity. By the latter, I refer to the fact that the 'final beneficiary'[11] (G3) is not identical to the initial benefactor (G1). And this has of course a connection with the *multilateral* character of the intergenerational context underlined above. In short, reciprocation is oriented towards an individual or a generation which is initially only a third party. And each of these reciprocation steps can be connected together to form a chain involving the successive generations. This may allow for a transitive approach to intergenerational justice.

As to the second model, it differs from the descending one by the direction of the transfers it involves. It goes in the opposite direction, which explains why I call it the *ascending* model. In its justificatory form, it states that G3 owes something to G2 because G2 has transferred something to G1. The substantive form adds that *G3 owes to G2 at least as much as what G1 transferred earlier to G1*. Such a model, especially in its justificatory form, is relevant for example to account for the logic of pay-as-you go pension schemes. The fact that an active generation owes something to another generation that is just reaching

---

[10] Note the connection between this (i.e. 'justifying the existence' and 'defining the content') and the distinction we drew above between source of obligation and source of inspiration.

[11] This is of course too rough since as soon as we abandon the model, such a four-generations world is itself anchored to an indefinite number of past and future generations.

retirement age is justified here by the fact that the latter cohort did the same for its own parents during its own active life.

However, the relevance of this ascending model in accounting for our intergenerational obligations in pay-as-you-go pension schemes is challenged by advocates of the idea of *double* reciprocity.[12] This is the only one of our three models that involves *direct* rather than indirect reciprocity. In other words, the initial contributor is also the final beneficiary in the context of a bi-directional relationship (whereas the two other models are mono-directional). Those who defend this model claim that our children's obligation to pay for our retirement benefits should not at all be conceived as a reciprocation of the fact that we would have done the same for our own parents in the past (ascending model). Instead, as Cosandey states:

> ... the only true contribution to retirement benefits is the money invested to the benefit of the next generation. Contributions paid to the benefit of the previous generation represent a duty for any citizen and should not give rise to new rights. They reimburse a debt that each of us has towards the previous generation, for having been taken care of during our own childhood.[13]

In short, paying the pension of our parents is not in reply to what they did themselves to the benefit of their own parents. It is rather in reply to what they did to us in terms of investing in our own education.

Before proceeding with an examination of three key objections to these models, let us add two points, one of a conceptual nature and the other of a rather practical one. The conceptual point is that we should not confuse the 'descending/ascending' distinction with the 'prospective/retrospective' one.[14] It is one thing to decide whether we transfer something *forward* (to the next generation) or *backward* (to the previous one). It is another to decide about whether *past* (actual) or *future* (expected) transfers should serve as a reference point in defining how much we owe to the generation to which we are making the transfer. To put things differently, it is one thing to ask 'in which direction should I reciprocate?'. It is another to ask 'when I reciprocate, which transfer should I take as a baseline to assess what I owe back?'. The 'descending/ascending' distinction has to do with the direction of transfers whereas the 'prospective/retrospective' distinction has to do with the temporal location of the reference transfer. In retrospective models, the reference transfer

---

[12] These are Cosandey's (2003) words. Bichot (1999) developed earlier arguments going in the same direction. However, he considers the notion of 'double reciprocity' as inappropriate (*in litt.*). We use it here to preserve a reference to Cosandey's view, even if the idea of 'direct reciprocity' is probably more appropriate. See as well Bichot (1980) and (1982).

[13] Cosandey (2003: 21) (our translation).   [14] See Kolm (2000: 30).

precedes the transfer that we are trying to define in terms of content. And in prospective models, we are taking as a reference transfer one that did not yet take place.

To illustrate this, let me take a substantive ascending model. It is presented in Table 4.1 in its retrospective form: G3 can find out what it owes to G2 by looking at what G2 did to G1. When it comes to the justificatory form of the ascending model, we will tend to use indifferently the retrospective and the prospective form. Moreover, the prospective form of the justificatory ascending model may have at least two advantages. First, when it comes to justifying the obligations of G3 towards G2 in specific cases in which G2 is a 'free lunch' generation (e.g. the very first generation to have benefitted from the establishment of a pay-as-you-go pension scheme), there is by definition no relevant G2-to-G1 transfer that could serve as a reference transfer. In theory at least, the only available strategy in such cases is to refer to the promise of a future transfer from G4 to G3. Second, leaving aside the free lunch generation(s) hypothesis, mutually disinterested people may be motivationally more concerned about securing their future pension through ascending transfers by the next generation than about making sure that promises made by others in the past be kept. For the promise we may be referring to could be one made by G1 to G2 claiming that G3 would do the same to G2. This being said, when it comes to the *substantive* form of an ascending model, the retrospective version is much more helpful since it provides us with a transfer that is certain because it already took place and that can serve as a secure reference point to define what the pivotal generation will now owe to the previous one. This equally holds for the descending model. This is why in the rest of this chapter, I shall assume that the retrospective versions are the standard

Table 4.1. The three models of intergenerational reciprocity and their two forms

	Justificatory	Substantive
Descending	G2 owes something to G3 because G1 transferred something to G2	G2 owes G3 at least as much as what G1 transferred to G2
Ascending	G3 owes something to G2 because G2 transferred something to G1	G3 owes G2 at least as much as what G2 transferred to G1
Double	G2 owes something to G1 because G1 transferred something to G2	G2 owes G1 at least as much as what G1 transferred to G2

ones, which is not always the case in practice, e.g. when it comes to the pension debate.

As to the more practical point, it has to do with the comparison between the ascending and the double models and their relative plausibility. I shall return to this point below (section 4). At this stage, it is worth emphasizing that despite the claim of defenders of double reciprocity—notably regarding the demo-insensitivity of the ascending model—the ability of the former model to serve as a normative guideline for intergenerational transfers will depend on factors such as the importance of education or people's life expectancy. Imagine for example a society in which children study normally but in which most people die before reaching the age of pension (if any). In such a society, the educational transfers will necessarily be much larger than those regarding pension benefits. In a double reciprocity model, if the two types of transfers are not equivalent, it will not be possible to end up with a plausible account.

2. Barry's challenge

Having presented the three central models of intergenerational reciprocity, let us consider a first challenge, faced more specifically by their *justificatory form*. The challenge is well expressed by Brian Barry:

If someone offers me a toffee apple, out of the blue, and I accept it, does my enjoyment of the toffee apple create even the tiniest obligation to distribute toffee apples to others? I do not see that it does.[15]

What we are asked to answer is why the mere fact of receiving something from someone would justify an *obligation* falling on me to give something back—regardless of whether empirical social sciences would actually show that people do (or not) *feel obliged* to reciprocate, of *feel bad* if they don't reciprocate. And we may indeed be willing to conclude that there is no way

---

[15] Barry (1989: 232). Nozick has the same kind of objection: 'So the fact that we partially are "social products" in that we benefit from current patterns and forms created by the multitudinous actions of a long string of long-forgotten people (...) does not create in us a general floating debt which the current society can collect and use as it will' (1974: 95). We do not examine here a more specific form of this objection that has to do more with the justification of the obligations of end-of-chain generations (first generation in the descending model, last generation in the ascending model). Note here that the first generation problem is relevant both to reciprocity-based views (as a generation having received nothing from an earlier one) and for contractarian theories (as a generation allegedly unable to benefit from the cooperation with later generations). See also Gardiner (Chapter 3 of this volume)) and Attas (Chapter 7 of this volume).

to justify an obligation of justice to give back. This may take several forms. We may of course conclude that we have no intergenerational obligations. We may also want to claim that what is at stake is not justice but mere gratitude. This could be Hobbes's position:

> As Justice dependeth on Antecedent Covenant; so does GRATITUDE depend on Antecedent Grace; that is to say, Antecedent Free-gift: and is the fourth Law of Nature; which may be conceived in this Forme, *That a man which receiveth Benefit from another of meer Grace, Endeavour that he which giveth it, have no reasonable cause to repent him of his good will.*[16]

A third way would consist instead in claiming that there is an obligation of justice, but that our obligation to give back does not originate in the fact of having received something. For example, a theory of justice such as maximin (luck) egalitarianism would claim that it is not what we received, but rather the concern that members of the next generation do not end up with circumstances worse than ours that justifies the need for descending transfers. In the absence of such transfers, members of other generations may end up with circumstances worse than ours, due to no fault of their own. So, the reasons underlying intergenerational transfers for an egalitarian clearly differ from those that may be invoked by a reciprocity defender, notwithstanding the fact that both rest with concerns of justice.

How to address Barry's challenge while remaining faithful to the idea that our intergenerational obligations are real obligations and that they constitute obligations of justice? An attempt at saving the reciprocity-based approach would need to come up with an account that would add a reason to the mere fact of having benefited from a transfer, such that the obligation to give back would amount to an obligation of justice. Let us consider for a moment the view that mere insistence on the idea of reciprocity is not enough to properly address Barry's challenge. We would therefore want to explore two approaches that are *prima facie* compatible with the reciprocity approach and which may help to support it. One is phrased in terms of collective intergenerational property and oriented towards the idea of an obligation towards future people. The other rests on a notion of free-riding and focuses directly on the (ascending) idea of obligations towards dead people. Both approaches can actually complement each other.

---

[16] Hobbes (1651: 209). For another example, in the realm of intellectual property: 'as we enjoy great advantages from the inventions of others, we should be glad of an opportunity to serve others by any inventions of ours; and this we should do freely and generously' (Benjamin Franklin, quoted in Boyle, 2003: n. 98).

128 AXEL GOSSERIES

Proprietarian metaphors

According to the proprietarian family of approaches, we do not fully and exclusively own as a generation what we inherited from the previous generation. This lack of full property is what will justify the existence of an obligation to give back to its owner what we are simply not entitled to freely dispose of. Such proprietarian approach comes in various forms. According to one possible metaphor, following the famous native American proverb,[17] what the current generation detains is actually supposed to have been lent to it by the next generations, which presupposes that the full collective ownership of our heritage (broadly taken) is constantly slipping into the hands of non yet existing, *future* generations. The same happens when we use the *usufruct* metaphor rather than the one of a loan. Again, the existing generations are either usufructuaries or borrowers and their entitlement ceases as soon as they die. As to future generations, the metaphor suggests that they would only keep the full property (in both cases) as long as they do not come into existence. The difficulty, present in both metaphors, is that in order to justify an obligation to keep (and transfer) something to future people, we need to ascribe ownership rights to people who don't exist yet, on objects that do currently exist. The same difficulty also arises when we rely on the co-ownership metaphor, rather than the loan or the usufruct one.

This calls for a set of four remarks, two of a more technical nature, followed by two more serious difficulties. First, while these analogies may be relevant to support the descending model, they are far less so for the ascending or double models. This suggests that it is unlikely that a single proprietarian analogy could automatically serve to support the three models altogether. Second, once we examine their legal regime in detail, each of these proprietarian metaphors have their specific limitations.[18] For instance, in case of a loan, in principle it is the very same good that we borrowed that should be restituted, which is not possible whenever we are dealing with non-renewable resources. Similarly, usufruct only applies to what are called fruits rather than products. Fossils fuels clearly belong to the latter category, not to the former. As to co-ownership models, they would in principle require the agreement of each and every co-owner, including future generations.

Third, and more importantly, suppose that we manage to characterize the nature of our intergenerational reciprocity obligations through the prism of

---

[17] 'Treat the earth well: it was not given to you by your parents, it was loaned to you by your children. We do not inherit the earth from our ancestors, we borrow it from our children' (various sources).

[18] Thanks to A.-P. André-Dumont and G.-F. Raneri for discussions on this point.

ownership-related ideas. The problem is that the existence of such ownership rights may need to be justified in turn. This is an uneasy task. One may want to refer to the will of God, as Locke did.[19] Another, more original strategy, consists in relying on the will of (some of) the earlier generations. This approach can be found in the work of Léon Bourgeois.[20] His strategy consists in producing a historical argument involving the following claim. Let us start with a minimalistic (normative) assumption such that the first generation was the exclusive owner of the Earth. This means that we could have had a scenario such that each generation would bequeath to the next what it owned as an exclusive owner, without any further condition. Let us now introduce a second (factual) assumption: we can plausibly claim that at least some of the generations that preceded us bequeathed what they had inherited from the previous generations with the view that it would belong to *all* future generations. If this is true for at least some of the generations that preceded us, it means that even assuming that the first generation was the exclusive owner of what it had, our heritage will be progressively collectivized (intergenerationally speaking) through the action of possibly just a few generations. And of course, the more such a collectivist intention can be found among recent generations just preceding ours, the more it will restrict our own freedom regarding what we inherited.

It is thus possible to justify the existence of an entitlement of all coming generations on what we inherited from the previous generations. This can be done through reference to an actual intention, either of God (Locke) or of some of the preceding generations (Bourgeois). And this can of course be done independently, by providing and defending a full theory of justice in line with our well-considered intuitions. But there is a fourth and quite decisive point to be made here. The logic of reciprocity insists on the contribution of each of us and on the idea that the reason why I owe something back is due to the fact that I received something in the first place. The ownership-based logic works differently since the reason why I owe something back has nothing to do with the fact that I received something. It has to do with the fact that

---

[19] Locke (1690, First treatise, §88). See as well in the same vein, referring to religion, Grégoire (1787: 132, our translation): 'Children of the Gospel, the religion that you are professing encompasses, through the links of love, all the mortals not only from all countries, but even from all centuries. Is it religion's fault if you ignore your duties towards posterity? It requires that, moved by the very fate of future generations, you would prepare the happiness of those who are still sleeping in nothingness, and who will only come to existence when you will be sleeping in dust'. My thanks to J.-M. Chaumont for pointing me to this.

[20] For further developments: Gosseries (2004: 161s). Compare: 'The improvements made by the dead form a debt against the living, who take the benefit of them. This debt cannot be otherwise discharged than by a proportionate obedience to the will of the authors of the improvements' (Madison, 1790).

what I possess is not (fully) mine. Hence, even if entitlement-based accounts of our obligation to transfer may coincide on their substantive claims with the reciprocity-based models, they would still misrepresent the very logic at work in the latter models. Can we do better than that?

Reciprocity and free-riding

In order to answer this question, let us look at a second possible option, consisting this time in turning more directly to the idea of obligation towards dead people and in relying on a revisited notion of free-riding. The idea consists here in accounting for our obligation to reciprocate, not on the ground of an obligation to give back a good that would not be (exclusively) ours, but rather on the basis of an obligation not to end up being a free-rider to the detriment of earlier generations. At first sight, one could think that the idea of free-riding should not be relied upon whenever the goods transferred from one generation to the next are of a rival type, i.e. whose enjoyment by one individual necessarily entails a reduction in the possibilities of enjoyment by others of the very same good (e.g. a car or a house). Yet, in the case of descending reciprocity (not under the two other models), a notion of free-riding could be usefully relied upon, even in the presence of rival goods, which is clearly the case for all non-renewable resources for example. Here is an account, in two steps. First, I discuss issues of scope of free-riding. Then I focus more specifically on the idea of free-riding with respect to dead people.

Let me begin with the assumption that free-riding obtains whenever a person derives a net benefit from the fruits of someone else's labour, the latter being fully voluntary, without diminishing in any sense the enjoyment that this other person derives from this good. Let us then define in general terms the scope of free-riding, considering on the one hand a non-rival good and a rival one on the other. First, if a good is both non-rival and of a strictly natural origin (e.g. sunlight, as opposed to public lighting with electricity), we clearly fall *outside* the scope of a notion of free-riding since we do not free-ride on anyone's contribution (given the natural origin of the good). In contrast, if this good is both non-rival as well as a product of human activity, we find ourselves in the *standard* scope of the concept of free-riding. We will then be concerned about whether, given the extent to which a person consumes this good, she has contributed enough or in excess to its production. *Ex hypothesi*, again, this good is assumed to result from the activity of third parties that voluntarily engaged in such a productive effort. It is because the concept of free-riding has to do with the production-consumption relationship (rather than focusing merely on consumption) that it is still capable of identifying injustices even if the good is non-rival.

Second—remaining within the realm of this free-riding-oriented analysis—suppose this time a *rival* good, and one that is man-made rather than of natural origin. In such a case, we could be tempted to consider this situation as laying outside the material scope of the concept of free-riding. Our claim is that this would be an incorrect analysis. The hypothesis here is that any rival good whose beneficiary would not be its producer belongs to the potential scope of the concept of free-riding, understood as referring to a contribution insufficient once we consider the voluntary production effort by others regarding this good. We generally tend *not* to analyse rival goods through the prism of free-riding. This is probably due to the fact that—contrary to what happens with non-rival goods—free-riding is not in this case the only concept available to account for our intuitions of injustice. For whenever a good exhibits rivalry, we can perfectly analyse the possible injustice of its consumer's behaviour, not only under the free-riding framework, but through the angle of a concept of deprivation (total or partial). In other words, we are able to check whether my consumption of this good unfairly deprives others from something. And we will tend to translate this with concepts such as theft or possibly exploitation (in the neo-marxian sense).

To put things differently, the key point here—of a psychologico-moral nature—is that accounts resting on the notion of deprivation tend to produce a sense of injustice much stronger than those flowing from an idea of insufficient contribution. Whenever both types of analysis (deprivation-based or free-riding oriented) are simultaneously available (which is the case for non-natural rival goods, not for non-rival ones), the first type (deprivation-based) will tend to outshine, to *dominate* the second type (insufficient contribution). This may nourish the mistaken impression that the latter would simply not be applicable to such cases. My view is that the concept of free-riding remains an available resource for the analysis of fair consumption of rival goods. A consumer could be *both* a thief and a free-rider. This is my first key hypothesis, having to do with the proper definition of free-riding's material scope. Let us call it the *coexistence hypothesis*, by reference to the two possible analysis in terms of justice of the consumption of a rival good. One refers to the impact of my consumption on the possibility for others to consume the same good (deprivation). The other focuses on the relationship between my consumption and the share that should have been mine in the production of this good (free-riding).

Coming now more specifically to the intergenerational realm, there are various ways of articulating generations and free-riding.[21] The one that is of interest to us here requires that we focus on a set of producers who became

---

[21] For another illustration: Gosseries (2006).

unable to consume the good they produced. Let us consider a good with objective features such that it could be rival. It would be man-made but its actual producers would now be *dead*. Think for example about a castle, inherited from your ancestors, and resulting from the hard work of seven generations of family members, all of them dead by now. It is clearly a rival good, not only towards the other members of my own generation (some would definitely enjoy living in such a castle), but also towards the coming generations (hoping that my own enjoyment of the castle will not reduce the enjoyment they could derive from it, had I not existed). In contrast, this good is *not* rival towards past generations. In other words, it is not rival towards all. Its degradation through my fault would not deprive earlier generations from any degree of enjoyment of this good that they could have had in my absence. And this is so even for those who believe that the dead do exist in a certain sense, since the latter sense would not in all plausibility entail their ability to enjoy material goods. However, it could be meaningful to claim that by destroying the castle or even by letting it fall apart,[22] the present generation would be free-riding on earlier generations. For it would take advantage, without adding anything itself, of the efforts they would voluntarily have put in this castle. The hypothesis would thus be: for this kind of good, the analysis in terms of free-riding could remain relevant, notwithstanding the fact that those on whom we are free-riding are now dead. At the same time, the idea of deprivation would not be available here for, when it comes to our relationship with dead people, the good we are dealing with exhibits the characteristics of a non-rival good. The obligation to reciprocate to the next generation would thus result from an obligation not to free-ride to the detriment of earlier generations.

Let me clarify this a bit further through a set of remarks. *First*, the idea is that for a certain number of goods, the death of one of the producers also leads to his death as a consumer. It then renders the good *non-rival towards that person*, since the latter is not a potential consumer anymore. My own consumption of this good is not at all able to deprive her from the enjoyment of the good. This presupposes the acceptance of the idea that someone may *exist* without being able to (fully) consume a given good. This is the case whenever a product's life

---

[22] There is a difference between degrading a good (i.e. worsening its situation as compared to a world in which I would not exist) and letting it fall apart (i.e. not doing anything to protect it from the effects of time). If we take as a reference point 'the world as it would be in my absence', we are unable to account for any obligations to actively care for degradable goods. Of course, from a free-riding perspective, the degree of my obligation to actively care for the good will have to be adjusted to the extent to which I derive any benefits from this good. If I merely inherited it without deriving any enjoyment from it, a free-riding-based account would be unable to criticize an inactive castle owner. See also *infra*.

expectancy extends beyond the death of its producer(s). However, the situation of dead people does not constitute the only possible illustration. Let us think about a vegetarian producer of cow meat (whose vegetarianism would rest on reasons that do not require from all of us not to consume meat). These cows are objectively rival 'goods'. Yet, they are not rival towards all. This being said, it is worth insisting on the fact that for those who consider that dead people do exist, some of the goods we inherited may remain rival *even towards the dead*. For example, if the paternity of a discovery can be recognized as a good, the fact that someone else would abusively claim the paternity of one of Einstein's inventions for example, could be seen as a potential source of deprivation (recognition deprivation) to the detriment of Einstein himself. For this type of goods, and provided that we accept the idea that the dead do exist in a given sense, Einstein's death will not entail that this good would become non-rival.

This leads us to a second remark. Deprivation-focused theories of justice, but also those that rest on a notion of free-riding (be it broadened) towards the dead *necessarily* presuppose that the dead do exist in at least a weak sense and that they could be affected by the consequences of actions taking place after their death. This is an important limitation of such a type of approach, as we indicated elsewhere.[23] A proprietarian approach à la Bourgeois would also be vulnerable to such a difficulty, as it rests on the idea of respecting the will of the dead. An egalitarian theory would in contrast escape this kind of difficulty.

Our third remark consists in underlining that whenever we use a notion of 'free-riding to the detriment of', we still rely on a notion of cost. It does not have to do with an opportunity cost that my consumption would impose on someone else's potential consumption. The cost rather has to do with the additional production cost resulting from my non-contribution to the production effort by others, bearing in mind that we are talking about voluntary production efforts by others. The question we need to ask ourselves is then the following: would the notion of free-riding not be also vulnerable to death's consequences, as is the case with the problem of deprivation? Death would remove the possibility of deprivation. But it would also remove the possibility of compensating people for costs that they would have incurred, be it voluntarily. This move should be resisted, for a reason illustrated by the following progression.

Suppose a closed world with two generations. Jo and Jack are contemporaries and we know that Jack will not have children. Jo produces a good alone but Jack would have been perfectly able to help him at the time of production.

---

[23] Gosseries (2004: ch. 2).

Jack then consumes part of that good without having contributed at all to its production, but also without having at all imposed such a production. Yet, there is a sense in which Jack imposed (by abstention) on Jo production costs that were higher than if the former had helped the latter. Let us now consider a slightly different situation in which Jack was born on exactly the same day as Jo's death. This means that Jack was absolutely unable to help Jo to produce this good. It would thus be inappropriate to consider him as a free-rider, at least in a sense that would have a minimally normative dimension.[24]

We could of course stop here. This would disregard the fact that the intergenerational space is an open one. It is open to the future. Jack will himself be followed by Jerry, who will himself be followed by Jim, etc. If the goods that have been produced are durable to a relatively significant extent (which is often the case), the non-contemporaneity of the potential producers does not mean that the 'production' effort of this good could not be pursued as time goes, a maintenance stage following the production stage. If this is so, we can re-consider the situation as follows. If Jack does not prolong to the benefit of Jerry the effort launched by Jo, he will be a free-rider towards Jo, not because the production costs (strictly understood) could have been lessened by Jack's contribution (although even that could be challenged), but rather because the production costs will have been incurred partly in vain if Jack simply does not care about preserving the good resulting from Jo's effort. When it comes to dealing with dead people, the nature of free-riding would thus be slightly different than in more common cases. Yet, it would still make some sense to claim that while not depriving the dead of the enjoyment of a good, the fact that his efforts have been allowed to become vain (by not caring about what he produced or by consuming alone a good that was aimed at the whole succession of coming generations) may affect this dead person.

It is thus clear that under such an analysis, free-riding towards the dead brings us back to the proprietarian approach defining our obligations towards coming generations. The proprietarian and the free-riding approach can thus overlap significantly, even if the former does not necessarily imply the latter. Rejecting the proprietarian approach when it comes to our relationship with the dead (because of the unavailability of deprivation-based accounts in such cases) does not entail that it should be rejected when it comes to our relationships with coming generations. Nor does it entail that we could not bring together the idea of free-riding towards dead people with a proprietarian definition of our obligations towards the next generations, considering or not the former as a foundation for the latter. Doing so however would certainly mean that the

---

[24] See however above n. 22.

apparent elegance of the descending reciprocity model would as a matter of fact hide the dual nature of its underlying justifications.

Let me add as well that the notion of free-riding will only be relevant for the fraction of our generational bequest that can be regarded as the fruit of earlier generation's labour. In contrast, the notion of e.g. collective property for example extends to the whole of our heritage, be it man-made or not, including untouched natural goods. Unless we ascribe an over-extensive scope to the notion of man-made goods, it follows that the idea of free-riding can only offer an *incomplete* account of the idea of descending reciprocity.[25]

Let me thus conclude on Barry's objection. It is not easy to dig underneath the three models of reciprocity in search of further justifications. And it is not certain at all that reformulations of the logic of reciprocity in terms of collective property or free-riding do full justice to the idea, do account for it, and really bring added value to the debate. At the same time, this does not need to be read as a sign of the weakness of reciprocity-based views. Any theory of justice will as some point hit a level at which it becomes too hard to dig deeper in order to identify even more fundamental intuitions at work.

3. The Problem of Direction

The objection we have just dealt with had to do with the justificatory versions of our three reciprocity-based models. Another objection has to do with whether reciprocity-based views are able to justify the *direction* of reciprocation in each case, i.e. why it should be ascending or descending.[26] This challenge potentially affects both justificatory and substantive forms. For, as a matter of theory, the 'initial transfer' to the current generation could in fact always be reciprocated in one of three possible directions: in an ascending manner (from the current to the previous generation), in a descending one (from the current to the next one), or through self-reciprocation (towards some members within the current generation).[27] A reciprocity-based model will thus only be robust if it is able to tell us why reciprocation should only follow one of these three directions, rather than the two other ones. From this perspective, how do our three models behave?

Let us envisage first the exclusion of self-reciprociation, i.e. reciprocation of what was transferred by another generation to the members of one's own

---

[25] See also *infra*, n. 33.   [26] See e.g. de-Shalit (1995: 99).

[27] Note that this distinction among three possible *directions* does not fully overlap with the three general models. Self-reciprocation is not the equivalent of the double reciprocity model.

generation. A relevant intuition here could be that it is at least as fair to transfer part of the basket of goods inherited from the previous generation to the least well-off members of our own generation, rather than to the next generation. From the perspective of a theory of reciprocity, this may lead to the fact that those least well-off members of our own generation would end up having benefitted from net transfers, to the extent that they would not have reciprocated as much as what they received from the previous generation. Self-reciprocation is thus incompatible, both at the individual and at the generational level with the prohibition on net transfers, and more specifically with the prohibition on people ending up being net beneficiaries. All three reciprocity-based models are quite robust when it comes to the rejection of self-reciprocation.

Are they equally so when it comes to the two other options excluded by the models, i.e. ascending reciprocation in the case of the descending model, and descending reciprocation when it comes to the ascending and double models? From this perspective, the descending model is equally robust once we consider it carefully. For, suppose a world involving a stationary population (the size of each generation remaining constant) and let us assume that G1 transferred 10 units to G2 who would have transferred 10 units to G3. Imagine now that G3 decides to transfer only 8 units to G4 and 2 units back to G2. G3 would certainly not end up being a net beneficiary since it would clearly have emptied its debt. Moreover, such option involving partial ascending reciprocation is a perfectly possible one in practice. For example, we can easily reciprocate something to our own parents in terms of health care or other non-durable goods. The problem, however, is that in this hypothesis, G2 will end up being a net beneficiary, which is problematic from the perspective of a reciprocity-based view as defined narrowly above. In a sense, by not following the descending direction, G3 will *force* G2 to end up having violated the reciprocity rule, for example if the latter is unable, because of her age, to reciprocate back to G3 the equivalent of what gives her the status of a net beneficiary. The descending model is thus especially robust insofar as the objection from direction is concerned, since the reciprocity-based logic allows us to exclude the two alternative options, namely, self-reciprocation and ascending reciprocation.

We still need to address the challenge when it comes to understanding why the ascending and the double reciprocity models would be able to exclude the option of descending reciprocation. The answer here is that if G2 decides to reciprocate to G3 rather than to G1 part of what had been transferred to it by G1, the latter will actually find itself in the position of a net contributor. The possibility of a descending transfer in this case will lead to a situation in which the previous generation will be forced to end up, not in the position of a net beneficiary, but rather of a net contributor, which is at least as problematic from the perspective of a reciprocity-based theory. To conclude, it turns out that our three reciprocity-based models are quite robust against the objection from direction.

4. Demographic Change

Let us finally consider a third difficulty. It is the most serious one. It becomes apparent when we take seriously the fact that a population will fluctuate from one generation to another. Are such fluctuations irrelevant when it comes to defining the nature of our obligations towards our neighbouring generations? Admittedly, this problem will not affect each and every type of intergenerational transfers.[28] And yet, the general public is right to be concerned with such population issues in connection with intergenerational transfers. An obvious illustration is the funding of our pension schemes as well as of health care for the elderly, which leads to special concerns when the reduction in birth rates is associated with an increase in life expectancy. Similarly, some of us are concerned with the ability of the planet to stand the agressions of a growing world population. As to the philosophical literature, it is rich in developments at the meta-ethical level,[29] but far less at the level of our substantive obligations of justice, probably in part because meta-ethical difficulties are often conceived as obstacles to advances at the substantive level. To put things differently, the philosophical litterature raises the question as to the conditions under which it is meaningful to claim that bringing to the world a larger population is more desirable than bringing about a smaller one. For example, if the number of people surrounding us, the size of our individual resources and the length of our lives affect in various ways our well-being, it is important to ask ourselves—*ex ante*—if it would not be fairer to bring to the world fewer children who would on average be happier, rather than more children whose average well-being would be lower. However, we are interested here in the *ex post* question: once this new generation has been brought to the world, its size should then be taken as given. Taking this for granted, we need to ask ourselves if the size of this population should affect

---

[28] The importance of transferring to the next generation democratic institutions, a culture of trust among people, etc is of course crucial as well. Such expectations of transfer should not be affected by the relative size of the generations at stake.

[29] See e.g. Arrhenius (2000), and also Chapter 12 in this volume.

the size and nature of the obligations of its surrounding generations towards it, as well as the size and nature of its own obligations towards the generations that surround it.

Under this *ex post* angle, there are two families of theories of intergenerational justice. The theories belonging to the first set tend to adjust what one generation owes to the other to the relative size of these populations, as opposed to merely to the size of the transfers that have or will take place, or to other factors. We refer to these theories as 'demo-sensitive' (or 'demo-reactive'). In theory, such demo-sensitivity could vary both in terms of degree and sign. In contrast, other theories will define what is owed to another generation exclusively by looking at the basket of goods that was or will be transferred to a generation, and perhaps as well on the basis of other factors, but certainly *regardless* of the relative size of the various neighbouring generations. We refer to the latter as 'demo-insensitive'.

A distributivist theory of the maximin egalitarian type for instance will certainly be demo-sensitive. It will probably require from one generation having decided to reproduce itself at a rate higher than the replacement rate, to transfer more—on aggregate—than it inherited from the previous generation. The goal is to make sure that the current generation and the next one will turn out having benefited, per capita, from an equivalent bequest. The demo-sensitive nature of such a theory results directly from the underlying logic according to which intergenerational transfers should aim at making sure that one generation does not end up having been disadvantaged by her cohortal circumstances.

The basic hypothesis that I wish to test here is the following : the very logic of reciprocity would exclude that our three theories be demo-sensitive. We have seen, while responding to the objection from direction, that the prohibition on forcing a person (or a generation) to end up being either a net beneficiary (in the case of descending reciprocity) or a net contributor (in the case of ascending and double reciprocity) played a key role in accounting for the robustness of such models. In the present case, the central idea would be the latter, i.e. the one according to which one should not force a person (or a generation) to end up being a net contributor. As was already said, the logic of reciprocity consists in getting rid of one's debts, regardless of *how many* people will be led to benefit from it. If I give back as much as what I received, this will suffice to exhaust or cancel out my obligations, even if it means that, in case of population growth, a larger number of people will have to share the same amount of resources. The latter conclusion is problematic, for it would allow, in full compliance with this definition of justice, in the context of a model of descending reciprocity, for a gradual impoverishment per head, as new generations come on board. This problem is often overlooked by those who consider reciprocity-based theories of intergenerational justice as intuitively attractive.

Our question is therefore the following: is it correct to consider that the reciprocity-based models are demo-insensitive? We will answer it in two steps, looking successively at theories of *indirect* reciprocity, and then at the double reciprocity model. Among the various possible demographic scenarios (e.g. non-linear decline or growth, baby-boom followed by a baby-bust, and conversely), we will focus each time on one single demographic scenario that leads to a requirement of justice that is either inconsistent or counter-intuitive.

The descending and ascending models

The simplest case involves a population increase with a *descending* model. Here, the difficulty is obvious since reciprocity allows us to leave the next generation in a situation less favourable per capita than ours. Because of the absence of an obligation to be a net contributor and the prohibition on imposing on other people to be net contributors, if the population doubles, there is no obligation on us to double the size of the basket of goods transferred to the next generation. This does not constitute a source of internal inconsistency. However, as it is compatible with the gradual impoverishment of humankind, generation after generation, it may be counter-intuitive, especially for opportunity/luck egalitarians. This is so because in such a case the members of a later generation may end up with having inherited an average productive potential (hence *circumstances*) worse than the one of earlier generations, due to demographic *choices* made by earlier generations.

Consider then the way in which the *ascending* model reacts in case of population decrease. Let me refer more specifically to the retrospective version of the ascending model, in which what G3 owes G2 corresponds to what G2 transferred in the past to G1, rather than to what G4 will transfer to G3 in the future. Imagine for a moment that our population decreases by 50 per cent at each generational step, and let us look at two sub-cases that have some connection with Musgravian pension models of 'fixed replacement rate' and 'fixed contribution rate'.[30] First case: if each member of G2 has invested 10 units in funding the pensions of G1, each member of G3 will in turn have to invest 20 units in funding the pensions of G2, and so on. This allows us to prevent the members of G2 from ending up being net contributors. Moreover, at first sight, the generational chain being open, it is possible, provided that

[30] See Musgrave (1981).

each generation progressively increases its contribution, to still comply with the idea that no member of generations ulterior to G2 would be constrained to end up being a net contributor. However, it will soon become clear that such an increase in contribution rate, allowing—*ceteris paribus*—the level of pension benefits to be kept constant *and* avoiding the violation, at least at the beginning, of the rule prohibiting the imposition of net contribution, will soon lead to a situation that is not economically sustainable. And it will necessarily lead at the end of the day to a violation of this very same principle.

Alternatively, one could consider that if each member of G2 has invested 10 units in funding G1's pensions, each member of G3 should in fact do the same towards G2. In such a case, the contribution rate could remain sustainable in the long-term. However, the level of pension benefits of the members of each generation would gradually decrease because of our scenario of demographic decrease. Each of us will then end up having contributed more (to the benefit of the earlier generation) than we will have received in return (from the next generation). The challenge that an ascending model needs to address in case of population decline is not only that this model would lead to counter-intuitive conclusions for those who defend approaches that differ from the reciprocity-based one. Rather, it is a problem *internal* to the theory, since it consists in its inability to propose in such a case a plausible transfer rule that does not violate in one way or another the principle according to which one should not be forced to end up as a net contributor in the intergenerational chain. The ascending model thus looks unable, in case of demographic decline, to propose a rule that would not end up violating this principle.[31]

---

[31] One possible way out of the difficulties faced by the descending and—more importantly—by the ascending one could consist in trying to include the demographic variable in the assessment of the size of our intergenerational transfers. Let us first look at what this would lead to in the case of a *descending* model. The idea would consist in arguing that 'making children' is as much a contribution as 'inventing new technologies', or 'setting up new types of institutions with long-term effects'. Children would therefore no longer be seen as future end beneficiaries of transfers, but rather as part of the very basket of goods being transferred from one generation to the next. Such an approach turns out, however, not to be very promising. For if a reproduction rate superior to the replacement rate were to be considered as a positive and higher transfer than the one done by the previous generation, it would then allow for a proportional reduction in other transfers (e.g. in terms of natural resources). This would just further worsen the problem identified above, in case of a growing population. In contrast, if this reproduction rate were perceived as adding an extra burden on the next generation, and would then have to be substracted when it comes to assessing the size of the basket transferred, the problem identified above would of course be lessened. But this would amount to denying completely the fact that, *ceteris paribus*, raising more children generates for a particular generation more costs than raising fewer children, and would in principle correspond to the idea of a more important transfer than the reverse. The strategy thus finally ends up being *ad hoc*, and not at all embedded in the very logic of reciprocity. Hence, it turns out that integrating the reproduction rate as a variable of the transfer itself rather than as a characteristic of the generational groups at stake looks quite inappropriate in the context of a descending model. What about an ascending one? It seems more difficult for the latter

The indirect demo-sensitivity of double reciprocity

Is double reciprocity more prone to integrate the demographic dimension, than the two indirect and unidirectional models? One reason for suspecting this is that defenders of double reciprocity are themselves motivated by a demographic concern. Bichot (1989) or Cosandey (2003) defend this view out of concern for an alleged anti-natalist incentive that would be built-in in some of the pension funding regimes. They consider as a misrepresentation the idea of viewing our contribution to pension benefits as a reciprocation by those who are now active, of the equivalent of what we paid ourselves to our own parents *in terms of contribution to pension benefits* (which is what the ascending model implies). As a matter of fact, for these authors, we should see such ascending transfers as in return for descending transfers, hence as an instance of *direct* reciprocity. More precisely, such ascending transfers would in fact reciprocate the education spendings that we made to the benefit of those who are now constituting the active population. Following such a line of argument, it becomes perfectly meaningful, *intragenerationnally*, to consider that those who did not (or less) make such descending transfers (typically through raising their children) would not be entitled (or less so) to ascending transfers on the part of the next generation. In other words, it would be unfair for non-parents not to compensate the fact that parents are contributing twice (intergenerationnally speaking), i.e. on the one hand, through part of the income of their labour, by funding the retirement benefits of their own parents, and on the other, this time through their parental activities, by raising future active people without whom future pensions would simply have no future, even in the case of funded pension schemes.

It follows that the double reciprocity model *is* demo-sensitive since if we have fewer children, we are contributing less to the future of pensions and we are therefore less entitled to an ascending transfer in return. Add to this the fact that defenders of double reciprocity consider that pension schemes that do not adjust their benefits or contributions to the number of children are not only unjust towards parents, but contribute by themselves by not providing the right incentives, to the demographic problem that they are facing. What matters even more to us here is that *mutatis mutandis*, we could shift from the intraganerational level (parents v. non-parents) to the intergenerational one ('rabbit' v. 'non-rabbit' generations), defending the view that a generation

---

to integrate such a dimension because of a problem of direction. For reproducing ourselves at a given rate, be it analysed as a benefit or as a burden, will constitute at best a *descending* transfer. So, whatever its sign, its direction will be a descending one. Since the descending model only involves descending transfers, it is unable to be modified in that way.

reprocuding itself at a rate lower than the rate of another one would only be entitled to lesser ascending transfers.[32] Hence, the double reciprocity model is demo-sensitive since it entails at the intergenerational level that 'rabbit' generations would be entitled to larger ascending transfers, simply because their descending transfers, i.e. their spending, would be larger.

To go a little bit further into this, if G2 doubles its population while its own parents (G1) had been reproducing strictly at the replacement rate, G2 would be entitled to a pension twice as large as the one of G1 (both in terms of aggregate size and per head), because it transferred twice as much to the benefit of its own children (i.e. G3). Conversely, if G2 decides to reproduce itself at a rate leading to a division in two of the next generation's population, as compared to its own population, it should be ready to accept a related reduction in ascending transfers (from G3 to G2) equivalent to the reduction in descending transfers (from G2 to G1) that could follow. It is clear that a person having two times fewer children does not necessarily divide up her education expenses by two when compared to those of her neighbour. Yet, the double reciprocity model exhibits a certain consistency in the demographic fluctuation scenarios envisaged here. It illustrates the possibility of a demo-sensitive model that would not necessarily violate the prohibition on imposing net transfers.

This being said, the double reciprocity model exhibits both a specificity as well as an important difficulty from the perspective of demographic fluctuations. Let us consider its specificity first. Its nature can easily be understood once we compare the demo-sensitivity of the double reciprocity model and the one of an egalitarian model. There are differences at two levels. First, the reason why an egalitarian theory is demo-sensitive, even when dealing with transfers taking place in only *one* direction (e.g. descending ones) has to do with the fact that such a theory is not indifferent to the nature and the number of beneficiaries of such transfers. In contrast, it is the very *bi-directionality* of the double reciprocity model that renders it demo-sensitive.

Second, still at the level of specificities, the egalitarian approach is demo-sensitive in a *direct* way, even if it will tend to treat differently descending and ascending transfers in a context of demographic fluctuations. For it is problematic for an egalitarian to reduce descending transfers per head if a generation *chooses* to reproduce above the replacement rate. In contrast, reducing ascending transfers because a generation *happens to be* smaller than the previous one is not necessarily problematic if the gap from the replacement rate can be ascribed to the choices of the generation assumed to benefit

---

[32] We would then come closer to Musgrave's 'fixed contribution rate' than to his 'fixed replacement rate' model. See Musgrave (1981).

from such ascending transfers. This would be the case at least with a luck egalitarianism relying on the choice/circumstance distinction. In contrast, the bi-directionality of the double reciprocity model only renders it demo-sensitive in an *indirect* and *not necessarily proportional* way, because the adjustment focuses on the relative size of the respective transfers rather than on the number of children as such. Indeed, what plays a key role in the case of double reciprocity is not so much the fact of 'producing' children as such in the physical sense. It is rather the fact that we invest in educating them, which means that we invested (which leads to the need for transfers in return) and that this educational investment allowed for the emergence of future active people (which allows for such a transfer in return). However, it is possible that the marginal rate of investment per child be a decreasing one. In the same line, it is not always true that having no children at all entails less investment in the education of the next generation. It follows that the adjustment of ascending transfers would not follow linearly the fluctuations in reproduction rate, for it is on the size of descending transfers (based on the number of contributors, not of beneficiaries) that it needs to be adjusted. This is not illogical from a reciprocity-based perspective. And it is also not counter-intuitive, even if it can become so once the egalitarian perspective is taken seriously.

Besides such a specificity of the double reciprocity model, there is also a problem, resulting this time from the *incomplete* nature of the double reciprocity model's material scope.[33] For if having fewer children may (but needs not always) mean that less will be invested in terms of education, it

---

[33] Such incompleteness/incomprehensiveness has to do with the model's (in)ability to cover by itself the whole material domain of intergenerational transfers. The key difficulty raised by the notion of incompleteness has to do with whether one of the three models can be considered more complete than the two others. The challenge to the ascending and double models is to integrate descending transfers of natural resources as well as those resulting from the use of the human capital of all the previous generations. The ascending model is clearly incapable to do so since such descending transfers are not even considered. As to the double reciprocity model, it could only take descending transfers into account if it were possible to reciprocate in an ascending manner the equivalent of what was transferred in a descending way. Since what is transferred in a descending way not only covers the natural heritage but also the fruit of part of the investment of *all* the previous generations (taken together), it seems absurd to require an ascending reciprocation from *each* generation of the equivalent of the fruit of the effort of *all* past generations as well as of nature. This would be far too demanding. This problem results in part from the fact that the double reciprocity model is not open towards the future in a way that would allow for net transfers without violating the requirement of reciprocity, as we saw above. Moreover, an accumulation compatible with a prohibition on net transfers is also jeopardized. Yet, it remains true that the descending model is not strictly more complete than the two other ones, as it ignores ascending transfers. However, perhaps the idea of completeness would refer rather to the idea of net transfers. A model would then be complete/comprehensive if it would leave room to more net transfers. The problem is that if descending transfers tend systematically to be of a larger magnitude than ascending transfers, it is then likely that the descending model is more adequate from this point of view, and to that extent less incomplete. See also above, text attached to n. 25.

could then justify lesser ascending transfers in return than in case of a 'rabbit' generation. Yet, we should bear in mind that we are dealing with a two-sided coin. Admittedly, if having fewer children may in many cases entail a lesser investment in educational terms, the consecutive reduction of ascending transfer will make sense. However, such a reproductive choice simultaneously entails that from the point of view of a set of rare goods such as space, natural resources, etc., each member of G3 will as a matter of fact inherit a basket per head much larger than what is inherited per head by G2. As a result, having fewer children also leads to transfering such types of resources in a *higher* proportion per head. Once we consider this, the reduction in ascending transfers appears less intuitively plausible. As we can see, even if it is indirectly or contingently demo-sensitive, the double reciprocity model is not necessarily devoid of difficulties in case of demographic fluctuations.

Conclusion

How should we conclude on our three models of intergenerational reciprocity, with regard to the three objections we just examined? We have shown first that Barry's objection is not decisive. As a matter of fact, it rather translates a difference in basic intuition compared to other approaches to intergenerational justice, such as Rawlsian egalitarianism. And it may be possible to reformulate in other languages, such as the one of property (and its derivates) or the one of rejection of free-riding, part of the intuitions at work in the reciprocity-based models.

We also indicated that the objection from direction revealed in fact an unexpected robustness of the reciprocity-based models. In contrast, it is probably the case of demographic fluctuations that constitute one of the most serious difficulties of such models comes to the front. Either the models are not demo-sensitive, which will lead to outcomes that are either counter-intuitive (when dealing with descending reciprocity), or inconsistent (in the case of ascending reciprocity). Or, as in the case of the double-reciprocity model, we have to face an approach that is indirectly demo-sensitive, but that, because of the incomplete nature of its material scope, also leads to trouble.

On top of having identified such difficulties, let us also emphasize the fact that in a context of demographic fluctuations, the possibility to transfer more to the next generation does not necessarily lead to a violation of the rule (key to the narrow notion of reciprocity relied upon here) according to which we should not impose on others the status of net beneficiaries.

This compatibility results from the fact that one of these reciprocity-based models—the descending one—is open towards the future. This may in turn lead to counter-intuitive results e.g. for egalitarians who would consider it potentially unjust to transfer more to the next generation (per head) than what we inherited from the previous generation.[34] But this is another story...

References

ARRHENIUS, G. (2000), *Future Generations. A Challenge for Moral Theory* (Uppsala: University Printers) (PhD Thesis).
BARRY, B. (1989), 'Justice as Reciprocity', in *Liberty and Justice* (Oxford: Oxford University Press), 211–41.
BICHOT, J. (1980), 'Le rôle du capital humain en matière de retraites et de prestations familiales', *Population*, 837–47.
—— (1982), 'Fonder un autre système de sécurité sociale sur un nouveau principe de justice commutative', *Droit social*, 9–10, 657–65.
—— (1999), *Retraites en péril* (Paris: Presses de Sciences-Po), 141.
BOURGEOIS, L. (1902), *Solidarité* (Paris: Armand Colin).
BOYLE, J. (2003), 'The Second Enclosure Movement and the Construction of the Public Domain', *Law and Contemporary Problems*, 66: 33–74.
CIGNO, A. (2005), 'A Constitutional Theory of the Family', IZA DP N° 1797 (Bonn), 26.
COSANDEY, D. (2003), *La faillite coupable des retraites. Comment nos assurances vieillesse font chuter la natalité*, (Paris: L'Harmattan), 164.
DE-SHALIT, A. (1995), *Why posterity matters. Environmental policies and future generations* (London/New York: Routledge).
DWORKIN, R. (2000), *Sovereign Virtue. The Theory and Practice of Equality* (Cambridge: Harvard University Press), 511.
GASPART, F., and GOSSERIES, A. (2007), 'Are Generational Savings Unjust?', *Politics, Philosophy and Economics*, 6/2: 193–217.
GOSSERIES, A. (2004), *Penser la justice entre les générations. De l'affaire Perruche à la réforme des retraites* (Paris: Aubier-Flammarion), 320.
—— (2006), 'Egalitarisme cosmopolite et effet de serre', *Les séminaires de l'IDDRI (Paris)*
GRÉGOIRE, H. (1787/1988), *Essai sur la régénération physique, morale et politique des juifs* (Paris: Flammarion) ('Champs' series), 219.
HOBBES, T., 1651 (1968), *Leviathan* (London: Penguin), 729.

---

[34] See Gosseries (2004: section 4). We have not been able to make here a detailed presentation of the egalitarian intergenerational theory. Those who are interested in this should refer themselves to Gosseries (2004: section 4) as well as to Gaspart & Gosseries (2007).

JEFFERSON, T. (1975), 'Letter to James Madison' (6 Sept. 1798), in M. D. Peterson (ed.), *The Portable Thomas Jefferson* (New York, Penguin Books), 444–51.

KOLM, S. (1984), *La bonne économie. La réciprocité générale* (Paris: PUF), 472.

—— (2000), 'Introduction', in L. -A. Gérard-valet, S. Kolm, and J. Mercier Ythier (eds.), *The Economics of Reciprocity, Giving and Altruism* (Basingstoke: MacMillan), 1–44.

—— (2006), 'Reciprocity: its scope, rationales and consequences', in S. Kolm and J. Mercier Ythier, *Handbook of the Economics of Giving, Altruism and Reciprocity* (vol. 1, Elsevier).

LAUWERS, L., and VALLENTYNE, P. (2004), 'Infinite Utilitarianism: More is Always Better', *Economics & Philosophy*, 20/2: 307–30.

LOCKE, J. 1690 (2003), *Two Treatises of Government* and *A Letter Concerning Toleration* (I. Shapiro, ed.) (New Haven/Londres: Yale University Press).

MADISON, J. (1790), Letter to Thomas Jefferson (Feb. 4). Available at: <http://www.familytales.org/dbDisplay.php?id=ltr_mad1668>

MASSON, A. (1999), 'Quelle solidarité intergénérationnelle?', *Notes de la Fondation Saint Simon* (Paris), n° 103.

MUSGRAVE, R. (1981), 'A Reappraisal of Financing Social Security', in (1986) *Public Finance in a Democratic Society. Vol. II: Fiscal Doctrine, Growth and Institutions* (New York, NYU Press).

NOZICK, R. (1974), *Anarchy, State and Utopia* (Oxford: Blackwell), 367.

RAWLS, J. (2001), *Justice as Fairness: A Restatement* (E. Kelly, ed.) (Cambridge (Mass): Harvard University Press), 214.

WADE-BENZONI, K. A. (2002), 'A Golden Rule Over Time: Reciprocity in Intergenerational Allocation Decisions', *Academy of Management Journal*, 45/5: 1011–28.

[13]

Life Extension versus Replacement

GUSTAF ARRHENIUS

ABSTRACT *It seems to be a widespread opinion that increasing the length of existing happy lives is better than creating new happy lives although the total welfare is the same in both cases, and that it may be better even when the total welfare is lower in the outcome with extended lives. I shall discuss two interesting suggestions that seem to support this idea, or so it has been argued. Firstly, the idea there is a positive level of well-being above which a life has to reach to have positive contributive value to a population, so-called Critical Level Utilitarianism. Secondly, the view that it makes an outcome worse if people are worse off than they otherwise could have been, a view I call Comparativism. I shall show that although these theories do capture some of our intuitions about the value of longevity, they contradict others, and they have a number of counterintuitive implications in other cases that we ultimately have to reject them.*

Introduction

It seems to be a widespread opinion that increasing the length of existing happy lives is better than creating new happy lives although the total welfare is the same in both cases, and that it may be better even when the total welfare is lower in the outcome with extended lives. I shall discuss two interesting suggestions that seem to support this idea. Firstly, the idea there is a positive level of well-being above which a life has to reach to have positive contributive value to a population. This view is usually called Critical Level Utilitarianism. Secondly, the view that it makes an outcome worse if people are worse off than they otherwise could have been. I shall call this view Comparativism.

Firstly, I shall describe what I call the pure case of life extension versus replacement. Then I shall very briefly describe some different views about the value of life extension and indicate why I think some of the arguments in favour and against life extension fail. I shall then turn to the implications of Critical Level Utilitarianism and Comparativism in regards to life extension and replacement, which is the main topic of this paper.

Life Extension versus Replacement: The Pure Case

Consider the figure below (Figure 1). The figure below shows two outcomes (or populations as I shall sometimes say): A and B. The width of each block represents the number of people, and the height represents their lifetime welfare. These outcomes could consist of all the lives that are causally affected by, or consequences of a certain action or series of actions (a policy). All the lives in the above figure have positive welfare, or, as we also could put it, have lives worth living.[1]

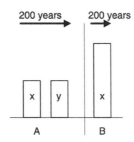

Figure 1.

In outcome A, there are five billion people, the x-people, who live for a 100 years, then another five billion people, the y-people, who live for a 100 years. In outcome B, there are five billion people, the x-people, who live for 200 years. There is the same welfare per year for everybody, thus the same total temporal welfare in both outcomes.

Outcome A is a case of replacement, since the x-people are being replaced by the y-people, whereas outcome B is a case of life extension, since the x-lives are extended. This is, of course, a very simplified and unrealistic case but it will make our discussion take a clearer form and work as a test case for different theories.

The outcomes above involve the same total amount of temporal welfare. According to some theories, it follows that there is the same total welfare in the outcomes, since total welfare is just a sum of temporal welfare. This is controversial, however, since it might be that some welfare components don't have a temporal location. The standard examples are accomplishments and posthumous fame. Such welfare components do increase an individual's lifetime welfare but not at any specific date, or so it sometimes argued. However, for our current discussion this doesn't matter much since we could just assume that the cases considered here are equally good in regards to such welfare components.[2] Hence, we are going to assume that the lifetime welfare of the B-people is double that of the A-people, and that the total welfare is the same in both outcomes.

Longevity could be non-instrumentally valuable in two ways: as an independent value apart from welfare or as a welfare component. In the latter case, longevity is another non-dated welfare component that will not show up if we only look at people's temporal welfare. Since the value of longevity is what we are investigating in this paper, we cannot assume that it is the same in the compared cases and we don't want to include it in the welfare depicted in the figures. So the welfare depicted in the figures does not include the eventual contribution of longevity to people's lifetime welfare. Thus, when we in the following refer to 'welfare', we have in mind temporal welfare and welfare from non-dated welfare sources other than longevity.

Which outcome, if any, is better? According to Hedonistic Total Utilitarianism, A and B are equally good since they involve the same amount of total temporal welfare, and according to Hedonism, all welfare components (pains and pleasures) are dated. Likewise for many consequentialist and deontological theories since they satisfy the following condition:

> *Neutrality*: If there is the same total welfare in two outcomes A and B, and there is perfect equality in A and B, then A and B are equally good (or choiceworthy), other things being equal.[3]

According to such theories, whether we should choose life extension or replacement depends only on empirical considerations regarding the probable effect of different policies on the total welfare, given that no other values are at stake. If life extension increases the total welfare, other things being equal, then that should be our policy, if it doesn't, then it shouldn't be. Of course, such estimates are likely to be very difficult since life extension with a hundred years or more over the average life expectancy in the affluent societies today might arguably alter the structure of those societies in quite a far-reaching way, not to talk about radical life extension and eternal life. I think Neutrality has much in its favour but I shall not consider it further in this paper.

According to some theories and suggestions, the *ceteris paribus* clause in Neutrality cannot be satisfied since there are some other values or structural features involved in the comparison between A and B that makes a difference between them. For example, some have argued in favour of life extension by appealing to a positive right to carry on living. Aubrey de Grey, for example, writes that '[h]uman rights do not get any more fundamental than the right to carry on living' and '... there is no moral distinction between ... acting to shorten someone's life and not acting to extend it'.[4]

Just postulating such a positive human right seems quite unsatisfactory, however, and it relies on an especially controversial denial of the act and omission doctrine. In essence, according to de Grey, we are complicit in the mass murder of old people by not providing them with the means for life extension. As he writes elsewhere, '[t]here may well be some sort of population explosion [from eliminating all deaths caused by ageing] ... but the first priority is to end the slaughter. Everything else is detail'.[5]

Some argue in favour of replacement by claiming that a too-long life or a life without death is a non-human life. Leon Kass, for example, claims that '... to argue that human life would be better without death is, I submit, to argue that human life would be better being something other than human'.[6] Clearly, such an argument doesn't touch moderate life extension. Moreover, it is unclear why an eternal life would be a non-human life and, if it is, why we should consider it a worse life than a human life. Arguably, such a non-human life could be better than a human life.

Average Utilitarianism yields that B is better than A since the average well-being is higher, and likewise for so-called compromise theories, which are combinations of Average and Total Utilitarianism and give some weight to the average utility in the compared outcomes. As others and I have shown elsewhere, however, Average Utilitarianism and its relatives have a number of very counterintuitive implications in different number cases so we can safely put them to the side.[7] For example, Average Utilitarianism implies that it can be better to add very bad lives to a population if it increases the average.

Critical-Level Utilitarianism

A better-developed effort in support of life extension is Critical Level Utilitarianism (CLU), as propounded by John Broome in a recent book.[8] In its simplest form, CLU is a modified version of Total Utilitarianism.[9] The contributive value of a person's life is her lifetime welfare minus a positive critical level. The value of a population is calculated by summing these differences for all individuals in the population. CLU could thus be written in the following form:

$$\text{CLU}(X) = \sum_{i=1}^{n}(u_i - k) \qquad n > 0$$

In the above formula, n is the population size of X and u_i is the numerical representation of the welfare of the i:th life in population X, and k is the critical level.

The critical level k is supposed to be the level at which it is axiologically neutral whether a life is created or not, what Broome calls 'the neutral level for existence'. Broome doesn't equate this level with the welfare level of a life that is neutral *for* a person, that is, neutral welfare, an option that the classical utilitarian would use. As he writes, '... the neutral level for existence is positive, once the zero of lifetime well-being is normalized at the level of a constantly neutral life'.[10] Hence, since the critical level is positive, the contributive value of lives with positive welfare below the critical level is negative.

What does CLU imply in regards to the case in Figure 1? Let w and $2w$ represent the lifetime welfare of the people in A and B respectively, and let $2n$ and n be the population size of A and B respectively. Then $\text{CLU}(A) - \text{CLU}(B) = 2n(w - k) - n(2w - k) = -nk$. Hence, CLU ranks B as better than A and thus supports life extension.

Notice that it is not essential to CLU's ranking of A and B that the x-people's extra welfare in outcome B appears in the form of longer lives. Even if the x-people only lived for a hundred years in outcome B, but with the same lifetime welfare as in the original case, CLU would still prefer B over A. In general, CLU favours that a given amount of welfare is spread among as few people as possible, and its implication in regards to life extension is a corollary of this general feature.[11]

Broome illustrates CLU's implications in respect to life extension with a choice between extending an already existing person's life or creating a new person. In his example, a couple can choose between extending their already existing child's life or having one more baby.[12] This can be seen a micro-version of the case in Figure 1.[13] Many people would probably, I take it, consider it obvious that we should extend the existing child's life instead of creating a new life, even if the total welfare would be the same in both cases. CLU seems to capture this intuition.

Nevertheless, I don't think CLU captures most people's intuition in the case of the couple's choice and life extension in general. For many people I think that the fundamental intuition is, roughly stated, that we should avoid making people worse off when no one else would benefit from it.[14] Let's call it the pointless harm intuition.

In the case of the couple's choice, if they don't extend their existing child's life, then she would be worse off. According to a commonly shared intuition, however, the new child doesn't benefit from being brought into existence. As Broome himself eloquently puts it in another context:

> [I]t cannot ever be *true* that it is better for a person that she lives than that she should never have lived at all. If it were better for a person that she lives than that she should never have lived at all, then if she had never lived at all, that would have been worse for her than if she had lived. But if she had never lived at all, there would have been no her for it to be worse for, so it could not have been worse for her.[15]

Broome's account of the value of longevity doesn't capture the pointless harm intuition, however, since it applies also to cases in which only the well-being of uniquely realisable people (that is, people who only exist in one of the possible outcomes) are at stake. In such cases, no one will be made worse or better off depending on our choice since their existence also depends on it. This could be the case, for example, when we evaluate future outcomes consisting of different people. CLU, however, would still prefer B over A even if there was no overlap and thus different people in A and B.[16]

The difference can be seen more clearly if we consider the following version of the couple's choice. Assume a couple can choose between extending their already existing child's life and having one more child with a short life (as short as the non-extended life of the existing child would be), or not extending their existing child's life and having a different extra child with a long life (as long as the extended life of the existing child would be). CLU is indifferent between these choices whereas most people, I surmise, would prefer the first option since then no one is made worse off.

Secondly, as Krister Bykvist has pointed out, the intuition involved in Broome's example about the couple's choice probably draws on our common sense idea about parental duties.[17] According to this, we have a special duty towards our already existing children which doesn't apply to the children we have not yet created. Hence, the intuition seems to be deontic rather than axiological in nature and is thus not an appropriate test case for an axiological theory.

Another aspect of CLU's support for life extension that some might like and other might find peculiar is its generality. For example, it prefers extremely long lives over very long lives. Assume that the people in outcome A in Figure 1 lives for five hundred years whereas the people in B lives for a thousand years. Still, CLU ranks B as better than A. Actually, Broome's seems a bit hesitant here since he writes that '[t]here may be limits to this intuition [the intuition that extension is better than replacement]. I am not sure we would think it better to prolong a 100-year-old person's life for another 100 years, rather than have a new person live for 100 years'.[18] But CLU doesn't leave room for such doubts, as its implication in the case in Figure 1 shows.

Moreover, CLU prefers long lives with horrible suffering rather than more lives with less suffering. Assume that the height of the blocks in Figure 1 represents people's negative welfare, their pain and suffering, so that the people in B suffer the most whereas the people in A suffer much less since they have shorter lives. Still, CLU would rank B as the best outcome. Actually, this could still be the case even if there was more total suffering in B. Those who believe that we should give extra moral weight to suffering, or to those that are worse off, will find this implication unacceptable.

Finally, there is a general problem with CLU which I think gives us a decisive reason to reject it, and this problem becomes extra pressing in the current context. CLU will only give the intuitively right result in the couple's choice if the critical level of existence is set very high. Even if the new child would have a very good life, many would think that this is not enough to make it better to let the existing child die, if the existing child would have a good future life.[19] Assume, for example, that if the couple doesn't have another baby, then their existing child will enjoy eighty very good years. If they do have another baby, then she will enjoy eighty very good years whereas the first child will only live for forty-one years. Still, even if the critical level is set as high as the welfare of a life enjoying forty very good years, CLU will recommend that the couple have another baby. Hence, the critical level has to be well above the welfare of the forty-year life to preserve our intuition in the couple's choice.

It is easy to show, however, that CLU has a very counterintuitive conclusion, which is especially disturbing if the critical level is set high. CLU implies that a population with negative welfare may be better than a population with positive welfare, a conclusion I have called the Sadistic Conclusion:[20]

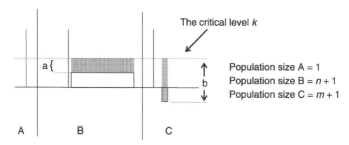

Figure 2.

In the above figure, the width of each block shows the number of people, and the height shows their welfare. Outcome A consists of one person with welfare well above the critical level. In outcome B, we have added n people with positive welfare x. Their welfare is a units below the critical level k, as indicated in the figure. The negative value of this addition is thus $n(x - k) = -na$ which is represented by the grey area in outcome B. In outcome C, m people with negative welfare y have been added. Their welfare is b units below the critical level, as indicated in the figure. The negative value of this addition is $m(-y - k) = -mb$ which is represented by the grey area in outcome C. Since $mb < na$ (the grey area in outcome C is smaller than the grey area in outcome B), it is better to add the people with negative welfare rather than the people with positive welfare, a clear case of the Sadistic Conclusion.

CLU implies especially troublesome versions of the Sadistic Conclusion:

> *The Very Sadistic Conclusion*: For any population of lives with very negative welfare, there is a population of lives with positive welfare which is *worse*, other things being equal.

There is always a population with sufficiently many people with positive welfare slightly below the critical level such that the total negative value of these people is greater than that of a given population made up of people with negative welfare. This holds irrespective of how much people suffer and of how many they are. Thus, CLU implies the Very Sadistic Conclusion. If the critical level is set above the welfare of a life consisting of forty very good years, then I find this implication utterly counterintuitive.

Comparativism

Let's turn to a more promising idea that several people have proposed to me in conversation in defence of the superiority of life extension over replacement: It makes an outcome worse if people are worse off than they otherwise could have been.[21] Another way to put it is to say that such people have a legitimate complaint or grievance and this makes the outcome worse. In addition to the well-being of everybody, we should take the badness of legitimate complaints, or what we will call comparative harms, into account. Moreover, a person is not harmed by not coming into existence since you have to exist in both of the compared outcomes to be harmed or to have a legitimate complaint. Let's call this view Comparativism. It can be more exactly described by the following two principles:

> *The Principle of Comparative Harm*: If a person exists in two alternative outcomes A and B, and if she would be worse off in terms of welfare in A as compared to B, then she would be comparatively harmed if A rather than B came about.
>
> *Comparativism*: The value of an outcome is determined by the total welfare and the comparative harm in the outcome.

Notice that the notion of 'comparative harm' is a technical notion that doesn't completely map onto our everyday use of 'harm'. For example, if you will enjoy an excellent life in both outcomes A and B but you are slightly less happy in B, then you are comparatively harmed if B came about, but many would hesitate to say that you are harmed in the ordinary language sense of 'harm' (there are many other examples). I could have used some other term to capture the idea that it makes an outcome worse if people are worse off than they otherwise could have been, but I think the technical notion of 'comparative harm' is sufficiently related to the ordinary notion of harm to justify its name.[22] For brevity, I will in the following sometimes use the term 'harm' and its cognates although I always have in mind 'comparative harm' in the above sense.

Moreover, nothing is yet said about how to calculate and aggregate the value of total welfare and comparative harm. The above formulation is open to many different ways of doing this. Intuitively, all such extension will imply that the more welfare, the better the outcome, other things being equal; and the more comparative harm, the worse the outcome, other things being equal.

Comparativism seems to give us an argument in favour of life extension. Consider again outcome A and B in Figure 1. In A, the x-people are harmed since they have only half of the welfare they enjoy in B. The y-people are not harmed in B since they don't exist in that outcome, and according to Comparativism, a person is not harmed by not coming into existence (recall that according to the Principle of Comparative Harm, you have to exist in both of the compared outcomes to be a candidate for harm). Consequently, although the total welfare is the same in both outcomes, A is worse in one respect since if it comes about, some people will be worse off than they could have been and thus there will be people who are harmed and can legitimately complain. Hence, since A and B are equally good in terms of people's well-being, but B is better in terms of comparative harms, B is better than A all things considered. In other words, life extension is better than replacement.

Notice that Comparativism not only gives support to extending lives that exist now, which I guess is the fundamental intuition in the pro-life-extension camp, but also future lives which exist in both of the compared future scenarios. In practice, this will not be a very common situation but consider the following case: A woman has the choice of either implanting two fertilised eggs or just one of them. If she implant both eggs, then her offspring are likely to live for a hundred years each. If she implants only one of them, then, because of a new therapy that can only safely be used when one egg is implanted, her child is likely to live for two hundred years. This case only involves future people but Comparativism would still recommend the latter option, given that the total well-being is roughly the same in both outcomes.

As with CLU, Comparativism's ranking of A and B doesn't turn on the fact that the x-people's extra welfare in outcome B appears in the form of longer lives. Again, if the x-people only lived for a hundred years in outcome B, but with the same lifetime welfare as in the original case, Comparativism would still prefer B over A. In general, Comparativism favours that a given amount of welfare is spread only among non-uniquely realisable people and not shared with uniquely realisable people.[23] Its implication in regards to life extension is a consequence of this general feature.[24]

Non-Transitivity

As we have so far formulated Comparativism, it has a serious flaw. Consider the following situation:

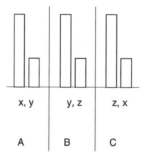

Figure 3.

The x- and y-people exist in outcome A, the y- and z-people exist in B, and the z- and x-people exist in C. Assume that all of these people have positive welfare, but that the y-people are better off in B as compared to A, the z-people are better off in C as compared to B, and the x-people are better off in A as compared to C.[25] All the outcomes in the figure are equally good in respect to the amounts of people's well-being. However, since the y-people are worse off in A as compared to B, the y-people would have a complaint if A came about. In this respect, A is worse than B. Consequently, all things considered, A is worse than B. The same reasoning yields that B is worse than C, and C is worse than A. But if A is worse than B, and B is worse than C, then transitivity yields that A is worse than C. Consequently, A is both better and worse than C, which cannot be true.

To meet this objection, one could argue that we should abandon transitivity of the relation 'better than', or that Comparativism should be couched in normative rather than axiological terms, and add the claim that there is no analogue to the transitivity of 'better than' for normative concepts. This wouldn't help much, partly because non-transitivity in the above case is just plainly counterintuitive (the intuitively correct result is that all the outcomes are equally good) and partly because non-transitive value orderings easily translate to moral dilemmas on the normative level. However, since I've discussed these latter problems at length elsewhere, and since there is another way of explicating Comparativism which doesn't imply non-transitive orderings, I shall not dwell on those details here.[26]

Here's one way to formulate Comparativism to avoid non-transitivity. When determining the value of an outcome we should consider both people's well-being and whether they are harmed in the sense of being worse off than they could have been. The value of an outcome is determined by the value of the total well-being in the outcome reduced by a factor that reflects whether people are harmed in the sense of being worse off than they could have been.[27]

Here's how this could be done. Assume that we represent well-being on a numerical scale and that the total well-being of the best-off people in Figure 3 is 10 units and the total well-being of the worst-off people is 5 units. Assume also that all the possible outcomes in the choice situation considered are those depicted in Figure 3. The value of outcome A would then be 15 minus some factor h that represents the fact that the y-people are worse off than they could have been. Intuitively, this factor should correspond to how much worse off the y-people are in A as compared to B. Similarly, the value of outcome B and C would be 15 minus h. Consequently, on this view all the outcomes in Figure 3 are ranked as equally good which seems to be the intuitively correct all things considered ranking in this case.

However, in regard to replacement versus life extension, this version of Comparativism picks B since the two outcomes are equally good in regard to people's welfare but A is worse in one respect since in A, some people are worse off than they otherwise could have been.

Dominated Outcomes

Although the reformulated version of Comparativism neatly captures some people intuitions regarding the value of life extension as compared to replacement and avoids the threat of non-transitivity, it also has implications that some people might consider counterintuitive. Consider the following three outcomes:

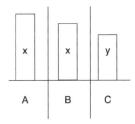

Figure 4.

There is the same number of people in all three outcomes in the figure above. Everyone in A is better off than everyone in B, and everyone in B is better off than everyone in C. Again, the x-people would be harmed if outcome B came about since they would be worse off than they otherwise could have been, i.e., if A would have been the case instead. Let h represent the total value of the harm done to the x-people in B. Let d represent the total difference in well-being between the x-people in B and the y-people in C. The difference in value between outcome B and C will then be d minus h.[28] Consequently, if h is greater than d, then Comparativism will rank C as better than B although everyone in the latter outcome is better off than everyone in the former. This seems a bit counterintuitive.

Yet, this result might not perturb the comparativists. They might say that since they believe in the negative value of comparative harm, they're willing to trade off some welfare to avoid such comparative harm. They might point to other non-welfarist axiologies such as desert theories where the value of an outcome is determined both by the receipt of welfare and the fit between receipt and desert. On such theories, there might be cases where we have to forego some welfare to achieve a better fit between receipt and desert.[29] Likewise for other pluralist axiologies.

Nevertheless, there are further related problems with this view if we turn to its normative implications. Assume some weak form of consequentialism, or consequentialist part of a deontological theory, to the effect that we ought to choose the best outcome in the cases currently under discussion.[30] Assume further that A is a very unlikely outcome. If we try to achieve A, we are most likely to fail and end up with C. If we aim at B or C, we will succeed. Still, Comparativism tells us that it would be wrong to choose B, just because there is an unlikely outcome A in the choice set.[31]

One might think that this problem can be fixed by letting the harm-factor depend on the probability of the better alternative. Instead of letting h represent the total value of the harm done to the x-people if we were to choose outcome B, it should be represented by ph, where p is the probability that A will be the case given that we choose A, and h is the harm done to the x-people were we to choose outcome B when we could have chosen A with certainty of success. The difference in value between outcome B and C will now be d minus ph so still, if ph is greater than d, which is clearly possible, then Comparativism will rank C as better than B although everyone is better off in B.

A better solution might be to let the harm-factor depend on people's expected welfare given a certain action which with certain probabilities brings about certain outcomes. On this view, people are harmed if their expected welfare is lower than it could have been given a different choice of action. Assume that if we choose an action a_A aiming at bringing about A, then the probability that A will be the case is 0.10 and the probability that C will be the case is 0.90, whereas if we choose action a_B, then B will be the case with certainty. Assume further that the total well-being in A is ten and in B eight. Then the x-people's expected welfare if we choose a_A is $0.10 \times 10 = 1$, whereas it is 1×8 were we to choose action a_B. Hence, on this formulation of Comparativism, the x-people are not harmed if we choose a_B since their expected welfare is higher if we choose that action rather than a_A. Hence, by switching to expected welfare and defining harm in terms of expected welfare, the problem of unlikely outcomes disappears.

On the other hand, if we went for a_A and A actually came about, then we would still have harmed the x-people and done the wrong thing since their expected welfare (at the time of the choice) were lower than it would have been had we chosen a_B, although they are better off since A rather than B actually came about. This might strike some as implausible but a possible rejoinder is to claim that it was wrong to choose a_A since that action exposed the x-people to a risk of getting nothing.[32]

This problem, however, is not peculiar to Comparativism but analogous to the old dispute among consequentialists regarding whether one should go for a formulation of consequentialism in terms of the actual or probable outcomes of actions, so I shall not discuss it further here.[33] It is noteworthy, however, that Comparativism seems more compatible with a probabilistic rather than an actualistic formulation of consequentialism.

Let me end this section with two other objections to Comparativism.[34] In Figure 3, Comparativism correctly ranked all the outcomes as equally good. One might object, however, that we cannot know this without knowing that exactly these three outcomes are the only ones available in the situation since, according to Comparativism, the value of an outcome depends on the set of possible outcomes in the situation. Suppose, for example, that there was another outcome D with only the x-people at level 15. This would not only yield that D was the best outcome in the situation but also change the ranking of A, B, and C, since the x-people in C will be more harmed than the y-people in A and the z-people in B. Hence, C will be ranked as worse than A and B.

The first objection is that it is absurd that one and the same outcome can both be worse than and equally as good as another outcome. This seems to be the case here since when D is not present in the set of outcomes, C is ranked as equally as good as A and B, whereas when D is present, C is ranked as worse than A and B. Hence, it looks like the same outcome, C, is both worse than and equally as good as A and B.

This would surely be absurd but the obvious rejoinder is to deny that these outcomes are the same outcomes. We can just partly individuate outcomes by the situation to which they belong. Hence, if we add another outcome to the situation described in Figure 3, then we have a new situations with, say, alternatives A', B', C' and D and it is B' which is better than C' which doesn't contradict that outcome B and C in the original situation are equally good.

The second objection is that in practice, we could never be epistemically justified in limiting the number of possible outcomes as we have done in the examples above. Hence, since the Comparativist ranking depends on the possible outcomes in the situation, we cannot be justified in believing in the ranking.

It is true that this makes Comparativism a bit special as an axiology since most axiologies, such as the axiological component of classical utilitarianism, yield context-insensitive rankings of outcomes. However, this problem appears for these theories on the normative level, since which outcome is the best one, and thus the one we ought to choose, depends on which other outcomes that are available in the situation. Hence, this alleged particular problem with Comparativism reduces to the old problem of whether consequentialist theories ought to be and can be action guiding and is thus no special problem for Comparativism. The same standard responses come in handy here. For example, we could make a sharp distinction between criterion theories and decision methods and claim that Comparativism is a criterion theory that has no claim to be used as a decision method other than indirectly in the choice of which decision methods that we should use.[35]

Anti-Egalitarianism

Here's a more problematic case for the Comparativist:

The Energy Policy Case: A country is facing a choice between implementing a certain energy policy (alternative A) or not (alternative B). Were this country to implement this policy, then there would be an increase in the welfare of the presently existing people of this country (the x-people) since they will live for a longer time. On the other hand, this increase would be counterbalanced by the harm the waste from this energy system will cause in the lives of people in the future (the y-people) by shortening their lives. The existence of these future people is contingent upon the implementation of this energy policy. If the country doesn't implement this energy policy, other people will exist in the future (the z-people) with the same good quality and length of life as the x-people. The advantages and disadvantages of other effects of this policy balance out.[36]

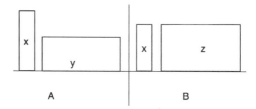

Figure 5.

In the above Energy Policy Case, assume that the total difference in well-being for the x-people in the two outcomes equals the difference in well-being for the y- and z-people. We can also assume that the total (and thus average) length of life is the same in both outcomes. In other words, A and B involve the same number of people, the same total sum of well-being, and the same total length of life.

A reasonable and modest egalitarian (or prioritarian) consideration implies that B is better than A since they are equally good in regards to the total (and average) well-being but there is perfect equality in B whereas there is inequality in A. Comparativism implies, however, that A is better than B because the x-people would be harmed if we were to choose outcome B rather than A since they then would be worse off than they otherwise could have been. The y- and z-people, on the other hand, cannot be harmed in this way since they are uniquely realisable (i.e. their existence depends on our choice and you cannot be harmed by not coming into existence according to Comparativism). Consequently, there is a tension between Comparativism and a reasonable egalitarian consideration.

Even if we lower the total welfare in A by reducing the longevity, and thus the welfare, of the y-people, Comparativism would rank A as better than B as long as the lower total welfare in A is counteracted by the comparative harm in B. Hence, Comparativism yields that an outcome with lower total well-being, lower total (and average) length of life, and inequality can be better than an outcome with higher total well-being and perfect equality.

Again, however, I think the comparativist can reply that since they believe in the negative value of comparative harm, they're willing to trade off some welfare to avoid such comparative harm. Moreover, if we also take comparative harm into account, then outcome B is also an unequal outcome since although people have the same welfare, the x-people are harmed.

Nevertheless, the point is that as a support for life extension, the above implication is a bit odd. If we are in favour of life extension, why should we opt for the alternative with less total and average longevity and with an unequal distribution of longevity? So this case shows that there is a conflict between intuitions regarding life extension and Comparativism.[37]

Future Populations and Trade-offs

Lastly, Comparativism might not deliver all the goods that the life extension proponents want. For instance, in all cases involving only uniquely realisable people, that is, situations in which there are different people in all outcomes, Comparativism determines the ranking by the total sum of people's welfare since such cases don't involve any comparative harm. Consequently, like Total Utilitarianism, in respect to future populations where there is no overlap of individuals in the compared populations, it will imply that A and B in Figure 1 are equally good. Moreover, it implies that for any population of 200-year lives, there is a better population in which, say, everybody has 50-years of life, since with enough people, there will be a greater total sum of well-being in such a population.

These might be acceptable implications for some life extension proponents, however, since what matters to them is that if lives are not extended, some existing people will be worse off than they otherwise could have been. This is of course exactly the intuition that Comparativism tries to capture. Nevertheless, it will imply similar conclusions even in cases that involve overlaps and thus involve great losses in longevity for non-uniquely realisable people, including existing people.

Here's a numerical illustration of this point (see Figure 6).[38]

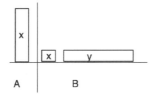

Figure 6.

Assume that we have a choice between outcome A with ten persons, the presently existing x-people, and outcome B with the x-people and an additional two hundred persons, the y-people. In outcome A, the x-people have very high lifetime welfare because of their long lives. Assume that this high welfare corresponds to ten units of welfare. Consequently, the value of outcome A is 10 × 10 = 100.

In outcome B, the x- and y-people have very low positive lifetime welfare because of their short lives. Assume that this very low welfare corresponds to one unit of welfare. Since the x-people have much lower welfare in B, they are harmed by in B. Assume that the harm factor for each x-person corresponds to her difference in welfare between outcome A and B. Thus, the value of the harm to the x-people in B is 10 × (−9) = −90 whereas the value of their welfare is 10 × 1 = 10. Taken all together, the value of the x-people in outcome B is 10 − 90 = −80. However, since there are also two hundred y-persons in outcome B, the total value of outcome B, according to Comparativism, is 200 − 80 = 120 which is greater than the value of A. Hence,

Comparativism here opts for the outcome with short lives, outcome B, although it involves a great loss in welfare and longevity for the existing people. In this respect Comparativism doesn't give a strong support for life extension over replacement.

One might think that this result depends on the weight given to comparative harm. However, as long as the harm factor is represented by a finite number (that is, as long as we don't give lexical priority to comparative harm), Comparativism will have the above implication. Here's a general demonstration:

Assume that h is a positive finite number that represents the weight given to the comparative harm of an individual due to the fact that she is worse off than she could have been. Let A consist of n non-uniquely realisable persons with very high welfare u_1 (because of their long lives). Let B consist of a mixed population of n uniquely and m non-uniquely realisable people with very low positive welfare u_2 (because of their short lives). The value of A is thus nu_1 and the value of B is $n(u_2 - h) + mu_2$. Now, for any value of h, there is an m such that $nu_1 < n(u_2 - h) + mu_2$, that is, a value of m that makes B better than A, namely $m > n(u_1 - u_2 + h)/u_2$.

Of course, how strong support Comparativism will give for life extension over replacement depends on the negative weight given to comparative harm. If we give lexical priority to avoiding comparative harm, then life extension will always be better than replacement. Given such an extreme negative weight on comparative harms, however, we will face extremely counterintuitive versions of the cases described in Figures 4 and 5.

For example, consider Figure 5 again and assume that there is only one x-person (or only one x-person with lower welfare in B as compared to A) but a vast number of y- and z-people. Assume further that the y-people in A only have lives barely worth living, and that the x-person's welfare in B is just slightly lower than in A (for example, one extra pin prick in her left thumb on her fifth birthday). The z-people in B have the same welfare as the x-people, that is, very high welfare. Still, if we give lexical priority to avoiding comparative harms, A is better than B.[39]

Likewise, consider a version of the case depicted in Figure 4 in which the y-people in C have lives barely worth living and only one of the x-people have slightly lower welfare in outcome B as compared to outcome A. Again, if we give lexical priority to avoiding comparative harms, C is better than B.

Comparativism as a support for life extension might be caught in a dilemma here. If it gives a great negative weight to comparative harm, then it will give a strong support for life extension but imply clearly unacceptable version of the cases described in Figures 4 and 5. It can avoid these counterintuitive implications if it puts a small negative weight on comparative harm, but then it will give a very weak support for life extension. It seems hard to find an acceptable way out of this dilemma.[40]

Gustaf Arrhenius, Department of Philosophy, Stockholm University, The Swedish Collegium for Advanced Study, CERSES (UMR CNRS 8137), Université Paris Descartes
Gustaf.Arrhenius@philosophy.su.se

NOTES

1 We shall say that a life has neutral welfare if and only if it has the same welfare as a life without any good or bad welfare components, and that a life has positive (negative) welfare if and only if it has higher (lower)

welfare than a life with neutral welfare. A hedonist, for example, would typically say that pain is bad and pleasure is good for a person, and that a life without any pain and pleasure has neutral welfare. This definition can be combined with other welfarist axiologies, such as desire and objective list theories. There are a number of alternative definitions of a life with positive (negative, neutral) welfare in the literature. For a discussion of these, see G. Arrhenius, *Future Generations: A Challenge for Moral Theory* (Uppsala: University Printers, 2000a) and J. Broome, *Ethics out of Economics* (Cambridge: Cambridge University Press, 1999). Cf. D. Parfit, *Reasons and Persons* (Oxford: Clarendon Press, 1984), p. 358. Notice also that the welfare shown by the height of the figures incorporates all possible sources of welfare in life, including the eventual loss of welfare due to the frustration of future oriented preferences that death brings about, or the happiness generated by having children, and so forth. See also the discussion below.

2 Alternatively, we could disperse the value of such components evenly throughout a person life. See J. Broome, *Weighing Lives* (Oxford: Oxford University Press, 2004), for a discussion of this strategy. Another reason to resist making a person lifetime welfare a mere sum of temporal welfare is that this view yields counterintuitive results when one compares lives where both the length and the temporal welfare vary (see e.g. G. Arrhenius, 'Superiority in value', *Philosophical Studies* 123 (2005): 97–114). I don't have space to consider these problems further here.

3 We have included a ceteris paribus clause in the formulation of the above condition. The idea is that people's welfare and longevity is the only axiologically and deontically relevant aspect which may be different in the compared populations, and that the compared populations are roughly equally good in regard to other axiologically and deontically relevant aspects. There are neither any constraints (for example, promise-keeping) nor options (for example, great personal sacrifice for the agent which is beyond the call of duty), nor any non-welfarist values in the outcomes (for example, cultural diversity) that give us a reason to (not) choose one or the other of the involved outcomes. The only reasons for choosing one or the other of the involved outcomes arise from the welfare and the longevity of the lives in the involved populations.

4 A. de Grey, 'Life extension, human rights, and the rational refinement of repugnance', *Journal of Medical Ethics* 31,11 (2005): 659–663.

5 A. de Grey (2007) 'Why we should do all we can to hasten the defeat of human aging', http://www.sens.org/concerns.htm#opop, accessed 25 July 2007.

6 L. Kass, 'L'chaim and its limits: why not immortality?', *First Things* May 2001 available at: http://www.firstthings.com/article.php3?id_article=2188

7 See Arrhenius (2000a) op. cit., section 3.3; G. Arrhenius, 'An impossibility theorem for welfarist axiologies', *Economics & Philosophy* 16 (2000b): 247–266; and Parfit (1984) op. cit., section 143.

8 Broome (2004) op. cit.

9 See Broome (2004) op. cit. This theory was first proposed in C. Blackorby & D. Donaldson, 'Social criteria for evaluating population change', *Journal of Public Economics* 25 (1984): 13–33. See also C. Blackorby, W. Bossert & D. Donaldson, 'Critical-level utilitarianism and the population-ethics dilemma', *Economics & Philosophy* 13 (1997): 197–230. These authors also propose a more refined version of CLU according to which the contributive value of people's welfare is dampened by a strictly concave function. Another version, favoured by Broome, introduces incommensurability among some populations. These modifications have no relevance for the arguments made here.

10 Broome (2004) op. cit., p. 259.

11 For more on CLU's implications in population ethics, see Arrhenius (2000a, b) op. cit.

12 Broome (2004) op. cit., pp. 8–9, 259.

13 I'll point out a crucial difference below.

14 Three other possibilities are that we should give priority to presently, necessarily, or actually existing people just because they are presently, necessarily, or actually existing. I discuss these views at length in the context of population ethics in Arrhenius (2000a) op. cit. and G. Arrhenius (2006b) 'The moral status of potential people', mimeo (available at http://people.su.se/~guarr/), and shall say nothing more of them here due to space constraint. In a comment on Broome's example, K. Bykvist, 'The good, the bad, and the ethically neutral', *Economics & Philosophy* 23 (2007): 97–106 at p. 104, writes that '... I think it is crucial to many people that the case is about extending the life of an already existing individual. This means that if the life is not extended then there is someone who will be worse off' (emphasis in original). The first sentence seems to indicate that Bykvist thinks that the intuition is about presently existing individuals, whereas the second expresses what I think is the source of the intuition.

15 Broome (1999) op. cit., ch. 10, p. 168 (emphasis in original). See also Parfit (1984) op. cit., pp. 395, 489; D. Heyd, 'Procreation and value: can ethics deal with futurity problems?', *Philosophia* 19 (1988): 157–161;

and K. Bykvist, 'The benefits of coming into existence', *Philosophical Studies* 135 (2006): 335–362. Cf. J. Narveson, 'Utilitarianism and new generations', *Mind* 76 (1967): 62–72 at p. 67: 'If you ask, "whose happiness has been increased as a result of his being born?", the answer is that nobody's has. . . . Remember that the question we must ask about him is not whether he is happy but whether he is happier as a result of being born. And if put this way, we see that again we have a piece of nonsense on our hands if we suppose the answer is either "yes" or "no". For if it is, then with whom, or with what, are we comparing his new state of bliss? Is the child, perhaps, happier than he used to be before he was born? Or happier than his alter ego? Obviously, there can be no sensible answer here' (emphasis in original).
16 For the same point, see Bykvist (2007) op. cit., p. 104.
17 Bykvist (2007) op. cit., p. 104.
18 Broome (2004) op. cit., p. 108.
19 The same point is made, I think, in Bykvist (2007) op. cit., p. 104.
20 See Arrhenius (2000ab) op. cit.
21 Private communication with, among others, Julian Savulescu and Nick Boström. Andrew Williams also suggested this possibility to handle certain problems in population ethics. Similar ideas are put forward in T. Hope (2003) 'Physicians' duties and the non-identity problem', mimeo, Oxford University; L. Meyer, 'Intergenerational justice', The Stanford Encyclopedia of Philosophy (Summer 2003 Edition), Edward N. Zalta (ed.), URL = <http://plato.stanford.edu/archives/sum2003/entries/justice-intergenerational/>; M. Roberts, *Child versus Childmaker: Future Persons and Present Duties in Ethics and the Law* (Rowman & Littlefield, 1998); and M. Roberts, 'The non-identity fallacy: harm, probability and another look at Parfit's depletion example', *Utilitas* 19, 3 (2007): 267–311.
22 An analogy would be the difference between the notion of the 'consequence of an action' in ordinary language and in the formulation of consequentialism (usually the whole possible world that would be the case if the action were performed).
23 For more on Comparativism's implications in population ethics, see Arrhenius (2000a, 2006b) op. cit. and G. Arrhenius, 'The person affecting restriction, comparativism, and the moral status of potential people', *Ethical Perspectives* 3–4 (2003a): 185–195.
24 Comparativism also share with CLU that it favours extremely long lives over long lives, although only in respect to non-uniquely realisable lives.
25 L. S. Temkin, 'Intransitivity and the mere addition paradox', *Philosophy & Public Affairs* 16, 2 (1987): 138–187 at pp. 168–9, uses a similar example to illustrate the intransitivity of the so called 'Person Affecting Restriction'.
26 G. See Arrhenius, 'The paradoxes of future generations and normative theory' in J. Ryberg & T. Tännsjö (eds.) *The Repugnant Conclusion* (Dordrecht: Kluwer Academic, 2005). Another option is to claim that the only thing we can say about this case is that B is better than A for the y-people, C is better than B for the z-people, and so forth, and that we cannot say anything at all about the all things considered ranking of these outcomes. In other words, extensive incomparability would appear in all cases involving uniquely realisable people (people that exist in some but not all of the compared outcomes). Apart from counterintuitive implications of this move (it seems reasonable to claim that the outcomes above are equally good and it seems daft to claim that the outcomes involved in the Energy Policy Case discussed below, are incomparable), it wouldn't be very helpful in the context of medical ethics and other practical contexts where we have to make a choice.
27 Alternatively, we could represent the value of an outcome with an ordered pair (w, h) in which w represents the total well-being in the outcome and h represents the total harm in the outcome. Such a representation would leave open the possibility that comparative harm has lexical priority over total welfare in the ranking of outcomes. As I shall discuss below, such a view is not very attractive.
28 Assume that the total well-being in C is m and in B thus $m + d$. The difference in value between B and C is then $(m + d - h) - m = d - h$.
29 See F. Feldman, *Utilitarianism, Hedonism, and Desert: Essays in Moral Philosophy* (Cambridge: Cambridge University Press, 1997); G. Arrhenius, 'Feldman's desert-adjusted utilitarianism and population ethics', *Utilitas* 15, 2 (2003b): 225–236; G. Arrhenius, 'Desert as fit: an axiomatic analysis' in R. Feldman, K. McDaniel, J. R. Raibley & M. J. Zimmerman (eds.) *The Good, the Right, Life and Death: Essays in Honor of Fred Feldman* (Aldershot: Ashgate, 2006a); and G. Arrhenius, 'Meritarian axiologies and distributive justice' in T. Rønnow-Rasmussen, B. Petersson, J. Josefsson & D. Egonsson (eds.) *Hommage à Wlodek: Philosophical Papers Dedicated to Wlodek Rabinowicz* (2007) (www.fil.lu.se/hommageawlodek/).
30 The kind of consequentialism I have in mind is what we could call Ceteris Paribus Act-Consequentialism: Other things being equal, an action is right (obligatory) if and only if its outcome is at least as good as

(better than) that of every alternative. An action is wrong if and only if it is not right. In other words, if a choice situation doesn't involve actions that are right or wrong by virtue of a certain deontic constraint or option, then the normative status of the actions are determined by the value of their respective outcomes. Most deontologists accept this form of consequentialism. For a discussion, see Arrhenius (2005).
31 Strictly speaking, Comparativism in conjunction with consequentialism has this implication. For the sake of brevity, I omit this qualification below.
32 Another interesting possibility, suggested to me by an anonymous referee, is to claim that people are comparatively harmed if and only if they are worse off than they could have been both in terms of expected and actual welfare. According to this view, if we choose a_A and A actually came about, then the x-people are not harmed since their actual welfare is maximised. A problem for such a theory, however, is that its normative prescriptions are a bit unclear. Does it direct us to choose a_A or a_B?
33 See, for example E. Carlson, *Consequentialism Reconsidered* (Dordrecht: Kluwer Academic Publisher, 1995) and F. Feldman, 'Actual utility, the objection from impracticality, and the move to expected utility', *Philosophical Studies* 129, 1 (2006): 49–79.
34 I'm indebted to John Broome for pressing these two points.
35 See R. E. Bales, 'Act-utilitarianism: account of right-making characteristic or decision-making procedure?', *American Philosophical Quarterly* 8, 3 (1971): for an excellent treatment of this issue. See also D. Brink, 'Utilitarian morality and the personal point of view', *Journal of Philosophy*, 83, 8 (1986): 421–7.
36 Cf. Parfit (1984), pp. 371–2.
37 I'm grateful to Speranta Dumitru for pressing this point.
38 This is basically a micro-version of Parfit's famous 'Repugnant Conclusion'. See Parfit (1984), ch. 17.
39 One could also construct examples in which the y-people have horrible tormented lives. However, such counterexamples could be avoided by revising Comparativism such that it counts as being comparatively harmed if you are born into a life not worth living and there is an alternative in which you're not brought into existence. I'm grateful to an anonymous referee for pressing this point.
40 I would like to thank Margaret Battin, Nick Boström, Dan Brock, Speranta Dumitru, Nir Eyal, Julian Savulescu, Torbjörn Tännsjö, Dan Wikler, and especially John Broome and Krister Bykvist for fruitful discussions and comments. The comments from the editors and one of the anonymous reviewers were also very useful. Earlier versions of this paper were presented at Enhance: The Ethics of Human Enhancement, IAB Satellite Conference, 8th World Congress of Bioethics, Beijing, August 2006; Oxford Medical Humanities Forum, Oxford University, November 2006; and at James Martin Advanced Research Seminar, Faculty of Philosophy, Oxford University, December 2006. I would like to thank the participants at these occasions for their stimulating criticism. Thanks also to Oxford Uehiro Centre for Practical Ethics for being such a generous host during some of the time when this paper were written. Financial support from the Bank of Sweden Tercentenary Foundation and the Swedish Collegium for Advanced Study is gratefully acknowledged.

[14]

THE PURE INTERGENERATIONAL PROBLEM[1]

Stephen M. Gardiner

> "[T]he part that covers how we affect future generations ... is the most important part of our moral theory, since the next few centuries will be the most important in human history."
> —Derek Parfit, *Reasons and Persons*, 351

Often the best way to make progress in solving a philosophical problem is to offer a robust account of the problem itself. Here I try to do that for a core issue of temporal moral distance.[2] I believe that the distant future poses a severe moral problem, the nature and extent of which has not yet been adequately appreciated. My main aim in this paper is to give a brief, initial account of this problem and its main features.[3] I will also argue for three claims about its status. First, it is the main concern of distinctively *intergenerational* ethics.[4] It explains both (a) why conceiving of the ethics of the future in terms of generations makes moral sense, and (b) what is distinctive about generational issues. Second, it occurs in a pure, long-term form manifest across human history and global populations, but also in degenerate forms which apply to shorter time periods and to social institutions. Third, it is manifest in the real world. In practice, it is neither rendered inert by fortuitous circumstance, nor overwhelmed by other future-oriented difficulties.

I. The Problem with 'Generations'

Ethical issues concerning future people are usually conceived of as problems of future generations. But this practice requires defence. For it makes two important assumptions: first, that it is both possible and useful to divide all those who will exist into groups of contemporaries; and second, that this is the morally salient way of conceiving of them. But neither of these claims is obviously correct.

Consider first the attempt to divide humanity as a while into generations. For one thing, this faces a significant *prima facie* objection. For individuals do not come into and out of existence as temporally discrete classes. On the contrary, there is a continuum of entry and exit. For another, this fact has practical importance. First, there is the question of appropriate starting-points. It might make a big difference to one's views about generational matters *when* one chooses to say that a generation begins, since particular people and particular events belong to different generations depending on this choice.[5] In practice, much talk of generations seems to be based on major historical and social events, such as World War II, and the so-called Baby Boom. But it is not clear why such divisions should be morally relevant. Second, there are potentially issues of overlap. For example, one generation may be physically present during the "time" of another generation (and affected by what occurs); and individuals have different life-spans, so that some people's entire lives may occur within a single generation, whereas others may overlap with three or four. Third, there is the matter of individuating generations. For example, some people define a generation in terms of replacement (e.g., the amount of time it takes for children to take the place of their parents); others in terms of the possibility of mutual interaction (future people whom those presently alive will not live to meet); and occasionally the excluded group is people not presently alive. But it makes a great deal of difference which period one has in mind. The first suggests new generations at intervals of about 30 years,[6] the second roughly 200 years, and the last about 100.

These concerns imply that choices of both generational units and starting-points require specific defence. These are nontrivial tasks. They make a considerable difference to how one conceives of both intergenerational and intragenerational issues, and especially those of intergenerational justice. But there is also a more general worry. Some rationale is needed for seeking to divide humanity into temporal classes in the first place. We must ask why might it be useful to speak of ethical obligations to future people in generational terms.

My proposal will be that the use of the concept of a generation to structure talk of ethics and the future can be made sense of indirectly. Categorization in terms of generations gains its point from the need to confront a certain kind of severe moral problem which is itself conceived of in generational terms. Given this, an account of intergenerational justice is one which provides an answer to the severe problem, since that is the point of a distinctively intergenerational theory. One advantage of this approach will be that it can explain and accommodate the use of intergenerational language across divergent temporal settings.

II. The Pure Intergenerational Problem

Let me begin by sketching the problem in its starkest form, with a schematic example. Imagine a world which consists of a sequence of groups of inhabitants over a length of time. Suppose that each group is temporally distinct, no group has any causal impact on any previous group, each group is concerned solely with its own interests, and the interests of earlier groups are independent of the interests of later groups (but not *vice versa*). Imagine then that each group has access to goods which are temporally diffuse in a particular way: they give modest benefits to the group which produces them, but impose high costs on all later groups. Under the given conditions, we would expect each group to produce such goods. Hence, we would expect earlier groups to impose uncompensated costs on later groups, and for those further along in the sequence to receive escalating burdens, since the costs will be compounded over time. Intuitively, such a world poses a problem of fairness.[7] I shall call this problem, 'the Pure Intergenerational Problem' (PIP).

The PIP is a problem of a particularly challenging kind. For it has a particularly harsh structure, and one which makes it unusually difficult to resolve. These facts can be brought out by comparison with a more familiar kind of problem, the Prisoner's Dilemma, or Tragedy of the Commons.[8] A Prisoner's Dilemma can roughly be characterized as follows.[9] Imagine a group of individuals trying to decide whether or not to engage in a polluting activity. Their situation might be characterized by the following two features:

> (PD1) It is *collectively rational* to cooperate and restrict overall pollution: each agent prefers the outcome produced by everyone restricting their individual pollution over the outcome produced by no one doing so.

> (PD2) It is *individually rational* not to restrict one's own pollution: when each agent has the power to decide whether or not she will restrict, each (rationally) prefers not to do so, whatever the others do.

Such situations are paradoxical because it is better for all parties to cooperate than to defect (given PD1), but the structure of the situation undermines their doing so (given PD2). In particular, PD2 makes it the case that individuals acting rationally in terms of their own interests collectively undermine that interest.

The prisoner's Dilemma is a serious kind of problem. But the PIP is worse. There are two main reasons. The first is that the claims which characterize the PIP are worse than the parallel claims for the Prisoner's Dilemma. The PIP claims are:

> (PIP1) It is *collectively rational* for most generations to cooperate: (almost) every generation prefers the outcome produced by everyone restricting pollution over the outcome produced by everyone overpolluting.[10]

> (PIP2) It is *individually rational* for all generations not to cooperate: when each generation has the power to decide whether or not it will overpollute, each generation (rationally) prefers to overpollute, whatever the others do

Now, the claims about individual rationality arise because parties lack effective means through which to ensure that the behavior of others is cooperative so long as theirs is. But PIP2 is worse than PD2 because the underlying rationale for it is more intractable. PD2 typically arises because there are contingent obstacles to cooperation (e.g., the inability to come together to make a contract, the lack of a coercive power to enforce a contract); hence, PD2 might be rendered false by removing such contingencies. But the reasons for PIP2 are not contingent. If a collective agreement is in the interest of a given group, it is because it does not want to suffer the ill-effects of the activities of its predecessors. But at the point that each generation has the power to pollute, it is no longer subject to action by its predecessors—by definition, they no longer exist,[11] and have already either overpolluted or abstained.[12]

In the case of collective rationality, PIP1 is also much worse than PD1. In PD1, it is in everyone's interest not to overpollute. But in PIP1 this is not the case. First, cooperation is not in the interests of the first group in the sequence. It is being asked to refrain from polluting activity which is beneficial to itself simply for the sake of future groups. If it is motivated simply by self-interest, therefore, it will overpollute. Second, cooperation is in the interests of any given group if and only if the groups which precede it also cooperate and do not overpollute. But then the asymmetrical position of the first group threatens to undermine the rationale for cooperation. For the problem of the first group is iterated. If the first group does overpollute, then it makes it the case that the second group has nothing to gain from cooperation, and so, under the egoistic assumption, will itself overpollute. But this makes it the case that the third group has nothing to gain from cooperation, and so on, for all the other groups in the sequence.

The second reason that the PIP is worse than the Prisoner's Dilemma is that it is more resistant to solution. Typical solutions to the Prisoner's Dilemma involve appeal to the broad self-interest of the parties, or to some notion of reciprocity. But these solutions do not work for PIP. For one thing, appeals to broad self-interest characteristically make reference to a wider context of interaction where mutual advantage is possible. But there is no such wider context under the PIP scenario, and mutual benefit is ruled out by the causal circumstances. Similarly, the possibility of reciprocity is ruled out by the description of the scenario.[13]

III. The Features of the PIP

We have established that the PIP is a serious problem. Still, the conditions for its manifestation appear to be stringent. Hence, it is probably rarely (if ever) instantiated in its pure form. Nevertheless, it is useful as a paradigm, since the basic structural ideas have force even under some common deviations from the idealized conditions. To show this, and to give a more detailed account of the problem itself, I will now analyze its features in a little more detail.

The first feature is *temporal asymmetry*. The PIP envisages groups of people who can be represented as a sequence of temporally distinct classes. Categorization in terms of such groups grounds the use of the term 'generations' in the PIP.[14]

Now, the first feature of the PIP does not yet justify using the language of generations to describe *our* problems with the future.[15] For, as we have already noted, human beings do not pop into and out of existence in distinct, fully-formed, temporal groups. Hence, for human situations, we need some other account of group differentiation. This account emerges from the second and third characteristics.

The second feature of the PIP is *causal asymmetry*. Earlier groups have a power to impose costs on later groups (including severe costs affecting their basic life circumstances),[16] whereas future groups have no causal power over them.[17] Causal asymmetry is the central feature from the point of view of describing the phenomenon as *generational*: it plays the role of individuating generations, and so makes talk of generations appropriate.[18] Given this, whether the PIP has any application depends not on whether people come in temporally distinct classes—they clearly do not—but whether there are causal asymmetries of the relevant type[19] between groups in the temporal sequence. Causal asymmetry is the primary notion. For on this account, a generation is a group which has a place in the temporal sequence and which stands in the basic causal relations with predecessors and successors described by the causal asymmetry.

Now, this account of generations has an important implication. For it suggests that the basic problem of fairness persists even if the relevant asymmetries cannot be assigned to rigidly separated groups, but the passage from generation to generation is more fluid. Consider the following. In the pure model, groups have constant membership over time and there is no overlap. But these conditions might be relaxed in various ways without altering much of the central causal structure of the problem. For example, a relevantly similar asymmetric causal relation may hold between groups whose core members remain the same, even if at the margins both add and shed members, in some cases to other groups (as when the older members of the first join the second).[20] Given this, the problem of the continuum need not imply that the PIP has no application to the human case.[21]

The third feature of the PIP is *asymmetric independence of interests*: the interests of earlier groups are independent of the interests of groups which succeed them. In particular, earlier groups have nothing to gain from the activities or attitudes of later groups (though, of course, later groups have a substantial amount to gain from earlier groups). This feature is important because it rules out any possibility of intertemporal exchange for mutual advantage.

In the PIP, asymmetric independence of interests is an independently posited feature. But it is tempting to think that this might be unnecessary, because perhaps one can claim that asymmetric independence follows directly from causal asymmetry. Two reasons for this claim spring to mind. First, the main cause of independence is presumably the lack of potential for reciprocity. But this depends on the causal asymmetry: if there can be no causal effects of later on earlier groups, then the later groups are unable to reciprocate in any way. Second, one might think that reciprocation is impossible for a more pragmatic reason: there is nothing that the later groups could give that the earlier could not take in any case.

However, the connection between causal asymmetry and asymmetric independence is less tight than the above account suggests. First, relationships characterized by reciprocity and mutual advantage narrowly conceived are not the only kind possible between different temporal groups. One possibility would be that groups pass on benefits through a scheme of indirect reciprocity—the first benefits the second, the second the third, and so on. Another is that earlier generations pass on benefits as gifts to the future, with the prospect of "receiving" gratitude in return. Neither requires backwards causation. Second, it is not strictly true that there is nothing that later groups can offer which the earlier are not in a position to take. For some goods are time-dependent: they are not available until later, and essentially so. Examples might include the respect or approval of future groups, or the continuation of projects and a group history.

These exceptions to the extent that causal asymmetry implies asymmetric independence are of practical importance. For they imply that asymmetric independence is likely to be false, strictly-speaking, in the real world. Still, it is questionable whether it is *substantially* false, in the sense that it simplifies in a way which undermines the point at issue. For what is important for the PIP is that the present interests of the current generation—i.e., those interests that they can secure for themselves by overconsuming—dominate any benefits they might expect to receive from the future and which depend on their not overconsuming. And this still seems empirically likely.[22] Hence, a degenerate form of the PIP is likely to have application.[23]

The fourth feature of the PIP is that groups are *exclusively self-interested*. This is part of the idealization. But it becomes more problematic when applied to real-world cases. For it seems clear that we do not simply want to assume that actual individuals are exclusively self-interested. For one thing, it is implausible. For another, we will want to allow for altruistic and other motives if the PIP is to have a practical solution.[24]

In fact, it seems that the applicability of the intergenerational problem does not require strong egoistic assumptions. First, whatever the truth about individuals, it seems likely that in many contexts generational groups will be dominantly concerned with the interests of those in their generation.[25] Second, the structure of the intergenerational problem does not require egoism *per se*. All that is required is concerns which are time-indexed, in the sense that they depend for their realization only on events and actions occurring before any future generations come into existence. Third, the time-indexed concerns need not be the only concerns agents have. In practice, the problem arises simply if they are the ones which are *operative*. For example, it seems highly plausible that most of the unreflective consumption decisions of individuals in the present generation are dominantly time-indexed.

The fifth feature of the PIP is that it involves *temporally diffuse goods* of a certain kind: they involve modest present benefits for the generation that engages in the activity and large costs for future generations. Now, the focus on such goods is designed to illustrate the problem in its most uncontroversial form.[26] But from the point of view of application, it is worth noting that many deviations from this make little difference to the basic intergenerational issue. For example, consider the following possibilities. First, there is an issue even if the present benefit exceeds the deferred cost in magnitude, because on most theories of justice distribution matters independently of overall utility.[27] Second, a similar problem arises for present costs needed to secure future benefits. Under the other PIP conditions, justified projects of this kind will tend to be undersubscribed. Third, the PIP envisages costs iterated over future groups. But a degenerate form of the problem arises even if costs are inflicted on only some future groups.

The final feature of the PIP is its *sequential* aspect. This is important because it gives rise to the iteration aspect of the PIP, which emerges from the first generation's lack of incentive not to overpollute. But we might note that even this feature can accommodate some deviations. First, even two generations are sufficient to give a basic version of the intergenerational issue. Second, groups do not need to be temporally proximate to each other in a continuous sequence for the problem to occur. Imagine, for example, a temporal sequence of causally asymmetric groups ABCDE, each of which is temporally proximate to the previous one. Given the right causal facts, the generational sequence relevant to the PIP may be ACE, rather than ABCDE.

IV. Applications & Complications

My discussion of the basic features of the PIP and the extent to which they can accommodate deviations has necessarily been preliminary and incomplete. Still, it suffices to show that empirical cases with structures close to the PIP are likely to arise in practice, so that PIP may be a serious practical problem. In this section, I will suggest three schematic areas where we might expect to see degenerate forms of the PIP.

The closest approximations to the PIP are likely to be found if one adopts the widest definition of future generation mentioned earlier: that future generations are those future people whom those presently alive will not live to meet.[28] Such situations seem to arise in a number of real-world cases. (One prominent example would be certain long-term implications of climate change.[29]) Still, it is clear that most issues usually described as intergenerational do not fit the wide definition. Hence, for the PIP to be relevant to most of our problems with future generations it will have to address narrower definitions of 'generation', and so deal with cases of temporal overlap between different groups.

The application of the PIP is less clear in situations where there is overlap. Nevertheless, I believe that a degenerate form still persists in such cases. Let me begin by distinguishing two kinds of overlap. The first is related to a usage of 'future generations' mentioned earlier, where future generations are those generations whose members have not yet been born. This use allows for a weak kind of overlap, namely cases where present people will exist at the same time as future people, but those future people are not yet present. The second kind of overlap is stronger. It allows for members of one group to be present alongside members of another when relevant decisions are being made. This corresponds to the use of 'generation' to mark the period needed for effective replacement of parents by their children.

The simultaneous physical presence of different generations naturally requires some distinction of groups based on factors other than temporal isolation. But here the PIP model is on firm ground. For the causal asymmetry feature both provides and explains that distinction. First, in the weak overlap case, the present generation retains the strong form of causal asymmetry present in the PIP until the first group of future people is born. (Then it reverts to the strong overlap case.) Second, even with strong overlap, there is a relevant causal asymmetry. For parents retain a strong power over their children until they grow up and achieve some kind of independence. Indeed, this is presumably what gives the narrower definition of generations its point: "replacement" means taking on the rights and responsibilities of adulthood, and that requires coming to approximate causal parity.[30]

So far, then, the PIP seems useful in explaining the degenerate cases. But perhaps we should consider whether the peculiar features of overlap undermine its overall application. If they are to do so, this will presumably be through their effects on the relationship between the generations (narrowly conceived). The two main factors seem to be potential reciprocity and personal attachment, both of which are thought to be impossible in the PIP. Hence, let us now consider each in turn, concentrating on the weak overlap case.

The PIP explicitly rules out reciprocity, through the assumption of asymmetric independence of interests, which ensures that earlier generations have nothing to gain from their successors. But this assumption is unlikely to be true in cases of both strong and weak overlap. Given this, for most real-world cases it is presumably true that the potential for reciprocity makes some difference, and that this difference increases with the extent of overlap.

Still, we must be careful not to overstate matters. First, many overlapping future people will have limited opportunities to benefit us much: e.g., they will still be too young; we will be too old. (This is especially so in weak overlap cases.) It may also be true that, though there is overlap, this is not when the problem is bad, or when complaints can be made. Second, there are two kinds of scenarios in these cases. In the first, the later group may eventually attain causal symmetry. It would then be able to subject the earlier group to reprisals. This would presumably have some effect on the behavior of earlier groups. Still, it is not clear that it would actually pay the later group to withhold cooperation for the sake of past bad treatment once it actually achieves causal parity, when this withholding damages its interests still further.[31] So, the effect may be limited. In the second kind of scenario, the later group may eventually attain a reversed causal asymmetry, where they have the upperhand. Here, earlier groups know that they will eventually be at the mercy of their successors.[32] Now, this undoubtably has a strong influence when it occurs, and it undermines the application of the PIP. Still, it is doubtful to what extent it characterizes many contemporary relationships between generations. So, the PIP will remain relevant in a range of cases.[33] Third, important though these factors are, they are limited by the fact that earlier groups can determine many of the circumstances within which the choices of later groups will be made.[34]

In conclusion, then, it seems that by itself reciprocity does not provide much ground for optimism. There are reasons to suspect that many overlap cases will retain much of the driving structure of the PIP.

The second main complicating feature of overlap is the possibility of personal attachment. The idea here seems to be that attachment can ground strong concern with the power to override (or modify) self-interest. Still, even if this is right, there are several problems in this case. For one thing, the model seems to presume that attachment occurs only on contact; but contact might be a long time coming, and so too late.[35] For another, it is not clear that attachment would give concern with the necessary emphasis on the long-term prospects of the future person, rather than on her short- to medium-term well-being.[36]

We can conclude then that though issues of reciprocity and attachment complicate the relevance of the PIP to the human case, they are unlikely to undermine it completely. Rather, they seem to make it clear that the crucial issue with overlapping generations is not *when* those who will live when we have gone appear, but the extent of our *present* concern for their well-being. Thus, the PIP remains relevant. For it models the self- and temporally-directed concerns which impact on the efficacy of such concern.

This point can be made more vivid with a particular kind of example. The relevance of degenerate forms of the PIP is perhaps most stark in one area where there is quite strong overlap. Institutions are often set up so as to produce a temporal sequence of groups with (a) asymmetrical power over others and (b) extremely limited time-horizons. This is especially noticeable with some of the most important institutions, such as governments and large corporations. Here, the presence of the second factor is obvious. Governments are focused on their impacts over limited terms of office, particularly as they affect their ability to win the next election; corporations are often focused on the dividends likely to be produced in the immediate years ahead, not the further implications of their actions. But the first factor is also present because such institutions are typically headed by elites, who are predominantly people in their mid-forties to mid-sixties. The time horizons during which the impacts of their policies on their institutions or people has significant effects is often much longer than the time they will be around to experience those effects.[37] Furthermore, even within these groups, there is diminishing institutional loyalty, and much moving around. Hence, often what is important is to make a good, highly visible, short-term impact at a given institution, as a way to move on. And this results in an incentive to ignore the long-term impacts of policy.

V. Mitigating and Complicating Factors

If I am right about its centrality and pervasiveness, why has the PIP not been emphasized before? There seem to be two main reasons: first, it has not seemed pressing in practice; second, other significant theoretical problems tend to make its presence obscure. In this section, I will briefly address these matters.

One possible response to the PIP is to claim that, assuming continued economic growth, people in the future will already be better off than the present generation, so that there is no immediate danger of affecting them for the worse. The basic idea here is that current economic activity tends to result in improved capital stock and infrastructure which are then passed on to the next generation. So, the self-interested behavior of the present generation actually tends to have good results for future people. There is an *invisible hand*.

There is something to this argument. But we must be cautious about its import.[38] Most importantly for our purposes, it relies on a set of bold empirical claims. The PIP assumes that there are temporally-diffuse goods which bring benefits for the present generation but impose costs on future generations. But the invisible-hand argument assumes that overall human activities are temporally-diffuse in a different, very beneficial way: they have long-term benefits as well as short-term benefits, and the long-term benefits are larger (so that the future is always better off).[39]

Now, if the empirical claim of the invisible-hand argument were true, this would be a good thing from the point of view of intergenerational justice. And I believe that it has been true to a substantial extent, at least in the recent history of the more developed nations. Still, we should not get overly carried away by this fact. For it seems unlikely that it holds to the degree necessary to undermine the relevance of the PIP. For one thing, at least some goods, and some very important goods, like climate stability, are temporally diffuse in the PIP sense. And their magnitude is potentially such as to overwhelm other (and purely economic) gains. For another, to the extent that it is present, the invisible hand appears to operate only under certain complex and advantageous background conditions which are themselves maintained by a social structure partially constituted by a legal and moral framework. Since the presence of such conditions hardly characterizes all countries and all periods of the world's history, we presumably have obligations to maintain such a framework, and the possibility of the PIP will play a role in explaining the form and import of those obligations.[40]

The second reason why the PIP tends to be obscured is *future uncertainty*. In particular, we do not know the technology, the general circumstances, nor the preferences of future people. Now, some writers seem to regard these problems as both definitional of future-generations problems and fairly crippling. They also seem to undermine the manifestation of the PIP. If it is impossible to know what will count as a cost in the future, then one cannot see the present generation as generating the relevantly temporally-diffuse goods.

Still, the uncertainty problem seems to me overstated. First, the importance and extent of technological changes is overemphasized. Whilst it is true that the internet, mobile phones and other luxury goods may not even have been conceivable in the late nineteenth century, it is also the case that basic human needs for food, water, shelter and health remain both largely unchanged and under threat in many parts of the world, in ways depressingly reminiscent of earlier centuries. Second, the uncertainty issue is not essentially or characteristically generational. There are already large problems with uncertainty with much shorter time horizons: e.g., in our own lives, in assessing what our long-term preferences might be; and in public policy, with the use of biotechnology in agriculture. Finally, the most worrying problems involving future people do not fit this mould. They are issues of large-scale environmental degradation and resource depletion. In such cases, there are not serious problems of technological uncertainty, or uncertainty about future preferences.[41]

The third complicating issue is that *we determine the very existence of future generations*. This suggests that the present generation has some control over the obligations it is under.[42] Now, I cannot attempt a full analysis of this complication here. But I will make four brief comments. First, in practice, creation issues arise only rarely. Hence, they do not undermine the general applicability of the PIP.[43] Second, in circumstances where they do arise, the really salient question is often whether the present generation has any obligation to bring a certain number of future people into existence. The PIP analysis attempts no answer to this question. But if the answer is 'yes', the PIP might help to explain why either too many or too few people are created. Third, those who believe that the creation issue poses large ethical problems tend not to think that it undermines our ethical obligations to the future. They will therefore still be concerned about the impact of the PIP on those obligations.[44] Finally, the creation issue is not specifically generational. It does not require dividing people into distinct generational groups; and, though it does involve *the act of generation* in a literal sense, the most relevant ethical consideration seems not to be one of intergenerational fairness, but to concern whether and to what extent the person created will have a worthwhile life.

VI. Conclusion

I have argued for three claims. First, there is a core intergenerational problem of fairness which defines the central issue of distinctively intergenerational ethics. Second, the nature of this problem can accommodate and justify the standard variations in our usage of the language of "generations." Third, it is manifest in a number of impure forms in the real world, and in particular is not overwhelmed by the presence of other problems often thought of as distinctively intergenerational.

I have also suggested that the problem has an especially challenging structure. But the point of my analysis is not to undermine ethical behavior towards the future, nor to show that it is impossible. Rather, it is to motivate further theoretical investigation of our obligations to future people, by reminding us that in practice present generations are vulnerable to corruption, in virtue of our asymmetric causal power and time-dependent interests.

Stephen M. Gardiner
University of Utah

Notes

1. This paper was written whilst I was a Visiting Fellow at the University of Melbourne Division of the ARC Special Research Centre for Applied Philosophy and Public Ethics (CAPPE). I am grateful to the Centre for its support, and especially to its Director, Professor C. A. J. (Tony) Coady, for the invitation to spend time in such a pleasant and productive academic environment. I am also grateful to the University of Canterbury, New Zealand, for Study Leave on that occasion. For very helpful comments on the paper, I would like to thank Roger Crisp, Leslie Francis, Neil Levy and Deen Chatterjee.

2. Roughly speaking, there are two main types of moral-distance problem: spatial and temporal. Both are severe. Spatial moral distance seems to get most of the attention. But it is not clear why this should be so. Offhand, problems of temporal moral distance seem likely to be worse. For example: there are more people in the future; pictures of their suffering cannot appear on the TV news to shock us into action; and there are no major charities devoted to protecting their interests as such. (We might also note that actual problems with the distant future often involve a spatial element as well.)

3. It may be possible to adapt my account of the intergenerational problem so as to illuminate problems of spatial moral distance. Perhaps it might even provide the basis for an overall analysis of "the problem of moral distance."

4. My position contrasts with that of Bryan Norton. Norton says:

> The philosophical problem of what we owe the future is not a single, monolithic problem, but rather an inter-related cluster of problems. For convenience, we group these sub-problems into three categories and give them somewhat descriptive names. They are; (1) *the distance problem*—how far into the future do our moral obligations extend? . . . (2) *the ignorance problem*—who will future people be and how can we identify them? And, how can we know what they will want or need, or what rights they will insist on? . . . and (3) *the typology of effects problem*—how can we determine which of our actions truly have moral implications for the future?

(Norton, "Ecology and Opportunity: Intergenerational Equity and Sustainable Options," in Andrew Dobson, ed., *Fairness and Futurity* (Oxford: Oxford University Press, 1998) 118–50, at 123–24. See also, Norton, "Future Obligations, Obligations to" *Encyclopaedia of Bioethics*, 2nd ed'n. (New York: Macmillan Reference, 1995)). I do not want to claim that the problem of future generations is monolithic, nor would I deny that Norton's perceptive classification of sub-problems is useful. But I do think (a) that none of the subproblems Norton identifies is exclusive to future-generations issues, and (b) that even collectively they fail to make clear why ethical issues concerning the future should be conceived of in generational terms. My account, on the other hand, explains why there is a distinctively intergenerational problem about the future. (Writers who may see the fundamental issue in terms close to my own include Robert Goodin, "The Sustainability Ethic: Political, Not Just Moral," *Journal of Applied Philosophy*, vol. 16, no. 3 (1999), 247–54, and John O'Neill, "Future Generations: Present Harms," *Philosophy* 1993; 68(263): 35–51: at 46–50.)

5. For example, say that one assumes that a new generation appears every 30 years. It might make a significant difference whether one chooses to speak of the 1941–1970 and 1971–2000 generations, or the 1921–1950 and 1951–1980 generations, or the 1931–1960 and 1961–1990 generations. For example, the third of these puts the 1960s cultural revolution in one generation, and WWI in another; the first does not.

6. But notice that much here depends on what replacement is taken to consist in. If to replace is to be a village elder, generations may be much longer; if it is simply to provide a net income to the family rather than a net loss, in some societies it will occur in late childhood.

7. Suppose we assume that fairness requires some kind of impartiality between affected parties. The world envisioned violates impartiality by allowing for costs to be visited on future groups for the benefit of earlier groups, even when there is no compensation, and where the benefits are small and the costs large and potentially catastrophic.

Now, some will claim that the initial intuition that future generations pose a problem of fairness turns out to be mistaken. In particular, it may be said, invoking Derek Parfit's Non-Identity Problem (NIP), that "people in later generations would not have existed were it not for the consumptive practices of their predecessors, so if anything they have a reason to be grateful rather than any complaint based on fairness." Hence, one might follow Parfit, and conceive of the problem as one of utility.

But I think this is too hasty. First, even Parfit may agree that there is a *presumption* in favour of treating future generations' issues as fairness problems. (It is just that this presumption is overturned once one is convinced by the NIP.) And this is what I argue for here. Second, many future-generations problems arise in cases where the NIP does not apply. In these cases, the language of fairness will still be apt *unless* one is independently convinced *both* that the NIP is a serious problem, *and* that it casts a shadow over how we should treat all future-generations cases. Third, there are reasons not to be convinced by either claim. (Unfortunately, there is not space to pursue these matters adequately here, though I do make a couple of additional remarks in note 10, and towards the end of the paper.) For Parfit's views, see *Reasons and Persons* (Oxford, 1985).

8. Some of the material in this section is drawn from my "The Real Tragedy of the Commons," *Philosophy and Public Affairs*, 2001.

9. For ease of exposition, I shall make the comparison in terms of a paradigm case, that of a problem of overpollution. Nothing depends on the case being of this form.

10. Proponents of the Non-Identity Problem may assert that (PIP1) is often false. For in non-identity cases, "any generation will in fact prefer that its predecessors have overpolluted," since otherwise that generation will not have existed. Alas, I cannot give a full response to this complaint here. Still, a few, all-too-brief, remarks may be helpful.

First, I emphasize again that the NIP cases are only a subset of the cases to which the PIP is relevant. So, the relevance of the PIP does not stand or fall with what is said about the NIP cases. (Furthermore, for identity cases, the generation produced by overpollution is the same as that produced by restricting pollution. In that case, (PIP1) holds.)

Second, the NIP complaint rests on the idea that in non-identity cases a generation will prefer to exist with overpollution rather than not to exist at all. In non-identity cases, the policies of overpollution and restricting pollution produce different groups of people at some time in the future, t. Call the group produced by restricting pollution A, and that produced by overpollution B. Consider now the situation of A and B with respect to (PIP1). Clearly, A prefer restricting pollution, since they believe it to be justified from an impartial point of view (as Parfit would claim too), and it allows them to come into existence in a situation where there is no unfairness to them. Hence, A do not dissent from (PIP1). The problem is with B. The NIP claim is that B will prefer overpollution, since their existence depends on it. Hence, B appear to contradict (PIP1).

But we should not be too quick to accept this conclusion. *One* issue—since (PIP1) refers to generations—is what counts as a distinct generation. Are A and B *considered together* (perhaps with others) a generation? Or does each count as a *separate* generation? The NIP-based objection to (PIP1) appears to assume the latter. (PIP1) is only made false if a distinct generation prefers overpollution. If B is a distinct generation, then (PIP1) might be straightforwardly false. But is B a distinct generation? Arguably, it is not. A generation seems to be a group which occupies a given temporal period, or one which is in a given causal relationship to its predecessors and successors. But these characterizations seem to yield *those who might be alive* at time *t*, and so are affected by the decisions of the present generation. This includes A and B. So, the question becomes, does the generation comprised of the possible peoples A and B accept (PIP1)? But then we need a way of forming a joint attitude, of A and B (and whoever else may turn up), toward (PIP1). It is not completely clear how one is to do this. (Having to do it does not itself resolve the question either for or against (PIP1): we already know that, taken independently, A accept, and [by hypothesis at this point] B dissent.) But at least one account suggests that the method will favor (PIP1). Suppose one is sympathetic to Rawlsian accounts of fairness. The relevant question to ask B (and A) might then be whether they prefer overpollution to restricted pollution from behind an appropriate veil of ignorance. But there it looks reasonable to suppose that both will accept (PIP1).

11. We have assumed that each group is temporally distinct.

12. Typically, of course, the Prisoner's Dilemma is made very much less problematic if there is a sequence of games to be played out involving the very same parties. This is not possible in the PIP; and there iteration makes the overall problem worse.

13. These considerations imply that the PIP is worse than PD in a further way. Historically, the most influential accounts of fairness or justice have relied crucially on the idea of mutual advantage, as providing either the central point of a theory of justice, or at least the best way of modelling fairness. But the PIP resists both forms of analysis. See, for example, Brian Barry, "The Circumstances of Justice and Future Generations," in R. I. Sikora and Brian Barry, eds., *Obligations to Future Generations* (Temple, 1978) 204–48; reprinted in John O'Neill *et al.*, *Environmental Ethics and Philosophy*.

14. Of course, usually the term 'generation' might be assumed to imply some genetic, familial, or community connection between the successors and their forebears. Still, whilst it is true that this characteristic makes the problem more vivid to those involved, and that it may provide some of the grounds for a solution in many cases, it is not crucial to the problem as such. The basic problem arises between groups of moral agents. From this point of view, there need be no connection between them other than that supplied by the problem itself. Hence, it is possible that the future groups might be from other nations, or even other planets.

15. After writing this paper, I came across an article by Tim Mulgan which describes a situation which resembles the PIP in having rigid temporal group differentiation. Mulgan proposes a minimal test for political theories. Political theories must justify at least some obligations to future generations in what he calls the Mayfly Case. There, generations of mayflies are rigidly differentiated over time. See Mulgan, "A Minimal Test for Political Theories," *Philosophia*, 2001.

16. There is also the power to decide whether future generations exist and which individuals will constitute them. I defer discussion of this problem until the final section.

17. It could be said that the emergence of this kind of problem is recent, and concerns the emergence of certain technologies. But this seems false. Earlier generations have always had the ability to have profound effects on later generations. What has changed is that interests are now more likely to be divergent.

18. Initially it might appear that causal asymmetry simply follows from the temporal asymmetry, given the temporal closure of the past. In this case, temporal asymmetry would be the primary theoretical notion. But it is not. For a generation is not just any randomly

chosen group from within the temporal sequence. It must satisfy a further criterion. Causal asymmetry provides this criterion.

19. There may be other interesting causal asymmetries. Some will count as degenerate cases of the PIP; others will not. But I will leave such questions aside here, since the point of the present paper is not to provide a taxonomy of either intergenerational problems or group dynamics more generally.

20. Even a persistence of numerically-identical core members may not be required. In some contexts, the dominance of a given set of ideals or interests may be sufficient to ground talk of a distinct generation. (E.g., in practice we often speak of a "new generation" or "second generation" of cars or politicians even when there is no presumption that the previous generation contained a core, persisting set of members.) Still, in future-generation cases we are typically concerned with the interests of individuals, so we do expect the core-group assumption to hold.

21. I shall say more about this later, when we consider the issue of overlapping generations.

22. Consider a paradigm case. The benefits to the present generation from energy consumption are likely to be large, secure, tangible and immediate, whereas the benefits from abstaining for the sake of the esteem of future generations are likely to be relatively small, uncertain, intangible and deferred. Furthermore, some benefits of reputation will not depend on the present generation not overconsuming. For example, some of the uses of energy consumption might be for cultural or scientific projects which themselves endear the present to the future in some respects.

23. In addition, it is not clear that it would be desirable for things to be different. For example, suppose some course of action could ensure a large and long-lived reputational gain for the present generation. This would likely be only for some correspondingly large project. But this would imply large investment (e.g., in the building of pyramids, a major space program, etc.). We could perhaps devote ourselves to these but it would probably be to the detriment of the welfare of both current and future people. So, it is not obviously desirable. (Furthermore, later people might be able to do such things better, and more cheaply, in any case.) On a related issue, see Nick Bostrom, "Astronomical Waste: The opportunity Cost of Delayed Technological Development," *Utilitas* (forthcoming).

24. This is not to deny that the PIP would remain a useful analytical tool even under the assumption of egoism.

25. I have in mind here Hume's observation, that though people are not self-interested, they do tend to be much more concerned with those close to them (friends, family, those in their immediate community), than those more distant. Often, generational groups will reflect those connections, so that the self-interest assumption will apply to those groups. (We might also say that some overconsumption has little to do with "interests" *per se*. Arguably, much overconsumption is caused by desires such as to indulge, or amuse, such as relatives show towards children. I thank Leslie Francis for discussion on this issue.)

26. Paradigm examples of environmental degradation seem to fit the basic pattern of temporally diffuse goods postulated in the PIP. Climate change caused by anthropogenic carbon dioxide emissions is a particularly good example. In climate change, the bad effects of energy consumption on climate stability are largely deferred, since they are extremely long-term, whereas the good effects are immediate and accrue largely to the current generation.

27. Furthermore, the deferred cost may be of a different, more fundamental kind than the present benefit (e.g., if the latter involves luxury consumption goods, and the former some basic harm, such as an incapacitation or disease). Indeed, we should note that from the point of view of the other features of PIP, the temporally diffuse good could be such that the deferred costs are extremely high (and concern the basic necessities of life), and

THE PURE INTERGENERATIONAL PROBLEM

the present benefits extremely low (and concern luxuries). For if earlier groups are indifferent to later groups, then relative magnitudes do not matter. These are the most serious cases from the practical point of view.

28. This should be unsurprising, since the wide definition of future people is the one which approximates most closely to the causal asymmetry condition of the PIP.

29. For example, over time global warming is expected to produce a melting of the West Antarctic Ice Sheet, which will ultimately produce a rise in global sea-level of around seven meters. But the Intergovernmental Panel on Climate Change predicts that this will occur gradually, and that most of the rise will occur after the present century and over the course of more than a thousand years. Similarly, there is some likelihood that climate change will cause the Thermohaline Circulation to shut down, cutting off the Gulf Stream to Western Europe. But the IPCC doubts that this will occur before 2100 (though it expects some weakening). See I.P.C.C., *Climate Change 2001: The Scientific Report* (Cambridge: Cambridge University Press, 2001).

30. Indeed, without this account, it is difficult to grasp either the meaning or the importance of "replacement" as a criterion for generation-individuation.

31. It may, of course, pay to pretend earlier on that this is what one will do, in order to extract benefits.

32. This is, no doubt, one of the reasons why some intergenerational problems are becoming more visible and pronounced. In earlier times the old were extremely dependent on the young. But they are much less so in many countries now.

33. A related problem arises here, that of obligations to the past. I cannot address that issue here.

34. Manipulation is obviously a concern. But even without this, the general circumstances for later groups will almost necessarily include the fact that at least some of the behavior of earlier towards later generations will have been beneficial. (For example, minimal nurturing behavior is necessary to their very survival long enough to gain significant causal power.) So, future groups will necessarily have at least mixed views about their relationship with their predecessors, and so be correspondingly reluctant to take punitive action against them for their transgressions.

35. If contact is not required, then "personal attachment" must be carefully distinguished from moral motives which imply direct concern for the future individuals. Such motives must presumably be part of any solution to the PIP and its manifestations.

36. There is no reason to assume that such concern is an all-or-nothing affair. Instead, what seems likely is that it is graduated. On the one hand, we are generally less concerned with those whom we will never meet, than with those not yet alive with whom there will be overlap, and less concerned with these than with people currently around. But, on the other hand, even when there is overlap, and we care about the well-being of at least some of the people who remain after we are dead, that concern tends to be less than our concern for individuals around now (even when the same people are at issue) and to decline over temporal distance.

37. A good example of this might be the Canadian rush to ratify the Kyoto Protocol, which journalists say has more to do with the current Prime Minister's wish to pose a difficult problem for his successor, a political rival, than any policy conviction. See Anne McIlroy, "Gas-guzzling Canada Divided Over Rush to Kyoto," *Guardian Weekly*, (Nov. 7, 2002). McIlroy says:

> The internal politics are treacherous ... So why the rush? Why anger the provinces? Why forge ahead without preparation? The simplest explanation is that Chrétien won't be around to implement the protocol. He has announced he will retire early in 2004, and there is pressure on

him to leave earlier. His heir apparent is his arch-rival and former finance minister, Paul Martin. If he wins the leadership and becomes prime minister, it is Martin who will have to decide whether to increase taxes on oil and gas. He is the one who will have to cope with any economic fallout from ratifying Kyoto. . . . Much of Chrétien's energy in the past few years has been devoted to sticking it to Martin. . . . But the idea of leaving Martin holding the bag for Kyoto isn't the only motivating factor for Chrétien. He has always spent more energy trying to look good on global warming—more specifically trying to look better than the US on the issue—than doing anything about it. In 1997, as Kyoto was being negotiated, the prime minister based Canada's strategy on a desire to best the Americans. The US has now abandoned Kyoto. By ratifying it, Chrétien will be able to leave office knowing he "beat" the Americans.

38. For one thing, it is subject to a number of well-known objections and qualifications. First, it relies on the assumption of continued economic growth. But growth is not an inevitable fact of economic life: human history has not always been characterized by it, nor has the history of particular regions. Hence, it seems likely that there is an invisible hand in this sense only under certain contingent circumstances. So, the PIP is only inoperative, if it is, under some conditions. Second, the argument focuses on narrowly economic benefits. It assumes (a) that there are not long-term noneconomic costs of economic growth (such as environmental costs) which outweigh the gains, or are not compensated for by a larger stock of capital; and (b) that the sole concern for future generations is economic, rather than for, say, stable political or social institutions. Third, evidence about growth itself says nothing about the distribution of wealth. So, we cannot tell, for example, whether the future growth (fortuitously) benefits future people in one part of the world only at the expense of future (or present) people in another part.

39. Also, it presumably assumes that the long-term benefits cannot be converted into short-term benefits for the current generation—otherwise we would need to account for why they do not do so—or that such benefits can be achieved through no specific attention to the PIP problem.

40. In some sense, the presence and extent of the invisible hand are a matter of fortuitous chance. Since in itself it relies purely on the self-interested motivations of the present generation, we must be especially wary of limitations to and deviations from the empirical circumstances. The PIP explains why.

41. It is very difficult to believe that scientists will come up with a climate stabilization device, or that future people will prefer climate instability to stability.

42. Not only can they control whether there is anyone to have such obligations *to*, but also the extent of those obligations: e.g., if they control the number of future people, they might control which goods really count as temporally-diffuse in the relevant sense. (The Non-Identity Problem rears its head again here. It allegedly suggests that we cannot harm future generations. Hence, some might argue that future generations raise no issues of distributive justice, so that even if the PIP applies, it poses no moral issue, and so is not a "problem.")

43. One reason turns on the variety of ways in which one might understand the term 'generation'. Another is that we have reasonable projections of global population for the next fifty years or so, and a reasonable grasp of the underlying trends. These suggest that world population for the next century or so will be substantially above that of the present. Other things being equal, this would increase our obligations to the future.

44. See Parfit. I have something to say about whether Parfit's Non-Identity problem undermines the application of the PIP in n. 10 (above). I hope to deal with the NIP more fully in a later paper.

[15]

Climate change and the duties of the advantaged

Simon Caney*

Department of Politics and International Relations and Magdalen College, University of Oxford, UK

> Climate change poses grave threats to many people, including the most vulnerable. This prompts the question of who should bear the burden of combating 'dangerous' climate change. Many appeal to the Polluter Pays Principle. I argue that it should play an important role in any adequate analysis of the responsibility to combat climate change, but suggest that it suffers from three limitations and that it needs to be revised. I then consider the Ability to Pay Principle and consider four objections to this principle. I suggest that, when suitably modified, it can supplement the Polluter Pays Principle.

> **Keywords:** climate change; duties; polluter pays principle; ability to pay principle

It is widely (though not universally) acknowledged that the earth's climate is undergoing profound changes and, moreover, that these changes are, to a large extent, the result of human activity. These changes are predicted to have profound and undesirable effects on people's standard of living, including most notably the standard of living of the most vulnerable and weak. The ill effects will include raised sea-levels which, in turn, destroy habitable land, human settlements and infrastructure. They will, in addition, expose some to greater risks of 'storm-surges'. The increased global warming will induce other malign effects, including higher deaths from drought and malnutrition. In addition to this the increased temperatures will increase the numbers of those exposed to infectious diseases, such as malaria, dengue and cholera. Higher temperatures will also result in death by heat stress. Climate change will, moreover, bring increased rainfall for some areas and this too will issue in harmful effects, causing destructive flooding. Finally, the majority of scientific experts hold that climate change heralds unpredictable weather events and such freak events will threaten human buildings and infrastructure.[1]

This raises the question of who should bear the burdens of dealing with climate change. One can identify at least two principles:

---

*Email: simon.caney@magd.ox.ac.uk

- those who caused the problem should pay (the Polluter Pays Principle – PPP);
- those who have the greatest ability to pay (the Ability to Pay Principle – ATP).[2]

Many discussions focus on the Polluter Pays Principle.[3] In what follows I want to chronicle some of its limitations and argue that a version of the Ability to Pay Principle must play a crucial role.

Before doing so, it is worth clarifying what I mean by 'bearing the burdens of global climate change'. We can distinguish between (at least) two different kinds of duty. First, one might say that there is a duty to cut back on activities which cause climate change. To use the language employed by the Intergovernmental Panel on Climate Change (IPCC), this duty requires people to engage in 'mitigation'. The duties involved would include, for example, a duty to reduce emissions of greenhouse gases (where these include carbon dioxide, methane, nitrous oxide, hydrofluorocarbons (HFCs), perfluorocarbons (PFCs), and sulfur hexafluoride (SF6)). It would, in particular, require cutting back emissions of carbon dioxide. In practice, this would require persons to adopt policies such as reducing air travel, driving less, insulating one's house more efficiently, using less electricity, and so on. The duty to prevent further climate change could also comprise creating and protecting carbon sinks. Let us call this first kind of duty a 'duty of mitigation'. A second kind of duty is the duty to devote resources to protect people from the ill effects of climate change. To employ the usage of the IPCC, this duty is a duty to facilitate and support 'adaptation' to climate change. Let us call this a 'duty of adaptation'. This duty would involve spending money on the following types of activity: building sea-walls which will protect those who live and work near the coast from sea-level rise and from storm surges; subsidizing people to move away from threatened coastal settlements; spending more money inoculating people from infectious diseases; supporting irrigation systems in drought-prone areas; sending overseas aid to victims of malnutrition; and so on.

It is widely recognized that, whatever happens, some adaptation is required. The emission of greenhouse gases has reached such a level and has been taking place for such a long time (since the industrial revolution) that even if emissions levels were dramatically cut there would still inevitably be an increase in temperature and in sea-levels. As a recent statement of the national academies of science of 11 countries (including those of the USA, India, China, Germany and the UK) reports

> Carbon dioxide can remain in the atmosphere for many decades. Even with possible lowered emission rates we will be experiencing the impacts of climate change throughout the twenty-first century and beyond. ... Major parts of the climate system respond slowly to changes in greenhouse gas concentrations.

Even if greenhouse gas emissions were stabilised instantly at today's levels, the climate would still continue to change as it adapts to the increased emission of recent decades.[4]

Furthermore, the distinguished scientist, Michael Mann, has recently stated that 'we're already committed to 50 to 100 years of warming and several centuries of sea-level rise, simply from the amount of greenhouse gases we've already put in the atmosphere' (Appell 2005, p. 23). Indeed recent research has found that '[s]ea level is likely to continue rising for more than 1000 years after greenhouse gas concentrations have been stabilised, so that with even a sizeable mitigation effort adaptation is also likely to be needed' (Lowe et al. 2006, p. 35). A policy of mitigation is, therefore, not sufficient.[5] To prevent climate change from jeopardizing the interests of persons some resources will be need to be spent on adaptation.

It is also widely, though not unanimously, accepted that a policy of mitigation is necessary and that one cannot simply rely on adaptation.[6] The need to engage in mitigation has been further underscored by the latest research. For example, recent studies have shown that the West Antarctic Ice Sheet (WAIS) and the Greenland Ice Sheet are both less stable than previously assumed and if these melt they will have severe and dangerous effects on sea-levels.[7] In addition, recent research has found that the Atlantic Thermohaline Circulation is under threat and if this shuts down this will have severe effects on human life.[8] There is, then, an urgent need for a reduction in greenhouse gas emissions to prevent further increases in the earth's temperature and increasing sea-levels. A full account of the duty to bear the burden of climate change must, thus, include both a duty to engage in mitigation and a duty to spend resources enabling persons to adapt to climate change.

Who should bear these burdens?

The 'Polluter Pays' Principle and two concerns

Consider, first, the view that the polluter should pay. This has an immediate intuitive appeal and should play a role in any plausible account of who should pay the price for addressing climate change. It is a strongly held view that if an actor causes pollution (through, say, releasing radioactive waste or emitting dangerous fumes) then that actor is morally responsible for dealing with the ensuing costs to others. The Polluter Pays Principle is, note, a backward-looking or historical principle. Drawing on this principle, it follows that those who contribute to climate change (either by using up excessive amounts of fossil fuels or by deforestation) should make amends for this. If, for example, they have used excessive amounts of greenhouse gases then, ceteris paribus, it is fair to require them to cut back their emissions accordingly (and/or to devote resources enabling the potential victims to adapt to dangerous climate change). This approach has been canvassed by a number of developing countries, most notably Brazil. In a proposal it submitted to the deliberations of the United Nations Framework Convention on Climate Change (UNFCCC) it argued that countries which had emitted more greenhouse gases should bear a greater responsibility in combating climate change.[9] This proposal was subsequently referred to the Subsidiary Body for Scientific and Technological Advice (SBSTA) and it seems unlikely to come into effect.[10] Our question, though, is whether the principle at heart is a valid one.

I shall argue that the Polluter Pays Principle should be supplemented by an additional principle, but before I do so it is important to consider two concerns that might be raised about the Polluter Pays Principle.

Objection 1

One concern that might be raised about the Polluter Pays Principle concerns its practicality. A critic might emphasize the extent of uncertainty in climate science and draw attention to two factors in particular. (1) The first concerns the uncertain nature of the estimated ill effects. The projections of the IPCC, for example, reasonably enough, take the form of projecting that a phenomenon P will increase by between x% and y%. The Third Assessment Report estimates, for example, that between 1990 and 2100 sea-levels will rise by between 0.09 metres and 0.88 metres and the temperature will increase by between 1.4 and 5.8° Celsius (Ahmad *et al.* 2001, p. 3). In addition it regards some of its projections as more confident than others and employs a five-point scale indicating various degrees of confidence (ranging from 95% confidence to 5% confidence) (Schneider and Sarukhan 2001, p. 79). It is hard, then, to specify how much harm will result from this and hence difficult to make people pay in proportion to their causal impact on a problem. For further illustration of this problem consider the category of persons who are suffering from 'water-stress'. On some projections, between 1.1 and 2.8 billion of these people will suffer further reductions in their access to water by 2050 and on other projections the estimate is that between 0.7 and 1.2 billion people will experience a decrease in access to water in this time period (Arnell 2006, p. 167). Estimating the extent of the harm caused by global climate change is therefore immensely difficult. (2) Consider now a second aspect. Take sea-levels again. Sir John Houghton reports that sea-levels are expected to rise by just under two metres by 2100 in Bangladesh, but he adds that without climate change there would be soil erosion anyway and only 70cm of this rise will result from anthropogenic climate change (Houghton 2004, p. 150). If this is so, we then need to ascertain what damage would result from a 70cm rise alone. To gain any non-arbitrary view here would seem to be next to impossible – yet, it is required to implement the Polluter Pays Principle. The key point is that to apply the Polluter Pays Principle we need to be able to specify the harm done and trace it back to the causal actors and where either the nature of the harm is uncertain or unpredictable (point

1) or the link between the climate change and the harm is uncertain (point 2) then this cannot be done.[11]

How serious is this problem? And how damaging is it to the Polluter Pays Principle? Three points can be made in reply. First, one might just reply that the preceding practical problems do not call into question, or undermine in any way, the moral force of the principle. What they reveal is that it is difficult to apply and in seeking to implement it we should be aware of the immense practical problems involved. In themselves, though, they do not establish that the principle is morally implausible. The lessons to be learned from the objection are, then, not that the principle should be rejected but that caution should be exercised when applying it and that we cannot hope for too much exactitude.

Second, it bears noting that climate modellers believe that they are making considerable progress in developing the capacity for the detection and attribution of climate change. Some are increasingly confident that it will be possible to attribute specific events to climate change.[12] For example, Peter Stott, Daithi Stone and Myles Allen have argued that one can attribute the heatwave that occurred in Europe in the summer of 2003 to human forcing (Stott *et al*. 2004).

Third, and finally, it is important to recognize that the problem does not only affect the Polluter Pays Principle. It affects it more acutely but actually all principles which ascribe duties for combating climate change are affected by this problem. To see why this is the case, it is useful to return to the distinction between the 'duty of mitigation' and the 'duty of adaptation'. Consider, first, the duty to fund adaptation. The Polluter Pays Principle is undoubtedly at a disadvantage when compared with alternative principles, such as the Ability to Pay Principle. This can be seen if we consider rising sea-levels again and ask who should finance the process of adaptation needed to ensure that rising sea-levels do not harm people's vital interests. The Polluter Pays Principle, *by its very nature*, must ascertain who caused how much harm and, as such, it must become embroiled in the complex historical problems noted above. It must do this to ascertain who the duty bearers are and the size of their duty. An Ability to Pay approach, by contrast, does not need to enquire into the causes of dangerous climate change in order to determine who should pay for the necessary adaptation. It need not get embroiled in issues surrounding the historical causes for climate change because all it needs to know are, first, what kind of adaptation measures are required and, second, who are the most advantaged. In light of this, a historical approach, like the Polluter Pays Principle, can, therefore, be said to be less practical than competing approaches such as the Ability to Pay Principle.

However, note that the problems of determining cause and effect also affect *all* principles determining who should bear the burdens of climate change. This can be seen if we consider the duty to engage in mitigation. The reason is straightforward: any account of the duty to prevent harms must employ an accurate account of which activities cause those harms and by how much. So even if one adopts an Ability to Pay approach one needs to know the extent of the harms caused by dangerous climate change and what causes those harms. Performance of the duty to mitigate requires this knowledge. It is only once one has this information that one can then specify what the wealthiest must do to perform their duty to prevent dangerous climate change. So *any* theory concerned with preventing further harmful climate change cannot avoid the complex causal issues raised above. The problem is, therefore, not particular to the Polluter Pays approach and, as such, does not give us reason to reject that approach in preference to another one.

Objection 2

Consider now a second challenge to the Polluter Pays Principle. One worry about applying the Polluter Pays Principle to global climate change is that some people were excusably ignorant of the fact that their activities may lead to dangerous climate change. As such it would be unfair to make them pay. They knew not what they were doing and, moreover, their ignorance is excusable.

A number of different counter-arguments might be made in response to this argument. One can identify at least five possibilities. These hold that the 'excusable ignorance' argument does not invalidate or limit the application of the Polluter Pays Principle to climate change because:

Reply (1): ever since the 1990s, it has been widely known that methane, nitrous oxide, hydrofluorocarbons, perfluorocarbons, and sulfur hexafluoride cause climate change.[13]

Reply (2): ever since a pre-1990 date, it has been widely known that carbon emissions *might* cause climate change and agents should have acted according to the 'precautionary principle'.

Reply (3): those responsible for emitting excessive amounts of greenhouse gases have continued to do so even when they have been made aware of the consequences of their actions so the fact that they were excusably ignorant before does not exempt them from being paying for the emissions that they generated when excusably ignorant.[14]

Reply (4): we should adopt a strict liability principle where this holds that if people engage in activities which jeopardize other people's fundamental interests by emitting excessive amounts of greenhouse gases then they should bear the costs of their actions even if they were excusably ignorant of the effects of their actions (see Neumayer 2000, p. 188; Shue 1999, pp. 535–536).

Reply (5): we should adopt a modified strict liability principle where this holds that if people engage in activities which jeopardize other people's fundamental interests by emitting excessive amounts of greenhouse gases, then they should bear the costs of their actions even if they were excusably ignorant of the effects of their actions if *they have benefited from those harmful activities* (see Baer 2006, p. 136; Gosseries 2004, pp. 40–41).[15]

Let us consider each of these responses. Reply (1) clearly has force now and from sometime in the last 15 or so years. However, its obvious limitation is that it cannot cover emissions that precede whatever cut-off date we specify as the date after which one cannot plead excusable ignorance. Given this, let us consider reply (2). This can reach further back into the past than reply (1) but it is hard to say with any specificity the date from which it can be applied. In addition to this, one important question that arises is whether persons who *had reason to think* that greenhouse gases *might* cause climate change should pay the same amount for the consequences of their action as persons who *knew* that greenhouse gases *did* cause climate change. Intuitively this seems wrong but then how much less should those who violate the precautionary principle pay? There is no obvious answer.

Consider now reply (3). Its thesis is that if people would not have cut back on their emissions even if they had not been excusably ignorant then the fact that they were indeed excusably ignorant does not exonerate them. Since they would have emitted just as much anyway, whether or not they were aware of the causes of climate change, their excusable ignorance is not germane: they are required to pay for their emissions. Now reply (3) is hard to dispute on empirical grounds. Those who have known about the effects of their carbon-intensive practices have not engaged in mitigation. Indeed emissions have continued to increase year after year. For example, carbon dioxide emissions stemming from fossil fuel use and industry have grown by more than 3% per annum during the 2000–2004 period (as compared to 1.1% per annum between 1990 and 1999) (Rapauch *et al.* 2007, p. 10288). One might, though, object to reply (3) on procedural grounds. Even if one had overwhelming reason to think that people would not have cut back on their emissions if they had known earlier and so would have acted wrongly, one is not entitled to treat them as if they have in fact acted wrongly. For they have not and it would be a violation of procedural justice to treat them as if they had. They should be given a fair chance to act correctly and reply (3) denies them this.

Given this one might adopt reply (4) and affirm a principle of strict liability. This, however, seems to me to fail to do justice to potential duty-bearers. Any compelling theory of justice must accommodate both the concerns of the rights-bearers (we wish that our rights be upheld) and the concerns of the duty-bearers (the duties entailed by the rights should not be unreasonable). However, an unqualified strict liability approach subordinates the perspectives of the rights-bearers over potential duty-bearers. The latter can plausibly complain 'why should we pay when we had no idea that our activities were having this effect and, furthermore, when we could not have been expected to know that our activities were harmful?' Reply (4) is, thus, unfair on the potential duty-bearers.

One might, however, revise reply (4) in light of this objection. Consider, again, the problem with reply (4). Suppose, for example, that by treading on a spot on the ground one causes harm to others on the other side of the globe and suppose that one could not be expected to know that this happens. Pace the argument of the last paragraph, one may conclude here that it is unfair to insist that the person who causes the harm should pay the cost. Now suppose, however, that the person who treads on the spot on the ground derives a benefit from this activity. The behaviour that causes the harm to others also brings them benefits. This considerably changes the situation. In particular, the complaint that it is unfair to make them pay for effects they could not have anticipated loses its force here because, and to the extent that, they have also benefited from this harmful behaviour. This leads us towards reply (5).

However, reply (5) is, as it stands, not quite right because it makes no reference to the size of the benefit. It says simply that where someone has engaged in activities that have a harmful effect that they could not have foreseen then they are liable as long as they have benefited. But it would be implausible to say that they are liable for massive costs even if they only benefited slightly. In line with this, I suggest the following:

Reply (6): we should adopt a modified strict liability principle where this holds that if people engage in activities which jeopardize other people's fundamental interests by emitting excessive amounts of greenhouse gases then (i) they should bear the costs of their actions even if they were excusably ignorant of the effects of their actions if *they have benefited from those harmful activities* and (ii) *their costs should correspond to the benefits they have derived*.[16]

This version of strict liability clearly accommodates the point of view of the duty-bearer for it prevents cases arising where the potential duty-bearer is made to pay large costs even though they have derived only minimal gains. It is, therefore, superior to replies (4) and (5). However, since those who have emitted high levels of greenhouse gases have in fact also benefited considerably from them this principle, in practice, has considerable bite and would impose duties on very many people in industrialised economies. It thus provides considerable protection to the potential victims of dangerous climate change.

Reply (6) thus gives us the resources to meet the argument from 'excusable ignorance'. The Polluter Pays Principle may rightfully apply to those who are excusably ignorant of the consequences of their climate endangering activities if, because, and to the extent that they have benefited from their high emissions.

The 'Polluter Pays' Principle – three limitations

Having addressed two challenges to the application of the Polluter Pays Principle to global climate change we may now consider three more serious problems. One problem with the Polluter Pays Principle is that it cannot cope with the effects on the climate that result from the emissions of earlier generations. On most accounts, carbon dioxide emissions began to rise during the industrial revolution and continued to rise throughout the nineteenth and twentieth century. This means, though, that some of the polluters, and hence some of the duty-bearers, are dead and we therefore need to ascribe the duty to address their emissions to someone else. The principle that the polluter should pay obviously needs supplementation when the polluter no longer exists (Caney 2005, p. 756).

Now when assessing this objection we should bear in mind that the most marked increase in greenhouse gas emissions has taken place over the last 35 years or so. Indeed, it has recently been found that '[s]ince 1751 approximately 329 billion tons of carbon have been released to the atmosphere from the consumption of fossil fuels and cement production. Half of these emissions have occurred since the mid 1970s' (Boden *et al.* 2009). Carbon emissions from fossil fuel burning, cement manufacture and gas flaring rose from 1630 million metric tons of carbon in 1950 (which amounts to 0.64 metric tons of carbon per capita) to 4076 million metric tons of carbon in 1970 (1.10 metric tons per capita). By 1980, 5332 million metric tons of carbon were released (which equates to 1.20 metric tons per capita) and by 2006 the total emissions were a staggering 8230 million metric tons (1.25 metric tons of carbon per capita) (Boden *et al.* 2009). Carbon emissions thus increased more than five-fold between 1950 and 2006. This notwithstanding, most accounts recognise that there was a pronounced and significant increase between 1840 and the mid-twentieth century. For example, emissions rose from a mere eight million metric tons in 1800 to 33 million metric tons in 1840, rising further to 932 million metric tons by 1920 and reaching 1630 million metric tons by 1950 (Boden and Marland 2009). And, of course, many of those causally responsible during the period from 1840 to 1950 (and indeed later) are dead so the Polluter Pays Principle cannot be applied to their emissions. The Polluter Pays Principle is, thus, incomplete.

A second problem with the Polluter Pays Principle arises if and when some climate change occurs which does not stem from human activity. Climate scientists overwhelmingly contend that human activity is the major driver of the current and projected climate change. However, their formulations also often allow that human activity may not be the sole cause of climate change. The 'Summary for Policymakers' in the IPCC's *Climate Change 2001: Synthesis Report* reports, for example, that '*most* of the warming observed over the last 50 years is attributable to human activities' (Watson *et al.* 2001, p. 5, emphasis added). How should we think about any warming that is not anthropogenic? A proponent of the Polluter Pays Principle faces a dilemma here. *Either* she holds that people should be protected against *all* malign climate change (where doing so is not unduly demanding) but then, if this is the case, she needs to go beyond a pure Polluter Pays approach and find some criterion for apportioning the remaining responsibility. She needs, that is, to find some principle to tell us who should bear that portion of the cost of dealing with harmful climate change that stems from non-anthropogenic causes. *Or*, she commits herself to a purist version of the Polluter Pays Principle, which holds that the Polluter Pays Principle is the *only* fair principle for determining duties and hence the only climate change that should be covered is that stemming from human activity. On this view, then, the harm resulting from non-human activities should go unaddressed. But this is implausible. Our concern about climate change (including non-anthropogenic climate change) stems from its impacts on people's lives (their exposure to drought, malnutrition, flooding, disease, heat stress and so forth). Given this, we have reason to be concerned about non-anthropogenic climate change. Someone might claim that climate change that has been imposed by other people is worse in some sense than non-human-induced climate change but it would be odd to think that non-anthropogenic climate change is of no concern at all. From the point of view of the victim, what matters is that dangerous climate change damages one's vital interests. The view that persons are entitled to protection from anthropogenic climate change and not from non-anthropogenic climate change is thus untenable. But if we accept this then an additional principle is required. The proponent of the PPP thus faces a dilemma. Either we ignore non-anthropogenic climate change, but this is morally questionable. Or we call for protection against all malign climate change, but if this is the case an additional principle is required to attribute responsibilities to deal with non-human-induced climate change.[17]

A third, and final, point bears noting. We tend to assume that to make the polluter pay is in practice often to make the affluent pay. That we do so is understandable because industrialised countries like the USA and European countries have traditionally been the highest emitters of greenhouse gases. However, there is not a perfect correlation between high emissions and wealth, and in some instances making people pay in proportion to their emissions would perpetuate the poverty of some and reduce others to poverty. This is true, for example, for many in China and India.

The view that China should not be subject to a strict application of the Polluter Pays Principle is, however, resisted by some. They argue, for example, that China's emissions are now greater than those of the USA so it should bear responsibility for those emissions. In support of this claim they might appeal to a recent report from the Netherlands Environmental Assessment Agency, according to which in 2006 China's total CO_2 emissions were 6,220 million tonnes whereas the USA's CO_2 emissions in that year were 5,801 million tonnes (Nature 2007, p. 1038). China is, moreover, not alone, and India's emissions are considerable. A critic may therefore resist the idea that developing countries should be partially exempted from the Polluter Pays Principle.

This counter-argument is, however, unpersuasive for several reasons. First, the figures cited above refer only to the total amount CO_2 of emitted. China has, however, a much larger population than the USA. China's population in 2006 was 1,323.6 million people as opposed to the USA's 301 million. Thus China's per capita emissions in 2006 were 4.7 tonnes of CO_2 per capita rather than the USA's staggering 19.3 tonnes per capita (Nature 2007, p. 1038). The same point applies if we look further than China. For example, in 2004 the developing countries (including China and India) comprised 80% of the world's population but emitted only 41% of the world's emissions (Rapauch et al. 2007, p. 10292). Second, however, the argument under consideration is inappropriate because the standard of living in China is much lower than the USA and it is wrong to impose mitigation duties on some if that jeopardizes their ability to attain a decent standard of living.[18] Third, the second point can be generalised further. And it is worth making the more general point that it would be a mistake to determine who should bear the burden of climate change in isolation from an analysis of their general economic entitlements. So if one holds, as I do, that people should not fall beneath a certain standard of living then the Polluter Pays Principle should be qualified to prevent it being the case that people are made to pay for emissions needed for their fundamental survival.[19]

These points do not – and are not intended to – establish that the Polluter Pays Principle should be abandoned when determining the duties of prevention and adaptation. They point to ways in which the Polluter Pays Principle must be supplemented with an additional principle (or set of principles). They establish that we need a principle of justice to deal with what we might term the Remainder, where I use this term to refer to harmful climate changes that stems from (a) the emissions of earlier generations, (b) non-human-induced climate change, and (c) the (legitimate) emissions of the disadvantaged.

The 'Ability to Pay' Principle

How should we deal with the Remainder? In this section I want to argue that the Remainder should be filled by an 'Ability to Pay' approach. Stated formally, this approach states that the duty to address some problem (in this case, bearing the burdens of climate change) should be borne by the wealthy, and, moreover, that the duty should increase in line with an agent's wealth.[20] In principle, the Ability to Pay approach is indifferent to who caused a harm: its emphasis is on who can rectify that harm. So by contrast with the Polluter Pays Principle it is a forward-looking, rather than a backward-looking, principle. To appraise the plausibility of the Ability to Pay Principle and to help us refine it consider several objections that might be levelled against it.

A: Objection 1 – why should I pay for something that is not my fault?

First, the advantaged might argue that it is unfair to make them cut back on emissions (and/or pay for adaptation) since the climate change in question (the Remainder) is, *ex hypothesi*, not their fault. To adopt an Ability to Pay component, they complain, is to make them bear a burden for something that is no fault of their own.

This objection, however, does not unsettle the use of the Ability to Pay principle. The objection rests on the following assumption: it is wrong that some bear a burden for a problem that is not of their doing. This assumption seems to me highly implausible but the most important point to make in this context is that whatever happens some will be bearing a burden that it is not their fault. To see this consider three options. We might say that the advantaged should pay (option 1) or that the poor should pay (option 2). In both cases, however, some would be bearing a burden that stems from a problem that is not of their doing. We might then hold that nothing should be done (what is termed 'business as usual'): this is option 3. But this too imposes a burden on some because of something that is not of their doing – for in this case victims of climate change (many of whom will be future generations) will have to bear a burden that stems from a problem that they did not cause. So all of the available options violate the assumption. It cannot therefore be used to invalidate an Ability to Pay approach.

We can go further. Reflecting on the three-option scenario just envisaged brings out the intuitive appeal of the Ability to Pay approach. Consider the three options again. In the first place we might hold that the poor should pay. However, to make the least well-off pay in a world where others are able to pay and still live a very affluent life seems perverse. In light of this, we might say that global warming should remain unaddressed. But this too seems unfair – especially on the poor members of some regions (such as Bangladesh, small island states and the Nile Delta) because they are particularly vulnerable to climate change. This leaves one group – the advantaged – and they have less cause for complaint than either of the other two groups.[21] The most advantaged are most able to pay the price without sacrificing any reasonable interests: therefore, they are under a duty to do so.

B: Objection 2 – isn't it counter-intuitive to ignore the historical record?

Consider now a second objection to an Ability to Pay component. A pure Ability to Pay approach holds that the only criterion for apportioning responsibility for bearing a burden is who can best bear that burden. This purist approach is, however, vulnerable to the objection that, by giving no place to the historical genesis of a problem, it ignores a morally relevant consideration. As noted above, an Ability to Pay approach is wholly forward-looking. As such, though, it is in conflict with a deep conviction that who should bear the burdens of climate change cannot be wholly divorced from an understanding of the historical origin of the problem. A wholly forward-looking approach, it might be argued, is out of kilter with some of our deepest moral convictions.

Two responses are available to proponents of the Ability to Pay principle. First, they might dismiss the intuition and bite the (counter-intuitive) bullet. Second, they might seek to accommodate the objection being raised. I shall pursue this second strategy. I propose the following position as an initial step in the right direction:

> **ATP***: The duties to bear the Remainder should be borne by the wealthy but we should distinguish between two groups – (i) those whose wealth came about in ways which endangered the Earth's climate and (ii) those whose wealth came about in ways which did not endanger the Earth's climate – and we should apportion greater responsibility to (i) than to (ii).[22]

To elaborate further: (i) refers to currently alive people whose holdings resulted from a historical process that involved excessively high emissions. So if a person owns £200,000 and if this is the case because their grandparents acquired this wealth in a climate-endangering way then that person would fall into category (i). The key point is that somewhere along the historical chain of events leading them to own their current holdings there have been climate injustices. Those in category (i), then, have received wealth because of the commission of injustices. For convenience's sake I shall term those who belong to category (i) as 'dirty developers' and those in category (ii) as 'clean developers' (even though some of those in category (i) might themselves not have emitted excessive levels of greenhouse gases).

This qualified version of the Ability to Pay has intuitive appeal but can we say more in its favour? I think we can. My suggestion is that those whose wealth did not come about in a climate-endangering way can provide more reasons to justify their wealth (and thereby to resist the claim that they should devote resources to ameliorating climate change) than those whose wealth did come about in a climate-endangering way. They have more reasons at their disposal to justify their view that they should not have to pay for the mitigation and adaptation costs needed to address the ill effects of climate change. The argument can best be illustrated by comparing two people. Suppose that we are apportioning responsibilities for addressing climate change. Imagine that there are two people, A and B, and suppose that they are equally wealthy. The historical process that lead to A's possession of her current wealth is one that involves excessive carbon emissions. (She thus falls into category (i) of the **ATP***.) B's wealth, by contrast, has not come about in climate-endangering ways. Suppose now that someone proposes that A and B should bear part of the burden of dealing with climate change and should do so equally. They will no doubt adduce various reasons to resist this demand. Familiar reasons would include:

(1) taxing the wealthy undermines economic growth because it reduces the incentive to engage in wealth-creation (the economic growth argument).

(2) taxing the wealthy restricts the liberty of the wealthy (the liberty argument).
(3) taxing the wealthy is unfair because they are entitled to their wealth, in virtue of the fact that it came about in a just way (the entitlement argument).

They might also, no doubt, adduce other reasons. Now the relevant point is this: B can invoke all of these reasons in support of her position whereas A can only invoke reasons (1) and (2). *Ex hypothesi*, A cannot invoke an entitlement-based argument in support of her position because her wealth did not come about in a just way. She therefore has less cause for complaint than B. The point can be put in another way: the significance of historic wrongs (like excessive carbon emissions or highly damaging deforestation) is that they discredit historical arguments that take the form 'we're entitled to X because our possession of X came about in a just way'.[23] Now insofar as we are concerned about historic injustices we should ask less of clean developers than dirty developers.

To further determine the plausibility or otherwise of **ATP*** let us consider two additional challenges to it.

C: Objection 3 – why should 'clean developers' pay anything?

Someone might dispute **ATP*** on the grounds that none of the burden should be borne by wealthy persons if their wealth did not come about in a climate-endangering way. The proposal in other words is to delete category (ii) from **ATP***. On this proposal the duty to bear the burden of the Remainder should fall squarely on those privileged members of the world whose wealth came about in a climate-endangering way. This criticism thus posits a challenge: why should the wealthy pay anything if their wealth came about through clean development?

A number of points can be made in reply. First, there are familiar cases where we think that a person is obligated to assist others even when they played no part in the other's poverty or sickness. In such cases we think that a positive duty falls on those able to help. For example, if someone sitting next to you at a table suddenly becomes seriously ill and you're well placed to help, then we tend to think that you should do so. It would be an odd person who refused to aid on the basis that they did not cause this harm. Even if people disagree with Peter Singer's claim that persons are obligated to aid others up and until the point that the cost to them of giving is greater than the benefit received, there is a fixed conviction that there is a duty to aid to some extent (Singer 1972). This leads to a second point: resistance to the idea that those who did not cause a problem can nonetheless be obligated often stems from a concern that they will be subject to unduly demanding duties. But there is, of course, no reason why this need be the case. One can respond to this concern by affirming positive duties on those able to pay so long as it is not too demanding. Third, and finally, as is commonly argued, the best account of what is wrong with causing a harm to befall others appeals to the importance of being able to pursue their interests. But, if it is morally important that persons can pursue their interests, then it entails not just that there is a duty not to harm those interests but also a duty to aid those who are vulnerable.[24] If we hold that there is a duty not to harm someone because such harms leave people unable to advance their fundamental interests then this suggests that we care about people being able to advance their fundamental interests. But if we hold this, it surely entails a positive duty on the behalf of others to advance those interests. The first objection to **ATP*** thus fails.

D: Objection 4 – why focus solely on previous climate injustice?

Let us consider, now, an additional and final objection. This time the concern is with the contention that greater responsibilities should be borne by wealthy persons whose wealth came about in *a climate-endangering way*. Why, a critic might ask, should the Ability to Pay Principle focus solely on 'those whose wealth came about in a climate-endangering way' rather than 'those whose wealth came about in an unjust way'? Imagine, for example, that some have wealth and that they do so because their ancestors participated in the slave trade (and I am assuming that that did not involve high carbon emissions or methane emissions and so on). Or consider those whose current affluence has arisen because they have inherited wealth from ancestors who appropriated land from indigenous peoples (and, again, let us assume that they did not emit high levels of carbon emissions and did not engage in deforestation). Their current holdings are thus based to some extent on a history of injustice: can it not be said of them that they have less claim on their current wealth? Furthermore, the critic might argue, the reasoning adduced in support of the **ATP*** (in particular the argument comparing the clean developer B with the dirty developer A) does not in fact support **ATP***. Let me explain. The argument in question compared A and B and made the point that A could muster less reasons on behalf of their claim to retain their wealth: in particular they could not employ an entitlement-based theory in their defence. But, and this is the key point, the same point could be made about those whose wealth came about because of the slave trade or political corruption or economic imperialism. They too cannot use an entitlement-based theory to defend their current holdings. Thus the normative rationale for **ATP*** actually entails that greater responsibility should be borne by the wealthy whose wealth came about in unjust ways. In light of this line of reasoning, we should revise **ATP*** (and the way in which it defines category (ii)) so that it reads as follows:

> **ATP****: The duties to bear the Remainder should be borne by the wealthy but we should distinguish between two groups – (i) those whose wealth came about

in unjust ways and (ii) those whose wealth came about in ways which were not unjust – and we should apportion greater responsibility to (i) than to (ii).

Given the argument mooted for **ATP*** (i.e. the comparison of A and B above) we should prefer **ATP**** to **ATP***.

Several further comments about **ATP**** are in order. First, someone might argue that it is particularly fitting that those whose holdings stem from a climate injustice make recompense for that particular wrong. Consider, for example, someone whose wealth stems from the fact that their grandparents collaborated with the slave trade: one might think it particularly appropriate that they deal with the contemporary ill effects of slavery. Or consider someone whose wealth came about because their ancestors appropriated wealth from Jews during the Second World War: one might think it appropriate that they address anti-semitism. **ATP**** accommodates such an intuition but it does not make it mandatory. It would allow those whose wealth stems from injustice to discharge their duties in this specific way but it does not require this kind of action. Second, in distinguishing between (i) and (ii) I am not committed to claiming that many or indeed any people fall into category (i). **ATP**** does not assume that there are in fact people in both categories. My point is to establish the morally relevant considerations and categories, not to make an empirical claim. Third, we should record that the **ATP**** needs to be stated more precisely. We need, for example, to say how the duty should be shared among the two groups mentioned. By what formula or rule? In the meantime, however, I hope that the preceding arguments make a persuasive case for **ATP****.

Before considering some implications of the view defended here, it is worth providing a statement of my conclusions. Thus far I have argued for two main positive conclusions. First, I have accepted a qualified version of the Polluter Pays Principle where this holds that

> Principle 1: Persons should bear the burden of climate change that they have caused so long as doing so does not push them beneath a decent standard of living (the *Poverty-Sensitive Polluter Pays Principle*).

Second, however, I have argued that the Polluter Pays Principle cannot cover all aspects of the problem (non-anthropogenic climate change, the emissions of the poor, and the emissions of past generations – what I have termed the Remainder). This leads to my second positive claim. For I have argued that

> Principle 2: The duties to bear the Remainder should be borne by the wealthy but we should distinguish between two groups – (i) those whose wealth came about in unjust ways, and (ii) those whose wealth did not come about in unjust ways – and we should apportion greater responsibility to (i) than to (ii). (*the History-Sensitive Ability to Pay Principle*).

The view defended, then, is a hybrid one that combines two separate principles.

The implications of the hybrid model

This provides the theoretical framework within which I think we should address climate change. I now want to describe it more fully and then explore its practical implications.

Let us begin then by fleshing out these two principles further. Three points are in order. First, nothing has been said so far on who the bearers of these duties are. Many thinkers and commentators treat 'countries' as the bearers of the duties of prevention and adaptation. This, no doubt, is in part a reflection of the fact that much of the focus on combating climate change is on international treaties like the Kyoto Protocol. It is, however, a consequence of the view defended above that the duties outlined above fall not just on states but also on other types of actor. For example, the logic of the *Poverty-Sensitive Polluter Pays Principle* is that all (sufficiently affluent) agents who are causally responsible for high emissions are under an obligation to cut back their emissions according (and/or spend money on adaptation). Now many actors other than national governments play a causal role. These include, for example, (1) individuals for individuals can choose whether to fly or not, what car to drive, how much heating or air-conditioning to use and so on. They also include (2) firms. Firms can frequently choose how much energy they need to consume, how much transportation to employ, the extent of building insulation, the level of heating and so on. They also include (3) sub-state political authorities like cities or the member states of federal systems like the USA. This level of analysis is often neglected, but recent research for the Pew Center on Global Climate Change has revealed how different states in the United States of America pursue quite different policies on climate change. States can exert considerable control over many areas that bear on greenhouse gas emissions (passing regulations on household goods; requiring use of renewable energy sources; restricting carbon emissions of power plants) and some states have pursued more aggressive mitigation policies than others (Pew Center 2006). To give some examples: Connecticut, Maine, Massachusetts, New Hampshire, New York, Rhode Island, and Vermont have pledged themselves to reducing greenhouse gas (GHG) emissions to 10% lower than 1990 levels by 2020. California has committed itself to reducing GHG emissions to 1990 levels by 2020 and New Mexico has pledged to reduce its GHG emissions to 10% lower than its 2000 level by 2020 (Fischer and Constanza 2005, p. 301). Other states have been far less active.[25] A final category of actors who play a causal role in generating climate change is, (4), international financial institutions (who often incentivise environmentally harmful economic growth). The duties generated by the *Poverty-Sensitive Polluter Pays Principle* thus fall to all these kind of actors. The same is true of the **ATP****. The thought underlying the latter is that those able to pay have a duty to do so and hence this duty falls too not simply on affluent 'states' but on any body that can possess wealth, such as individuals, corporations and so on.

220   S. Caney

Second, it is worth noting that although I have argued that the most advantaged have a leading responsibility to play, my argument also places duties on the least advantaged as well. For if they can develop in ways that do not involve high levels of fossil fuel combustion, and can do so without great cost to themselves, then it would be wrong for them to pursue a high emissions policy.

A third point also bears recording: it might be thought that my position justifies a policy according to which later generations pay for climate change. The thought here is that future generations will be wealthier than current generations and hence more able to pay; as such an 'ability to pay' criterion should allocate duties to them.[26] This, in effect, amounts to a policy of not preventing climate change for now and then trying at some point in the future both to prevent further climate change and also to adapt to the changes that have occurred. Although future people may well be better off than current people, I believe that it does not follow that an Ability to Pay Principle has the implication of postponing action into the future. There are at least two reasons for this. First, although future people may have more wealth, the costs will also be very much greater in the future. It will cost less to prevent the problem from arising than to allow it to arise and then seeking to adapt to it later.[27] Second, unless mitigation takes place now, there will be dangerous climate change to which people are unable to adapt. A failure to mitigate would therefore inevitably result in injury to some future people and it would be wrong knowingly to allow a wrong to occur with a view to seeking to compensate those wronged later. People should not be wronged in the first place. Mitigation now is thus not only cheaper than postponing action but it is also required if we are to respect people's fundamental interests.

Let us, finally, turn to the policy implications of the view defended on pp. 695–708. Different kinds of policy have been proposed to cut back on emissions. These include (among other things): (a) carbon quotas and trading policies, (b) carbon taxes, (c) clean development initiatives, and (d) adaptation programmes. Each of these instruments can be used in line with the view defended above. What is required is a set of measures that prevent people (within reason) from emitting excessive emissions, ensure that those who have emitted more than they should have done cut back their emissions and support adaptation, and that ensure that the most advantaged cover the Remainder. The policy instruments listed above can all serve these objectives.

(a) Consider first a system of carbon quotas and carbon trading. This approach is affirmed in Article 17 of the Kyoto Protocol and a system of carbon-trading (the EU Emissions Trading Scheme) came into effect on 1 January 2005.[28] Advocates of carbon trading often suggest that 'states' have quotas that they can use, or sell, but this is not the only option. Alternatively, one might suggest a scheme where permits are auctioned off to firms who then pass the costs on to the consumer and in which the proceeds are spent to further people's entitlements. Finally, some have proposed a system of individual quotas (what has been Domestic Tradable Quotas).[29] Now a quota-based system can, if effectively enforced, serve the goal of reducing carbon dioxide. Many who favour a system of quotas hold that everyone should have an equal per capita entitlement to emit carbon dioxide.[30] The account developed above would, however, dissent from this in several ways. First, following the Polluter Pays Principle it would hold that those who have in the near past emitted excessive amounts of carbon dioxide should have less now. Second, the arguments above claim that the least advantaged have a stronger claim to emit carbon dioxide than the advantaged. Third, I have argued that the most advantaged should bear the cost of the emissions of both past generations and of the disadvantaged, in which case it follows that the advantaged should not have an equal right to emit carbon dioxide. The key point I wish to make though is that the account developed above can be reflected by a system of emissions quotas and carbon trading.

(b) The view defended above can also, however, employ a system of taxes. In the first place, a system of carbon taxes can be utilised both to discourage people from exceeding their fair share and also to ensure that those who do exceed their fair share pay money in compensation (thereby making the polluter pay). Second, one can ensure that carbon taxes exempt the very poor. In virtue of both of these features, carbon taxes can realize what I termed the *Poverty-Sensitive Polluter Pays Principle* (as defined on p. 708). Third, as proponents of carbon taxes often observe, carbon taxes can produce a 'double dividend'. So as well as discouraging high emissions they can generate funds – funds that can be spent on adaptation.[31] Finally, and moving away from carbon taxes, a system of progressive taxation can be implemented in countries with an extensive history of industrialisation to ensure that the most advantaged pay for those types of climate change not covered by the Polluter Pays Principle (which is what would be required by the *History-Sensitive Ability to Pay Principle* defended above).

The key point to observe then is that the principles I have defended can be implemented via either a 'cap and trade' system of carbon trading or a system of carbon (and other) taxes. Though the principles I defend are rather complex the preceding discussion shows how taxes and trading schemes can be designed to approximate them.

(c) Note, further, that a successful programme of combating climate change must find ways that poor countries can develop and meet their legitimate needs without jeopardizing the earth's atmosphere. However to attain such sustainable development there must be financial schemes which both stimulate research and development of clean technology and which also ensure that such clean technology is transferred from rich to poor countries.[32] This, however, requires funding and this again requires us to turn to the Hybrid View.

(d) Finally, the Hybrid View can determine who should fund adaptation. As was noted earlier, adaptation is necessary. It is widely recognised that the global poor will be highly vulnerable to dangerous climate and therefore their adaptive capacity needs to be developed. Applying the Hybrid View, it is clear that the global poor themselves should not bear the cost. The Poverty-Sensitive Polluter Pays Principle would exempt them (either because of their poverty and/or because their emissions are very low) and since they are disadvantaged they would also be exempted by the Ability to Pay component. There therefore needs to be a global adaptation fund that is funded by those who have emitted excessive amounts of GHGs and by the advantaged of the world.

Conclusion

It is time to conclude. This paper has examined the question of who should bear the burdens of climate change. It would be convenient if we could rely on a simple formula to answer this question. I have argued, however, that no such simple formula is available. The truth is rather more complex than any crude slogan. To answer to the question we need to draw on qualified versions of the Polluter Pays Principle and the Ability to Pay Principle.

Acknowledgements

Earlier versions of this paper were presented at the 'Global Inequalities, Local Injustices' Seminar Series, University of Oxford (November 2005); the Political Theory Seminar, University of Newcastle (November 2005); the Symposium on 'Democracy, Equality and Justice', the British Academy (December 2005); the 11th International Social Justice Conference of the International Society for Justice Research, Humboldt University, Berlin (August 2006); the Conference on 'Global Justice and Climate Change', University of Reading (October 2006); and the Oxford-Princeton 'Global Justice Seminar', at Princeton University (March 2007). I am grateful to members of all the audiences for comments and thank, in particular, Arthur Applbaum, Paul Baer, Brian Barry, Paula Casal, Steve Gardiner, Wilfried Hinsch, Brad Hooker, Andy Hurrell, Vijay Joshi, Peter Jones, Robert Keohane, Melissa Lane, Stephen Macedo, David Miller, Sue Mendus, Lukas Meyer, Helen Milner, Kieran Oberman, Onora O'Neill, Philippe van Parijs, Alan Patten, James Pattison, Jennifer Pitts, Dominic Roser, Henry Shue and Andrew Williams. I am especially grateful to Derek Bell, Matthew Clayton and Edward Page for discussions of the view defended here. This research was conducted as part of an Arts and Humanities Research Council (AHRC) research grant on 'Global Justice and the Environment' and I am grateful to the AHRC for its support. I completed this essay while holding a Leverhulme Research Fellowship and I am grateful to the Leverhulme Trust for its support.

Notes

1. For excellent empirical data on all these see McCarthy et al. (2001), Schellnhuber et al. (2006), Parry et al. (2007).
2. This list is not exhaustive. A third principle holds that those who have benefited from industrialization, and/or from climate change itself, should pay (the Beneficiary Pays Principle – BPP). I have criticised this principle elsewhere and will not

discuss it here. For a defence of the view see Gosseries (2004). For criticism see Caney (2006, pp. 471–476).
3. For defences of this kind of approach see Neumayer (2000) and Shue (1999, pp. 533–537). Shue himself prefers not to describe his position as a polluter pays principle (p. 534) but his position conforms to the PPP as I interpret it.
4. Joint Science Academies' Statement: Global Response to Climate Change (2005).
5. See, further, Hare and Meinshausen (2006).
6. Some, like Bjørn Lomborg, have contested this, arguing that prevention will cost too much and will yield too little. See Lomborg (2001, pp. 305–318, especially p. 318). Lomborg's arguments are, however, unpersuasive. For a good critique see Cole (2003).
7. For discussion of the West Antarctic Ice Sheet see Rapley (2006, pp. 25–27). For discussion of the Greenland Ice sheet see Lowe *et al.* (2006, pp. 29–36).
8. For good discussions of the Atlantic Thermohaline Circulation see Schlesinger *et al.* (2006, pp. 37–47) and Wood *et al.* (2006, pp. 49–54). See also Vellinga and Wood (2002).
9. See 'Paper No. 1 Brazil: Proposed Elements of a Protocol to the United Nations Framework Convention on Climate Change, Presented by Brazil in Response to the Berlin Mandate', Item 3 of the Provisional Agenda of the Seventh Session of the Ad Hoc Group on the Berlin Mandate, FCCC/AGBM/1997/MISC.1/Add.3, 30 May 1997.
10. See the SBSTA's 'Progress Report on the Review of the Scientific and Methodological Aspects of the Proposal by Brazil', Item 4 of the Provisional Agenda of the Fourteenth Session of the SBSTA, Bonn, FCCC/SBSTA/2001/INF.2, 10 July 2001.
11. For further extended analysis on the uncertainties in determining causal responsibility see den Elzen and Schaeffer (2002).
12. See, for example, Allen (2003), Allen and Lord (2004), and Allen *et al.* (2007).
13. This kind of response has been made by a number of different thinkers, though they do not always agree on the date after which the plea of excusable ignorance is inappropriate. See, for example, Singer (2002, p. 34), who proposes 1990 as the cut-off date, and Neumayer (2000, p. 188), who suggests that the cut-off date should be in the mid-1980s. Shue also makes this kind of response but does not specify a key date after which one cannot claim excusable ignorance (Shue 1999, p. 536).
14. I am grateful to Andrew Williams for pressing this response when I presented this paper at the British Academy.
15. This reply is also suggested in passing by Peter Singer (2002, p. 34). Singer, however, does not press the point and in a desire to construct a principle that might enjoy support among industrialised countries he makes no further use of the idea of strict liability in his argument.
16. In his illuminating analysis, Axel Gosseries (2004) also mentions the relevance of the size of the benefit that the excusably ignorant perpetrator receives from their harmful act to the issue of whether (and by how much) that perpetrator owes (2004, pp. 40–41). However, it is not clear from his discussion of liability incurred when excusably ignorant what criteria determine the relationship between the amount of benefit received and the size of the duty owed. On my account, the cost that can be demanded should correspond to the benefit actually enjoyed. It is not clear from Gosseries' account whether he would concur and what he says suggests that he would not (2004, p. 41).
17. This point is made by Edward Page. As he rightly says a PP approach cannot cope where climate change is 'entirely nonanthropogenic in origin' (Page 2006, p. 169.

cf also p. 172). Actually we do not need to imagine a case where it is *wholly* anthropogenic to see the limitations of the Polluter Pays Principle for even if non-anthropogenic causes are *part* of the cause then the Polluter Pays Principle is incomplete.

18. Some make a second kind of argument. They point out that the increase in carbon emissions is most marked in developing countries like China and India. This is true. To take 2004 again, 73% of the increase in emissions came from the 80% of the earth's population that come from developing countries (Raupach et al. 2007, p. 10292). However, this does not entail that the Polluter Pays Principle should be applied in full force to China and India. First, as argued in the text above, whether this increase in emissions is justified or not depends in part on the material needs of the Chinese people and the extent to which the increase in emissions is necessary to meet these. Second, even if we ignore this first point, a high rate of increase is not the relevant benchmark anyway. For one needs to know China's absolute level of emissions (per capita), not the rate of increase. So if the increase is great but the level of emissions is still low, then what should inform policy is the fact that the quantity of emissions (per capita) is low.

19. See also Shue's affirmation of a 'guaranteed minimum' principle (1999, pp. 540–544). For an important defence of 'sufficiency' see Frankfurt (1987).

20. See here Shue's affirmation of an 'ability to pay' principle (Shue 1999, pp. 537–540, especially p. 537). (For further discussions where Shue has argued that the wealthy should bear the mitigation and adaptation costs of climate change and that the poor be given less demanding duties see: Shue 1993, pp. 42–43, 56, 58; Shue 1994, pp. 343–366; Shue 1995, pp. 250–257.) Darrel Moellendorf also argues that the Ability to Pay Principle should play a role. In particular, he argues that it is needed to cover the fact that the Polluter Pays Principle cannot deal with the emissions of the dead. See his succinct but perceptive treatment: Moellendorf (2002, pp. 97–100).

21. For an earlier statement of this argument see Caney (2005, pp. 771–772). For a closely related line of reasoning see Moellendorf (2002, p. 100).

22. For a similar, but nonetheless distinct, position see Page's illuminating reflections in *Climate change, justice and future generations* (2006, pp.172–173). Page's suggestion is that there should be 'some "discount" in what is required of the better off when their behaviour is not [the] cause of the problem' (p.172). His view, however, differs from ATP* in several fundamental respects. First, ATP* applies this modified Ability to Pay approach simply to the climate change covered by the Remainder and not to all climate change. Second, Page's claim is that '"ability to pay" arguments gain at least some of their plausibility from the implicit assumption that those who have the ability to solve environmental problems are generally responsible for them' (p. 173). ATP*, by contrast, does not claim this. It contends that those who have the ability to pay have an even greater responsibility if, and because, they have inherited wealth and resources that were produced in a way that involved very high emissions (*even though they themselves were not 'responsible for' those emissions*). Such people are obligated (for ATP*) not because they have emitted high levels themselves (for they might not have) but because they are wealthy and that wealth stems from the excessive emissions of earlier generations.

23. See, further, Caney (2006).

24. This is brought out nicely by Allen Buchanan (2004, pp. 89–92).

25. In addition to this, recent research has shown that the policies pursued by city councils often has a marked impact on climate change. Some cities, for example, belong to the Cities for Climate Protection (CCP) programme and through it adopt

policies that cut emissions. See Betsill and Bulkeley (2004) and Bulkeley and Betsill (2005).
26. I am grateful to Vijay Joshi for raising this issue.
27. This view is strongly confirmed by Sir Nicholas Stern (2007)
28. For Article 17 of The Kyoto Protocol see: http://unfccc.int/resource/docs/convkp/kpeng.html.
29. See Starkey and Anderson (2005); Fleming (2006).
30. See Baer *et al.* (2000); Neumayer (2000, pp. 185–192); Athanasiou and Baer (2002, especially pp. 76–97).
31. One recent study finds, for example, that if a tax of $21 for each metric ton of carbon were universally adopted then it would generate $130 billion per annum. See Sandmo (2005, p. 48).
32. This point should not be confused with support for the 'clean development mechanism' that is articulated in Article 12 of the Kyoto Protocol *(http://unfccc.int/resource/docs/convkp/kpeng.html)*. The latter is, I have argued elsewhere, profoundly flawed. For the reasons why see my paper 'Markets, morality and climate change: what, if anything, is wrong with emissions trading?' (Caney forthcoming).

Notes on contributor

Simon Caney is Professor of Political Theory and Fellow and Tutor in Politics at Magdalen College, University of Oxford. He is the author of *Justice beyond borders: a global political theory* (Oxford University Press, 2005). He is currently working on two books – *Global justice and climate change* (with Derek Bell – under contract to Oxford University Press) and *On cosmopolitanism* (under contract to Oxford University Press). From 2008 to 2011 he will hold an ESRC Climate Change Leadership Fellowship.

References

Ahmad, Q.K. *et al.*, 2001. Summary for policymakers. *In:* J. McCarthy *et al.*, eds. *Climate change 2001: impacts, adaptation, and vulnerability.* Cambridge: Cambridge University Press.
Allen, M., 2003. Liability for climate change: will it ever be possible to sue anyone for damaging the climate? *Nature,* 421 (6926), 891–892.
Allen, M. and Lord, R., 2004. The blame game: who will pay for the damaging consequences of climate change? *Nature,* 432 (7017), 551–552.
Allen, M. *et al.*, 2007. Scientific challenges in the attribution of harm to human influence on climate. *University of Pennsylvania law review,* 155 (6), 1353–1400.
Appell, D., 2005. Behind the hockey stick. *Scientific American,* 292 (3), 23–24.
Arnell, N., 2006. Climate change and water resources: a global perspective. *In:* H. Schellnhuber *et al.*, eds. *Avoiding dangerous climate change.* Cambridge: Cambridge University Press, 167–175.
Athanasiou, T. and Baer, P., 2002. *Dead heat: global justice and global warming.* New York: Seven Stories Press.
Baer, P., 2006. Adaptation: who pays whom?. *In:* N. Adger, *et al.*, eds. *Fairness in adaptation to climate change.* Cambridge MA: MIT Press, 131–156.
Baer, P., *et al.*, 2000. Equity and greenhouse gas responsibility. *Science* 289 (29), 2287.

Betsill, M. and Bulkeley, H., 2004. Transnational networks and global environmental governance: the cities for climate protection program. *International studies quarterly*, 48 (2), 471–93.

Boden, T. and Marland, G., 2009. Global CO_2 emissions from fossil-fuel burning, cement manufacture, and gas flaring: 1751–2006. Carbon Dioxide Information Analysis Center, Oak Ridge National Laboratory, Oak Ridge, TN. At http://cdiac.ornl.gov/ftp/ndp030/global.1751_2006.ems.

Boden, T.A., Marland, G. and Andres, R.J., 2009. Global, regional, and national fossil-fuel CO_2 emissions. Carbon Dioxide Information Analysis Center, Oak Ridge National Laboratory, US Department of Energy, Oak Ridge, TN. At http://cdiac.ornl.gov/trends/emis/tre_glob.html.

Buchanan, A., 2004. *Justice, legitimacy, and self-determination: moral foundations for international law*. Oxford: Oxford University Press.

Bulkeley, H. and Betsill, M., 2005. Rethinking sustainable cities: multilevel governance and the 'urban' politics of climate change. *Environmental politics*, 14 (1), 42–63.

Caney, S., 2005. Cosmopolitan justice, responsibility and global climate change. *Leiden journal of international law*, 18 (4), 747–775.

Caney, S., 2006. Environmental degradation, reparations and the moral significance of history. *Journal of social philosophy*, 37 (3), 464–482.

Caney, S., forthcoming. Markets, morality and climate change: what, if anything, is wrong with emissions trading?.

Cole, M., 2003. Environmental optimists, environmental pessimists and the real state of the world – an article examining *The skeptical environmentalist: measuring the real state of the world* by Bjorn Lomborg. *Economic journal*, 113 (488), 362–380.

den Elzen, M. and Schaeffer, M., 2002. Responsibility for past and future global warming: uncertainties in attributing anthropogenic climate change. *Climatic change*, 54 (1–2), 29–73.

Fleming, D., 2006. *Energy and the common purpose: descending the energy staircase with tradable energy quotas (TEQs)* at: http://www.teqs.net/book/teqs.pdf.

Fisher, B. and Costanza, R., 2005. Regional commitment to reducing emissions. *Nature*, 438 (7066), 301–302.

Frankfurt, H., 1987. Equality as a moral ideal. *Ethics*, 98 (1), 21–43.

Gosseries, A., 2004. Historical emissions and free-riding. *Ethical perspectives*, 11 (1), 36–60.

Hare, B. and Meinshausen, M., 2006. How much warming are we committed to and how much can be avoided?. *Climatic change* 75 (1–2), 111–149.

Houghton, Sir John, 2004. *Global warming: the complete briefing*. 3rd ed. Cambridge: Cambridge University Press.

Joint Science Academies' Statement: Global Response to Climate Change, 2005. Available from: http://www.royalsoc.ac.uk/displaypagedoc.asp?id=20742.

Lomborg, B., 2001. *The skeptical environmentalist: measuring the real state of the world*. Cambridge: Cambridge University Press.

Lowe, J., et al., 2006. The role of sea-level rise and the Greenland ice sheet in dangerous climate change: implications for the stabilisation of climate. *In:* H. Schellnhuber, et al., eds. *Avoiding dangerous climate change*. Cambridge: Cambridge University Press.

McCarthy, J., et al., eds. 2001. *Climate change 2001: impacts, adaptation, and vulnerability – contribution of working group II to the third assessment report of the Intergovernmental Panel on Climate Change*. Cambridge: Cambridge University Press.

Moellendorf, D., 2002. *Cosmopolitan justice*. Boulder, CO: Westview Press.

Nature, 2007. Gas Exchange: CO_2 emissions 1990–2006. *Nature,* 447 (7148), 1038.
Neumayer, E., 2000. In defence of historical accountability for greenhouse gas emissions. *Ecological economics* 33 (2), 185–192.
Page, E., 2006. *Climate change, justice and future generations.* Cheltenham: Edward Elgar.
Parry, M.L. et al., eds. 2007. *Climate change 2007: impacts, adaptation and vulnerability – contribution of working group II to the fourth assessment report of the Intergovernmental Panel on Climate Change.* Cambridge: Cambridge University Press.
Pew Center on Global Climate Change, 2006. *Climate change 101: state action.* http://www.pewclimate.org/docUploads/101%5FStates%2Epdf
Rapley, C., 2006. The Antarctic ice sheet and sea level rise. *In:* H. Schellnhuber, eds. *Avoiding dangerous climate change.* Cambridge: Cambridge University Press.
Raupach, M. et al., 2007. Global and regional drivers of accelerating CO_2 emissions. *Proceedings of the National Academy of Sciences of the United States of America,* 104 (24), 10288–10293.
Sandmo, A., 2005. Environmental taxation and revenue for development. *In:* A.B. Atkinson, ed. *New sources of development finance.* Oxford: Oxford University Press, 33–57.
Schellnhuber, H. et al., eds. 2006. *Avoiding dangerous climate change.* Cambridge: Cambridge University Press.
Schlesinger, M. et al., 2006. Assessing the risk of a collapse of the Atlantic thermohaline circulation. *In:* H. Schellnhuber et al., eds., 2006. *Avoiding dangerous climate change.* Cambridge: Cambridge University Press.
Schneider, S. and Sarukhan, J., 2001. Overview of impacts, adaptation, and vulnerability to climate change. *In:* J. McCarthy et al., eds. *Climate change 2001: impacts, adaptation, and vulnerability.* Cambridge: Cambridge University Press.
Shue, H., 1993. Subsistence emissions and luxury emissions. *Law and policy* 15 (1), 39–59.
Shue, H., 1994. After you: may action by the rich be contingent upon action by the poor? *Indiana journal of global legal studies,* 1 (2), 343–366.
Shue, H., 1995. Avoidable necessity: global warming, international fairness, and alternative energy. *In: Theory and practice:* NOMOS XXXVII. New York and London: New York University Press.
Shue, H., 1999. Global environment and international inequality. *International affairs,* 75 (3), 531–545.
Singer, P, 1972. Famine, affluence, and morality. *Philosophy & public affairs* 1 (3), 229–243.
Singer, P., 2002. *One world: the ethics of globalization.* New Haven and London: Yale University Press.
Starkey, R. and Anderson, K., 2005. Domestic tradable quotas: a policy instrument for reducing greenhouse gas emissions from energy use. Tyndall Centre for Climate Change Research: Technical Report No. 39. http://www.tyndall.ac. uk/sites/default/files/Domestic%20Tradeable%20Quotas%20%20A%20policy %20instrument%20for%20reducing%20greenhouse%20gas%20emissions% 20from%20energy%20use%20(tr39).pdf.
Stern, Sir Nicholas, 2007. *The economics of climate change: the Stern Review.* Cambridge: Cambridge University Press.
Stott, P.A., Stone, D.A. and Allen, M.R., 2004. Human contribution to the European heatwave of 2003. *Nature,* 432 (7017), 610–614.
Vellinga, M. and Wood, R., 2002. Global climatic impacts of a collapse of the Atlantic thermohaline circulation. *Climatic change,* 54 (3), 251–267.

228   S. Caney

Watson, R., *et al.,* 2001. Summary for policymakers. *In:* R. Watson and the Core Writing Team, eds, *Climate change 2001: synthesis report: contribution of working groups I, II and III to the third assessment report of the Intergovernmental Panel on Climate Change.* Cambridge: Cambridge University Press.

Wood, R., *et al.,* 2006. Towards a risk assessment for shutdown of the Atlantic thermohaline circulation. *In:* H. Schellnhuber *et al.,* eds., *Avoiding dangerous climate change.* Cambridge: Cambridge University Press, 49–54.

Part III
Normative Significance of Historical Injustices and their Consequences

[16]

THE NEW INDIAN CLAIMS AND ORIGINAL RIGHTS TO LAND

David Lyons

1. The New Indian Claims

Most Americans take this country's possession of its territory for granted, even though we all know that a great deal of its land was wrested by force or fraud from those who occupied it before the Europeans came—from Native Americans, who were dispossessed and either massacred or subjugated, the survivors displaced from their homelands and in large part consigned to live on shrinking reservations. The monumental theft of land that was involved in the European conquest of America is regarded as a neutral fact about the past with little, if any, practical bearing on the present.

It is that attitude that I ask you now to suspend, if you have not done so already. I assume here not only that the socially weak and disadvantaged condition of Native Americans in our society represents a wrong it is incumbent on us to right, but also that their dispossession may call for significant rectification. I shall concentrate on the latter issue because the serious possibility of radical social surgery to correct it must now be contemplated. The unthinkable idea of giving the land back to the Indians has suddenly become thinkable.

Early in its constitutional career, in 1790, Congress passed the Indian Nonintercourse Act, which requires that all transfers of lands from Indians to others be approved by the federal government. The Act was modified from time to time over the next forty-odd years, but it was not changed in any relevant respect, and it remains in effect today.[1] Its purpose is clear. It was meant to guarantee security to Native Americans against fraudulent acquisition by others of the Indians' allotments of land. Such guarantees were plainly needed. By 1790, expropriation had been practiced by

Europeans for nearly two centuries. Fraudulent land acquisitions by colonists had been a source of friction between them and the British government, which occasionally leaned towards protecting Native Americans. Security for Indian land was an important bargaining point during the Revolutionary War, when Indian support or at least neutrality was desperately needed by the rebellious colonists. The Nonintercourse Act of 1790 pledged federal security for Indian land holdings. Under it, the federal government is bound to act as guardian or trustee, overseeing all transfers of Indian lands, including those to states and other branches of government as well as to private parties.

Several suits that have recently been initiated by American Indian tribes for recovery of lands held by them when the Nonintercourse Act took effect in 1790 invoke this law. It is alleged that certain transactions by which lands were subsequently lost to them are invalid because federal approval was neither sought nor obtained in those cases. Those historical facts have not been contested.

A great deal is at stake. Some of the suits concern hundreds, others thousands, of acres. The largest tract, claimed by the Penobscot and Passamaquoddy tribes, amounts to twelve and a half million acres in Maine, comprises more than half the state, and has a value estimated at twenty-five billion dollars.[2]

In some cases, recovery of the lands is being effected smoothly, as in Gay Head, on Martha's Vineyard, off Cape Cod, where voters have approved the transfer of about two hundred fifty acres back to the Wampanoag. But that is an atypical case, since the land is undeveloped and has always been reserved for public use, which is what the Gay Head branch of the Wampanoag wish to secure it for, and about half the voting residents are Wampanoag descendants. More typical, perhaps, is the claim in Mashpee, on Cape Cod, where another branch of the Wampanoag is seeking to recover jurisdiction over about seventeen thousand acres, comprising most of the town of Mashpee, in an area that is currently undergoing rapid commercial development. That suit has thrown a cloud over land titles, freezing real estate transactions and development. Since Indian lands are not subject to local taxation, it has also disrupted the sale of municipal bonds. The professed aim of the claimants is reportedly not to dispossess current homeowners or active businesses. A prime objective is to regain lost hunting and fishing rights; another is to reassert control over the portion of the land that remains undeveloped, in order to inhibit such development. Almost all of the undeveloped land at issue in these suits, however, has passed into private hands. Consider the situation in Maine. Although the claims there embrace populated areas, including whole cities and towns, they chiefly concern, and the tribes appear chiefly interested in, vast tracts that are not only undeveloped but are, unlike the Mashpee claim, unlikely to undergo any ordinary commercial development. For these are mainly huge forest reserves that are owned by paper companies and related interests.

These lands will not be returned to the Indians without a bitter struggle. At first the claims were not taken seriously. But once they began to receive favorable attention in the federal courts, current owners—especially the large landed interests in Maine—began to mobilize a political campaign against recovery by the Indians.

Their concern and the subsequent political maneuvering is understandable. Federal court decisions have affirmed federal responsibility in such cases, whether or not the federal government has officially recognized the tribes in question,[3] and they have dismissed as inapplicable the various standard defenses, such as adverse possession (which invokes a statute of limitations on claims), laches (which invokes a similar doctrine in the law of equity), and estoppel by sale (which would use the prior transactions as a bar to recovery).[4] The law seems clear: any title to Indian land that has been obtained without explicit federal approval is null and void.

It does not follow—either legally or morally—that all of the land in question must be returned to the Indians. But an observer might well suppose that some, at least, of the lands should be restored to them. I wish to examine that idea, not only to help us in determining what justice requires, but also to evaluate some lines of reasoning in support of and in opposition to it. For the most natural arguments that might initially be advanced on both sides of the issue—arguments that appear to be implicit in the rhetoric already surrounding these cases—center on what we, following Robert Nozick,[5] might call "historical" considerations affecting social justice. These cases give us an opportunity to scrutinize Nozick's conception of justice and, more generally, the idea of a right to property.

2. The Historical Entitlement Arguments

Suppose that one is aware of the current plight of Native Americans and its background. This might understandably make one sympathetic to the new land claims. But it is incumbent on one to ask: What are the moral foundations of such claims? How can they be defended, not so much in a court of law as in the court of conscience?

One natural (one might almost say naive) way of reasoning about the claims is this. Native Americans were the first human occupants of this land. Before the European invasion of America, the land belonged to them. In the course of that invasion and its aftermath, the land was illicitly taken from them. The rightful owners of the land were dispossessed. The current owners lack a well-founded right to the land, which now lies illicitly in their hands. Ideally, the land should be restored to its rightful owners. This may be impractical; compromises might have to be made. But the original wrong can most easily be righted by returning the land to them—or by returning it wherever that is feasible.

This sort of argument turns upon the idea of original acquisition and, somewhat less directly, on the idea of legitimate transfer. Without original acquisition by the Indians, they might have had no rights to the land that dispossession was capable of violating. The argument concerns legitimate transfer by claiming that the transfers by which the Indians lost the lands were illegitimate.

The argument also assumes that rectification in these cases is, at least in principle, most straightforward. Injustice is corrected, justice is done, by restoring the land to its original and still rightful owners. That is a most important feature of the argument. For, if correct, it means that we can avoid getting bogged down in the uncharted territory of compensatory or reparative justice. Without that assumption, the problem has no easy solution, even in theory.

A frequent reply to the current claims is that one cannot simply ignore two hundred years of history. Those who now possess the land did not, in fact, secure it illicitly. They obtained it from others, by purchase, gift, and inheritance. To find illicit land transfers, we would have to trace the chain of transactions back several generations. But all of that is, by now, dead history. Somewhere along the line, custom and settled expectation generated new rights to the land. And it is these rights, not some long extinguished "original" right, that must now be enforced.

This line of reasoning has much in common with the usual defenses against claims whose foundations go far back into the past. The defense of adverse possession, for example, rests on the rule that one cannot validly reclaim property after a certain period of time has passed, during which one has registered no complaint about another's misappropriation. Such a defense has been ruled inapplicable to the current cases, as we have seen. But that is not decisive here, when we are concerned with the moral foundations for such claims; it might simply amount to a legal technicality, which has only limited implications about what is right and what is wrong. If adverse possession is in general a reasonable defense against such claims, it might be legally inapplicable here only because of a strange quirk in the law. But I shall not pursue that complex matter now. Any defense against such claims is also likely to rely upon inheritance, and this issue will be more central to our concerns in this paper.

In what follows, my purpose will be to challenge these naive arguments, on both sides of the issue, by throwing doubt upon property rights as we usually think of them. I shall suggest that property rights, including rights to land, are thinner and much more flexible, or variable with circumstances, than these arguments allow. If that is so, our whole way of looking at such matters may require radical revision.

Let me relate this now to Nozick's theory of justice. We are dealing here with property, on which Nozick concentrates, and the particular issues in the case correspond to major aspects of his theory—acquisition and transfer. The two main elements of Nozick's theory are what he calls "the principle of justice in acquisition" and "the principle of justice in transfer." The former concerns the circumstances in which one can acquire rights to things by appropriating them. The latter concerns the ways in which one can receive rights from others, such as gifts, inheritance, and exchange.

Many textbook theories of justice ignore historical factors, especially those involving voluntary transfer. Some theories imply, for example, that I possess a thing unjustly unless I can be said to merit or deserve it. Nozick reminds us, however, that justice does not frown upon gifts and favors, charity and generosity, and fair bargains. One can obtain things by such means without meriting or deserving them—and yet without any injustice being done.

Historical factors are thus relevant to justice, and any adequate theory must accommodate them. It does not follow (nor is it true) that Nozick's theory alone is capable of accommodating them. In fact, Nozick goes to the opposite extreme, exaggerating the role of historical considerations.

Nozick defends the following thesis: to establish the moral foundations for one's ownership of a thing, it may not be necessary to show that one's ownership fits into some preferred social pattern, such as equality. It may suffice to show that one obtained the thing in accordance with the principle of justice in acquisition or the principle of justice in transfer. This is significant because voluntary transfers can upset preexisting patterns of distribution, such as equality. If the results of such transfers are unobjectionable, then patterns cannot exhaust the important truths about social justice.

Nozick's examples tend to show that historical factors are relevant to matters of justice, independently of other factors. That is an important point; but Nozick tries to stretch it further. From the claim that historical factors are relevant he seems to infer that they are the only factors relevant to justice, that all other considerations are irrelevant, such as merit and desert and the relative distribution of benefits and burdens in society. But the latter simply does not follow from the former, and it may very well be false.

In this paper I shall argue that Nozick's theory incorporates another exaggeration—the notion that property rights, once legitimately acquired, are virtually unaffected by circumstances. I shall then show how this undermines the historical entitlement arguments concerning Indian land claims. But I argue, finally, that it does not defeat the current claims.

3. Original Acquisition

Let us first consider the idea of original rights to land. How are such rights to be understood? Locke is one of the few writers to discuss the subject, so it seems reasonable to begin with his view of it.[6]

Locke says that one acquires property, originally, by "mixing one's labor" with an unowned thing, or something that belongs to all humanity in common. (§27) Locke clearly means us to take this notion of "mixing one's labor" with a thing very loosely—to cover, for example, one's picking up an acorn with a view to eating it. (§28) But, as Nozick observes,[7] there are problems with this notion. The limits of what I can acquire in this way are radically indeterminate. If no one yet owns them, can I make the oceans my own property by simply stirring water at the shore? More fundamentally, it is not clear why mixing my labor with a thing that I do not own is a way of acquiring that thing rather than a way of losing my labor.

When Locke applies his general theory to the acquisition of land he obtains a doctrine that is at least much clearer. He says that one must cultivate the soil, make it productive agriculturally, and be able to consume its products. (§32) Mixing one's labor with a parcel of land in this way removes it from the common stock of land that has been provided for all humanity and gives one original title to it.

This cultivation test seems natural enough—so long as we assume that cultivation is the only proper way of using land. But a moment's reflection reminds us that, even for the purpose of obtaining food, land can effectively be used in other ways—hunting, gathering, and herding, for example. And, of course, land can be used in ways unrelated to food production. Locke was aware of this. How, then, did he justify his narrow cultivation test?

His reasoning is suggested by the following passage which Locke had added to the collected edition of his works:

> [H]e who appropriates land to himself by his labor does not lessen but increase the common stock of mankind; for the provisions serving to the support of human life produced by one acre of enclosed and cultivated land are—to speak much within compass—ten times more than those which are yielded by an acre of land of equal richness lying waste in common. And therefore he that encloses land, and has a greater plenty of the conveniences of life from ten acres than he could have from a hundred left to nature, may truly be said to give ninety acres to mankind; for his labor now supplies him with provisions out of ten acres which were by the product of a hundred lying in common. (§37)

Locke maintains, moreover, that "there is land enough in the world to suffice double the inhabitants," provided it be cultivated. (§36) By his reckoning, there is not a fifth enough land for all the people of the world if none of it is cultivated. The argument therefore seems to be that, by enclosing and cultivating land, one actually performs a service to others. If I appropriate and cultivate only so much land as I require for my own subsistence, I thereby release land to others that I would have needed to support myself by hunting on it or gathering food from it. Cultivation involves the far more efficient use of land, from which all benefit. Most important, the failure to cultivate suitable land results in privation for a corresponding number of people.

Nozick appears to reject Locke's theory about the original acquisition of land. The argument suggests a utilitarian rationale for property rights, which Nozick regards as unacceptable. And, even within its utilitarian framework, the argument is not very promising as a way of showing that cultivation is the only legitimate basis for acquiring unowned land. The empirical premises of the argument are dubious, and alternative grounds of appropriation seem possible. More importantly, Nozick, as we have seen, raises skeptical doubts about Locke's general theory of property acquisition.

Nozick's alternative account appears to be that appropriation alone is sufficient for the legitimate acquisition of property, provided that a certain condition is satisfied. Nozick calls this the "Lockean proviso"; this is a requirement Locke included in his own theory, that "enough and as good" of whatever is being appropriated be left for others. (§27) If enough and as good land is left for others when one appropriates land, the appropriation is legitimate, justice is done, and one acquires a right to the land. Otherwise the appropriation is illegitimate and one acquires no right to the land.

Let us suppose, for the sake of argument, that some sort of right to land can be established, and also that Native Americans established original rights to land in the Americas before the European invasion, land that was later taken illicitly by some of the invaders. The question we must face is, what difference that can make today.

The argument invoking original rights to land in support of the current Indian land claims assumes that original rights are very stable. They are unaffected by changes in circumstances, because they are still valid today despite the passage of history. They are also largely independent of the institutions that are internal to a society. That is to say, they do not merely regulate relations within a community, but also relations between the community and the outside world. For these original rights are supposed to set limits on the conduct of persons outside Indian society; they are supposed to be valid claims relative to nonassimilating Europeans.

It may be useful here to distinguish between two different kinds of moral rights to property. There may be morally defensible property rights within a given social system, taking into account the laws and other social rules governing property and the general circumstances of the community. The moral justification of claims couched in terms of such rights makes essential reference to social rules and circumstances. For the reasons just given, it is doubtful that original rights to land can be of this type. At least, the arguments invoking them ignore radical shifts in circumstances and fail to explain how ancient Indian institutions have a direct bearing on current claims to land. The original rights to land that are invoked would seem to be strictly nonconventional and inherently stable rights, which are not relative to social rules or circumstances.

I shall argue here that moral rights to property are not so stable.

4. Inheritance

I can best begin by considering the inheritability of rights. This is an appropriate point of departure because Nozick takes for granted that property rights are inheritable, and inheritance would seem to be involved in the argument concerning the current claims. After discussing inheritance, I shall go on to consider other common features of property rights.

Inheritance may appear to be a factor in the naive argument supporting the Indian claims because the current members of the tribes that are suing for recovery of lands once held by them are not the same individuals who belonged to those tribes when the land was acquired or when the contested transfers were made. The current members are descendents of those individuals. If the current members have valid claims to the land, claims deriving from their ancestors' original rights, it would seem that those rights must have been passed down through the generations by means of inheritance.

That is, interestingly, not the case. The current claims are being made, not on behalf of individual Native Americans who are supposed to have inherited ordinary property rights in land (or shares in a land-owning company) from their ancestors, but rather on behalf of entire tribes collectively. The land was originally held in common by the tribes, and that is how the land would be recovered. A tribe is a continuously existing entity, like a nation, that spans the relevant generations of human beings. Its ownership of land is like the possession by a nation of its territory. Its ownership need not be thought of as involving transfer from one individual to another by inheritance or any other means.

So inheritance would not seem to be an element in the Indian claims based on original rights. That gives us one way of distinguishing between the opposing arguments—for inheritance is almost certainly an element in the arguments on the other side. Most of the land in question has long been in private hands. It is virtually certain that inheritance has been involved in transfers from one generation to another since the contested transfers took place. It is, admittedly, conceivable that land (or shares in a land-owning company) should be transferred from one individual to another over an indefinite period without inheritance entering the picture. But it is extremely unlikely in the current cases. So, if inheritance is suspect, then some of the objections to the current claims—those based upon inheritance—are suspect too.

I wish to throw some moral doubt on claims based upon inheritance; but that is a secondary purpose. What I mainly wish to show is that inheritability cannot be an essential feature of moral rights to property. This is because the moral acceptability of inheritance is relative to circumstances. And I wish to do this, not by rejecting historical factors affecting justice, but rather by developing them beyond the point at which Nozick stopped. My argument will not be that inheritance is morally objectionable from a nonhistorical point of view (that may well be true, but will not be considered here). My argument will be that inheritance can undermine justice in transfer, and thus can be objectionable from an *historical* point of view.

Nozick's idea is that transfers are legitimate and their outcomes are consequently morally unobjectionable when they are voluntary and do not violate the Lockean proviso. The theoretical model for this idea has been provided by John Rawls, who distinguishes between "perfect" and "imperfect" procedural justice, on the one hand, and "pure" procedural justice on the other.[8] Perfect and imperfect procedural justice are virtues of transactions based upon the real or likely outcomes of the transactions. Pure procedural justice is a virtue of transactions that derives from the character of the processes themselves. Thus, the results of a lottery are morally unobjectionable when the lottery itself has certain characteristics and is consequently fair. Bargains and agreements can be judged in this way too. Their outcomes are morally unobjectionable when the bargains and agreements themselves are fair. I am not sure whether the applicable notion of fairness is captured by Nozick's requirement that transfers be voluntary and not violate the Lockean proviso; but I doubt it. At any rate, bargains and agreements are not fair unless fraud as well as force is absent and the parties are (roughly speaking) equal and informed as well as free.

Now, one trouble with inheritance is that it often promotes concentrations of wealth and power. This is *not* an egalitarian objection. My point is, rather, that concentrated wealth and power is able to impose its will on smaller and weaker parties, thus creating bargains, agreements, exchanges, and social arrangements generally that are unfair. Extremes of power undermine the legitimacy of social processes, and the outcomes cannot be assumed to be morally unobjectionable. (If they are unobjectionable that will be so by virtue of nonhistorical considerations.) In such circumstances, inheritance promotes injustice in transfer. Embedding inheritance into property rights would therefore create internal difficulties for historical principles.

Claims and Original Rights

I do not mean to suggest that inheritance is intrinsically objectionable. The effects to which I refer are clearly relative to social conditions. Inheritance will have such consequences in some circumstances and not in others. Specific rules governing inheritance may thus be justified in some circumstances. But it is implausible to suppose that inheritance is morally fundamental. Specific rules governing inheritance could not be incorporated into a basic principle of justice in transfer.

Nozick appears to assume that inheritance is an indispensable feature of private property. He discusses original acquisition in such terms, as if one could not acquire property that was not permanent and inheritable. The alternative possibility is never considered. But that is surely a mistake. The idea of a right to property does not entail that it be inheritable. That is simply one possible form that property rights can take.

And, of course, inheritance as we know it is a straightforwardly conventional arrangement, a certain type of economic institution. Its moral justification is the justification of an institution, which must take social circumstances into account. An heir can morally defend his claim to some (conventionally) inherited thing only by appealing to the rules of such an institution. His claim is morally successful, so to speak, only if the institution itself is morally defensible. Nozick does not seem to look at inheritance in this way. He seems to assume that an heir could defend his claim to some inherited thing without making any reference to laws and other social rules. He appears to assume, more generally, that the morally supportable property rights that we have correspond precisely to moral rights that do not presuppose any laws or other social rules. That is another mistake, based perhaps on a failure to distinguish between morally defensible property rights within a given social system, the justification of which is relative to social rules and circumstances, and moral rights to property that are not relative to social rules or circumstances.

We can conclude, then, that moral rights to property are not necessarily inheritable. We should accordingly observe (although this seems to have no direct bearing on the current Indian claims, for reasons already noted) that original rights to land or other property cannot be assumed to be inheritable. Furthermore, the given defenses against the current Indian claims are suspect so far as they rely upon inheritance. For our society contains concentrated wealth and power, which does impose its will on others, and inheritance contributes to those conditions.[9] Property rights affected by inheritance are thus subject to further moral scrutiny.

5. The Lockean Proviso

What I wish to suggest now is that other typical features of property rights as we know them are morally defensible only relative to circumstances and therefore cannot be assumed parts of stable rights to land or other property, and cannot be morally fundamental.

Nozick himself, surprisingly, appears to admit as much. The contents, at least, of a property right are relative to circumstances. How I may transfer or use, or deal with others' use of, a thing that I have previously acquired depends on how my behavior would affect others. Nozick develops this point in terms of the Lockean proviso, which was introduced to regulate original acquisition and now is extended to regulate property rights much more extensively.

It will be recalled that Locke's proviso was that "enough and as good" of whatever is being appropriated be left for others. Nozick does not regard this formulation as satisfactory, perhaps because it does not cover certain sorts of cases. "The crucial point," he says, "is whether appropriation of an unowned object worsens the situation of others."[10] That is the sufficient condition, Nozick thinks, to place upon legitimate appropriation. If one does not worsen the situation of others, one acquires the right to a thing one has appropriated.

But, in Nozick's view, the Lockean proviso has an "historical shadow,"[11] making arguments like the following possible. Suppose that I am landless in a world with much land that has already been appropriated but little that remains unowned. Suppose further that I cannot appropriate land for my own use and enjoyment without leaving enough and as good for others, that is, without worsening others' situation, because there is simply not that much to go around. If that were so, then it might be argued that the last persons to appropriate land worsened the situation of others, me in particular, and by similar reasoning that *all* prior acts of land appropriation are now illicit because they worsened the situation of others. For scarce resources, such reasoning might seem to show that private acquisition is simply illegitimate.[12]

Nozick wishes to meet this objection apparently because he wishes to defend private acquisition, even of scarce resources. He seems so preoccupied with that objective that he fails to draw attention to the odd, retrospective character of these lines of reasoning. The objection is supposed to show that *past* acts of appropriation are *now* to be regarded as illicit because acts of appropriation now would violate the Lockean proviso. But the problem now might result entirely from changes in circumstances, such as a decrease in the amount of usable land or an increase in the population. In such a case, the prior acts of *appropriation* could not plausibly be said to have violated the Lockean proviso.

Nozick's treatment of the "historical shadow" of the Lockean proviso, here and elsewhere, makes clear that his concern is not just with acquisition but more generally with the effects of continuing private ownership on others. It is not that *acquiring* the land violated the Lockean proviso but that *keeping* it appears to do so. Even if the original acquisition was perfectly legitimate, retention of the property might worsen others' situation in the same kind of way that the Lockean proviso is intended to prevent. The underlying idea is that property arrangements must accommodate the basic needs and interests (Nozick would probably say the rights) of others.

Nozick then seems to reason as follows. The argument against original acquisition or retention of scarce resources goes through only if we assume that property rights entail the right to exclusive use and enjoyment. But others' situation is not worsened by appropriation or retention if that assumption is rejected. In order to protect his assumption that property rights should be permanent and bequeathable, Nozick is prepared to modify the contents of such rights, or rather to make their contents variable with circumstances. This comes out most clearly in the following passage:

> Each owner's title to his holding includes the historical shadow of the Lockean proviso in appropriation. This excludes his transferring it into an agglomeration that does violate the Lockean proviso, and excludes his using it in a way, in coordination with others or independently of them, so as to violate the proviso by making the situation of others worse than their baseline situation. Once it is known that someone's ownership runs afoul of the Lockean proviso, there are stringent limits on what he may do with (what it is difficult any longer unreservedly to call) "his property." Thus a person may not appropriate the only water hole in a desert and charge what he will. Nor may he charge what he will if he possesses one, and unfortunately it chances that all the water holes in the desert dry up, except for his. This unfortunate circumstance, admittedly no fault of his, brings into operation the Lockean proviso and limits his property rights. Similarly, an owner's property right in the only island in the area does not allow him to order a castaway from a shipwreck off his

island as a trespasser, for this would violate the Lockean proviso.[13]

This passage indicates that, while Nozick places a great deal of weight upon the notion that a prior claim is a superior claim, he does not wish to ignore the valid claims of those who might suffer merely because their needs arise later. It should be noted now that similar considerations apply to inheritance, though Nozick does not make the connection. Inheritance can work so as to worsen the situation of others, and then property rights must be modified accordingly.

But my objection to inheritance was more far-reaching. Nozick wishes to retain rights and let them be passed down through inheritance by eliminating exclusive use and restricting other forms of transfer. This segregation of inheritance from other forms of transfer seems arbitrary: if the other forms of transfer can be restricted, then so can inheritance. Inheritance is not an *essential* feature of property rights. Similar reasoning shows the same thing about other normal features of property rights, such as transfer by gift or exchange and exclusive use and enjoyment: these are not *essential* features of property rights. Or, if they are essential features of property rights, then property rights are inherently unstable. One cannot have it both ways—not, at least, if one thinks that justice must accommodate the basic needs and interests of others.

6. The Instability of Property Rights

Now I wish to suggest that property rights may be even more unstable than has so far been argued. Let us expand on an example that Nozick uses. Suppose that we are occupants of an isolated island. We have arranged to use the land and all its other resources among ourselves, and we live comfortably, with some less perishable goods set aside for rainless seasons. One day, a party of castaways from a shipwreck are washed up on our shore. They are uninvited but also involuntary guests. There is no prospect for their safe removal, and they have no resources beyond their capacity to work. But they are also unaggressive. What are we to do? Nozick would agree that we may not drive them back into the sea just because they come with no rights to anything on our island. Nor may we merely allow them to stay without sharing our resources with them. It is incumbent on us to share with them—whether we like the idea or not—even if that means that we enjoy a lowered standard of living as a consequence.

Do the new islanders acquire any rights to things on the island? Nozick seems to imply that they acquire only such rights as is required to meet their minimal needs.[14] And they acquire no property rights—except, say, what they might acquire through our charity or in exchange for their labor. We retain all our original rights, though our exercise of them, or their contents, has become restricted.

But this is not entirely satisfactory, for reasons we have considered before in connection with inheritance. How are the new islanders supposed to live for the indefinite future on our island? Unless they have equal access to its resources, they may well be condemned to an economically and socially subordinate position. In some circumstances, at least, justice would not smile gladly on such a prospect—even justice within an historical theory like Nozick's. For they might then be cheated and exploited because of their poor bargaining position and lack of social power. Justice requires the establishment and maintenance of background conditions for fair bargains and agreements and for fair social arrangements generally. This may well require that we share with them more radically than Nozick might envisage.

One cannot say, a priori, what form such sharing would have to take. One possibility is this. Suppose that we original islanders held our resources in private parcels. If we all agreed to this arrangement, and it served us well, no one suffering as a consequence, then it may have been beyond reproach. But, once the newcomers are present, economic arrangements must be adjusted to accommodate the increased demand upon our resources, the complications arising from a changed population, and so forth. It is not beyond the realm of possibility that, under the new conditions, a system of private property will serve us very badly, while shared property, with carefully managed use and enjoyment, would serve us well. Such a change might be accomplished voluntarily, in which case Nozick would presumably have no objection. But it is conceivable that a private property holdout among the original islanders would properly be obliged to cooperate, against his will, and be required to place his resouces, along with everyone else's, in a common pool. This suggests that property rights themselves, and not just their exercise or contents, are relative to circumstances.

But that inference is not irresistible, and for all practical purposes it might make no difference which way we describe the situation—

as a modification of our original rights or as a redistribution of property. The question is whether the original islanders retain some latent, prior claim to their original holdings, which entitles them to recover their original property (so far as that might be possible) when conditions change again.

To explore this possibility, suppose that our island is volcanic and occasionally rises from the sea with the consequence that a greater land surface becomes available to its inhabitants. Suppose that, after the arrival of the new islanders, we eliminated private property in land and managed its exploitation collectively. Then, one day, during our current generation, the land rises due to volcanic activity, providing a new doughnut-shaped area available for settlement and exploitation. It might be the case that under these circumstances private ownership of land would once again be satisfactory and that everyone elects to adopt that system. The question then is whether we original islanders have a superior claim to property within the portion of the island that we originally occupied. If so, it looks as if there is a definite point in Nozick's suggestion that we continue ascribing the original property rights to their original holders, so long as they have not relinquished them of their own free will.

Now, I do not wish to deny that our original occupation of the center of the island might provide good and sufficient reasons for returning that part to us when redistribution is effected once again. It may be assumed that we grew up in that part of the island and regard it as our home, that we would be less happy elsewhere, which is not true of the later arrivals on the islands. Such factors are undoubtedly relevant to a *humane* as well as fair redistribution of the land. But it is not clear that they amount to *rights*.

To see this, consider a case in which such sentimental attachments are missing and in which the idea of a prior claim consequently appears pointless and absurd. Suppose (expanding on another example of Nozick's) that the sole source of fresh water on the island is a set of virtually identical water holes at some distance from our dwellings. Through custom each family had exclusive use of its own water hole. One day all of the water holes but one dry up. As a consequence, the water from this hole must be shared by all the islanders. If this condition continued indefinitely, the water hole might amount, in effect, to common property. But is that mere appearance? Suppose that after a while the other water holes are unexpectedly replenished and become good natural sources of water once again. It is reasonably concluded that each family should once again have exclusive use of its own water hole. Suppose, however, that the water holes are literally indistinguishable without some conventional signs indicating their respective family assignments. When all the holes but one dried up, the signs were not maintained, and now that all the water holes are flourishing once more, we find that they are almost indistinguishable. Since all the water holes are equidistant to each person's home, all are equally usable, and they have no distinguishing features, there is no point in any family invoking a prior claim to recover its original water hole. No one, presumably, has sentimental attachment to a water hole. If one somehow acquired such an attachment, then our humanity might require that the person's feelings be respected. But that seems a far cry from a claim of right.

Examples of this sort suggest that property rights are not stable even within a single generation. They can be extinguished without being voluntarily transferred. The very persistence of a right to property such as land, and not just its content, is relative to circumstances.

If we wish to identify a right to property such as land that is not relative to circumstances, then we must make the right itself inherently more flexible and responsive to circumstances. Locke's proviso suggests a possible model for beginning to construct such a right. Its core would be conduct that is not harmful or dangerous to others (or, as Nozick might prefer, conduct that does not encroach upon or violate others' rights). To this we add an obligation upon others not to interfere with such conduct. This yields a full right of action, composed of what jurists have called "liberty-rights," to do certain things, which are protected by "claim-rights," not to be treated by others in certain ways, the latter correlating with others' obligations not to interfere. A minimal right to land may be seen, initially at least, as a special case of such a right of action, so long as Locke's proviso is satisfied. For, if enough and as good is left for others—or, more generally, others' situation is not worsened by one's appropriation of a parcel for, say, use and occupation—then one may be said to have the liberty-right to use and occupy the land and others the obligation not to interfere with such use and occupation. As conditions change, of course, the *concrete implications* of such a right can vary. Most important, such a right would *not* imply a permanent *title* to the parcel of land.

I am uncertain whether one can have any fuller right to property, such as land, independently of laws and other social rules. Within a given social setting, one might acquire morally defensible rights to land and other property, but only so long as the institutions involved are themselves morally defensible.

7. Applications

Let us now consider a variant of our original example. Suppose that the castaways who arrive upon our shore are not friendly and cooperative but aggressive and domineering. We try to be hospitable but they do not reciprocate. They cheat us, kill many of us, and force the survivors to reside in a small area of the island, away from our homes, while they appropriate a disproportionately large part, including the most desirable sectors, for themselves.

What does justice call for in such a case? It cannot require less for us than it would have done in our original example, when it required that we share with the newcomers. We too have a right to a fair share of the island's resources. If justice requires more, then it may well include compensation from the piratical invaders for the wrongs we have suffered at their hands. We may be too weak to secure our rights; but that does not invalidate our claims.

Suppose that we are too weak and that we pass from the scene without justice being done. Once we are dead, it is impossible to compensate *us* for the wrongs *we* have suffered. Likewise, once the invaders die away, the wrongdoers cannot contribute to any rectification that justice may require.

Consider now the claims of our descendents, and for this purpose imagine two alternative (or possibly successive) historical developments. In the first continuation of our island's story we imagine that our descendants continue to be subjugated, cheated, and denied a fair share of the island's resources, and continue to reside in that portion of the island that was earlier assigned to us, their departed ancestors. They too have valid claims, analogous to those we had that were never respected. For justice requires that they receive not only a fair share of the island's resources but also, we may assume, compensation for the wrongs they themselves have suffered in being deprived during their lifetime of that fair share.

In the second continuation of our island's history, we imagine that enlightenment finally spreads across the island. The descendants of the piratical invaders come to live in harmony with our own descendants, so that no one is deprived of a fair share of the island's resources. Can we assume that any of our descendants, in this happy sequel to our unhappy history, have additional claims

Claims and Original Rights

against the others on the island, the descendants of the piratical invaders? I do not see how we can. If the generation in question has been deprived of no part of its own fair share of the island's resources, if they suffer no continuing disadvantage owing to the legacy of the former system on the island, what relevant matter might have been overlooked? The wrong that was done to us, the wrong that was never rectified, cannot now be corrected. That part of history is irrelevant to their current claims.

It is important to see now that similar considerations apply to the former case, the first and less happy continuation of our current example. Our subjugated descendants have claims to a fair share of the island's resources and to compensation for wrongs done them by a system on the island that deprives them of that fair share. That system and thus their deprivation and their claims are rooted, *causally and historically,* in the wrongs that we, their ancestors, suffered at the hands of the invaders. But this is not to say that their claims are *normatively* derived from ours, that they inherited our original rights, or that their claims for compensation are claims for correction of wrongs that were done to us, as distinct from wrongs that have been done to them.

My metaphor and its moral may by now by obvious. Let the island be America and the original islanders Native Americans, to whom all the land may be said initially to belong. If those who had landed on these shores had been impoverished outcasts from Europe, unaggressive and cooperative, with no resources save their labor power and no place else to go, it would have been incumbent on their hosts not only to share their resources with them but also to reshape their social arrangements to accommodate the new members of their universe. For the purpose of this general point, it makes no difference how the original occupants of the land had used it, how they had divided it up, how they conceived of property rights, whether they held it individually or collectively, and so on.

That is not, of course, the way things happened, and so history developed much more like the unhappy history in the example of this section and its first, unhappy continuation. Native Americans by and large tried to be hospitable to their uninvited and unexpected guests, but the guests did not generally reciprocate. To be sure, some of the guests were impoverished, some were outcasts, some were unable to leave once they had arrived, and some, perhaps, would have been prepared to form an integrated society or to settle contentedly on limited tracts set aside for them by their hosts. But too many acted rather as invaders, slavers, and conquerors, who proceeded by force and by fraud to appropriate the land and to eliminate or drive out the people living here.

I do not wish to deny any of this or to minimize the wrongs that were done. I most especially do not mean to deny or to minimize the valid claims of Native Americans living today. My point is that their claims are unlikely to derive normatively from their ancestors' original rights. The original rights of Native Americans were no more sacrosanct than anyone else's. From the fact that they had morally defensible claims two hundred or four hundred years ago it cannot be inferred that those claims persist. But the initial argument assumes just that; it assumes that circumstances had no effect on those rights.

8. The New Indian Claims Reconsidered

Native Americans have systematically been discriminated against in our society. They have a valid claim to a fair share of its resources as well as to social and economic opportunities. They also have a valid claim to compensation for unjust deprivation that the *current* generation has suffered from past injustices. But it is highly doubtful that they have any special claims based upon their distant ancestors' original occupation of the land. For circumstances have significantly changed. After the European dispossession of the Indians, waves of impoverished immigrants arrived on these shores in little better shape than castaways from a shipwreck. Most of the occupants of America today have had little, if anything, to do with dispossession of Native Americans. This does *not* mean that they have no complicity in a pattern of unjust deprivation of *current* Native Americans, for which compensation is required. But that is another matter entirely, and a much more complex matter too.

I suggest, therefore, that the current Indian land claims be viewed, not as invoking an original right to the land, a right that has been passed down to current Native Americans and that now needs to be enforced, but rather as an occasion for rectifying current inequities (some of which, of course, may trace back causally to the dispossession of Native Americans and the aftermath).

Now that I have made my major points, I must try to note some complications.

One set of complications turns upon the fact that the current Indian claims are being made on behalf of tribes rather than private persons. Tribes originally held the land, and a tribe, like a nation, can hold a right over generations. This has some bearing on the current claims. It does not affect my main point, which was not just that inheritance is suspect but more generally that moral rights to land are inherently unstable or variable with circumstances. We cannot assume that rights held generations ago, even if they were held by tribes, have persisted to this day. But this aspect of the cases is relevant to claims invoking the notion of *compensation* for wrongs done. Some past wrongs can no longer be corrected, but some can. It may be impossible to compensate the ancestors of current Native Americans for wrongs that they suffered long ago, but it may be possible to compensate tribes for past wrongs done them. If the *tribes* were wronged, those wrongs may well have involved violations of original rights, even if those rights did not survive the changing circumstances and did not persist into the current generation. If tribes can indeed be wronged, and such wrongs are subject to compensation, then the current claims can be supported by related considerations: this sort of argument transcends the valid claims of current Native Americans for compensation in view of wrongs done to them as individual human beings. I do not wish to deny such possibilities here. They require careful and systematic examination.

The tribal character of the current claims is relevant in other respects too, which raise complex and difficult issues. I have noted, for example, that one aim of the current suits appears to be not mere ownership of the land but control over its development. There is the prospect of conflict between the interests of Native Americans in preserving undeveloped land and others who wish to develop it, build on it, live and work on it. This is not like the conflict between conservationists and developers. For the Native Americans involved are seeking to rebuild a way of life that turns upon certain ways of dealing with the land, and an issue here is the right to inhibit development (which may involve sorely needed jobs, and not just profits) based on the right to secure a culture.

That brings us to a central argument favoring the current claims. And it is important to support the current claims, since radical steps have been threatened to undermine them, including retrospective legislation.

One thing that makes the claims under the Nonintercourse Act so important is that they appear to be legally well-founded. Unlike past calls for reparations for black Americans, in view of the legacy of slavery and discrimination, the current claims under the Nonintercourse Act turn upon existing law. Radical new legislation or executive action is not needed to sustain them.

But it may reasonably be urged that these cases test the sincerity of our historical commitments. The federal government long ago assumed "fiduciary" responsibility for securing Indian lands and protecting Native American interests. It has however adhered to the law chiefly when that worked to the Indians' disadvantage. Now, when at last Native Americans have marshalled the legal resources to secure some lost benefits, the threat is that the law will not be followed. Even handed fairness would seem to require that the federal government live up to its past commitments and not retroactively change the rules just when it would undermine Indian interests to do so.

Beyond this, it may dutifully be observed that justice would not be done by simply returning all the lands in question to the tribes now claiming them. This would impose enormous burdens on small home owners and small businesses without sufficient reason. It seems, in any case, that undeveloped land is the primary target of the tribes, the other land being unavoidably blanketed in under the legal claims. The federal government should work to negotiate a satisfactory settlement. This is what the tribes have been seeking for some time.

If a settlement results in burdens on individuals or states, it would seem reasonable for the federal government to assume responsibility for compensation too. For the federal government not only has greater resources than the several states, some of which are hardly affluent; it was also negligent, under its own law, in failing to oversee the transfers of land and in thus failing to discharge its legal responsibilities as trustee. The responsibility for righting such wrongs and for paying what it costs to do so should not be allowed to fall on the nearest and perhaps most vulnerable parties, but should be shared by society at large.

These costs will be of two types. First, cash payments are being sought, in addition to the lands, for back rents and damages. (These claims, incidentally, appear immune to attack by retroactive legislation.) Second, cash settlements will undoubtedly be made in lieu of some land that might otherwise be recovered. That seems a sensible solution for much developed land within the tracts in question, and a solution that the Indian tribes are quite willing to achieve. Such costs should be borne by the federal rather than by individual state governments.

Claims under the Indian Nonintercourse Act are different from

Claims and Original Rights 271

some other claims that Native Americans may make for recovery of land, since the former turn upon plainly illegal transactions while the latter may involve marginally legal but unjustifiable acts by the federal government. The rhetoric that I have anatomized in this paper does not distinguish between these cases. I do not mean to suggest that the claims are unsupportable because the rhetoric is unilluminating. The point is rather that the claims are stronger then the rhetoric may suggest. My purpose here has been to challenge certain ways of thinking about moral rights to property—ways that are typically invoked to secure unjust holdings. Property rights are not sacrosanct. They must bend to the needs and interests of human beings.[15]

NOTES

1. 25 U.S.C.A. §177.
2. On the Maine cases in particular see Robert McLaughlin, "Giving it back to the Indians," *Atlantic Monthly* (February 1977): 70–85; more generally see *Akwesasne Notes* 9 (early Spring 1977): 18–21.
3. Joint Tribal Council of the Passamoquoddy Tribe v. Rogers C. B. Morton, 528 F. 2d 370 (1975).
4. Narragansett Tribe of Indians v. Southern Rhode Island Development Corporation, 418 F. Supp. 798 (1976).
5. See his "Distributive Justice," *Philosophy and Public Affairs* 3 (Fall 1973): 45–126, especially Section I, 46–78. This essay was later published as Chapter 7 of Nozick's *Anarchy, State, and Utopia* (New York: Basic Books, 1974).
6. John Locke, *The Second Treatise on Government*, Chapter V ("Of Property"). (Citations in the text are to numbered sections of the work.)
7. On Locke's theory, see Nozick, "Distributive Justice," 70ff.
8. See *A Theory of Justice* (Cambridge, Mass.: Harvard University Press, 1971), 85–87.
9. For example, by helping to fix vast wealth within a very limited number of families, and thus helping to establish permanent power elites.
10. "Distributive Justice," 72.
11. "Distributive Justice," 76.
12. "Distributive Justice," 72.
13. "Distributive Justice," 76.
14. "Distributive Justice," 75–77.
15. Earlier versions of this paper were read at The Catholic University of America, Hamilton College, and the University of Vermont. I would like to thank those who commented on those occasions for their helpful criticisms and suggestions. I would also like to thank John

Fischer, Stephen Massey, Robert Summers, and William Wilcox for comments, as well as the readers for *Social Theory and Practice,* and Matthew Lyons for research on the historical background of the cases under discussion here.

David Lyons
Department of Philosophy
Cornell University

[17]

Superseding Historic Injustice*

Jeremy Waldron

I. INJUSTICE AND HISTORY

The history of white settlers' dealings with the aboriginal peoples of Australia, New Zealand, and North America is largely a history of injustice. People, or whole peoples, were attacked, defrauded, and expropriated; their lands were stolen and their lives were ruined. What are we to do about these injustices? We know what we should think about them: they are to be studied and condemned, remembered and lamented. But morality is a practical matter, and judgments of 'just' and 'unjust' like all moral judgments have implications for action. To say that a future act open to us now would be unjust is to commit ourselves to avoiding it. But what of past injustice? What is the practical importance now of a judgment that injustice occurred in the past?

In the first instance the question is one of metaethics. Moral judgments are prescriptive in their illocutionary force; they purport to guide choices.[1] But since the only choices we can guide are choices in front of us, judgments about the past must look beyond the particular events that are their ostensible subject matter. The best explanation

---

* An earlier version of this article was presented in 1990 at the annual conference of the New Zealand division of the Australasian Association of Philosophy. I am grateful to Graham Oddie for his invitation to attend that conference and to the Waitangi Foundation for their support. A later version was presented as a public lecture at Boalt Hall, University of California. I am particularly grateful to Robert Cooter, Meir Dan-Cohen, Einer Elhauge, Sanford Kadish, David Lewis, Richard Mulgan, Carol Sanger, Joseph Sax, Andrew Sharp, Henry Shue, and the editors and referees of this journal for their criticisms and suggestions.

1. Opinions differ in metaethics about whether this illocutionary function provides a complete explanation of the distinctively moral meaning of the words 'right,' 'wrong,' 'unjust,' etc. For the view that it does, see R. M. Hare, *The Language of Morals* (Oxford: Clarendon, 1952). But most moral philosophers concede that even if it is not the whole story, still it is an essential part of the explanation of the meaning of such words that they have this prescriptive function. The few philosophers who deny this do so purely because of the embarrassment it poses for their realist claims that moral judgments are nothing but judgments about matters of fact. For examples, see Michael Moore, "Moral 'Reality'" (*Wisconsin Law Review* [1982], pp. 1061–1156); and David Brink, *Moral Realism and the Foundations of Ethics* (Cambridge: Cambridge University Press, 1989), chap. 3.

of this relies on universalizability. When I make a moral judgment about an event E, I do so not in terms of the irreducible particularity of E but on the basis of some feature of E that other events might share. In saying, for example, "E was unjust," I am saying, "There is something about E and the circumstances in which it is performed, such that any act of that kind performed in such circumstances would be unjust." I am not so much prescribing the avoidance of E itself (a prescription that makes no sense if E is in the past), but prescribing the avoidance of E-type events. If E involved breaking a promise, or taking advantage of someone's credulity, then our condemnation of it commits us to a similar condemnation of breaches of faith or exploitation in the present. Though E occurred 150 years ago, to condemn it is to express a determination now that in the choices we face, we will avoid actions of this kind.[2]

The point of doing this is not that we learn new and better standards for our lives from the judgments we make about the past. Unless we had those standards already, we would not make those judgments. But our moral understanding of the past is often a way of bringing to imaginative life the full implications of principles to which we are already in theory committed. To be disposed to act morally, it is not enough to be equipped with a list of appropriate principles. One also needs a sense of the type of situation in which these things may suddenly be at stake, the temptations that might lead one to betray them, and the circumstances and entanglements that make otherwise virtuous people start acting viciously. That is what history provides: a lesson about what it is like for people just like us—human, all too human—to face real moral danger.

Beyond that, there is an importance to the historical recollection of injustice that has to do with identity and contingency. It is a well-known characteristic of great injustice that those who suffer it go to their deaths with the conviction that these things must not be forgotten. It is easy to misread that as vain desire for vindication, a futile threat of infamy upon the perpetrators of an atrocity. But perhaps the determination to remember is bound up with the desire to sustain a specific character as a person or community against a background of infinite possibility. That *this* happened rather that *that*—that people were massacred (though they need not have been), that lands were taken (though they might have been bought fairly), that promises were broken (though they might have been kept)—the historic record has a fragility that consists, for large part, in the sheer contingency of what happened in the past. What happened might have been otherwise,

---

2. For this understanding of moral judgments made about the past, and for the assumed interaction between prescriptivity and universalizability, see R. M. Hare, *Freedom and Reason* (Oxford: Clarendon, 1963).

and, just because of that, it is not something one can reason back to if what actually took place has been forgotten or concealed.[3]

Each person establishes a sense of herself in terms of her ability to identify the subject or agency of her present thinking with that of certain acts and events that took place in the past, and in terms of her ability to hold fast to a distinction between memory so understood and wishes, fantasies, or various other ideas of things that might have happened but did not.[4] But remembrance in this sense is equally important to communities—families, tribes, nations, parties—that is, to human entities that exist often for much longer than individual men and women. To neglect the historical record is to do violence to this identity and thus to the community that it sustains. And since communities help generate a deeper sense of identity for the individuals they comprise, neglecting or expunging the historical record is a way of undermining and insulting individuals as well.

When we are told to let bygones be bygones, we need to bear in mind also that the forgetfulness being urged on us is seldom the blank slate of historical oblivion. Thinking quickly fills up the vacuum with plausible tales of self-satisfaction, on the one side, and self-deprecation on the other. Those who as a matter of fact benefited from their ancestors' injustice will persuade themselves readily enough that their good fortune is due to the virtue of their race, while the descendants of their victims may too easily accept the story that they and their kind were always good for nothing. In the face of all this, only the deliberate enterprise of recollection (the enterprise we call "history"), coupled with the most determined sense that there is a difference between what happened and what we would like to think happened, can sustain the moral and cultural reality of self and community.

The topic of this article is reparation. But before I embark on my main discussion, I want to mention the role that the payment of money (or the return of lands or artifacts) may play in the embodiment of communal remembrance. Quite apart from any attempt genuinely to compensate victims or offset their losses, reparations may symbolize a society's undertaking not to forget or deny that a particular injustice took place, and to respect and help sustain a dignified sense of identity-in-memory for the people affected. A prominent recent example of this is the payment of token sums of compensation by the American government to the survivors of Japanese-American families uprooted, interned, and concentrated in 1942. The point of these payments was not to make up for the loss of home, business, opportunity, and standing

---

3. For a moving discussion, see Hannah Arendt, "Truth and Politics," in her collection *Between Past and Future: Six Exercises in Political Thought* (New York: Viking, 1968).

4. John Locke, *An Essay concerning Human Understanding*, bk. 2, chap. 27, secs. 9–10, ed. John Yolton (London: Everyman's Library, 1965), vol. 1, pp. 280 ff.; see also Stuart Hampshire, *Thought and Action* (London: Chatto & Windus, 1970).

in the community which these people suffered at the hands of their fellow citizens, nor was it to make up for the discomfort and degradation of their internment. If that were the aim, much more would be necessary. The point was to mark—with something that counts in the United States—a clear public recognition that this injustice did happen, that it was the American people and their government that inflicted it, and that these people were among its victims. The payments give an earnest of good faith and sincerity to that acknowledgment. Like the gift I buy for someone I have stood up, the payment is a method of putting oneself out, or going out of one's way, to apologize. It is no objection to this that the payments are purely symbolic. Since identity is bound up with symbolism, a symbolic gesture may be as important to people as any material compensation.

II. THE COUNTERFACTUAL APPROACH TO REPARATION

I turn now to the view that a judgment about past injustice generates a demand for full and not merely symbolic reparation—a demand not just for remembrance but for substantial transfers of land, wealth, and resources in an effort actually to rectify past wrongs. I want to examine the difficulties that these demands give rise to, particularly when they conflict with other claims that may be made in the name of justice on the land, wealth, and resources in question.

It may seem as though the demand is hopeless from the start. What is it to correct an injustice? How can we reverse the past? If we are talking about injustice that took place several generations ago, surely there is nothing we can do now to heal the lives of the actual victims, to make them less miserable or to reduce their suffering. The only experiences we can affect are those of people living now and those who will live in the future.

But though these are obvious truths, we may miss something if we repeat them too often. To stand on the premise that the past cannot be changed is to ignore the fact that people and communities live whole lives, not just series of momentary events, and that an injustice may blight, not just hurt, such a life. Individuals make plans and they see themselves as living partly for the sake of their posterity; they build not only for themselves but for future generations. Whole communities may subsist for periods much longer than individual lifetimes. How they fare at a given stage and what they can offer in the way of culture, aspiration, and morale may depend very much on the present effect of events that took place several generations ealier. Thus, part of the moral significance of a past event has to do with the difference it makes to the present.

But then there is a sense in which we can affect the moral significance of past action. Even if we cannot alter the action itself we may be able to interfere with the normal course of its consequences. The present surely looks different now from the way the present would look if a given injustice of the past had not occurred. Why not therefore change the present so that it looks more like the present that would have obtained in the absence of the injustice? Why not make it now as though the injustice had not happened, for all that its occurrence in the past is immutable and undeniable?

This is the approach taken by Robert Nozick in his account of the role played by a principle of rectification in a theory of historic entitlement:

> This principle uses historical information about previous situations and injustices done in them (as defined by the first two principles of justice [namely, justice in acquisition and justice in transfer] and rights against interference), and information about the actual course of events that flowed from these injustices, until the present, and it yields a description (or descriptions) of holdings in the society. The principle of rectification presumably will make use of its best estimate of subjunctive information about what would have occurred (or a probability distribution over what might have occurred, using the expected value) if the injustice had not taken place. If the actual description of holdings turns out to be one of the descriptions yielded by the principle, then one of the descriptions yielded must be realized.[5]

The trouble with this approach is the difficulty we have in saying what would have happened if some event (which did occur) had not taken place. To a certain extent we can appeal to causal laws or, more crudely, the normal course of events. We take a description of the actual world, with its history and natural laws intact, up until the problematic event of injustice (which we shall call event 'E'). In the actual course of events, what followed E (events F, G, and H) is simply what results from applying natural laws to E as an initial condition. For example, if E was your seizure of the only water hole in the desert just as I was about to slake my thirst, then F—the event that follows E—would be what happens normally when one person is deprived of water and another is not: you live and I die. So, in our counterfactual reasoning, we replace E with its closest just counterpart, $E+$ (say, we share the water hole), and we apply the laws of nature to that to see what would have happened next. Presumably what would have happened next is that we both slake our thirst and both survive. The same laws of nature that yield F given E, yield a different sequel $F+$ given

---

5. Robert Nozick, *Anarchy, State, and Utopia* (Oxford: Blackwell, 1974), pp. 152–53. To this passage, Nozick appends the following footnote: "If the principle of recodification of violations of the first two principles yields more than one description of holdings, then some choice must be made as to which of these is to be realized. Perhaps the sort of considerations about distributive justice and equality that I argue against play a legitmate role in this subsidary choice" (p. 153n.).

the just alternative $E+$ and further sequels $G+$ and $H+$ on the basis of that.[6] The task of rectification then is to take some present event or situation over which we do have control (e.g., H, a distribution of resources obtaining now) and alter it so that it conforms as closely as possible to its counterpart $H+$—the situation that would obtain now if $E+$ rather than E had occurred.

But what if some of the events in the sequel to $E+$ are exercises of human choice rather than the inexorable working out of natural laws? Is it possible to say counterfactually how choices subsequent to $E+$ would have been made, so that we can determine what state of affairs ($H+$) would obtain now in a society of autonomous choosers, but for the problematic injustice? Suppose that if E had not occurred, you would have made me a fair offer to form a partnership to cultivate land near the oasis? How are we to know whether I would have accepted the offer? Had I accepted it, I might have acquired wealth that I would not otherwise have had and with it the opportunity to engage in other transactions. How are we to know which transactions I would have chosen to engage in? The problem quickly becomes intractable particularly where the counterfactual sequence $\{E+, F+, G+, H+\}$ is imagined to extend over several generations, and where the range of choices available at a given stage depends on the choices that would have been taken at some earlier stage.

This is not a mere academic difficulty. Suppose (counterfactually) that a certain piece of land had not been wrongfully appropriated from some Maori group in New Zealand in 1865. Then we must ask ourselves, What would the tribal owners of that land have done with it, if wrongful appropriation had not taken place? To ask this question is to ask how people would have exercised their freedom if they had had a real choice. Would they have hung on to the land and passed it on to future generations of the tribe? Or would they have sold it— but this time for a fair price—to the first honest settler who came along?[7] And, if the latter, what would he have done with it? Sold it again? Passed it on to his children? Lost it in a poker game?

---

6. We could of course imagine a world in which not only $E+$ occurs instead of E but also in which the laws of nature are different (e.g., living beings can survive and flourish without water). But those worlds are of limited practical interest. The reason why we choose (in David Lewis's terminology) the closest possible world in which $E+$ occurs, and why 'closest' includes 'same laws of nature' is that that is the world which ought to have been in the contemplation of the agent who faced the choice between E and $E+$. See David Lewis, *Counterfactuals* (Cambridge, Mass.: Harvard University Press, 1973).

7. Often the injustice complained of is that some renegade member of the tribe disposed of tribal land as though it were his own private property. So if a piece of land is indeed tribally owned and its alienation prohibited by tribal custom, is there any point in asking how it would have been disposed of if the injustice of this individual's alienation of it had not occurred? Surely we ought to assume that, if the land had not

10   *Ethics   October 1992*

Part of our difficulty in answering these questions is our uncertainty about what we are doing when we try to make guesses about the way in which free will would have been exercised. The status of counterfactual reasoning about the exercise of human freedom is unclear. I do not mean that the exercise of human choice is necessarily unpredictable. We make predictions all the time about how people will exercise their freedom. But it is not clear why our best prediction on such a matter should have moral authority in the sort of speculations we are considering.

Suppose that I am attempting to predict how my aunt will dispose of her estate. My best guess, based on all the evidence, is that having no dependents she will leave it to Amnesty International, well known as her one cherished cause. In fact, my aunt surprises everyone by leaving everything to an obscure home for stray dogs that she has only just heard of. My prediction is confounded. But the important point is the following. Even though my prediction was reasonable, even though it was based on the best available evidence, it is her whimsical decision that carries the day. My guess has no normative authority whatever with regard to the disposition of her estate. All that matters is what she eventually chooses.

If this is true of decision making in the real world, then I think it plays havoc with the idea that, normatively, the appropriate thing to do in the rectification of injustice is to make rational and informed guesses about how people would have exercised their freedom in a hypothetical world. For if such guesses carry no moral weight in the real world, why should any moral weight be associated with their use in counterfactual speculation?

This is not an epistemic difficulty. It is not that there is some fact of the matter (what this person would have chosen to do with her goods if things had been different) and our difficulty lies in discovering

---

been wrongfully disposed of, it would have remained the property of the tribe. So, it might be thought, there should be no difficulty in showing that the counterfactual approach requires its present restoration to the tribe. Unfortunately, things are more complicated than that. There are two other things that might have happened if the injustice had not taken place. The members of the tribe might have decided, in the exercise of their powers as communal owners, to sell some of the land. Or the members of the tribe might have decided, in an exercise of sovereignty over their own laws and customs, to abrogate the system of communal property. Both possibilities need to be taken into account in any realistic reconstruction of what would have happened if the injustice had not taken place. The second is particularly important. All societies change their customs and laws, including their property laws, from time to time, and there is every reason to imagine such change as a probable and reasonable response to new circumstances and conditions on the part of such flexible and resourceful polities as Maori tribes, for example. If we are honestly inquiring into what would have happened in a just world, we have to take at least the possibility of such adaptive exercises of sovereignty into account.

what that is. The thing about freedom is that there is no fact of the matter anywhere until the choice has been made. It is the act of choosing that has authority, not the existence as such of the chosen option.

Of course there are situations in which we do think it acceptable to substitute our best guess about what a person would have done for that person's actual choice. If my aunt's investments have been entrusted to me, and there is a crisis in the stock market while she is abroad and incommunicado, I must do what I figure she would have done: hold the stocks in the companies to which she has a sentimental attachment and sell the rest. Maybe she would have acted whimsically and done the opposite, but as her trustee this is morally the best I can do. By doing this I adopt in effect a rational choice approach to the decision: given what I know about her preferences, I act in a way that will maximize her utility. She might have acted perversely or she might not. But given that her hypothetical consent is my only warrant to act in this matter at all, I can do nothing except choose rationally to give content to the hypothesis.

Now we are unlikely to be able to reach conclusions this determinate in applying the rational choice approach to aboriginal land claims. We will probably not be in a position to say that selling to Q rather than to R would have been the rational thing for P to do if he had not been forcibly dispossessed, and that selling to S rather than T would have been the rational thing for Q to do if P had sold the land to him rather than to R, and so on down a reconstructed chain of entitlement. But broader conclusions may be available. Suppose P enjoyed a certain level of utility derived from his holdings, U_E, just before the events complained of took place. Then any rational choice reconstruction about what would have happened but for the injustice will maintain P's utility at that level at least. No rational chooser enters a voluntary transaction to make himself worse off. So any account of what would have happened had all transactions been voluntary will require P to emerge at least as well off as he was at the beginning of the story. If in actual reality he is worse off, the counterfactual approach will require that he be restored to a level at or above U_E. By making our rational choice assumptions airy enough, we can reach similar conclusions about the well-being of P's descendants and the well-being of the person who dispossessed P and of his descendants as well. And these conclusions are likely to match our intuitions: if the injustice had not taken place, the descendants of those who suffered it would be better off than they are and descendants of those who perpetrated it would be somewhat worse off than they are. So a transfer from the latter to the former seems justified.

However, several difficulties remain. One concerns what might be called the contagion of injustice. Suppose I possess a piece of land which I inherited from my father who bought it from his sister-in-law who bought it from a settler who obtained it in the mid-nineteenth century from a fraudulent transaction with a member of the Maori tribe. The counterfactual approach to reparation suggests that some transfer from me to the surviving members of the tribe may be required in order to bring the present state of affairs closer to the state of affairs that would have obtained if the fraud had not been perpetrated. Unfortunately we cannot leave the matter there. My neighbor may be in possession of a similar piece of land whose pedigree, considered in itself, is impeccable: there is no fraud, no coercion, no expropriation in the history of her holding. Still the price my neighbor (and her predecessors in title) paid for her land is likely to have been affected by the low price that was paid for my land (on account of the original fraud). Thus, rectification of the injustice will involve an adjustment of her holding as well. We cannot assume that rectificatory transfers will be confined to those who have had dealings with tainted holdings. All present holdings are called in question by this business of winding the film back to the injustice, changing that frame (from E to $E+$), and then winding the film forward to see what results. If one person behaves unjustly, particularly in the context of a market, the injustice will have an effect not only on her immediate victim, but—via the price mechanism—on all those who trade in the market in question. Some will gain and some will lose as a result of the injustice, and any attempt at rectification—any attempt to implement the state of affairs that would have obtained but for the injustice—will involve interfering with those holdings as well.

Worse still, the events of justice and injustice may make a considerable difference in who exists at a later time. We cannot simply hold the dramatis personae constant in our speculations. Children may be conceived and born, and leave descendants, who would not have existed if the injustice had not occurred. Short of putting them to death for their repugnancy to our counterfactuals, the present approach offers no guidance at all as to how their claims are to be dealt with.

A more general difficulty has to do with our application of rational choice in counterfactual reconstruction. People can and often do act freely to their own disadvantage, and usually when they do, they are held to the result. A man who actually loses his land in a reckless though voluntary wager and who accepts the justice of the outcome may be entitled to wonder why, in the attention we pay to aboriginal reparations, we insulate people from the possibility of similar vicissitudes. He may say, "If we are going to reconstruct a history of rational choice, let us do so for all holdings, giving everyone what they would have had if they had never acted voluntarily to their own disadvantage. Maybe that will lead to a more just world. But if we are not prepared to do that, if we insist that it is alright, from the point of view of justice, to leave a person like me stuck with the results of his actual choices, it may be more consistent to admit that we simply can't say what (by the same token) justice now requires in the case of those whose ancestors were wrongfully dispossessed."

The dilemma is a difficult one. On the one hand, there is nothing normatively conclusive about rational choice predictions. Why should the exaction of specific reparation in the real world be oriented to what the idealized agents of rational choice would have secured for themselves in a hypothetical world? On the other hand, hypothetical rational choice is essential to our normative thinking about justice. Modern contractarian theories consist almost entirely of asking what the people of a society would have agreed to in the way of institutions governing the distribution of resources, had they been consulted.[8] But it is characteristic of such approaches that they are holistic, systemic, and structural rather than local and specific in their conclusions and recommendations. We deploy the counterfactuals of modern contractarianism to evaluate the entire basic structure of a society, not to evaluate some particular distribution among a subset of its members.[9]

The issue is particularly acute because the reparations that these counterfactuals support are likely to have a wide effect on holdings across the board. The case is quite different from the simple situation of my aunt's investments, where I ask only what she would have done with her capital and do not attempt to redistribute a whole array of different people's holdings. Reparation of historic injustice really is redistributive: it moves resources from one person to another. It seems unfair to do this on a basis that reconstructs a profile of holdings by attributing rational choice motivations to only some, and not all, of the parties who are affected.

Ultimately, what is raised here is the question of whether it is possible to rectify particular injustices without undertaking a comprehensive redistribution that addresses all claims of justice that may be made. The counterfactual approach aims to bring the present state of affairs as close as possible to the state of affairs that would have obtained if some specifically identified injustice had not occurred. But why stop there? Why be content merely to bring about the state of affairs that would have ensued if this injustice had not occurred? Why not try to make things even better than they would have been if that particular unjust transaction, or any unjust transaction, had not taken

---

8. See John Rawls, *A Theory of Justice* (Oxford: Oxford University Press, 1971); and T. M. Scanlon, "Contractualism and Utilitarianism" in *Utilitarianism and Beyond,* ed. Amartya Sen and Bernard Williams (Cambridge: Cambridge University Press, 1986).

9. See Rawls, p. 7. For the distinction between holistic and piecemeal uses of contractarian models, see Kim Scheppele and Jeremy Waldron, "Contractarian Methods in Political and Legal Evaluation," *Yale Journal of Law and Humanities* 3 (1991): 206–10.

place? Are we so sure that a smooth transition, untainted by particular injustice, from some early nineteenth-century status quo ante would leave us now where we actually want to be? Quite apart from particular frauds and expropriations, things were not marvelous in the nineteenth century. Many people lacked access to any significant resources, and many people had much more than what one might regard as a fair share. Why take all that as the baseline for our present reconstruction?

III. THE PERPETUATION AND REMISSION OF INJUSTICE

So far we have focused on the effects of isolated acts of injustice like event E, events that took place firmly in the past. But we are seldom so fortunate as to confront injustice in discrete doses. The world we know is characterized by patterns of injustice, by standing arrangements—rules, laws, regimes, and other institutions—that operate unjustly day after day. Though the establishment of such an arrangement was an unjust event when it took place in the past, its injustice then consisted primarily in the injustice it promised for the future. To judge that establishment unjust is to commit oneself to putting a stop to the ongoing situation; it is a commitment to prevent the perpetuation of the injustice that the law or the institution embodies; it is to commit oneself to its remission.

Suppose someone stole my car yesterday. That is an unjust act that took place at a certain place and at a certain time: at 9:30 A.M. on September 5, my car was stolen from the parking lot. Clearly anyone committed to the prevention of injustice should have tried to stop the theft taking place. But once the car has been driven nefariously out of the parking lot, the matter does not end there. For now there is a continuing injustice: I lack possession of an automobile to which I am entitled, and the thief possesses an automobile to which she is not entitled. Taking the car away from the thief and returning it to me, the rightful owner, is not a way of compensating me for an injustice that took place in the past; it is a way of remitting an injustice that is ongoing into the present. Phrases like 'Let bygones be bygones' are inappropriate here. The loss of my car is not a bygone: it is a continuing state of affairs.

The implications of this example are clear for the historic cases we are considering. Instead of regarding the expropriation of aboriginal lands as an isolated act of injustice that took place at a certain time now relegated firmly to the past, we may think of it as a persisting injustice. The injustice persists, and it is perpetuated by the legal system as long as the land that was expropriated is not returned to those from whom it was taken. On this model, the rectification of injustice is a much simpler matter than the approach we discussed in the previous section. We do not have to engage in any counterfactual speculation. We simply give the property back to the person or group from whom it was taken and thus put an end to what would otherwise be its continued expropriation.

Difficulties arise of course if the original owner has died, for then there is no one to whom the property can be restored. We could give it to her heirs and successors, but in doing so we are already setting off down the counterfactual road, reckoning that this is what the proprietor's wish would have been had she had control of her property. Fortunately, that difficulty is obviated in the case of many aboriginal claims: usually the property is owned by a tribe, a nation, or a community—some entity that endures over time in spite of mortality of its individual members. It is this enduring entity that has been dispossessed, and the same entity is on hand now more than a hundred years later to claim its heritage.

What, if any, are the difficulties with this approach? It does not involve any of the problems of counterfactual reasoning that we identified earlier, but does it face any other problems? As I see it, the main difficulty is the following. Are we sure that the entitlement that was originally violated all those years ago is an entitlement that survives into the present? The approach we are considering depends on the claim that the right that was violated when white settlers first seized the land can be identified as a right that is still being violated today by settlers' successors in title. Their possession of the land today is said to be as wrongful vis-à-vis the present tribal owners as the original expropriation. Can this view be justified?

It is widely believed that some rights are capable of "fading" in their moral importance by virtue of the passage of time and by the sheer persistence of what was originally a wrongful infringement. In the law of property, we recognize doctrines of prescription and adverse possession. In criminal procedure and in torts, we think it important to have statutes of limitations. The familiarity of these doctrines no doubt contributes to the widespread belief that, after several generations have passed, certain wrongs are simply not worth correcting. Think of the earlier example of the theft of my automobile. Certainly, the car should be returned if the thief is discovered within weeks or months of the incident. But what if she is never caught? What if the stolen car remains in her family for decades and is eventually passed down as an heirloom to her children and grandchildren? Are we so sure that when the circumstances of its acquisition eventually come to light, it should be returned without further ado to me or my estate?

The view that a violated entitlement can "fade" with time may seem unfair. The injustice complained of is precisely that the rightful owner has been dispossessed. It seems harsh if the fact of her dispossession is used as a way of weakening her claim. It may also seem to involve some moral hazard by providing an incentive for wrongdoers to cling to their ill-gotten gains, in the hope that the entitlement they violated will fade away because of their adverse possession.

Still, the view that certain rights are prescriptable has a number of things to be said in its favor. Some are simply pragmatic. Statutes of limitations are inspired as much by procedural difficulties about evidence and memory, as by any doctrine about rights. It is hard to establish what happened if we are enquiring into the events that occurred decades or generations ago. There are nonprocedural pragmatic arguments also. For better or worse, people build up structures of expectation around the resources that are actually under their control. If a person controls a resource over a long enough period, then she and others may organize their lives and their economic activity around the premise that that resource is "hers," without much regard to the distant provenance of her entitlement. Upsetting these expectations in the name of restitutive justice is bound to be costly and disruptive.[10]

There may be reasons of principle as well. One set of reasons has to do with changes in background social and economic circumstances. If the requirements of justice are sensitive to circumstances such as the size of the population or the incidence of scarcity, then there is no guarantee that those requirements (and the rights that they constitute) will remain constant in relation to a given resource or piece of land as the decades and generations go by. I shall deal with this in detail in the next section of this article.

The other reason entitlements may fade has to do with the basis of the rights themselves. Theories of historic entitlement, like the theory of John Locke or the theory sketched more recently by Robert Nozick, focus on the establishment of an intimate relation between a person and a resource as the basis of property rights.[11] A person works with an object, shaping and modifying it, so that it becomes imbued with part of her personality; it comes to contain a part of herself. But if the right is taken out of her hands for a long period, the intimacy of that relation may evaporate.

Whether this happens depends partly on what we take to be the morally important relation between the person and the thing. In John Locke's theory, the relation is described as mixing one's labor.[12] A

---

10. Hence the insistence of Jeremy Bentham on absolute security of expectations as the proper basis of a utilitarian theory of property. See the extract from Jeremy Bentham, *Principles of the Civil Code*, in *Property: Mainstream and Critical Positions*, ed. C. B. MacPherson (Oxford: Blackwell, 1978), pp. 42–58.

11. John Locke, *Two Treatises of Government* (1689), ed. Peter Laslett (Cambridge: Cambridge University Press, 1988), bk. 2, chap. 5; Nozick, chap. 7. There is a comprehensive discussion of this approach in Jeremy Waldron, *The Right to Private Property* (Oxford: Clarendon, 1988), chaps. 6, 7.

12. Locke, *Two Treatises*, bk. 2, chap. 5, sec. 27.

person mixes her labor with a piece of land, and the land comes to embody her efforts; that labor is now like a jewel embedded in the land for all time. So anyone who takes hold of the land is necessarily taking hold of the jewel. And no one can doubt that the jewel—the labor—continues to belong to the original person who invested it. So even if a hundred years of adverse possession go by, the land still contains the labor—and thus part of the personality—of that individual. The labor is intrinsically and essentially hers, though embedded in an object that has been out of her possession for all that time. As long as the personality of this individual commands our moral respect, she is always entitled to demand this part of it back.[13]

Unfortunately, as I have argued elsewhere, the Lockean image of labor (whether it is individual or cooperative) being literally embedded or mixed in an object is incoherent.[14] Even if it did make sense, the idea would be far too strong to do the work its proponents want it to do. For it would it be impossible to explain how property rights thus acquired could be alienable—how they could be transferred, through sale or gift, from one person to another—without offense to the personality of the original acquirer. If a resource, once labored on, contains for all time a fragment of the laborer's personality, how can that same resource be held legitimately by someone to whom that laborer has chosen to transfer it? Not only that, but how can that second entitlement (the entitlement of the transferee) have anything like the moral force of the original entitlement?[15] Does a fragment of the transferee's personality replace the original nugget of labor in the object? If it does (and if we can make sense of the idea that this is possible), then surely we cannot dismiss out of hand the possibility that an expropriator may also in time replace the original embedded labor of the person she expropriated with something of her own.

In recent years, historical entitlement has been found its most able and consistent defender in Robert Nozick, and some reliance on Nozick's approach is almost inevitable for any defender of historic reparations.[16] But Nozick also dismissed the conundrums of Locke's theory about the "mixing of labor." He retained the form of a Lockean approach—insisting that an adequate theory of justice must be founded

---

13. It is not hard to see how this could be adapted to express a conclusion about the labor and the identity or personality of a whole community. A community takes possession of a resource by investing the labor of its members. The resource now contains something of the community's spirit and personality. And this is what the community is claiming back when it demands the restoration of stolen lands.

14. See Jeremy Waldron, "Two Worries about Mixing One's Labor," *Philosophical Quarterly* 33 (1983): 37–44; and Waldron, *Right to Private Property*, pp. 171–94. See also the criticisms of Locke's idea in Nozick, pp. 174–75.

15. For a full elaboration of this problem, see Waldron, *Right to Private Property*, pp. 259–62.

16. Nozick, chap. 7.

on some principle of unilateral acquisition—without telling us much about the content of that principle or how it might be justified.[17] However, the task of filling in the content cannot be indefinitely postponed because the substance and justification of a principle of acquisition will partly determine what we can do with it. Do entitlements based on acquisition fade over time, or can we appeal to them generations later as a basis for reparation? We cannot answer this question until we know what the entitlement theorist proposes to put in the place of the incoherent Lockean idea.

If we abandon Locke's image of the mixing of labor, the most plausible account of initial acquisition goes like this. An individual, P, who takes possession of an object or a piece of land and who works on it, alters it, and uses it, makes it in effect a part of her life, a pivotal point in her thinking, planning, and action. She shapes it in a certain way—ploughing it, for example, or practicing good husbandry in her hunting over it—so as to allow it to perform a certain role in her life and activity not only now but in the future. If someone else, Q, comes along and seizes the land, taking it from P without her consent, then the whole structure of action is disrupted. P's planning and the structure of P's action are destroyed and replaced by that of Q. Moreover, P did not have to do anything equivalent to this disruption in order to establish the resource as the center of her life. Before P took it, shaped it, etc., the resource was the center of nobody's life. But when Q took it, it was already the center of P's. This asymmetry between the first and subsequent appropriator is the basis of P's historical entitlement and the basis of its moral priority. It is the reason why we say that Q's taking is wrong in a way that P's original appropriation was not, despite the fact that both parties are seeking to realize their autonomous purposes in the resource.

If any defense of historical entitlement is possible, it is going to be something along those lines. But—unfortunately—if this sort of line is taken, then we have a justification for historical entitlement that is vulnerable to prescription, a justification that is weakened by the historic persistence of dispossession, a justification that does fade over time. If something was taken from me decades ago, the claim that it now forms the center of my life and that it is still indispensable to the

17. There were good reasons for this reticence: it was worth focusing for a while on the question of what the basic shape of a theory of justice should be. As Nozick put it, "I am as well aware as anyone of how sketchy my discussion of the entitlement theory has been. But I no more believe that we need to have formulated a complete alternative theory in order to reject Rawls's undeniably great advance over utilitarianism, than Rawls needed a complete alternative theory before he could reject utilitarianism. What more does one need or can one have, than a sketch of a plausible alternative view, which from its very different perspective highlights the inadequacies of the best existing well-worked-out theory?" (Nozick, p. 230).

exercise of my autonomy is much less credible. For I must have developed some structure of subsistence. And that will be where my efforts have gone and where my planning and my practical thinking have been focused. I may of course yearn for the lost resource and spend a lot of time wishing that I had it back. I may even organize my life around the campaign for its restoration. But that is not the same thing as the basis of the original claim. The original entitlement is based on the idea that I have organized my life around the use of this object, not that I have organized my life around the specific project of hanging on to it or getting it back.

It may be objected that this argument furnishes an incentive to anyone who is inclined to violate another's rights. She knows that if she steals resources and hangs on to the proceeds, her victim will have to reorder his life and, once he does, he will no longer be in a position to claim that the stolen resources should be restored because of their centrality to his plans. But I do not see how this difficulty can be avoided, unless we introduce a different theory of the basis of property entitlements. We cannot pretend that a long-stolen resource continues to play a part in the original owner's life when in fact it does not, merely in order to avoid the moral hazard of this incentive effect. What the objection shows, I think, is that the normal line of argument for property entitlements based on autonomy is simply insufficient to establish imprescriptible rights. And what the failure of Locke's argument shows is that any case for making property rights fully imprescriptible is likely to run into other serious difficulties.

Historical entitlement theories are most impressive when moral entitlement is conjoined with present possession. Then it seems plausible to suggest that continued possession of the object might be indispensable to the possessor's autonomy and that an attack on possession is an attack on autonomy. But when the conjunction is disrupted, particularly when, as in the cases we are considering, it is disrupted for a considerable period of time, the claim looks much shakier.

I think this argument is important, by the way, but not always conclusive. It may not apply so clearly to cases where the dispossessed subject is a tribe or community, rather than an individual, and where the holding of which it has been dispossessed is particularly important for its sense of identity as a community. Many of the aboriginal claims, in New Zealand, Australia, and North America, have to do with burial grounds or lands which have some other symbolic or religious significance. Religions and cultural traditions we know are very resilient, and the claim that the lost lands form the center of a present way of life—and remain sacred objects despite their loss—may be as credible a hundred years on as it was at the time of the dispossession. In this regard, claims that land of religious significance should be returned to its original owners may have an edge over claims for the return of lands whose significance for them is mainly material or economic. Over the decades people are likely to have developed new modes of subsistence, making the claim that the land is crucial to their present way of life less credible in the economic case than in the religious case.

IV. CIRCUMSTANCES AND SUPERSESSION

I mentioned two ways in which an entitlement might be vulnerable to the passage of time. As well as the one we have just considered, there is also an important point to be made about changes in background circumstances that occur in the period after the original violation. I have in mind changes in population, changes in resource availability, occurrence of famine or ecological disaster, and so on. To assess these cases we have to ask questions about the relation between justice and background circumstances. Is justice relative to circumstances? Do entitlements change as circumstances change? If so, does the significance of past injustice change also? Or should we simply say that once something becomes mine it remains mine (and so it remains wrong for you to keep it), no matter what else happens in the world?

It is difficult to resist the conclusion that entitlements are sensitive to circumstances. Certainly, the level of our concern for various human predicaments is sensitive to the circumstances that constitute those predicaments. One's concern about poverty, for example, varies depending on the extent of the opportunities available to the poor: to be poor but to have some opportunity for amelioration is to be in a better predicament than to be poor with no opportunities at all. Similarly, our concern for the homeless may vary with the season of the year or the climate of the state in which they live. And these are not just fluctuations in subjective response: they are circumstantially sensitive variations in what we would take to be the appropriate level of concern. Now, the (appropriate) level of our concern about such predicaments is directly related to the burden of justification that must be shouldered by those who defend property rights. If an individual makes a claim to the exclusive use or possession of some resources in our territory, then the difficulty of sustaining that claim will clearly have some relation to the level of our concern about the plight of other persons who will have to be excluded from the resources if the claim is recognized. The only theory of property entitlement that would be totally immune to variations in background circumstances would be one that did not accept any burden of justification in relation to our real concerns.

We can express this claim about sensitivity to circumstances as follows. In the case of almost every putative entitlement, it is possible to imagine a pair of different circumstances, C_1 and C_2, such that the entitlement can only barely be justified in C_1 and cannot be justified at all in C_2. The shift from C_1 to C_2 represents a tipping point so far as the justification of the entitlement is concerned.

If this is accepted it clearly makes a difference to the original acquisition of property rights. A scale of acquisition that might be appropriate in a plentiful environment with a small population may be quite inappropriate in the same environment with a large population, or with the same population once natural resources have become depleted. In a plentiful environment with a small population, an individual appropriation of land makes no one worse off. As John Locke put it, "He that leaves as much as another can make use of, does as good as take nothing at all. No Body could think himself injur'd by the drinking of another Man, though he took a good Draught, who had a whole River of the same Water left him to quench his thirst. And the case of Land and Water, where there is enough of both, is perfectly the same."[18] But as Locke also recognized, the picture changed once the population increased to the point where scarcity was felt. If one person's appropriation cast a shadow on the survival prospects of others, then it evidently raised questions of a moral character that were not raised when resources were as plentiful as water in a river.[19] One does not need the exact formulation of a "Lockean proviso" to see this. It is simply that there are real and felt moral concerns in the one case that have to be addressed which are not present in the other.

The same point is recognized by Robert Nozick. The principle of acquisition that forms the linchpin of his theory depends for its acceptability on the claim that individual appropriations of previously unowned goods do not worsen anybody's situation.[20] (Nozick wishes, as far as possible, to present initial acquisition in the same light of Pareto improvement as consensual transfer.) We need not worry about the exact details of this proviso or of the various Lockean and Nozickian formulations of it.[21] What is clear is that in any plausible theory of historic entitlement, there is some spectrum of social circumstances, relating to the effect a putative acquisition would have on the prospects and life chances of other people, such that the further one goes along this spectrum the less inclined we are to say that the acquisition in question generates legitimate rights.

So far I have talked about one acquisitive act, A_1, taking place in one set of circumstances, C_1, and another acquisitive act, A_2, taking place in different circumstances, C_2. I have said that circumstances may make a difference so that the conditions for the moral legitimacy of A_2 may be different from the conditions for the moral legitimacy of A_1 (even though, considered in themselves, A_1 and A_2 are the same type of act). However, we know that acquisition is not an isolated act.

18. Locke, *Two Treatises*, bk. 2, sec. 33.
19. Ibid., bk. 2, secs. 36 ff.
20. Nozick, pp. 174 ff.
21. But see the discussion in Jeremy Waldron, "Enough and as Good Left for Others," *Philosophical Quarterly* 29 (1979): 319–28.

By laboring on a resource, the would-be acquirer not only takes it now but also purports to appropriate it permanently. The effect of her acquisition continues to be felt long after the acquisitive action has taken place. What happens, then, if circumstances change after the moment of the acquisitive act but during the time that the act has effect, that is, during the period of ownership to which the acquisitive action gives rise? A person performs acquisitive act A_1, in circumstances C_1 that make it legitimate. She establishes a title for herself (and her successors) that endures through time. During that time circumstances change, so that conditions C_2 now obtain, and conditions C_2 are such that an equivalent act of appropriation would not be legitimate. What effect does this change have on the legitimacy of the title founded by action A_1?

The answer has to be that it calls the legitimacy of that title into question. We can reach this conclusion by two routes.

The first and most straightforward argument is that property entitlements constrain us over a period of time, and they do so continually in the sense that they constantly call for action in support of them or they constantly involve action undertaken in their exercise. Day after day, an owner performs acts whose legitimacy is based on her entitlement; if she did not have the entitlement, she would have no right to perform these acts. Also, day after day, the owner faces explicit or implicit challenges from others, wanting to use her resource; if she did not have the entitlement to rely on she would not be in a moral position to rebut or resist these challenges. So each time she exercises her right and each time she resists an encroachment, she relies on the entitlement founded by A_1. At each of those times, the legitimacy of what she does depends on the appropriateness of her entitlement as a moral right at that time. So long as circumstances remain unchanged or so long as any changes are broadly consonant with the necessary conditions for the legitimacy of her entitlement, the fact that her claim is, so to speak, renewed day after day is not a worry. Its renewal is automatic. But if circumstances change radically in the way we have been envisaging, the continued application of her entitlement cannot be taken for granted.

The second line of argument is a response to an objection that might be made. Someone might object as follows:

> Surely if the original appropriation were legitimate, the conditions of its legitimacy would take into account the normal vicissitudes of human life including the prospect that things might change, goods become scarce, etc. To say that P acquires an entitlement by A_1 is surely to say that she acquires an entitlement that endures even in the face of changing circumstances. That is why we subject A_1 to such strict scrutiny, for its purports to found an enduring entitlement, not a temporary and circumstantially vul-

nerable one. The test for initial appropriation should be severe and morally rigorous, but if A_1 passes this test, it should not have to face further scrutiny later simply because conditions are not the same.

Here is the response to this objection. Maybe it is a good thing for the test of the initial acquisition, A_1, to take into account the possibility that conditions may change and therefore only to certify entitlements that survive that consideration. But it surely cannot be the upshot of this that, in circumstances C_1, only those acquisitions are certified that would be valid in all circumstances including C_2. That would be wasteful and pointless: why shouldn't people act as though goods are plentiful, at least when they are plentiful?

No. If a rigorous test of initial acquisition does take future vicissitudes into account, it will do so in a more subtle way. What it will do is provide ab initio, in the terms of the entitlement, that the exact array of rights, liberties, and powers is to be circumstantially sensitive. Thus, what P acquires through A_1, are rights that entitle her to do one set of things in C_1, and another, perhaps more restricted, set of things in C_2. So, as before, the net effect of P's entitlement does vary, depending on the circumstances. If, for example, P acquires an oasis in conditions of plenty, she acquires (i) a right to use it freely and exclude others from its use so long as water remains plentiful in the territory, and (ii) a duty to share it with others on some fair basis if ever water becomes scarce. The right that is (permanently) acquired through A_1 is thus circumstantially sensitive in the actions it licenses.

If all this is accepted so far as justice in acquisition is concerned, it must also apply to issues and allegations of injustice. Suppose a person has legitimately acquired an object in circumstances of plenty, C_1, and another person comes along and snatches it from her. That act of snatching, we may say, is an injustice. But the very same action of snatching an already appropriated object may not be wrong in a different set of circumstances, C_2, where desperate scarcity has set in and the snatcher has no other means of staying alive. One and the same type of action may be injustice in one set of circumstances and not injustice in another.[22]

---

22. The point can be borne out by comparing the following passages from Locke's *Two Treatises*. The first follows on from the statement about conditions of plenty that was quoted a page or two earlier: "He that has as good left for his Improvement, as was already taken up, needed not complain, ought not to meddle with what was already improved by another's Labour: If he did, 'tis plain he desired the benefit of another's Pains, which he had no right to, and not the Ground which God had given him in common with others to labour on, and whereof there was good left, as that already possessed." But the second passage raises the specter of scarcity: "God . . . has given no one of his Children such a Property, in his peculiar Portion of the things of this World, but that he has given his needy Brother a Right to the Surplusage of his Goods;

I hope it is clear where the argument is going. I said that the burden of justifying an exclusive entitlement depends (in part) on the impact of others' interests of being excluded from the resources in question and that that impact is likely to vary as circumstances change. Similarly an acquisition which is legitimate in one set of circumstances may not be legitimate in another set of circumstances. From this I inferred that an initially legitimate acquisition may become illegitimate or have its legitimacy restricted (as the basis of an ongoing entitlement) at a later time on account of a change in circumstances. By exactly similar reasoning, it seems possible that an act which counted as an injustice when it was committed in circumstances C_1 may be transformed, so far as its ongoing effect is concerned, into a just situation if circumstances change in the meantime from C_1 to C_2. When this happens, I shall say the injustice has been *superseded*.

Consider the following example.[23] On the savanna, a number of groups appropriate water holes, in conditions where it is known that there are enough water holes for each group. So long as these conditions obtain, it seems reasonable for the members of given group, P, to use the water hole they have appropriated without asking permission of other groups with whom they share the plains; and it may even seem reasonable for them to exclude members of other groups from the casual use of their water holes, saying to them, "You have your own water hole. Go off and use that, and leave ours alone." But suppose there is an ecological disaster, and all the water holes dry up except the one that the members of P are using. Then in these changed circumstances, notwithstanding the legitimacy of their original appropriation, it is no longer in order for P to exclude others from their water hole. Indeed it may no longer be in order for members of P to casually use "their own" water hole in the way they did before. In the new circumstances, it may be incumbent on them to draw up a rationing scheme that allows for the needs of everyone in the territory to be satisfied from this one resource. Changing circumstances can have an effect on ownership rights notwithstanding the moral legitimacy of the original appropriation.

Next, suppose as before that in circumstances of plenty various groups on the savanna are legitimately in possession of their respective water holes. One day, motivated purely by greed, members of group

---

so that it cannot justly be denied him, when his pressing Wants call for it." An action which may be condemned in one set of circumstances as the covetous meddling of someone too lazy to fend for herself, becomes in another set of circumstances the exercise of a right, which may not be resisted by the initial appropriator.

23. The example is suggested by David Lyons, "The New Indian Claims and Original Rights to Land," in *Reading Nozick*, ed. J. Paul (Oxford: Blackwell, 1982), p. 371.

Q descend on the water hole possessed by group P and insist on sharing that with them. (What's more they do not allow reciprocity; they do not allow members of P to share any water hole that was legitimately in the possession of Q.) That is an injustice. But then circumstances change, and all the water holes of the territory dry up except the one that originally belonged to P. The members of group Q are already sharing that water hole on the basis of their earlier incursion. But now that circumstances have changed, they are entitled to share that water hole; it no longer counts as an injustice. It is in fact part of what justice now requires. The initial injustice by Q against P has been superseded by circumstances.

Once again, it may be objected that this reasoning generates a moral hazard—an incentive for wrongdoers to seize others' lands confident in the knowledge that if they hang on to them wrongfully for long enough their possession may eventually become rightful.[24] But the argument of this section is not that the passage of time per se supersedes all claims of injustice. Rather, the argument is that claims about justice and injustice must be responsive to changes in circumstances. Suppose there had been no injustice: still, a change in circumstances (such as a great increase in world population) might justify our forcing the aboriginal inhabitants of some territory to share their land with others. If this is so, then the same change in circumstances in the real world can justify our saying that the others' occupation of some of their lands, which was previously wrongful, may become morally permissible. There is no moral hazard in this supersession because the aboriginal inhabitants would have had to share their lands, whether the original injustice had taken place or not.

I do not think this possibility—of the supersession of past injustice—can be denied, except at the cost of making one's theory of historical entitlement utterly impervious to variations in the circumstance in which holdings are acquired and withheld from others. If circumstances make a difference to what counts as a just acquisition, then they must make a difference also to what counts as an unjust incursion. And if they make a difference to that, then in principle we must concede that a change in circumstances can affect whether a particular continuation if adverse possession remains an injustice or not.

Of course, from the fact that supersession is a possibility, it does not follow that it always happens. Everything depends on which circumstances are taken to be morally significant and how as matter of fact circumstances have changed. It may be that some of the historic injustices that concern us have not been superseded and that, even under modern circumstances, the possession of certain aboriginal lands

---

24. I am grateful to Carol Sanger for this formulation of the objection.

by the descendants of those who expropriated their original owners remains a crying injustice. My argument is not intended to rule that out. But there have been huge changes since North America and Australasia were settled by white colonists. The population has increased manyfold, and most of the descendants of the colonists, unlike their ancestors, have nowhere else to go. We cannot be sure that these changes in circumstances supersede the injustice of their continued possession of aboriginal lands, but it would not be surprising if they did. The facts that have changed are exactly the sort of facts one would expect to make a difference to the justice of a set of entitlements over resources.

V. CONCLUSION

It is important that defenders of aboriginal claims face up to the possibility of the supersession of historic injustice. Even if this particular thesis about supersession is mistaken, some account has to be given of the impact on aboriginal claims and on the reparation of generations-old injustices of the demographic and ecological changes that have taken place.

Apart from anything else, the changes that have taken place over the past two hundred years mean that the costs of respecting primeval entitlements are much greater now than they were in 1800. Two hundred years ago, a small aboriginal group could have exclusive domination of "a large and fruitful Territory"[25] without much prejudice to the needs and interests of very many other human beings. Today, such exclusive rights would mean many people going hungry who might otherwise be fed and many people living in poverty who might otherwise have an opportunity to make a decent life. Irrespective of the occurrence of past injustice, this imbalance would have to be rectified sooner or later. That is the basis for my argument that claims about historic injustice predicated on the status quo ante may be superseded by our determination to distribute the resources of the world in a way that is fair to all of its existing inhabitants.

Behind the thesis of supersession lies a determination to focus upon present and prospective costs—the suffering and the deprivation over which we still have some control. The idea is that any conception of justice which is to be made practically relevant for the way we act now must be a scheme that takes into account modern circumstances and the way those affect the conditions under which people presently live their lives. Arguments for reparation take as conclusive claims of entitlement oriented toward circumstances that are radically different from those we actually face: claims of entitlement based on the habitation of a territory by a small fraction of its present population, and claims

---

25. The phrase is from Locke, *Two Treatises*, bk. 2, sec. 41.

of entitlement based on the determination to ignore the present dispersal of persons and peoples on the face of the earth, simply because the historic mechanisms of such dispersal were savagely implicated in injustice. And yet, here we all are. The present circumstances are the ones that are real: it is in the actual world that people starve or are hurt or degraded if the demands of justice in relation to their circumstances are not met. Justice, we say, is a matter of the greatest importance. But the importance to be accorded it is relative to what may actually happen if justice is not done, not to what might have happened if injustice in the past had been avoided.

I want to end by emphasizing two points that qualify or clarify this thesis of the supersession of historic injustice. First, what I have said applies only if an honest attempt is being made to arrange things justly for the future. If no such attempt is being made, there is nothing to overwhelm or supersede the enterprise of reparation. My thesis is not intended as a defense of complacency or inactivity, and to the extent that opponents of reparation are complacent about the injustice of the status quo, their resistance is rightly condemned. Repairing historic injustice is, as we have seen, a difficult business and, as a matter of fact, it is almost always undertaken by people of good will. The only thing that can trump that enterprise is an honest and committed resolve to do justice for the future, a resolve to address present circumstances in a way that respects the claims and needs of everyone.

Second, my thesis is not that such resolve has priority over all rectificatory actions. I claim only that it has priority over reparation which might carry us in a direction contrary to that which is indicated by a prospective theory of justice. Often and understandably, claims based on reparation and claims based on forward-looking principles will coincide, for, as we saw in Section III above, past injustice is not without its present effects. It is a fact that many of the descendants of those who were defrauded and expropriated live demoralized in lives of relative poverty—relative, that is, to the descendants of those who defrauded them. If the relief of poverty and the more equal distribution of resources is the aim of a prospective theory of justice, it is likely that the effect of rectifying past wrongs will carry us some distance in this direction. All the same, it is worth stressing that it is the impulse to justice now that should lead the way in this process, not the reparation of something whose wrongness is understood primarily in relation to conditions that no longer obtain.

Entitlements that fade with time, counterfactuals that are impossible to verify, injustices that are overtaken by circumstances—all this is a bit distant, I am afraid, from the simple conviction that, if something was wrongly taken, it must be right to give it back. The arguments I have made may seem to deflate a lot of the honest enthusiasm that surrounds aboriginal claims and the hope that now for the first time in centuries we may be ready to do justice to people and peoples whom we have perennially maltreated. The arguments may also seem to compromise justice unnecessarily, as they shift from the straightforward logic of compensation to an arcane and calculative casuistry that tries to balance incommensurable claims.

But societies are not simple circumstances, and it does not detract one bit from the importance of justice nor from the force of the duties it generates to insist that its requirements are complex and that they may be sensitive to differences in circumstance. Even the members of a modern society not afflicted by a history like ours would find the demands of justice difficult to discern and hard to weigh: the modern discussion of the subject, with the utopian cast of its "perfect compliance" assumptions, has made that at least clear.[26] It is true that in many cases the complexity of these issues does not diminish our ability to recognize acts of injustice—stark and awful—like direct expropriation and genocide. The fallacy lies in thinking that the directness of such perception and the outrage that attends it translate into simple and straightforward certainty about what is to be done once such injustices have occurred.

"First come, first served." "We were here first." These simplicities have always been unpleasant ways of denying present aspirations or resisting current claims of need. They become no more pleasant, and in the end no more persuasive, by being associated with respect for aboriginal peoples or revulsion from the violence and expropriation that have disfigured our history.

---

26. For the assumption of "perfect compliance," see Rawls, pp. 8–9.

[18]

THE APOLOGY PARADOX

By Janna Thompson

An outbreak of apology has swept the globe. Bill Clinton has apologized for slavery, Tony Blair for British policy during the Irish potato famine. The Canadian government has apologized to indigenous communities for breaking up their families and to Japanese Canadians for putting their families in internment camps during World War II. The Vatican has apologized for its failure to condemn the Nazi treatment of Jews, Queen Elizabeth for the British exploitation of the Maoris. The Japanese government has apologized to Korean women who were forced into prostitution during World War II, and some former government officials in South Africa have apologized for their behaviour during the period of apartheid. Though the Australian Prime Minister has refused to apologize for past treatment of Aborigines, many Australians have taken it upon themselves to make an apology. But does it make sense to say 'Sorry'? Can it be done without hypocrisy? The following paradox suggests that there is something wrong with the exercise of apologizing for what our ancestors did, or something wrong with common assumptions about such apologies.

I. THE PARADOX

1. We should apologize for what our ancestors did to indigenous people, or the blacks, or the Jews, or the Irish, etc.
2. If we are really sorry for the deeds of our ancestors then we regret that they did what they did.

This step requires that we understand what 'Sorry' means in the way we understand it when we apologize for our own actions. We regret the bad deed; we wish that we had not done it, and our apology is taken as a sign of remorse. If we apologize without remorse, then we are being hypocritical. Even if remorse is out of place when we are apologizing for deeds done by others, surely regret is appropriate and necessary.

3. If we regret that our ancestors did their unjust deeds, then we prefer that they had not been done.
4. But if our ancestors had not done what they did to indigenous people, to the blacks, the Jews, the Irish, then the history of our country, indeed the history of the world, would have been significantly different from what it has been, and we would probably not exist.

This step makes use of a plausible point made by Derek Parfit about the contingency of persons.[1] Our actions, and the events that influence them, determine not only the conditions of life of our offspring, but also who they are. Even minor events can bring into being individuals who would not otherwise have existed, and after a few generations the number of people whose existence depends on such contingencies becomes very large.

A major historical event or institution of the past, like slavery and the slave trade, the dispossession of indigenous people in Canada, the United States and Australia, apartheid in South Africa, the Irish potato famine or the Holocaust, had an effect on the lives of large numbers of people. It influenced where they moved, whom they met, whether they emigrated, and the overall pattern of their lives – and, as a result, what children they had. It is not unreasonable to think that almost everyone now alive in the United States, Israel, Australia, Canada, Britain and South Africa would not be here if these events had not happened or these practices had not existed. Relatively minor historical occurrences, like the Australian and Canadian practice of taking children away from indigenous families and raising or educating them in special institutions, would not have played such a large role in determining who exists. Nevertheless since even relatively minor events can have an effect on what individuals are brought into being, and this effect is magnified over several generations, it would be rash for Australians and Canadians to assume that their coming into existence did not depend upon these policies.

5. Most of us are glad to be alive. We think it a good thing that we came into existence. That is, we prefer the world's being such that we exist.
6. This means that we cannot regret that those deeds or practices happened on which our existence depended, or probably depended. For if the deeds had not been done then the world would (probably) have been such that we would not exist.

[1] D. Parfit, *Reasons and Persons* (Oxford: Clarendon Press, 1984), p. 352.

7. Therefore we cannot sincerely apologize for the wrongs done by our ancestors, and we should not do so.

II. PROPOSED SOLUTIONS TO THE PARADOX

Some may think that the obvious solution is to endorse the last step, and thus reject the first: we should not apologize for the deeds of our ancestors. But this suggestion is not very attractive. The fact is that many of us are sorry for the unjust deeds of our ancestors. Being sorry is a very natural moral response to learning about the harm they did. Not responding in this way, it seems to me, would demonstrate a lack of moral sensibility. Furthermore, the paradox applies to the regrets of the descendants of victims of dispossession, neglect or atrocity. Descendants of slaves, of victims of apartheid, of indigenous people who were dispossessed, or of those who emigrated because of the potato famine, or the children of Holocaust survivors, would not now be in existence if these injustices had not been done. But it seems reasonable, even inevitable, for these descendants to regret that injustices were done to their ancestors. The question is how they can do this while preferring that the world should be such that they exist.[2]

Some may say that there is no paradox once we understand that the one who apologizes is a state or an institution, not particular individuals. There is no reason why an institution or community cannot regret what it did. The trouble is that individuals have to be the ones who issue these apologies, and those they represent are expected to endorse them; and the problem remains of how they can do this sincerely. Which particular individuals exist may not matter as far as the existence of a state is concerned, but it matters to those who act on behalf of the state or to its present citizens. In any case, whether leaders officially apologize or not, many individuals are apt to regret what their ancestors did or suffered.

Another response is to admit the paradoxical result of saying 'Sorry', while insisting that it does not matter. We do regret some of the deeds done by our ancestors without being sorry that we are alive. If this amounts to inconsistency, so be it. Not being sorry for the unjust deeds of our ancestors would be a worse failing. Nevertheless the existence of inconsistency leads to an uncertainty about how our apologies should be understood. It would be better if we did have a non-paradoxical interpretation of what we mean.

[2] Neil Thomason has suggested to me that the paradox may be more accurately understood as being about regret for bad things that have happened in the past rather than about apology.

It might be argued that no inconsistency exists when proper attention is paid to intension. I can consistently regret the happening of an action, process or practice under one description ('the practice of apartheid') and not regret it under another ('series of events on which my existence depends') – just as I can consistently believe that the Morning Star is Venus, and at the same time that the Evening Star is not Venus. However, whether my beliefs are consistent or inconsistent depends upon what I know or believe about the world. If I know that the Morning Star is the same as the Evening Star, then my beliefs *are* inconsistent. If I know, or have good reason to believe, that the practice of apartheid is identical to the series of events on which my existence depends, then my regret is paradoxical.

It could be argued that it is the sixth step that should be rejected. Utilitarians in particular might make this move. They might argue that the happiness of ourselves and our co-existents must be weighed and compared with the happiness that would now exist if the bad deeds had not been done. If it is total happiness that counts and not who has it, then we might well be forced to conclude that it would be better if history had been different in a way that would have resulted in our not being born. But the calculations required would be more than merely difficult (since, presumably, all other possible historical events that might have happened if the bad deeds had not been done would have to be weighed in the balance). In any case, the kind of utilitarianism that insists on maximizing total happiness is subject to serious objections (as Parfit also points out, pp. 387ff.).

Apart from the utilitarian position, it does seem reasonable that some people might sincerely wish that something had never happened, even though they recognize that if it had not, they (and their friends, family and associates) would not exist. They may consider that the destruction caused to their community (or by their ancestors to someone else's community) was so great that it would be better if they had never been born rather than that this destruction should have occurred. However, I suspect that most of us cannot sincerely take this position in respect to what our ancestors did.

Another alternative is to reject the second step. It might be argued that official apologies such as those made by Clinton, Blair and other leaders should not be interpreted as expressing regret about what was done by people in the past. They are forward- rather than backward-looking. They are meant to signal the beginning of a new relation with descendants of those who were harmed, or to alleviate the psychological damage suffered by members of a group with a historical grievance.[3] They are a way of

---

[3] 'Reparations may symbolize a society's undertaking not to forget or deny that a particular injustice took place, and to respect and help sustain a dignified sense of identity-in-memory for the people affected': J. Waldron, 'Superseding Historical Injustice', *Ethics*, 103 (1992), p. 6.

making a commitment to justice, of recognizing members of a disadvantaged group as equal citizens, or they are an expression of the intention to act more justly than did people of the past.

These ideas about how to understand what official apologies mean, or ought to mean, are plausible, but they cannot tell the full story. If the intention to act justly in the future is signalled by saying 'Sorry', then the ability of the words uttered to convey this message surely depends upon their being interpreted as an apology – as an expression of regret for what was done in the past. To use the distinction made by J.L. Austin in *How to Do Things with Words*, making an apology can be a perlocutionary act intended to have a certain effect in a particular situation. But its ability to have that effect depends upon it being the kind of illocutionary act that it is – in this case, having the force of an apology. In any case, many of those who have apologized for wrongs of the past, for example, those Australians who offered their private apologies, were not signalling a new era of justice for wronged people. As ordinary citizens they were not in a position to do this. But they did intend to say that they were sorry.

Nevertheless it might be argued that the meaning of saying 'Sorry' is not properly described in the second and/or third steps of the paradox. Perhaps what we mean to convey is not regret but simply our recognition that certain acts performed in the past were wrong. But this idea is not appealing. What we want is a way of understanding our action as an apology, and surely anything that counts as apologizing has to be understood as expressing regret. More promising is the suggestion that regretting that something occurred does not mean that we prefer that it had not happened. It merely means that we wish it had not.[4] People can wish for something incompatible with their preferences, for something impossible or even nonsensical. I can wish that I could fly like a bird, that daylight in winter lasted as long as daylight in summer, or that I could marry Mr Fitzwilliam Darcy. So why can I not wish that my ancestors had not done their evil deed, even though I think it likely that my existence depends upon it?

There are wishes and wishes. Some wishes are fanciful, acts of imagination that do not commit the wisher to a desire that the wish may come true or to a regret that the event wished for did not happen, or even to a belief that it is (or was) possible for it to happen. I am struck by how exhilarating it would be to soar above the treetops, or how pleasant to ski after tea. Or I express an opinion about what I would like to do or be in an imagined world (not necessarily a possible one). It would be inappropriate for my friends to suggest that I take hang-gliding lessons, to give me a lecture on astronomy, or tell me that I cannot marry a fictional character. It would be

---

[4] Tim Oakley made this suggestion.

inappropriate for them to point out that the wish is inconsistent with some of my beliefs and preferences. However, some wishes do express preferences. If in a conversation about politics I say that I wish that there were greater equality in our society, or that NATO had not bombed Belgrade, I shall be understood as expressing a preference – saying what I would like to be the case or what I would have preferred. If I have said something on another occasion that seems to contradict my utterance, or if I am ignorant about relevant facts, then it is appropriate for others to accuse me of inconsistency or ignorance. A wish of preference, unlike a wish of fancy, commits the wisher to preferring that the wish should come true, or to preferring that the world had been such that it had come true, and thus to the logical implications of these preferences. It is hard to interpret the wish that my ancestors had not committed an injustice as anything other than a wish of preference. In having this wish I am not engaging in an act of fancy or expressing a view about an imaginary world in which they did not do the deed. I prefer that they had not done it in this world.

It is not plausible to interpret our regrets concerning the deeds of our ancestors as a wish of fancy. But there is another way of arguing that apologizing does not commit us to preferring that a deed had not been done, at least as this is usually understood. Many people feel uncomfortable or even apologetic about benefiting from an injustice even when they had no responsibility for it. They are sorry that the good things that they now possess came to them because of a past injustice. They do not regret that they have these things, but that they came to have them in the way they did. An apology could be interpreted as an expression of this kind of regret. So interpreted it is not, strictly speaking, an apology *for* the deeds of our ancestors or an expression of regret that they happened. Rather it is an apology *concerning* deeds of the past, and the regret expressed is that we owe our existence and other things we enjoy to the injustices of our ancestors. Our preference is for a possible world in which our existence did not depend on these deeds.

It seems to me that this is the best solution. Nevertheless it requires that we must reinterpret what we are doing when we apologize or regret past injustices. It implies that we are not doing what many of us thought we were doing – apologizing for the deeds themselves and preferring that they had not happened. For this reason, many will find it implausible. However, the paradox requires us to reinterpret what we are doing when we apologize for deeds of the past, and the reinterpretation I am recommending seems not so drastic or counter-intuitive as those I have rejected.

La Trobe University

[19]

Transgenerational Compensation

GEORGE SHER

Many people believe that compensation is owed for the effects of certain wrongs that took place more than a generation ago—the slave trade, for example, and the appropriation of aboriginal lands. It is also widely believed that to compensate someone for a wrong is to make him as well off as he would be if it had not been done.[1] Taken together, these claims appear to imply that we owe it to the current descendants of victims of wrongs done more than a generation ago to (try to) make them as well off as they would now be if those wrongs had not been done. Although doing this would require far more counterfactual knowledge than we can ever have, such compensation remains, in the eyes of many, a compelling theoretical ideal.[2] However, according to others, its intelligibility is compromised by the fact that many descendants of the original victims who were conceived after they were wronged would not have

---

I am grateful to Emily Fox Gordon, Donald Morrison, Hanoch Sheinman, the participants in conferences on historical justice in Berlin and Riverside, California, and the Editors of *Philosophy & Public Affairs*, for helpful suggestions concerning this article. When I presented the paper at the Riverside conference, I discovered that one of the other speakers, Bernard Boxill, had independently arrived at an argument similar to the one presented in Section III. Boxill's paper, which has since appeared in *The Journal of Ethics*, is cited in another context in n. 21.

1. This view of compensation is succinctly expressed by Anthony T. Kronman: "The aim of compensation is to put the injured party in the position he would have been in if the invasion of his legally protected interest had not occurred. So stated, the principle of compensation determines the damages for a tortious injury as well as for breach of contractual obligation." See Anthony T. Kronman, "Specific Performance," *University of Chicago Law Review* 45 (1978): 355–82, p. 360, n. 38. The view is also influential among philosophers; Robert Nozick's well-known formulation is quoted in the text below.

2. Those who appear to accept this ideal include many who argue that African Americans are owed reparations for slavery and its aftermath. Some examples: "What harm was done to Khalea's nine-year-old friend, and millions like her, was done long ago for profit, and with her country's complicity. Now it must properly be the country's responsibility to undo the damage and make victims like Khalea's friend whole." See Randall Robinson,

existed if the wrongs had not been done.³ This fact is said to threaten our ability to compensate because it seems incoherent to ask how much better off someone would be in a situation in which he would not even exist.⁴

This, clearly, is a fundamental challenge to the ideal of transgenerational compensatory justice. However, although the challenge has been discussed by various philosophers, myself included, it has received comparatively little attention; and neither, in my opinion, has it been adequately met. Thus, with some trepidation, I propose to revisit the issue here. In the article's first section, I will bring out an unnoticed distinction between two versions of the problem; in the second, I will criticize two previously proposed solutions; in the third and fourth, I will open up a new approach that appears to hold more promise. Although the new approach does not quite vindicate the intuition that persons can be owed compensation for wrongs done more than a generation ago, it does imply that in the great majority of cases that elicit such intuitions, the current descendants of the original victims are owed compensation for later wrongs that are non-contingently connected to the original wrongs.

The Debt: What America Owes to Blacks (New York: Dutton, 2000), p. 223; "Whites owe blacks money, roughly several trillion dollars.... While most of the debt is owed to poor blacks, all blacks have been victimized by centuries of economic injustice in ways the benefit whites in the top 30 percent." See Richard F. America, *Paying the Social Debt: What White America Owes Black America* (Westport, Conn.: Praeger, 1993), p. 4; "Since millions of Africans were transported across the sea and enslaved in the Caribbean and America for more than two centuries, what method of calculating loss will be employed?... [T]he overarching principle for establishing loss might be determined by ascertaining the negative effects on the natural development of people, that is the physical, psychological, economic, and educational toll must be evaluated." See Molefi Kete Asante, "The African American Warrant for Reparations," in *Should America Pay? Slavery and the Raging Debate on Reparations*, ed. Raymond A. Winbush (New York: Amistad, 2003), pp. 9–10.

3. In what follows, I will use the term "descendant" to refer only to those children, grandchildren, and so on of the original victims who were conceived after the original victims were wronged.

4. As one of the Editors of *Philosophy & Public Affairs* has pointed out, it is also possible to defend reparations not as a way of elevating the descendants of the original victims of slavery to the levels of well-being that they would have enjoyed in its absence, but rather, and more simply, as a way to "acknowledge and make up for the wrong done." If this approach can avoid reliance on the counterfactuals whose intelligibility is in question, it will not be vulnerable to the threat I have described.

Transgenerational Compensation

I

In *Anarchy, State, and Utopia*, Robert Nozick sums up the standard view of compensation as follows:

> Something fully compensates a person for a loss if and only if it makes him no worse off than he otherwise would have been; it compensates person X for person Y's action A if X is no worse off receiving it, Y having done A, than X would have been without receiving it if Y had not done A.[5]

Because implementing this formula requires raising X's level of well-being in the actual world, in which A occurred, to the level X would have enjoyed in A's absence, the formula evidently presumes that X himself exists in both contexts. This is the presumption that is said to be problematic whenever A was performed before X was conceived. But why, exactly, is the presumption viewed as problematic?

In fact, the case against it has been developed in two quite different ways. As far as I know, these two arguments have never been explicitly distinguished. Both for reasons of analytical clarity and because certain rejoinders (including the one I will propose) are not equally effective against both arguments, I begin by spelling out the difference between them.

The first of the two arguments is an appeal to probabilities. Its points of departure are, first, that each existing person would not have existed if the spermatozoon that fertilized the ovum from which he developed had not done so and, second, that that sperm would *not* have fertilized that egg if the person's father and mother either had not met or had not copulated exactly when and in the manner they did. Because each male ejaculation contains hundreds of millions of sperm cells, it follows that "any trivial difference affecting conception would ... [bring] it about

---

5. Robert Nozick, *Anarchy, State, and Utopia* (New York: Basic Books, 1974), p. 57. As Nozick states it, this formula does not specify the requirements for the rectification of injustice because it contains no implication that Y's action A, for which X is to be compensated, was *wrong*. However, the formula will specify the requirements for the rectification of injustice if we replace the phrase "Y's action A" with the more explicit "Y's *wrongful* action A"; and I shall from now on assume this substitution to be made.

that a different individual is conceived."[6] Thus, given "a significant harm that disrupts the life of the original victim"[7]—given, for example, the victim's forcible removal from Africa to America by slave traders—it is overwhelmingly likely that the victim's children *would* have been different individuals if the wrong that caused the harm had not been done. Because of this, and because the divergence between the world as it is and as it would have been in the wrong's absence can be expected to increase with each generation, we may confidently assert that

> [w]ere we to project the 200 years of our country's history in a rectified movie, the cast of characters would surely differ significantly from the existing cast. Had our ancestors lived and moved in a rectified version of our history, quite likely many of us would not be alive today.[8]

Thus, for the typical descendant of a person who was wrongfully harmed a generation or more ago, there is simply no answer to the question of how well off *he* would now be if the original wrong had not been done.

According to the argument I have just summarized, the reason the actual descendants of the past victims of wrongdoing would probably not have existed in the absence of the original wrongs is that the relevant sperms would probably not have fertilized the relevant eggs. This suggests that if, improbably, the same sperm and egg that in fact developed into one of the actual descendants *had* also managed to unite in the absence of the original wrong, then the person into whom the fertilized egg developed *would* have been identical to the relevant actual descendant. That this possibility is at least theoretically open is conceded by the (understated) "quite likely" in the quoted passage. By contrast, the second argument for the non-existence of the current descendants purports entirely to rule the possibility out.

Because this second argument is generally couched in the language of possible worlds, I will, in summarizing it, use that language as well.

---

6. Christopher Morris, "Existential Limits to the Rectification of Past Wrongs," *American Philosophical Quarterly* 21 (1984): 175–82, at p. 177.

7. Ibid.

8. Lawrence Davis, "Comments on Nozick's Entitlement Theory," *The Journal of Philosophy* 73 (1976): 836–44, at p. 842. See also Onora O'Neill, "Rights to Compensation," *Social Philosophy and Policy* 5 (1987): 72–87, at pp. 80–82.

The argument relies on a certain account of the possible worlds that are relevant to the truth of counterfactuals and a corresponding account of what makes persons in these possible worlds identical to actual ones. To identify the possible world that is relevant to the counterfactual "if E1 had occurred at t1, then E2 would have occurred at t2," the argument asks us to imagine a world that is identical to the actual world until t1, in which E1 occurs at t1 as it does *not* in the actual world, and in which all subsequent events unfold in accordance with the prevailing causal laws. If in this alternative world E2 occurs at t2, then the counterfactual is true; otherwise, it is false. Whether a given actual person is *identical* to anyone in the alternative world depends on whether that actual person is transtemporally identical to any pre-t1 person to whom some person in the alternative world is also transtemporally identical. If this condition is met—if the actual and the alternative world are both "branches" of what was once a single world and a person in each is transtemporally identical to a single pre-branching person—then the actual person also exists in the alternative world; otherwise, he does not.

Even in hasty summary, this way of thinking about the relevant counterfactuals and possible worlds has an obvious power and appeal. If we accept it, however, then we must indeed acknowledge that no current descendant of any victim of a wrong done more than a generation ago could possibly have existed in the wrong's absence. The reasoning, as I elaborated it some years ago, runs as follows:

> [S]uppose now that [the wrong act] A is performed *before* X begins to exist as a person. In such a case, any A-less world will have to diverge from the actual world before X begins to exist as a person as well. Because of this, the X who subsequently begins to exist in the actual world will be unable to stand in the branching relation to any inhabitant of the relevant A-less world. A fortiori, X will be unable to stand in the branching relation to any *better-off* inhabitant of the relevant A-less world.[9]

Because X's non-existence in the relevant possible world follows logically from the proposed account, this argument's conclusion is far stronger than that of its probabilistic predecessor.

---

9. George Sher, "Compensation and Transworld Personal Identity," *The Monist* 62 (1979): 378–91, at p. 384.

II

Although the two arguments that I just distinguished are not identical in scope,[10] the success of either would effectively undermine the intelligibility of the vast majority of the counterfactuals that transgenerational compensation requires. For this reason, some who favor transgenerational compensation have advanced proposals aimed at preserving the intelligibility of the relevant counterfactuals. Of these proposals, a first is to build the existence of the current actual descendants of the original victims right into the description of the possible worlds that determine whether the counterfactuals are true; a second is to drop the requirement that the individuals to be compensated be the very ones who would have been better off in the absence of the original wrong. Although I once thought that both proposals held promise, I now think they both fail. Here, in brief, are my reasons.

The first proposal, which seeks to replace the claim that the relevant possible worlds are the closest ones in which the original wrongs are absent with the more complicated claim that they are the closest worlds in which the wrongs are absent *and the descendants of the original victims exist*, has been clearly articulated by A. John Simmons. Here is how Simmons puts it:

> The best analysis of the counterfactual above, I think, sees it as equivalent to: "In those possible worlds in which I (or my counterpart) exist and my parents do not have all of their property stolen (before my conception), I have an easier life as a child (than that which I had in the actual world)." Since there certainly *are* such possible worlds (i.e., since . . . the absence of the theft could not be claimed to *necessarily*

---

10. To arrive at a case in which the implications of the arguments differ, imagine an embezzling victim who does not discover his loss until after his child is conceived. Because this victim's pre-conception behavior is unaffected by the embezzlement, we may safely assume that the sperm and egg that in fact unite to become his child would also have united if the embezzlement had not taken place. For this reason, the first argument does not preclude compensating the child for the embezzlement's effects. By contrast, the second argument does preclude compensating the child; for even if the embezzlement does not affect which sperm unites with which egg, a world in which it does not occur must diverge from the actual world before the child is conceived. For this reason, that world cannot contain any person who is transtemporally identical to an earlier person who is also transtemporally identical to the actual child.

exclude my existence [or the existence of my counterpart]), the counterfactual at issue will be perfectly capable of being true.[11]

Because Simmons takes the existence of the original victims' descendants to be part of the description of the relevant possible worlds, the non-identity problem is, for him, no problem at all.

But is Simmons really entitled to say that the absence of the original wrong "could not be claimed *necessarily* to exclude" the current descendants of the original victims? It seems, on the contrary, that most descendants of the original victims *will* necessarily be excluded if we adopt the "branching" criterion of personal identity across possible worlds. According to that criterion, an actual person is only identical to a possible one if they are both transtemporally identical to a single pre-branching person. This means that no actual person can be identical to any person in any possible world that branched off from the actual world before the actual person's conception. However, if a given wrong was done before a current descendant of one of its victims was conceived, then a world without the wrong must indeed have branched off before that descendant's conception. Hence, at best, Simmons's strategy will only succeed if we reject the branching criterion of personal identity across possible worlds.

To anyone sympathetic to the branching criterion, the natural inference to draw from this is that we should reject Simmons' strategy. Not everyone *is* sympathetic to the branching criterion, however, so it is worth pointing out that Simmons's problems do not end here. Even if we substitute a criterion that *does* allow possible worlds that lack the original wrong but nevertheless contain the victims' current descendants, the relevance of such worlds to compensation will remain problematic if they are sufficiently remote from the actual world.

If this problem is not immediately apparent, it is probably because the wrongdoing in Simmons's own example—the theft of his parents' property before he is conceived—is so localized that we can easily

---

11. A. John Simmons, "Historical Rights and Fair Shares," *Law and Philosophy* 14 (1995): 149–84, at pp. 178–79, n. 41. For further brief mention of this strategy, see my "Ancient Wrongs and Modern Rights," *Philosophy & Public Affairs* 10 (1981): 3–17, at p. 8, and the introduction to my *Approximate Justice: Studies in Non-Ideal Theory* (Lanham, Maryland: Rowman and Littlefield, 1997), p. 5. (The latter work also contains versions of "Ancient Wrongs and Modern Rights" and "Compensation and Transworld Personal Identity.")

envision a world from which it is absent but in which little else is (initially) changed. However, things become far murkier when we try to imagine the closest possible world that contains the child of two people who in the actual world were thrown together by the social upheaval associated with some massive injustice such as the slave trade or the Holocaust. Where such an injustice is concerned, every close possible world from which the *injustice* is absent may also be one from which the *child* is absent. If it is, then the question of whether the child is owed compensation may be radically indeterminate.

An illustration may be helpful here. Suppose that in the actual world, the father of a child born into slavery was originally abducted by slave traders from a remote village in southern Africa; and suppose the child's mother was originally abducted from an equally remote village in the north. Suppose, further, that until the slave traders arrived, each village was so isolated that its inhabitants never ventured far abroad. Given the situation as described, there is no ordinary course of events that would have led to the child's conception if the slave traders had not appeared. There are, of course, innumerable possible worlds in which the slave traders do not appear but the child *is* nevertheless conceived, but none are worlds in which "things not directly affected by the wrong [have] in its absence . . . gone on more or less as they in fact did."[12] Because each relevant world differs from the actual world not only in the wrong's absence but also in the addition of one or another adventitious sequence of events sufficient to bring the man and woman together, we find, when we scrutinize these worlds, that we have no real grip on which one is closest to the actual world.

For should we say that the closest relevant world is one in which the man and woman each become the first in their respective villages to set out in search of adventure, grow wealthy in their travels and meet, and have the child in conditions that give him a far better life than he has as a slave? Is it, instead, a world in which the man and woman are driven from their respective villages by famine and drought, meet after surviving hardships that ruin the man's health and drive the woman half mad, and raise the child under conditions that make his lot even *worse* than that of a slave? Is it a world in which the slave traders are replaced by recruiters who lure the man and woman to America where they meet,

12. Simmons, "Historical Rights and Fair Shares," p. 158.

live as impoverished sharecroppers, and raise the child in conditions so straitened as to be indistinguishable from slavery? How, even in principle, could we settle the question of which of these worlds is closest to the actual world? Given how distant from actuality each one is, how much could it matter if one of them *were* marginally closer than the others?

The other strategy for avoiding the non-identity problem that I want to consider is that of dropping the requirement that the individuals to be compensated be the very ones who would have been better off in the absence of the original wrong. This strategy may seem appealing if, first, we cannot find a way to refute the claim that many descendants of the victims of past injustices would not have existed in the absence of those injustices, but, second, we also cannot rid ourselves of the conviction that many of those descendants are now owed compensation. To eliminate the inconsistency in our belief-system, we may be tempted to take the baseline that determines whether the current descendants are owed compensation to be not the level of well-being that *they themselves* would have enjoyed in the absence of the injustice, but rather the levels of well-being of certain other people who exist either in the actual world or in the alternative world in which the injustice has not been done.

This is the position I took in the paper from which I quoted above. I proposed, there, that when a person's low level of well-being can be traced to a previous wrong in whose absence he would not exist, the level of well-being that determines whether he is owed compensation is not the one that he would have enjoyed in any alternative world but rather that of certain related others: perhaps "the average person or the average member of [his] society,"[13] perhaps "all the descendants of [his] antecedents who would have existed if the act which harmed him had not been performed."[14] However, in retrospect, I think these and all similar proposals are highly implausible.

What any such proposal would require, but what I see no way of providing, is a principled explanation of *why* anyone's claims to compensation should depend on any facts about the well-being of any actual or possible others. When a given wrong has caused someone to exist at a certain level of well-being, the significance of the fact that he himself

---

13. "Compensation and Transworld Personal Identity," p. 389.
14. Ibid.

would have been better off in the wrong's absence is to establish that the wrong has made him worse off. By contrast, neither the fact that certain other individuals are currently better off than he is nor the fact that certain others would have been better off in the wrong's absence has any comparable significance. Even if those who would have been better off in the wrong's absence are all descendants of the relevant person's ancestors, the gap between their well-being and his own would only imply that the wrong had made him worse off if, absurdly, having the same ancestors were sufficient to establish personal identity across possible worlds.

These considerations do not render it incoherent to say that persons can be owed compensation for past wrongs that have caused them to be less well off than others; but they do mean that any convincing version of that claim must be backed by an explanation of why it holds. At least offhand, the obvious explanations are, first, that wrongs that make people worse off than others often also cause them to be less well off than they themselves would otherwise be, and, second, that any inequalities that result from such wrongs are objectionable just in themselves. However, if a proponent of the current proposal were to opt for the first explanation, then his account would beg the question against the non-identity problem, while if he were to opt for the second, then he would be vulnerable to the objection, advanced by Christopher Morris against my own earlier essay, that instead of defending transgenerational compensation he has merely "transformed compensation into redistribution."[15] If there is a further explanation that avoids both difficulties, I must confess that I do not see it.

III

Neither the strategies just discussed nor any others that have appeared in the literature seem likely to defeat the non-identity problem. Hence, the history of the discussion so far may appear to favor the conclusion, drawn by Morris from the argument's probabilistic version[16] and by Michael Levin from its non-probabilistic version,[17] that the ideal of

---

15. Morris, "Existential Limits to the Rectification of Past Wrongs," p. 178.
16. Ibid., p. 177.
17. Michael Levin, "Reverse Discrimination, Shackled Runners, and Personal Identity," *Philosophical Studies* 37 (1980): 139–49, p. 143.

transgenerational compensation is simply incoherent. However, we are not yet forced to abandon the intuitions that support that ideal; for at least one further move appears to hold some promise.

Put briefly and (too) abstractly, the line of argument I want to explore is that (1) the unrectified wrongs of previous generations are systematically correlated with certain wrongs done *within* the current generation, and that (2) what look like claims to be compensated for the earlier wrongs are in fact claims to be compensated for the associated recent wrongs—wrongs which, having been done within the current generation, do not give rise to the non-identity problem. To give content to this argument, I shall now elaborate and briefly defend each claim in turn.

1. In saying that the unrectified wrongs of previous generations are systematically correlated with further wrongs done in this one, I do not mean merely that certain types of unjust acts have been performed both in previous generations and in the current generation. Although this claim is no doubt true—witness the persistence of racial discrimination in the United States—it is irrelevant to our concerns because a duty to compensate for an earlier injustice is generally not discharged by compensating for a later injustice of the same type. If Y maliciously destroys X's bicycle at t_1 and then returns to destroy X's stereo at t_2, Y cannot make things right by simply buying X a new stereo. Y must buy X a new bicycle too. Hence, where different tokens of the same type of injustice are concerned, the obligation to compensate for an injustice done at one time cannot be discharged simply by compensating for an injustice done at another.

But being of the same type is not the only way in which injustices done at different times can be related. A different and more relevant pattern of relationship is suggested by Jeremy Waldron's observation that

> [i]nstead of regarding the expropriation of aboriginal lands as an isolated act of injustice that took place at a certain time now relegated firmly to the past, we may think of it as a persisting injustice. The injustice persists, and it is perpetuated by the legal system as long as the land that was expropriated is not returned to those from whom it was taken.[18]

---

18. Jeremy Waldron, "Superseding Historical Injustice," *Ethics* 103 (1992): 4–28, at p. 14.

Although Waldron himself speaks of the original expropriation as a single injustice that persists until it is rectified, we may, with at least as much propriety, speak of the subsequent ongoing failure to return the land as a sequence of injustices each of which is *distinct* from the original unjust expropriation. Indeed, this alternative description actually seems *more* appropriate, given that injustices are individuated in part by their perpetrators and that those who are in a position to return the land always may, and after a certain point must, be different from those who originally expropriated it. It is the relation between these two sorts of wrongs—between an original wrong and the subsequent wrong of failing to rectify it—that I have in mind when I say that the unrectified wrongs of past generations are systematically correlated with certain wrongs done within the current generation.

2. Given this correlation, an obvious strategy for avoiding the non-identity problem is to say that where the child of an original victim of injustice is concerned, the wrong for which he is owed compensation is not the original one, which was done before he was conceived, but rather some subsequent wrongful failure to compensate *for* the original wrong that takes place *after* he is conceived. If we can relocate the compensable wrong to a point within the child's lifetime, then we can guarantee that the child himself *would* have existed if that wrong had not been done. However, to this obvious strategy, there is what may seem an equally obvious objection: namely, that if the child of the original victim would not have existed in the absence of the original injustice, then that child was never owed compensation *for* the original injustice, and hence was not treated unjustly by any subsequent failure to provide it. In light of this objection, is the strategy of avoiding the problem by relocating the time of the compensable wrong not doomed from the start?

In fact, it is not; for even if the post-conception wrong for which the child is owed compensation cannot be a wrongful failure to compensate *him*, it still may be a wrongful failure to compensate his *parent*. Because the child's parent *was* an original victim of the injustice, he clearly would have existed if the injustice had not been done. Thus, the child's parent, unlike the child himself, can indeed be owed compensation for the original injustice. If he is, then he is done a further wrong when he is *not* compensated, and this further wrong, having been repeated at every moment since the original injustice, has a fortiori been repeated at every moment since the child was conceived. Because it is perfectly coherent to say that the child would be better off if one of these post-conception wrongs had not been done, it must also be coherent to say that the child is owed compensation for that post-conception wrong's effects.

Is the latter claim merely coherent, or might it also be true? To see that it may well be true, we need only remind ourselves that if the wrong of not compensating the parent after the child's conception had not been done, the result would have been an improvement not only in the parent's level of well-being but also in the parent's ability to provide for the child. Hence, given only the uncontroversial assumption that improvements in the ability of parents to provide for their children are generally accompanied by improvements in what is provided, it follows that the child probably *would* have been better off if the wrong of not compensating his parent after he was conceived had not been done.

Because the wrongful failure to compensate the parent after the child's conception has probably made the child worse off, the child may well be owed some compensation for its effects. However, the question of *how much* compensation the child might be owed is trickier; for that depends on a number of further considerations including (a) how much better off the parent would have been after the child's conception if the original wrong had not been done; (b) how much, in addition to what the parent was then owed as compensation for the original wrong, he was owed as compensation for the further injustice of withholding it; and (c) how much better off fully compensating the parent after the child's conception would have made the child in the normal course of events. Given the tangle of empirical and conceptual questions that these considerations raise, the only thing we can conclude with certainty is that the child is likely to be owed at least some compensation for the wrongful failure to compensate his parent after he was conceived.

Because this result is so vague, it may seem unlikely that the amount of compensation that the child is owed for the wrongful failure to compensate his parent will match the amount that we take him to be owed as compensation for the original injustice. A disparity between these amounts would be troubling because it would undermine the plausibility of the proposal that what looks like the child's claim to be compensated for the original injustice is really a claim to be compensated for the more recent one. However, in fact, there is no disparity; for because there is no truth of the matter about how much better off the child would have been in the absence of the original injustice, there is also no definite amount that the child appears, on reflection, to be owed as compensation for it. Because the only definite intuition is that the child is owed *something*, my proposal captures this intuition whenever compensating the parent would have made the child at least somewhat better off. It does not capture the intuition in the relatively few cases in which compensating the parent would *not* have made the child better off; but because such cases are both infrequent and hard to identify, our intuitions about them may simply be an overgeneralization from the more usual situation.[19] Thus, all in all, the objection that my conclusion is too vague to capture our intuitions has very little bite.

So far, I have argued only that we can avoid the non-identity problem when we are dealing with persons who are a single generation removed from the original injustice. The argument I have made, however, can clearly be generalized. If the child of an original victim of an injustice can be owed compensation for a wrongful failure to compensate that victim after the child is conceived, then the grandchild of the original victim can in turn be owed compensation for a wrongful failure to compensate the *child* after the *grandchild* is conceived; and the same holds, mutatis mutandis, for the original victim's great-grandchild, great-great-grandchild, and so on. This of course does not mean that the descendants of the victims of ancient wrongs must be owed as much compensation as are the descendants of the victims of recent ones—there is, I think, independent reason to believe that they generally are not[20]—but it does mean that if we can solve the non-identity problem

---

19. By thus acknowledging that it is hard to determine whether, and if so to what degree, any given parent would have benefitted his child if he had been compensated, I may appear to imply that such counterfactuals are no less indeterminate than the ones upon which Simmons's approach was seen to rest. However, the problem with the different stories about how the parents of a child born into slavery might have met in a world without slavery was that they all involved such massive departures from actuality that no one of them seemed any better suited than any of the others to support a counterfactual about how well off the child would have been. For this reason, I concluded that there was simply no (morally significant) truth of the matter. By contrast, in the current case, the indeterminacy is merely epistemic: if any counterfactuals can be true—and to deny this would be to reject the presupposition upon which all claims to compensation rest—then counterfactuals about what particular individuals would have done if compensated are surely among them.

20. My reasons can be found in "Ancient Wrongs and Modern Rights." For related discussion, see David Lyons, "The New Indian Claims and the Original Rights to Land," *Social Theory and Practice* 4 (1977): 249–72 and Waldron, "Superseding Historical Injustice."

for the first generation after an injustice, then we can also solve it for each succeeding generation.

IV

My main aim has been to sketch a theoretical account of how (something like) transgenerational compensation might be possible despite the non-identity problem. That aim, I hope, has been achieved. Even if it has, however, there are certain contexts in which compensation is not obviously inappropriate, yet in which the proposed account appears to fail. To assess the threat that such contexts pose, I will end by briefly examining three problematic types of case, which will be discussed in ascending order of difficulty.

The first problematic type of case is one in which the original victim dies before his child is conceived. If, for instance, someone's sexual exertions cause him to suffer a fatal heart attack just before the child's conception, or someone is killed in an automobile accident after making a sperm or egg donation but before the scheduled artificial insemination or fertilization can take place, then there is no moment at which the child and the original victim both exist. Hence, a fortiori, there is no moment at which the child exists and the original victim is wrongfully denied compensation for the original injustice. Thus, if the child's being owed compensation depends on his having been made worse off by a wrongful failure to compensate his parent at some point after his conception, then the child cannot be owed compensation here.[21] But is it

---

21. Some authors, when discussing what is owed to the children of the uncompensated victims of wrongdoing, have attempted to detach the grounds for compensating those children from the claim that they would have been better off if the original victims *had* been compensated. Their thinking is that if the original victim was owed a certain amount as compensation, then that amount is part of his rightful estate and so is owed to his actual descendants for reasons independent of whether they would have better off if he had been compensated. This proposal, which has been advanced by Stephen Kershnar, "Are the Descendants of Slaves Owed Compensation for Slavery?" *Journal of Applied Philosophy* 16 (1999): 95–101, and by Bernard Boxill, "A Lockean Argument for Black Reparations," *The Journal of Ethics* 7 (2003): 63–91, would if successful enable us to make sense of transgenerational compensation without addressing the non-identity problem. However, although I cannot argue the point here, I strongly doubt that the proposal *is* successful. To cite just one difficulty, I think there are serious problems with the claim that the original victim is morally if not legally the "owner" of whatever compensation he is owed but has not received. If this claim cannot be defended, then the argument's conclusion, that the ownership of any compensation owed the original victim automatically passes to whichever persons are his actual heirs, will not be defensible either.

really plausible to take the child's eligibility for compensation to depend on whether his parent dies just before or just after he is conceived?

This question draws its force from our sense that the timing of the child's conception should not matter this much, that if he can be made worse off by a wrong done just after his conception, then he also can be made worse off by a wrong done just before it. However, precisely because the difficulty has this source, the natural way to accommodate it is simply to adopt a criterion of personal identity across possible worlds that does *not* treat such differences in timing as crucial. Of the criteria that we have discussed, the branching criterion does make the timing of the wrong crucial, since the moment at which the wrong occurs is the moment at which a world without it branches away from the actual world. By contrast, the same-sperm-and-egg criterion does *not* make the timing of the wrong crucial, since by that criterion what matters is only whether the very sperm and egg that unite in the actual world that contains the wrong would also unite in a world without it. Thus, properly understood, what this first type of case shows is not that there is any problem with my proposal that what the child is owed compensation for are the effects of the wrongful failure to compensate his parent, but only that that proposal will not capture all of our intuitions unless it is coupled with a same-sperm-and-egg criterion of personal identity across possible worlds rather than a branching criterion.

At first glance, this rejoinder may not seem entirely satisfactory, since we can also imagine a case in which the same heart attack or accident that kills the original victim before the child's conception has the further effect of determining which sperm unites with which egg. As one of the editors of *Philosophy & Public Affairs* has dryly noted, "one might expect the experience of someone suffering a fatal heart attack during lovemaking with you to have some effect on one's pattern of behavior." However, what follows from this (obviously correct) observation is not that the uncompensated heart attack victim would have had a different child if he had been compensated, but only that he would have had a different child if he had not had a heart attack. This is entirely consistent with my claim that the actual child—the one who is in fact conceived after the heart attack—would also have existed, but would have been better off, if the original victim had been compensated *before* the heart attack.

Transgenerational Compensation

Consider, next, a type of case in which, as above, the original victim dies before the child is conceived, but in which, in addition, the original victim's being compensated at any moment prior to his death would have resulted in the child's *not being* conceived. One way to flesh out this possibility is to suppose that if the victim had been compensated, then he would have used part of the proceeds to purchase contraception for use in the sexual encounter that precipitated his heart attack. Alternatively, we may suppose that the victim's failure to secure compensation was both what induced him to seek solace by donating to the sperm bank and the occasion of the deep depression that led him to take his own life immediately after attempting to secure the only immortality to which he was still able to aspire.

In this type of case as in the first, the original victim dies before the child is conceived. Thus, here again, there is no post-conception failure (or simultaneous-with-conception failure) to compensate the original victim in the absence of which the child would be better off. However, in the current type of case, the child also would not have come into existence if the original victim had been compensated *before* what is in fact the moment of conception, and so there is also no *pre*-conception failure to compensate the original victim in the absence of which the child would be better off. Because these two possibilities are exhaustive, they jointly rule out the possibility that there is *any* failure to compensate the original victim in the absence of which the child would be better off. Hence, where cases of this second type are concerned, my account really does imply that the child is not owed compensation.

Just how damaging this implication is will depend on how strong an intuition we have that the child *is* owed compensation. We clearly have no such intuition in the sperm- or egg-donation case; for if the original victim is merely the source of the sperm that eventually fertilizes an unknown woman's egg or the egg that is eventually fertilized by an unknown man's sperm, then even if the original victim had lived, it is immensely unlikely either that that victim would either have done anything to provide for the resulting child or stood in any significant moral relation to it. The intuition's absence is less clear in the heart attack case, since here we *can* presume both that the original victim would have provided for his child if he had lived and that he would have provided for the child at a higher level if he had lived and been compensated (but the contraceptive had failed) than if he had lived and *not* been compensated. However, because this comparison turns on a new and unlikely supposition (the contraceptive failure) that is extrinsic to the original case, its moral significance is at best unclear. Thus, here again, the implication that the child is owed no compensation may be one that we can simply accept.[22]

Although the first two types of case are undoubtedly problematic, they do not, in my opinion, seriously threaten the account I have proposed. However, the last type of case that I will consider is threatening indeed, and I can at the moment see no fully satisfactory way of dealing with it. Thus, to conclude my discussion, I will simply lay out the difficulty as I see it.

The seriously problematic type of case is one in which the effects of the original wrong that intuitively appear to give the child a claim to compensation are causally independent of any recent failure to compensate the original victim. As a simple example, consider a case in which either the original injustice or a subsequent unjust failure to compensate for it irremediably worsens the original victim's character when he is young, and in which his child, conceived many years later, is treated badly as a result. Here compensating the original victim after the child's conception, or even slightly before it, will have no effect at all on how the child is treated. By then the original victim's character will long have been formed, and so compensating him will not improve his treatment of the child. Morever, if the original victim had been compensated early enough to forestall the deterioration of his character, then his subsequent behavior would surely have been different enough to prevent that particular child from being conceived. Because the child has therefore not been made worse off by the effects of any wrong in whose absence

---

22. A further variant of the heart attack case, in which the heart attack itself is not only the cause of the relevant sperm's uniting with the relevant egg but also an effect of the victim's stress at not being compensated, requires different treatment again. At first glance, this may appear to be another of the cases in which compensating the original victim at any point while he was alive would have prevented his actual child from coming into existence. However, as long as there was any interval at all between the time at which the accumulated stresses rendered the heart attack inevitable and the time of the heart attack itself, there must also be a series of wrongful failures to compensate the victim in whose absence his actual child—the one who is conceived as a result of the heart attack—would still have existed but would have been better off. Because the relevant counterfactual can therefore be true, this variant is not a counterexample to my account at all.

he still would exist, we are again forced to conclude that he cannot be owed compensation.

As in the previous type of case, we cannot here avoid the difficulty by adjusting the time of the relevant wrongful failure to compensate the original victim. However, unlike cases of the previous type, at least some cases with the current structure *do* appear to elicit firm intuitions that the child is now owed compensation. We may not have a firm intuition to that effect when the child's poor treatment is due to the original victim's bad character, since even if the original victim was himself corrupted by the original injustice, we may feel that he alone is responsible for any harm he subsequently does. However, the intuition that the child is owed compensation becomes stronger when we take the relevant effect of the original injustice to consist not of the original victim's moral corruption, but rather of his justifiably coming to believe that the deck is stacked heavily against him and so acquiring a demoralized, defeatist attitude. It becomes stronger yet when we substitute the effect of fostering, within the group to which the original victim belongs, a broader set of attitudes that are unconducive to happiness, achievement, or success.

To reconcile the proposed account with this final type of case, I must either offer a reason to discount any intuition that the original victim's child is here owed compensation or else argue that despite appearances, there *is* some recent wrongful failure to compensate for the original injustice in whose absence he would be better off. A possible way of pursuing the first strategy is to stress the degree to which the causal sequence that runs from the original injustice to the child's current low level of well-being is mediated by the choices of others; a possible way of pursuing the second is to argue that the attitudes in which those mediating choices are grounded are harmful to their possessors as well as the child, and that the failure to eliminate them after the child's conception is therefore itself a wrongful failure to compensate for the original wrong's effects. However, before we could develop either proposal (and, a fortiori, before we could adjudicate between them), we would have to address a number of hard questions both about responsibility and about the relations between persons and their attitudes and traits. These topics, clearly, require far more discussion than can be provided here. Thus, for now, my conclusion is simply that the best response to the non-identity problem may be one whose implications coincide only imperfectly with our intuitions about when transgenerational compensation is warranted.

V

This article offers a technical solution to a technical problem. It seeks to explain how we can make sense of the idea that someone can be owed compensation for the effects of a wrong in whose absence he would never have existed. Because the case for compensating such individuals has turned out to rest on at least two different counterfactuals—because, for example, the case for compensating the child of an original victim has been seen to depend partly on how much better off that victim would have been if he had been compensated after the child's conception, partly on how much better off the child would have been if the victim had then been compensated—the proposed account does not advance, but if anything sets back further, our ability to acquire enough information to know how much any actual individual is owed. However, because we had no hope of acquiring that much knowledge in any event, the additional layer of impracticality is not significant. Moreover, in another respect, the account may actually represent a practical advance; for by revealing the normative structure of a coherent ideal of transgenerational compensation, it compels us to confront the practical implications of the inscrutability of the counterfactuals upon which the ideal rests. Should we react to our irremediable ignorance by abandoning the goal of compensating for wrongs that go back more than a generation? Should we instead seek a workable approximation of what we can never know? If the latter, what principles would determine whether our approximation was close enough? These are the hard theoretical questions about practice to which an adequate solution to the non-identity problem is a mere (though indispensable) preliminary.

[20]

Who Can Be Wronged?

RAHUL KUMAR

I. INTRODUCTION

Imagine that a child is born with severe restrictions on the quality of her life, and that her parents might have prevented such an outcome if they had taken certain precautions prior to conception.[1] Depending on how certain other relevant considerations are filled out, such as how reasonable it was to have expected the child's parents to have taken the necessary pre-conception measures and what the circumstances were that resulted in their failure to do so, many are inclined to believe that it is at least arguable that the child has been wronged by her parents' failure. Those who are skeptical of this possibility, however, argue that the intuitive appeal of this line of thought is a result of overlooking a further relevant consideration: that taking the appropriate precautions would have significantly delayed conception.[2] Drawing upon the lesson of what Derek Parfit has labeled the *non-identity problem*, they argue that the legitimacy of a person's claim to have been wronged requires that the psycho-physical identity of the wronged not be what it is because of the

---

Early versions of this article were presented at the University of Washington (Seattle), the Harvard Program for Ethics and the Professions, a meeting of the PHILAMORE group, and the BSET Conference at the University of Reading. Thanks to the participants on these occasions for helpful discussions of the material. For invaluable conversations that helped me clarify my position, I am particularly indebted to Samuel Freeman, Maggie Little, Lukas Meyer, Derek Parfit, Tim Scanlon, David Silver, Gopal Sreenivasan, and Andrew Williams. Many thanks are also owed to an anonymous reader for *Philosophy & Public Affairs* for extensive and insightful written comments that resulted in innumerable improvements to all aspects of the paper.

1. Assume that her prospects, though limited, are good enough that the child's life is certainly objectively worth living.

2. A nice statement of the skeptical position is advanced in A. Buchanan, D. W. Brock, N. Daniels, and D. Wilker, *From Chance to Choice: Genetics and Justice* (Cambridge: Cambridge University Press, 2000), pp. 226–57.

wrongdoing.[3] On this view, a person can only claim to have been wronged by the conduct or decision of another if she has been harmed as a result of the relevant conduct or decision, and that a person is harmed if and only if she is left worse-off than she otherwise would have been. The very possibility of being left worse-off than one otherwise would have been requires that the psycho-physical identity of the person on whose behalf the claim is being made remain fixed between the world as it is and the counter-factual world to which it is to be compared. For this reason, it is argued, the fact that the taking of appropriate precautions would have significantly altered the timing of conception must be a morally relevant consideration, because the time of conception is an identity-fixing consideration.

In this discussion, I argue that the skeptical position about the *possibility* of wronging in such cases is not warranted. Whether or not the child has in fact been wronged requires the filling in of further facts concerning, e.g., the circumstances of the parents' failure to have taken appropriate precautions, and substantive moral argument to show the expectation that they take such precautions to have been a reasonable one. The matter cannot be settled by conceptual fiat.

For purposes of argument, I accept that the fact of the parents' failure to take appropriate pre-conception precautions is a consideration that is relevant for fixing the child's psycho-physical personal identity. What I take to be mistaken is the idea that the kinds of considerations identified by the non-identity problem, concerning the fixity of psycho-physical personal identity, are morally relevant for reasoning about whether or not one person has been wronged by another. The idea is mistaken, I suggest, irrespective of whether or not one also takes such considerations to be irrelevant for understanding what it is to have been harmed. Key to this argument is the distinction between the wronging and the harming of another. The kinds of considerations that are relevant for determining whether or not a person has been harmed have primarily to do with the state of the person who claims to have been harmed. Whether or not another has wronged one, on the other hand, has primarily to do with facts concerning the character of the wrongdoer's regulation of her conduct with respect to how she has related to the wronged.

---

3. See Derek Parfit, *Reasons and Persons* (Oxford: Oxford University Press, 1984), pp. 351–79.

Who Can Be Wronged?

By accepting, for the sake of argument, the metaphysical presuppositions of the non-identity problem, I do not mean to suggest that they cannot be fruitfully challenged. Rather, what I will argue is that the moral relevance of the considerations to which the non-identity problem draws attention depends upon an understanding of *wronging* that incorporates certain ideas about moral reasoning that have a natural home in consequentialist accounts of moral reasoning. In particular, the idea that the fundamental kinds of considerations that are relevant for determining whether or not one has been wronged have to do with outcomes, or more generally, with *what happens*, is taken to be an uncontroversial matter. As an implicit component of the skeptic's argument, this consequentialist-influenced approach to the explication of what it is to have been wronged is assumed but not defended. My claim is that if one instead adopts a plausible, distinctively non-consequentialist characterization of reasoning about wronging, it turns out that considerations concerning the fixity of psycho-physical personal identity can be shown to be of no moral relevance. This alternative characterization can also be fruitfully used to develop a plausible rationale for how it is possible for the child to have been wronged by her parents' failure to pursue appropriate precautions. The non-identity problem, then, need not be taken to pose a challenge to reasonably common convictions concerning who can be wronged.

The non-identity problem, I believe, only presents a serious challenge to common intuitions concerning who can be wronged when one accepts the idea that a person having been wronged necessarily requires that the wronged be left worse-off than she would have been had the wrongdoing not taken place. Call this the *outcome approach* to understanding the idea of wronging, as it is one that is most likely to appeal to those who are generally inclined to take facts about outcomes as fundamental for understanding moral wrongness. There are, however, also further considerations that are relevant to an account of its intuitive appeal.

Towards this end, consider first the standard consequentialist characterization of objective moral wrongness. It takes the fundamental relevant considerations for moral reasoning to be those that concern the aggregate value of the outcome that was brought about in comparison to others that could have been brought about. Moral wrongs in this sense are impersonal wrongs; what is objectionable is bringing about a worse outcome, regardless of whether or not it is worse *for* any particular individual.

Appeals to having been *wronged*, on the other hand, concern a distinct sense of moral wrongness, one at work in contexts where the claim is not impersonal, but is made by, or on behalf of, an individual who is the *victim* of the wrongdoing. Being wronged as a distinct category of moral wrongness is an idea closely associated with non-consequentialism; consequentialists do not generally accept that there is such a distinct category. The outcome approach to explicating wrongs in this distinct sense is one, however, that retains consequentialist remnants, insofar as it treats a claim to have been wronged as fundamentally having to do with how the outcome that has been brought about is *worse for the particular person wronged*, rather than being worse in impersonal or aggregative terms. The intuitive appeal of this approach is often bolstered by presenting it as the view that a person has been wronged only if she has been harmed, and that a person is harmed if and only if she is left worse-off than she otherwise would have been. The characterization of 'harm' here takes it to be a necessarily comparative concept, but neither it nor any concept of harm is an essential element to this approach.[4] What is necessary for a claim to have been wronged, on these terms, is that the counter-factual judgment, that a person has been left worse-off than she otherwise would have been had the wronging not occurred, be a plausible one.

As an account of what it is to be wronged, this approach has its intuitive appeal. A claim to have been wronged suggests that something has been done to the claimant, such that it is appropriate to think of her as the victim of the wrongdoing. The suggestion that the claimant's complaint must necessarily have to do with how she has been left worse-off (in some morally significant way) than she otherwise would have been, is a powerful way of spelling out this intuitive appeal. Connecting the

---

4. The widespread understanding of harm amongst consequentialists as an essentially comparative concept suggests that the way they often understand harm is as a catchall for the class of considerations they countenance as morally significant. This class includes considerations that have nothing to do with how the concept is typically employed, e.g., the view may count very well-off people as 'harmed' because they were not made as well-off as they might have been. Though such failures may be morally significant according to the consequentialist, they are not the kind of consideration that intuitively come to mind when one thinks of harms. "Harms" on this view, at least intuitively, have to do with a significant *setback* to one's goals or interests, in contrast to merely advancing them less than one had hoped. Hence, it should be noted just how revisionist the consequentialist use of "harm" has turned out to be.

idea of being left 'worse-off in some morally significant way' with the concept of harm further bolsters the conviction that there is something 'right' about this approach.

On closer scrutiny, however, it proves to be inadequate. The root of its inadequacy has to do with a commitment that is fundamental, though no doubt not exclusive, to the outcome approach, namely the accounting for what it is to be wronged in terms of what has *happened* to the victim. Can't a person have been wronged without anything having happened to her? Isn't it conceivable that she may be left no worse-off as a result of having been wronged?

Consider, for example, the case of a drunk driver who comes swerving along the street where you happen to be taking a late evening stroll, thereby momentarily imperiling your life. Luckily, nothing *happens* to you; the whole incident takes place so quickly, you don't even have time to be frightened. You are not, therefore, in any way worse-off as a result of your life having been put at risk. As the risk did not in fact blossom into an actual harm, or end up setting back one's interests in any way, any talk of one having been left worse-off as a result of the drunk driver's conduct would be, in this case, misplaced.

But there is nothing suspect about the claim that one has been wronged by the drunk driver (expressed, perhaps, as resentment of him or anger directed towards him), simply in virtue of his having, without justification, taken your life in his hands by exposing you, even briefly, to so serious a risk. An adequate analysis of being wronged ought to be able to make good sense of our intuitions in this kind of case, rather than identify them as suspect because they do not involve anyone being left worse-off, or harmed.

Being left worse-off as a result of having been wronged is not, of course, an unusual occurrence. It turns out, however, that the consequentialist analysis fares no better in making sense of claims to have been wronged in examples which do involve something happening to the victim. Such claims have a distinctive character that simply cannot be accounted for in terms of considerations having to do with what has happened to a person, such as having been harmed.

Take, for example, the case of the hiker who steps on an animal trap lying on the trail, resulting in a serious injury to her foot. She has certainly been harmed, but it would be intuitively odd to assess the incident as one in which she has been wronged. Say, however, that it turns out that trap lying on the trail was not a fluke occurrence, but was in fact placed on the trail by the owner of the property that the trail traverses, as a way of discouraging hikers from venturing on to her land. This variation to the example makes no difference to what has happened to the hiker; her injury is no worse, nor is she generally worse-off because the trap lying in the trail turned out to be the result of the property owner's machinations. The difference such added information does make is that it justifies her claiming the incident to be one in which she was not only harmed, but one in which she has been *wronged*. Why this is so is difficult to make good sense of using the resources of any approach, like the outcome approach, to understanding interpersonal wrongdoing that takes the fundamental class of relevant considerations to be about outcomes.

The outcome approach, then, proves to be intuitively dubious quite apart from its revisionist implications concerning who can be wronged that stem from its endorsement of the non-identity problem. For it fails to isolate the kinds of considerations that are intuitively relevant for assessing whether a person's conduct constitutes a distinctively *moral* transgression, of the kind for which a person may be held accountable. It may be that a person's conduct has resulted in harm befalling another, or another being born in a bad-off state, whose status as a harmed being turns on what one takes to be the most plausible account of the nature of harm.[5] Settling a question of whether or not conduct has resulted in harm will not, however, intuitively settle whether the conduct was morally faulty. Conduct may result in another being harmed without it being a moral violation, and a person's conduct may be correctly assessed as morally defective even though it did not resulted in anyone being harmed. The kinds of considerations that I take to be intuitively relevant for assessing the morality of a person's conduct are those having to do with the character of the conduct itself, taken apart from its consequences. It is to these kinds of considerations that I believe one is directed in thinking about whether a person has been *wronged*. And as these considerations do not concern outcomes, it is reasonable to think that conclusions concerning wronging may not be sensitive to the same kinds of counter-factual considerations that can cast doubt on certain intuitive judgments concerning whether or not a person has been harmed.

---

5. I have in mind here questions concerning the plausibility of a counter-factual analysis of whether or not a person has been harmed. See the helpful discussion of this matter in Seana Shiffrin, "Wrongful Life, Procreative Responsibility, and the Significance of Harm," *Legal Theory* 5 (1999): 117–48.

The non-consequentialist conviction, broadly stated, is that *what one does* has an intrinsic significance in moral reasoning that is independent of *what happens* as a result of what one does. It is to the moral significance of what the wrongdoer has done, or more precisely, how the wrongdoer has related to the wronged (quite apart from the consequences for the victim), that the non-consequentialist turns in order to account for the distinctive character of a claim to have been wronged.

Now, a plausible characterization of the relation between wrongdoer and wronged needs to be one in which the former's offense is fundamentally an offense against the latter. This is to suggest that the basis of the offense should fundamentally focus on why the wrong in question constitutes a failure of the wrongdoer to respect the status of the wronged as a being worthy of respect. The outcome approach's appeal to the victim having been made *worse-off* as a result of having been wronged appears to satisfy this desideratum quite nicely, despite the approach's dubious overall plausibility. The challenge for a non-consequentialist account of wronging, that can be shown to be invulnerable to the non-identity problem, is to avoid cashing out the basis of the victim's complaint against the wrongdoer in counter-factual terms.

The resources of Scanlonian contractualism are helpful for illustrating a plausible non-consequentialist approach to the characterization of what it is to have been wronged that both evades the non-identity problem and vindicates commonsense convictions concerning who can be wronged.[6] The argument I put forward does not, however, require acceptance of the entire contractualist account of wronging. Although the argument does have implications for how contractualism ought to be understood, its role here is primarily as a helpful vehicle for illustrating a general non-consequentialist strategy for deflating the challenge of the non-identity problem.

II. REASONING ABOUT WRONGING: THE CONTRACTUALIST APPROACH

Contractualism aims to provide a plausible framework for explicating the rationales of the principles, or normative standards, of that aspect of morality concerned with the regulation of interpersonal conduct and

---

6. See T. M. Scanlon, *What We Owe to Each Other* (Cambridge: Harvard University Press, 1998).

consideration. Relating to one another on terms of mutual respect for one another's value as persons requires compliance with these principles.

Though the moral wrongs of this domain are those having to do with one person having *wronged* another person by having related to her in a certain way, the view does not characterize a claim of having been wronged as requiring an appeal to how one has been (or stands to be) made *worse-off* than one otherwise would have been. Rather, a claim to have been wronged requires that certain *legitimate expectations*, to which one is entitled in virtue of a valid moral principle, have been violated.

The interpersonal role of moral principles, as contractualism characterizes it, is analogous to that of laws in a legal system: they fix what the general terms are for relating to one another on a basis of mutual respect for one another's value as persons, by establishing certain legitimate expectations concerning consideration and conduct between persons.[7] What can be legitimately expected of one varies, of course, according to the character of the relationship one stands in with respect to another person. A relationship of a particular kind can, in fact, be distinguished from others on the basis of the distinctive cluster of legitimate expectations that is characteristic of that kind of relationship, the regulation of one's conduct in light of which is at least partially constitutive of what it is to stand in a relationship of that particular kind with respect to another.[8]

The appeal to "persons" here should be understood to be an appeal to a specific *normative* ideal of the person, the salient characteristic of which is the capacity for rational self-governance in pursuit of a meaningful life. Following Scanlon, this normative ideal of the *rational self-governor* should be understood to comprise two distinct claims: First, that persons are creatures capable of recognizing, and acting upon, reasons. This places them amongst a select group of those animals capable of intentional action. Second, that persons "have the capacity to select among the various ways there is reason to want a life to go, and therefore to govern and live that life in an active sense."[9] The capacity to select among reasons is a specific way of exercising a general capacity to

---

7. "Legitimate expectations" is used here as a term of art, insofar as the expectations are normative, not psychological.

8. On this point, see my "Defending the Moral Moderate: Contractualism and Commonsense," *Philosophy & Public Affairs* 28 (2000): 275–309.

9. Scanlon, p. 105.

reflect upon one's reasons, often referred to as the capacity to form *second-order* beliefs, or rational attitudes, about one's beliefs and attitudes. In other words, a person has the capacity not only to be guided by her beliefs about reasons, but also to reflect upon whether her beliefs are correct, select among her beliefs in ways that allow her to shape her life in distinctive ways, and reflect upon the quality of her selections. It is this general capacity, without which self-knowledge would not be possible, which distinguishes persons from other animals capable of intentional behavior. More importantly, it is in virtue of this capacity that there is the possibility of what Philippa Foot refers to as "second-order evil" in human life, which has to do with "the *consciousness* of being disregarded, lonely or oppressed."[10] The capacity to be conscious of reasons results, then, in a distinct kind of vulnerability, a vulnerability to what another's reasons, or reasoning, concerning how it is appropriate to relate to oneself, says about oneself.

One person wronging another, then, requires that the wrongdoer has, without adequate excuse or justification, violated certain legitimate expectations with which the wronged party was entitled, in virtue of her value as a person, to have expected her to comply. Returning to the previous example, a rough account of why the drunk driver has wronged the pedestrian ought to appeal to the failure to comply with the pedestrian's legitimate expectation of the driver that she operate her vehicle in a manner conducive to keeping the risk at which others are put as a result of her activity within certain acceptable limits.

Note that to have "not complied" with certain legitimate expectations should be read broadly in this context: it is not just a matter of having failed to conduct oneself in a certain way. It can also be understood as a failure to have been responsive to certain considerations that it was legitimate to expect one to have been responsive, or to have taken into account considerations that it was reasonable to have expected one to have disregarded as irrelevant for one's deliberations at that time. For example, your best friend may be the person best qualified for a position, and that is a good reason to hire her; to hire her because she is your best friend, however, is to wrong her. She may be your friend, but where professional matters are concerned, she is entitled to expect you to relate to

---

10. Philippa Foot, "Rationality and Virtue" in *Norms, Values, and Society*, ed. Herlinde Pauer-Studer (Netherlands: Kluwer, 1994), p. 210.

her as a fellow professional, assessing her on the basis of her qualifications as a professional.

This is only to gesture at the possibilities that might count as ways of culpably failing to comply with the legitimate expectations that another may be entitled to have of one, and in so failing, of wronging her. The essential point to note here is that the contractualist characterization of being wronged emphasizes the culpable failure of the wrongdoer, rather than how the wrongdoer has left the wronged worse-off than she otherwise would have been. A claim to have been wronged, then, does not require making the kind of counter-factual appeal that would leave it vulnerable to the challenge of the non-identity problem.

The contractualist account is not, however, insensitive to the importance of the intuitions that underwrite the appeal of analyzing wronging in terms of counter-factual claims. Recall that the intuition is that for a person to have been wronged, the grounds for the complaint against the wrongdoer must appeal to how the wrong in question has resulted in the wronged being made *worse-off* than she otherwise would have been. In more general terms, the idea is that a formal characterization of claiming to have been wronged ought to restrict the range of considerations that might be appealed to as the basis for a particular claim of having wronged another to those that concern the negative implications *for the victim* of the wrongdoing.

This thought finds expression in the contractualist analysis of wronging through its *individual reasons restriction*, which isolates as morally relevant for the justification of principles that regulate individual relations only those considerations that have a bearing upon the recognition of the status of a person as one capable of rational self-government.[11] The restriction should be read broadly enough to encompass considerations that anyone has reason to care about in the early stages of the developmental path that generally results in the realization of the capacity for rational self-governance.

Some such relevant considerations will not relate to an individual's current or future welfare. Rather, they may concern the requisites for

11. In *What We Owe to Each Other*, Scanlon puts forward a restriction of this kind. He calls it the "personal reasons restriction." Though I agree with the substance of the restriction, I worry that his term can be very misleading. I discuss this in "Reasonable Reasons in Contractualist Moral Argument" (manuscript).

interpersonal relations on terms of mutual respect. This is important for contractualism's claim to be able to account for how it is that a person can be *wronged* without being *harmed*. One person may wrong another without leaving that person worse-off through such things as insults, humiliations, intentional slights, "looking through a person," expressions of a lack of trust, many kinds of paternalism, and, in general, interfering with an aspect of a person's life over which she rightly has sole sovereignty. For though one may not have made the other worse-off, the way in which one has related to the other may still express a failure to have appropriately recognized and taken account of a person's value as capable of rational self-governance. A person can be wronged, then, simply in virtue of how she figures, or does not figure, in how one is rationally disposed to relate to her.

The denial of the value of one's humanity may sound abstract. But, in fact, we see its effects every day: the way in which some are treated or seen by others can undermine a person's sense of her own worth, dignity, self-confidence, and so forth, resulting in inferiority complexes, a sense of worthlessness, abasement, despair, and other kinds of general diminution of a person's capacity for independent agency. Note, though, that these are only common consequences of having been wronged, not the grounds for claiming to have been wronged. Harm, then, may result from being wronged without being the basis of a claim to have been wronged. A wrongdoing need not, in fact, have any consequences of this kind for it to be true that a wronging has transpired, and for the wronging in question to be one that is seriously objectionable.

The individual reasons restriction is essential for contractualism's being able to do justice to the initial intuition that a person's being wronged consists in something having been done to *her*, the force of which needs to be accounted for in light of the implications for *her life*. It does so by securing the connection between culpably failing to comply with the legitimate expectations of another—or *wronging* another—and a failure to have appropriately recognized her status as a person in one's understanding of how it is appropriate to relate to her. While rejecting the idea that having been wronged has to do with having been left worse-off, then, contractualism can be understood as recognizing the importance of the intuition to which this idea appeals, namely that to be an instance of a wronging, an action must be such that it can make the kind of difference to a person that can be appealed to as a basis of a claim to have been wronged.

III. THE NON-IDENTITY *PROBLEM*?

In directing attention to the violation of legitimate expectations as the basis of a claim to have been wronged, contractualism implicitly shifts the focus from what has *happened* to the person wronged to *what was done*. The shift in focus is the crucial move that makes it possible to then declare contractualism to be immune to the non-identity problem.

A declaration of immunity may, however, be thought to be somewhat hasty. Contractualism claims that being wronged has to do with the culpable violation of certain legitimate expectations, compliance with which was owed to one in virtue of one's status as a person. But in the relevant kind of case, i.e., pre-conception negligence cases, it is not obvious that it makes sense to speak of a child having been wronged by a culpable failure to comply with certain legitimate expectations. How can there be an issue concerning one's failure to have complied with the legitimate expectations of a person if, at the time of acting, there was no determinate person to whom compliance with those expectations was owed? Insofar as a particular person did not exist at the time of the relevant conduct, *she* cannot claim to have been wronged by that conduct, especially in light of the fact that, had it not been for the course of conduct about which she believes she has a legitimate complaint, she would never have even come into being. The challenge of the non-identity problem has not, it appears, been evaded, as it is easily recast in contractualist terms: how can one have wronged another when there was no "other" who stood to be wronged by one's conduct at the time of that conduct, and who is now the particular person she is because of the conduct in virtue of which she takes herself to have been wronged?

To see how the resources of contractualism may be marshaled to respond to this challenge, start by considering a quite ordinary case of thinking about what one owes another. Say, for instance, that it has been a long day, and you are feeling tired and would like to go home. What stops you from doing so is that a student has made an appointment to come and see you about some difficulties writing a term paper that is soon due. You know that waiting to see the student and properly working through her problems will keep you at your desk for at least another two hours. You begin to wonder whether there are any steps you can take that would make it morally permissible for you to go home and see the student tomorrow.

Your thinking about what it may be permissible to do can be characterized in contractualist terms as reflecting upon the principles that are relevant for the regulation of promises between teachers and students. Principles, in contractualism, roughly fix what a person, understood here as a *type*, is entitled to expect of another person, in certain *types of situation*, as a matter of respect for her status as a person. Your conclusions, then, concerning what may be legitimately expected of you, under the circumstances, are not specific to yourself as a teacher and the particular student who is coming to see you. Rather, they are conclusions concerning what, in a certain type of situation, a student may legitimately expect of a teacher.

A "type" of person is not, of course, a substantive individual, any more than a "type" of situation is an actual situation.[12] Rather, the "types" in question are simply normatively significant sets of characteristics, whose instantiation together may be found in actual, substantial, individuals, and in the actual situations in which individuals find themselves. An individual, for instance, is a token of the basic type "person" insofar as those facts that are picked out by the type description "person" are true of her.[13] Other type descriptions will be applicable to an individual insofar as that individual exemplifies those characteristics identified as relevant by a different type descriptions, e.g., an individual will count as a student insofar as the kinds of facts isolated as relevant by the type description "student" are true of her. What an individual may legitimately expect of others, and what may be legitimately demanded of her, at a given time turns on both (a) what expectations can in fact be defended on the basis of the relevant principle, and (b) the relevant type descriptions that happen to fit her and her circumstances at that time.

The basic "type" description in contractualism can be understood to be that of the "person," as an individual capable of rational self-governance in pursuit of a meaningful life. Many principles, however, will be concerned

---

12. In general, I take talk of "types" in this discussion to be a convenient way of making singular reference without reference to particulars.
13. The appeal to "facts" here should be broadly construed, so as to include facts about the kinds of relationships one stands in with respect to others.

with the regulation of specific forms of relationship that persons can stand in with respect to one another. Consider, for example,

> M: Those individuals responsible for a child's, or other dependent person's, welfare are morally required not to let her suffer a serious harm or disability or a serious loss of happiness or good, that they could have prevented without imposing substantial burdens or costs or loss of benefits on themselves or others.[14]

Principle M concerns the regulation of the relationship that caretakers and their dependents stand in with respect to one another. To the extent that the facts justify taking one to stand in such a relationship to another in, e.g., the role of caretaker, one has reason to take oneself to be bound to comply with certain legitimate expectations to which the relevant dependent is entitled. The expectations established on the basis of *Principle M* do not, of course, hold between persons generally, but only between those whom it is appropriate to take as standing in a relationship of caretaker and dependent with respect to one another.

Now, in the most familiar situations, one knows the others with respect to whom one stands in a certain kind of normatively significant relation, e.g., those who stand in a relation as dependents, as particular persons. For purposes of thinking about what one is entitled to expect of another, however, knowledge of the particular identity of the other is not essential. What is essential is that one has reason to take the other to be of a certain type. Facts concerning the identity of the other in virtue of which she is a particular token of a certain type may be helpful for refining one's understanding of what one owes the other, but are not essential. One has reason, then, to take another to be bound to one as a dependent just in case the relevant facts support one standing in such a relationship with respect to the other. The only knowledge of the other that is necessary here is that of it being reasonable to take her to be a certain type, whatever else may turn out to be true of her in virtue of which she is a particular token of the relevant type.

There is nothing mysterious about "taking another to be of a certain type." To do so amounts to nothing more than the reasonable attribution to another of the kinds of interests and legitimate concerns that characterize the concerns and interests that one capable of rational

---

14. Buchanan et al., p. 226.

self-government might have in a relation of that kind. For example, taking another to be of the type "child" is to have reason to attribute to the other the legitimate concerns of one who is at least potentially capable of rational self-government, concerning how she is related to by others in the early stages of development towards the realization of a capacity for rational self-government. Reflection, then, concerning what, by way of consideration and conduct, one is entitled to expect of another requires only that the other be identifiable in normative terms—those appealed to in certain type descriptions. That the particular psychophysical identity of the person in question, at the point in time at which compliance with the duty is required, may still be an indeterminate matter turns out to be of no consequence, as the other retains her standing as a certain type to whom certain duties are owed regardless of what her token identity turns out to be.[15]

Consider, for example, a couple thinking about what steps they would have to pursue if they decide to go ahead and conceive a child. At this point, what they know is that if they decide to pursue having a child, their relation to the intended child will be that of caretakers to a dependent.[16] They will stand in such a relation to the child in virtue of the influence that it will be reasonable to take their decisions and attentiveness to the interests of the child to have in determining the extent to which the child is at risk of being born with severely limiting disabilities, diseases, etc. Having a ready grasp of the legitimate expectations that attach to role of caretaker of a child, as roughly articulated by *Principle M*, they see that one thing that can be legitimately expected of them is that they undergo various pre-conception tests, in order to minimize the risk of their child being born with limiting disabilities or diseases. The justification for requiring risk-minimizing measures of this kind appeals to the relevant concerns of the normative ideal of persons presupposed by the contractualist framework of reasoning. Culpably failing to complete

---

15. Assuming, of course, that at some point in the developmental process there will be a metaphysical fact of the matter concerning identity.

16. Although the example is one that concerns the wronging of a victim who stands in a special relationship to the wrongdoer, standing in a particular, or special kind, of relationship to another is not fundamental, on this view, for the possibility of being wronged by another. What is fundamental is that one is entitled to certain legitimate expectations concerning consideration and conduct in one's relations with other persons, in virtue of one's status as a person.

the required pre-conception testing would be to wrong their child, for it is their child whom they would be putting at risk by their failure. Note that nothing in this line of reasoning relies on specific considerations that are sensitive to variations in the particular psycho-physical identity of the child.

The initial challenge questioned the sense of holding a person accountable for having culpably failed to comply with the legitimate expectations of another, and who is, in a significant sense, the person she is now as a consequence of the alleged wrongdoing. The challenge proves, however, to be illusory, as it relies on a crucial misunderstanding of the character of legitimate expectations in contractualism. Legitimate expectations are expectations to which a person is entitled; a violation of legitimate expectations, then, is a violation of entitlement.

What is important for concluding that a person has wronged another, then, is that the *wrongdoer* have been in a position to understand what other persons are entitled (in virtue of the principles that constitute the moral system) to expect of her in terms of respectful conduct and consideration. There may be, therefore, a considerable temporal gap between the time when the entitlement to a claim to have been wronged is created (by the failure of the wrongdoer to comply with legitimate expectations) and there being a particular person entitled to make the claim, insofar as she is a token of the relevant type.[17]

There is no special problem for contractualism, then, concerning how one can have wronged one's child as a result of a culpable failure to pursue appropriate pre-conception testing. To be so bound to one's child, as caretaker to dependent, it need only be true that (a) one intends to conceive a child, and (b) one has reason to take it to be the case that the intended, but yet to be conceived, child will be of the type required for her to owe it to the child to take appropriate measures to protect its welfare, regardless of what its particular token identity turns out to be.

This last point should not be taken to be one that has straightforward implications for, say, the moral permissibility of abortion; e.g., it does

---

17. It is possible, of course, that no such particular individual ever does come into existence. This, however, does not change the fact that the culpable negligence created an entitlement, such that, had there been a relevant particular individual, she would have been justified in claiming herself to have been wronged.

not follow that the abortion of a fetus in cases where conception was not involuntary is morally prohibited. Relating to a child on terms of respect for the child includes being accountable for taking appropriate account of its legitimate concerns even at a stage where 'the child' is only the potential for the coming into being of one who has the potential to develop into a rational self-governor. The principle of due care that is relevant here, though, is only one of a system of moral principles. It is not incompatible with other principles that concern the contours of a caretaker's entitlement to take steps to terminate the caretaker–dependent relationship. How the entitlement to terminate is to be justified, as well as the kinds of considerations that are relevant for the appropriate exercise of the entitlement, is a matter that requires investigation into the relevant principles governing the justifiable termination of a fetus, as well as attention to other questions of value that are not primarily of concern because of their bearing on interpersonal relations.

What the discussion does suggest, however, is that it is reasonable to think that there will be important constraints on how one relates to one's child even at the early stage of the developmental process where the child has only the potential to develop a capacity for rational self-government. One may, therefore, be entitled to *terminate* the caretaker–dependent relationship with one's child, but as long as one allows the relationship to continue, it may be that one is *not* entitled to *interfere* in certain ways with the child's development. It is certainly plausible to think, for instance, that deliberately circumventing a developmental process that there is reason to think will result in a being with a potential for developing a capacity for rational self-governance, such that the being continues to develop, but along lines that will not result in the development of a potential for a capacity for self-governance, would count, on the basis of the relevant principle, as an instance of wronging one's child.[18] Nothing said in this discussion can be taken to settle this matter; all it does is suggest that there are interpersonal moral standards that require articulation in order to better illuminate, and perhaps settle, questions concerning, e.g., how it is permissible to relate to one's child in the very early, embryonic stages of the development process.

18. Thanks are owed here to a reader for *Philosophy & Public Affairs* who pressed me on the questions addressed in this paragraph.

IV. WRONGDOING AS IRRESPONSIBILITY

On the proposed view, a child's claim to have been wronged owing to pre-conception negligence, for example, should focus on the way in which the alleged wrongdoers risked the child's health by culpably failing to comply with standards of due care which the child, whose development was under their control, was entitled to have expected them to successfully comply. A great deal depends here, of course, upon the demand, given the circumstances and the importance of compliance for the health of the child, having been a reasonable one. It is also crucial to the case that failure to comply with the relevant standards be a culpable failure, e.g., a consequence of their negligence.

No doubt determining whether or not a failure counts as a morally culpable failure is a difficult judgment to make. What the present line of analysis clarifies is that what makes such cases hard to assess is the difficulty inherent in making subtle assessments concerning whether or not a person's failure to comply with a certain standard of due care was a culpable, or blameworthy, failure, or whether there are exculpatory considerations that tell against culpability. The challenge they present has nothing to do with a variance in psycho-physical identity that renders certain counter-factual claims as unavailable.

One important implication of this approach for thinking about how a child can be wronged by pre-conception negligence is that a child's claim to have been wronged could be valid whether or not she has been born worse-off than she otherwise would have been. If, for instance, a case can be made against a child's parents that they culpably failed to pursue pre-conception testing, then they have wronged their child by exposing the child to avoidable risk, whether or not the risk ends up materializing as harm. Exposing the child to such risks involved an exercise of authority with respect to the child's interests to which the parents were not entitled.

It does seem, though, that both the fact of negligence, and the child's being badly off, are relevant to commonsense intuitions about this kind of case. There are at least two reasons why this is not surprising. First, that a child has been born in a badly off state is often an important element in the evidentiary basis for there having been pre-conception negligence. Second, the association of this kind of case with civil lawsuits can mislead, insofar as it invites one to think about questions of liability, and how liability is to be fixed, if at all, in such a case. The contractualist analysis of wrongdoing, however, is in the first instance only concerned with questions of *culpability* for having wronged another, not *liability*. That is, the kinds of considerations whose identification as relevant for moral assessment with which contractualism is primarily concerned are those having to do with whether or not one has in fact wronged another, an issue of culpability. These considerations are, in principle, distinct from those it might identify as relevant for fixing issues of liability, which concern the kinds of burdens that a wrongdoer can justifiably be asked to bear because of her wrongdoing. Contractualism's denial of the relevance of facts concerning harm for determining whether or not a person has been wronged should not, therefore, be taken to be a rejection of the relevance of such considerations for thinking about the costs the wrongdoer must bear as a consequence of her wrongdoing.

The last point makes explicit that the analysis of wronging offered here aims to illuminate only a certain class of claims that a wronged party may be entitled to press against a wrongdoer. These are claims by the wronged for *acknowledgment* of the wrong done to her by the wrongdoer. This may make the analysis of less interest for thinking about wronging in legal contexts, but does not diminish its importance for the illumination of issues concerning the morality of interpersonal relations, where the value of acknowledgment has an intuitively natural home.[19]

V. CONCLUSION

The non-identity problem only poses a threat to commonsense moral convictions concerning who can, in principle, be wronged, if the basis of an individual's claim to have been wronged is understood to be rooted in what has happened to her as a result of how a wrongdoer has related to her. To side-step the problem, I have suggested, one must fully embrace the non-consequentialist commitment to the maxim that the focus of an investigation into a claim of having been wronged should be

---

19. For some discussion of the moral importance of the acknowledgment of wrongdoing, see Rahul Kumar and David Silver, "The Legacy of Injustice: Wronging the Future, Responsibility for the Past" in *Historical Justice*, ed. Lukas H. Meyer (Baden-Baden: Nomos, 2003).

put squarely on the character of the wrongdoer's conduct, rather than the consequences for the wronged of that conduct. In particular, the wrongdoer's conduct needs to be assessed as a failure to live up to her responsibilities with respect to the wronged. The relevant questions, then, should concern whether or not the failure was indeed a culpable failure, how best to characterize the failure, and what the justification might be for holding the wrongdoer to be accountable.

Questions concerning who can be wronged are not in any way being dismissed here as somehow misconceived, or absurd. Such questions are clearly of great moral importance. What is being suggested is that they should be approached as questions that concern the scope, and the justification for the scope, of interpersonal accountability. Thinking about who can be wronged should direct us, then, not towards a discussion of the metaphysics of identity and the theory of counter-factuals, but towards the theory of responsibility.

[21]

On Benefiting from Injustice

DANIEL BUTT

How do we acquire moral obligations to others? The most straightforward cases are those where we acquire obligations as the result of particular actions which we voluntarily perform. If I promise you that I will trim your hedge, I face a moral obligation to uphold my promise, and in the absence of some morally significant countervailing reason, I should indeed cut your hedge. Moral obligations which arise as a result of wrongdoing, as a function of corrective justice, are typically thought to be of a similar nature. If I set fire to your hedge, I owe you compensation: both for the damage caused to your property and for any directly related losses you may have suffered as a consequence of my actions. It is more controversial, although not uncommon, to suggest that agents can acquire moral obligations as a result of the actions of others. Cases of rescue are an obvious example: if another individual is pushed into a pond and is about to drown, and I (and only I) can rescue her at no risk and little cost to myself, many would maintain that I face an obligation to save her. This obligation may impose costs upon me (which may be unrecoverable), but it mandates me regardless of the fact that I have done nothing to bring this obligation upon myself, other than happening (blamelessly) to be in a particular place at a particular time. The case of how an agent may be said to acquire moral obligations involuntarily is particularly important in philosophical consideration of present day obligations arising from historic injustice. One commonly expressed claim has it that agents can acquire rectificatory obligations as a result of *benefiting* from acts of injustice committed by others, such as their ancestors. Judith Jarvis Thomson makes the case in the context of the debate over positive discrimination, maintaining that it is not inappropriate to impose costs upon young white males, even though 'no doubt few, if any, have, themselves, individually, done any wrongs to blacks and women,' since 'they have profited from the wrongs the community did.'[1] More generally, claims that various Western nations owe compensation to their former colonies as a consequence of the (disputed) fact that they are benefiting from colonialism and/or from slavery in the present day are commonplace.

This article examines, and defends, the claim that agents can acquire rectificatory obligations through involuntarily benefiting from acts of injustice.[2] I start, in Part I, by considering David Miller's article 'Distributing Responsibilities,'[3] which focuses on the distribution of duties of assistance, in cases where it is accepted that someone ought to provide assistance to those in need but where it is controversial upon whom the costs of assistance should fall. Miller proposes four morally relevant forms of connection with the victims of injustice which can give rise to moral obligations to assist — I propose that benefiting from the plight of those in desperate need, however involuntarily, constitutes an additional morally relevant form of connection. Part Two goes further, and argues that moral agents can possess compensatory obligations as a result of involuntarily benefiting from injustice even when the victims of injustice do not need to be lifted above some minimal threshold level of well-being.

I Miller on duties of assistance

In 'Distributing Responsibilities,' David Miller seeks to address what he calls 'the problem of remedial responsibility,' which he defines as follows:

> To be remedially responsible for a bad situation means to have a special obligation to put the bad situation right, in other words to be picked out, either individually or along with others, as having a responsibility towards the deprived or suffering party that is not shared equally among all agents.[4]

---

1 Judith Jarvis Thomson, 'Preferential Hiring,' in *Rights, Restitution and Risk: Essays in Moral Theory* (London: Harvard University Press 1986) 135-53, at 152

2 I use 'involuntary' here, and throughout, to indicate that the benefits in question are not voluntarily acquired or accepted, in that they are conferred upon those who receive the benefits without an exercise of the will on the part of the beneficiaries.

3 David Miller, 'Distributing Responsibilities,' *Journal of Political Philosophy* 9 (2001) 453-71

4 Miller, 'Distributing Responsibilities,' 454

The kinds of 'bad situation' Miller has in mind are those where individuals or groups are below some minimal threshold of well-being, such as Iraqi children who are malnourished and lack access to proper medical care. In such cases, Miller supposes that it is not in question whether the situation requires a remedy, given that it is possible that a remedy could be given;[5] the interesting question is who it is that should do the remedying (in the absence of an institutional mechanism for formally assigning responsibility.) His aim is to find a principle, or set of principles, for assigning this responsibility 'which carries moral weight, so that we can say that agents who fail to discharge their remedial responsibilities act wrongly and may properly be sanctioned.'[6] His methodology here makes explicit reference to our existing intuitive beliefs as to who it is that properly bears these responsibilities: his aim is to 'lay out principles for distributing responsibilities that we hope will command widespread agreement.'[7] He considers four different approaches that seemingly find support in the real world: based upon causal or on moral responsibility for the occurrence of the condition; on capacity for remedying the condition and on communal obligations to the affected party or parties. He concludes that no single approach can give a full account of who should remedy the situation in any given situation — using a single principle results in intuitively unpalatable outcomes. Instead, he argues for a 'connection theory,' whereby any of the four relations listed above may establish a sufficiently strong link between parties to allocate remedial responsibility. Which principle is to be invoked in a given case will depend upon its particular characteristics, so that 'when connections have to be weighed against each other, we can do no more than appeal to our shared moral intuitions about which is the stronger.'[8]

In this section I accept the idea of the connection theory, but argue for a fifth possible ground for the acquisition of remedial responsibility, specifically that of receiving benefits from the occurrence in question. My claim is that it is possible to think of cases where this form of

---

5 This is consistent with his argument in *On Nationality* (Oxford: Clarendon Press 1995), in which he outlines a theory of basic rights with correlative obligations regardless of nationality. These are principally conceived of as rights to forbearance, 'but may also include rights to provision, for example in cases where a natural shortage of resources means that people will starve or suffer bodily injury if others do not provide for them' (74).

6 Miller, 'Distributing Responsibilities,' 454

7 Miller, 'Distributing Responsibilities,' 454

8 Miller, 'Distributing Responsibilities,' 469

132 *Daniel Butt*

connection seems intuitively to give rise to remedial responsibilities, even though other forms of connection, as listed by Miller, are also present.

Consider the following example. Four people, A, B, C and D, live on a remote island; each one possesses one quarter of the land. All four are entirely self-sufficient, and their landholdings are separated by high fences. There is little or no contact between the four. The only crop which will grow on the island is the extremely versatile Polychrestos plant, whose root can be used to produce a wide variety of different dishes, as well as providing raw materials for clothing and other household essentials. The Polychrestos plant's root grows underground and is harvested each autumn, and must not be disturbed at any other part of the year. Although this means that the size of the crop will only be revealed at harvest time, the climate on the island is extremely constant, and the island's underground river distributes water evenly throughout the island's soil. Nonetheless, the Polychrestos plant is a high maintenance crop; and the size of the underground portion of the plant therefore is strictly correlated to the amount of care the overground portion of the plant receives. In order for each person to support herself, she must produce 200 kilos of root per year. A is a very hard-working, industrious type, whose agricultural efforts, from dawn to dusk each day, mean that she produces 700 kilos per annum, allowing her to eat very well and produce a wide range of leisure products. B, C and D are rather laid-back in their approach to agriculture, and work just five hours a day to produce the minimum 200 kilos a year. After a year of this, however, D, a rather unsavoury character, decides she does not want to work even five hours each day. Unknown to all the others, she diverts the underground river away from B and C's sections of land, so that her land receives all of their water, boosting, she hopes, her own crop considerably. When harvest time comes, there are a number of surprises. A harvests her regulation 700 kilos. C's land has had no water, and consequently she has no crop. She is destitute, despite her efforts over the past year. It also emerges that D (no water engineer) has in fact diverted the water away from her own land as well as that of C, and B, far from having a failed crop, has been the beneficiary. To her surprise, she harvests 400 kilos. D is also destitute, and in rage and despair hangs herself with a rope fashioned from the last of the previous year's Polychrestos crop. This leaves the problem of C. Without her year's produce, C will die unless A and B provide her with the necessary 200 kilos. How should the remedial responsibilities be distributed? There appear to be no ties of community between the individuals, and neither is either causally or morally responsible for C's fate — that responsibility, in both senses, lies with D. This seems to leave us only with capacity — who is better placed to remedy C's situation? Either A or B could transfer the necessary 200 kilos to C, while retaining at least 200 kilos themselves, but evidently A's extra level of resources mean that her capacity is the greater. As such, on Miller's account, A has the greater connection to C and bears the remedial responsibility. Yet does not such a conclusion seem intuitively objectionable? Miller notes of the capacity approach that, 'its exclusive focus on the present necessarily blinds it to historical considerations'[9] — it does not consider how the resources which are to be redistributed came about. In this case, D's actions conferred benefits upon B. Should we not hold that B's improved position, which has come about as a direct result of C's worsened position, constitutes just the sort of 'morally relevant relation' between parties which might be considered when we ask who should bear remedial responsibilities?

Thus, one could formulate the following claim in relation to remedial responsibilities:

> *If the events which cause agent C to fall below the morally relevant threshold confer benefits upon agent B, then the fact of the receipt of these benefits, however involuntary, establishes a morally relevant connection between C and B, which may give rise to remedial obligations on the part of B.*

It is key that the claim only states that receipt of benefits *may* give rise to remedial obligations. As with Miller's four other forms of morally relevant connection, in cases where more than one party is relevantly connected to the suffering agent we must use our moral intuitions to determine either which party bears the primary responsibility, or how the costs should be shared amongst different parties. My claim in this section is simply that benefiting from injustice constitutes a fifth form of morally relevant connection to go alongside Miller's existing four, which may give rise to remedial responsibilities in certain circumstances. This improves the existing typology in two ways. The first is that it responds directly to the problems that Miller cites with the capacity problem, in that it identifies a class of resources which may be available for remedying a situation — those which have arisen elsewhere as a result of that situation — which do not have a problematic history, in that it is hard to link them to their present owners by any kind of desert claim. But furthermore, there are independent moral reasons for supposing that such resources should be redistributed. It is not so much that they represent a class of neutral resources which can be safely redistributed,

---

9 Miller, 'Distributing Responsibilities,' 461

as that, insofar as they represent the 'fruits of injustice,' they may be seen as distortions within the overall scheme of distribution. This can be seen by examining Miller's account of when it is that different relations amongst the four he identifies become relevant in determining remedial responsibility. It is not always the case that this allocation of responsibility should turn on, for example, the extent to which different parties can effectively remedy the situation, and the costs they will bear in doing so. Thus in some cases there are 'independent moral reasons' for assigning remedial responsibility to a particular agent, and this applies most obviously when A is morally responsible for P's injury, when there may be two such reasons. These essentially stem from the concept of corrective justice. The first of these is that.

> ... first, where A has unjustly benefited from the injury he has inflicted on P — he has stolen something of P's or exploited him, for example — then if A is made to compensate P by returning what he has taken or in some way undoing the damage he has inflicted, then this will help to cancel out A's unjust gain, and so restore justice between them.[10]

Secondly, even if A has not benefited from his actions, he has wronged P, and owes P compensation. Our concern here is with the first of these reasons. We need not think that the only circumstances where a party enjoys an 'unjust gain' are those whereby she gains as a result of acting unjustly. In a legal context, for example, the category of 'unjust enrichment by subtraction' within the law of restitution is principally concerned with those circumstances whereby injustice in distribution arises despite the absence of wrongdoing; in the case, for example, of a mistaken payment.[11] It is possible to see the changes in distribution that emerge as a result of injustice as (to use Nickel's term) 'distortions' in the overall scheme of distribution, even if the party who has benefited has acted legitimately and has not committed any wrongdoing. Such cases may be seen as falling squarely within the preserve of corrective justice, defined by Nickel as, 'the matter of people having those things that they deserve and are entitled to, or otherwise ought to have, and compensation serves justice by preventing and undoing actions that would prevent people from having those things.'[12] Such an approach evidently serves an Aristotelian conception of justice as the maintenance of an

---

10 Miller, 'Distributing Responsibilities,' 470

11 See Andrew Burrows, *The Law of Restitution* (London: Butterworths 1993), 16-23.

12 James W. Nickel, 'Justice in Compensation,' *William and Mary Law Review* **18** (1976) 379-88, at 382

equilibrium of goods between members of society.[13] If corrective justice is seen in this way, then, as Coleman writes, 'rectification ... is a matter of justice when it is necessary to protect a distribution of holdings (or entitlements) from distortions which arise from unjust enrichments and wrongful losses. The principle of corrective justice requires the annulments of both wrongful gains and losses.'[14] The claim here, then, is that insofar as a third party directly benefits from unjust action and the victim suffers, a distortion in the fair scheme of distribution is created. Insofar as pinning remedial obligations on benefiting third parties seeks to correct this distortion, it appears that we have independent moral reasons for the allocation of responsibilities.

II Benefiting from injustice and compensation for wrongs

It has been argued that the receipt of benefits — however involuntary — stemming from an act of injustice can confer remedial obligations upon a moral agent. The arguments put forward so far, however, apply only to a particular kind of remedial responsibility, namely responsibility for fulfilling duties of assistance. In such cases, it is a given that assistance should be given by someone; the question is who it should be. There is no question of not imposing a burden on *someone*. But such 'bad situations' are not the only ones which may be thought to be in potential need of remedy. What of 'bad situations' where one party is wronged and harmed by another, but not so badly harmed as to fall below a minimal level of welfare sufficient to bring duties of assistance into play? Might a third party who benefits from the injustice in such cases potentially acquire compensatory obligations? In speaking of 'victims of injustice' here, I mean to refer to people who have been both wronged and harmed by the actions of another agent or agents. The 'bad situation' here is not defined in terms of some independently derived minimal level of welfare, an absolute criterion; rather, it involves the position of the victim of injustice relative to a counterfactual position, which may be defined crudely as that where the

---

13 For discussion of this in a legal context, see Lon L. Fuller and William R. Purdue Jr., 'The Reliance Interest in Contract Damages,' *Yale Law Journal* 46 (1936) 52-96. See also Ellen Frankel Paul's discussion in 'Set-Asides, Reparations and Compensatory Justice,' *NOMOS XXXIII: Compensatory Justice*, John W. Chapman, ed. (New York: New York University Press 1991) 97-139 at 98-104.

14 Jules L. Coleman, *Markets, Morals and the Law* (Cambridge: Cambridge University Press 1988), 185

injured party would have been had the unjust action never occurred.[15] If we assume that the harm suffered is not sufficient to bring the victim below our welfare threshold, then why should we believe that anyone not responsible for causing the harm should have obligations to remedy it? Doing so seems to run counter to the common law principle of 'risk bearing,' which holds that losses should generally lie where they fall.[16] Cane defends the principle thus:

> The shifting of a loss — or making one person compensate another for some misfortune — involves an alteration of the *status quo* and so it involves administrative expense. Therefore (it is usually asserted), the onus is on those who wish to shift a loss to justify the shift. Unless there is some good reason for shifting a loss, it should be left to lie where it falls.[17]

This position assumes an account of distributive justice that is generally happy to allow individuals to suffer losses without requiring that others pay compensation to make up for their losses. So the question is whether, within such an account, the fact that an innocent third party has benefited from another's wrongdoing gives us a good reason to shift some or all of the victim's losses to the third party. It is my belief that we lack a coherent set of principles to answer this question. For example, having just cited a common law principle, it is interesting to see how various different branches of legal theory cope with the problem. Consider, first of all, the case of accident liability in tort law, which determines under what circumstances agents should be liable to pay compensation to the victims of accidents. There is no real consideration here given to the concept of benefit at all. There is certainly debate over when parties who cause an accident should pay compensation for the costs of the accident, but this most usually involves a disagreement over the moral legitimacy or otherwise of strict tort liability, which holds that compensation is due if one is causally responsible for an accident, even if one is not at fault.[18] The alternatives to models which place liability on those responsible for the accident are those which place it either on a particular group who

---

15 Though see the argument in Part III relating to morally relevant counterfactuals.

16 See Jules L. Coleman, 'Justice and the Argument for No-Fault,' *Social Theory and Practice* 3 (1974) 161-80, at 161.

17 Peter Cane, *Atiyah's Accidents, Compensation and the Law* (London: Butterworths 1993), 355

18 See Coleman, 'The Morality of Strict Tort Liability,' *William and Mary Law Review* 18 (1976) 259-286 and Honoré, 'Responsibility and Luck,' *Law Quarterly Review* 104 (1988) 530-53.

are most likely to cause such accidents, under a principle of risk-sharing (such as when motorists as a group are held responsible for the costs of traffic accidents), or on society as a whole, under a principle of loss-distribution, which broadly stems from communitarian obligations.[19] So no reference is made to the possibility of consideration of third party benefits. Mention has already been made of the concept of unjust enrichment under the law of restitution, according to which, it is maintained, the law protects one person from being unjustly enriched at another's expense. This seems clearly applicable to the present case, and yet the extent to which claims may be made under this general principle are (broadly speaking) limited to cases where one party has either freely accepted a particular benefit or has possession of or legal title to a particular item of property or sum of money to which another party has a strong moral entitlement. For reasons which will be discussed later, moves to claim that an agent might acquire obligations through the involuntary receipt of a benefit in kind are severely restricted. Finally, in the area of criminal law, a slightly different approach is taken to the subject of possessing stolen goods. If I have been given or have bought for a cheap price an item of stolen property in good-faith, I may reasonably be said to have benefited from an act of injustice. The question of what should happen next varies for different kinds of property, and in different legal jurisdictions. In some cases, the beneficiary has to return the item, receiving no compensation even if she has purchased it in good faith. Clearly, this might leave the (one-time) beneficiary of an injustice paying the greatest price for the injustice, and being worse off than she was prior to the injustice. In other cases it is the victim who is held liable for these costs, and the beneficiary keeps the property in question.[20]

---

19 Thus Bernard Boxhill argues that community membership is sufficient to ground obligations of compensation to victims on the part of the community as a whole. Such a commitment is, he maintains, implicit in the community's social contract; so he writes, 'The case for rights of compensation depends ... on the fact that the individuals involved are members of a single community, the very existence of which should imply a tacit agreement on the part of the whole to bear the costs of compensation' (Boxhill, 'The Morality of Reparation,' in Gross, ed., *Reverse Discrimination* [Buffalo: Prometheus 1977] 270-8, at 272).

20 Saul Levmore, 'Variety and Uniformity in the Treatment of the Good-Faith Purchaser,' *Journal of Legal Studies* 16 (1987) 43-65. Levmore attributes the wide variety of practice he identifies in the treatment of good-faith purchasers of stolen goods to the existence of uncertainty or reasonable disagreement about the behavioural effects of alternative legal rules: 'some reasonable people might favor the innocent owner, some might prefer the innocent purchaser, and others might split between the two on the basis of time passed, place of purchase, or both' (57).

Given the variable legal treatment of the issue, we must look to its theoretical underpinning. The most common way that moral agents are said to acquire compensatory obligations is through what is sometimes called 'the fault principle.' In broad terms, this is the idea that those who are responsible for injuring other parties bear a moral responsibility to compensate the victims of their actions, precisely because it is their fault that the injuries in question occurred. Once it is established what would compensate the injured party, the guilty party has a moral obligation to so act, insofar as they are able to do so. Evidently, this is the understanding of moral responsibility discussed by Miller in the previous section, and, as before, it seems clear that this should generally be the primary response to acts of injustice and is in most cases the ideal response. However, what of circumstances where the parties who were actually responsible for the act of injustice do not or cannot fulfil their obligations? For some writers this is the end of the matter, and any suggestion of the acquisition of compensatory obligations without fault is simply unacceptable. Thus O'Neill writes:

> some laissez faire liberals are dubious about rights to compensation except where the individuals who inflicted wrong are identifiable and obliged to compensate for the injuries they inflicted. On such views rights to compensation are symmetrical with rights to punish, in that they are absent when there is no wrongdoer, or no identifiable wrongdoer. Just compensation presupposes an injuring as well as an injured party.[21]

As it stands, such a position is too strong, as it rules out the possibility that non-offenders may acquire compensatory obligations through prior agreements that one party will cover another's losses in the event of them suffering particular harms. This may be either as a result of a contractual arrangement, as in the case of buying insurance, or simply as a result of a promise or commitment, such as when a government sets up an agency to compensate victims of crime for their injuries. Such schemes are not normally seen as justifiable if they actually allow the offender to escape responsibility, but rather act as a safety net to compensate victims should they not receive their due from the offender. Thus, for example, car insurance should not protect one from a conviction for dangerous driving, nor from subsequent claims for damages, but covers one for accidental harm one causes and for any harms one may suffer through accident or the fault of others. This is simply a case of a special obligation,

---

21 Onora O'Neill, 'Rights to Compensation,' *Social Philosophy and Policy* 5 (1987) 72-87, at 77

of the same nature as a promise. As such, the obligation is essentially voluntaristic.

The issue becomes controversial, then, when it is claimed compensatory obligations can be acquired involuntarily. As noted above, the question of the involuntary receipt of benefits has been explicitly invoked in the context of discussions of the normative justifications of reverse discrimination as a compensatory response to injustice. A frequently cited example comes from the writing of Judith Jarvis Thomson. She concedes that practices of reverse discrimination in hiring impose costs upon the (say) white males who are affected by them, but she argues that this is not necessarily unjust:

> of course choosing this way [reverse discrimination] of making amends means that the costs are imposed on the young male applicants who are turned away. And so it should be noticed that it is not entirely inappropriate that those applicants should pay the costs. No doubt few, if any, have, themselves, individually, done any wrongs to blacks and women. But they have profited from the wrongs the community did. Many may actually have been direct beneficiaries of policies which excluded or downgraded blacks and women — perhaps in school admissions, perhaps elsewhere; and even those who did not directly benefit in this way had, at any rate, the advantage in the competition which comes of confidence in one's full membership, and of one's rights being recognized as a matter of course.[22]

The principle at stake seems to be that, by benefiting from an act of injustice, one can acquire obligations towards the victims of that injustice. This is not an uncontroversial conclusion, and it has been strongly criticised by Robert Fullinwider. Fullinwider claims that the passage cited above reflects a particular moral principle, 'he who benefits from a wrong must help pay for the wrong.'[23] Fullinwider claims that this is

---

22 Thomson, 'Preferential Hiring,' 152. This position, insofar as it relates to the benefit acquired by a group rather than by individuals, obviously raises important questions as to the distribution of compensatory burdens within the benefiting group, which Thomson only addresses fleetingly. For criticism, see Jones, 'On the Justifiability of Reverse Discrimination' in Gross, ed., *Reverse Discrimination*, 348-57. Others have questioned the extent to which all white males do in fact benefit from their societal identity. For defence of the proposition, see Charles R. Lawrence III and Mari J. Matsuda, *We Won't Go Back: Making the Case for Affirmative Action* (Boston: Houghton Mifflin Company 1997). For opposition, see Gertrude Ezorsky, *Racism and Justice: The Case for Affirmative Action* (Ithaca: Cornell University Press 1991), 83-4.

23 This is the version of the principle given in Fullinwider's 1980 book, *The Reverse Discrimination Controversy* (Totowa, NJ: Rowman and Littlefield 1980). It replaces the more commonly cited 'he who benefits from a wrong shall pay for the wrong' from his 1975 article, 'Preferential Hiring and Compensation,' *Social Theory and Practice* 3 (1975) 307-20.

'surely suspect as an acceptable moral principle,' suggesting that only 'he who wrongs another shall pay for the wrong' is justifiable as a principle of compensatory justice.[24] To illustrate his case he uses the following example:

> While I am away on vacation, my neighbour contracts with a construction company to repair his driveway. He instructs the workers to come to his address, where they will find a note describing the driveway to be repaired. An enemy of my neighbour, aware, somehow, of this arrangement, substitutes for my neighbour's instructions a note describing *my* driveway. The construction crew, having been paid in advance, shows up on the appointed day while my neighbour is at work, finds the letter, and faithfully following the instructions, paves my driveway.[25]

It is clear that in this case the neighbour is a victim of his enemy's unjust act, and has a valid claim against him. But what is to be done in the absence of the enemy? Fullinwider rejects the conclusion, which he believes follows from the principle of compensatory justice he attributes to Thomson, that I am obliged to pay my neighbour for his driveway, contending that to do so would constitute an act of moral supererogation: a laudable act certainly, but not one which is required by a moral obligation. The key point for Fullinwider is that the receipt of the benefit in this case is *involuntary*. Perhaps the situation is different with regard to those who willingly accept benefits stemming from injustice: 'If I knowingly and voluntarily benefit from wrongs done to others, though I do not commit the wrong myself, then perhaps it is true to say that I am less than innocent of these wrongs, and perhaps it is morally fitting that I bear some of the costs of compensation.'[26] But those who involuntarily receive benefits bear no compensatory obligations.

This takes us to the heart of the issue. Is Fullinwider right about the involuntary receipt of benefits? It seems to me that he is not, and that the power of his example derives from a confusion over how extensive compensatory obligations stemming from injustice should be.

So let us return to the drive. The crucial question here seems to stem from my attitude towards my newly re-surfaced drive. Let us suppose that the drive cost my neighbour £500. I have not, however, benefited

---

24 Fullinwider, 'Preferential Hiring and Compensation' in Steven M. Cahn, *The Affirmative Action Debate* (New York: Routledge 2002) 68-78, at 75

25 Fullinwider, 'Preferential Hiring and Compensation,' 75-6

26 Fullinwider, 'Preferential Hiring and Compensation,' 76. This point mirrors the legal doctrine of free acceptance. See Birks, *An Introduction to the Law of Restitution* (Oxford: Clarendon Press 1989), 265ff.

financially, as the re-surfacing has added no value to my property.[27] But let us also assume that I have indeed derived overall benefit from the experience, in that I prefer my new drive to my old one. This is not to say, of course, that I would necessarily have been willing to pay £500 to have it re-surfaced. Let us suppose that, had the drive re-surfacer knocked on my door the day before and offered to re-surface my drive for £500, I would have refused.[28] Asking me to pay £500 in this circumstance does seem unfair, since to do so would leave me worse off than I would have been had the whole experience not taken place. I would, in truth, have become the victim of the piece. But this is not the only alternative open to us. Imagine that the drive re-surfacer had in fact offered to do my drive for £200. This is considerably below the going rate, and I may well have leapt at the opportunity. If this was indeed the case, and I am correspondingly (at least) £200 better off on the basis of my own evaluation, then is it unreasonable to say that I should pay £200 to my neighbour? After all, I am still benefiting from the whole transaction; to use economic terminology, I am on a higher utility curve than before. We may well think that I do not (necessarily) owe my neighbour £500, but it does not necessarily follow from this that I owe him nothing at all. Certainly I am innocent of wrongdoing towards him at this point. But might it not be that our moral relationship, the balance between the two of us, will be altered if I materially benefit from my neighbour's unrectified experience of injustice without making any effort to offset his losses?

Fullinwider's example seems initially powerful due to its 'all or nothing' character. However, one can have compensatory obligations to X without having an obligation to compensate X fully. Thomson's point in relation to affirmative action, if it is to succeed, must be that the situation of white males even after policies of affirmative action have been put into place is better than it would have been had past and recent injustice not occurred; they derive a net benefit from their social position even when such policies have been enacted. Clearly, the principle 'he who benefits from a wrong shall pay for the wrong,' which Fullinwider initially erroneously attributes to Thomson, is nonsense, given that the benefit one receives from the wrong might be utterly marginal, whereas

---

27 Perhaps I rent my house on a long-term lease. Or perhaps the re-surfacing has been cosmetic rather than structural. I am grateful to Hillel Steiner for helping to clarify this point.

28 Fullinwider assumes this to be the case: 'Presumably I valued other things more dearly than having my own driveway repaired; otherwise I would have done it myself' (*The Reverse Discrimination Controversy*, 39).

the cost of paying for it might be monumental. So the compensatory obligations of the beneficiaries of injustice can be limited to paying compensation up to the point where they are no longer beneficiaries of the injustice in question. Nor is it necessarily the case that a beneficiary need pay anything at all, given that other parties (most notably, the agent responsible for the act in question) may have prior obligations which fully compensate the victims, leaving no work for the beneficiary to do.[29] Insofar as the receipt of benefits does give rise to a principle, it can only be as demanding as, 'she who benefits from a wrong may have obligations to (help to) pay for the wrong, insofar as doing so does not leave her worse off than had the wrong not occurred.' Interestingly, this follows closely a parallel argument within the literature on political obligation, over the extent to which the involuntary receipt of benefits provided by the state can ground obligations to obey the law. Jonathan Wolff, for example, disputes the extent to which this can be the case on the basis that, for some people, the benefits the state provides are not worth the price the state extracts: i.e. acceptance of political obligations. Thus he writes (of the fairness account of political obligation):

> a revised account does not appeal to the idea that the mere receipt of benefits is sufficient to create obligations.... Rather obligations are generated for an individual only if an individual receives a *net* benefit according to his or her subjective scale of valuation.[30]

---

29 Generally, it seems to me that we should see the obligations of offender to victim as conceptually prior to any compensatory obligations other parties might have. O'Neill argues that only when compensation is forthcoming from offender to victim can restitution, in the sense of the restoration of the moral relationship between the parties, occur. As such, compensation is always a second-best response to an incidence of injustice. Thus there is a temptation to introduce lexical priority here, and hold that third parties only acquire compensatory obligations when offenders cannot or will not fulfil their own obligations. However, some may prefer to extend Miller's 'connection theory' into this area, and maintain that this is only a presumptive priority. It is quite possible to think of circumstances where relatively minor wrongs could have massive consequences, in that one party could lose and a third party could gain huge amounts, but where the offender makes no material gain at all, or even an overall loss (should, for example, her plans go awry). It is not necessarily clear that the offender should foot all of this bill, even if she is able to, when such an obvious distortion has entered into the distributive scheme. Nonetheless, even Fullinwider's revised formula, 'he who benefits from a wrong must help pay for a wrong' is far too strong here, as in many cases of wrongdoing when a third party benefits, the entire burden of compensation will fall on the wrongdoer.

30 Jonathan Wolff, 'Political Obligation, Fairness and Independence,' *Ratio* 8 (1995) 87-99, at 96. This point can be used in the context of Nozick's famous account of the community public address system, whereby it is claimed that one has an obligation

It is my contention that compensatory obligations can be generated in a similar fashion. Moral agents can have obligations to compensate victims of injustice if they are benefiting and the victims are suffering from the automatic effects of the act of injustice in question. It is crucial to the argument that the losses and benefits in question arise from injustice, which is to say wrong-doing by other agents. The individual's duty not to benefit from another's suffering when that suffering is a result of injustice stems from one's moral condemnation of the unjust act itself. In consequence, a duty to disgorge (in compensation) the benefits one gains as a result of injustice follows from one's duty not to so benefit. My claim is that taking our nature as moral agents seriously requires not only that we be willing not to commit acts of injustice ourselves, but that we hold a genuine aversion to injustice and its lasting effects. We make a conceptual error if we condemn a given action as unjust, but are not willing to reverse or mitigate its effects on the grounds that it has benefited us. The refusal undermines the condemnation. The belief that certain acts are wrong and should not be performed on account of their harmful consequences commits one to endorse the application of corrective justice to seek to undo the effects of injustice, insofar as doing so does not render oneself a victim, by making one worse off overall. Being a moral agent means being committed to the idea that justice should prevail over injustice. Losses which others suffer as a result of the unjust actions of other persons cannot be dismissed as arbitrary or simply unfortunate: they create distortions within the scheme of fair distribution. If no one else is willing or able to make up these losses, then the duty falls to those who are benefiting from the distortions in question.[31]

It is useful here to consider Janna Thompson's work on the nature of apologies for historic wrongs. Thompson's query is what it means to say that one is 'sorry' that a particular event occurred. She identifies what she calls, 'the apology paradox': if we owe our existence to a given act of injustice, and if we are happy that we are alive, how can we meaning-

---

to contribute a day's labour to the system on the grounds that one has benefited from it, even though one voted against its institution. See *Anarchy, State, and Utopia* (New York: Basic Books 1974), 93-5. The burden becomes less onerous if the proviso that one receives *net* benefit is included, which is to say that one has benefited even after doing one's day of service. Nozick's initial example has such force because we imagine the possibility of an individual who has indeed benefited from the system, but not to the extent that he would receive a net benefit from having listened to the system and provided a day's labour.

31 My exposition of this section of the argument is deeply endebted to an anonymous referee for the *Canadian Journal of Philosophy*.

fully say that we regret the act of injustice that brought our very existence about? And if we do not regret the act of injustice, how can we apologise for it? Thompson argues that we need to reinterpret what we are actually doing when we apologise for historic injustice:

> Many people feel uncomfortable or even apologetic about benefiting from an injustice even when they had no responsibility for it. They are sorry that the good things they now possess came to them because of a past injustice. They do not regret that they have these things, but that they came to have them in the way they did. An apology could be interpreted as an expression of this kind of regret. So interpreted it is not, strictly speaking, an apology *for* the deeds of our ancestors or an expression of regret that they happened. Rather, it is an apology *concerning* deeds of the past, and the regret expressed is that we owe our existence and other things we enjoy to the injustices of our ancestors. Our preference is for a possible world in which our existence did not depend on these deeds.[32]

The claim here is not that we should regret our own existence, insofar as it stems from historic injustice, but that we should regret the fact that our existence is a result of unjust rather than just actions. We would prefer a world where both we existed and where our ancestors had not acted unjustly. But if we accept (as I think we should) all that Thompson says, are we not obliged in fact to do rather more than simply regret the fact that the world is as it is, and issue an apology in recognition of this fact? If we actually wish that we were in a different kind of world, and think that such a world would be more just than our current world, surely it follows that we should seek to make our world more similar to the counterfactual world in question? Thompson specifically refers to 'our existence and other things we enjoy.' But while we obviously cannot alter the fact that we have come into existence, we do have control over those 'things we enjoy' which are transferable resources. Suppose that, through the intervention of an unknown enemy, the estate of A's parents is left to B in their will rather than to A, as A's parents had intended. A would surely be entitled to feel aggrieved if B expressed her sorrow at what had taken place, and expressed the wish that they lived in a counterfactual world where the event had never happened, while still retaining the estate. My point is not just that B's expressed sentiments seem empty; it is that they are incompatible with her subsequent actions. If our moral condemnation of injustice, our regret that injustice has occurred, is to be taken seriously, it must be matched by action to remedy the effects of injustice, insofar as they persist as the automatic effects of

---

[32] Janna Thompson, 'The Apology Paradox,' *The Philosophical Quarterly* 50 (2000) 470-5, at 475

injustice. We are right to feel guilty at benefiting from others' misfortune, precisely because this suggests that we have not fulfilled our compensatory obligations.

One final point in this section. In his article 'Superseding Historic Injustice,' Jeremy Waldron refers to what he calls the 'contagion of injustice.'[33] The interdependence of different parties, both domestically and internationally, and their involvement in, for example, market transactions makes it likely that many people may, to an extent, have benefited as a result of a given act of injustice. It follows from the preceding argument that such people collectively possess a duty to put the situation right, insofar as doing so does not leave them worse off than if the injustice had not occurred. So it might well be argued, for example, that the West as a whole has benefited from the injustices of the colonial period, and so even those countries which did not directly act as colonial powers may have compensatory duties in the current day. When considered at a domestic level, the likelihood that many and diverse innocent third parties may have benefited from a given act of injustice may in some cases make the fulfillment of the ensuing collective duties at best onerous, and at times practically impossible. This might well be thought to provide an argument for an automatic, government-sponsored scheme for compensation for the victims of crime. But this notwithstanding, we might nonetheless think that some duties may appear more pressing to some beneficiaries of injustice than to others. This relates to the earlier claim that recognising one's duties amounts to a condemnation of the previous act of injustice, and a kind of determination that injustice should not prevail. It seems to me that the parties who should feel this most strongly are those people who were intended to benefit from the act of injustice. Consider, yet again, the example of the driveway. Suppose that the purpose of the evil note leaver was not only to harm my neighbour, but also to benefit me specifically. Insofar as I have in fact benefited from his actions, he has achieved his aim and injustice, as it were, has triumphed. This is true not only in the sense that a distortion in the fair scheme of distribution remains, but also in the sense that what has resulted is the precise unfair distribution which the perpetrator of injustice intended. This has relevance in an intergenerational context, in that it is often a major aim of those who seek to gain advantage to improve the prospects of their descendants, and relevance in an international context, as frequently the motivation for international wrongdoing is to benefit one's nation, understood as a historic commu-

---

33 Waldron, 'Superseding Historic Injustice,' *Ethics* **103** (1992) 4-28, at 11

nity which exists through time. There is, then, a sense in which it might not be wholly accurate to see some innocent persons or groups as genuinely third parties in relation to injustice. Their position is more involved or implicated than this. It is not a necessary condition of having these duties that it was intended that we benefit from the act of injustice, but it may be that we can see our moral duties more clearly when this is indeed the case.

III From theory to practice — problems of measuring benefit

It has been claimed that insofar as moral agents have benefited from the wrongdoing of others, they may have obligations to compensate the victims of this wrongdoing. Undoubted complications arise, however, when we come to consider what it means to say that a given agent has indeed benefited from a given act of injustice. Thus far, the argument has concerned clear cases where one party suffers and another party benefits as an automatic result of an instance of injustice. As such, it is clearly dependent upon an understanding of what it means for a person or persons to so benefit, and for another to be disadvantaged. Such an assessment relies upon some kind of counterfactual calculation, whereby the actual world, following an act of injustice, is compared to an alternative, possible world where injustice is absent. The earlier example of the Polychrestos harvest is deliberately simplified in order to make calculations of the counterfactual seem uncomplicated: the relevant counterfactual is the world where D does not direct the underground river and B, C and D each harvest 200 kilos after 5 hours of work each day. The case is straightforward because the sole difference between the actual, unjust world and the just counterfactual world can be described as the automatic effect of the act of injustice. B has not done anything to deserve the extra 200 kilos she has gained, nor can it be maintained that C is at fault in any way, or has worked less hard than she would have done had the act of injustice not occurred. So it seems relatively unproblematic to propose a transfer of 200 kilos from B to C. The driveway example is relevantly similar in this regard — all the difference between the actual world after the note switch and the counterfactual world where no injustice occurred can be attributed to the direct results of the dastardly actions of my neighbour's enemy.

The real world is rarely as straightforward as this. Arguments relating to benefiting from injustice often consider the lasting effects of historic actions, committed some considerable time in the past. Calculations of advantage and disadvantage stemming from historic injustice will, of necessity, have to refer to complicated counterfactuals. The question of how such counterfactual calculations should be made is undoubtedly a very important question within compensatory justice, and I consider it at length elsewhere.[34] There are an infinite number of ways in which history might have unfolded had injustice not occurred, and so the challenge for the theorist is to identify the 'morally relevant' counterfactual which can be used to assess gain and loss. The claim of this article is simply that, once the appropriate counterfactual has been identified, those who can be seen to have benefited as a result of injustice may bear compensatory duties to those who have been disadvantaged. This argument is quite distinct from the separate question of which counterfactual should apply in a given case, but it is worth suggesting that the most plausible candidates will be those which allow an approximation of the automatic effects of injustice, which should be remedied, while still holding persons accountable for their actions and omissions following an act of injustice. So, for example, George Sher has argued that justice may not, in some cases, require individuals to be brought to the level of well-being they would have if injustice had not befallen them if we hold them to be at least partially responsible for their failure to recover from the effects of injustice. Sher uses the example of a student who is unjustly denied a place at law school. Had this not occurred, the student would have become a prominent lawyer with a high degree of prestige and a high salary. Instead, he allows himself to be discouraged by his rejection and does not reapply the next year, and so has a far inferior life. If we hold the candidate to be partially at fault for his situation for not reapplying, then we might suggest that at least part of his disadvantage relative to the injustice-free counterfactual is not a result of the 'automatic effects' of the act of injustice, but rather because of his own omission. An extreme example will make the point: suppose that one day, when I am walking to the shops, I encounter my childhood nemesis, the boy who bullied me at school. Reverting to type, he trips me up and I fall over. As a result of this, I decide that the world is against me, and I elect to spend the rest of my days skulking in my house brooding upon my misfortune, instead of pursuing my successful and lucrative career as a popular circus performer. Now, in such a case I have been treated

---

34 See Butt, *Rectifying International Injustice: Principles of Compensation and Restitution Between Nations* (Oxford University Press, 2009) as well as the discussion in George Sher, 'Ancient Wrongs and Modern Rights,' *Philosophy and Public Affairs* **10** (1980) 3-17; A. John Simmons, 'Historical Rights and Fair Shares,' in Simmons, *Justification and Legitimacy: Essays on Rights and Obligations* (Cambridge: Cambridge University Press 2001), 222-48; and Joel Feinberg, 'Wrongful Life and the Counterfactual Element in Harming,' in *Freedom and Fulfillment: Philosophical Essays* (Princeton: Chichester 1992), 3-36.

unjustly, but the vast majority of the responsibility for the difference between my actual and counterfactual positions seems to lie at my door. The suggestion is that I have allowed a trivial incident to blight my life; in short, I should have got over it. Thus the difference between actual and counterfactual world is down to my omissions, and the normative counterfactual — what I 'should' have — is not the same as what I would actually have had if the unjust action in question had never occurred. If I neglect opportunities to acquire alternative entitlements, I cannot necessarily keep on blaming this on the original act of injustice. Sher goes on to link this claim to a more general scepticism concerning compensatory obligations stemming from historic wrongdoing:

> Where the initial wrong was done many hundreds of years ago, almost all of the difference between the victim's entitlements in the actual world and his entitlements in a rectified world can be expected to stem from the actions of various intervening agents in the two alternative worlds. Little or none of it will be the automatic effect of the initial wrong itself. Since compensation is warranted only for disparities in entitlements which *are* the automatic effect of the initial wrong act, this means that there will be little or nothing left to compensate for.[35]

The first point to make about this claim, as Simmons notes, is that it does not say that automatic effects of injustice necessarily *cannot* last over long periods of time, simply that it becomes harder to maintain that current disadvantage is the result of historic wrongdoing.[36] Sher himself acknowledges this point when he suggests that ancient wrongs to Native Americans and African Americans within the US may be atypical in that they have made it very hard for the descendants of the originally injured parties to acquire alternative entitlements. Secondly, we should be careful when blaming the lingering effects of historic injustice on the omissions of the victims not to underestimate the profound impact which injustice can have upon its victims, even when they do make reasonable efforts to 'get over' its effects. Of relevance here are Jeremy Waldron's comments concerning the significance of historic wrongs to national and group identity.[37] Insofar as injustice compromises the self-determination of a people, it can have a profound effect upon the national identity of members of the nation, and may indeed damage the ability of the nation to govern itself subsequent to the act of injustice. In cases where the ability of nations to adapt and prosper has itself been affected by historic

---

35 Sher, 'Ancient Wrongs and Modern Rights,' 13

36 Simmons, 'Historical Rights and Fair Shares,' 171n.

37 Waldron, 'Superseding Historic Injustice,' 6

injustice, the extent to which they should be deemed responsible for their omissions must be accordingly limited. In any case, the point to be underlined for the sake of the present article is that it is the automatic effects of injustice, however calculated, with which we are primarily concerned.

The identification of the morally relevant counterfactual is only half the problem, however, when it comes to making judgments as to advantage and disadvantage. Thus far, the calculation of what constitutes a benefit has been presented as either uncontroversial, as in the Polychrestos case, or as being subjective in that it depends upon the extent to which the putative beneficiaries believe that they have themselves benefited, as in the driveway case. That calculations of advantage will often turn upon the subjective preferences of those concerned does undoubtedly have complications for the application of the theory. It suggests that it would be very difficult to ground legal rights to compensation in a variety of such cases, as is demonstrated by existing laws on unjust enrichment. Seeking restitution in a legal context simply because another has been unjustly enriched at one's expense is difficult in the absence of free acceptance of the benefit in question, because of the problem of subjective devaluation. This is an argument based upon the premiss, 'that benefits in kind have value to a particular individual only so far as he chooses to give them value. What matters is his choice.' So what constitutes a benefit is up to the individual and is an inherently subjective manner: 'Some people like their poodles permed. Others abhor permed poodles.'[38] Only in the case where one party actually receives money can it be taken for granted that she has benefited, since its nature as a medium of exchange is taken to mean that is beneficial by definition: 'Where the defendant received money, it will be impossible on all ordinary facts for him to argue that he was not enriched. For money is the very measure of enrichment.'[39] To refer to the previous example; one could not hold the owner of the new driveway legally liable for the costs to his neighbour, because there is no way for an external agent to determine the degree of benefit the owner has received. There is nothing inherently unreasonable about his claiming that he has received no benefit from the experience whatsoever, and in fact preferred the drive as it was. Even if it is the case that the re-surfacing has unambiguously added to the value of his property, he still has to live with his unfavoured driveway until

---

38 Birks, *The Foundations of Unjust Enrichment* (Wellington: Victoria University Press 2002), 95

39 Birks, *The Law of Restitution*, 109

such a time as he sells his house, and it is quite conceivable that this experience might make him worse off overall, even if he eventually receives a higher price for his property. So it may be that, even if one accepts the moral force that attaches itself to benefiting from injustice, there is no way that rights stemming from such obligations can, in many cases, be written into the law, since defendants would simply have to claim that they did not consider themselves to have received benefit to avoid legal obligations. Two things follow from this. First, and most obviously, the topic becomes more a matter of moral than legal obligation, unsuitable for codification into positive law. Benefiting from historical injustice may not present a sound way to ground claims against an unwilling putative beneficiary due to the problem of subjective devaluation. But there is no problem with claiming that moral agents must honestly ask themselves to what extent they have themselves benefited from injustice, and assess their moral obligations accordingly. This is not, of course, to say that the question is not a matter of public policy, but simply that it becomes a moral and a political question, of what ought to be done in policy terms, rather than of what one has to do in order to fulfill one's legal obligations. When the beneficiaries are not individuals, with particular likes and dislikes, but collective entities such as peoples or corporations, it may in any case be easier to make an objective assessment of well-being, and hence of advantage and disadvantage, by reference to material considerations. Such entities will have to debate and decide upon the actions they think it is right to pursue given their circumstances.[40]

Second, it might be that a discourse of 'rights to compensation' on the parts of victims is simply misplaced in this context, and we should

---

[40] It should be noted here that the fact that the extent to which an individual benefits from a given action will, to a large extent, depend upon the subjective preferences of the agent does not necessarily mean that an individual cannot be mistaken concerning the degree of benefit which they have in fact received. Suppose it is the case both that a) I prefer, in aesthetic terms, my old driveway to my present driveway, and that b) the new driveway adds considerably to the value of my house. If I am not aware of (b), then it may be that I have in fact gained a net benefit from the act of injustice, but mistakenly believe that I have not. (Of course, it is still possible that even though I am ignorant of (b), my dislike of my new driveway is so great that I am not compensated by the increase in my property's value, and so have not benefited overall.) In such a case, I do possess compensatory obligations to my neighbour, even though I am not aware of it. Whether or not I am culpable here, in moral terms, depends on whether we think I am negligent in failing to be aware of the true nature of the lasting effects of injustice. As noted above, I do believe that moral agents face a duty to scrutinise actively the nature and provenance of their place in the world.

instead focus upon a duty based model, where initiatives of compensatory justice gain momentum not from the political protests of victims, but from critical reflection by benefiting moral agents as to the provenance of their advantages. Such an approach might address problems which Onora O'Neill has identified with rights-centred accounts of compensatory justice. She writes:

> When we ask what our rights are we no doubt assume that we and others are agents, but our first question is to ask what ought to be done for us, what we ought to receive from others. When we ask what our obligations are we begin by asking what we ought to do.... [The rights-centred approach] invites a conception of oneself and others above all as victims, rather than as doers or citizens; it distracts allocation away from capacity for acting... Only the weak and powerless have reason to make the perspective of recipience and rights their primary concern.[41]

Insofar as those who have benefited from injustice are not the weak and powerless, this duty-based model is surely the approach they should adopt.

One final point arises. Throughout this article, I have sought to depict the involuntary beneficiaries of injustice as innocent third parties, even if their advantage was the motive of the wrongdoer. This is the correct way to address the problem in a purely theoretical sense. Throughout, the beneficiaries of injustice have been presented as if they have only just received the benefits in question. A and B, we might imagine, are considering C's plight as they survey their freshly harvested Polychrestos crop. The surprised owner of the repaired driveway has just come home from work and is trying to work out what to do next. In such cases, the beneficiaries in question truly are innocent third parties. But, if it is accepted that they at this point have rectificatory obligations to others, then they are innocent only insofar as they act reasonably promptly to fulfil the said obligations. A third party who benefits from injustice but does nothing to repair the plight of the victim, when it is clear that no other party is likely to act, is not an innocent bystander; she is acting unjustly in relation to the victim and so becomes a wrongdoer herself. Fullinwider states the principle succinctly in outlining the case against his own position:

> Possession of illicit benefits undermines one's claim to 'innocence.' The wrongful possession serves the same function as personal fault, it makes one liable to pay appropriate compensation.[42]

---

41 Onora O'Neill, 'Rights to Compensation,' 84

42 Fullinwider, *The Reverse Discrimination Controversy*, 37

This argument is of great significance when it comes to considering real world compensation claims, precisely because they typically respond to acts of injustice which have already occurred, sometimes some distance in the past, and for which no one has paid compensation. In such cases, the argument is not simply that an innocent third party has moral obligations towards victims still feeling the effects of the act of injustice. It further holds that the third parties are themselves guilty of compounding the act of injustice by withholding due compensation, which is to say that they have acted unjustly to the victim and so may owe them compensation over and above that which would have been required had they acted correctly initially. This suggests an alternative vision of historical injustice; instead of seeing it as something which fades with time, perhaps we should see its continued non-rectification as a gigantic perpetuation of the injustice itself, locking successive generations into compensatory obligations which, in their turn, are not met.[43] At the very least, it suggests an urgent need to consider the source of our present-day advantages — and to consider at what expense to others they were procured.[44]

Received February 2004
Revised October 2005
Revised April 2006

---

43 I address this possibility in Butt, 'Nations, Overlapping Generations and Historic Injustice,' *American Philosophical Quarterly* 43 (2006) 357-67.

44 I would like to thank the following for their comments on this article: Clare Chambers, Francesca Galligan, Robert Goodin, Dan McDermott, David Miller, Jon Quong, Henry Shue, Hillel Steiner, Zofia Stemplowska, Adam Swift and anonymous referees from the *Canadian Journal of Philosophy*. I would also like to thank participants of the Nuffield College Workshop in Political Theory in Oxford.

[22]

Climate justice and historical emissions

Lukas H. Meyer[a]* and Dominic Roser[b]

[a]*University of Graz, Austria;* [b]*University of Zürich, Switzerland*

> Climate change can be interpreted as a unique case of historical injustice involving issues of both intergenerational and global justice. We split the issue into two separate questions. First, how should emission rights be distributed? Second, who should come up for the costs of coping with climate change? We regard the first question as being an issue of pure distributive justice and argue on prioritarian grounds that the developing world should receive higher per capita emission rights than the developed world. This is justified by the fact that the latter already owns a larger share of benefits associated with emission generating activities because of its past record of industrialisation. The second question appears to be an issue of compensatory justice. After defining what we mean by compensation, we show that different kinds of compensatory principles run into problems when used to justify payments by historical emitters of the North to people suffering from climate change in the South. As an alternative, we propose to view payments from wealthy countries for adaptation to climate change in vulnerable countries rather as a measure based on concerns of global distributive justice.
>
> **Keywords:** intergenerational justice; global justice; climate change; historical emissions

Introduction

Climate change can be seen as a unique case of historical injustice involving a complex intersection of global and intergenerational justice. It also involves a diversity of goods and bads: first, the benefits of engaging in emission generating activities, such as driving cars, growing rice, or engaging in deforestation;[1,2] second, the climate damages which are a side effect of these activities; and third, payments which allow for adaptation measures to these climate damages. Some of the notable features of the climate change issue are: first, in the past it was predominantly the North which created climate change. Second, due to various factors the South is more vulnerable to climate change. Third, much of the climate change that is caused by emissions materialises with a time lag of several decades after the occurrence of those emissions.

---

*Corresponding author. Email: lukas.meyer@uni-graz.at

The structure of the problem suggests that the just distribution of emission rights on the one hand and a fair way of dealing with climate damages on the other is a rather complex matter. It differs from the standard problem of how to respond to historical injustices[2] where we often face the problem that earlier generations of one community wronged earlier generations of another community and today's generations of both communities are now looking for an adequate way of responding to this historical fact. In the climate change debate, however, we are faced with the situation that earlier generations of one community (the North) *directly* effect something to the detriment of later generations of the other community (the South).[3] It also differs from some other cases of historical justice in that it is not a problem of exclusively one generation/community being wronged and exclusively another generation/community having committed the wrongs and/or wrongfully benefiting. Rather, victims, wrongdoers, and beneficiaries are dispersed (but unequally so) among different communities and generations. It also differs from other instances of historical injustice in that the activity that constitutes the wrong (that is: emitting) is not something that is wrong *per se* such as genocide or slavery, but rather is only wrongful when done excessively.

We propose to disentangle this combination of questions of intergenerational and global justice posed by climate change by splitting it up:

What level of present emissions can be justified on a global scale? This is a question that we do not answer in this article. We simply presuppose that a justifiable global quota can be determined in some way.[4] While considerations of self-interest, international justice and the significance of the relations between humans and the rest of nature may play a role in determining such a quota, we think that the consideration that yields the most stringent constraint on the size of the justifiable quota is intergenerational justice.

How should this global quota be split up among the present population of the planet? This is the question concerned with the mitigation burden (section 2).

Who should pay for the damages that are caused by emissions, in particular assuming that people have not stayed and will not stay within their fair shares as determined in section 2? This is the question concerned with the adaptation burden (section 3).

We simplify strongly by always referring to the contrast between countries of the South and the North.[5] The distinction between these two regions relies on the fact that there is a correlation – partly based on causal interdependencies – between (1) having emitted more in the past, (2) having more benefits grounded in past emissions, (3) being less vulnerable to climate change, and (4) being wealthier in general. Even though we rely on the simplified perfect correlation for the purpose of our discussion, our argument becomes most relevant where the correlation is not perfect (e.g. a poor country with high past emissions or a wealthy country with high vulnerability). The reason is that any argument that ascribes higher duties to some regions than to others will be based on one of the four features from above. If those features all coincide in the North almost any argument will then ascribe higher duties to the North. In such a case, the sole purpose of the argument consists in the determination of the exact *extent* of the duty of the North. If, however, the four features do not coincide in some countries, analyzing *how exactly* the higher duties of some countries are to be *justified* then becomes more relevant.

Another complication that we bracket is the fact that the size of climate damages is not only determined by emissions. Responsibility for exposing people to climate damages lies also with those who contribute, possibly wrongfully, to vulnerabillity (where vulnerability is understood as the degree to which people are susceptible to suffer from and unable to cope with a given level of climate change). A fuller treatment of compensatory justice in climate change would have to include those who enhance vulnerability as possibly standing under a duty to pay and, where contributing to one's own vulnerability is at stake, as reducing their right to receive payments. Accounting for vulnerability creation, however, is a difficult matter: What level of enhancing vulnerability (or, respectively: what level of failing to engage in measures which decrease vulnerability) are sufficiently high so as to generate a compensatory duty? What kind of activities count as vulnerability creation – does any policy, for example, which limits economic growth qualify? We consider these intricate issues to be problems for another day and focus this text on emissions as the salient cause to climate damages.

Prioritarian distribution of emission rights

In this section we will ask how emission rights should be split up among the present-day global population. We assume that some justifiable global quota has been determined which now must be dealt out to the countries on this planet. We are interested in a fair *initial* allocation of emission rights which may then be changed by subsequent trade.

Determining a fair distribution of emission rights is of high relevance in current climate policy. If the international community decides to cap total emissions then the emissions allowed under this cap *have* to be distributed in some way or other. As the right to emit was unlimited before the cap turned it into a scarce good, there is no pre-existing default distribution of this asset (worth billions of dollars) on which one could fall back in case no distribution was agreed upon. In the Kyoto Protocol a cap was agreed on only for the industrialised countries, with the US ultimately not ratifying the agreement. In general, though, even with Kyoto enacted, the industrialised countries still have higher per capita emissions than the developing countries, which have

232   L.H. Meyer and D. Roser

no limits on emissions. The political philosopher interested in the pattern according to which emissions were dealt out to industrialised nations under the Kyoto Protocol must be disappointed, however. The distribution was not based on the application of any clear-cut and explicit criterion of distributive justice but rather reflects political negotiation[6] in that a strong element of grandfathering[7] is discernible.[8]

The good to be distributed and the standard to be applied

We will judge the initial allocation of tradable emission rights according to prioritarian standards and we must be careful to state clearly what exactly *the good* is to which we apply these standards.[9] We will often use a rough shorthand and simply speak of distributing emissions while obviously what is up for distribution are tradable emission *rights* and not emissions themselves. The goods to which prioritarian standards are applied are, however, the *benefits* that the use of emission rights makes possible and not the emission rights themselves. Emission rights are beneficial because they allow for what we call emission-generating activities such as producing industrial commodities, subsistence farming, or flying to go on vacations.[10] So, what the shorthand of 'distributing emissions' ultimately amounts to is distributing (*by* distributing emission rights) the benefits of engaging in emission-generating activities. Or, *very* roughly but more intuitively, we could say that *by* distributing emission rights we are distributing economic progress – 'very roughly', because, first, economic progress of course does not capture everything that is beneficial about emission-generating activities (sometimes economic progress is not even itself something beneficial), and, second, because there is no one-to-one relationship between emissions and economic progress as some draw much more economic output from the same amount of emissions than others.

We will judge the distribution of goods according to the priority view. This view can be seen as aiming at taking into account the intuitions behind egalitarianism and sufficientarianism in the most plausible way.[11] It is the view that benefiting people matters regardless of how much others have and that we should give greater weight to benefits for people who are badly off than to benefits for people who are well off.

There are two options for applying the priority view to a single good. This can be called a problem of 'local justice',[12] that is, a problem of the just distribution of a certain slice (in our case: emission rights or adaptation costs) of the whole universe of goods. According to the first option the fair distribution of the good is determined as though the distribution of other goods was completely faded out from our view. According to the second option the currently existing unequal background distribution of other goods is taken as given and the fair distribution of the specific good in question is determined in light of it.

Both options are problematic. The largest problem of the first option is that if one is concerned with justice it then seems unnatural to be concerned with the just distribution of some one specific good in abstraction from the highly unequal background distribution of other goods. The problem with the second option is that it would yield a very simple answer: give all the emission rights to the South. However, it seems less than reasonable to aim at bringing the *overall* distribution of goods closer to the ideal by adjusting the distribution of only *one* particular good.

One might want to respond to these problems by denying that we can meaningfully ask how a certain single resource should be distributed; instead, questions of distributive justice can only meaningfully be raised concerning a whole bundle of goods such as, say, natural resources or primary goods (or even: only about the design of institutions affecting the distribution of those goods). However, whether we like it or not, political reality currently hands us such problems of fair distribution of certain specific goods in our non-ideal world. Currently, it is not an issue of much political relevance of how to globally redistribute, say, natural resources or *all* goods in general but the determination of the distribution of the newly created emission rights in contrast is an issue which *cannot* be escaped.

We will rely on the first option when discussing the just distribution of emission rights, i.e. we will in general abstract from the background distribution. The importance of relying on the first option is diminished by the fact that the second option only strengthens, and in no way weakens, the general conclusion we draw, which is that the North should shoulder a larger burden than it does today.

Taking historical emissions into account

We want to argue that, based on prioritarian premises, the historical inequality in emissions gives us reason to tilt the present allocation of emission rights in favour of the South in the sense that its per capita emission rights should be higher than in the North. The difference in historical emissions between the North and the South is far from negligible. Developed countries were responsible for more than three times as many emissions between 1850 and 2002 than developing countries[13] while the latter host a much larger part of humanity. In the policy arena a counterbalance to the historical inequality in emissions was most prominently discussed under the heading of the 'Brazilian Proposal' (1997).[14] The Brazilian Proposal received little support. More generally, there is quite some resistance to counterbalancing past emissions. Frequently heard objections include the following three points:

The first objection states that currently living people should not be made responsible for the acts of their ancestors and should not be put at a disadvantage simply because the people inhabiting their country before them emitted too much.

The second objection states that one can only be blamed for a certain act if one knows – or is liable to know – of the harmful effects of the act, and it is debatable whether knowledge of the harmful effect of emissions was sufficiently widespread until recently.

The third objection points to the relevance of the non-identity problem; no one can claim to be worse off or better off than she would be had another climate policy been pursued in the sufficiently distant past.

Note that each of the objections attacks emissions caused up to different dates of the past. The first concerns emissions by people who are now dead; the second, emissions, say, before the first IPCC report in 1990;[15] and the third emissions (and policies influencing emissions) so early as to be a determining factor of the number and identity of people living today.

There are, however, two ways of taking (part of) past emissions into account that are not susceptible to the three objections. The first way turns on what we consider the relevant units of concern and, in particular, what temporal extension they have. If as prioritarians we do not demand a just distribution of emission benefits at each point in time but rather over the whole lifespan of individuals[16] then one part of past emissions enters very naturally into the fair deal concerning the present distribution of emission rights; namely, the emissions that occurred during the life of the presently living. The simple idea is that people of the North already enjoyed much benefits associated with emissions during their lifetime and therefore a larger part of the remaining benefits should go to people in the South, which gives them the opportunity to 'catch up'.

The first and third objections obviously do not speak against this way of taking past emissions into account. The second objection has no bite either: the above argument does not justify higher emission rights for the South as compensation for past wrongdoing of the North but rather by the idea of realising a just distribution of emission benefits over the lifetime of individuals. If an individual of the North already has used up his share, it does not matter whether he did so knowingly and wrongfully or not.[17]

The second justifiable way of taking past emissions into account for the determination of the presently fair shares relies on the fact that we do not want to achieve a just distribution of *emissions* but rather of *benefits of emissions*. And since the industrialisation of the ancestors of the people currently living in the North yields benefits up to today and much more so for people of the North than the South, this has to be taken into account even if the emissions were caused by people who are now dead.

The first two objections obviously do not speak against this way of taking past emissions into account. The third objection has no bite either: we do not claim that people of the South are worse off than they would have been without emissions in the distant past and neither do we claim that people of the North benefit from industrialisation in the distant past in the sense of being better off than they would have been had there been no industrialisation. They only benefit in the sense that since their conception they have enjoyed being brought up in an industrialised world while others cannot enjoy such circumstances. If there is at present more 'economic progress to be given away' (that is: emission rights to be distributed which allow for the emissions that accompany economic progress), and if we want to hand out shares of economic progress – taken here as the main benefit associated with emissions – according to prioritarian standards then people of the South should get a disproportionate share of emission rights because people of the North have already received a large part of their share by inheritance from their ancestors.

Against this second way of taking the past into account it might also be objected that it is questionable that the receipt of benefits generates any obligations at all, in particular if the benefits were 'imposed' rather than voluntarily accepted, as is the case with being born into an industrialised world. The answer to this worry is that we do *not* rely on the premise that inheriting emission benefits generates obligations to give something to others *in turn*. The argument only presupposes that those who were born with a large 'slice of the pie' have a smaller claim when it comes to splitting up the rest of the pie.

So, our conclusion is that based on the unequal benefits enjoyed by people in the North and the South certain parts of past emissions should be taken into account for the purpose of distributing emissions rights today.[18] Not all inequality in historical emissions should be taken into account, however; those emissions that belonged to people who are now dead and which yield no benefits for the currently living should be written off.

We can now look at the general reason why the three objections do not pose any problem for our two ways of taking past emissions into account. All three objections rely on the idea that lower than equal shares for the North must be grounded in the idea of compensation. The third objection denies that past emissions can be seen as harmful (or beneficial) and, so, if there is no harming (or benefiting), then no compensation is appropriate. The second objection claims that even if past emissions could be seen as harmful, they still cannot be seen as wrongful; as such, no compensation is owed. The first objection goes further in stating that even if past emissions were both harmful and wrongful, still, compensation is not owed, the reason being that compensation is something that the wrongdoer himself must pay and not his descendants.

Even if the objections were based on sound premises when applied to other positions, they have no bite here since our two ways of taking past emissions into account do not rely on the idea of compensation but consider the distribution of emission rights as a problem of pure distributive justice without any reference to harm or wrong.[19] The idea is simply

236   L.H. Meyer and D. Roser

to distribute the benefits associated with emission-generating activities according to the priority view among the presently living – and because people in the North start with a higher level of such benefits people of the South have priority when it comes to deal out the presently available emission rights.[20] This is not to say that the three objections are not important. They are important when it comes to the different question of fairness in adaptation (section 3).

A numerical illustration

To make the points of this chapter more comprehensible we will present the basic idea in a simple numerical illustration. Assume that we have two islands called 'North' and 'South'. Both islands consist of three persons: 'Old', 'Middle', and 'Young'. On both islands, Young is born after the death of Old. We have two time-periods: period I and II.

The question is: presupposing the emissions of period I, how should emission rights be distributed in period II among the North and the South? We assume that each island is able and willing to fairly distribute its emission rights internally. An important assumption is that two units of emissions in the North in period I create two units of benefit for the North in period I, and one unit of benefit for the North in period II (assume for example that the two units of emission were used in period I for (i) an airplane flight into vacation and (ii) the building of a school: the airplane flight is beneficial only at the time of the emission while the school building yields a benefit in both periods). The same applies to the South. We assume that the South emitted eight units in period I and the North emitted 12 units in period I.

Assume that there are 10 units of emissions to be distributed in period II. How many should the North get and how many should the South get accord-

Benefits associated with emissions **from** period I **in**

	Period I	Period II
For North-Old	6	
For North-Middle	6	3
For North-Young		3
For South-Old	4	
For South-Middle	4	2
For South-Young		2

Figure 1.

ing to our reasoning? People in the North alive in period II already own 12 emission benefits. Six of those 12 benefits are those that North-Middle enjoyed in period I (our first way of taking the past into account) and the other six benefits are those that North-Middle and North-Young enjoy in period II as a result of the Northern emissions in period I (our second way of taking the past into account). People in the South alive in period II in contrast only own eight emission benefits (4+2 from South-Middle and 2 from South-Young).

So, our argument says that of the 10 emission benefits to be distributed, the North should get three (together with its 12 benefits this sums up to 15) and the South should get seven (together with its eight benefits this sums up to 15 as well). Given that these emission rights are fairly distributed internally within each island,[21] distributive justice among the people alive in period II is created in such a way. Not all past emissions have been taken into account: The inequality of emissions benefits between North-Old and South-Old in period I will forever remain without relevance.

What would this mean in practice for a post-Kyoto treaty? Enacting the fair solution demands allocating a share of emissions to each country that is either above or below the equal-per-capita share depending on whether the country has a lot or few benefits from past emissions. Countries, then, have to ensure that they internally distribute the mitigation burden fairly, which amounts to disproportionately burdening those citizens who already own many emission benefits. The most accurate way of approximating this is by each citizen's wealth, we submit.

At the country level, however, benefits from past emissions can not only be approximated by the country's wealth but also by a measure which adds up cumulative past emissions of a given country but discounts those emissions according to how far in the past they lie. The idea of such discounting is that emissions closer to the present yield more benefits for the presently living. Relying on such a measure as an approximation for benefits from past emissions instead of relying on wealth as an approximation amounts to either assuming that the current inhabitants of each country should be made responsible for how many benefits are drawn from a given amount of emissions in the past or else to make the simplifying assumption that everyone draws the same amount of benefits from a given amount of emissions. It also leaves open whether wealth is a good specification of what constitutes benefits from emission-generating activities.

Note that these ways of taking past emissions into account for the specification of the distribution of the mitigation burden are similar to but distinct from the Brazilian Proposal. The latter is the most prominent suggestion for taking past emissions into account. However, in its calculations it relied on the cumulative effect of emissions since 1840 on global average surface temperature, that is, it discounted past emissions not according to the benefits they yield today but according to how much damage they do.

238   L.H. Meyer and D. Roser

Who must pay for climate damages?

The last section discussed a fair deal concerning emissions as the *cause* of climate change and this section discusses a fair deal concerning climate change as the *effect* of these emissions, both with a special eye towards the relevance of the past. The costs of climate change have two aspects: first, the climate damages themselves, and second – since the impact of emissions not only depends on the level of climate change produced by them, but also in the human reaction to this change – the adaptation costs necessary to minimise or at least decrease climate damages. In this section our ultimate concern is justice concerning all costs – i.e. the adaptation costs *plus* the damages that remain even after optimal adaptation. But: since the damages themselves cannot be transferred from one person to another, justice concerning the whole costs of climate change will have to be reached by taking only the *one* aspect of who is responsible for adaptation costs as a variable under control of policy.

The issue of injustice concerning climate damages arises on two levels. First, the South will be hit harder by climate change. This is so independently of how much climate change occurs and who is causally responsible for it. It is likewise so even if only non-anthropogenic climate change occurred or if everybody in the past had stuck to their fair share of emissions. The most important reasons for the higher vulnerability of the South are geographical factors (e.g. the higher temperature independently of climate change), the higher reliance on agriculture and the lower adaptive capacities. Second, and independently of the first point, it is the case that people have exceeded and predictably will exceed their fair shares as determined in the last section. In any realistic scenario the North will have exceeded its share, and will have done so more than the South. In any case, we will presuppose that this is so in this section.

How should climate damages, and in particular the fact that the South will be particularly vulnerable to climate change while at the same time being causally less responsible for it, be dealt with from the point of view of justice? One answer that quickly comes to mind is that the South is owed compensation for its suffering and that the North as the main culprit for climate change should provide sufficient measures of compensation. This section will point out the problems of this view and suggests instead that we should view climate damages primarily as a reason for redistribution due to undeserved benefits and harms rather than compensation.

Distributive and compensatory justice

To argue for this conclusion we will first discuss compensation (in three versions) and then redistribution. One way to make the distinction between the basic idea of redistribution and compensation starts with the premise that there is some *baseline distribution* of goods that is just which is determined on the one hand by a certain criterion (such as the priority view, egalitarianism, or sufficientarianism or possibly simply the status quo distribution) and on the other hand by permissible changes to the distribution (as determined by the criterion) which someone experiences as a result of his own *responsible (and non-wrongful) choices*. Deviations from this baseline then call for two different kinds of reactions. In case the reaction the deviation calls for is *based on the wrongfulness* of what occurred, we are operating in the realm of *compensatory justice*. In case the reaction the deviation calls for is based on the idea of *evening out undeserved* benefits or harms (which are due to for example luck or harmful but non-wrongful actions), we are operating in the realm of *distributive justice*.

The basic idea is to ask: which duties to pay for adaptation to climate change rely for their justification on the wrongfulness of what was done, i.e. which duties can be traced back to the compensatory rationale? Any duties that cannot be so traced back will fall into the category of the redistributive rationale and will be regarded as grounded in the objective of levelling off undeserved benefits and harms. Whether payments for adaptation costs are justified on the basis of the compensatory or redistributive rationale will also help to determine the size of such payments.

Two remarks are appropriate. First, not everybody regards evening out undeserved benefits and harms through redistribution as a moral imperative; and some, namely sufficientarians, regard it as an imperative only up to the point where everybody has 'enough'. We will assume that undeserved benefits and harms should be evened out according to prioritarian standards, but we believe that the basic point of distinguishing compensatory and redistributive rationales remains interesting also for theorists who do not see undeserved benefits and harms as giving weighty reasons for redistribution.

Second, note that we are operating with such a narrow notion of compensation that it is not completely in line with the way the terminology is used in other contexts where the notion of compensation is also used for payments which are due to non-wrongful harm-doing. All we argue for is that it is an interesting question in the intergenerational context of climate change to separate payments based on wrongfulness from those not based on wrongfulness and, further, that the latter can be seen as based on other (namely, redistributive) concerns than the former.

We will distinguish three versions of compensatory payments depending on who has the duty to come up with them.[22] The most natural duty bearer for compensatory payments is the emitter of wrongful emissions himself: the *Emitter Pays Principle* (EmPP). A second version identifies the beneficiary of wrongful emissions as responsible for providing compensation: the *Beneficiary Pays Principle* (BePP). A third version ascribes the duty to pay compensation to the wrongdoing community: the *Community Pays Principle*

240   L.H. Meyer and D. Roser

	Benefits associated with emissions from period I in		Climate Damages associated with emissions from period I in	
	Period I	Period II	Period I	Period II
For North-Old	6		–	
For North-Middle	6	3	–	–5
For North-Young		3		–5
For South-Old	4		–	
For South-Middle	4	2	–	–10
For South-Young		2		–10

Figure 2.

(CoPP). In discussing these three principles, we will have to answer two questions for each principle: How plausible is it as a principle of compensatory justice in general? And: what kind of compensatory measures can it justify in the climate change context?

In order to illustrate more easily why compensatory measures are difficult to justify we will make use of the numerical example from the last section again. For this section, we add the assumption that the emissions from period I cause climate damages in period II, say five for people in the North and 10 for people in the South (Figure 2).

Compensatory justice and climate damages

There are six basic problems for justifying compensatory payments in the context of climate damages:

Potential payers might be dead.[23]
Potential payers might not have exceeded their fair shares.
Potential payers might have been (blamelessly) ignorant.
Potential recipients might (due to the non-identity problem) only be said to be harmed according to a threshold conception of harm.[24]
Potential payers might (due to the non-identity problem) not be said to have benefited.
Potential recipients might not be wrongfully harmed because climate change may also have non-anthropogenic sources.

First let us look at the principle that demands that the emitter must pay compensation for his wrongful emissions to those who are wronged (EmPP). There is not much doubt that in general (that is, disregarding whether it can usefully be applied to the climate change problem) the idea of such compensation is very well supported by our moral intuitions.[25] This is in contrast to BePP and CoPP where the principle itself is in need of some supporting arguments. The only dispute in the case of EmPP is whether it can justify compensatory payments for the specific case of climate damages or not.

If EmPP is put to the service of justifying compensatory payments one has to identify wrongful emitters and wrongfully harmed persons. Someone emits wrongfully if (1) he exceeded his fair share and (2) he knew or was liable to know about the harmfulness of his emissions. Someone is wrongfully harmed by emissions if he either is worse off due to wrongful emissions than he would otherwise have been or falls below the specified threshold of harm due to the wrongful emissions (or both).[26] Let us use the numerical example to look at what duties to pay compensation and what rights to receive compensation the EmPP can and cannot justify in period II:

North-Old and South-Old cannot have a duty to pay compensation because they are dead.

South-Middle (as well as South-Old) did not exceed its fair share and so must not pay.

North-Middle (as well as the other emitters from period I) might not have been aware, and might neither have been liable to be aware, of the problematic nature of its emissions and thus it can be excused by ignorance of wrongdoing.

North-Young and South-Young can only claim to be wronged – and claim with it a right to compensation – if they fall below the sufficientarian threshold of the threshold understanding of harm. They cannot be said to be harmed simply because climate quality is worse than it would be had there been less emissions in period I.

So, if one could legitimately be excused by ignorance in period I, then EmPP cannot identify *any* wrongful emitter at all to pay compensation payments. If not, it can still only ascribe compensatory duties to North-Middle (even though it is only one of four agents causally responsible for climate change in period II). EmPP also has some trouble in identifying wronged persons: In contrast to South-Middle (and North-Middle), South-Young (and North-Young) can only be said to be wronged – and thus be the rightful recipient of compensatory payments – if they fall below the sufficientarian threshold.

Of course, some assumptions that we made in the numerical model might be loosened and then some duty bearers or right bearers might be identified. First, period I could be defined as being at a point of time when the excuse of ignorance has no more force. Second, damages could be modelled as starting to materialise immediately after the emissions were produced and not only in the next period. Third, the South might also exceed its fair share. Fourth, one might doubt the relevance of the non-identity problem. Our purpose in making these strict assumptions, though, was to highlight all the problems that potentially come up when one makes an attempt at justifying compensatory payments based on EmPP.

Let us turn to the principle that demands that those who have *benefited* from wrongful emissions must pay compensation (BePP). First we have to ask whether it is a legitimate principle in general, that is, apart from the climate change question, to accrue benefits from a wrong imply accepting the duty of compensation. Applied to the issue of climate damages the question is the following: why should people who have committed no wrongful emissions but have only benefited (either from emission-generating activities or from climate change itself) have to pay compensation? Note that the people who received benefits from past emission-generating activities did not ask for these benefits; they were imposed on them, so to speak.

There is no completely obvious answer to the question of whether benefiting from wrongdoing creates a duty of compensation. The difficulty of judging this issue is based on two reasons. First, if one was benefited by a wrong this benefit is most definitely not *deserved*. It is deserved as little as any other benefit one receives by luck (if anything, it is deserved even less).[27] And based on considerations of distributive justice one can see *any* undeserved benefit (and harm) as calling for redistribution regardless of whether one received this benefit due to a wrongful action or brute luck. But what we are asking in discussing the BePP is whether the reception of benefits from a wrong implies a duty which for its justification presupposes the wrongness of the action and not whether it creates a duty of redistribution. The second reason why it is difficult to judge the BePP as a principle of compensatory justice is that in our daily lives we are not used to thinking about cases where the people who commit the wrong are not the ones who benefit from it.[28]

Still, the BePP has to be judged, even if it is difficult. On the one hand, there are clear examples where we do not judge benefiting from an injustice as calling for compensation. Note for example that everybody who uses an x-ray profits from how this technology was refined using data from Hiroshima.[29] On the other hand, there are intuitions to the contrary. Gosseries, for example, interprets benefiting from an action without paying the associated costs in terms of free-riding.[30] Present-day inhabitants of the North can be seen as transgenerational free-riders because they *currently* benefit from *past* emissions that impose costs on people *currently* living in the South. Importantly, Gosseries distinguishes two interpretations of the way in which free-riding can be seen as objectionable. The first interpretation relies on considerations of distributive justice and this is not the relevant case for the BePP. It is the idea sketched a few lines above that, of course, *any* undeserved benefits and harms can be seen as calling for redistribution – and benefits and harms due to injustice committed by others are simply *one* instance of undeserved benefits and harms. But if one relies on this interpretation it is difficult to see what is specific about benefiting from a wrongful action in contrast to benefiting from some other kind of action or event for which one is not responsible. All that one could possibly argue is that, intuitively, there seem to be weightier reasons to even out undeserved deviations from a just baseline that are due to a wrong than to even out undeserved deviations that are due to more general causes. The second interpretation of why free-riding is objectionable relies on what Gosseries calls 'interactive justice', which is similar to our conception of compensatory justice. It is the relevant case for making use of BePP to legitimise compensatory payments. This second way gains some plausibility if one regards benefiting from an action or a scheme or a policy as in some way involving an action, namely the action of willingly *accepting* being benefited by it. Accepting being benefited by wrongful emissions can possibly be seen as transferring (some of) the wrongdoer's duty of compensation to the beneficiary. Another basis for the position that benefiting from wrongdoing calls for compensation is proposed by Butt. He claims that condemnation of injustice implies not being willing to benefit from it while others suffer from it: 'My claim is that taking our nature as moral agents seriously requires not only that we be willing not to commit acts of injustice ourselves, but that we hold a genuine aversion to injustice and its lasting effects. We make a conceptual error if we condemn a given action as unjust, but are not willing to reverse or mitigate its effects on the grounds that it has benefited us.'[31]

Even though we are sceptical of the position that benefiting from wrongful actions not only gives rise to duties of redistribution but also to duties of compensation, we will not commit ourselves to a definite answer. Rather, we will note that *even if* the BePP could be defended as a principle in general, there is still something very questionable about applying it to climate damages. Due to the non-identity problem, North-Young and South-Young (who constitute the people who did not emit in Period I thereby causing climate damages in Period II) cannot be said to have benefited at all. Without past emissions they would not be worse off but rather not exist at all (this is problem e. from the above list). And even if the non-identity problem were irrelevant or could be shown to be of little practical relevance, there still remains an obstacle: if *voluntary acceptance* of benefits should prove to be a condition of their giving rise to compensatory duties, one would have to address the difficult issue of whether abstaining from emigrating from an industrialised country (or rejecting the benefits of living there in some other way) can really count as willingly accepting these benefits. Thus, although BePP seemingly has a larger base of possible duty bearers than the EmPP – not only the emitters themselves but anybody who benefited from the wrongful emissions – it is no more successful in identifying duty bearers than EmPP.

So, both EmPP and the more questionable BePP can only justify a small amount of compensatory measures or none at all. Let us now turn to the principle that demands that present-day members of a community must pay for the wrongs that past members of the community committed (CoPP). We will not commit ourselves to a certain view as to what the adequate specification of the community would be in the context of climate change but we will use countries or other communities with a legal form as the most suggestive examples.

Note that we in no way presuppose the collective *moral* responsibility of today's people living in the North for the emissions of their ancestors in the sense that the currently living would be able to incur blame or guilt for past wrongful emissions. We want to place our arguments firmly on normative individualist grounds. There are sound arguments, however, even on these grounds, to the effect that community membership can, in principle, be a reason to ascribe duties to presently living members of a transgenerational community to provide compensation for the wrongs committed by earlier members.[32]

People can value their membership in certain groups. Accordingly, they will be willing to accept standing under obligations of preserving the group to which they belong. People can have valid reasons for understanding themselves in such a way. First, the group to which they belong might exhibit a general value by being, say, a just or tolerant community. All people have reason to value belonging to such a community insofar as living in, say, a just society is – individually and collectively – of intrinsic value. The groups typically are transgenerational in character. If justice requires, inter alia, providing measures of restitution and compensation for wrongful harm-doing such transgenerational communities will be just, inter alia, by providing compensation to presently living victims of injustices that earlier members of the community committed. Second, people will value their membership in such groups for a further reason: the group might exhibit particular features that are highly relevant for the well-being of its members since they manifest particular ways of communal life. Due to these features of their group's culture people have access to particular options that are highly valuable to them given who they are: the particular culture of their group will often have shaped their social identity in decisive ways.

The two types of reasons for holding membership in one's community or polity to be valuable are interrelated: the intrinsic value of our being a member of a society will depend in part on the ways in which we relate to its particular features, yet we clearly do not attribute intrinsic value to just any society. Rather, for a society to have intrinsic value it will have to fulfil certain minimal requirements concerning its internal and external relations. What these minimal conditions amount to will depend on what universal and particularly weighty reasons for action people can be said to have. It seems plausible to suggest that people ought to value their membership in a society on the condition that their society is just to a reasonable degree. Thus, for them to be able to attribute intrinsic value to their membership, they will have to contribute to the creation and strengthening of the institutions that are necessary for their society fulfilling its obligations of justice. Arguably, among these obligations are those to provide measures of compensation for wrongs that were committed publicly (or even in the name of the community) by its members in the past.

So, given that the intrinsic value of communities is only present under certain conditions, one has reason to see to it that these conditions are fulfilled. And if one of those conditions is that present-day victims of historical injustice are compensated, one has reason based on valuing the community to do so. One's reasons can be partly understood to reflect the idea of a natural duty to justice: we all have the duty to support the realisation of justice and thus, if membership in a community, and the creation of adequate institutions in this community, and the support of the specific goal of compensation payments to victims of historical injustice are necessary prerequisites for justice becoming a reality, then one has a duty to work towards these goals. This is so not as a matter of personal preference of identifying with one's community but reflects categorical reasons: carrying out the natural duty of justice serves a good, the protection of which is thought to be of such importance that people are thought to have categorical reasons for doing so. At the same time, membership in the community is valued in part due to its specific features (its history and unique communal ways of life). When members of such communities fulfil their duties of justice, this will reflect their *wanting* to uphold a particular *self-understanding*, namely, that of being a participating member of their community. For they understand that they can wish to uphold the particular communal way of life of their society (based, in part, on its particular features) only if their society is sufficiently just. This, arguably, requires the provision of restitution and compensation for wrongs that were committed publicly (or even in the name of the community) by its members in the past.

So, the bottom line is that there are ways in which liberals relying on normative individualism can justify why present-day members of countries should accept the duty to make compensatory payments for wrongful emissions of earlier members of the country as demanded by CoPP. Thus, the scope of possible duty-bearers is extended so as to include North-Young and North-Middle paying for the wrong done by the emissions of North-Old. They do this as members of the community of the North.

However, compensatory payments along the lines of CoPP still only cover *wrongful* emissions. And thus, emissions made under ignorance about their harmful nature, and emissions that did not exceed the fair share, as well as non-anthropogenic causes of climate change all remain uncovered. Actually, reliance on CoPP can only complement EmPP and BePP in the sense that it escapes problem a. of the above list of problems (that is, potential polluters might be dead) with the other problems remaining unaffected.

246 L.H. Meyer and D. Roser

Redistribution as a response to climate damages

Compensation payments for climate damages are difficult to justify for the reasons offered above. And, more importantly, insofar as such arguments (for EmPP, BePP, or CoPP) actually succeed in justifying *some* compensatory measures, they only justify them for *part* of those who cause or suffer from climate change.

Still, the fact that the South has to carry such a large share of climate damages seems to be a situation that cries out for *some* kind of response. And of course, compensation (in the narrow sense of wrongdoers paying something to the wronged persons on the grounds of the injustice committed) is not the only kind of possible response. Rather, given that many effects of climate change can be seen as undeserved harms – and harms which go along with undeserved benefits for other persons – levelling off such effects *on the basis of a concern for distributive justice* is an equally plausible response. In assuming that the priority view is the correct kind of principle for distributing emission rights we assumed that principles of distributive justice do apply at the global level.[33] And consequently, we believe that principles of distributive justice can also be applied (at least to some degree) to the distribution of duties to pay for adaptation measures. Of course, to common moral intuition, demands of compensatory justice seem to have a stronger force than demands based simply on evening out undeserved benefits or harms, particularly at the global level.[34] We do not necessarily want to question that view. However, in the context of climate damages, compensation payments are only justifiable for such a small part of the problem that it is appropriate to direct attention primarily to the redistributive demands. The focus must be turned to sharing undeserved benefits and harms equitably rather than focusing on compensating wronged persons in view of the limited applicability of the latter enterprise.

In practice, a prioritarian redistributive scheme concerned with climate damages amounts to those who are lucky in terms of not being affected much by climate change assisting those who are unlucky in terms of being affected heavily. They owe this assistance *independently* of who caused climate change. Thus according to the redistributive approach to climate damages, even if, contrary to actual fact, it were historically the South that predominantly had created the climate problem, it would still be those vulnerable to a lesser extent who should support adaptive measures in those countries where people were more vulnerable.[35] Another way to install a prioritarian redistributive scheme concerned with climate damages would not only aim at a just pattern concerning this one specific good called 'climate damages' but rather take into account the whole background distribution of other goods.[36] This means making the wealthy assist those who are vulnerable to climate change, which would not make that much of a difference because wealth and low vulnerability are correlated to quite some degree.

In the real world this would mean that countries have to be ranked according to their vulnerability to climate change and those that are highly vulnerable get privileged access to the resources available in a global adaptation fund. The above argument suggests that such a fund would have to be paid for either by those who exhibit low vulnerability or by the wealthy. To some limited extent, it could also be financed by those who, despite all the problems mentioned in section *Compensatory justice and climate damages*, stand under duties to provide measures of compensation. Within countries, raising the money for such a global adaptation fund through progressive taxation could serve as an approximation for making the less vulnerable pay. At the intra-national level, aiming at additional redistribution from the hardly vulnerable to the highly vulnerable might take many different forms, such as government subsidies for adaptation measures in poor communities.

Conclusion

This chapter discussed a fair way of allocating the mitigation and adaptation costs associated with climate change, in particular in the light of the benefits and damages brought forth by past emissions. It presupposed a prioritarian theory of distributive justice and generally proceeded by abstracting from the background inequality existing in the real world. It first discussed mitigation and concluded that the South should get higher per capita emission rights than the North because it has less benefits associated with past emissions to start with. It then discussed who should pay for adaptation costs and argued that it is difficult to frame the duty of the North to those who are highly vulnerable as a duty of compensation; it should primarily be seen as a duty grounded in concerns of distributive justice.

Even though we separated the issues of mitigation and adaptation for analytical purposes, there might be ample reason to link the two issues, in particular when it comes to practical policy-making. In a 'local justice approach' there is no general guideline on which goods to discuss jointly and which goods to discuss separately, and it is of course not at all far-fetched to discuss the two climate change-related goods of emission rights and climate damages in conjunction, particularly given that we have shown that both primarily pose issues of distributive justice.[37] By treating mitigation and adaptation jointly, one could, for example, argue for assisting those with above average vulnerability through the specific 'currency' of emission rights. In linking adaptation and mitigation one could also take note of interdependencies, such as the need for economic progress (and thus the need for emission rights) in poor countries in order to diminish vulnerability (and thus adaptation costs). It is also desirable to link the discussion up more with the background distribution of other goods, which would in general strengthen the duties of the North even more and point to the need for linking development and climate policies, but would in addition also highlight the duties of wealthy individuals within poor countries.

Regardless of which goods are treated jointly both in the policy arena and for purposes of analytical discussion, the message stays the same that almost any argument on climate justice ascribes larger shortcomings to the North than the South in comparison with the ideally just state of affairs. Since there is not much to dispute concerning this general conclusion, the interest of any argument must lie in the *rationale* it gives for this conclusion. It has been the goal of this article to give a plausible justification for this widely accepted claim, in particular by stressing how past emission-generating activities yield unequal benefits and harms for the presently living – an inequality which generally calls for the application of distributive justice rather than compensatory justice.

Acknowledgements
We wish to thank Keith Bustos, Simon Caney, Axel Gosseries, Sarah Kenehan, Pranay Sanklecha and participants at the Manchester Political Theory Workshops for their helpful comments and criticisms.

Notes
1. For simplicity's sake, we refer also to deforestation and other ways of decreasing sinks as emission generating activities. An umbrella term which would more precisely capture both activities which add emissions to the atmosphere and activities which diminish the removal of emissions from the atmosphere would for example be 'emission concentration enhancing activities'.
2. By emissions we always refer to greenhouse gas emissions. In a more complete treatment one would not only cite greenhouse gas emissions as responsible for exposing people to climate damages, but also include the removal of sinks which absorb emissions (in particular deforestation) as well as activities which increase the vulnerability of people to a changed climate.
3. Cf. Gosseries (2004, p. 37). On the topic of historical injustice in general see Meyer (2004, 2005.)
4. One implication of this is that it makes one of the answers to historical injustice more difficult to sustain, namely the answer which argues that one should compensate descendants of wronged persons because those descendants were wronged in that their parents did not receive the appropriate compensation and that as a result of this lack of payments the descendants are worse off than they would be if the compensation to their parents had been paid (after their conception), see Sher (2005) and Meyer (2008, sec. 5.1)
5. For plausible attempts at answering this question, see e.g. Caney (2006b) or Page (2006).
6. When we speak of the North and the South we always implicitly either take those terms as an abbreviation for an individual of the North or the South or else we assume a two-stage process where in a first stage climate justice between the countries of the North and the South is determined after which each country will

then, in a second stage, internally distribute its mitigation and adaptation burdens fairly to individuals.
7. See Depledge (2002, p. 37).
8. Grandfathering refers to the scheme that grants high current emission rights to those with high past emissions. Because this scheme plays an important role in policy debates, it is important to deal with this proposal: see Meyer and Roser (2006, pp. 229ff.) If polluters are actually *entitled* to (a certain proportion of) the emissions level they have historically acquired, then there would be no scope for distributing emissions according to some pattern such as the priority view.
9. See Bartsch and Müller (2000, p. 227).
10. Some people speak of giving everyone a share of the *atmosphere* (Friends of the Earth 2006) or a share of the *climate* (Christian Aid 1999). This is less than precise since the issue is not more or less atmosphere or climate. Others speak of fairly distributing the *absorptive capacity of the atmosphere* (Neumayer 2000). This is not the best description of the good in question either because what is limited is not really the *capacity* of the atmosphere to *absorb greenhouse gases* but rather the willingness of humans to put up with the climate quality that ensues from high concentrations of greenhouse gases in the atmosphere.
11. Besides this, emissions can also be beneficial in a different way, namely through the climate change they cause: selected people (e.g. some farmers in Northern latitudes) profit from a warming world.
12. For a more extensive discussion see e.g. Meyer and Roser (2006), Casal (2007) and Holtug and Lippert-Rasmussen (2007).
13. See Gosseries' remark on this issue in Gosseries (2007) as well as similar remarks in Gosseries (2004). He relies on Elster (1992).
14. See Baumert *et al.* (2005, p.32)
15. For an overview see La Rovere *et al.* (2002)
16. Gosseries (2004) lists some salient dates which might serve as an alternative to 1990.
17. According to Holtug and Lippert-Rasmussen (2007, p. 10) most egalitarians find this latter option more plausible.
18. This approximate conclusion has to be qualified somewhat as a matter of transitory justice (cf. Gosseries 2007): *if* people were legitimately ignorant about the problematic nature of their emissions then *some* legitimate expectations accompany the ownership of their emission benefits.
19. Caney (2006a) argues that evening out inequalities in emissions over time relies on a collectivist framework. Note that by focusing on the *benefits* of past emissions enjoyed by the *presently living*, we can eschew this problem.
20. Note also that there is something peculiar about seeing mitigation as a kind of compensation for not mitigating: it can only be applied in the sense of seeing present mitigation as compensation for past lack of mitigation, but of course not in the synchronic fashion of seeing present mitigation as compensation for a lack of present mitigation. This is in contrast to paying for adaptation costs, which can be seen as compensation for a lack of present mitigation.
21. If the background distribution were taken into account (i.e. the second option) when determining the just distribution of emission rights according to prioritarian standards, we would be faced with a more complex picture but which most plausibly still ascribes much higher emission rights to the South. First, we would additionally have to take into account which countries can draw many benefits from emission rights, based on factors such as geographical circumstances and the current living standards. Second, the interaction between emission rights and the background

distribution would also have to be taken into account in that the allocation scheme can influence economic growth and population growth.

22. North-Young could blame North-Middle for emitting so much in period I as a result of which the whole North gets few emission rights in period II. North-Young might punish North-Middle for this by, for example, cutting its social security.

23. These distinctions and the discussion of problems associated with each principle in the context of climate change justice have been most helpfully introduced and discussed by Simon Caney (2005, 2006a) and Axel Gosseries (2004). In many ways our argument in this section is indebted to their interpretations and analyses.

24. By potential payers we mean people who were either causally responsible for climate change or who grew up in beneficial circumstances that are partly due to emission-generating activities. By potential recipients we mean people who grew up in a place which would exhibit more favourable living conditions if it were not for climate change.

25. The non-identity problem precludes us from saying that future people are harmed (or benefited) by actions that are necessary conditions of their existence (cf. Parfit 1984). This is so if we understand harm in the sense of being made worse off by an action than one would otherwise be. There is however another conception of harm which successfully evades the non-identity problem: by claiming that people can be said to be harmed by actions which make them fall below a certain pre-specified threshold, future people can also be said to be harmed by actions which are a necessary condition of their existence. For a treatment of these issues, see Meyer (2008).

26. Note that we distinguish this principle from 'polluter pays principles' (or also 'strict liability principles') by focusing *only* on wrongful emitters while the polluter pays principle or a strict liability principle or also Moellendorf's (2002, p. 98) causal principle make *any* emitter – whether wrongful or not – pay. Such principles, which make people pay who are causally responsible for emissions irrespective of their culpability, can obviously not serve as principles of compensatory justice in the narrow sense defined above. This is not to say, however, that *in practice* policies relying on such a polluter pays principle could never be justified for certain areas of environmental policy. It can legitimately be put into practice for three reasons:

(1) In practice, in some areas of environmental policy it might be difficult to hold wrongful and non-wrongful emitters apart; or the two categories might overlap to such a large degree that it would be too cumbersome to hold them apart. Thus, enacting a polluter pays principle might serve as an *approximation* for the policy, which demands compensation from wrongdoers.

(2) The policy might also serve as an *approximation* for a policy based on the redistributive rationale: because polluters often benefit from their polluting action, making them pay something to the harmed can be seen as evening out undeserved deviations from a just baseline.

(3) A third and completely unrelated justification is based on instrumental grounds in the following way: According to economists, making people pay for harmful activities sets the right incentives and thus generates efficiency. If emitters (who are assumed to act self-interestedly) have to bear the external costs that appear as side effects of their actions they will only perform an emitting action in case the benefits exceed the costs. Thus, in a society where emitters (whether wrongful or not) are made to pay, all and only those emitting actions will be performed that have a net benefit which brings forth efficiency. However, such an instrumental justification for making emitters pay has no necessary link to the

idea of compensatory or redistributive justice. This can also be seen by noting that such an instrumental justification in fact provides no rationale at all for why the emitters' payments should be handed over to the people harmed by the emissions. The principle's whole idea is to deter people from emitting on a non-optimal level by making them pay, where the optimal level of emissions is set by some pre-specified goals.
27. See note 25.
28. However, in our non-ideal world benefits from wrongdoing can bring an individual closer to the well-being he or she ideally ought to enjoy.
29. See Anwander (2005, p. 40).
30. *Ibid.*
31. See Gosseries (2004).
32. See Butt (2007, p. 143).
33. For an extensive treatment, see Meyer (2005), chapters IV and V.
34. See among others Pogge (1989).
35. See Miller (2004, p. 241, fn. 1) and Gosseries (2004, p. 55).
36. In terms of figure 3, enacting a prioritarian distribution between the North and the South of the specific good of climate damages would amount to a transfer of 5 units of benefits from the North to the South.
37. Cf. the second option from section. The good to be distributed and the standard to be applied.
38. In terms of figure 2, enacting a prioritarian distribution of both benefits and damages jointly would demand giving all the 10 emission rights which are up for distribution in period II to the South and in addition demanding a transfer of two units of benefits from the North to the South. This would leave the people in the South who are alive in period II taken together with zero net benefits and the same is true for the people in the North who are alive in period II taken together.

Notes on contributors

Lukas Meyer is Professor of Practical Philosophy at the University of Graz, Austria. He is the author of *Historische Gerechtigkeit* (de Gruyter, 2005). He is also the co-editor of *Intergenerational justice* (Oxford University Press, 2009), *Justice in time* (Nomos, 2004), *Rights, culture and the law* (Oxford University Press, 2003) and *Neukantianismus und Rechtsphilosophie* (Nomos, 2002), and author of more than 30 articles on political and moral philosophy, especially intergenerational justice.

Dominic Roser studied economics, philosophy, and politics at the Universities of Berne, Geneva, and Oxford, and has been a doctoral student at the University of Zurich in a programme on interdisciplinary ethics. His research interests are in political philosophy; more particularly, in climate justice and ethical issues pertaining to economics and the economy. He publishes articles on intergenerational justice, global justice and risk in climate policy as well as the normative standing of climate economics.

References

Anwander, N., 2005. Contributing and benefiting: two grounds for duties to the victims of injustice. *Ethics & international affairs,* 19(1), 39–45.

252   L.H. Meyer and D. Roser

Bartsch, U. and Müller, B., 2000. *Fossil fuels in a changing climate.* Oxford: Oxford University Press.

Baumert, K., Herzog, T. and Pershing, J., 2005. *Navigating the numbers: greenhouse gas data and international climate policy.* Washington, DC: World Resources Institute.

Butt, D., 2007. On benefiting from injustice. *Canadian journal of philosophy,* 37(1), 129–52.

Caney, S., 2005. Cosmopolitan justice, responsibility and global climate change. *Leiden journal of international law,* 18(4), 747–775.

Caney, S., 2006a. Environmental degradation, reparations, and the moral significance of history. *Journal of social philosophy,* 37(3), 464–482.

Caney, S., 2006b. Cosmopolitan justice, rights and global climate change, *The Canadian journal of law & jurisprudence,* 19(2), 255–278.

Casal, P., 2007. Why sufficiency is not enough. *Ethics,* 117(2), 296–326.

Christian Aid, 1999. *Who owes who? Climate change, debt, equity and survival,* http://www.jubileeresearch.org/ecological_debt/Reports/Who_owes_who.htm (accessed 21 February 2008).

Depledge, J., 2002. Continuing Kyoto: extending absolute emission caps to developing countries. *In*: K.A. Baumert, O. Blanchard, S. Llosa and J.F. Perkaus, eds. *Building on the Kyoto protocol: options for protecting the climate.* Washington, DC: World Resources Institute, 31–60.

Elster, J., 1992. *Local justice. How institutions allocate scarce goods and necessary burdens.* Cambridge: Cambridge University Press.

Friends of the Earth, 2006. *Climate justice: a fair share of the atmosphere,* http://www.foe.org.au/resources/publications/climate-justice/A%20fair%20share%20of%20the%20Atmosphere.pdf (accessed 21 February 2008).

Gosseries, A., 2004. Historical emissions and free riding. *Ethical perspectives,* 11(1), 36–60.

Gosseries, A., 2007. Cosmopolitan luck egalitarianism and climate change. *Canadian journal of philosophy supplementary volume,* 31, 279–309.

Holtug, N. and Lippert-Rasmussen, K., 2007. An introduction to contemporary egalitarianism. *In*: Holtug, Nils and Kasper Lippert-Rasmussen, eds. *Egalitarianism. New essays on the nature and value of equality.* Oxford: Oxford University Press, 1–38.

La Rovere, E., de Valente de Macedo, L., and Baumert, K., 2002. The Brazilian proposal on relative responsibility for global warming. *In*: K. Baumert, O. Blanchard, S. Llosa and J. Perkaus, eds. *Building on the Kyoto protocol: options for protecting the climate.* Washington, DC: World Resources Institute, 157–173.

Meyer, L., ed., 2004. *Justice in time. Responding to historical injustice.* Baden-Baden: Nomos.

Meyer, L., 2005. *Historische Gerechtigkeit.* Berlin and New York: de Gruyter.

Meyer, L., 2008. Intergenerational justice. *In*: E.N. Zalta, ed., *The Stanford encyclopedia of philosophy* (2008 edition, forthcoming), http://plato.stanford.edu/archives/sum2003/entries/justice-intergenerational.

Meyer, L. and Roser, D., 2006. Distributive justice and climate change, *Analyse & kritik,* 28(2), 223–249.

Miller, D., 2004. Holding nations responsible. *Ethics,* 114(2), 240–268.

Moellendorf, D. 2002. *Cosmopolitan justice.* Boulder, CO: Westview Press.

Neumayer, E. 2000. In defence of historical accountability for greenhouse gas emissions. *Ecological economics,* 33(2), 185–192.

Page, E.A., 2006. *Climate change, justice and future generations,* Cheltenham: Edward Elgar.

Parfit, D., 1984. *Reasons and persons.* Oxford: Clarendon Press.
Pogge, T., 1989. *Realizing Rawls.* Ithaca, NY: Cornell University Press.
Sher, G., 2005. Transgenerational compensation, *Philosophy & public affairs,* 33(2), 181–201.

Name Index

Adam and Eve 83
Ahmad, Q.K. 324
Allen, Myles 325
Appell, D. 323
Arnell, N. 324
Arneson, Richard 231
Arrhenius, Gustaf xvii, 283–96
Austin, J.L. 403

Bach, Johann Sebastian 137
Baer, P. 326
Bandura, A. 136
Barry, Brian xi, xvi, 183–207, 262, 263, 271, 280
Bartholet, Elizabeth 177
Baumert, K. xviii
Baumgartner, C. 141
Bayertz, K. 144
Beckerman, Wilfred 196, 197
Beitz, Charles 219, 220, 221
Benatar, D. xii
Bentham, Jeremy 3, 10
Bichot, J. 277
Birnbacher, Dieter xvi, 121–46
Blair, Tony 399, 402
Bobbitt, P. 130
Boden, T. 329
Bonaparte, Napoleon 26
Bourgeois, Leon 265, 269
Brooks, R.L. xiii
Broome, John xvii, 91–119, 285, 286, 287
Brundtland, G.H. xvii
Buchanan, A. xii
Butt, Daniel xiii, 445–68, 483
Bykvist, Krister 287

Calabresi, G. 130
Cane, Peter 452
Caney, Simon xvii, xix, xxi, 321–40
Casal, P. xvi
Christ, Jesus 126
Churchill, Winston 5
Clinton, Bill 399, 402
Coleman, Jules L. 451

Cosandey, D. 260, 277
Cowen, Tyler xvii, 103

Dasgupta, P. xvi
De George, R. xii
de Grey, Aubrey 285
de-Shalit, Avner 138, 189
DeGrazia, David 62, 70

Einstein, Albert 269
Elizabeth I, Queen of England 399
Eve and Adam 83

Feinberg, Joel xiv, 154, 155, 160, 171
Fishkin, J.S. xi
Flew, Anthony 3
Foot, Philippa 433
Fullinwider, Robert 455, 456, 457, 467

Gardiner, Stephen M. xv, 301–14
God 56, 265
Godwin, William 38
Goodin, Robert 205
Gosseries, Axel xii, xiv, xv, xvi, xx, 255–81, 326
Govier, T. xvi

Habermas, Jürgen 56
Hare, R.M. 122, 124
Herzen, Alexander 18
Heyd, David xi, xii, xvi, 55–73, 237
Hitler, Adolf 5
Hobbes, Thomas 263
Horace 131
Horkheimer, Max 79
Houghton, Sir John 324
Hume, D. 121, 126, 129

Jonas, Hans xvi, 127
Jones, Hiram 5

Kals, E. 137
Kant, Immanuel 18, 24, 25, 26, 27, 55, 56, 60, 121, 124, 243

Kass, Leon 285
Kavka, Gregory 66
Kripke, Saul 70
Kumar, Rahul xii 63, 64, 425–44

La Rovere, E. xx
Laslett, P. xi
Leibniz, Gottfried 70
Leopold, Aldo 137, 138
Levin, Michael 414
Locke, John 56, 265, 354, 355, 356, 358, 360, 361, 362, 365, 385, 386, 387, 388, 390
Lowe, J. 323
Lyons, David xiv, 349–72

Mann, Michael 323
Manning, R.E. 127
Marglin, Stephen 116
Marland, G. 329
McMahan, Jeff 62, 63
Meyer, Lukas H. xi–xxiv, 79–88, 225–50, 469–88
Mill, John Stuart xi, 3, 10, 184, 186, 198, 199
Miller, David 245, 446, 447, 448, 449, 450, 454
Minteer, B.A. 127
Moore, G.E. 203, 204
Morris, Christopher 414
Moses 70
Mulgan, Tim xiv, xvi, 63

Narveson, Jan xi, xvi, 3–13
Neumayer, E. 326
Newton, Isaac 43
Nickel, James W. 450
Nietzsche, Friedrich 130, 137
Nobel, Alfred 81, 82, 83, 84
Nozick, Robert 351, 353, 354, 355, 356, 357, 358, 359, 360, 361, 362, 363, 364, 365, 377, 385, 386, 390, 407

O'Neill, Onora 454, 467

Page, E. xxi
Parfit, Derek xi, xii, xvi, xvii, 23–50, 56, 57, 59, 60, 61, 63, 65, 66, 67, 68, 69, 103, 108, 109, 110, 111, 112, 227, 301, 400, 402, 425
Partridge, Ernest xiv, 139
Passmore, J. 137
Patton, P. xiv
Paul the Apostle 72

Pigou, A.C. 115, 116, 118
Pitcher, G. xiv
Plato 121
Pogge, Thomas 219, 220
Porritt, Jonathon 205
Posner, E.A. xix
Prichard, H.A. 121

Ramsey, Frank P. xi, 94
Rapauch, M. 327, 331
Rawls, John xi, xv, xvi, 15–22, 55, 56, 58, 59, 64, 65, 242, 358
Rawls, John 209–224
Raz, Joseph 246
Reiman, Jeffrey 64, 65, 66
Roberts, Melinda A. xii, 66, 67
Roser, Dominic xvi, xvii, xx, xxi, 225–50, 469–88
Ruben, David-Hillel 82, 83
Russell, Y. 127

Sarukhan, J. 324
Scanlon, Thomas W. 226, 232, 432
Schneider, S. 324
Schopenhauer, Arthur 124, 129
Sen, Amartya 213
Sher, George xiii, 405–24, 463, 464
Shiffrin, Seana Valentine xii, 151–82
Shue, H. xxi, 326
Sidgwick, Henry 60, 124, 203, 204
Simmons, A. John xii, 410, 411, 464
Simon, Julian 198
Singer, Peter xxi, 62, 63, 334
Smart, J.J.C. 3, 8, 9, 13
Socrates 83
Spinoza, Baruch 121
Stendhal 139
Stiglitz, Joseph 95
Stone, Daithi 325
Stott, Peter 325

Thompson, Janna xiii, xv, 399–404, 459, 460
Thomson, Judith Jarvis 455, 457
Tolstoy, Leo 26

Ulysses 141

Visser't Hooft, H.P. 137

Wade-Benzoni, K.A. 136
Waldron, Jeremy xiv, 373–97, 415, 416, 461, 464

Waluchow, Wil xiv
Wasserman, David 68
Watson, R. 329
Weisbach, D. xix
Weiss, E.B. 145

Wellman, C. xv
Williams, A. xvi
Williams, Bernard 121
Wolff, Jonathan 458
Woodward, James xii, 65